I0823056

THE FUTURE OF STORYTELLING

THE FUTURE OF STORYTELLING

How Immersive Experiences Are Transforming Our World

CHARLES MELCHER

Published By

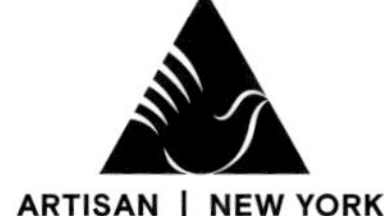

Produced By

Library of Congress Cataloging-in-Publication Data is on file.

Hardcover ISBN 978-1-64829-383-2
Ebook ISBN 978-1-64829-385-6

Published by Artisan, an imprint of Workman Publishing, a division of Hachette Book Group, Inc.
1290 Avenue of the Americas
New York, NY 10104
artisanbooks.com

Printed in China (IMSF) on responsibly sourced paper.

First printing, September 2025
10 9 8 7 6 5 4 3 2 1

To my mother and father, Barbara and James,
who instilled in me a love of stories and a
curiosity for learning.

And to my wife, Jessica, and son, Daniel,
who remind me every day that life is best when
experienced with those you love.

CONTENTS

ABOUT THIS BOOK'S COVER

In the future of storytelling, people won't just passively watch stories—they will live them, taking on different roles and playing many different characters. One way characters are established is through their costumes: Superheroes have capes, cowboys have hats, fairies have wings, et cetera.

Just like you can tell something about a character from their clothes, you can tell the character of a book by the costume it wears—its dust jacket. To express the idea that participants in the future of storytelling can have agency and embody many roles, I've created a book that can wear a variety of costumes. The dust jacket unfolds to reveal twelve interchangeable cover designs, ranging from sci-fi to romance to westerns, each reflective of a genre of stories you'll find featured inside. (See diagram, opposite.) As the reader, you get to personalize the cover by choosing which design best suits you; which reflects your taste, your mood, or your coffee-table decor.

To customize the cover, start by unfolding the trifold jacket completely so you can view all the designs. Each of the three panels has two cover designs, one on the front and one on the back, making for six covers each on both sides of the sheet. Since the folds are double scored, you can refold the three panels to select any one of the twelve covers for the front of the book. Voilá! You have now customized the book and made it your own!

THE STORY CONTINUES

The world of immersive storytelling is constantly changing, with new projects, creators, and forms arriving on the scene all the time. To join me in my ongoing discovery and stay up-to-date on the best examples of these amazing experiences, scan the QR code at left. And for engaging interviews with the creators and thought leaders shaping the future of storytelling, subscribe to and follow *The Future of StoryTelling* podcast wherever you get your podcasts.

HOW TO CUSTOMIZE THE COVER

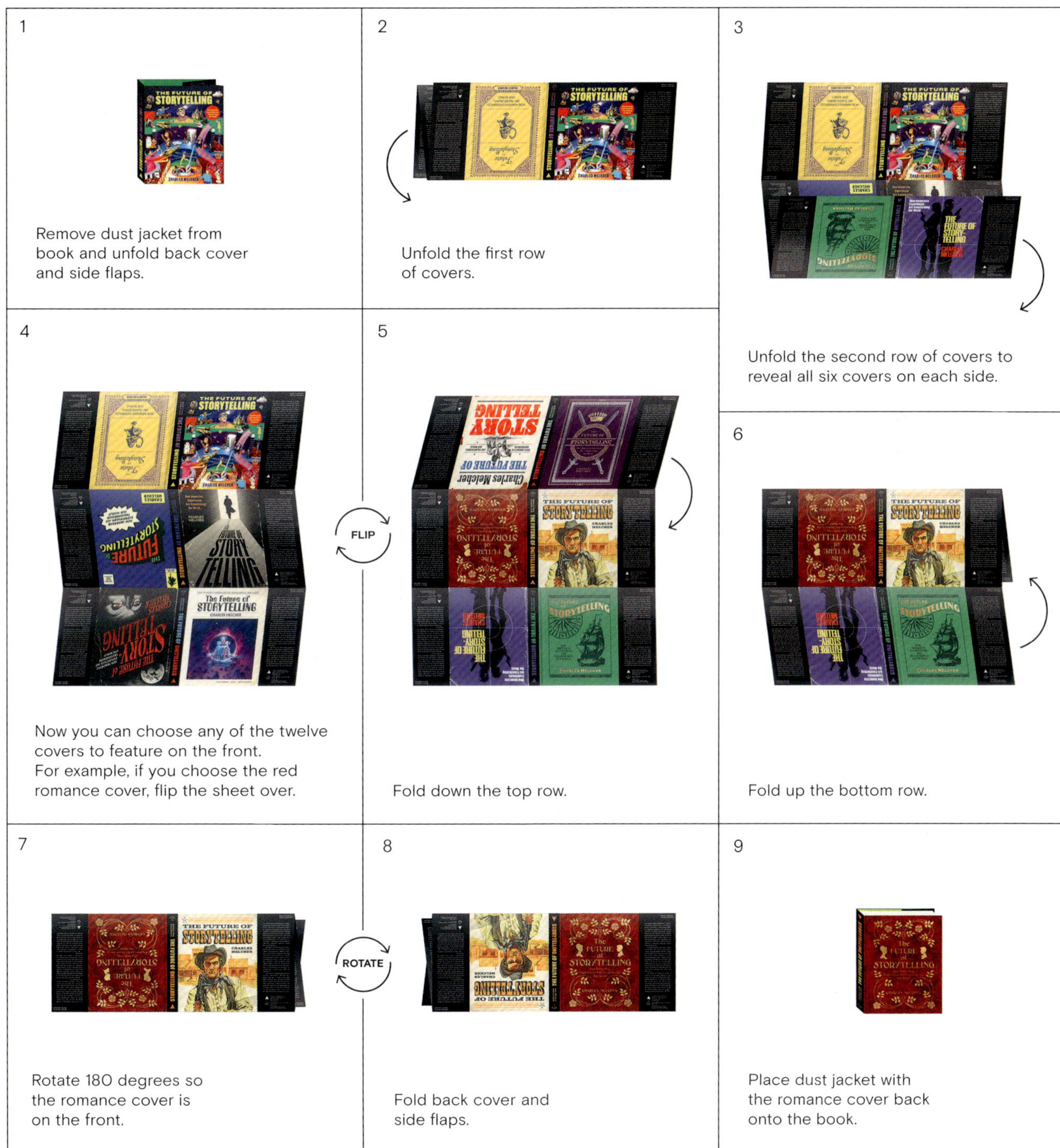

INTRODUCTION

When I was little, my parents used to read to me before bed. I loved snuggling up between their arms and the pages of a book. The stories fed my young imagination and transported me to far-off worlds, with their rich characters and vibrant illustrations. I *loved* books. So, you can imagine my dismay when, in first grade, while taking turns reading books from the *Dick and Jane* series with my classmates, I realized I couldn't decipher the squiggly black lines on the page. As the other kids giggled and I turned red with embarrassment, my frustration and panic grew. Much to my relief, it turned out that I wasn't slow or stupid; instead, after taking some tests, I learned that I had dyslexia. To address my disability, my school placed me in remedial reading classes with a special-ed teacher named Mrs. Schultz. Twice a week, we would meet in her office, which was no bigger than a closet, and sit there knee to knee. She would open a glass jar full of sand and pour it out onto a little tray that she set on my lap. I would shake the tray so the sand would flatten, and then our lesson would begin. She would hold up a card with the letter *B* on it and say *"B"* and sound out *"buh."* Then I'd have to repeat it back to her—*"B"* and *"buh"*—while drawing the letter *B* with my finger in the tray of sand. The lesson would continue with the letter *C*, and so on. Slowly, I learned the alphabet, and over several years I was able to catch up to my classmates with my reading and writing skills. By using multisensory reinforcement (sight, sound, touch), I discovered how to differentiate the letters and learn their sounds. I owe my ability to read to this kind of embodied learning.

Over time, my love of books expanded to many other forms of storytelling, including comics and graphic novels, photography, film, and video games. Ironically for a dyslexic person, after college I decided to go into publishing. But I brought to it my affinity for multisensory storytelling. In 1993, I started my own book packaging and publishing company, Melcher Media, and we quickly set ourselves apart by focusing on highly visual, beautifully produced and popular books that pushed the limits of the printed page. We created pop-up books for adults, accordion-fold books, books with hidden compartments, and books with sound chips. We even invented a new format for waterproof books (we called it DuraBooks™), for which we received a patent. Celebrities, artists, and other luminaries such as Eminem, Sarah Jessica Parker, and Secretary of State Madeleine Albright, along with companies like Nike, Harley-Davidson, and HBO came to us for help telling their stories in print. The company grew and thrived, boasting numerous bestsellers, award-winning designs, and a reputation for quality, creativity, and innovation. Business was good.

Then it all came crashing down.

The recession of 2008–2009 hit. Almost overnight, the world's interest in—and ability to pay for—beautifully produced books tanked. For me, this was devastating. Not only was my business in trouble, but the word on the street was that printed books were dying, too.

Meanwhile, social media (Facebook and Twitter) went mainstream, and smartphones and the mobile web took off with the success of Apple's iPhone 3 and App Store—which in turn led to an explosion of free and cheap content online. This was the dawn of self-publishing, audiobooks, e-books, and mobile apps. People began to realize that they didn't need the gatekeepers of the traditional media industries in order to get their stories out there and noticed. Social media had introduced features such as comment sections, like and share buttons, and so on. Because people could react to content in ways that were visible to others, they were no longer passive consumers of it. Now they were starting to play an active role in the stories they loved.

While some of my colleagues in book publishing were hiding under their desks hoping this whole digital thing would blow over, I saw opportunity. Books may have been (temporarily, we now know) dead, but stories were more alive than ever.

I decided it was time for Melcher Media to try its hand at digital storytelling. We had recently worked with Vice President Al Gore on his 2006 bestselling book, *An Inconvenient Truth,* and were about to embark on a sequel called *Our Choice.* I asked Mr. Gore if he would grant us the digital rights, and to my surprise he agreed to trust us. Then I found two talented young developers—one a UX designer and the other a coder—and invited them to partner with us to build an iOS mobile app as a companion to the book. It took our small team more than a year to build. The *Our Choice* app was filled with rich media, interactive infographics, and an elegant UX design, and most distinctly it used the sensors in the phone to allow for tactile and multisensory interaction with the content. We launched the app from the TED Conference stage in 2011. Soon thereafter, Steve Jobs and his team saw it, were impressed, and honored it with an Apple Design Award as one of the best-designed apps of the year. *Our Choice* became a top-grossing app in the App Store, and *Wired* magazine hailed it as "a model for the book of the future."

I had joined the two young developers as a founding partner in their new software company, Push Pop Press, and before the end of 2011, Facebook bought the company.

So, over the course of two years, I had gone from telling stories printed on dead trees to creating a successful app and becoming part of a software company that was sold to Facebook. Based on this experience, I walked into Melcher Media's weekly company meeting and announced to my team that: 1) We were no longer in the book business but instead in the *storytelling* business, and we would begin to work across multiple forms of media; and 2) We needed to find a new storytelling community, and the best way to do that was by building one. We would start a summit to gather the world's most innovative content creators, technologists, thought leaders, and marketers and get them networking, sharing best practices, and collaborating. This annual event was eventually named the Future of StoryTelling (FoST) Summit (see p. 290).

Featuring small, participatory roundtables with speakers, hands-on creative workshops, interactive exhibitions of cutting-edge technologies and immersive experiences, and captivating performances, the FoST Summit launched in 2012 by invitation only. The event quickly grew, and we soon added a FoST Festival that was open to the public. Within a few years, we went from a one-day experience for 300 guests to a week's worth of programming for nearly 6,000. It regularly drew some of the biggest names shaping storytelling in the twenty-first century as speakers, *Fortune* 100 companies as sponsors, and a devoted community of multi-hyphenate creators, makers, and marketers.

Along the way, FoST evolved into a multidisciplinary creative studio that produces content throughout the year, including apps, websites, films, VR/AR, events, and immersive experiences; storytelling workshops; curated exhibitions; a monthly newsletter, *FoST in Thought*; and the bi-weekly *Future of StoryTelling* podcast, where I get to interview some of the world's most interesting storytellers across a range of disciplines.

For the past fifteen years, my quest to find the people and technologies that are reinventing storytelling has often led me to some unexpected places—which is how I found myself, one evening in 2014, in a former mail-processing facility in London, taking in a performance of *The Drowned Man* by the immersive theater company Punchdrunk (see p. 40). I'd flown over specifically to see the show. The conceit was that you were in a Hollywood-like film studio where a movie was being shot. Upon entering, guests were given masks and asked to keep them on at all times and not to speak. Otherwise, there were no rules, and the nearly 600 guests were free to roam around the building like ghosts, either exploring the many intricately designed rooms or following specific actors as they performed scenes in different locations.

After a couple hours of wandering and watching, I grew tired and was thinking of calling it a night, when just then a beautiful young actress in a tight leopard-print dress and ruby-red lipstick drifted into the room. I chose to stay a little longer and see what unfolded. I followed her, along with some of the other guests, as she performed different scenes, until she ducked behind a door that I hadn't noticed. On a whim, I decided to see where she was headed, so I followed her. She was waiting for me on the other side and quickly shut the door behind me and locked it. She motioned for me to follow her down a hallway into a little office. There, she reached up and took off my mask. My cloak of invisibility had been removed, and I felt exposed, face-to-face with this actress, just the two of us.

She hung my mask on a coat rack and took a Humphrey Bogart-style trench coat off the hook. She put it on me, tying the belt and adjusting the collar just so, and then led me by the arm down a narrow corridor that got progressively darker until it was pitch black. Finally, she let go.

I was alone in the dark, every one of my senses on high alert. After what felt like a long time, I suddenly heard a voice over a loudspeaker yell, "Action!" followed by a popping sound and an explosion of light, then another pop and another burst of light. As my eyes adjusted, I realized I was surrounded by about thirty silver umbrellas, the kind photographers use to diffuse strobe lights. And then I saw her, the actress, starting to walk slowly toward me—but she was completely transformed. She had an intense, almost crazed look in her eyes. I was worried that she was no longer a friend but a foe—maybe even insane. As she drew closer to me, I froze, fearful that I was going to need to physically defend myself against her. She raised her hand up toward my neck and then laid it gently on my cheek. When she took another step forward, I could feel the warmth of her body up against mine. I could smell the sweetness of her perfume. Instinctively, my hands went around her waist.

As she looked longingly up into my eyes, I was no longer afraid of her—now I was afraid of *myself*. What role was I willing to play here? I'm a happily married man, but there I was, alone in a room with a beautiful starlet in my arms. While I contemplated whether to lean in for a kiss, I heard the same voice over the loudspeaker yell, "Cut!"

> Creators and audiences all over the world are embracing embodied, immersive stories, although the scale and breadth of this trend is still invisible to most.

and everything returned to pitch black. The actress moved away and I was alone, every part of my body shaking with excitement and uncertainty. Then I felt her hand on my arm, and she led me back down the corridor into the small office, where she removed my trench coat, hung it on the hook, and put my mask back on. Finally, as she was about to see me unceremoniously out the door, she stopped and whispered in my ear: "I think you would be great for the part." I was off again, left afloat among the hundreds of other ghosts in the building.

I'd entered the experience as a voyeur, but by the end, I was playing a role—in fact, I realized I had been auditioning for the role of the leading man. And as unsettling as it was, I loved it. For the rest of the weekend, I walked around London just a little bit taller, feeling like James Bond, with the sense that adventure might be waiting for me around any corner.

It was some weeks later that I found myself back in my office trying out the second-generation version of Kinect, the motion-controller peripheral for Microsoft's Xbox console. Using RGB cameras and infrared detectors and projectors, the Kinect was able to perform real-time gesture recognition and body/skeletal recognition. The device also included microphones that allowed for speech recognition and voice control. I have been a huge fan of video games since I was a kid playing *Space Invaders* on my Commodore PET home computer. The Kinect, however, offered something entirely unprecedented—the chance to get up off the couch and use my entire body to interact with what I was seeing on the screen without being tethered to a joystick or controller.

Both my *Drowned Man* and Kinect experiences made me realize that I was craving a new type of storytelling, one that is participatory, multisensory, interactive, and highly personal; stories that aren't confined within a screen, a pair of headphones, the words on a page, or a theatrical proscenium but exist all around us, engage with us, and even change based on our decisions. And I'm not alone: Creators and audiences all over the world are embracing embodied, immersive stories, although the scale and breadth of this trend is still invisible to most.

The exciting reality is that a revolution in storytelling is taking place, and it is going to have profound implications in almost every field. It's happening in the top-secret tech labs of Meta, Apple, and Google; in avant-garde performances at fringe theater festivals; in escape rooms housed in storefronts of suffering shopping malls; in cores of quantum supercomputers containing next-generation artificial intelligence; in the newest VR and AR headsets; and in centuries-old museums. It's happening at festivals like SXSW, Cannes Lions, and Comic-Con; in restaurants and bars; in old garages and abandoned bowling alleys; in Hollywood studios and Madison Avenue advertising agencies; on university campuses and at nonprofit organizations. It's happening in the middle of the desert in Nevada and on a palm-sized device that lives inside the pocket of nearly every person who will read this book.

So what are stories that immerse, embody, and respond to the audience called? Up until now, there wasn't a term that united these experiences, but I have come to call them *living stories*.

And for the past fifteen years, I've been incredibly lucky to get invited into the studios, labs, offices, and academic corridors where the future of living stories is being invented. And while people are still trying to figure out the techniques, technologies, and organic languages that will unlock living stories' full potential, I want to share what I've learned thus far so I can help businesses, creators, and audiences better understand and appreciate the future of storytelling.

I have come to believe that if we can understand the mechanics and unleash their full power, living stories have the potential to become more popular than Hollywood and gaming have ever been. Artists and storytellers have a new opportunity to serve their audiences by creating experiences in which the audience plays an active role. To me, this is one of the fundamental cultural, psychological, and technological transformations of the twenty-first century, embracing the shift from storytelling that was two-dimensional, fixed, passive, and disembodied to three-dimensional, agentic, responsive, and multisensory.

What I have learned after experiencing hundreds of living stories is that something beautiful happens when creators relinquish control of the narrative to their audience. Director Alejandro González Iñárritu, who wrote and directed the virtual-reality work *Carne y Arena* (see p. 22), calls this kind of immersive storytelling "the end of the dictatorship of the frame." The reason living stories are so powerful is that they engage not only our eyes and ears but our whole person. They gift us experiences that our brains and spinal cords are primed for, thanks to millions of years of evolution. You can feel your response to a living story in the hairs on the back of your neck, in the pit of your stomach, in the ache in your thighs as you move and choose, emote, and think through these experiences.

Just imagine: How different is it to read a book or see a movie about surviving a natural disaster than to believe in the moment that you did? How much more satisfying is it when you, not King Arthur, are able to pull the sword out of the stone? Stories have always provided us with a safe, instructive way to survive the world, as we observe characters making choices (often the wrong ones). With living stories, those characters are us, and we learn from the choices we make, and learn deeply, because we feel them throughout our own bodies. Living stories are a gateway to a more intense emotional life, to living more fully in the world.

The purpose of this book is not to undermine the traditional storytelling forms, like books, theater, and film—or to suggest that they should or will be replaced. I wrote it because of my love for living stories and my excitement for what these stories can and will do now and in the future, due to breakthroughs in technology, storycrafting, world-building, and our perpetual yearning for new paradigms.

As I've come to understand living stories more profoundly, I've identified six characteristics that define them. Living stories are agentic, immersive, embodied, responsive, social, and transformative. The chapters of this book are organized around each of these concepts. Not every living story exhibits all six of these characteristics, but the best of them do. Each one featured in this book has some degree of at least four.

In Chapter 1, I argue that the future of storytelling is agentic—defined by the audience's active participation and decision-making within the narrative. In living stories, the traditional passive role of the audience is being replaced by a new role in which individuals shape, influence, and even co-create the story. Agency transforms both the role of the audience and the experience—and challenges creators to design stories that are flexible and responsive. The rise of agentic storytelling marks a cultural shift toward shared authorship in the stories we tell.

I have come to believe that if we can understand the mechanics and unleash their full power, living stories have the potential to become more popular than Hollywood and gaming have ever been.

Chapter 2 explores how the future of storytelling is immersive, and I describe what I see as three categories of immersion: physical, participatory, and emotional. One of the foundational skills for immersive storytelling is the craft of world-building. Drawing on examples from master world-builders and immersive experiences like *Star Wars: Galaxy's Edge* (see p. 86) and Meow Wolf's *House of Eternal Return* (see p. 98), this chapter illuminates how thoughtful design, multisensory detail, and interactivity allow for rich narrative possibility and deep audience engagement.

Chapter 3 is about how living stories are embodied—they go beyond the sights and sounds of traditional media and are told through all the senses, even those of which we're unaware. Research shows that our bodies significantly shape memory and emotion, suggesting that storytelling that involves the whole body has a much greater impact than traditional two-dimensional media. Just as early filmmakers developed a new visual language of cinema, today's creators are beginning to invent a language of embodied storytelling—one that uses the full range of movement, touch, and sensation to craft narratives that resonate on a deeper, more human level.

I discuss how living stories are responsive in Chapter 4, that they adapt in real time to the actions, preferences, and emotions of each participant. Unlike traditional, fixed narratives, responsive stories engage the audience on a personal level, making the experience feel unique and intimate. I also highlight technological advances—such as generative AI, affective computing, and real-time emotion recognition—that are making personalized storytelling possible at scale. These tools promise to revolutionize narrative experiences by enabling content that dynamically adjusts based on the audience's mood, behavior, and even digital history. Responsive storytelling has the potential to turn every story into an individualized journey.

Chapter 5 argues that the future of storytelling is social, and that shared story experiences can foster meaningful human connection and counteract the isolation of modern life. Storytelling has always been inherently social—helping humans survive, learn, and emotionally connect. We are biologically wired to share stories. While social media can have the effect of alienating us from one another, new forms of entertainment that center collaboration and communication offer a way to bring people together again. Living stories don't just entertain; they build trust, empathy, and a sense of belonging so desperately needed on our increasingly divided planet.

Living stories have the power to create lasting change in how we see ourselves, others, and the world.

Living stories have the power to create lasting change in how we see ourselves, others, and the world. This kind of transformative change is the focus of Chapter 6. Drawing on lessons from live-action role-playing (LARP) games (see p. 298), this chapter explores how living stories can be vehicles for self-discovery. Deeply immersive experiences allowing the participant to walk in the shoes of the less fortunate can also evoke empathy that can lead to humanitarian impact. At their best, living stories can facilitate enduring emotional insights and perspective shifts.

There is, of course, some irony in writing (and reading) a book about a category of experience whose power lies specifically in its evolution beyond text. The truth is that many of the living stories you'll be introduced to in these pages must be seen, heard, felt—*lived*—to be believed. I strongly encourage you to go out and experience great living stories for yourself, and to get you started, this book also includes photos and descriptive text about nearly fifty best-in-class examples of some of my favorites from around the globe.

These are meant to celebrate both the projects themselves and the brilliant, creative people who brought them to life. They also document a history-in-the-making of this extraordinary new medium, one that I have had the great privilege to experience firsthand.

This evolution of storytelling we are witnessing today is ushering in a world of agentic, immersive, embodied, responsive, social, and transformative storytelling. The impacts of this shift will be profound and far-reaching. It will remake the storyteller and the audience into co-creators of narrative. It will transform industries beyond just media and entertainment—from education and advertising to retail and hospitality. It will change the way we learn, the way we're entertained, the way we think about ourselves, and the way we interact with one another. We will, at last, become the heroes of our own stories.

For storytellers, audiences, and stories themselves, it's an exciting time to be alive.

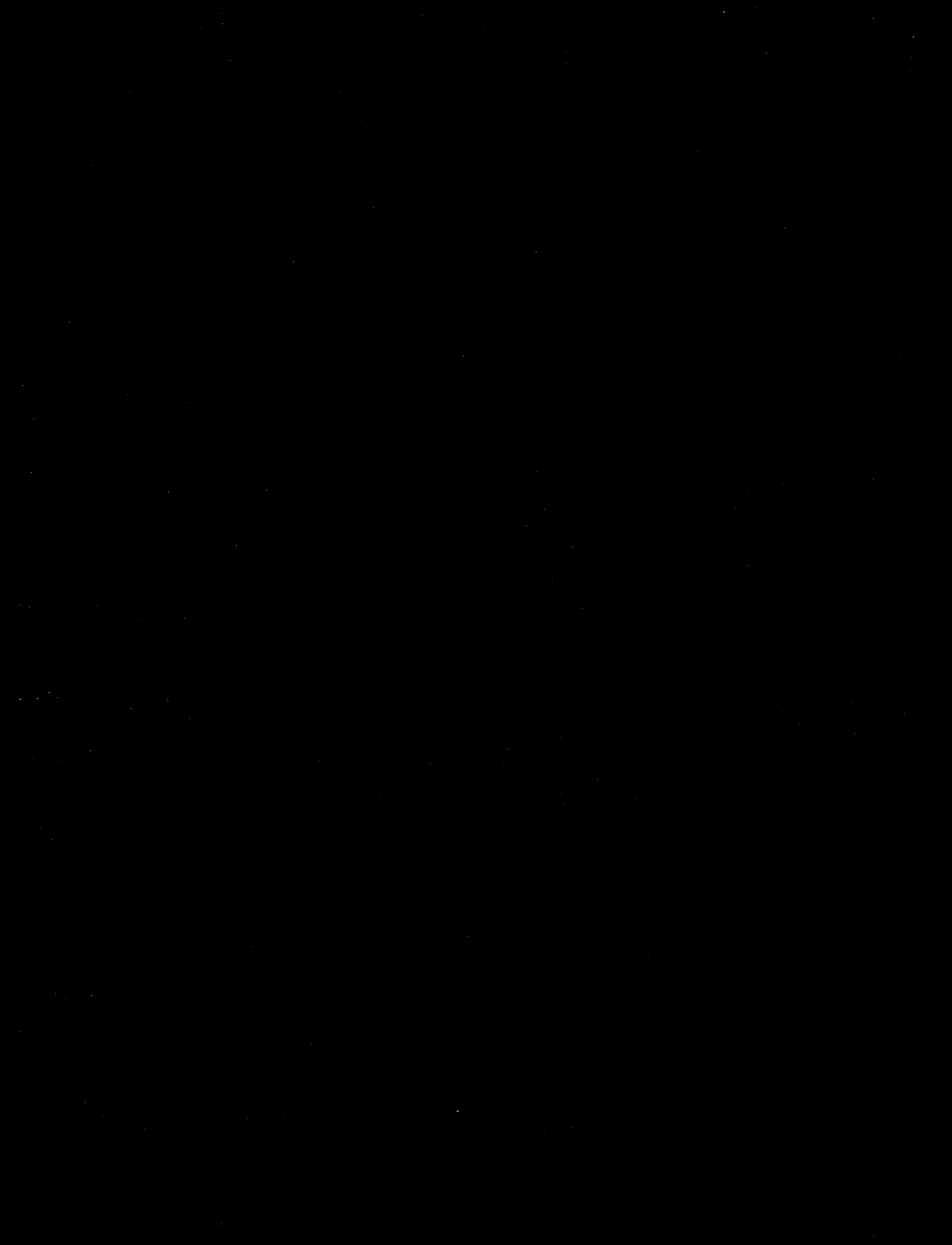

1

THE FUTURE OF STORYTELLING IS AGENTIC

It was February 2023, and I was in the desert. The sand of the desert floor was cold beneath my bare feet. It was just before dawn, and the glow of the coming sun mingled with the purple night on the horizon, framing the nearby shrubs and rock outcroppings in silhouette.

The air was alive with the chirps and whistles of desert birdsong, but otherwise, I seemed to be alone—until I caught the sounds of hushed voices, slowly drawing nearer, off to my left. I turned to see a small group heading toward me; I could catch just enough of their speech to know it was Spanish. As they approached, I made out several faces: men of various ages, women with downturned eyes, children in their arms and at their legs. The group moved with exhaustion, staggering, some limping. Many, like me, were barefoot.

As I watched them pass, I noticed a faint whirring in the distance. Before the sound had even fully registered, a helicopter appeared in the sky above, its spotlight blinding; then there were trucks, too, and from the trucks came men in combat gear, pointing rifles at the group of people, screaming at everyone to get on the ground. *The coyote,* they shouted over the chop and rushing wind of the copter blades, *where is the coyote?*

I naively believed that whatever was going on did not include me. I wasn't part of this group, just an observer who was clearly in the wrong place at the wrong time. As far as I could tell, nobody even knew I was there. But then the guns swung in my direction, and that sense of separation vanished. Before I knew it, there were two or three men on me, staring me down with the muzzles of their rifles. *Get on the ground! NOW!*

In that moment, the boundary between fiction and reality collapsed. It didn't matter that I was standing in a warehouse in Northern California wearing a VR headset, that the desert and the Spanish-speaking group of migrants and the military men and their weapons were all a fabrication. There was a gun in my face, and I had to make a decision.

I got on the ground. My hands met the cold, gritty sand of the desert floor.

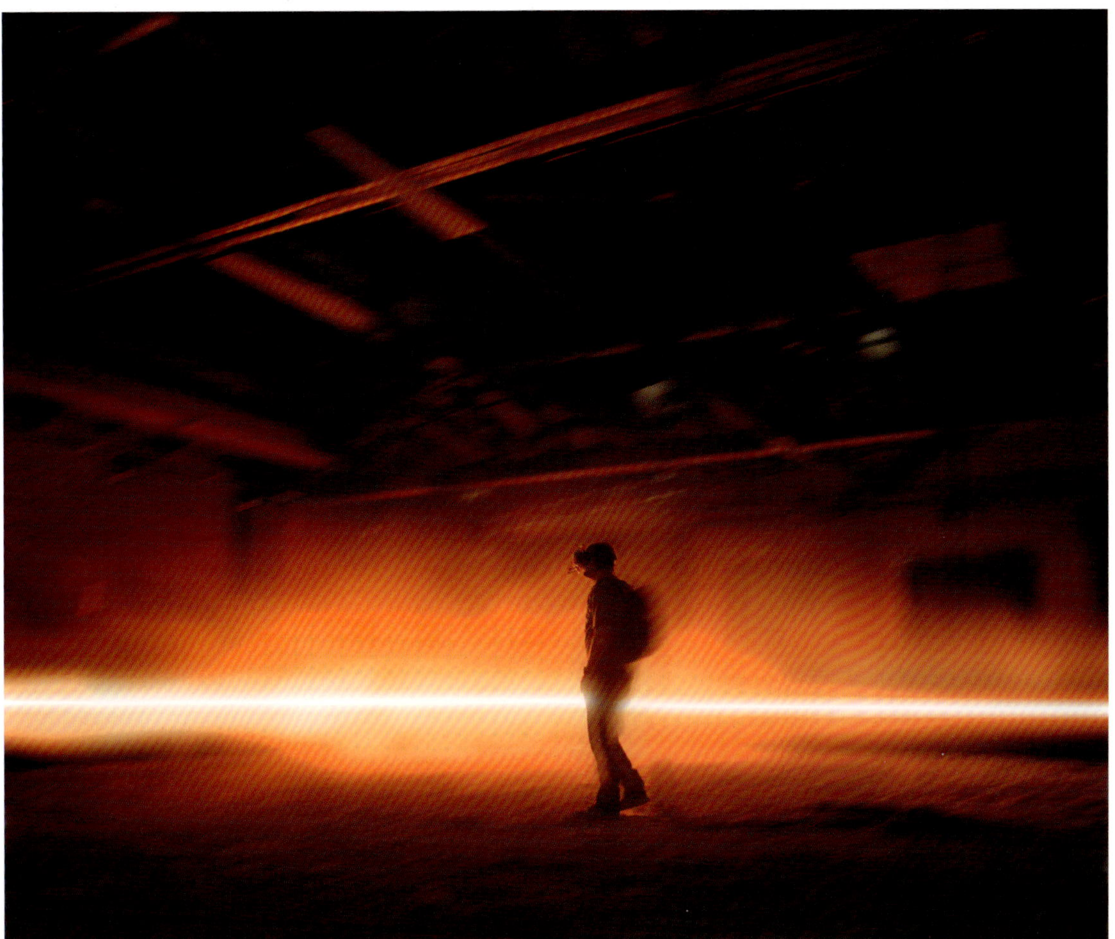

A participant wearing a VR headset walks barefoot through a desert in the *Carne y Arena* experience.

INVISIBLE NO MORE

What I experienced in that Bay Area warehouse on that February evening was Alejandro González Iñárritu's brilliant VR installation, *Carne y Arena*. The piece is based on the real lives of Mexican and Central American refugees and their attempts to cross the Mexican border into the United States, but the script is ultimately a work of fiction. Intellectually, I know this. When I recall the memories of that night, and the emotions it stirred, however, I'm not so sure. The second those border agents came at me, I felt wildly unsafe. My adrenaline surged. When I dropped to the ground, it was not play-acting. It was survival instinct. I was truly terrified.

Up until that moment, I had been working under the comfortable assumption that I was invisible, as I have so often been while on the receiving end of a story. I was a member of the audience, not an actor, not a migrant, and certainly not the coyote—as such, my role was supposed to be that of a passive recipient.

All that comfort disappeared in an instant. The Border Patrol officer was staring at *me*. The face his gun was pointed at was *mine*. And when you have a gun pointing at your face, inaction is not an option. I had to make a choice. I chose to drop to my knees.

The radical shift that occurred in that moment is that I was given agency. *Carne y Arena* was not the first story experience I'd had that provided me with agency, but it was one of the most impactful, in part because that agency came as a surprise. In most of today's VR experiences and live immersive productions, you're either a participant or you're not, and it's generally made very clear up front which is the case. But Iñárritu made a specific choice to surprise viewers with their own involvement. This worked well as a reflection of one of the themes of the story—human struggles anywhere concern humans everywhere—but it also worked as a meditation on our current cultural moment in storytelling. We, the audience, are being invited more and more to step directly into the stories we receive.

Giving us true agency—the power to make meaningful choices within the story environment—is a relatively new phenomenon, and one that transforms the nature of the audience itself.

Possessing agency is a profound change in how we as an audience experience storytelling. For much of modern history, the most the audience was able to do to interact with a story was clap or boo or perhaps throw cabbages (and even then, only in live theater). Giving us true agency—the power to make meaningful choices within the story environment—is a relatively new phenomenon, and one that transforms the nature of the audience itself. In an agentic story experience, it could be argued that there is no audience at all: By taking an active role in the unfolding story, the group that in traditional terms would be called the audience becomes something more akin to a troupe of actors, or even storytellers themselves.

THE LONG ROAD FROM *PONG* TO *CARNE Y ARENA*

I can vividly recall the first time I experienced agency in an immersive, virtual environment, decades before my foray into the simulated desert of *Carne y Arena*. I remember being completely floored by the experience and thrilled by the prospect of the exciting future that it signaled. I remember every single detail of the virtual world I had plunged into, although it wasn't particularly impressive: I was staring at a black screen, watching a white dot bounce between two white lines. The experience was called *Pong*, and it was magical.

I spent hundreds of hours batting that dot back and forth on my vertical dash of a paddle. And I wasn't alone: In 1972, when the very first *Pong* cabinet was installed in a bar in Sunnyvale, California, so many players stuffed so many quarters into the machine that within days its coin reservoir jammed and Atari had to send its designer, Al Alcorn, to install a bigger one.

Though they were unprecedented in the media landscape at the time, *Pong* and other early video games found eager audiences who were hungry to enter and control their virtual worlds. But while these nascent games afforded players agency in gameplay, they couldn't yet give players agency in narrative. It would take nearly a decade before a video game delivered any sort of storyline. While the mid-'70s saw the release of *Colossal Cave Adventure* and *Zork*, two early instances of interactive digital narratives, both were text adventures, closer to digital books than true video games, with no environment for the player to explore or visuals of any kind. *Donkey Kong*, released in 1981, is often cited as the first truly narrative video game, but even then, the story was extremely simple (random man rescues damsel in distress from large monkey) and entirely linear (players could not alter the narrative in any meaningful way with their choices).

In the decades since the release of *Donkey Kong*, video-game storytelling has made enormous progress—yet the games that deliver truly great, emotionally impactful stories are still few and far between. To this day, player choices often fall short of shaping the larger storyline in important ways, and outside of a few significant exceptions like *Baldur's Gate 3* (see p. 214) and *Red Dead Redemption 2*, that storyline itself tends to exist largely to move players from gameplay sequence to gameplay sequence. In his book *Extra Lives: Why Video Games Matter*, video-game writer and critic Tom Bissell imagines that when a game comes along that allows player decisions to have truly narrative-altering consequences, "an altogether new form of storytelling might be born: stories that, with your help, create themselves." However, he notes, a word already exists for such stories: "That word is *life*."

THE INVENTION OF THE ALPHABET AND THE DEATH OF STORYTELLING

Agency within stories feels like a new phenomenon, and I would argue that we are still very much in the process of figuring it out. But in fact, it may be more accurate to say that it's the original way of doing things. Anthropological research suggests that in the old days—the really old days, when our ancestors gathered around campfires—storytelling was not a passive experience at all. In the 1970s, University of Utah anthropologist Polly Wiessner studied the conversations of preliterate !Kung bushmen in the Kalahari Desert and found that 81 percent of their nighttime conversations were devoted to participatory storytelling, with chanting, call-and-response, and other interplay with the storyteller. Michael Wesch, a cultural anthropologist at Kansas State University, found a similar practice among preliterate tribes in Papua New Guinea. In their culture, he says, stories were "happenings," or shared participatory events. During a story, listeners "constantly nudged in with challenges and amendments, until at last, one would take over the lead as a storyteller, only to lose it to yet another challenger moments later. It was a communal, living experience."

Another way of looking at this kind of preliterate storytelling is as a form of co-creation. The audience had influence and agency over the story; indeed, in Papua New Guinea, audience members could quickly become the storytellers themselves.

This active, participatory storytelling was the norm for most of human history. People "lived inside their stories," Wesch says. "They were not things to be consumed but were platforms for connection, participation, spontaneity, mystery, immersion, and involvement."

In Papua New Guinea, as had happened earlier in other cultures, the oral tradition of storytelling was eventually dethroned when new tools for communication were introduced. "The new media arrived," Wesch says, "but here new media was not social media or smartphones, it was writing." Literacy transformed Papua New Guinean culture, and not always for the better. Thanks to the ideas spread by new religious writings, the old houses of communion and worship were abandoned. For the government, writing became the single source of truth—elevated above the actual patterns and traditions of the people—and communities were dramatically reshaped in service of this new truth. To make written record-keeping easier, Wesch says, formerly scattered villages "were burned and replanned...[with] houses in clean, straight rows, numbered to match the census book."

Wesch's point is that when the way we tell stories changes, *we* change—not only in how we communicate but also in how we understand ourselves and the world around us, and thus how we organize our thoughts, our society, and our culture.

The ancient orator and philosopher Socrates made a similar observation about the invention of writing. He famously practiced dialogues—two-way discussions—believing that only through conversation could you ever really understand somebody or get to the truth of a matter. In Plato's *Phaedrus*, Socrates says, "You might think [written words] spoke as if they had intelligence, but if you question them, wishing to know about their sayings, they always say only one and the same thing." When language is written down, it is stripped of the gestures, intonation, facial expressions, and responsiveness of the person giving life to the words. In this sense, it becomes dead language.

By extension, with the invention and spread of writing, storytelling also in some sense "died." It became static, no longer something you engaged in but rather something that you received passively. Words and stories were literally set in stone (cuneiform tablets), then in ink on papyrus, vellum, and eventually paper.

In his book *Orality and Literacy: The Technologizing of the Word*, the scholar Walter J. Ong writes that "more than any other single invention, writing has transformed human consciousness." According to Ong, writing things down allowed ideas and information to be stored, referenced, and worked on without relying on human memory, and thus allowed for more linear, analytical, and abstract thinking. As seen in Papua New Guinea, writing also produced a new hierarchy of knowledge—people relied on the information written in books and, in turn, on the authorities who had read (or written) those books.

By fixing and preserving knowledge, writing fostered entirely new ideas and standards of information, the birth of the scholarly tradition, and the wider development of critical thinking, among other advances. There's no question that the invention of writing has been a boon for humankind. But it also meant that our stories became fixed, static, and linear, leaving little room for the kind of dynamic, agentic storytelling we once did around campfires.

TWO-WAY MEDIA: A REVOLUTION IN STORYTELLING

At the individual level, the written word didn't profoundly affect many people's lives. For millennia, reading and writing remained skills largely reserved for the elite. It was the *printed* word that truly changed things, when, in 1448, Johannes Gutenberg invented the printing press. Suddenly, books were no longer handmade objects but mass-produced goods, and writing descended from the towers to the villages. By the year 1500, there were an estimated ten million printed books in Europe.

Print was the first true mass media and led to the invention of the newspaper, the magazine, and the novel. Later, the dawn of another game-changing piece of storytelling technology—the film camera—gave rise to another explosion in mass media with the advent of movies and television. With all these new mediums, storytelling was almost exclusively one-way: The audience sat (usually) and read, watched, or listened. Now they couldn't even throw a cabbage.

By the middle of the twentieth century, mass media had reached a formerly unimaginable scale. From 1940 to 1942, Hollywood movie studios together churned out approximately 700 movies; each week they sold an estimated sixty million tickets in a country whose population then was 130 million. In the '50s and '60s, movies lost their primacy to TV, and by the early '80s, multiple television broadcasts had reached more than 100 million simultaneous viewers in the United States (among them, the final episodes of *M*A*S*H* and *Roots* and the TV movie *The Day After*). Global events like the Olympics, the World Cup, and a British royal wedding have since reached worldwide audiences in the billions.

In this age of mass one-way media, the viewers were by and large passive, so much so that they were commonly derided as "couch potatoes." As media critic and scholar Clay Shirky notes in his book *Cognitive Surplus*, the audience had been seen as couch potatoes for so long that this arrangement could be mistaken for the natural order of things, "easy enough to explain by assuming we've wanted to be passive participants more than we wanted to be other things."

But around the turn of the twenty-first century, new tools and technologies began to upend the era of one-way entertainment. The rapid rise of the Web, social media, and mobile devices challenged the assumption that our natural state as media consumers was that of sofa-inhabiting, vegetable-like life-forms staring at screens. Studies showed that for the first time since television's widespread adoption, young people were watching less of it than their elders, choosing interactive media over media that, in Shirky's words, "presupposes pure consumption." Our passive consumption of media, he writes, turned out to be nothing more than "a set of accumulated accidents, accidents that are being undone as people start [using] new communications tools to do jobs older media simply can't do."

The invention of two-way media upended the old "couch potato" narrative and ushered in a whole new era—of people telling their own stories, building collaborative wikis about the stories of others, blogging, sharing photos and videos, firing back at writers in online comment sections, and making Internet profiles for their cats. Consumer technology—digital cameras, easy-to-use and inexpensive video editing tools, free blogging platforms—enabled almost anyone to speak to almost everyone.

More and more, we want to live our stories, not just hear, read, or watch them from the outside. We want to engage. We want to play a role.

All of this new, interactive technology prompted a new kind of audience to emerge. In 2006, amid this rapid reshaping of the media ecosystem, a journalism professor at New York University named Jay Rosen published a provocative essay on his blog *Press Think* titled "The People Formerly Known as the Audience." The essay was a manifesto, a declaration that the rules and expectations of media had changed:

> The people formerly known as the audience wish to inform media people of our existence, and of a shift in power that goes with the platform shift you've all heard about....
>
> The people formerly known as the audience are those who *were* on the receiving end of a media system that ran one way, in a broadcasting pattern, with high entry fees and a few firms competing to speak very loudly while the rest of the population listened in isolation from one another—and who *today* are not in a situation like that *at all*.

Rosen's essay captured the radical power shifts heralded by a new set of democratizing tools and platforms. Video, broadcasting, news, and publishing in general were all being disrupted—disintermediated—in real time. He was careful to point out that "the audience" still wanted their traditional "big media pleasures," their TV shows and blockbusters and favorite radio stations—but these alone, and in their traditional forms, would not suffice. The audience wanted more:

> We graduate from wanting media when we want it, to wanting it without the filler, to wanting media to be way better than it is, to publishing and broadcasting ourselves when it meets a need or sounds like fun....

Rosen focused on new content platforms and how they were rapidly democratizing the ability to publish and participate in what had long been a closed-off realm. But his declaration prophesied not only the riot of social media to come but also the waves we're now seeing in immersive experiences and living stories.

It's not just that people now make things that once only the media could. It's that we have come to expect that we can participate in real time. More and more, we want to live our stories, not just hear, read, or watch them from the outside. We want to engage. We want to play a role.

ENTER THE ACTIENCE

The word *audience,* from the Latin root for hearing, *audientia,* dates back to an age when stories were mostly oral and therefore experienced through listening. Even as media diversified and evolved, the word was appropriate enough—whether listening, watching, or reading, the audience has largely the same role. But living stories are not only about listening, watching, or reading. They are about *doing*; they both offer us agency and demand that we take action in order to complete the narrative. Those experiencing a living story should no more be called an "audience" than those eating food at a restaurant should be called "observers."

For fifteen years, I struggled to come up with a term that encompassed what this new kind of audience was. Taking a note from Janet Murray's brilliant book on narrative in the digital age, *Hamlet on the Holodeck,* I tried out "interactors," then "players," then "guests," and even—after reading Jay Rosen's article—"the people formerly known as the audience." None of these terms felt like an exact fit.

I finally realized that this new concept needed a new word. I coined the term *actience* to reflect that they are taking an *active* role in the work. You'll see me use this term throughout the book to talk about the audiences who come to living stories—audiences with agency who help co-create these narratives.

This new experience of possessing agency can be incredibly fun, engaging, and impactful. But aside from eliciting profound emotional responses from the individual audience member, having agency changes the role that the creator expects of the audience. Lyn Gardner, theater critic for *The Guardian*, noted in 2014 that in performances where the audience has a role, "perhaps we can no longer hide behind our passivity, claiming that what is happening has nothing to do with us. If the relationship between artists and audiences is built on a different kind of contract perhaps we, the audience, have to take responsibility."

As we, the actience, take on new roles, we will discover and build new skills. We are just beginning to learn our lines, to become familiar with these new avenues for self-expression.

CREATING FOR AGENCY

For millennia, storytellers have exerted near total control over their stories. These stories had a beginning, a middle, and an end, and their narratives did not offer the audience any say in the matter. Now a growing subset of storytellers working in forms such as VR and immersive theater has begun to rethink that old approach. They are letting their audiences make decisions, leaving room for them to create something new within the work, and providing opportunities to see a story from multiple points of view. This new paradigm requires creators to cede some power and control to the audience but at the same time depict their worlds in more detail than ever before. (We'll discuss how creators build detailed, immersive worlds in the next chapter.)

Alejandro González Iñárritu confronted this challenge in the production of *Carne y Arena*. Upon deciding that his audience should be able to freely walk around the simulated environment, he realized that his creative role had changed radically. "As a filmmaker, you are used to controlling the frame," he says. "Each frame is precious, right? Cinema is that little keyhole that you look through." In a sense, he now had less control over the audience's experience, because they could walk around and see the story from whatever angle they chose. But he also had to provide more detail than he would have in film. He describes this challenge using a hypothetical scene in a restaurant: "When you're shooting a guy in a restaurant, you know that behind the camera, there are a lot of people in the restaurant—but you can create that with sound....Here, I have to [show] the whole restaurant, and all the waiters, and everybody has to be in action." He found that he could no longer single out one main character in a scene and focus exclusively on them, because his audience would be able to focus on any character they chose. "It was super exciting," he says, "but super terrifying."

Video-game designers confronted these challenges decades ago, as player agency and open-world games became technically and economically feasible and soon wildly popular. Writing about agency on his blog *gamedesignskills.com*, game designer Alexander Brazie explaines, "Game designers create the bounds, defining what impact the players can have on the game world. Delivering on the promises of choice is no small task: In order for agency to be real, players must have the time, space, and resources to make those decisions and the game must showcase their consequences."

Creators of immersive experiences are addressing these same challenges. In living stories, they are no longer the sole authors of the work—more like mentors, collaborators, and co-creators. Their tasks now include helping the audience succeed at contributing to the story in a way that matters. They must develop a new level of trust for the audience, who will do things beyond the creators' control. Crafting a story without a single, canonical narrative is difficult, though. Creators must relinquish enough control to give players agency, but they also have to balance that with narrative coherence.

Felix Barrett—founder of Punchdrunk, creator of *Sleep No More* and *The Drowned Man*, and one of the legendary pioneers of immersive theater (see p. 40)—describes the challenges of designing a realm that allows for control and personalization: "How do you create an environment where [the audience] doesn't wake up from the dream? Over the years, we spent huge sums just making sure that no natural light could get in, because one crack of natural light would reveal the artifice and the bubble would burst. You architect your own evening." For Barrett, the story-crafting shift leads away from passive entertainment and toward something active, immediate, alive.

The Johnny Cash Project, created in 2010 by directors Chris Milk and Aaron Koblin in collaboration with Rick Rubin and Radical Media, is a great example of how to achieve balance between audience participation and narrative cohesion. The concept was straightforward: They invited Cash's fans to co-create a video for his final studio recording before he died, titled "Ain't No Grave."

After assembling a rough video from existing footage of Cash, the team designed a website where fans could choose and draw a single frame from that video using a web-based painting application. (To match the somber theme of the song, users were limited to a palette of black, white, and shades of gray.) This provided necessary narrative structure, but otherwise gave the audience free rein to create what they wanted. Clearly, it resonated: By September 2010, 250,000 fans from 172 countries around the world had created frames, and when the team released the final version later that year, more than 1.3 million people had contributed. Each time a visitor to the original site played the video, it would be assembled anew, using different fan-created frames; viewers could pause and vote for their favorites. Eventually, Milk and Koblin created a "Director's Cut" with 1,300 of the most popular frames alongside some of their own personal picks.

***The Johnny Cash Project* invited fans to contribute their own drawings to create, frame by frame, a tribute to the late country music legend.**

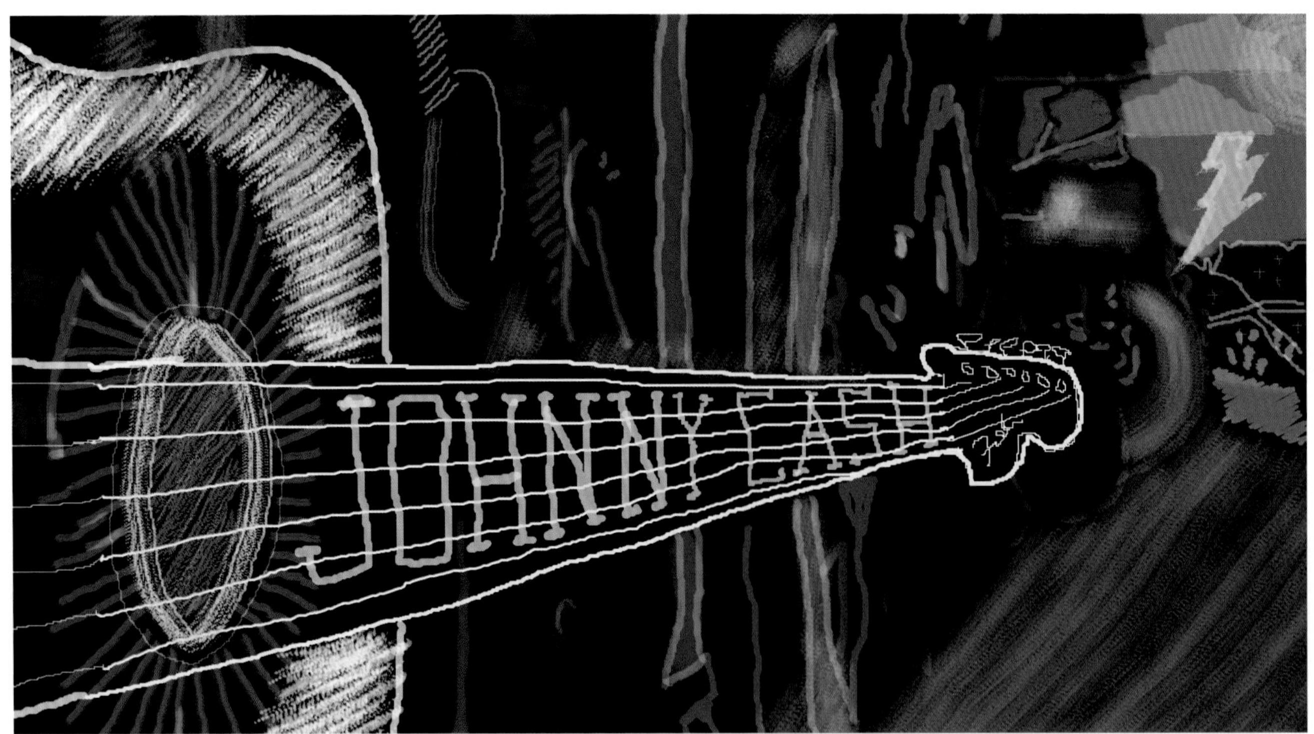

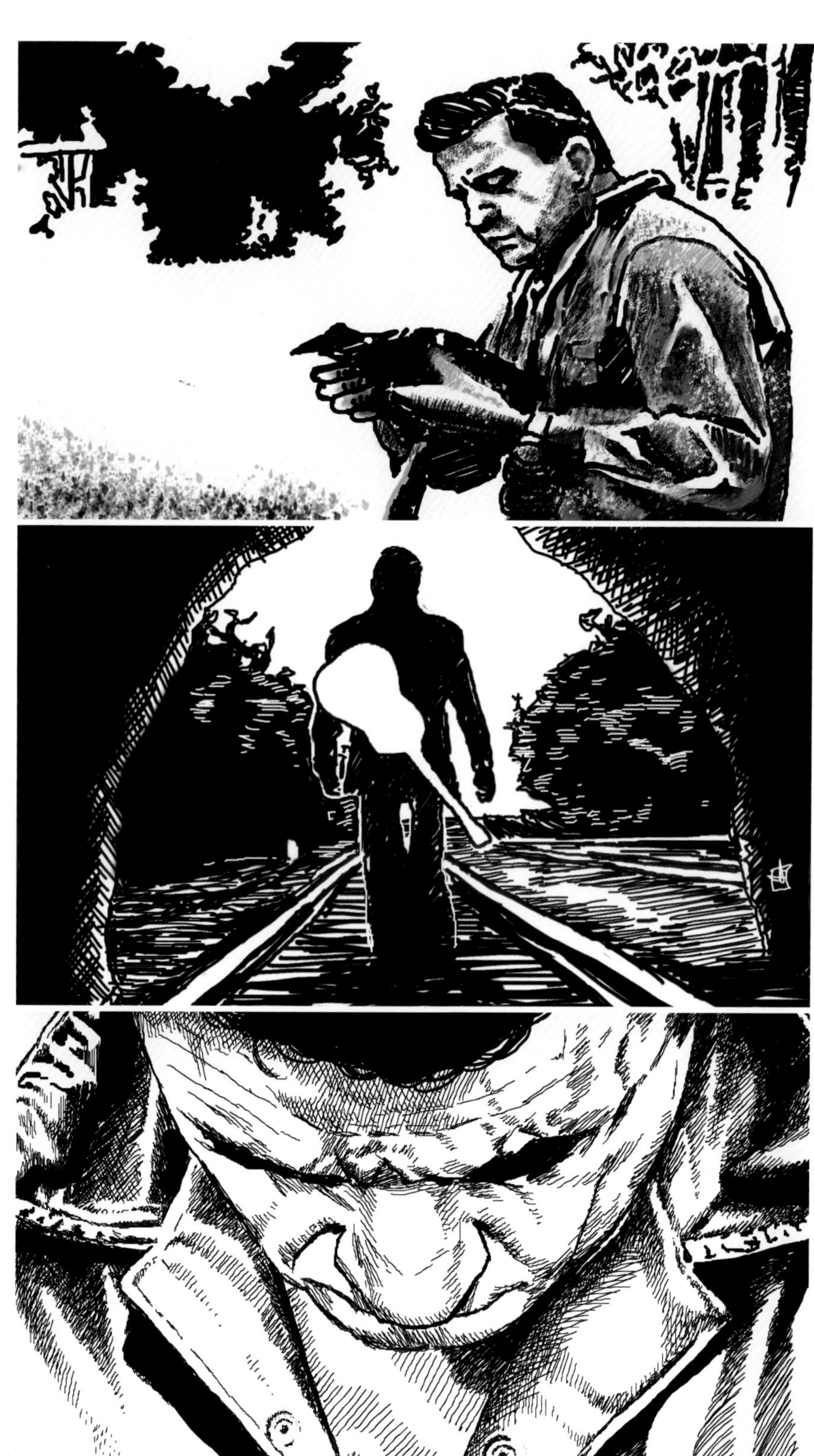
SANDOVAL'10

For Milk, the project revealed the powerful emotional impact that participatory stories could have on audiences. "What I saw with that project was that it was playing a more meaningful role in people's lives," he tells me. "Watching a music video on MTV or YouTube is three and a half minutes of your life. Maybe it tells a story that resonates with you, but it's very much a thing that comes and goes quickly. It's ephemeral. Whereas with *The Johnny Cash Project,* people were spending hours, even days, crafting one single frame of this larger collective portrait of Johnny Cash and talking about how meaningful it was in their life to participate in that. It really opened my eyes to how creating a conversation between the audience and the work led to a more meaningful relationship between the audience and that work."

"*The Johnny Cash Project*...really opened my eyes to how creating a conversation between the audience and the work led to a more meaningful relationship between the audience and that work." —CHRIS MILK

The term *crowdsourcing* was coined in 2006, but it has been part of Internet culture for much longer, as collaborative works like Wikipedia and Linux were built. What made Milk and Koblin's project so memorable was the integrity between form and content, and the ability to give the fans artistic voice to pay tribute to the musician they love. They embraced the chance to contribute to the project, to exert their own influence—small, yes, but equal to that of any other fan—over the video and, in some small way, over Cash's legacy. Milk's final cut is dark and moody, reflecting the intensity of Cash's artistry in his last years. "The work became a conversation," he says, "between the audience and the artist."

FREEING PROSPERO WITH A GAME ENGINE

In the final monologue of Shakespeare's *The Tempest,* the usurped duke Prospero, trapped on a barren island for twelve years, beseeches the audience to free him with their applause and cheers:

> But release me from my bands
> With the help of your good hands.
> Gentle breath of yours my sails
> Must fill, or else my project fails,
> Which was to please.

The play, thought to be Shakespeare's last solo work, has often been read as a commentary on the relationship between a storyteller, their characters, and their audience. Like Prospero, who had spent the play using his magical powers to control the lives of others, Shakespeare had spent his career bending his characters to his will and putting them in situations that suited his own dramatic aims. But here, in the final words of his final play, he acknowledged that all his powers were useless without an audience to believe in them. In the words of Samantha Gorman, cofounder of VR studio Tender Claws, "Essentially, Prospero was bowing out and saying, 'This cannot be completed or envisioned without you, my audience.'"

During the summer of 2020, at the height of the Covid-19 pandemic, Tender Claws premiered a VR experience based on *The Tempest*. The year before, they had built one called *The Under Presents* in which many of the virtual characters that players could meet were in fact "puppeted" by live actors in real time. "You'd be playing the game," explains Tender Claws cofounder Danny Cannizzaro, "and a live actor,

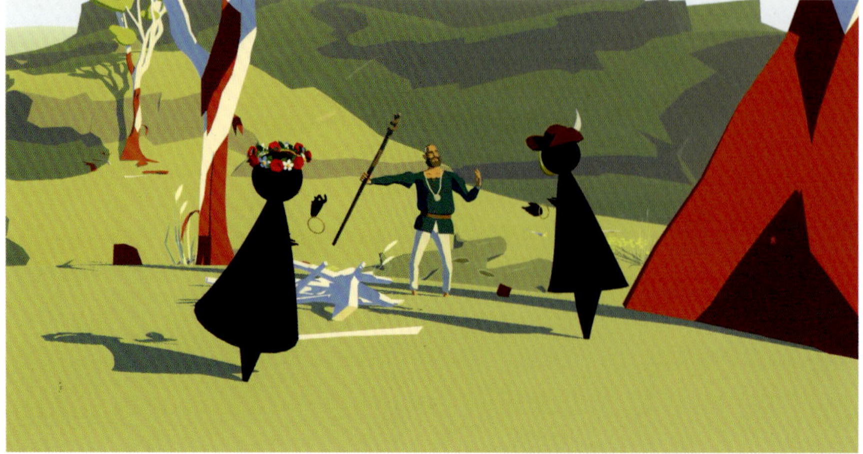

Participants in *The Under Presents: Tempest* had the ability to affect the workings of the virtual play—exploring settings, taking on quests, and interacting with live actors.

in a headset somewhere across the world, could pull you aside, deliver a monologue, set you off on a quest, or teach you a spell."

When the pandemic hit and many of their actor friends found themselves out of work, Gorman and Cannizzaro realized that with *The Under Presents* they had created the perfect platform for staging virtual plays. And what better play to adapt for a VR experience that would invite the audience to participate in the narrative than Shakespeare's famous meditation on the power dynamics of the theater?

In *The Under Presents: Tempest*, a small group of theatergoers was transported to a bonfire outside a mansion in the Hollywood Hills, where they met an actor who was set to play Prospero in a production of Shakespeare's play that was canceled thanks to the pandemic. The actor then guided the participants through an interactive reimagining of the play, using godlike powers to lead them through a variety of settings and all the while relying on them to complete the action taking place.

Tender Claws built in tools for their live actors to control aspects of the environment. "Each actor was not only in charge of the movement and the speaking of their character but was also acting as the lighting manager and the sound-cue person," Cannizzaro says. "They had powers over the world. They could cue moments, spawn objects—the whole virtual world became almost like an instrument they could play. In the final scene, the actor is literally conducting a storm."

In the next era of storytelling, storytellers, actors, and audiences will all have new roles to play, and everyone involved might have opportunities to exert control over the story. But giving some agency to the audience doesn't have to mean losing agency entirely as a storyteller. "We still feel like we're keeping a lot of authorial control," says Cannizzaro. "It's just instead of directly authoring a single experience, we're authoring a set of possibilities."

FROM ORALITY TO LITERACY TO . . . SOMETHING ELSE

All of these advances in participatory narrative, from social media to VR to experiments in hybrid digital and live experiences, have inaugurated a new era of human communication. Will the transition to agentic, immersive, two-way media be as far-reaching as the shift from orality to literacy? Will our brains be rewired, our sources of truth change, our society restructure? So far, each leap forward in media technology and presentation, from writing to the printing press to film and television to the Internet, has precipitated dramatic shifts in culture. Perhaps the next wave will have more in common with our origins as an oral culture than the written culture that followed.

In the grand epic of human history, we journeyed from a world where stories were communal, collaborative, participatory, and euphoric to a culture of passive audiences. Our agency within stories was stripped away. In this sense, the new era of living stories feels less like a sea change and more like a course correction.

When I tell Chris Milk about a powerful moment I had experienced in one of his VR pieces, he's quick to remind me that it didn't belong to him alone. "It was your moment too," he says. "It will forever be your story. The memory is not that of a story that you witnessed—it's a story that you lived."

Once upon a time, we humans sat around our campfires, creating and enacting and *living* our stories together. As the audience regains their agency, our imaginations are being unleashed. We are only now seeing the first hints of how this huge shift will change us, but it's clear how it's changed our stories: They have come back to life.

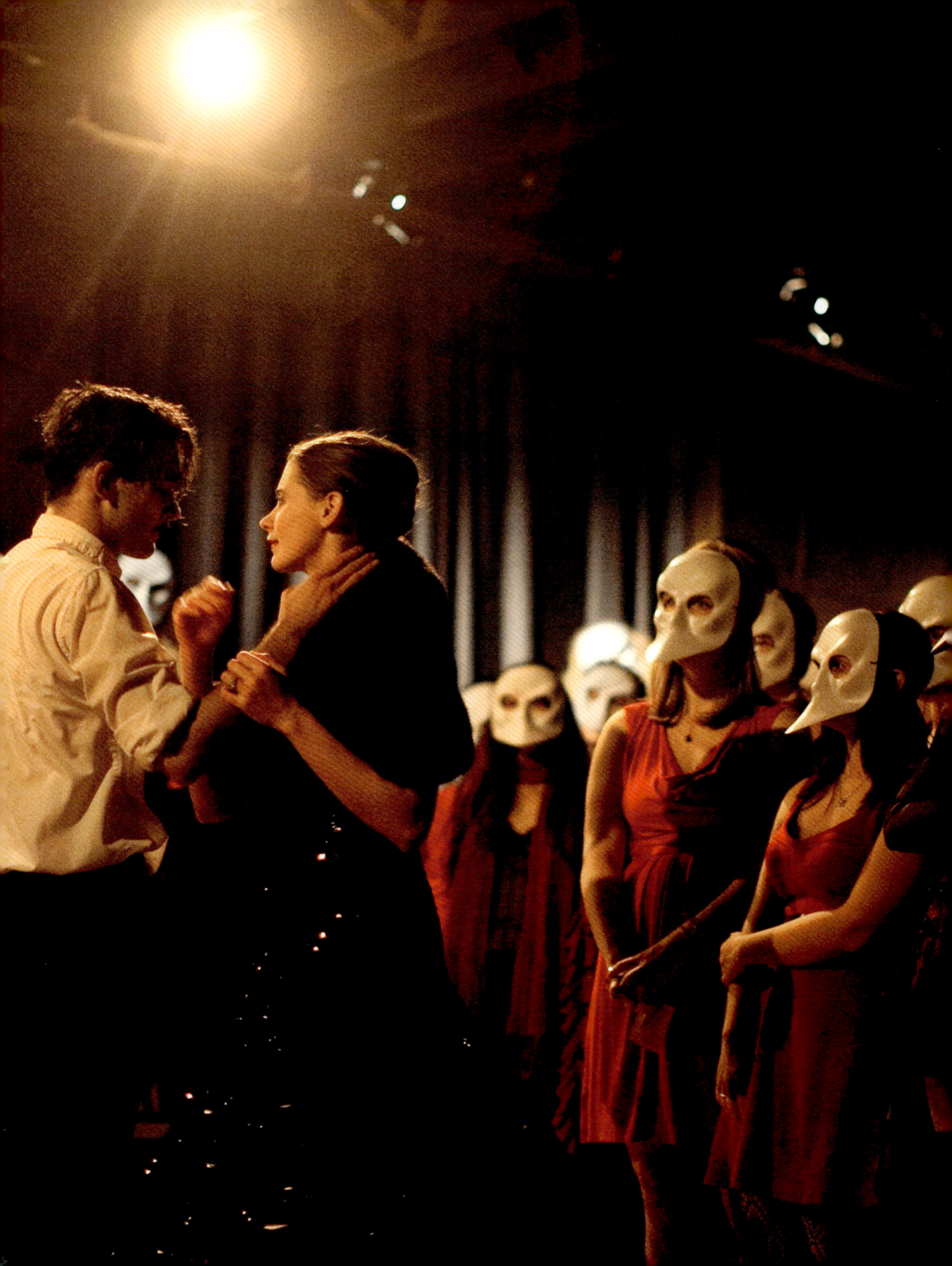

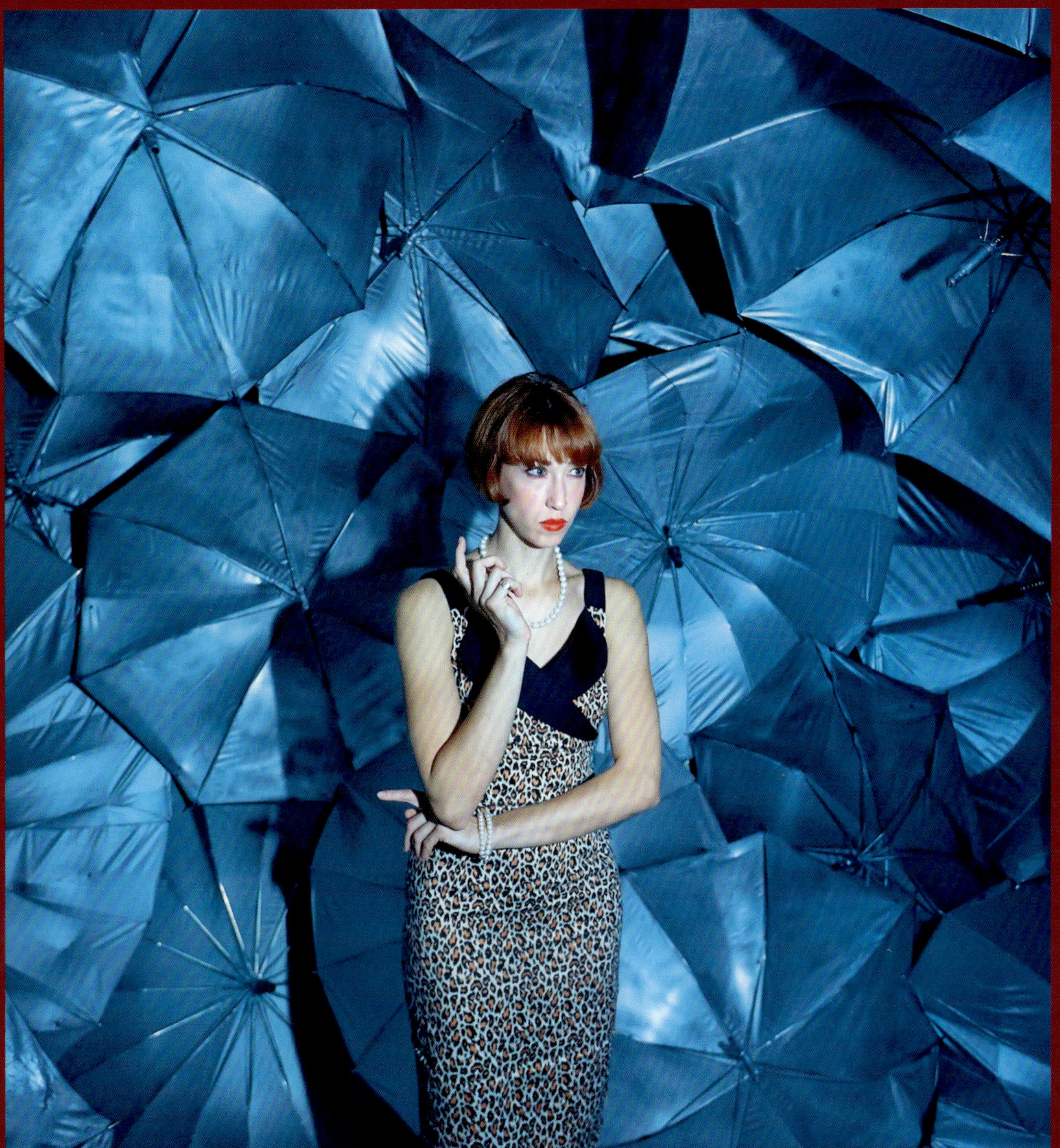

PUNCHDRUNK

When Felix Barrett founded Punchdrunk back in 2000, his goal was to "break the rules" of conventional theater, to make it feel daring and "dangerous" again. It was a daunting task for an art form practically as old as culture—and yet when the company's *Macbeth* adaptation, *Sleep No More*, opened in London in 2003, it became the spark that quickly ignited an entire movement of interactive theater. In a Punchdrunk production, there is no stage for performers alone to tread; no seats for the audience to passively sink into; no "fourth wall" to divide them from one another. Instead, a Punchdrunk production offers a whole world in which audiences can submerge themselves.

Interactive theater was not unheard of before Punchdrunk arrived on the scene, but Barrett pushed it a step further with "masked shows," the type of production for which his company is best known: evocative dance-filled dramas

In *The Drowned Man* (above) and *Sleep No More* (opposite), masked audience members were invited to observe and interact with unmasked actors.

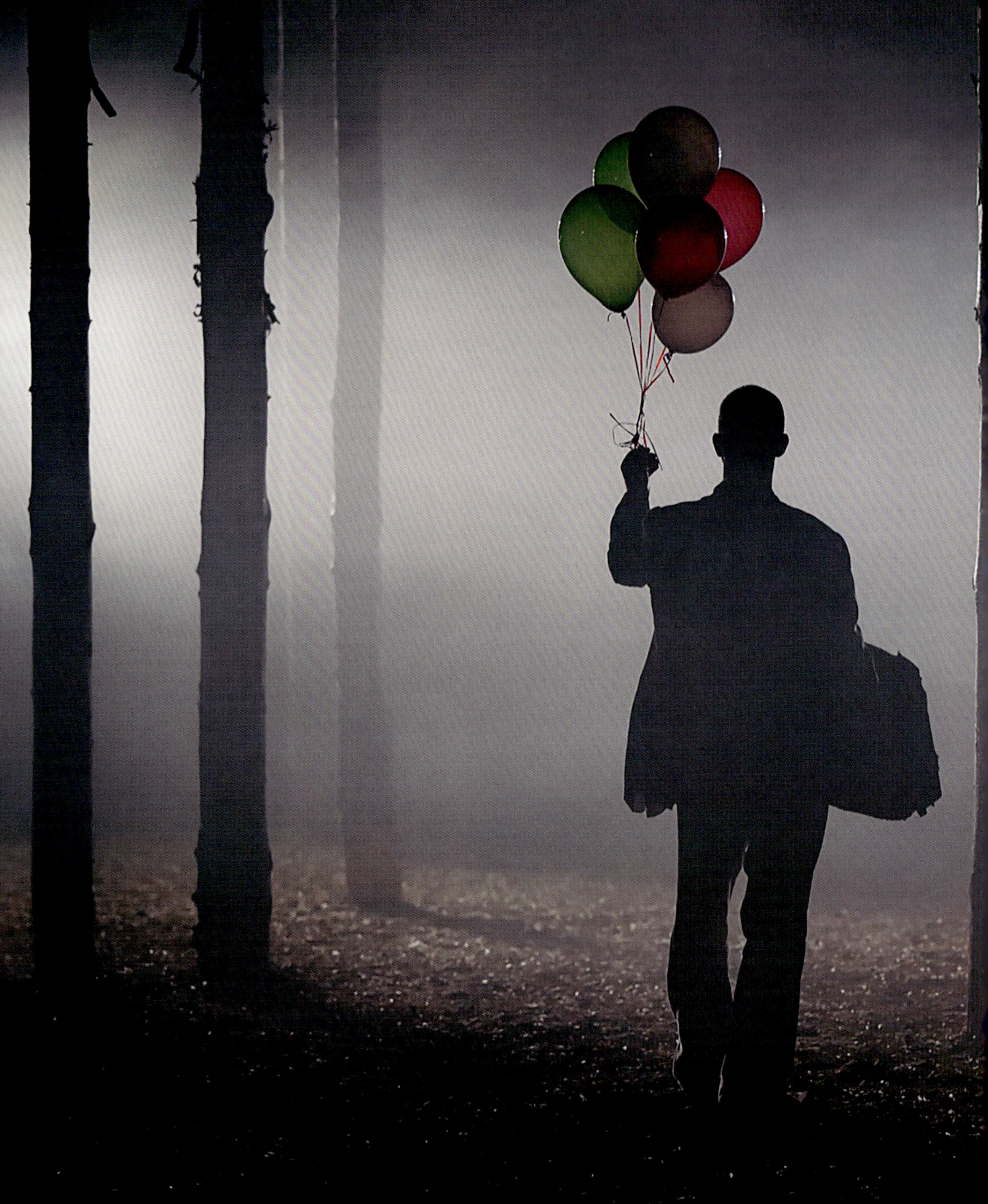

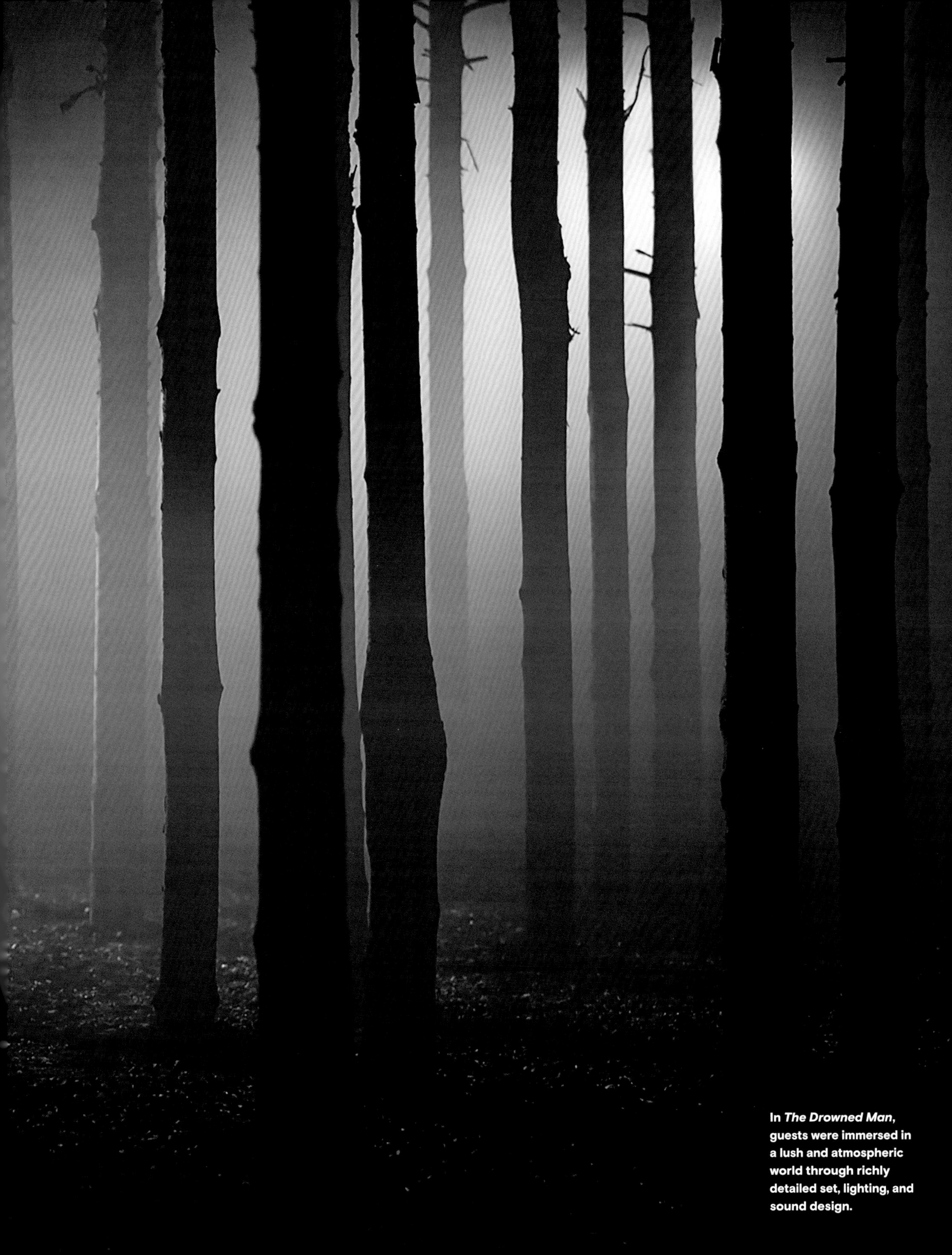

In *The Drowned Man*, guests were immersed in a lush and atmospheric world through richly detailed set, lighting, and sound design.

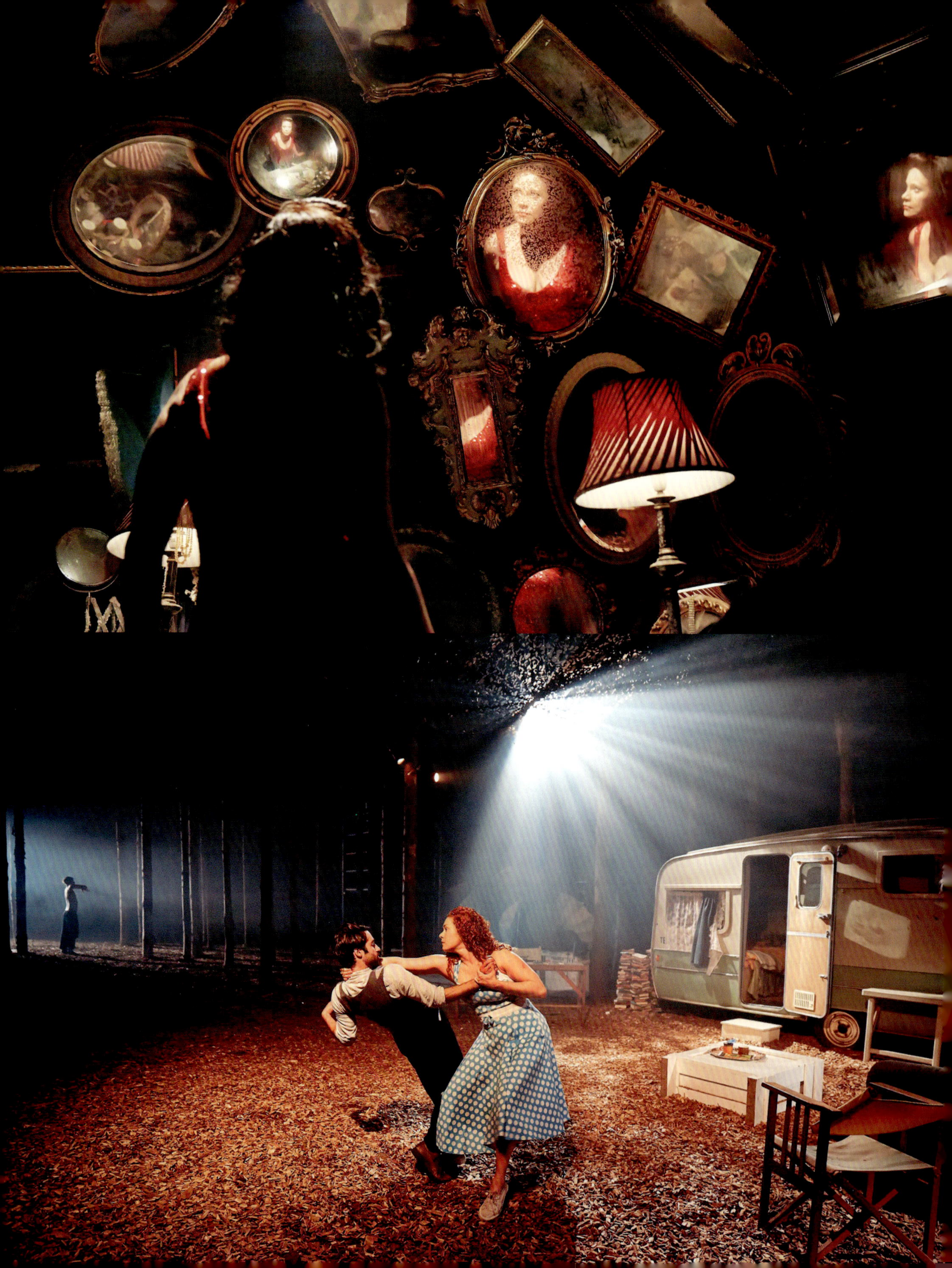

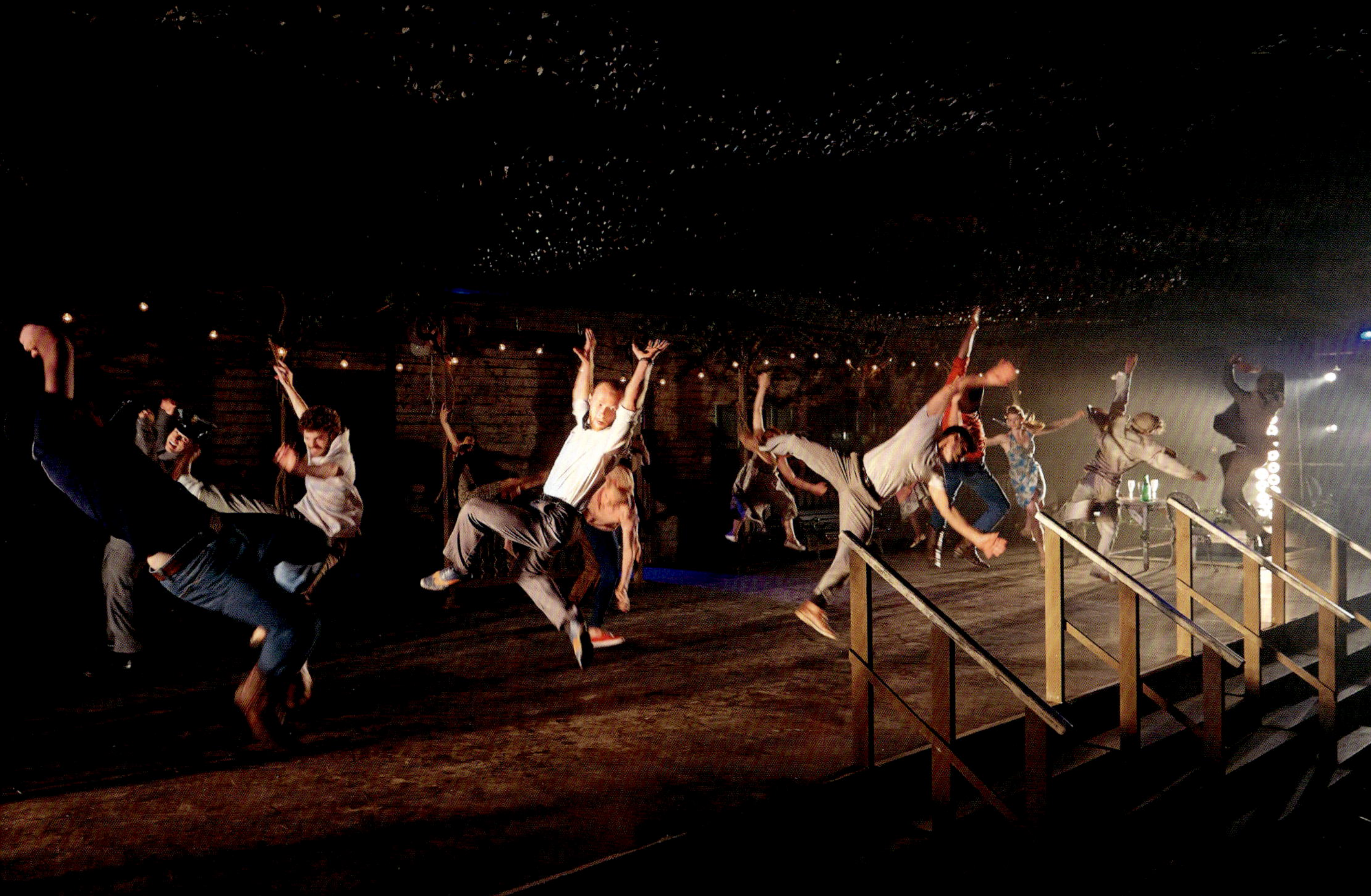

where the audience, clad in stark white masks, are allowed to wander freely through scenes and among the unmasked performers. With scant few directives aside from maintaining silence and keeping the mask on, participants are granted a level of agency that could make your head spin if all you knew before was the stiff etiquette of traditional theater. In *Sleep No More*, *The Drowned Man*, *The Burnt City*, and other masked Punchdrunk shows, the curtain dissolves as the stage expands over an enormous space (*Sleep No More*'s long-running New York incarnation, for example, occupied 100,000 square feet and allowed for some 450 audience members per show) filled with exquisitely detailed sets, props, dramatic lighting, and music that makes your hair stand on end. The mask is not just a costume: Functionally, it distinguishes audience members from the actors while also affording them some anonymity; psychologically, it frees participants from self-consciousness and the judgment of others, making them feel more daring and the experience more thrilling. Through the mask's eyes, participants witness characters darting from room to room, performing different fragments of their stories before disappearing again—and leaving the audience to decide if they want to follow. And if you're lucky enough to experience a rare one-on-one scene, where a cast member takes you aside in a secret place and removes your mask, you may find that you have become less of who you were before entering this world and more a part of the dream unfolding within.

It is a testament to Punchdrunk's magic that *Sleep No More*'s original six-week planned run continually extended for twelve years, which amounted to more than 5,000 performances between London, Boston, New York, and Shanghai, making it one of the most successful and influential immersive theater shows of all time. Those who had the opportunity to take part in one of these shows—whether once, twice, or dozens of times—will not soon forget their genre-defining power, nor will they want to miss any of Punchdrunk's future productions.

***The Drowned Man* told much of its story through dance.**

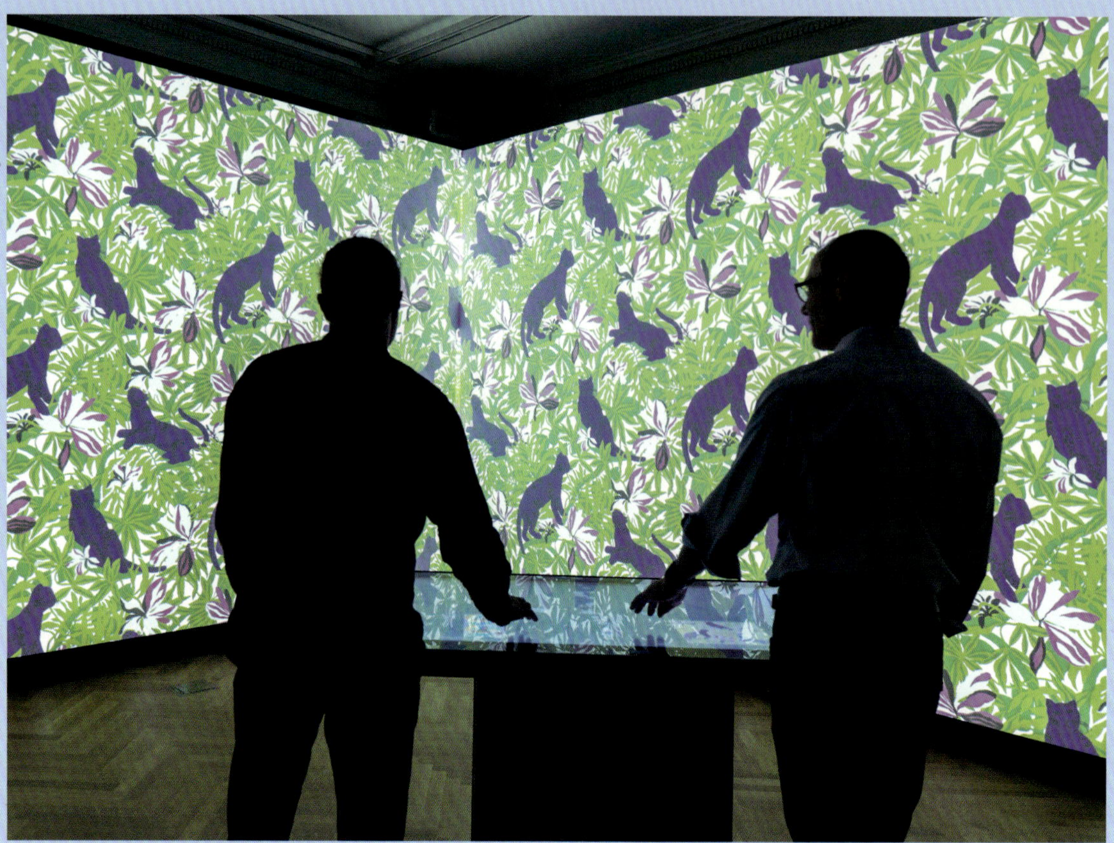

LOCAL PROJECTS

Local Projects is a boundary-breaking interactive design firm that collaborates with museums, brands, and public spaces to develop innovative approaches to storytelling. As founder Jake Barton puts it, "Our mix of creative technology and physical design delivers memorable experiences that stick with visitors." Since their founding in 2005, Local Projects has earned more than 100 major design awards, including the Interaction Design National Design Award, AIGA Design Competition for Effective Design, and *Fast Company*'s Design Studio of the Year.

Local Projects masterfully uses technology and physical interaction to deepen emotional connections to stories. For instance, they designed the world's first voice-activated museum dedicated to language, Planet Word in Washington, D.C. The museum's ten interactive exhibits bring words to life, including books that animate with projected visuals and cinematic narrations, a village filled with word-based mysteries and puzzles, and a kinetic sculpture showcasing conversations with native speakers of multiple languages. In the Word Worlds gallery, visitors can use a "smart paintbrush" to select a word and "paint" it. As they brush the walls, a projected landscape blooms with imagery that reveals the meaning of the chosen word. Each stroke of the paintbrush evolves the artwork, creating a dynamic, embodied vocabulary learning experience.

At the Cleveland Museum of Art's Gallery One, Local Projects was tasked with engaging a diverse audience, from art novices to seasoned experts. Their solution was a massive touchscreen wall that displays the gallery's collection, allowing visitors to explore the catalog by creative themes like color and shape. A swipe feature enables guests to save their favorite artworks from the large screen onto a tablet. Once satisfied with their selections, the app designs a custom tour, so museumgoers can navigate to their chosen pieces. Throughout the rest of the gallery, Local Projects incorporates

Clockwise from above: **Guests express their creativity through physical interactions with the collections at the Cooper Hewitt Smithsonian Design Museum, Greenwood Rising, and the Cleveland Museum of Art.**

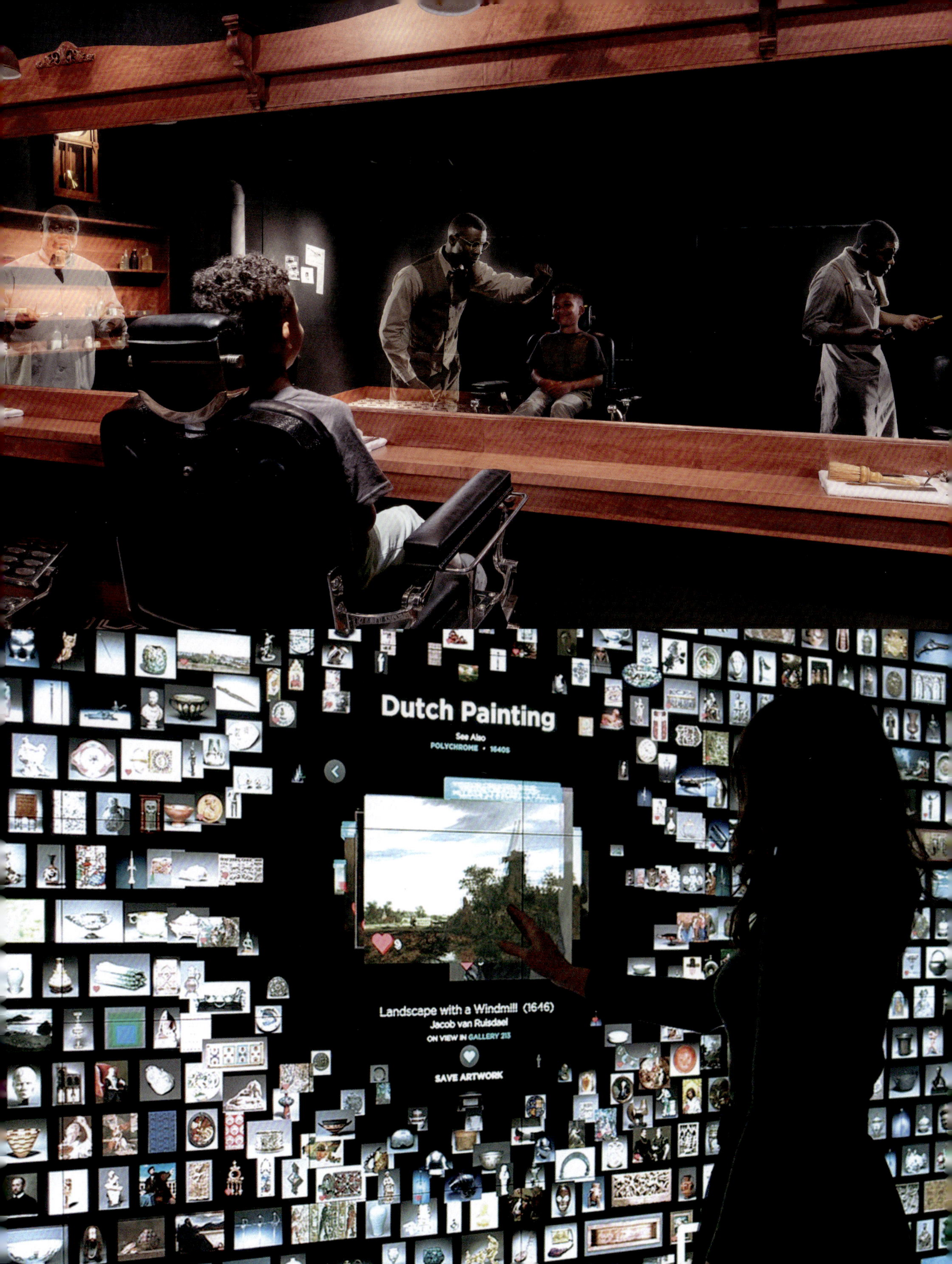
Dutch Painting
See Also
POLYCHROME • 1640S
Landscape with a Windmill (1646)
Jacob van Ruisdael
ON VIEW IN GALLERY 213
SAVE ARTWORK

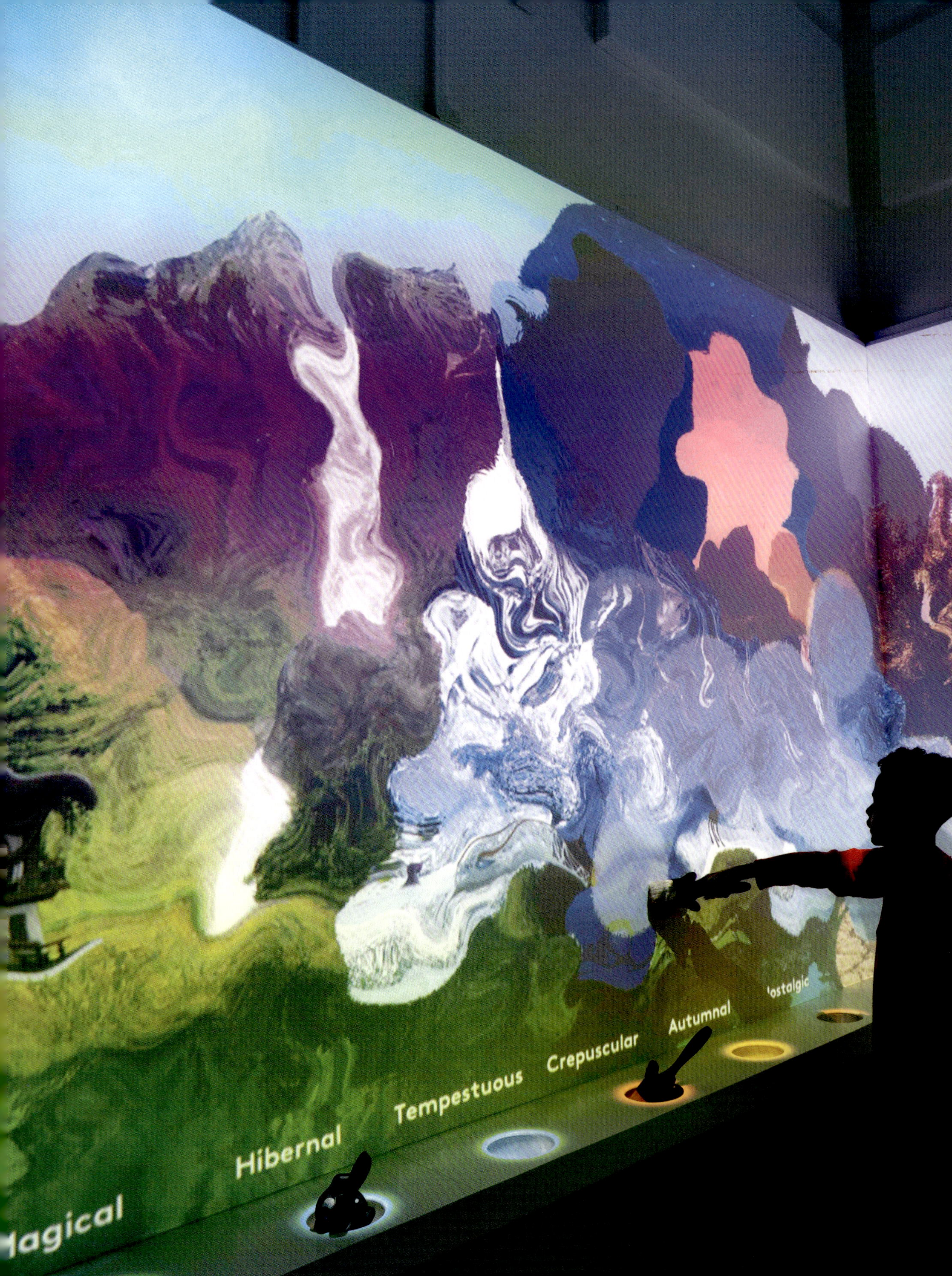
Hibernal
Tempestuous
Crepuscular
Autumnal

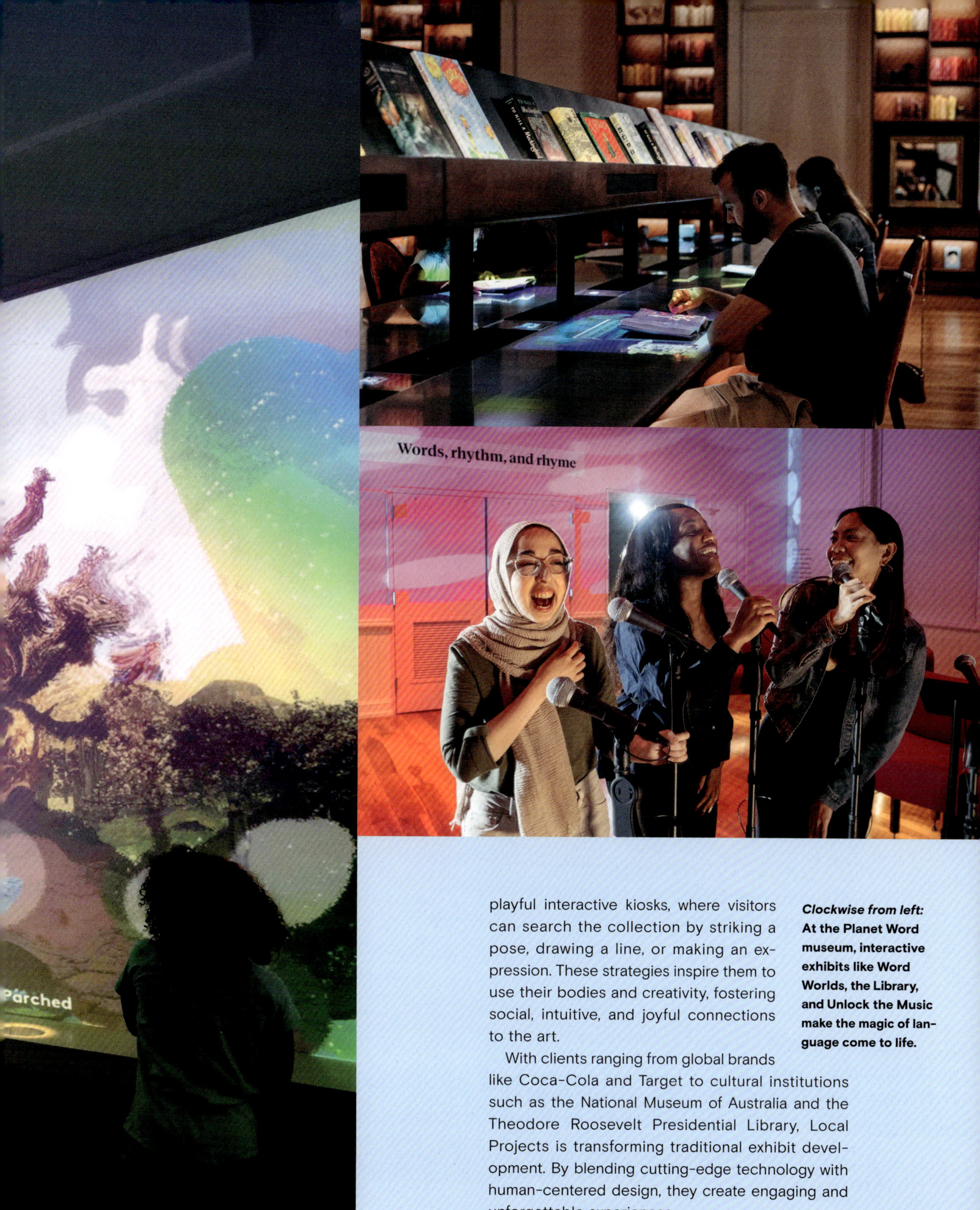

Clockwise from left: **At the Planet Word museum, interactive exhibits like Word Worlds, the Library, and Unlock the Music make the magic of language come to life.**

playful interactive kiosks, where visitors can search the collection by striking a pose, drawing a line, or making an expression. These strategies inspire them to use their bodies and creativity, fostering social, intuitive, and joyful connections to the art.

With clients ranging from global brands like Coca-Cola and Target to cultural institutions such as the National Museum of Australia and the Theodore Roosevelt Presidential Library, Local Projects is transforming traditional exhibit development. By blending cutting-edge technology with human-centered design, they create engaging and unforgettable experiences.

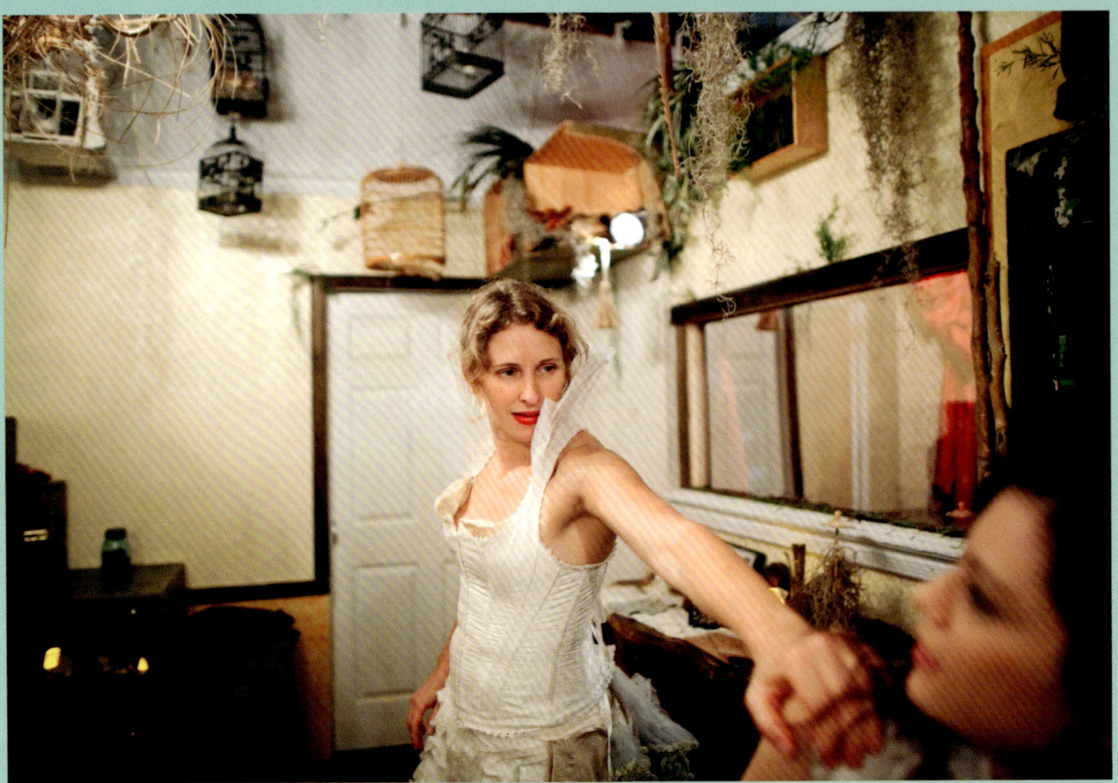

THEN SHE FELL

In a word, the work of Zach Morris, Tom Pearson, and Jennine Willet—collectively known as Third Rail Projects—is *intimate*. In *Then She Fell*, their exquisitely liminal production inspired by the life and writings of Lewis Carroll, participants were part of an audience no larger than fifteen people per show. The White Queen, the Mad Hatter, and other iconic characters took each guest by the hand, sometimes literally, to lead them through carefully choreographed narrative vignettes as a dance/scene partner. A participant might have been tucked in with a bedtime story, given a draught to drink, or asked to help Alice herself finish combing her hair. In many scenarios, participants could find themselves alone with a character, and the scene that unfolded felt as if it were being performed with them, as a duet or a dialogue, rather than for them.

Then She Fell earned renown in the theater community due to its unique design philosophy and the emotionally powerful experience that resulted. Morris, Pearson, and Willet wanted to treat the audience not as spectators or side characters but as key contributors. Each participant was thoughtfully invited in and treated with the utmost care so that they too could give their best performance. The depth of the engagement was left in each person's hands: Lean in and the story would embrace you; lean back and it would leave you be. Doors were opened, trust was built, and, ultimately, a genuine intimacy emerged.

In a revolutionary reimagining of creative control, Third Rail Projects' trio of director-choreographers leaves crucial aspects of their work at the mercy of the public, leading to a heightened experience for all involved. The show ran for seven years in Brooklyn, with an impressive 4,444 performances—a testament to the show's power and audiences' desire for participatory storytelling. Morris, Pearson, and Willet have since gone on to teach, consult, and produce more immersive site-specific work with collaborators like Lincoln Center and the Denver Center for the Performing Arts while maintaining the intimacy that makes their craft so notable.

***Clockwise from above:* Performances by characters such as the White Queen, Lewis Carroll, and Alice were highly choreographed to engage the audience and take full advantage of the tables, chairs, and walls of the intricate sets.**

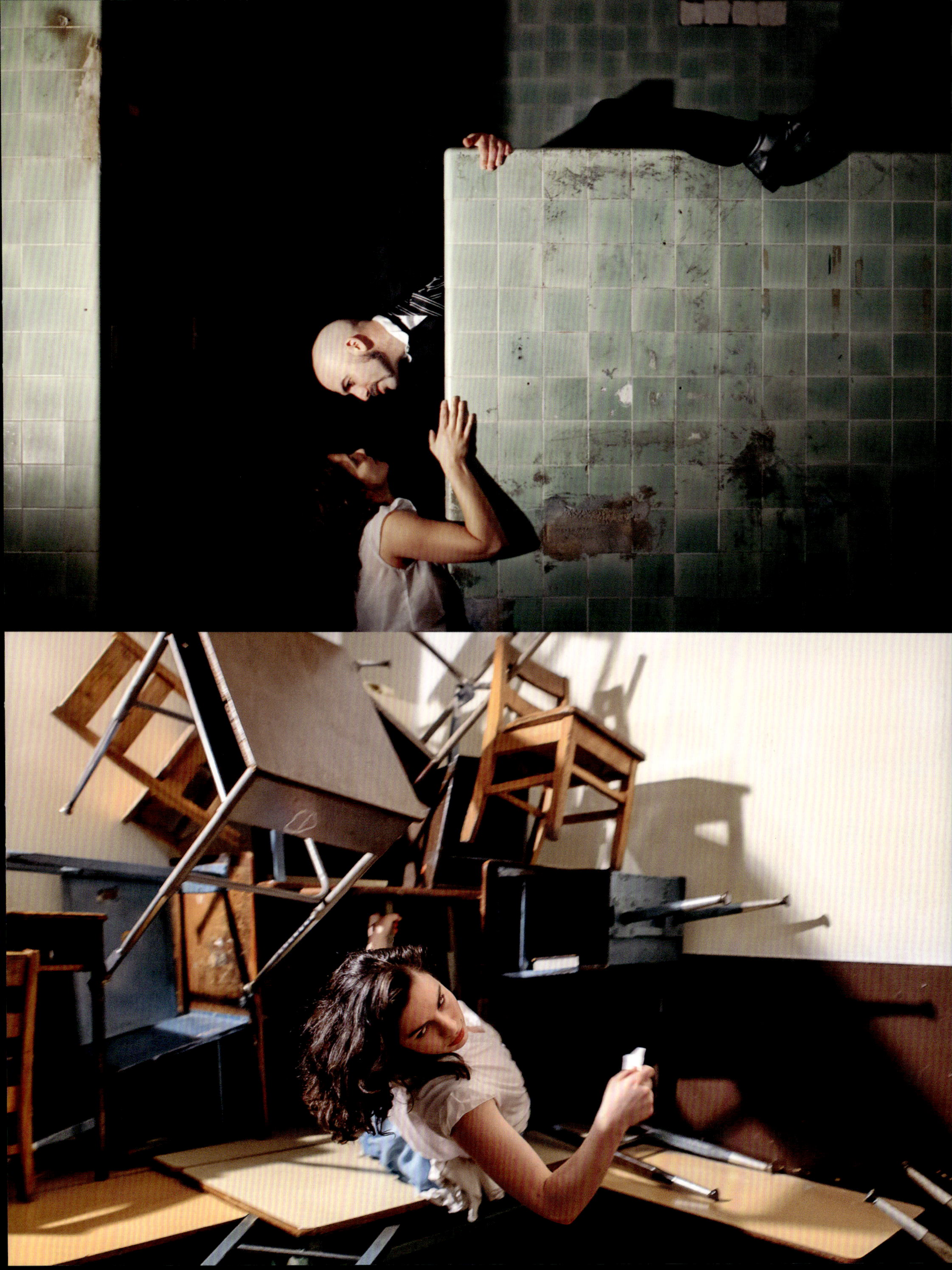

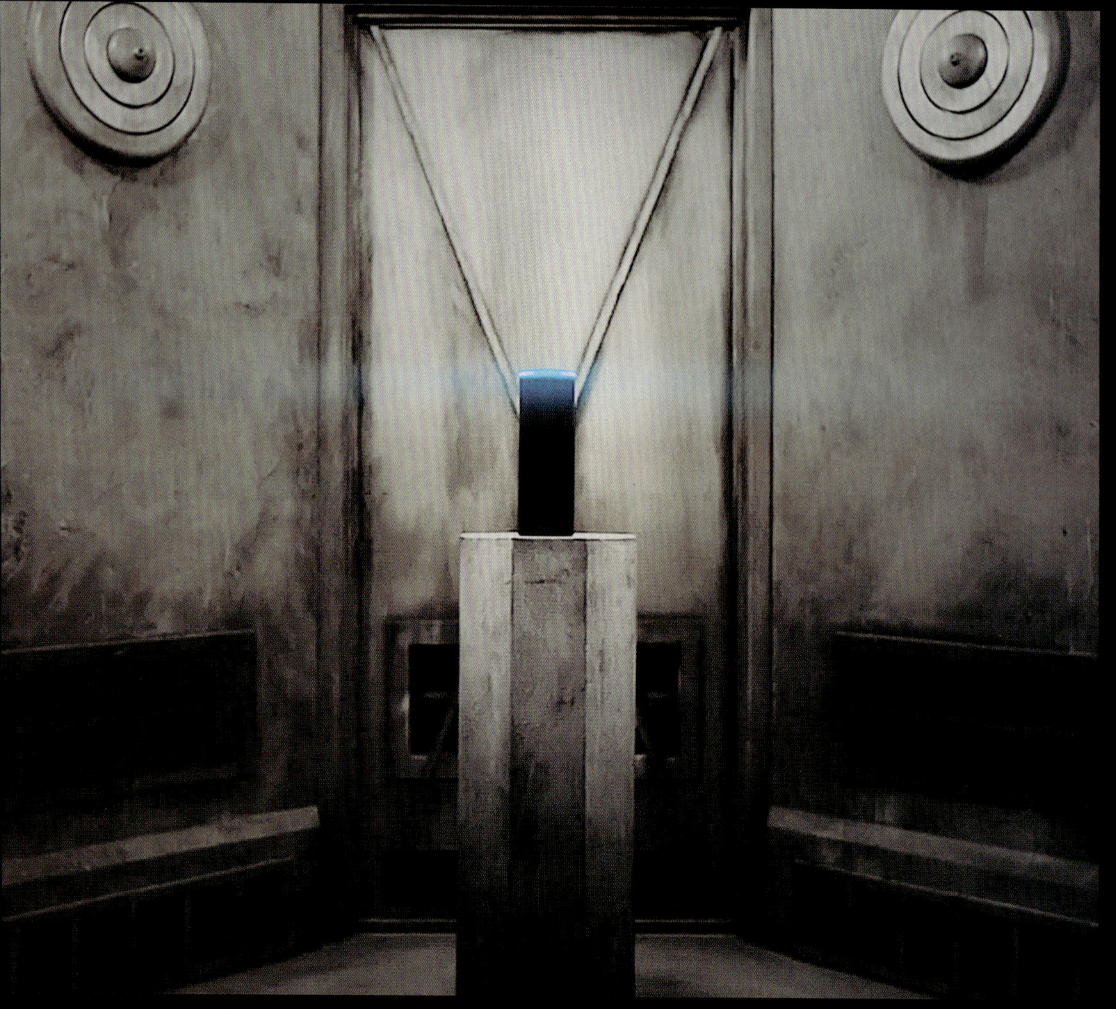

AMAZON ECHO ESCAPE

You're trapped in a room with a group of strangers, and only your voice can save you...specifically, your voice in conversation with Alexa. Amazon Echo Escape was a marketing activation experience produced by AKQA that introduced the public to the new Echo device. It debuted at New York Comic Con in 2017, becoming the hit of the convention with more than 5,000 people eager to participate.

Set in the world of *Tom Clancy's Jack Ryan*, the experience dropped participants into a thrilling high-stakes story where they had to utilize Alexa's voice-activated features to discover information, solve puzzles, control devices, and interact with live actors. The key, they soon discovered, was to figure out the most effective way to engage with Alexa: commanding her to turn off the lights to reveal a message only visible in ultraviolet, calling an informant played by an actor, or displaying the feed from a surveillance camera outside the building. This was no mere tech demo; this physically immersive, voice-activated interaction allowed users to directly communicate with Alexa's diverse functionalities, fostering an intuitive understanding of the product's capabilities.

Amazon and AKQA brilliantly crafted the experience to appeal to a marketing-resistant audience. By embedding the Echo's functionalities into a compelling escape-room narrative, they managed to introduce the device in an engaging, positive light, wherein Alexa was a trusted and helpful companion

***Above:* The centerpiece and main mechanic of the escape room, Amazon's Alexa. *Opposite:* Participants used Alexa to perform a variety of tasks, such as turning on a fan that scattered money throughout the room for players to examine, changing the light colors to reveal a hidden message, and communicating with fellow players while handcuffed.**

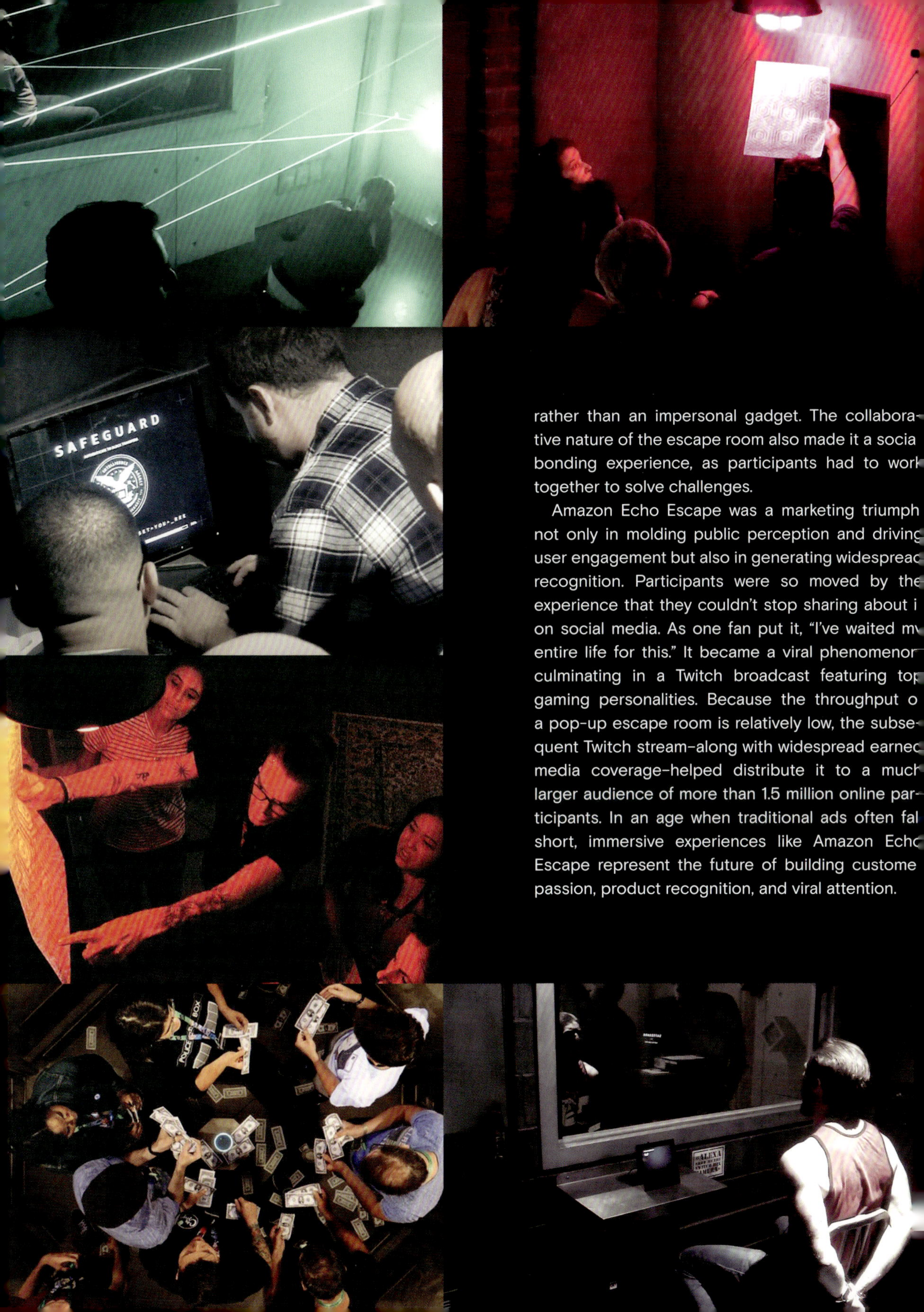

rather than an impersonal gadget. The collaborative nature of the escape room also made it a socia bonding experience, as participants had to work together to solve challenges.

Amazon Echo Escape was a marketing triumph not only in molding public perception and driving user engagement but also in generating widespreac recognition. Participants were so moved by the experience that they couldn't stop sharing about i on social media. As one fan put it, "I've waited my entire life for this." It became a viral phenomenon culminating in a Twitch broadcast featuring top gaming personalities. Because the throughput o a pop-up escape room is relatively low, the subsequent Twitch stream–along with widespread earnec media coverage–helped distribute it to a much larger audience of more than 1.5 million online participants. In an age when traditional ads often fal short, immersive experiences like Amazon Echo Escape represent the future of building custome passion, product recognition, and viral attention.

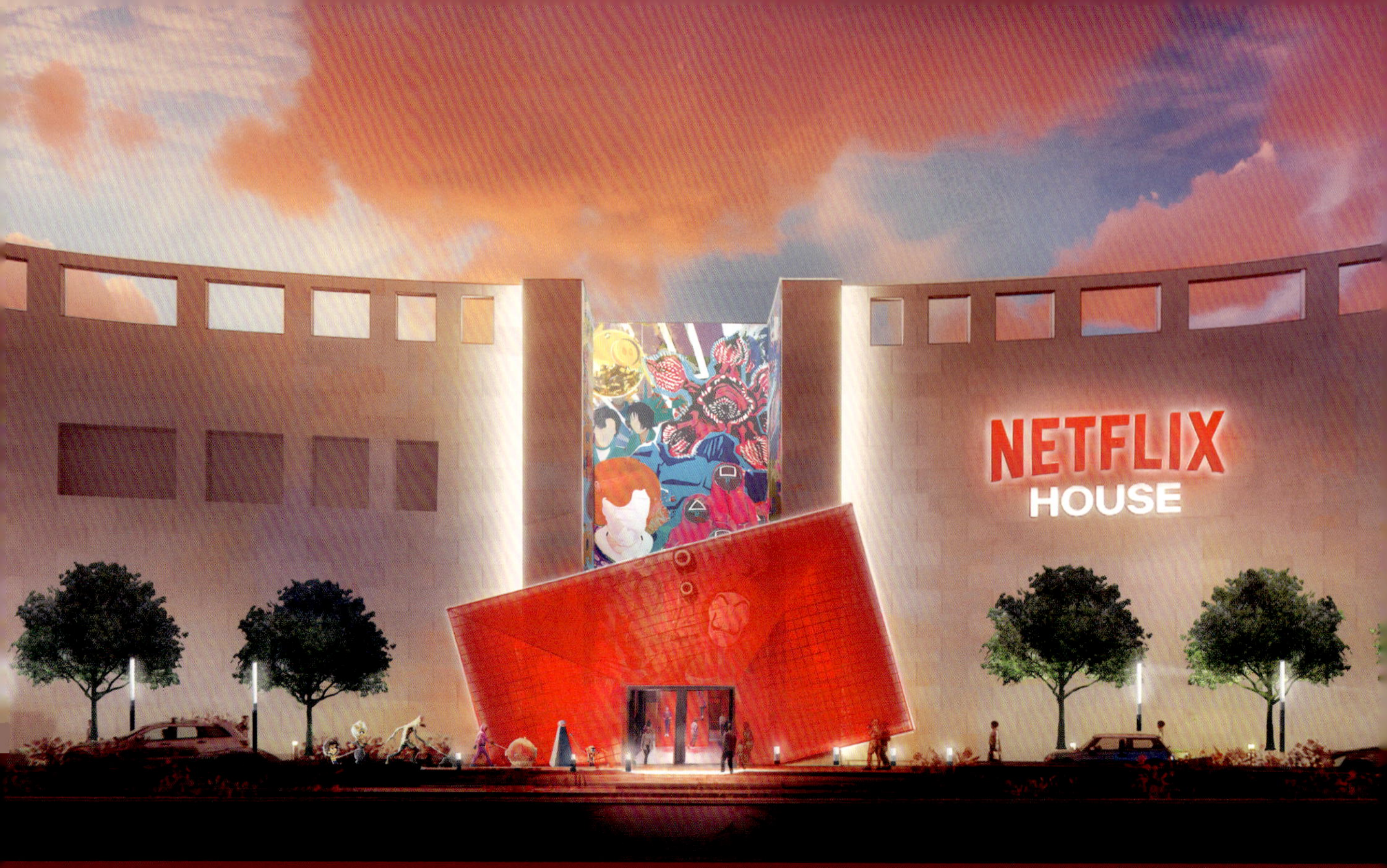

NETFLIX

Dance the night away at the Queen's Ball. Use your psychic powers to thwart the schemes of evil scientists and otherworldly monsters. Break into a vault and execute a bank heist. These are just a few of the fantasies that Netflix allows you to live out with immersive experiences dedicated to some of its biggest shows. Formerly confined to passive binge-watching, fans of *Bridgerton*, *Stranger Things*, *Money Heist*, and more can now have their own hero moment within the story worlds they love.

Clockwise from above: **An exterior view of the new home of Netflix experiences, Netflix House; guests at *Stranger Things: The Experience* posing for a photo on a set replicating one of the distinctive settings from the show; participants try out their psychic powers.**

The primary goal with these detailed immersive experiences isn't simply to sell tickets—though they are wildly popular. In the words of Netflix's head of live experiences, Greg Lombardo, their true aim is to give fans "more ways to love these stories and more ways to love Netflix." While shows may be between seasons, their corresponding experiences are running all over the world, feeding viewers' hunger for high-quality content that will keep them engaged with their favorite characters until the next batch of episodes is released.

Each Netflix immersive production is carefully planned to give guests an authentic role in the story world and allow for the ultimate fan wish fulfillment. Attendees at the *Bridgerton* Queen's Ball were encouraged to come dressed in Regency-era cosplay and had an opportunity to be presented to the Queen herself. In the *Stranger Things: The*

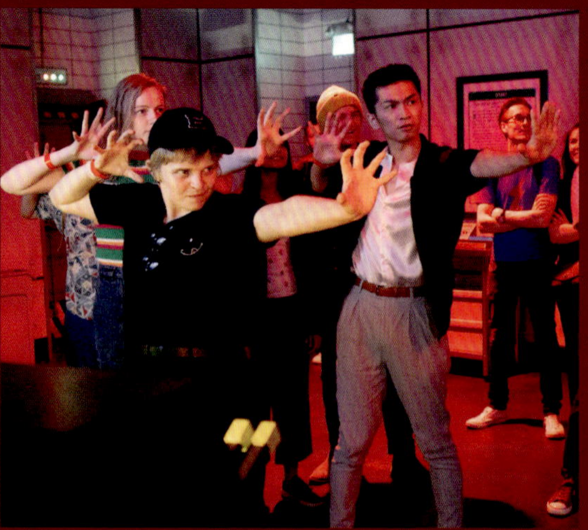

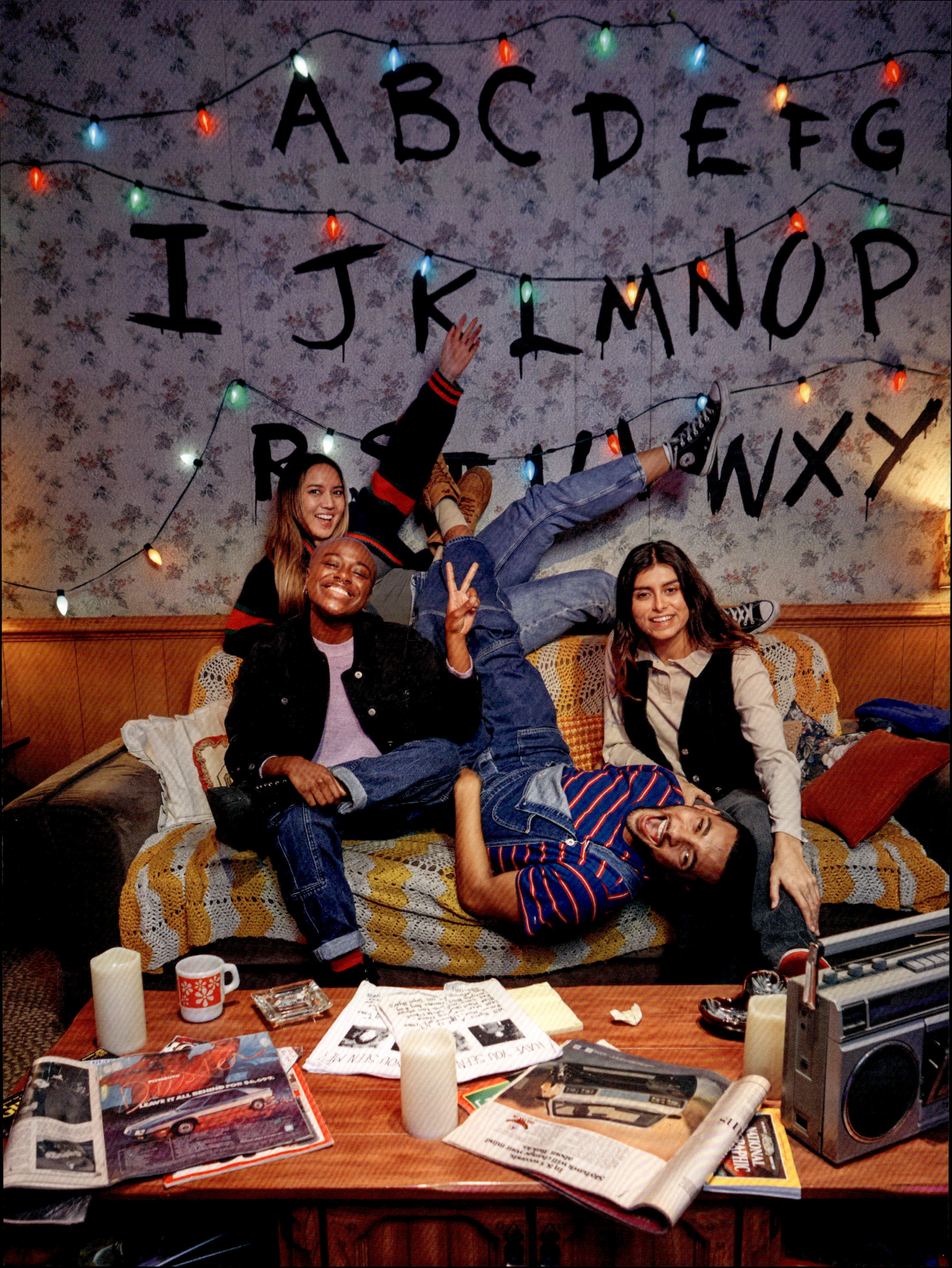

A B C D E F G
I J K L M N O P
W X Y

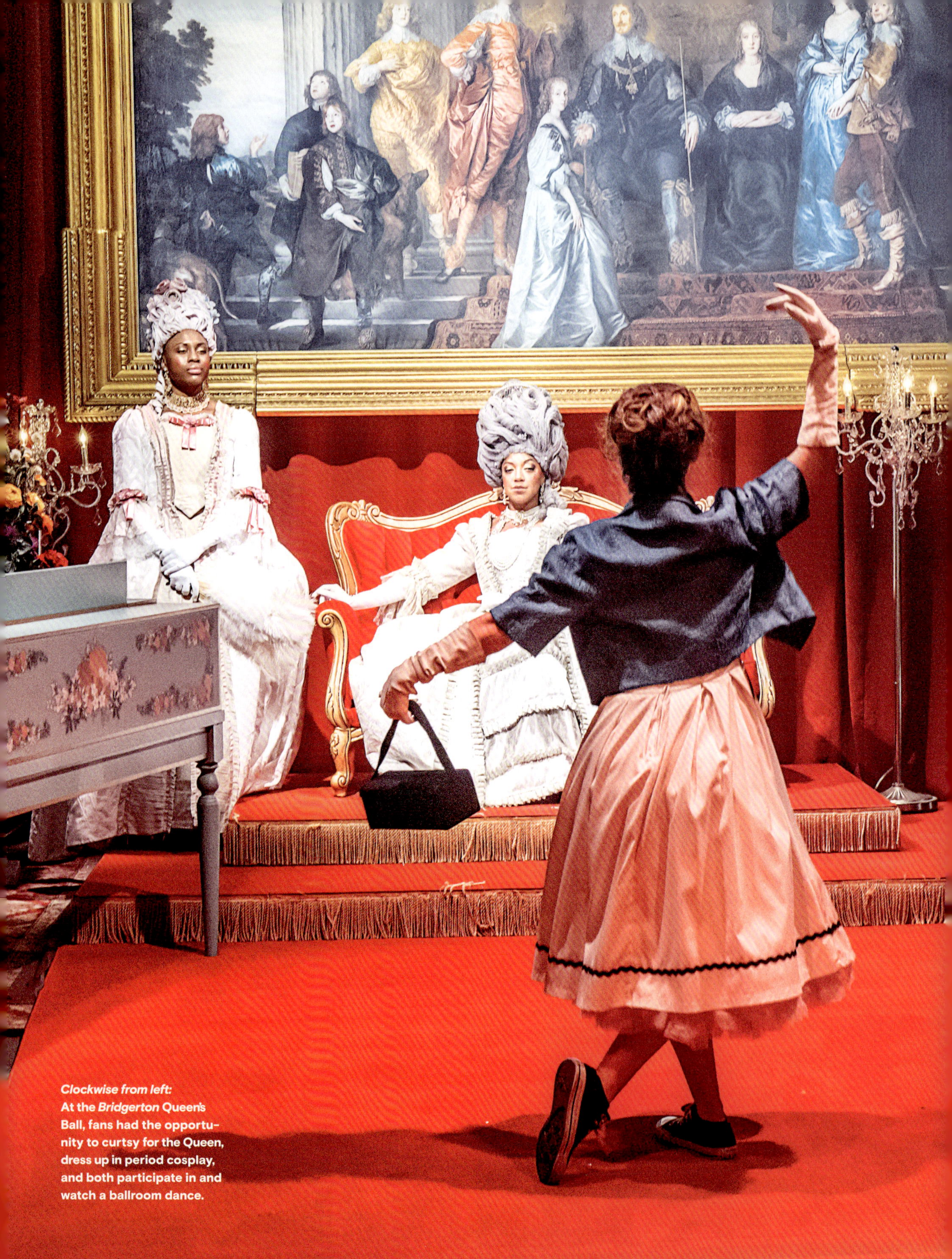

Clockwise from left:
At the *Bridgerton* Queen's Ball, fans had the opportunity to curtsy for the Queen, dress up in period cosplay, and both participate in and watch a ballroom dance.

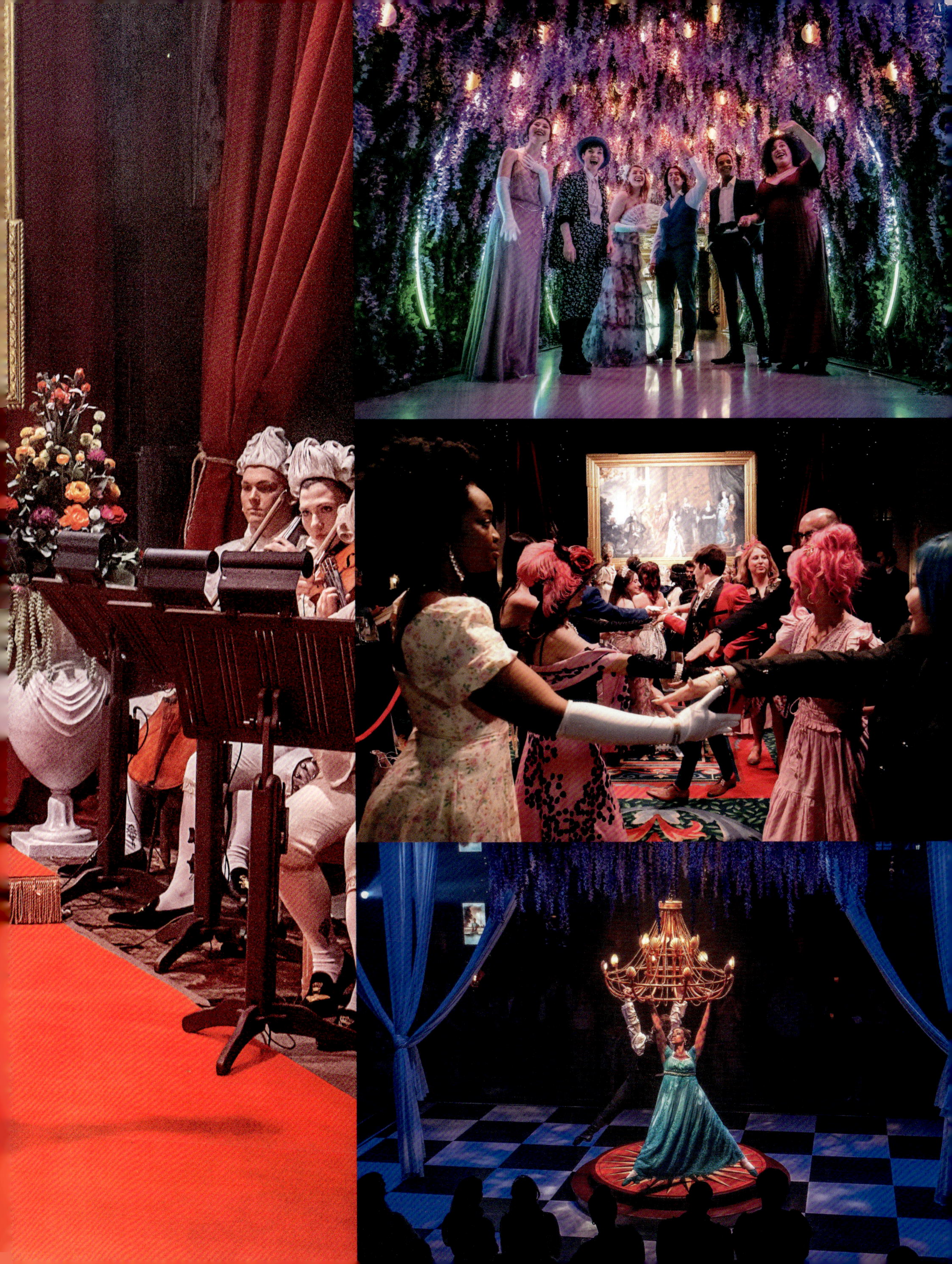

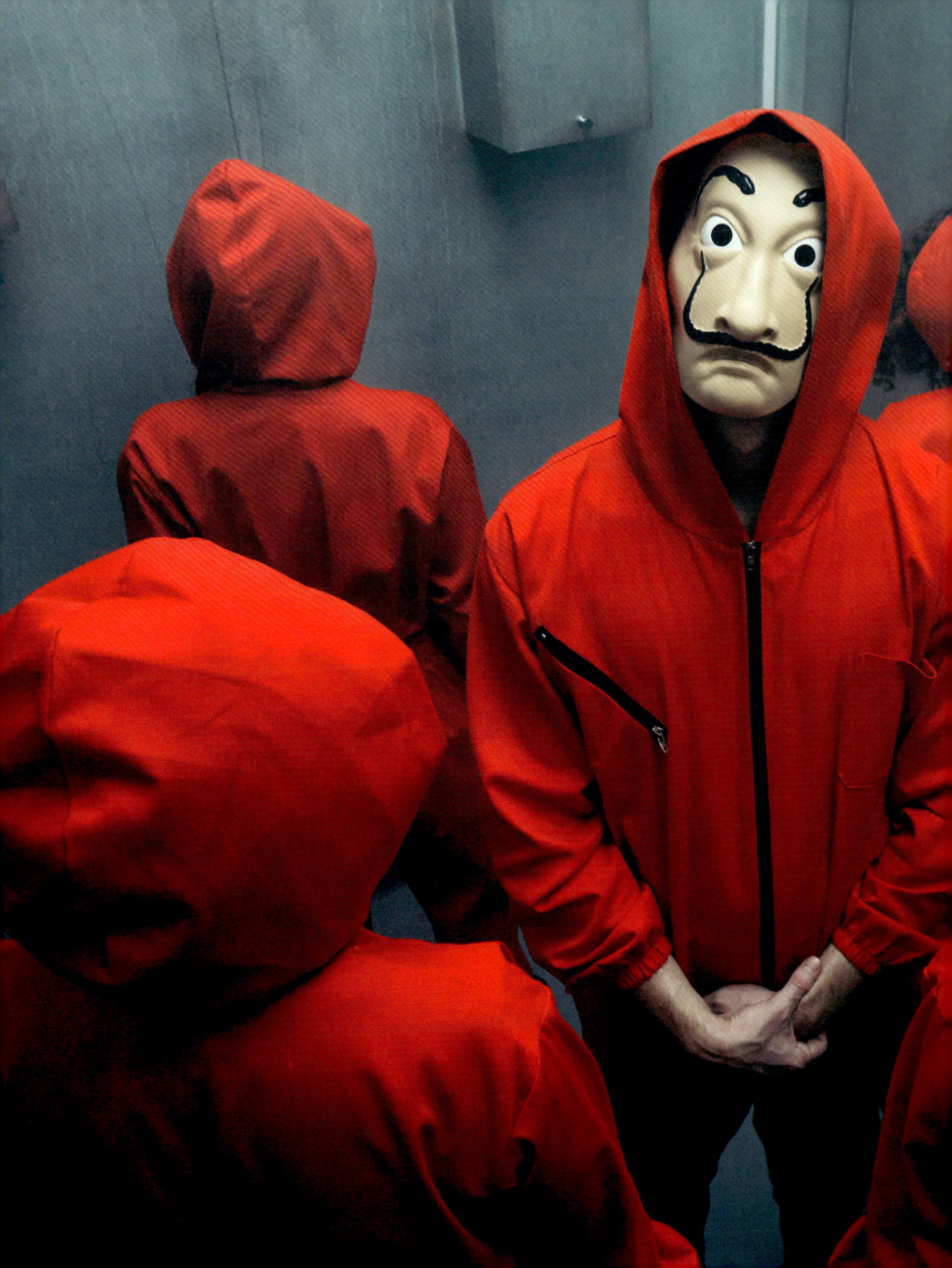

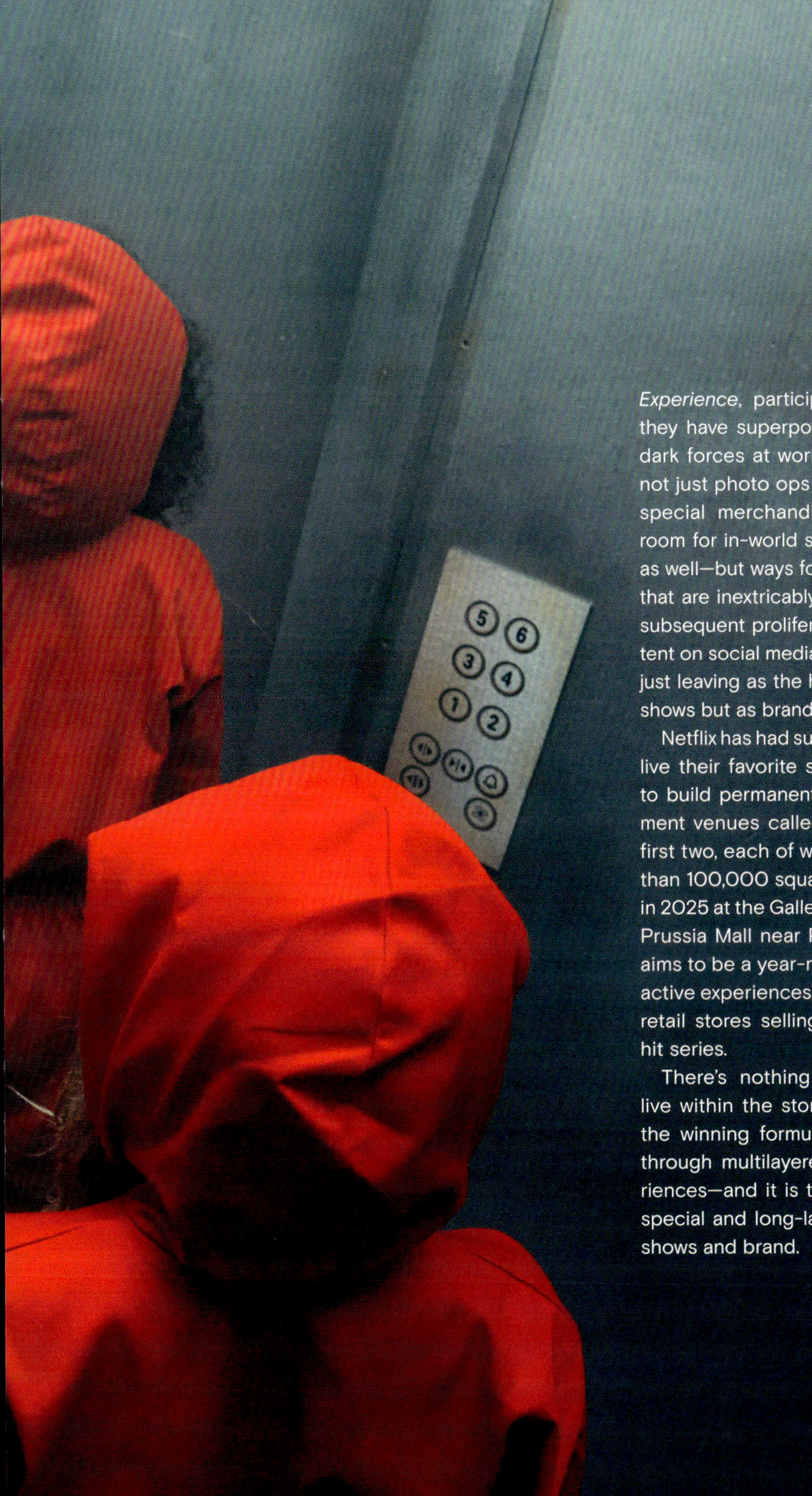

Experience, participants discover that, like Eleven, they have superpowers they can use to defeat the dark forces at work in Hawkins, Indiana. These are not just photo ops on staged sets or pop-ups with special merchandise—although there's plenty of room for in-world snapshots and souvenir shopping as well—but ways for fans to create lasting memories that are inextricably linked to Netflix shows. And the subsequent proliferation of experience-related content on social media suggests that participants aren't just leaving as the heroes of their favorite shows but as brand ambassadors, too.

Just like in the show, participants donned red jumpsuits and Salvador Dalí masks for Netflix's immersive *Money Heist* experience.

Netflix has had such success letting fans live their favorite stories that it decided to build permanent immersive entertainment venues called Netflix Houses. The first two, each of which will take up more than 100,000 square feet of space, are set to open in 2025 at the Galleria Dallas in Texas and the King of Prussia Mall near Philadelphia. Each Netflix House aims to be a year-round destination featuring interactive experiences, themed restaurants, games, and retail stores selling merchandise inspired by their hit series.

There's nothing that fans want more than to live within the stories they love. Netflix has found the winning formula for fulfilling these fantasies—through multilayered, active, and embodied experiences—and it is the perfect means for creating a special and long-lasting passion for the streamer's shows and brand.

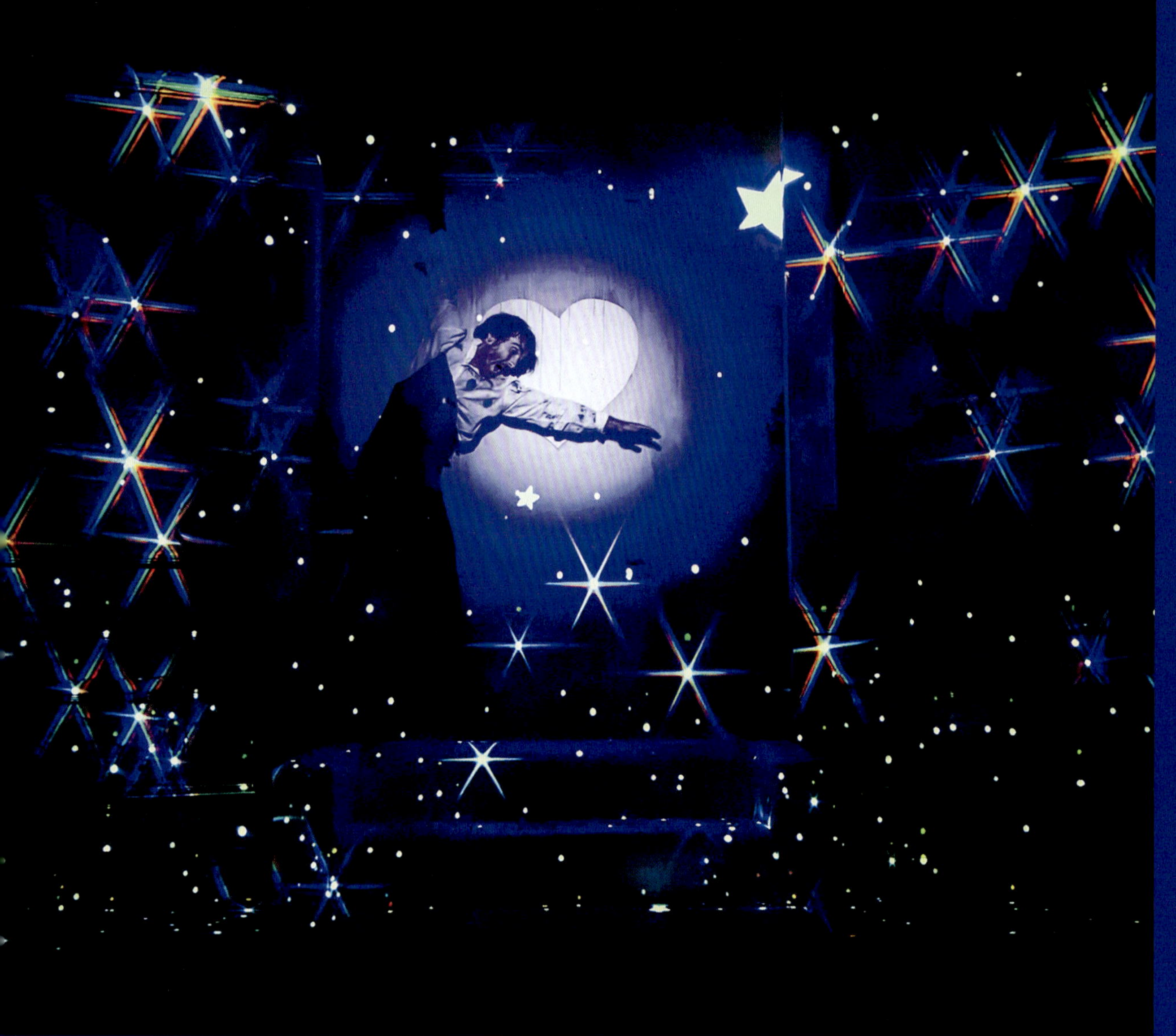

PARTICLE INK

Have you ever wanted to step inside an artist's imagination? Thanks to Particle Ink, you can do just that. Co-created by the visionary director and former Cirque du Soleil artist Dandy Punk, Particle Ink seamlessly blends 2-D and 3-D worlds through projection-mapped animation, augmented reality, dance, and acting to bring dreams to life. The innovative and groundbreaking work was recognized with a Thea Award for Outstanding Achievement in Immersive Live Experience in 2022 for its original Vegas show *Particle Ink: Speed of Dark*. In 2024, this ambitious project debuted a follow-up, *Particle Ink: House of Shattered Prisms*, at the Luxor Hotel & Casino on the Las Vegas Strip.

In *House of Shattered Prisms*, live performers interacted with projection-mapped animations, encountering characters, being swept away by cartoon oceans, and doing stunts around projected structures. As Dandy Punk once put it, "The projector is the perfect tool, since it enables a simple sketch, done on a piece of scrap paper, to become twenty feet tall and completely surround the audience." Ushers and characters guided the audience from room to room, following the dreamlike narrative about finding

The analog and digital played together in *House of Shattered Prisms*, allowing participants to step into the world of Particle Ink.

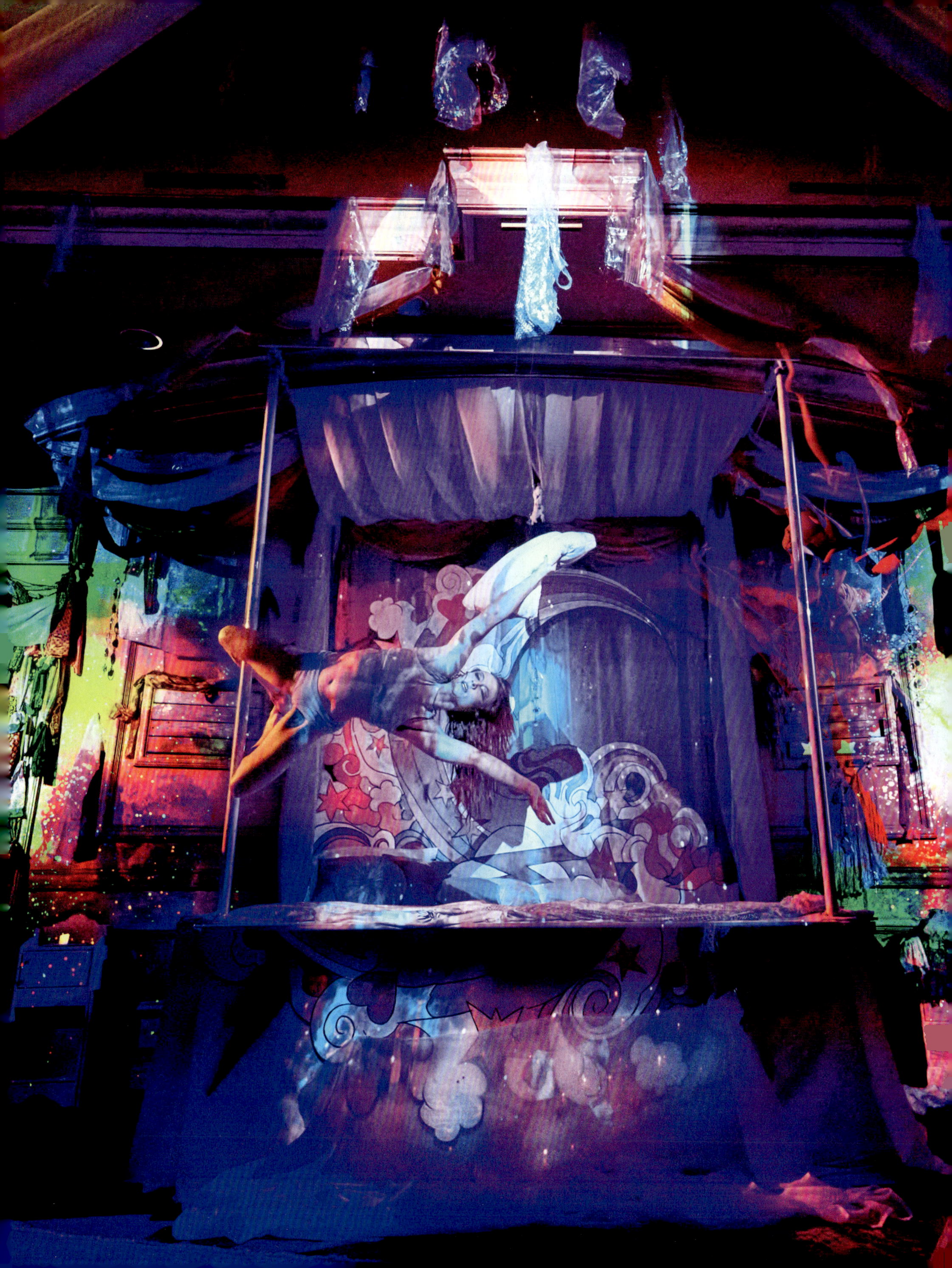

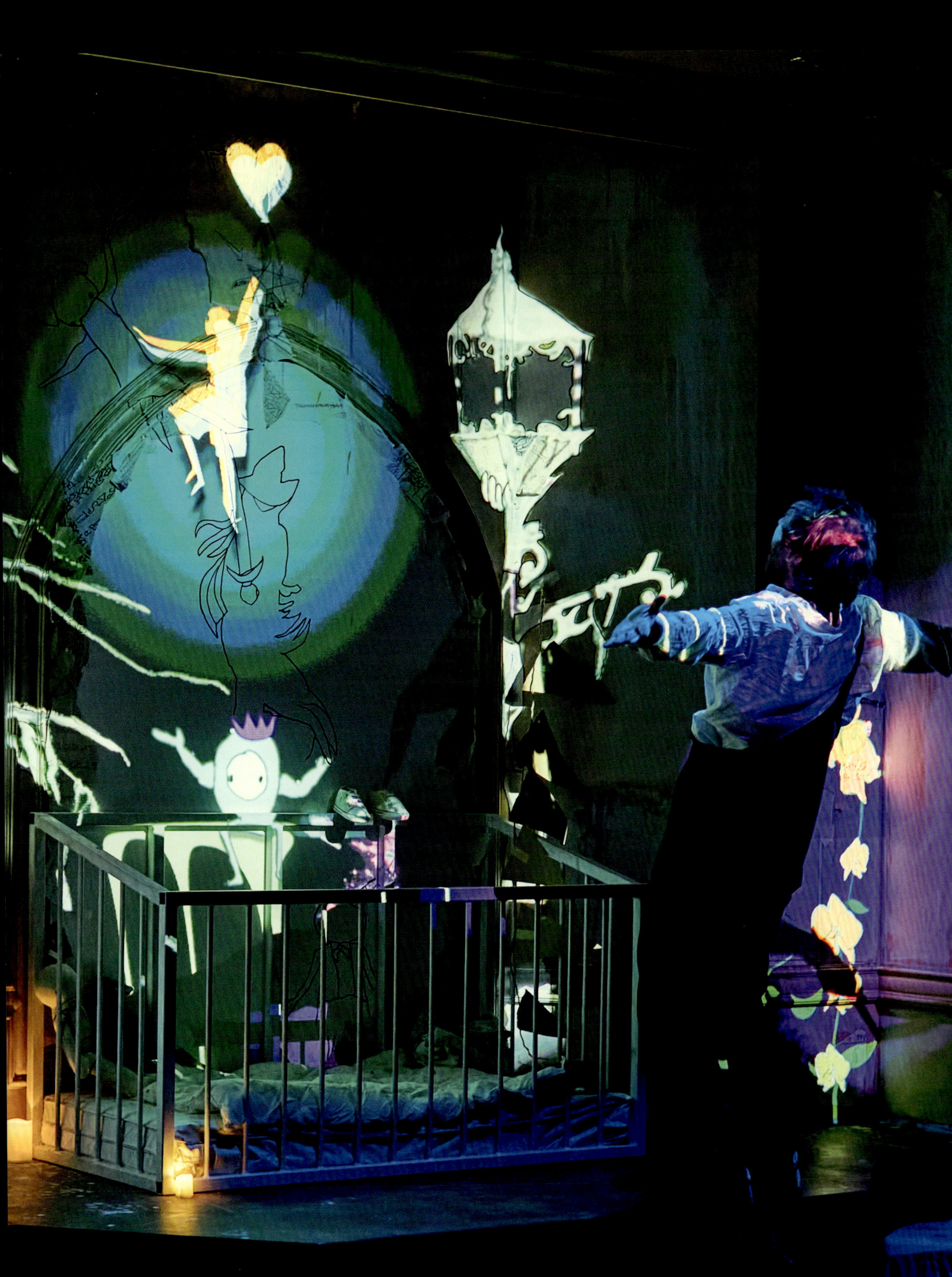

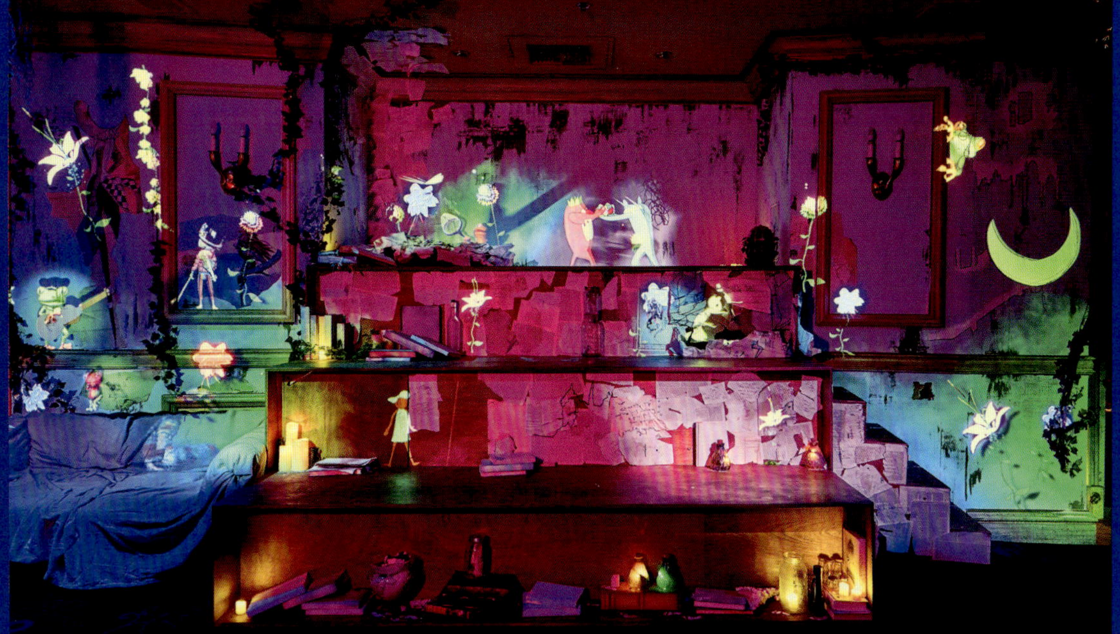

the light amid the darkness of life. The integration of three-dimensional set pieces further blurred the line between the real and the imagined.

During the day, the venue also hosted a separately ticketed experience called *Wanderlust*, a choose your own adventure where visitors could explore the rooms from the show at their own pace. Technology was cleverly woven into the experience: "Magic mirrors" in the form of tablets enabled you to place Particle Ink's animations in real space, and "spray paint cans," which were handheld digital devices, let you leave your mark on the walls with projected light and color. This collaboration of production studio Kaleidoco and visual art collective LightPoets, of which Dandy Punk is a founding member, allowed technology to enhance the narrative immersion, deepening the connection between the audience and the world of the so-called "2.5 dimension."

Particle Ink represents a new frontier in storytelling, intertwining the richness of animated and computer-generated worlds with the sensorial engagement of real spaces and the improvisation of live performers. It's a beautiful example of the power that can come from merging the digital and analog, where projections, augmented-reality overlays, and interactive technology combine with real sets, live performers, and opportunities for audience participation.

Particle Ink utilizes a mix of real sets, live actors, projections, and augmented reality to merge 2-D and 3-D elements into a richly vibrant and interactive story experience.

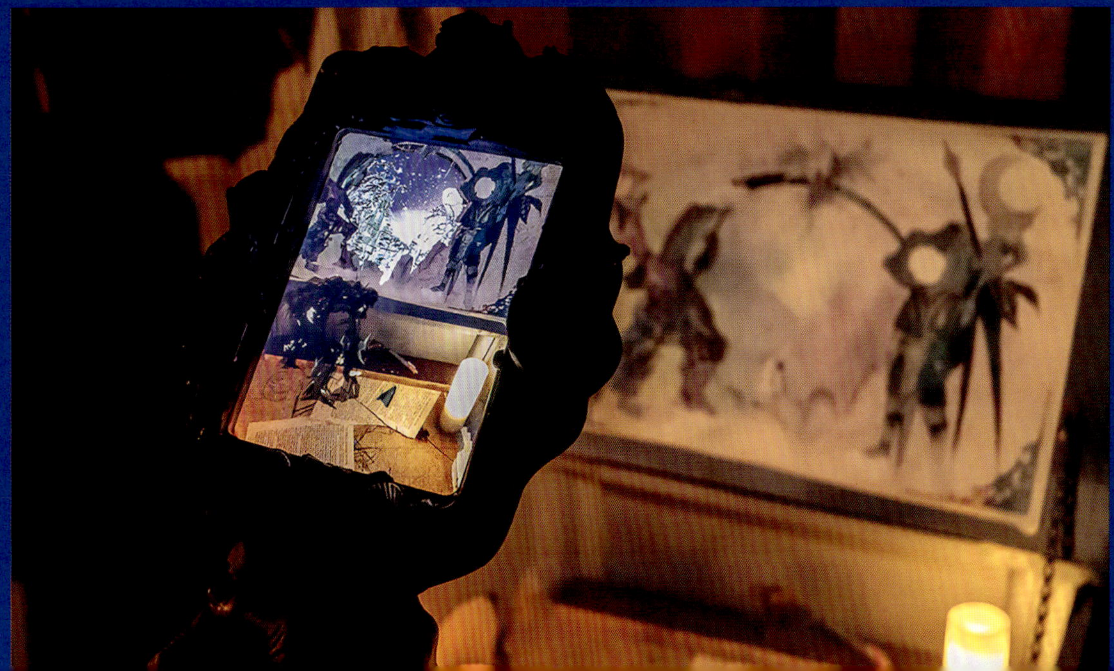

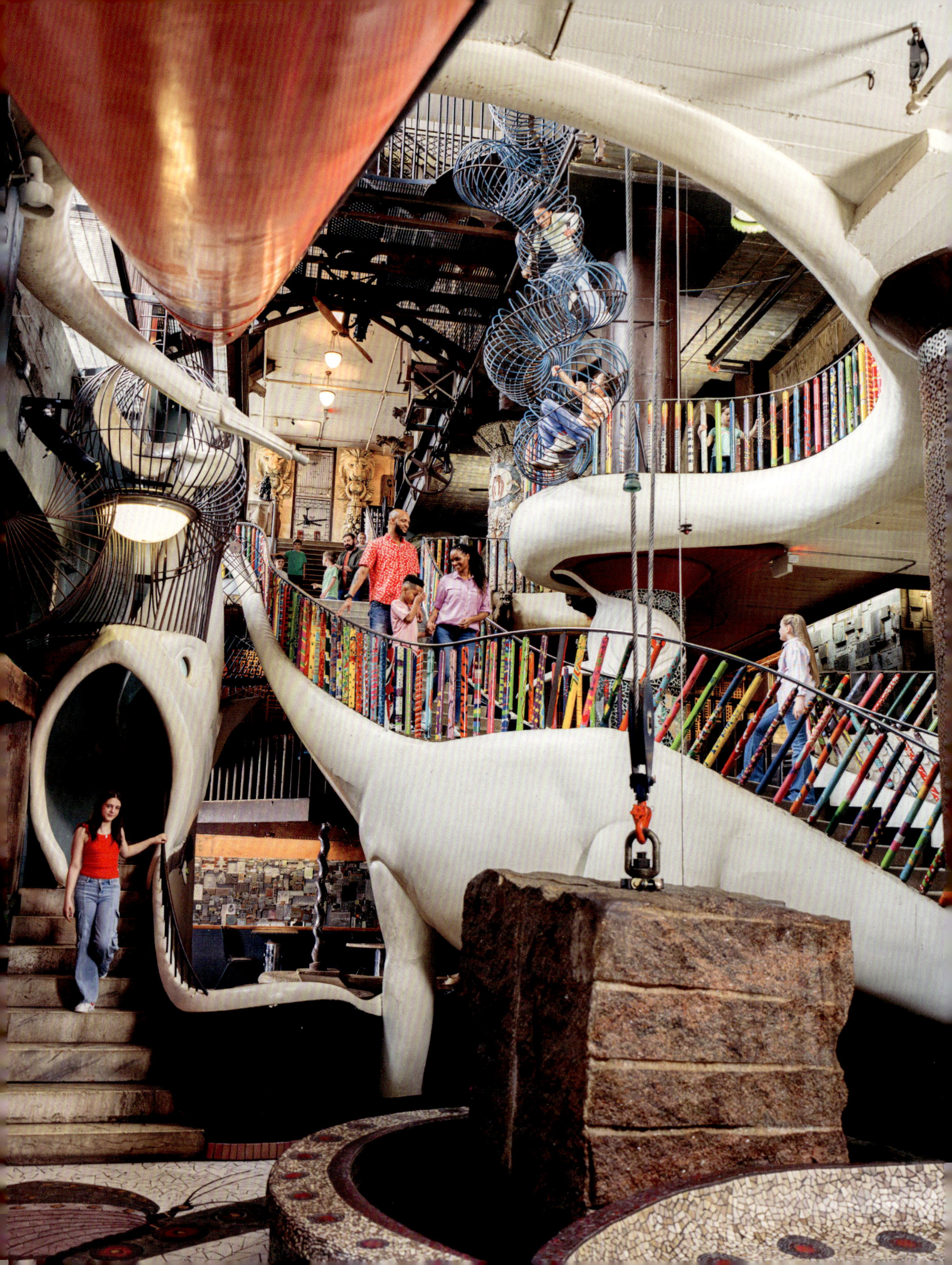

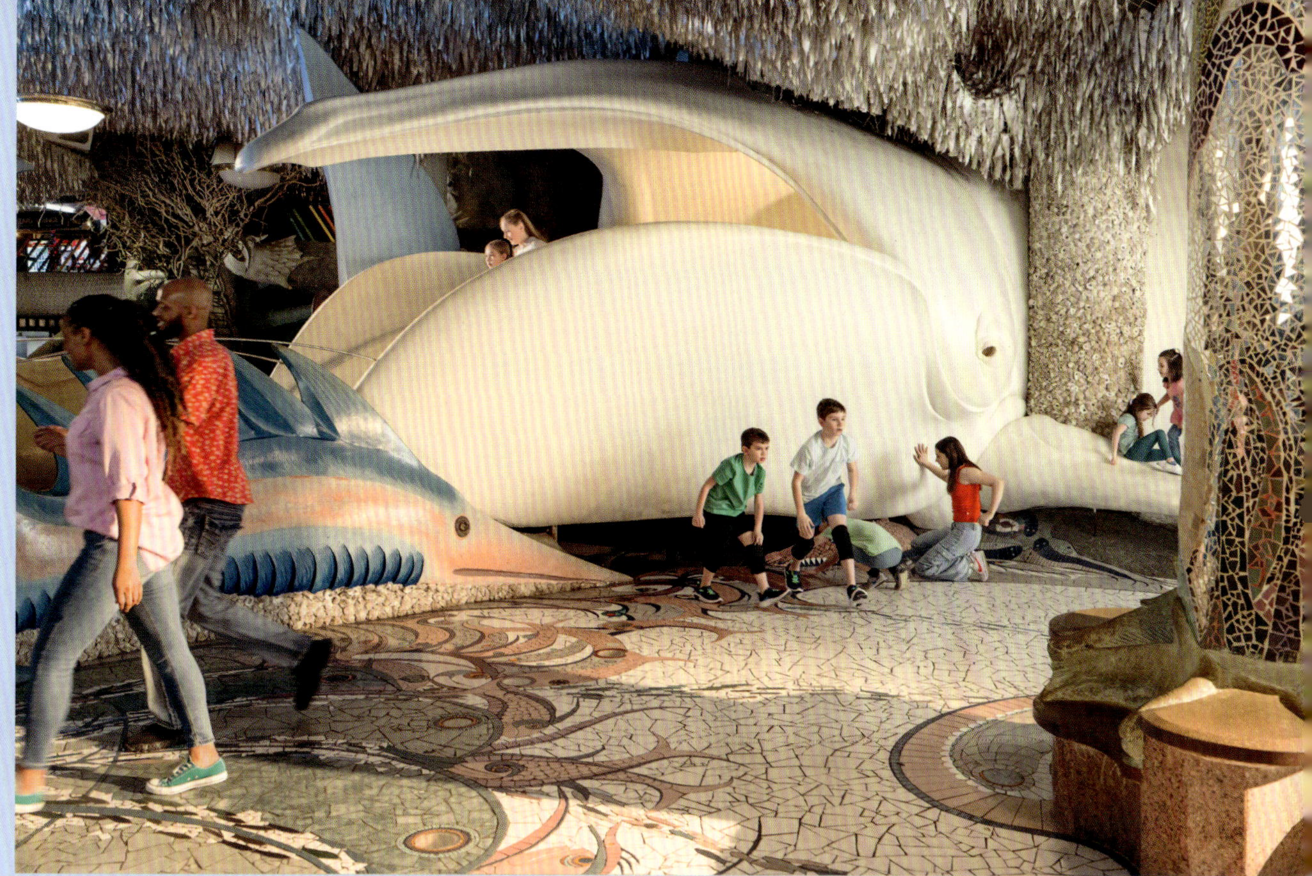

CITY MUSEUM

Downtown St. Louis's City Museum isn't just for looking at art—it's for engaging with it. Inside the 6,000-square-foot former shoe factory, visitors can explore imaginative installations that are spread across every inch of the repurposed building. You are encouraged to climb, crawl, slide, and play, sparking adventure, discovery, and delight through tactile interaction with the art.

When City Museum opened in 1997, its hands-on, boundary-breaking approach stood apart from traditional museum experiences. Bob Cassilly said that he and cofounder Gail Cassilly wanted to "build a space where you become the sculptures, the surroundings...so that all of your senses are affected." Using found materials such as facades from demolished buildings, old Twinkie and Ding Dong pans, and retired playground equipment, City Museum's team of artisans created a new architectural masterpiece. Decades after its opening, the venue continues to evolve as new artists add to its design. Spaces are torn out, rebuilt, and augmented over time, giving the museum a life of its own.

Throughout the ten floors and rooftop, visitors discover wonders at every turn. Winding caves in the basement contain treasures like huge dinosaur sculptures and a 1925 Wurlitzer organ. Towering tree trunks rise through all three stories of the Treehouse, where you can climb and slide. On the rooftop, a decommissioned school bus seems to hang off the building's edge, while a working 1940s Ferris wheel offers stunning views of the city.

Despite being made from an eclectic collection of repurposed materials, City Museum feels remarkably permanent. Its concrete, wrought-iron, tile, and wood structures stand as testaments to the masterful craftsmanship behind its creation.

As one of the world's first interactive, play-based museums, it paved the way for other institutions and experiences with its creative approach to immersing visitors in a physical world. Vince Kadlubek, a founder of Meow Wolf, cites City Museum as a key inspiration for their work. It remains a pioneer in embodied storytelling, inspiring guests to devise their own narratives through exploration and play.

***Above:* Visitors explore in and around the white whale sculpture, which contains tunnels to different areas of the museum. *Opposite:* The museum's main stairwell, where visitors can find art to touch, climb, and admire.**

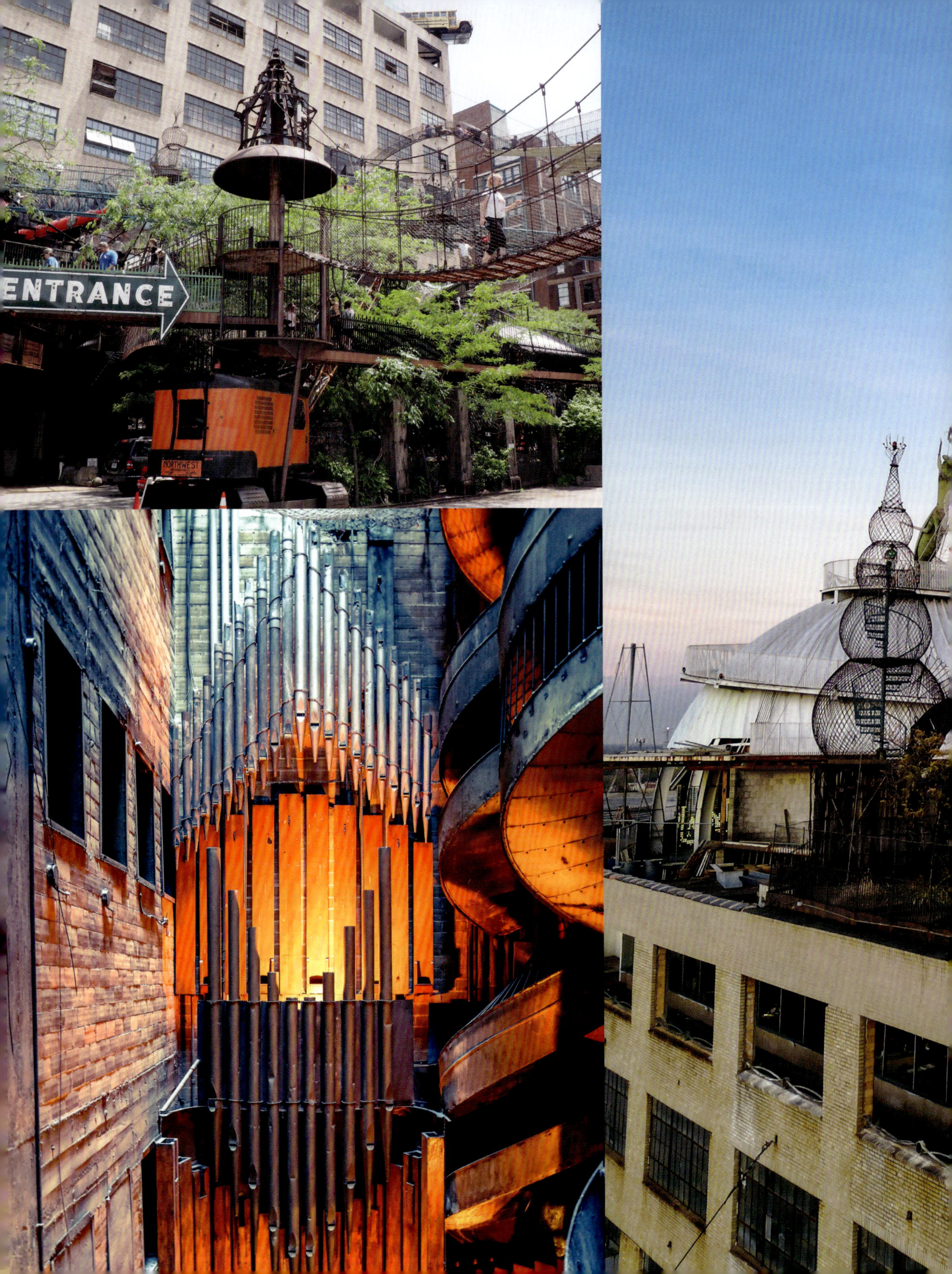
ENTRANCE
NORTHWEST

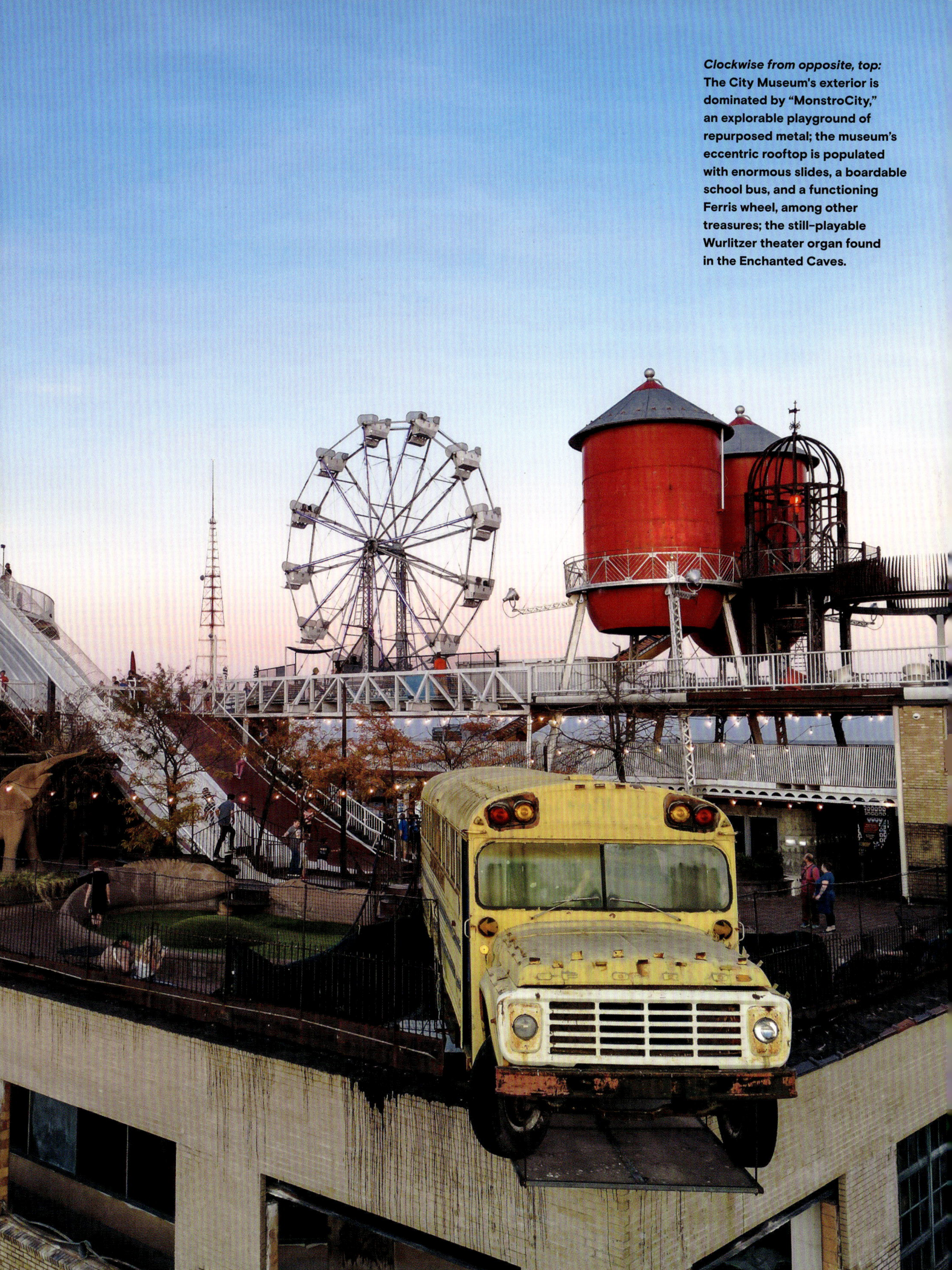

Clockwise from opposite, top: **The City Museum's exterior is dominated by "MonstroCity," an explorable playground of repurposed metal; the museum's eccentric rooftop is populated with enormous slides, a boardable school bus, and a functioning Ferris wheel, among other treasures; the still-playable Wurlitzer theater organ found in the Enchanted Caves.**

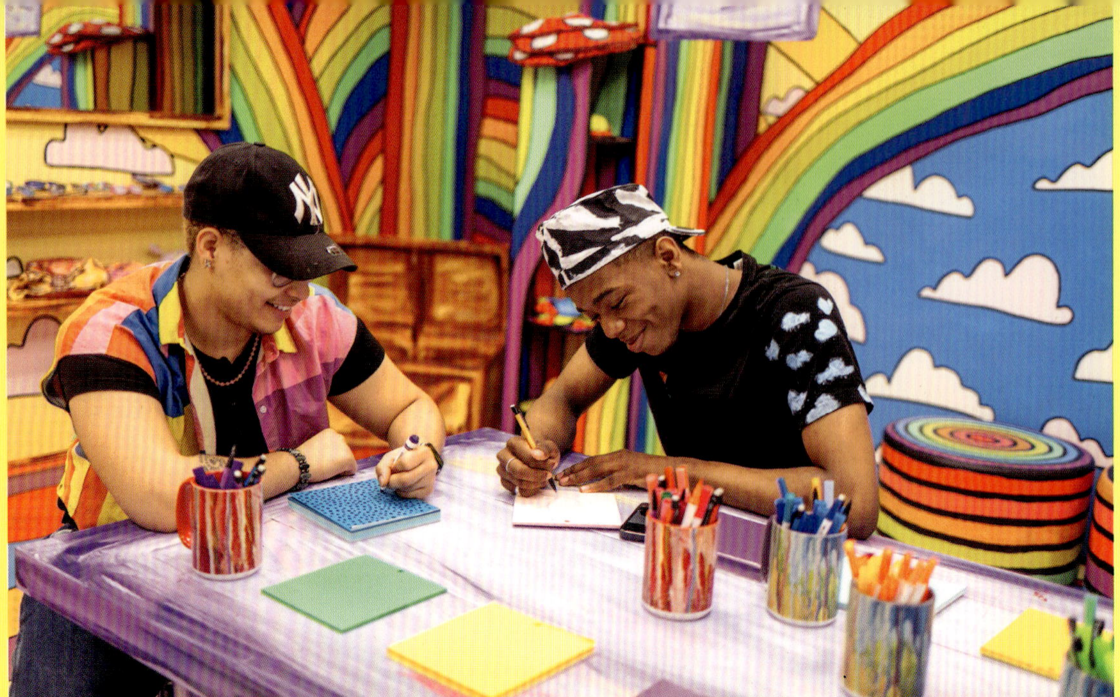

WONDERLAND DREAMS

Alexa Meade's immersive installation, *Wonderland Dreams*, was a handcrafted art experience that allowed visitors to enter into and interact with the artist's unique vision of a universe where imagination and creativity reign supreme.

Meade is best known for her distinctive artistic technique, in which she completely covers live subjects—models, their clothes, props, and even surroundings—in expressive and vibrant swirls of paint, transforming three-dimensional people and objects into 2-D paintings. This original approach to art-making evolved into *Wonderland Dreams*: an entire world rendered in Meade's style.

Wonderland Dreams began as a 4,000-square-foot installation in Beverly Hills in 2018 called *Immersed in Wonderland*, before growing into its 2022 iteration on Fifth Avenue in New York City. With the help of twenty assistants, Meade spent two months painting every surface of a 26,000-square-foot former Best Buy in Midtown Manhattan in her signature style. She and her team transformed the space into a living fantasy: a place where people could step off of the busy city streets and into a world of childlike wonder.

Composed of more than thirty installations, *Wonderland Dreams* was remarkably interactive, priding itself on letting visitors touch and play with the work in a way that no traditional gallery would dream of. Guests could try on various painted articles of clothing, like overcoats and top hats, and pose in "picture frames" that were themselves made of paint. In other rooms, they could craft a house of cards out of oversized playing cards, color their own roses to add to a garden of guest-contributed flowers, or hold a tea party worthy of the Mad Hatter with a multitude of carefully painted teacups, plates, and cakes. Houses shrank to the size of cupboards, and thrones grew to make even adults look small, giving guests the chance to play with optical illusions as they explored and took photos throughout the installation. Other spaces, such as the drawing studio and graffiti alley, encouraged them to express their creativity.

"At *Wonderland Dreams*, everyone who walks into the exhibit becomes part of this living work of art," Meade stated. More than 100,000 guests went down this rabbit hole of creativity over the course of its 2022–2023 run—and left a little more inspired and paint-splattered than when they came.

Clockwise from above: **Guests making their own artistic creations at *Wonderland Dreams*; visitors holding a Mad Hatter–esque tea party with fully painted tablewear and accessories like hats and jackets; the oversized Queen of Hearts Throne made those who sat in it look tiny.**

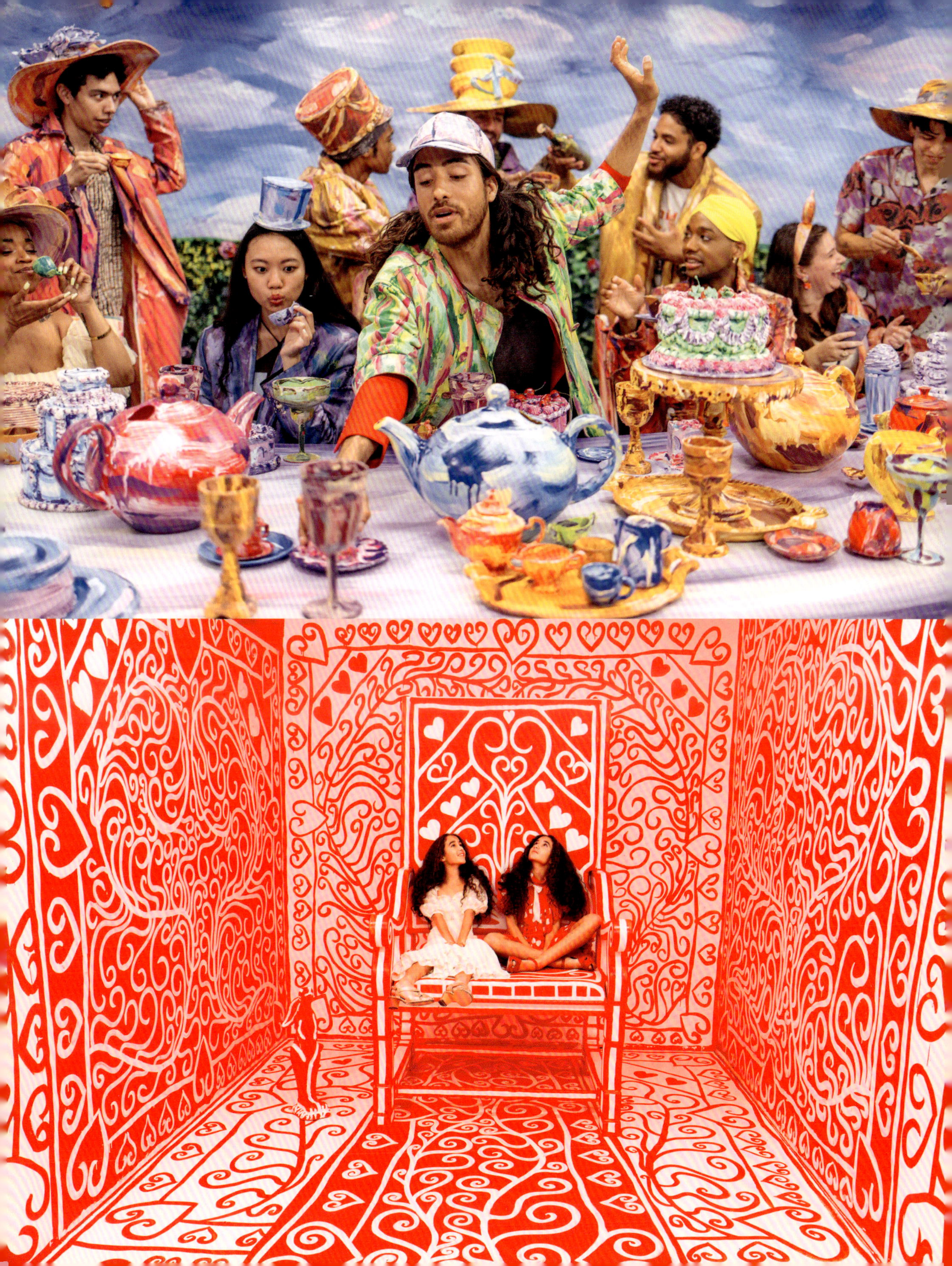

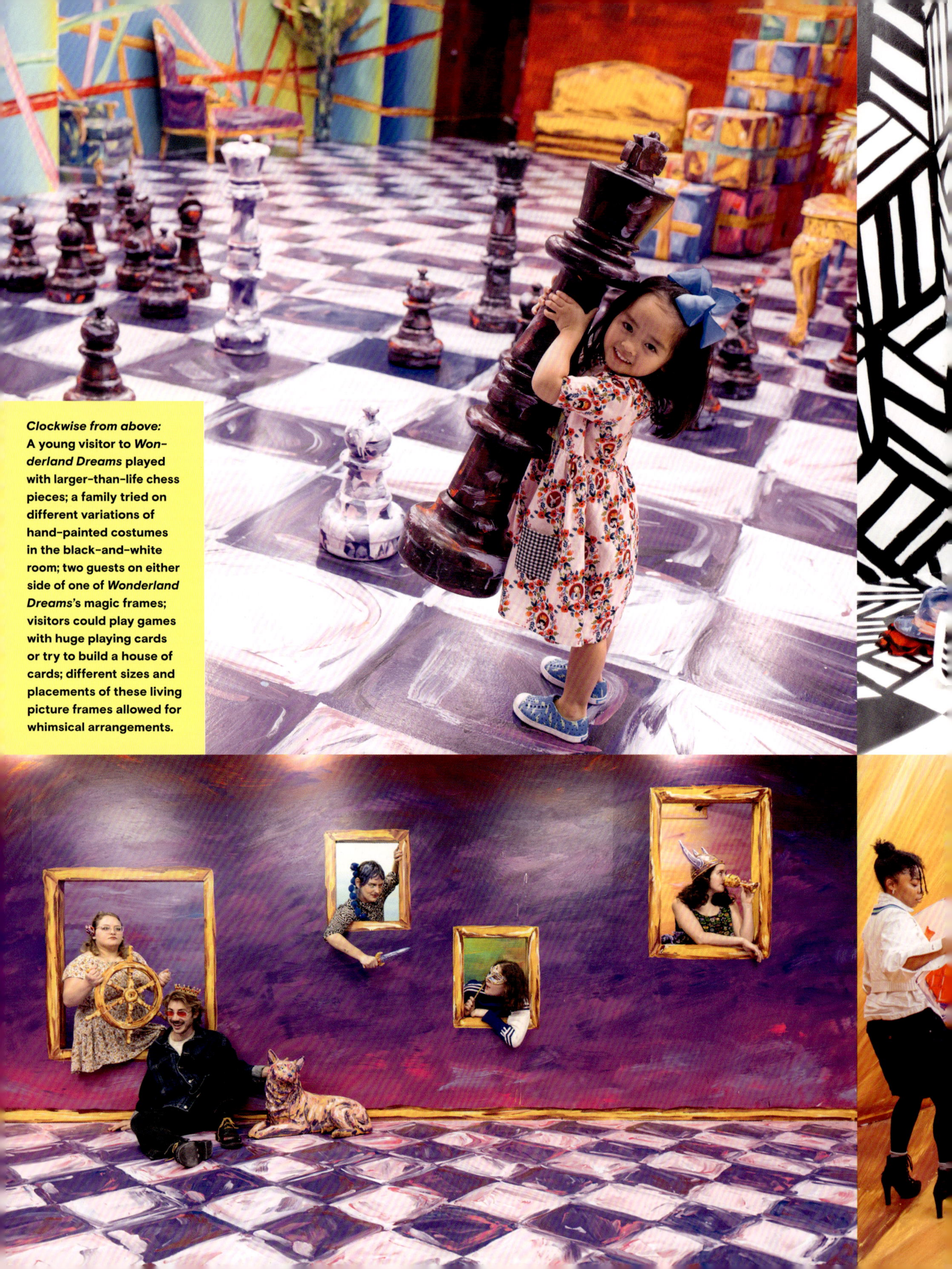

Clockwise from above: A young visitor to *Wonderland Dreams* played with larger-than-life chess pieces; a family tried on different variations of hand-painted costumes in the black-and-white room; two guests on either side of one of *Wonderland Dreams*'s magic frames; visitors could play games with huge playing cards or try to build a house of cards; different sizes and placements of these living picture frames allowed for whimsical arrangements.

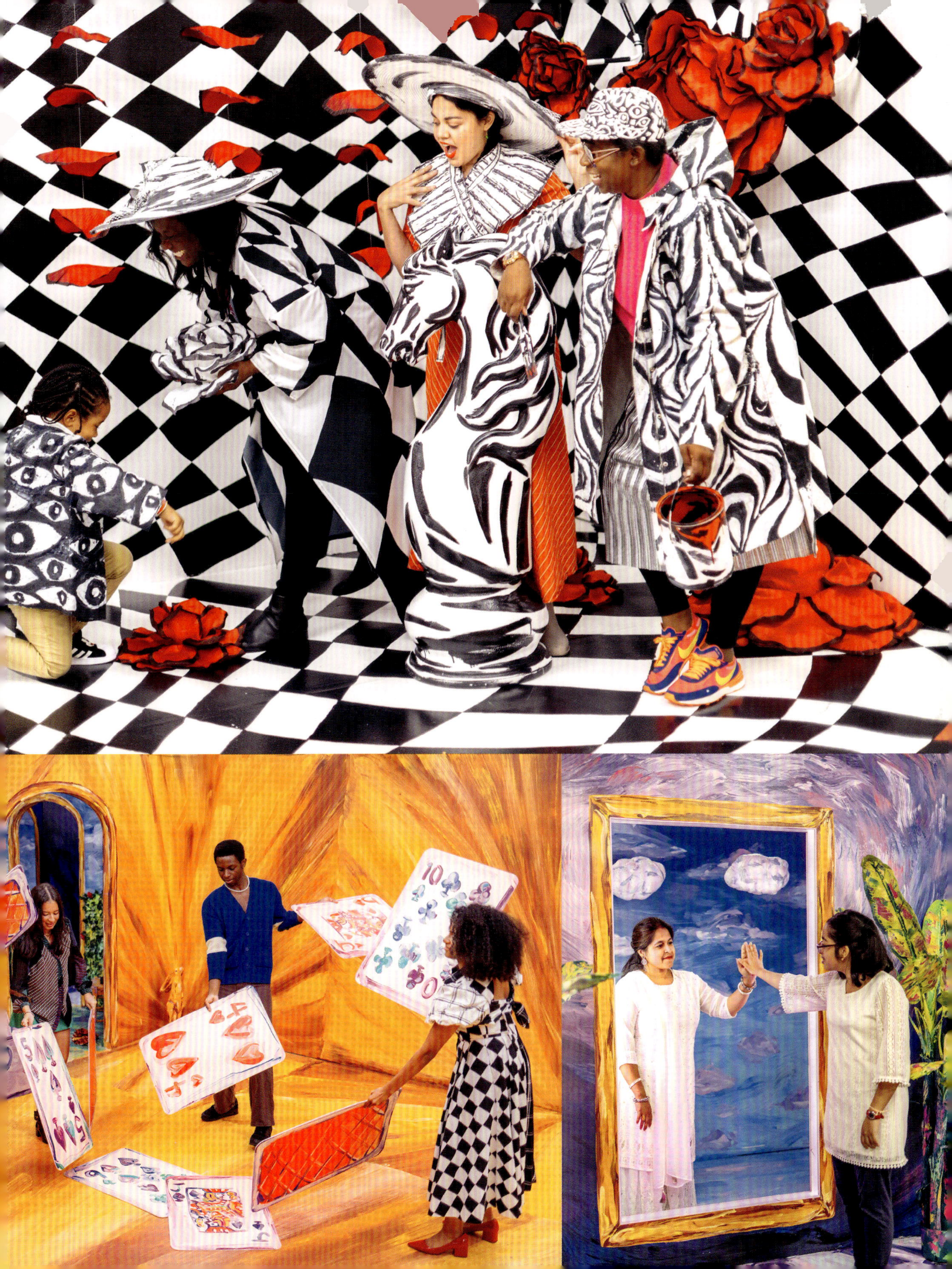

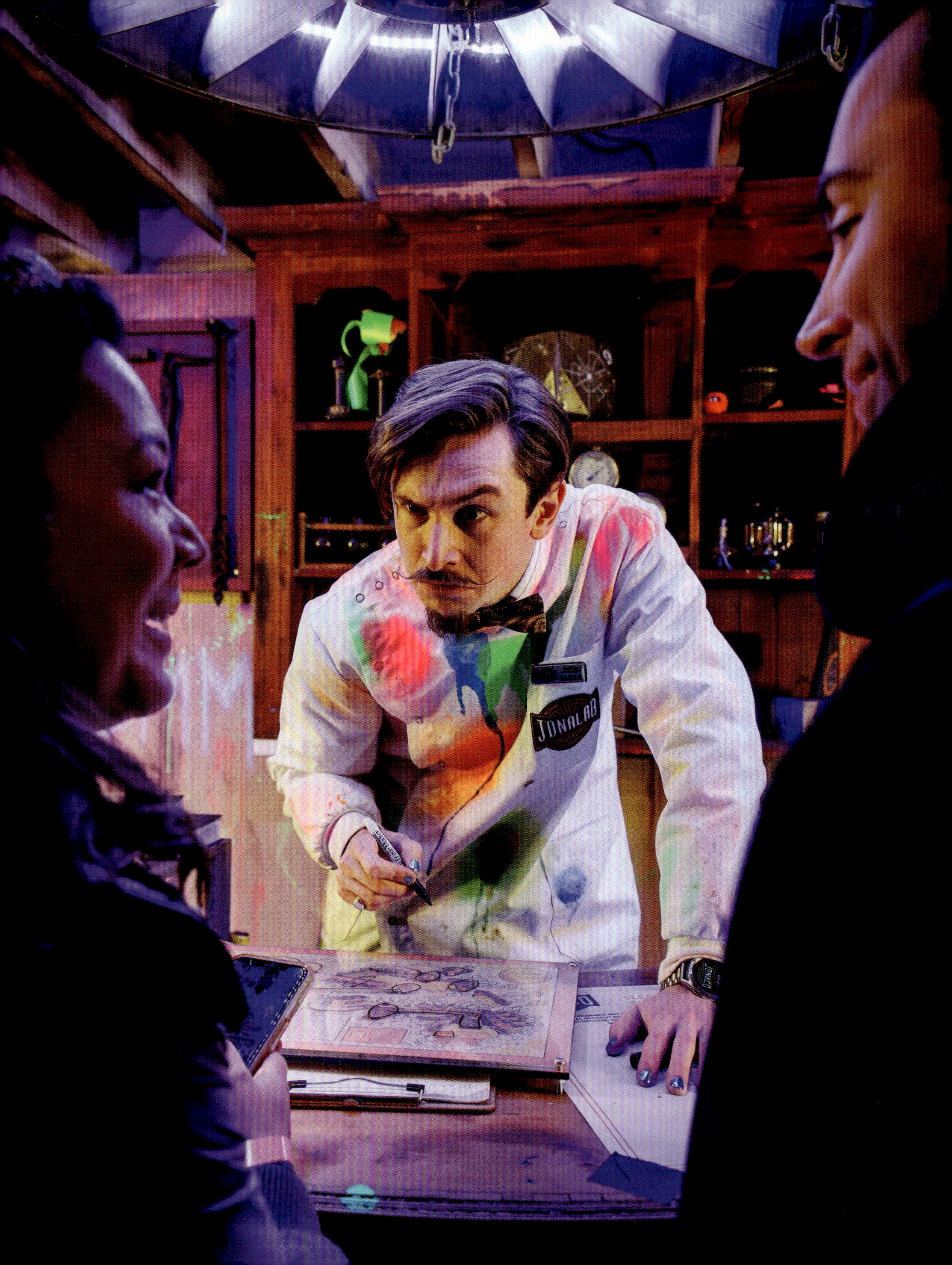
JONALAB

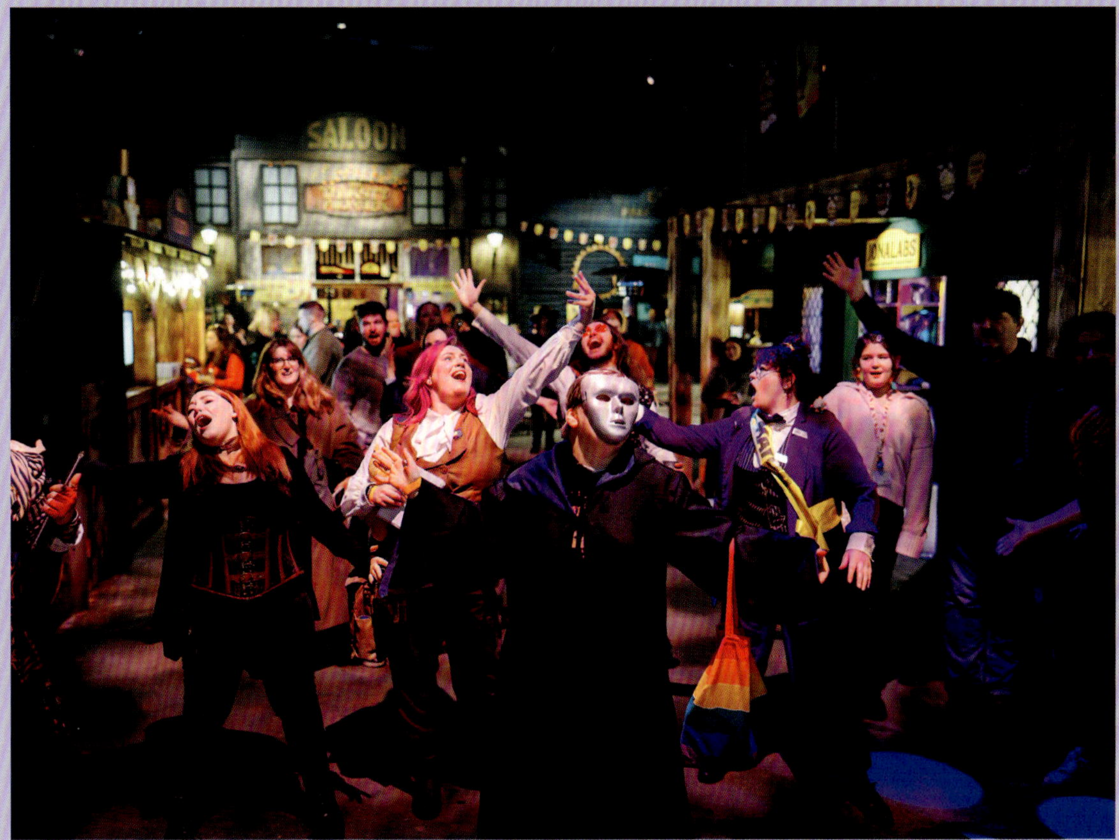

***Above:* The *Phantom Peak* cast breaks into song in the Old Town. *Opposite:* An actor playing mad scientist "Dr. Winter" interacting with guests.**

PHANTOM PEAK

Choose-your-own-adventure stories are taken to the next level at *Phantom Peak*, a sprawling 30,000-square-foot immersive attraction in London. Launched in 2022 by founders Nick Moran and Glen Hughes, the experience takes advantage of their escape-room and set-design expertise to bring a fully realized, fictional western town to life. Guests arrive as tourists during one of the town's rotating seasonal festivals, free to explore a world filled with story, humor, playfulness, and whimsical charm.

Across the venue, visitors can engage in a wide variety of narrative entertainment and activities, like completing puzzle-filled quests, chatting with eccentric townsfolk played by live actors, challenging friends in arcade games, and enjoying themed food and drink. *Phantom Peak* blends immersive theater, escape rooms, gaming, and F&B into an expansive and low-pressure adventure where guests truly have the autonomy to make the visit their own.

The experience is constantly evolving; the team develops ten new story-driven adventures for each of the four annual seasons. *Phantom Peak* calls these "trails": interactive, three-act stories guided by a custom app that gives guests clues and tracks their progress. While each "show" lasts about four hours, there's so much to uncover that most people complete one to three trails in a single visit. Even the menus change regularly to reflect each season's theme. With such an overload of activities, roughly 30 percent of visitors come back—an impressive figure in the world of immersive entertainment.

Phantom Peak's nimble production model is key to its success. The flexible tech platform enables efficient updates each season, while a cast of just thirteen actors makes the town come alive for up to 400 guests five times a week. *Phantom Peak* combines the benefits of analog and digital interaction to create a dynamic, richly layered realm. With its incredible variety, attention to detail, and emphasis on lighthearted fun, this isn't just a place you visit—it's a world you return to, again and again.

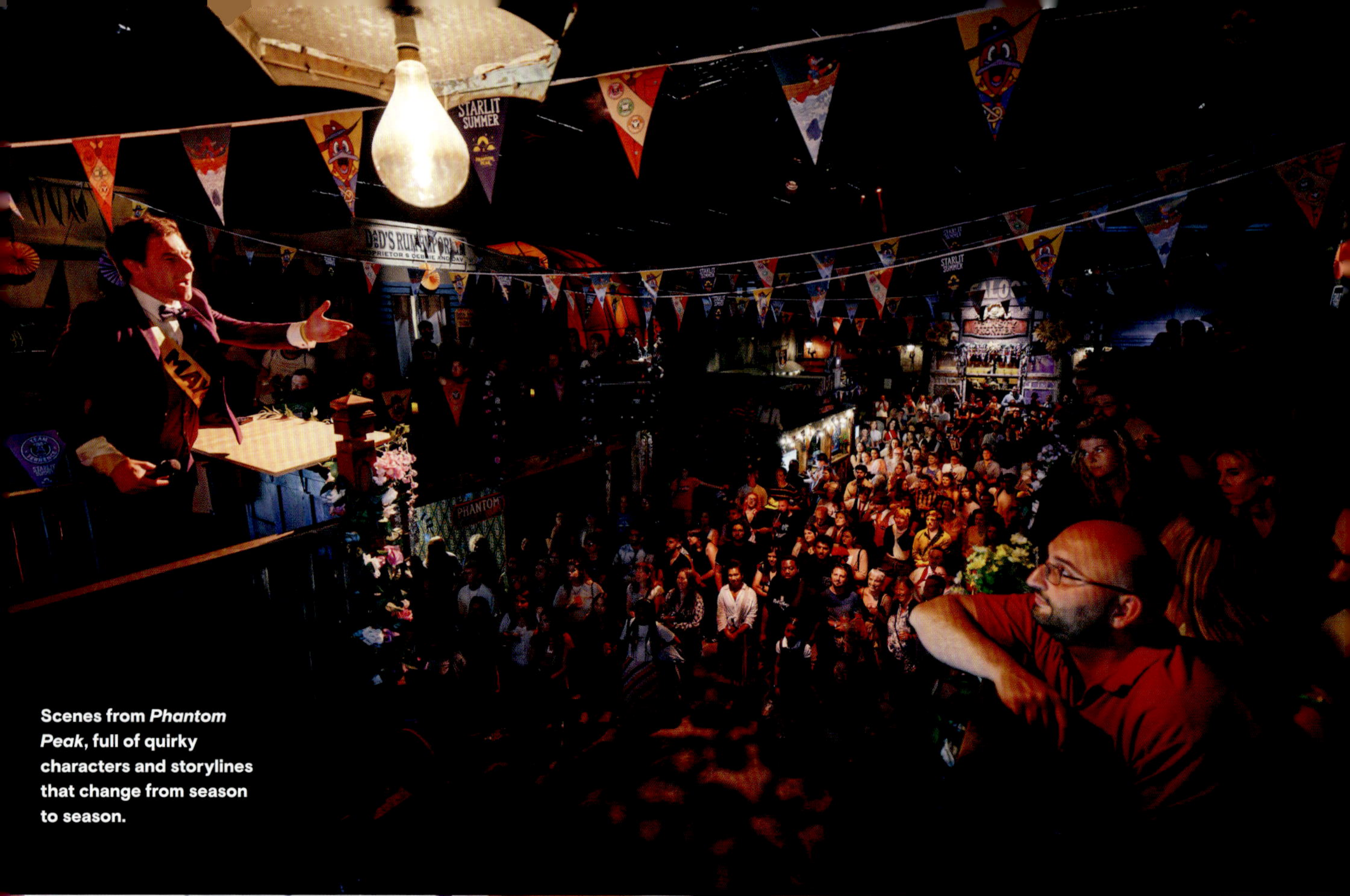

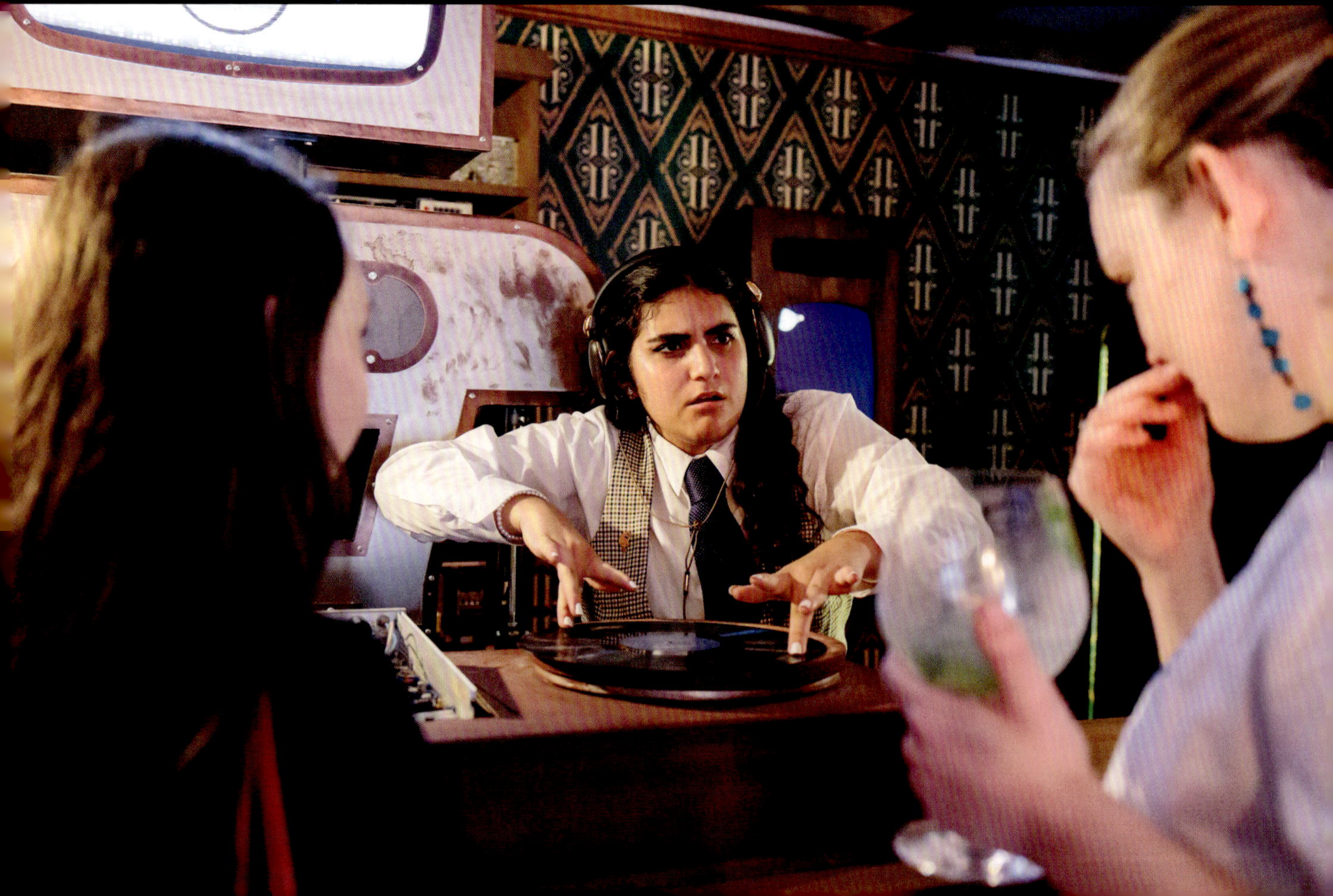

Scenes from *Phantom Peak*, full of quirky characters and storylines that change from season to season.

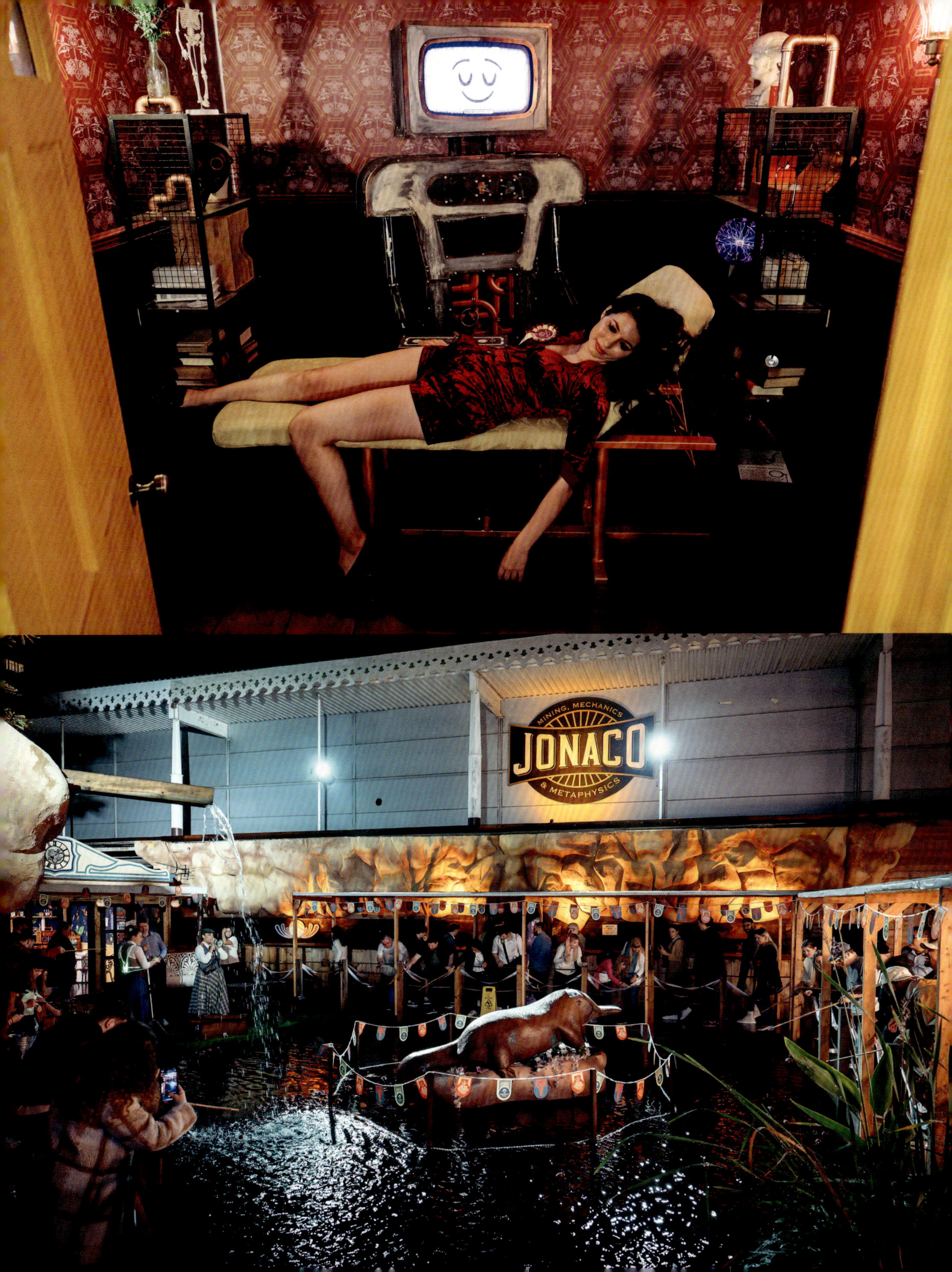
MINING, MECHANICS
JONACO
& METAPHYSICS

2

THE FUTURE OF STORYTELLING IS IMMERSIVE

Immersive. It's a word used so often that it's easy to gloss over it as a meaningless marketing buzzword. Movie theaters use the word to mean the movie will play on a larger screen. Google Maps' "immersive view" feature gives the user a 3-D rendering of a map. Cruises and all-inclusive hotels use the word to describe their vacation packages. The truth is that this is a difficult term to pin down—living stories creators use *immersive* to describe many different kinds of experiences and their effects on the actience.

The *Cambridge Dictionary* defines immersion as "the fact of becoming completely involved in something." True immersion is much more than simple attention capture. An experience is truly immersive when the actience can suspend their disbelief and imagine they're living in the story. To achieve this feat, living stories must stimulate the senses, invite active participation, and captivate the imagination; they must fully engage the hands, the head, and the heart.

True immersion is much more than simple attention capture. An experience is truly immersive when the actience can suspend their disbelief and imagine they're living in the story.

For this reason, I've created a framework that encompasses the three categories of immersion: physical, participatory, and emotional. Each of these categories exists on a spectrum.

Physical immersion is achieved when the body is fully engaged in the experience—when the actience is physically interacting with the environment in a multisensory way.

Participatory immersion is achieved when the actience can have an impact on the world, make decisions that have consequences, and affect the outcome of the story.

Emotional immersion is achieved when the actience is invested in the characters and narrative arc of the story world, and their experience leads to a sense of empathy, connection, and transformation.

There are endless combinations of these three categories of immersion that play out in various forms of entertainment. Movies can be highly emotionally immersive but low on physical and participatory immersion. Video games might rank high on participatory immersion but lack the emotional and physical elements. The best

SCALE OF IMMERSION

In this framework, there are three categories of immersion: physical, participatory, and emotional. This scale outlines five levels of immersion in each category, progressing from passive to total. You can use the scale as a guide in evaluating or designing immersive experiences. The best living stories achieve a high level in each category.

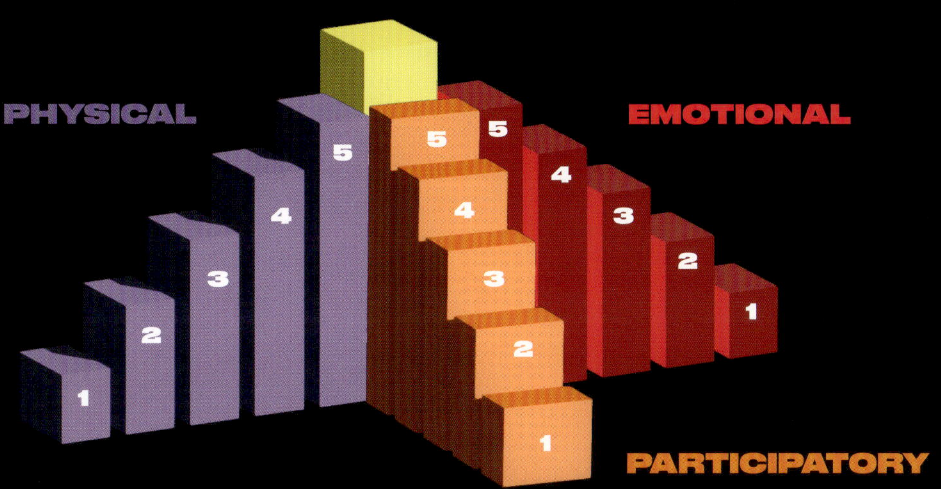

	1 PASSIVE	2 LIGHT	3 MODERATE	4 INTENSE	5 TOTAL
PHYSICAL	Observing a story using no more than one or two of the senses, such as watching TV.	Engaging in limited physical interaction, such as touching an object or walking through a space.	Participating in an experience with some physical effort, like climbing stairs or carrying something.	Engaging with an experience that requires significant physical effort or movement, like a VR game or an obstacle course.	Becoming completely engulfed in an experience that engages all of the senses and requires vigorous physical effort.
PARTICIPATORY	Observing an experience without actively engaging, such as listening to music in an elevator.	Engaging with an experience in a limited way, such as answering questions or interacting with a touch screen.	Participating in an experience to a significant degree, such as attending a hands-on workshop.	Fully engaging in an experience and actively contributing to it, such as playing a role in a theatrical production.	Becoming deeply involved in co-creating the experience, to the point where your actions have a noticeable and consequential effect on the outcome.
EMOTIONAL	Observing an experience with indifference or very little investment, such as driving by an outdoor advertisement.	Engaging with an experience enough to motivate your participation, such as watching a streaming series to the end.	Participating in an experience on an emotional level so that you suspend disbelief and care about characters' fates, such as when you're unable to put a novel down and feel sad when the story is over.	Engaging emotionally to the point where you feel a sense of real connection and investment in a narrative, such as imagining yourself in a character's role.	Engaging so deeply in an experience that it feels as if it is really happening to you. You feel the moral consequences of your decisions, and the lessons you learn can lead to lasting change.

living stories, on the other hand, succeed at creating high levels of participatory, physical, and emotional immersion.

Levels of immersion in traditional forms of media are dependent on the author's ability to create characters and plots that engage the audience's interest. Traditional stories tend to move through an arc, beginning with the exposition and ending with the denouement. And though authors can experiment with form, such stories are bound by the flat mediums, like the page, through which they're told.

But living stories are different. Because they have a physical and participatory component and are not necessarily linear, they begin not with narrative elements like exposition or conflict but with a world—a dynamic environment that can be discovered, explored, and even tested by its audience. You can think of the world as the "rules" of the experience, or the conditions under which the action can unfold. World-building is one of the primary tools living-stories creators use to produce high levels of immersion.

To be sure, authors of traditional stories also construct a world, just as living-stories creators construct narrative arcs and characters. Characters in the former type of story operate under a set of rules, no matter how fantastical. Consider, for instance, *Animal Farm* by George Orwell, a novel about a group of farm animals who overthrow their human farmer and try to form their own government. In the world of *Animal Farm*, animals can speak and think like humans, but pigs can't fly. Despite the absurd and unpredictable nature of the world, Orwell's characters adhere to its rules.

You can think of the world as the "rules" of the experience, or the conditions under which the action can unfold. World-building is one of the primary tools living-stories creators use to produce high levels of immersion.

With developments in storytelling technology, story worlds have room to grow more detailed and concrete. In a book, much of the world is left to the reader's imagination. Movies make worlds, in a certain sense, more real: A single frame can convey countless pages of description, and a world's physical laws, technological advancement, stylistic conventions, and biology might all be evident to the viewer within seconds. Tiny details that might require a paragraph of words to get just right—a certain type of bird fluttering among the treetops, the lettering style on the signs in a village—are understood in an instant. The advent of video games took world-building a step further by building worlds players could interact with, albeit in a limited way.

Today, storytellers working in immersive media are creating worlds that the audience can experience firsthand. The best immersive experiences erase thc “filter” of the medium, allowing the audience to inhabit and explore fictional worlds from the inside, achieving an immediacy that no traditional film or video game can match.

In living stories, every detail in the world is subject to inspection. The actience can approach any object, peer behind every door, interact with every character.

In these emerging mediums, which plunge the audience into an invented world with a hyper-realism rivaling real life, the art of world-building has never been more vital. Audiences may spend more time exploring the world, interacting with it and its characters, and derive more emotional impact from that experience than by just following its storylines. Just ask the attendees of Punchdrunk’s immersive theater production *Sleep No More* (see p. 40), many of whom didn’t even realize they were in an adaptation of Shakespeare’s *Macbeth*. As in a great literary work, where each word is essential to the ultimate meaning of the story, here every inch of the created world plays a role in constructing meaning.

This is a lesson for all creators of living stories. Detail is what makes creating any story—especially a living story—so daunting and so rewarding. In fiction, readers are not able to look around every corner of a scene. In living stories, every detail in the world is subject to inspection. The actience can approach any object, peer behind every door, interact with every character.

DETAILS THAT WRITE THE PLOT

To learn more about the craft of building immersive fictional worlds, I turned to one of the masters on the subject, Alex McDowell. McDowell is a legendary world-builder with decades of experience across film, live entertainment, and XR, as well as the founder and director of USC's World Building Institute and World Building Media Lab. He has contributed to the production design for some of Hollywood's biggest blockbusters of the past thirty years.

At the beginning of his career, McDowell hadn't set out to be a world-builder. Early on, he served as a production designer for music videos, and from there he graduated to feature films, developing a reputation in Hollywood through his work on *Fear and Loathing in Las Vegas* and *Fight Club*. His job as a production designer was to create the visual worlds of these films, collaborating with teams on everything from location scouting and set building to prop modeling and costume design.

I left my interview with McDowell convinced that the world of a living story should be detailed enough to inspire an amazing plot—not the other way around. But this is not how he first learned world-building. Early in his career, McDowell designed worlds the traditional way: based on scripts. In hindsight, he discovered a downside to that approach. His worlds during this period were "tunnel-shaped," he says, more like dioramas than full-fledged worlds. "The script is a path, and the tunnel follows the path," he tells me. "It's got trees and fields and houses and cities around it, but in a fairly consistent relationship to the linear pathway of the script."

That changed for McDowell when Steven Spielberg contacted him to work on *Minority Report*. From the beginning, Spielberg's approach was unique: He hired McDowell and the film's writer, Scott Frank, on the same day, asking McDowell to begin designing *Minority Report*'s world *before* its script even existed. Rather than designing

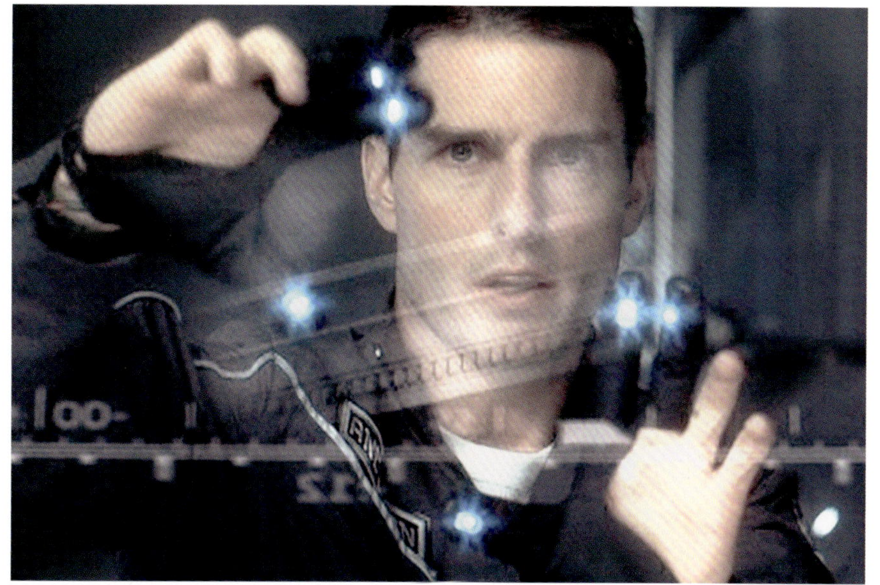

Tom Cruise as John Anderton, using hand gestures as a computer interface, one of many technological inventions that was first demonstrated through Alex McDowell's world-building for the film *Minority Report*.

sets to support a predetermined story, McDowell's job was to craft a comprehensive, richly detailed fictional world that would allow that story to flourish. He and his team met with top minds across a wide variety of fields to envision each detail of the future Washington, D.C., where the film takes place, from its buildings, vehicles, and roadways to its politics, culture, and history. By the time the work was done, says McDowell, they knew the city so intimately that "if Steven Spielberg had wanted Tom Cruise to turn left instead of right out of any doorway, we knew what was there."

You might question whether this level of detail is necessary, especially when much of it may not register for the audience. (How many moviegoers took note of the waste-management system in *Minority Report*?) But for those looking to create rich, living worlds that merit deep exploration, captivate audiences, and even support franchises, the devil is in the details.

Spielberg's world-first approach bore fruit: As McDowell and his team fleshed out the world of *Minority Report*, their designs began affecting the story. "The writers of *Minority Report* drew their inspiration for the script from the world," McDowell recalls. "Sequences like the vertical car chase evolved from our R&D into futuristic car designs that could move vertically. The writers had to consider how Tom Cruise gets to work in the morning, and what would happen if they combined a taxi cab with an elevator, turning it into a transportation system that moves vertically up buildings. Nobody asked us to build a car. It was just part of the fabric of the city."

Minority Report was a turning point for McDowell: He saw, for the first time, the profound impact that world-building could have on storytelling. A well-constructed world reunited siloed creatives. It enabled a robust interchange among artists, designers, directors, and writers that generated a richer final product. Perhaps most importantly, it provided a platform for the development of an infinite number of stories. *Minority Report* arrived in 2002, about a decade before Hollywood entered its current "franchise" era, but McDowell saw its potential. "*Minority Report* could have generated many different stories," he tells me. "When you understand a world deeply enough, stories spring almost effortlessly from that base world."

For McDowell, reaching that deep understanding comes through asking questions. The first questions are the broad, contextual ones that establish basic parameters: *Where are you, and when are you?* From there, the work—and the questions that drive it—proceed at multiple scales simultaneously, signifying that the smallest details of a world are often intimately connected to and reflective of its broadest workings. "We use the example of getting up in the morning and going to work," McDowell tells me. "By the time you've gone through the first two hours of your day, you've dealt with: *What is the size of your household? What's the structure of your social system? What are the economic conditions within which you're*

...in a future in which next-generation technologies or live production techniques can create multisensory, embodied, 3-D stories that are nearly indistinguishable from reality—we will need worlds, too, that match the depth and breadth of the one we actually live in.

living? What are you eating? Where did the food come from? There's an entire massive economic system based on what you have on your plate. Step outside the door. *What does your street corner look like? Do you get onto some kind of public transport or your own transport? And go to where?* In that very short time in a single day, every single aspect of that holistic world has had to deliver." McDowell refers to this process of examination through questions as "core-sampling," and as it progresses, the world "becomes more and more robust, at multiple scales—street corner, neighborhood, city, state, region—simultaneously." No stone is left unturned: McDowell's thorough exploration includes major categories such as culture, technology, biology, physics, language, and history, but also less obvious ones

"As a creator, you may not know the politics, the culture, the infrastructure of a world. But if those elements are not intact or coherent, your audience will sense it immediately." —ALEX McDOWELL

like fuel sources, education and policing systems, waste management, and building materials. The process is further supported by research to ensure that as the world develops, it stays logical and internally consistent.

McDowell's system may be an outlier in its scope and complexity. Nonetheless, I believe that his work should serve as an inspiration and a benchmark of what is possible in the field of world-building. At the highest end of the immersion scale—in a future in which next-generation technologies or live production techniques can create multisensory, embodied, 3-D stories that are nearly indistinguishable from reality—we will need worlds, too, that match the depth and breadth of the one we actually live in.

Ernest Hemingway described the necessity of detail in what's become known as the "iceberg theory." This says that a great story is like an iceberg floating in the ocean, with only a small portion—that which the author puts on the page—visible above the water. Though Hemingway's writing was spare, his stories were dense and rich with subsurface detail. Hemingway believed that the writer's deep knowledge of the story's world would affect the reader even more powerfully when implied or only vaguely suggested than if it were stated outright. Conversely, he wrote, "A writer who omits things because he does not know them only makes hollow places in his writing."

McDowell reinforces the idea that the strength of a fictional world is not its plot but rather its detail. He says, "As a creator, you may not know the politics, the culture, the infrastructure of a world. But if those elements are not intact and coherent, your audience will sense it immediately." Living stories can't afford the slightest omissions in detail, because the audience is certain to discover them.

Disney's *Star Wars: Galaxy's Edge* is rich with world-building details, from the scale replica of the Millennium Falcon *(top)* to the stained walls and equipment at Mubo's Droid Depot *(bottom)*.

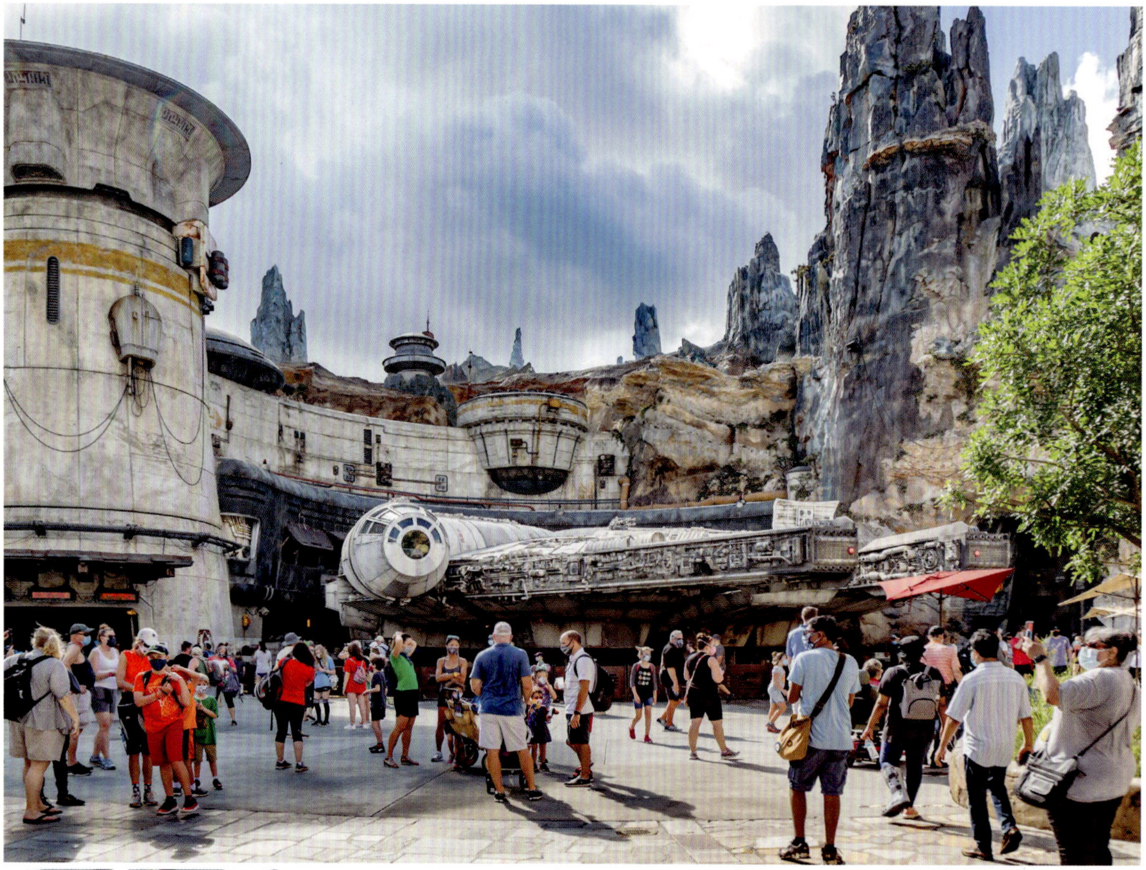

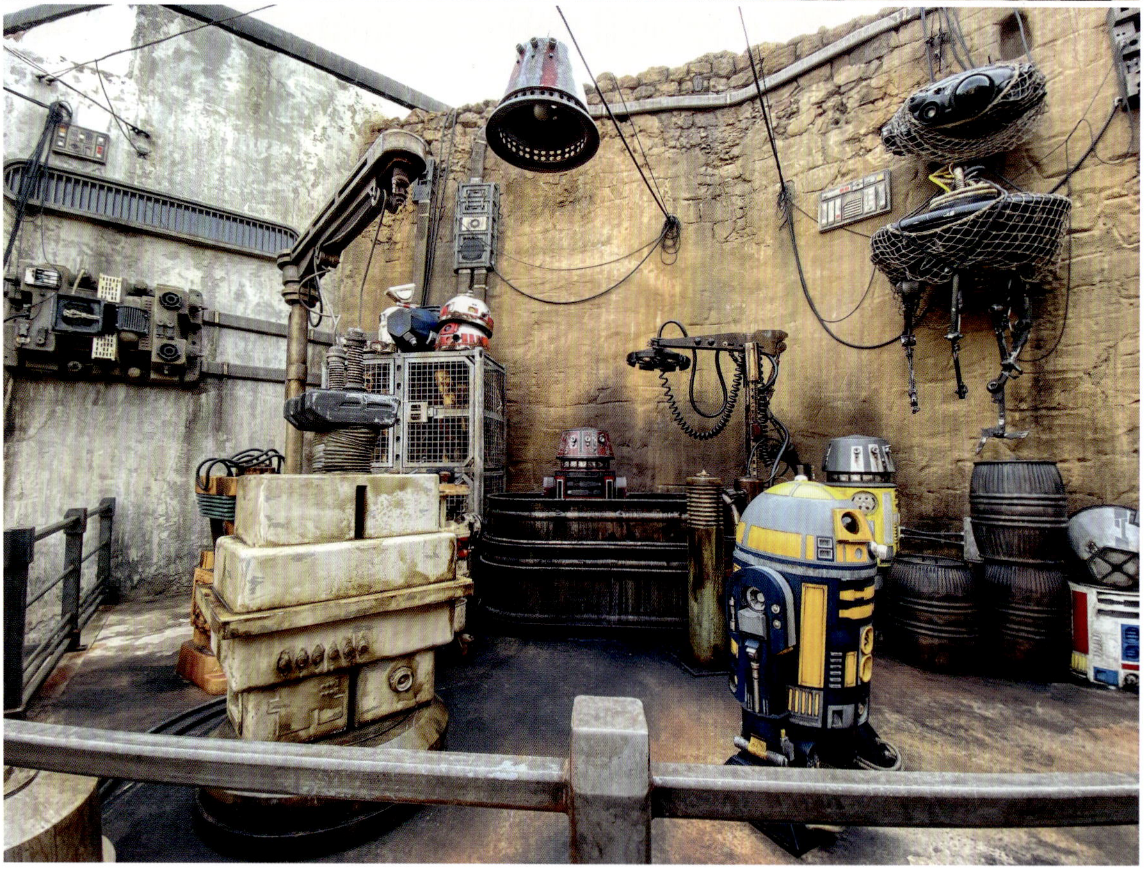

WORLD-BUILDING FOR LIVING STORIES

From the shape of a drawer handle and the creak of an old floorboard to the scent in a certain area, each sensory detail contributes to the resonance of a constructed world. To illustrate just a small sampling of the diverse methods available when world-building for living stories, let's take a closer look at two of the most extraordinary and richly detailed examples of our time: Disney's *Star Wars: Galaxy's Edge* and Meow Wolf's *House of Eternal Return* (see p. 98).

For *Galaxy's Edge*, the *Star Wars*–themed land that debuted at Walt Disney World Resort in Florida and Disneyland Resort in California in 2019, Disney wanted to give fans the feeling of truly living within their beloved franchise. Their approach was a drive for realism—not in the content of the story, of course, but in the construction of the world. Scott Trowbridge, creative executive for Walt Disney Imagineering, has more than thirty years of experience in building incredibly immersive, award-winning theme-park rides. Serving as creative lead on *Galaxy's Edge*, he describes how the smallest details and the full range of senses help achieve this realism: "The way things smell, the ground you're walking on, the texture of things you're feeling—all of that registers subconsciously. Even if guests don't actively consider these details, they would notice if they were absent. They just make things believable."

Galaxy's Edge brims with fine details. Black Spire Outpost, the fictional town that provides its setting, is a storied trading hub on the galactic frontier that plays host to all manner of spacefaring smugglers, outcasts, and adventurers. It has a rich past and an aesthetic reminiscent of the Middle East and North Africa, and to capture that atmosphere, Trowbridge's team visited Istanbul and Marrakech to study those cities' centuries-old bazaars. While their local tour guides directed their attention to famous mosques and palaces—or tried to—the team was busy photographing doorknobs and windowsills and taking rubbings of the textures of walls. Later, they used these captured details as inspiration to imbue Black Spire Outpost's fourteen acres with as much history—and story potential—as possible.

Seen through Trowbridge's eyes, every inch of the outpost has a story to tell. The transition from crumbling, aged facades to newer, cleaner buildings speaks to its shifting fortunes throughout its history. Regarding the choice to add some deep scrapes in the wall of a building at a street corner, Trowbridge explains, "As droids and carts come around here and they kind of cut the corner, they end up dragging and cutting into the wall." Most guests might not notice the scrapes or guess their cause, but in Trowbridge's words, "it has a reality to it that I think helps lend a feeling of history and authenticity to the whole place." The same goes for the scorched holes in the side of a building nearby, left by a long-ago blaster battle: "There are stories behind the fight that happened outside Oga's Cantina that left those blaster marks on the wall. We know those stories."

Trowbridge and his team may know those stories, but many of them are never delivered directly during a visit to *Galaxy's Edge*. Here, as with *Minority Report*, we see an "iceberg" method of world-building: The designers know far more than they share, and this profusion of knowledge distilled through the audience's awareness forms a world that feels deep, real, and alive, inviting the audience's curiosity while encouraging them to suspend their disbelief.

It also, crucially, provides fertile ground for developing an ecosystem of stories across media. For instance, visitors exploring the alleyway behind Mubo's Droid Depot in the Black Spire marketplace might pay attention to a number of powered-down droids half submerged in barrels of oil. "Mubo's giving these droids oil baths," Trowbridge explains. "Here on this dusty, outer-rim planet, it's hard to keep your droids in good shape." This detail serves to add depth to the world of *Galaxy's Edge*, as well as to spark curiosity about a character that audiences can then explore further in other forms of media. "If you really want to get a sense of Mubo's world, we've released VR experiences where you get to go on adventures with Mubo and visit some of the back rooms of his droid shop," Trowbridge says. "It's part of our connected storytelling approach, where you can visit the 'real world' here, and you can also meet some of these characters in comics, novels, games, and VR experiences." A rich world serves not only the primary narrative for which it's developed but also, potentially, a web of related stories that can take many different forms.

If *Galaxy's Edge* uses subtle details to create a sense of realism, Meow Wolf takes almost the opposite approach in their landmark installation, *House of Eternal Return*, a psychedelic playground in Santa Fe, New Mexico, that draws hundreds of thousands of visitors per year. While *Galaxy's Edge* asks visitors to suspend their disbelief by couching its sci-fi storytelling in relatable real-world detail, *House* confronts audiences with something unlike anything they've experienced, upending expectations at each turn. No suspension of disbelief is required here: This world is, thrillingly, unbelievable. While Meow Wolf's design approach is just as detailed as the Disney Imagineers', the former uses those details not to heighten a sense of reality but to intentionally distort it.

The world-building at *House of Eternal Return* is most apparent in the psychedelic imagery. Its colors and textures are often in direct opposition to what we would expect in reality: One cave-like room is adorned with fuzzy rainbow rocks, its ceiling dripping with wispy, transparent stalactites. Everything glows, from the twinkling LED

Meow Wolf's *House of Eternal Return* takes every opportunity to immerse guests in its psychedelic vision. People literally go down the rabbit hole through this portal to another dimension hidden in the laundry room dryer.

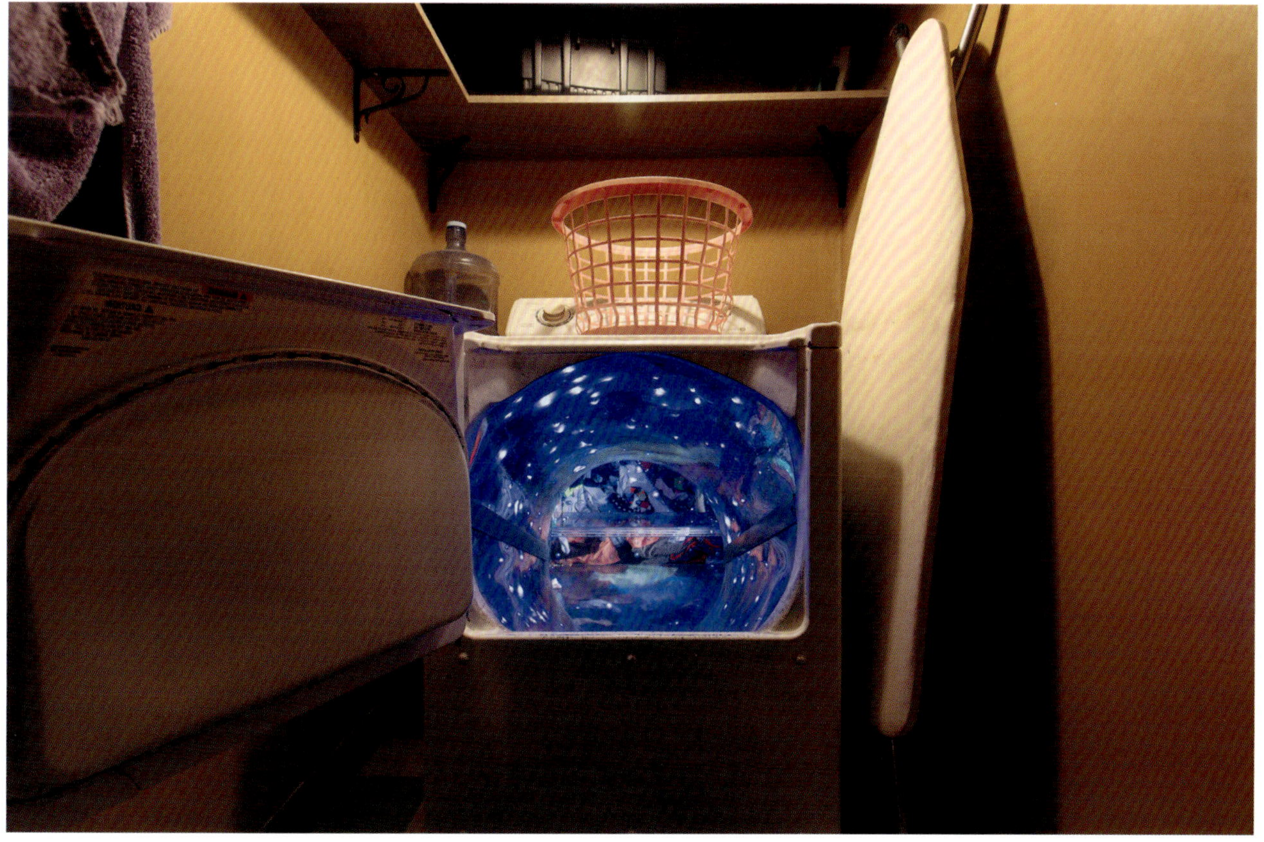

power lines strung between telephone poles in a central village to the luminescent blue mammoth skeleton half embedded in the wall of a nearby tunnel. Like Disney, Meow Wolf pays keen attention to flooring: Here, it's often decked out with undulating patterns reminiscent of optical illusions. Yet also like Disney, these details are complemented by subtler touches that work primarily on a subliminal level—such as the outright subversion of standard building dimensions. According to Meow Wolf cofounder and artistic visionary Vince Kadlubek, "A confusing, non-traditional layout is really important. So is using non-traditional dimensions. We like to play with odd numbers with regard to the sizes and angles of rooms. Same with heights: Rather than just having a ground floor and a mezzanine, we like to place in-between heights so there are levels you're not used to, entire floors at a height you're unaccustomed to." It's the physical equivalent of J. K. Rowling's Platform 9¾, a detail used to emphasize that this world is thoroughly different from the one you're leaving behind.

Like Alex McDowell and the Disney Imagineers, the Meow Wolf team started their world-building with scrupulous research. *How do things look in real life? How are they built? What materials are used? What are the standard dimensions of traditional construction?* Then, instead of following these conventions, the team upended them, creating a world that is strange and disorienting in ways both immediately obvious and vanishingly subtle. The subtler details are unlikely to be consciously registered by most visitors; rather, they work on a subconscious level to achieve the design goals of what's being built.

The uncommon building dimensions used at Meow Wolf also point to the unique way that living stories can affect our psyches. If you read a book, watch a movie, or play a video game in which a character enters a world with odd proportions, you may think, *What a strange place*. But when you walk through *House of Eternal Return*, you feel strange yourself. The atmosphere surrounds you completely, permeating your subconscious, shifting your mood just like a sudden change in weather.

A great writer may capture your imagination, and a great director may dazzle your eyes and ears, but a living storyteller has the opportunity to speak to your hands, head, and heart.

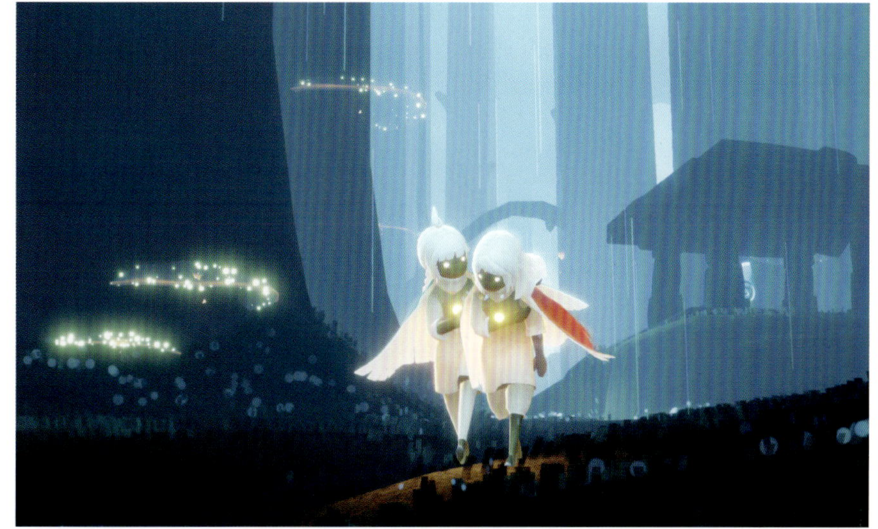

Unlike other online multiplayer games, ***Sky: Children of the Light*** **was consciously designed to foster compassion and generosity through a game mechanic that encourages players to give gifts.**

INTERACTIVE WORLD-BUILDING

Once a world-builder establishes their setting, they have to create the conditions for interaction within it. They must ask: *How does the actience participate in this world? What are they able to do and how will that make them feel? How can their actions affect the world and the stories occurring within it?*

The laws of interaction in an immersive world are as fundamental as the laws of physics in the real world. Just as a science-fiction writer may create a world with no gravity or where time moves in reverse, an immersive world-builder creates laws of interaction to reinforce or complicate the themes of that world's stories. Take, for example, *Sky: Children of the Light*, a 2019 open-world video game developed and published by Thatgamecompany. Its laws of interaction are striking. Though *Sky* is played online and allows gamers to interact in real time, they start the game with no text- or voice-chat functions, initially able to communicate only through gestures and gift-giving. Jenova Chen, Thatgamecompany cofounder and director of award-winning games *Cloud*, *Flower*, and *Journey*, attributes this design choice to a desire to capture the beauty of human relationships and combat the toxicity common to online gaming interactions. "In the end," he says, "it's about, how do you structure these virtual societies where interpersonal relationships can actually be nudged toward those positive qualities that human beings are already capable of?"

Sky is a free-to-play mobile game, and like many others of its kind, it generates money through microtransactions: Players spend real money on virtual in-game items, such as clothing, spells, potions, and musical instruments. Upon the game's release, Chen and his team found that its message of goodwill and compassion had a measurable impact: Players were buying large numbers of in-game items through microtransactions solely for the purpose of giving them to other players as gifts. In the first four years, 22 percent of *Sky*'s revenue from all merchandise, as well as 50 percent of all its season-pass sales, came via these gift purchases. It's a remarkable figure and an enticing vision: a world where 22 percent of all money spent in a video game is dedicated not to empowering the spender but to enriching the lives of others.

I've often wondered, as I've ventured through the idyllic world of *Sky*, wandered the playa at Burning Man (where the economy operates largely on principles of decommodification and gift-giving), and explored other story worlds with profound lessons to share, *Is our own world not, in some sense, a story that we all collectively co-create? And if so, couldn't we change the rules of our world to drive more positive, compassionate, and empathetic interactions?*

WHEN WORLDS COLLIDE

Perhaps the most exciting possibility of world-building is its potential to change the real world. This is exactly what *Minority Report* did: Many of the futuristic technologies first seen in the film have since become real fixtures in our daily lives, and Alex McDowell estimates that more than a hundred patents filed in the years since the movie's release can in some way be traced back to its influence.

McDowell and his team did not predict the future; rather, they saw nascent technologies and envisioned a world where those innovations had been successfully incorporated into daily life, which then inspired real-world product development. Similarly, the world of *Sky* helps its players envision and embrace, first in virtual environments, more positive modes of communication and interaction. In this sense, the *world* of a story—the set of design choices that create the physical, narrative, and interactive environments within which the story plays out—has as much potential to affect the hearts and minds of the audience as the plot beats, character arcs, and dialogue that make up the story itself. A carefully considered story world is not simply a container for narrative but a vehicle for meaning in its own right.

Vince Kadlubek, too, believes a well-crafted immersive world can change your life. *House of Eternal Return* is set up to look like a run-of-the-mill suburban home, until participants discover that hidden in the fridge and the laundry machine are portals to another dimension. For Kadlubek, this juxtaposition of the extraordinary with the mundane is the very core of Meow Wolf's art. "You start with something very relatable, like a fridge," he says. "Then, within that vehicle, you venture down the rabbit hole. If you can provide people with a familiar context and then break that context with new possibilities, they start to realize they have new possibilities within themselves. They realize that the refrigerator is completely different from what it seemed to be. And in that moment, people also realize that the world can be different from what it seems to be. And that *they* can be different from what they seem to be."

At their best, living stories have the power to change the lives of those who experience them, to bring communities together, and even, dare I say, to change the world. Whether it's Meow Wolf showing people new possibilities for themselves, *Sky: Children of the Light* helping to build a culture of generosity among online gamers, or *Minority Report* shepherding new technologies into being, it all starts with a world.

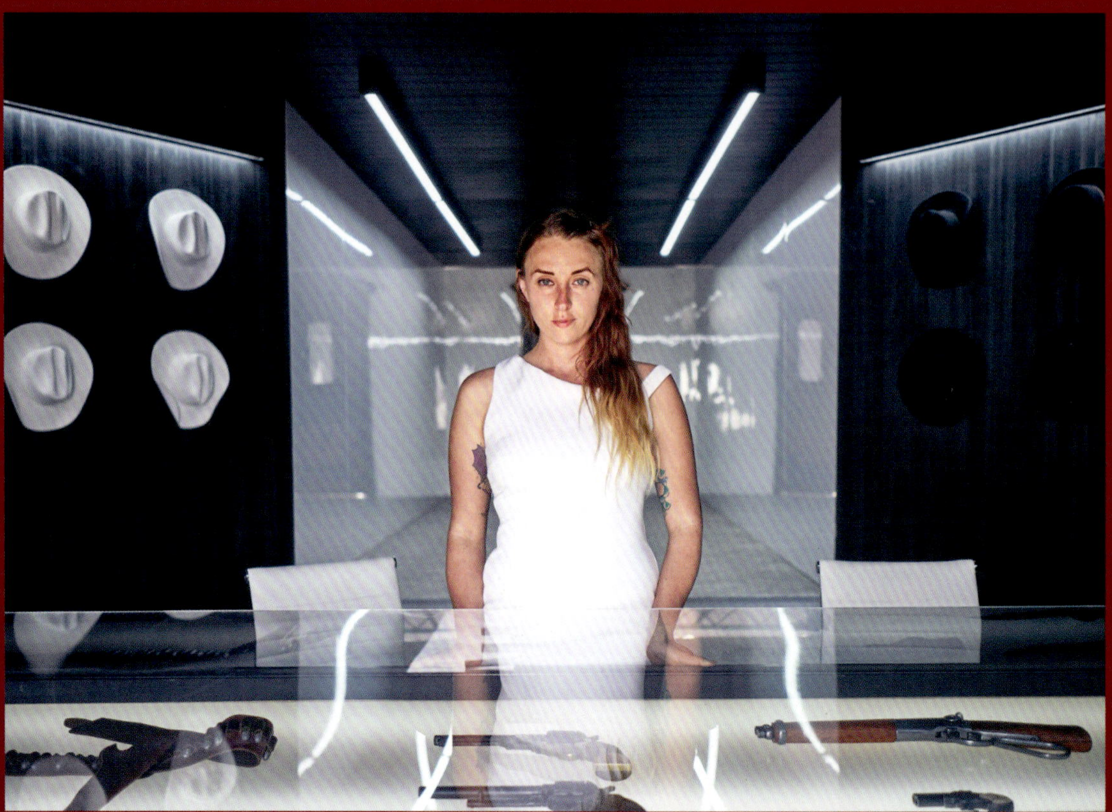

WESTWORLD: LIVE WITHOUT LIMITS

In 2018, HBO asked marketing agency Giant Spoon to help build excitement for the upcoming second season of the network's hit show *Westworld*. Giant Spoon came back with an ambitious proposal: to re-create an entire *Westworld* town as a massive immersive experience at the South by Southwest Festival in Austin. With HBO's approval, Giant Spoon worked alongside entertainment development company Mycotoo and creative marketing agency Glass Eye to transform a Texas ghost town into "Sweetwater," the show's fictional frontier-themed town, which would host 4,500 guests over the course of three days. The experience generated 1.9 billion social-media impressions and went on to win a Cannes Gold Lion, among many other awards.

From the moment guests stepped off the train into Sweetwater, their fate was in their own hands. Perhaps they ran into the town blacksmith, who let them know there was a letter waiting for them at the post office. That letter could have led them to embark on a series of adventures with dozens of potential outcomes—but what if they chose not to pick it up? Perhaps they headed to the saloon instead, where they might enlist in the search for a missing woman. Or perhaps they simply spent their day playing poker, drinking whiskey, and watching gunfights. As in the *Westworld* theme park from the show, here guests were not ushered down one path; the world was theirs to explore.

For Giant Spoon and their collaborators, re-creating Sweetwater was no small feat. Within the 90,000-square-foot town, eleven locations inspired by the show were brought to life in exacting detail, from the songs played on honky-tonk pianos down to the custom-printed wallpaper in the saloon. Sixty-six actors were hired to perform more than 400 pages of script alongside improvised interactions with guests. The experience quickly become the hottest ticket in town.

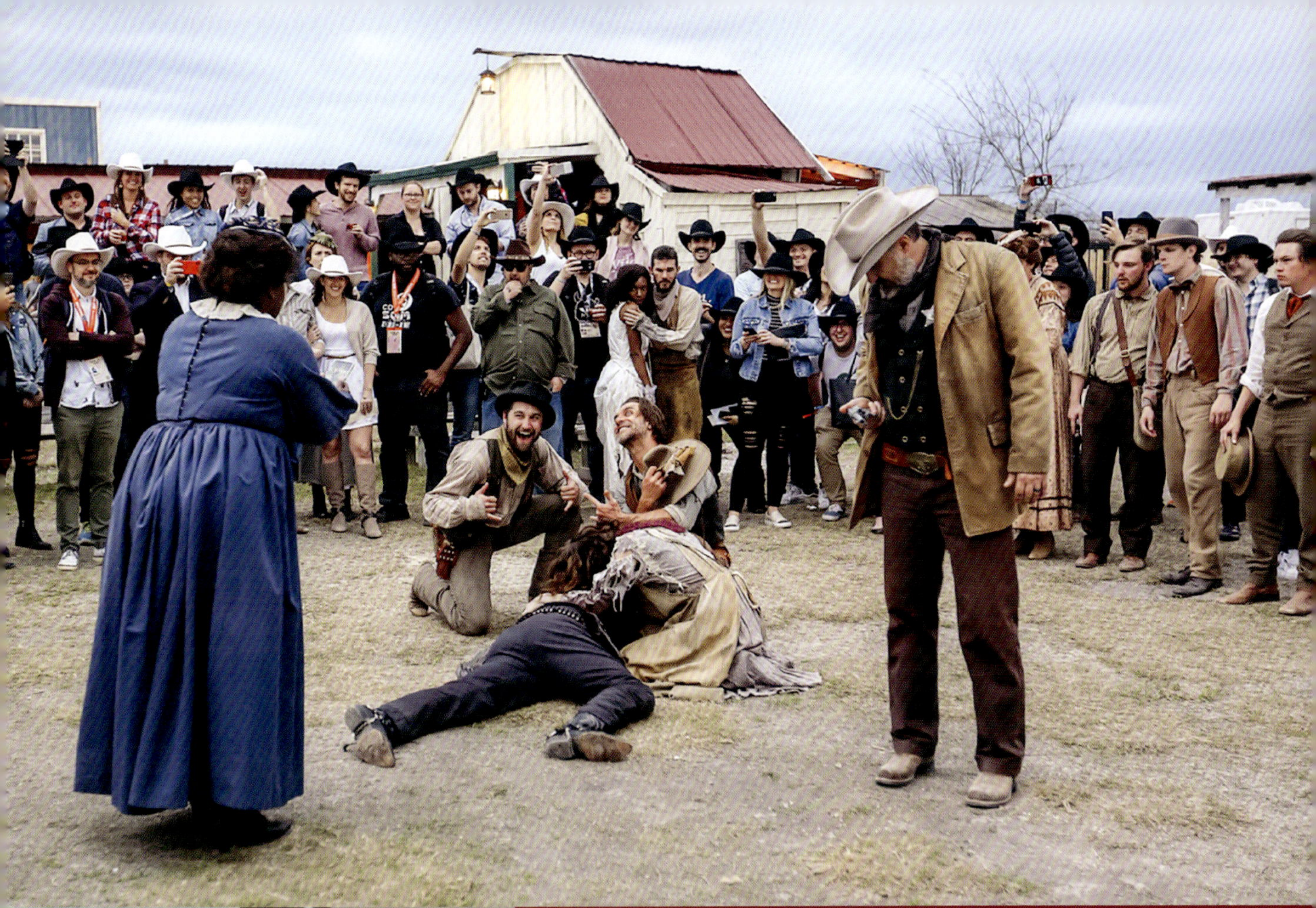

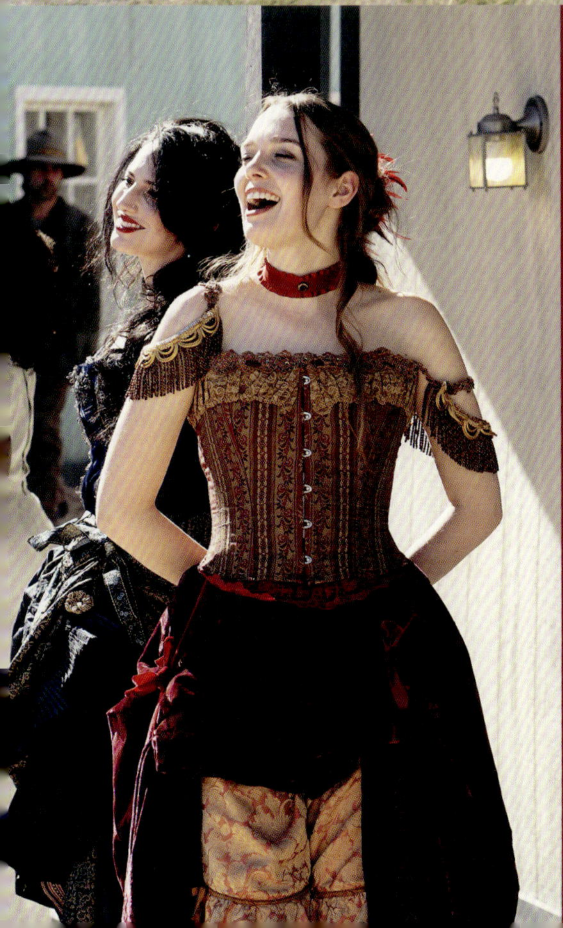

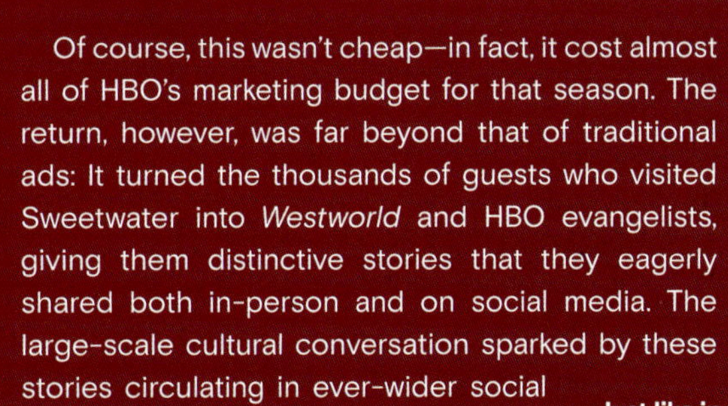

Of course, this wasn't cheap—in fact, it cost almost all of HBO's marketing budget for that season. The return, however, was far beyond that of traditional ads: It turned the thousands of guests who visited Sweetwater into *Westworld* and HBO evangelists, giving them distinctive stories that they eagerly shared both in-person and on social media. The large-scale cultural conversation sparked by these stories circulating in ever-wider social groups meant that millions more people heard about *Westworld* from their friends rather than from an ad agency, and the series garnered millions of dollars in earned media impressions.

As Giant Spoon cofounder Marc Simons says, "We're in the business of making brands more memorable." Certainly, with *Westworld: Live Without Limits*, their partnership with HBO gave fans a unique experience that they won't soon forget. Their efforts go a long way in showing that when it comes to marketing, immersive experiences can be a powerful and popular tool.

Just like in the show, guests at HBO's *Westworld* activation were transported from a slick futuristic set to a frontier town populated with costumed actors playing out various interactive storylines.

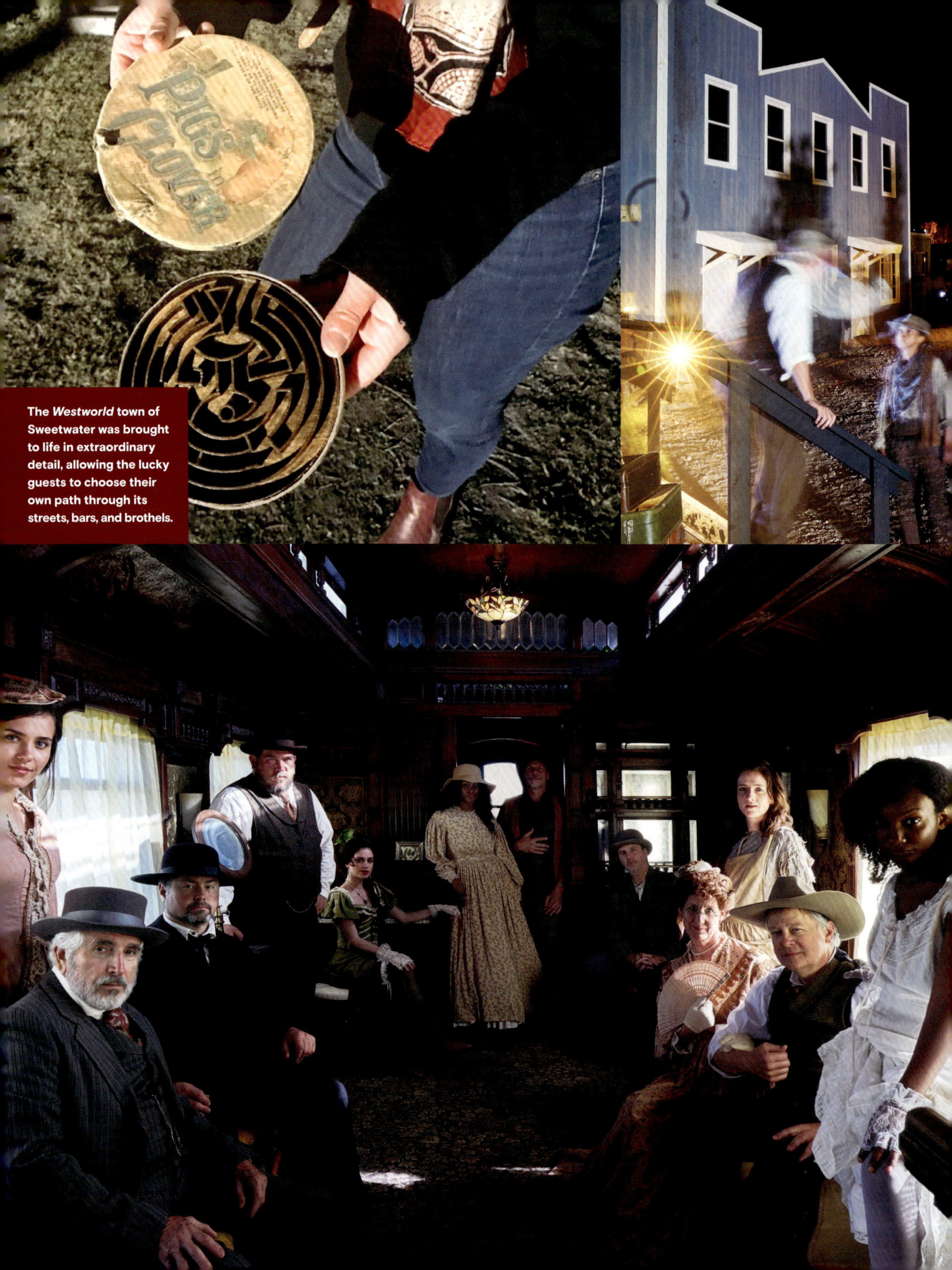

The *Westworld* town of Sweetwater was brought to life in extraordinary detail, allowing the lucky guests to choose their own path through its streets, bars, and brothels.

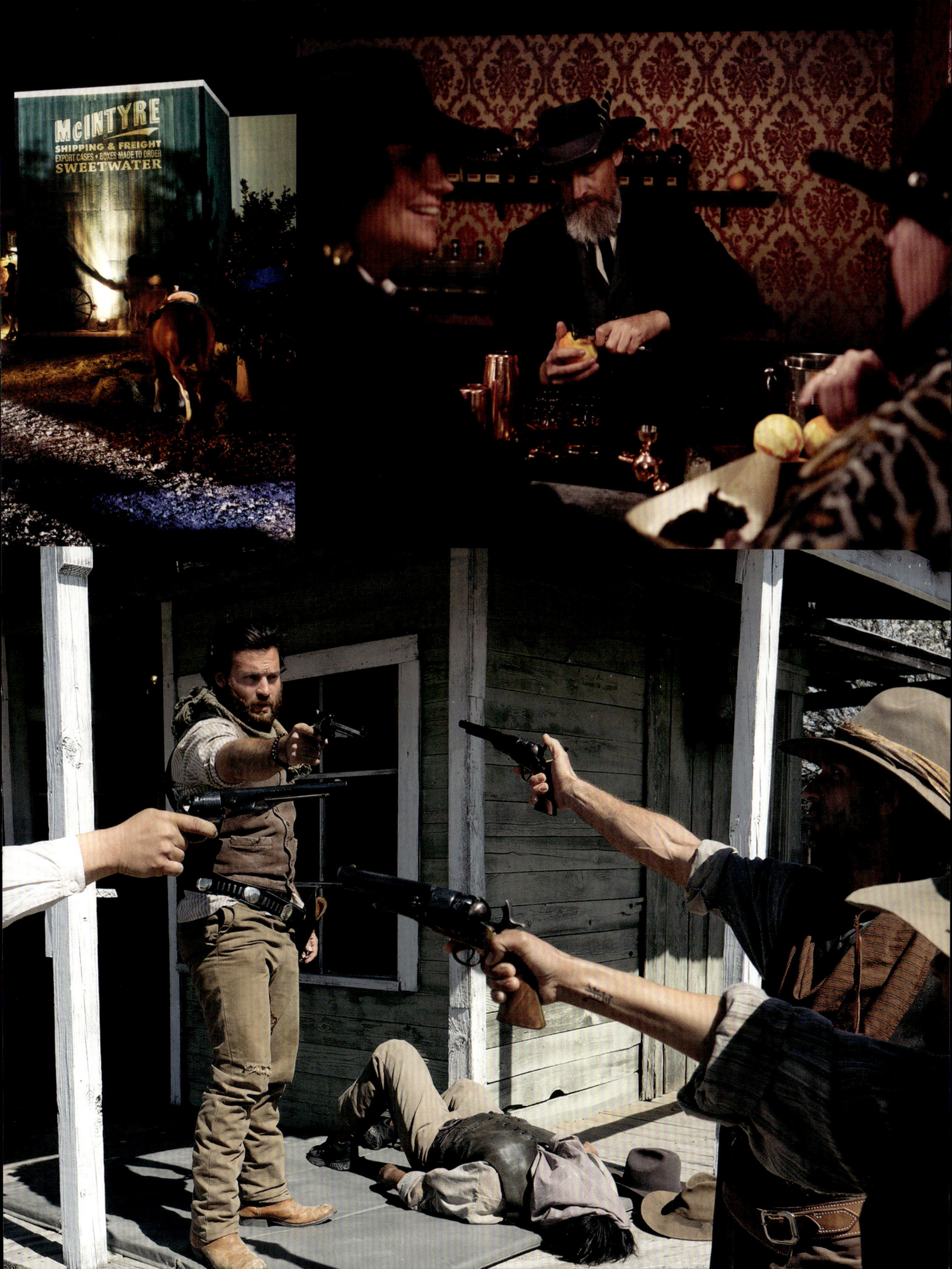
McINTYRE
SHIPPING & FREIGHT
EXPORT CASES • BOXES MADE TO ORDER
SWEETWATER

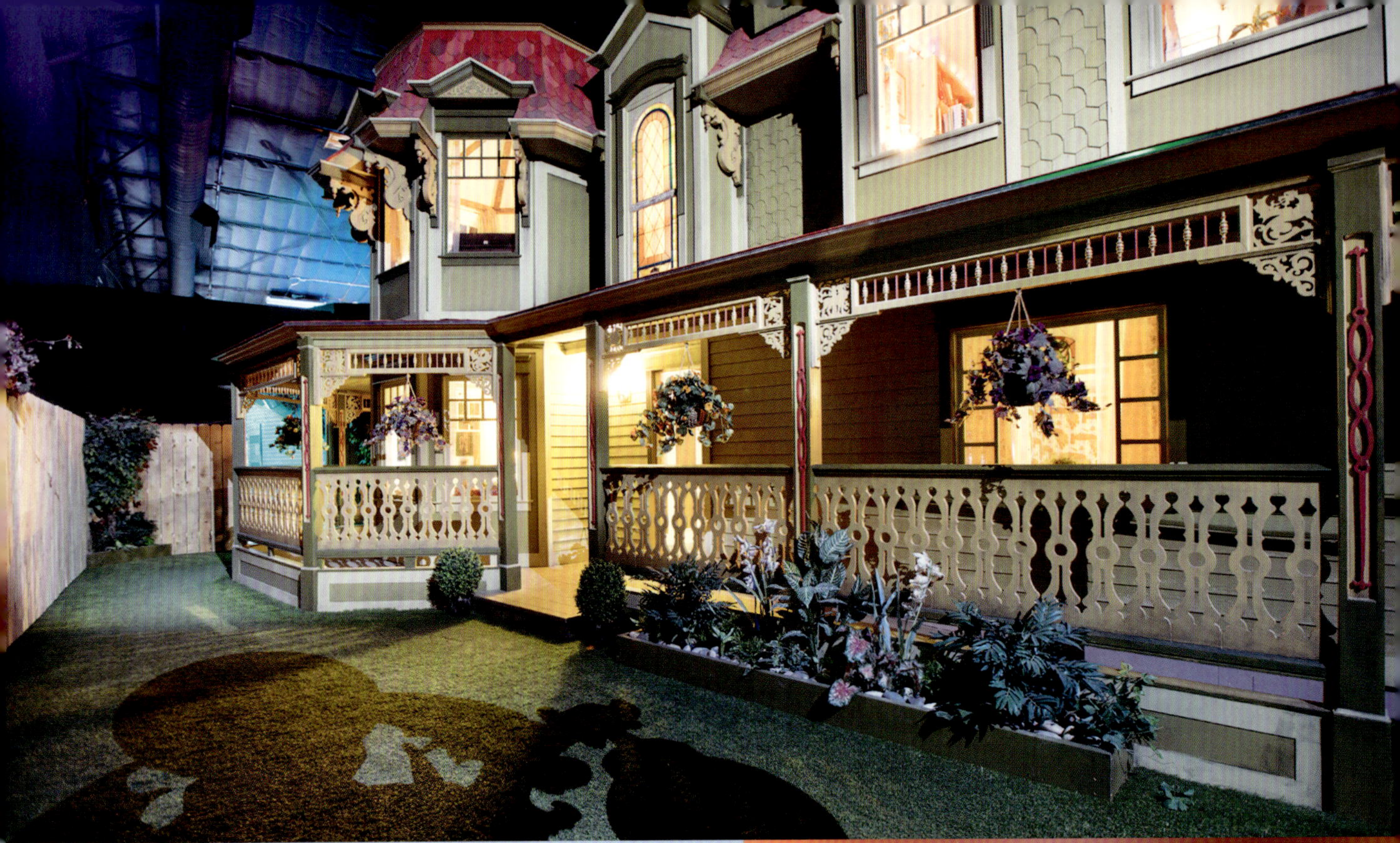

MEOW WOLF

In 2008, a group of outsider artists in Santa Fe came together to transform the ordinary into the extraordinary. Accustomed to pooling funds for studio space and diving through dumpsters for materials, the self-described "orphans of neglect" wanted to agitate the stodgy contemporary-art scene by making something weird. Calling themselves Meow Wolf, they began building elaborate worlds defined by a sense of infinite possibility.

The group soon accumulated a loyal following of fans, including *Game of Thrones* author George R. R. Martin. When Meow Wolf gathered to design their most ambitious work to date, Martin financed the collective's purchase and renovation of a disused bowling alley into an immersive experience. This first permanent project, *House of Eternal Return*, opened in 2016 and soon became a massive success. Cofounder Vince Kadlubek hoped for 150,000 visitors in the first year—but by the end of it, *House* had surpassed 450,000 guests and earned $6.8 million

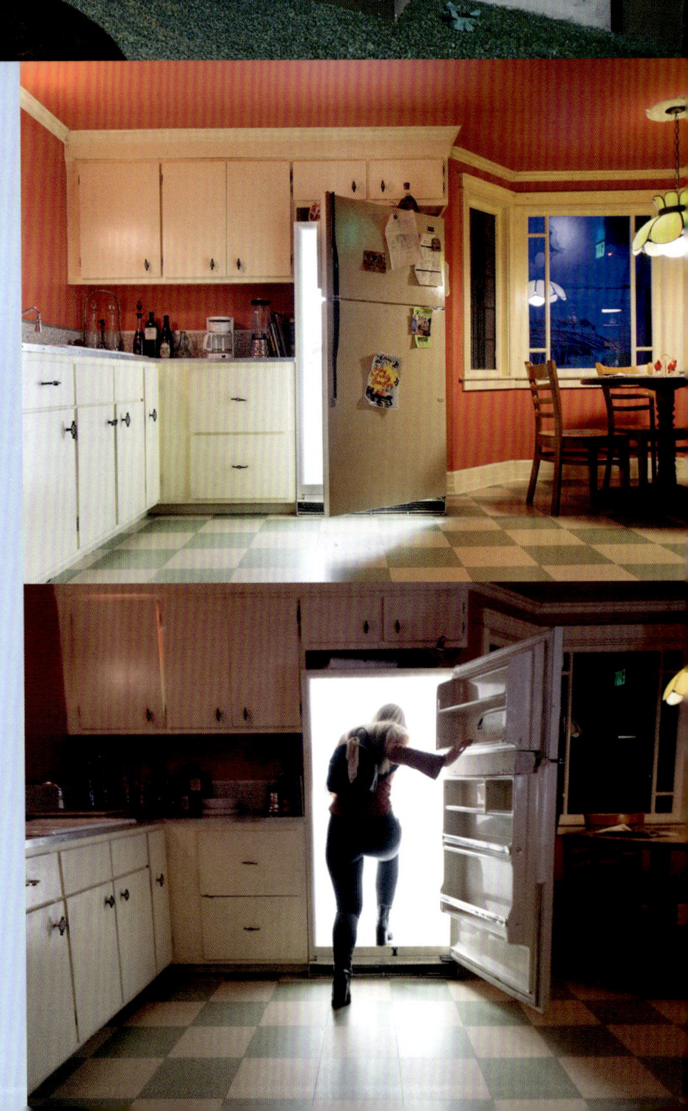

***This page:* Meow Wolf's *House of Eternal Return* in Santa Fe transports visitors from a normal Victorian home to a hallucinatory wonderland through a number of unlikely portals, such as the refrigerator.**

in revenue. Recognized with the prestigious Thea Award for Outstanding Achievement in Connected Immersion on a Limited Budget in 2017, *House* reached the milestone of one million visitors by 2018 and cemented its status as one of New Mexico's top attractions.

The eponymous house appears to be an ordinary Victorian home (albeit one inside a former bowling alley). Inside, there are no directions or signposts—instead, you're invited to follow your curiosity. As you explore, you discover photos, journals, and newspaper clippings strewn about, all alluding to something mysterious. Upon opening the refrigerator, you're blinded by white light: a portal. Climb inside and you'll leave behind the house's sleepy, traditional interior for a maze of secret passages, mind-bending art installations, and color-soaked environments, packed to the gills with delightful detail and interactive elements at every turn. The experience is also densely layered: You have the option to simply enjoy the visual feast or dig deep into the mystery and uncover hidden layers of story throughout.

House's incredible success was just the beginning. Meow Wolf raised more than $150 million in 2019 for expansion across America and opened additional permanent locations in Denver, Las Vegas, a Dallas suburb, and Houston, with two more announced in Los Angeles and New York. But while these Santa Fe artists may no longer be outsiders, their founding philosophy hasn't changed. Each experience takes you out of the everyday and plunges you into a fantastic universe unbound by the laws of propriety, logic, and even physics. There, the world operates differently: Where our society prioritizes predictability and safety, Meow Wolf primes you to be constantly surprised and adventurous. Regardless of your age, when you're confronted with a fridge that can take you to another dimension, you're encouraged to unleash your inner child. Meow Wolf can even teach you to keep that open mind once you leave—after all, if household appliances can be interdimensional portals and orphans of neglect can become internationally respected artists, isn't anything possible?

***This page:* "The Forest" within *House of Eternal Return*, full of magical flora and fauna.**

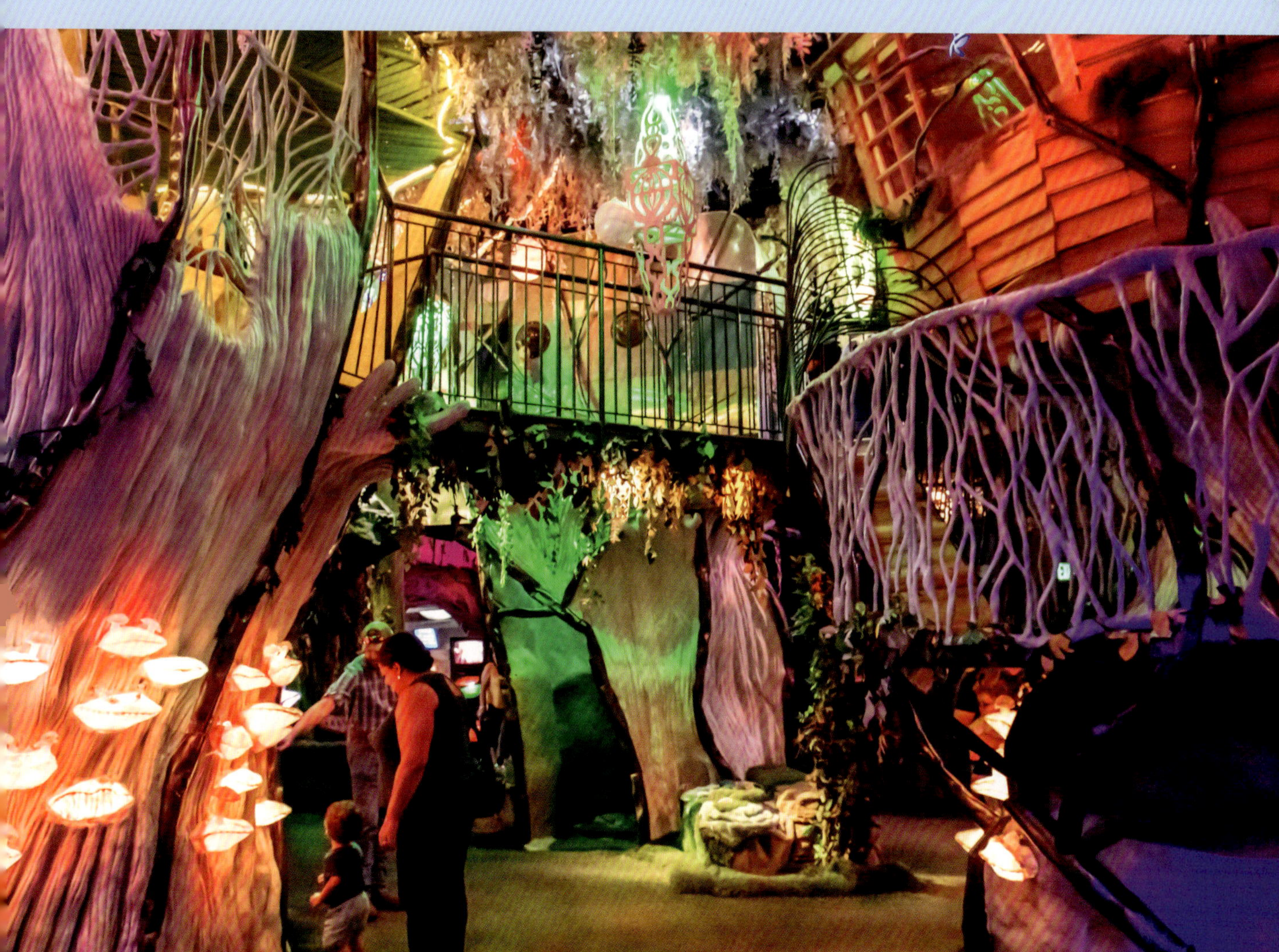

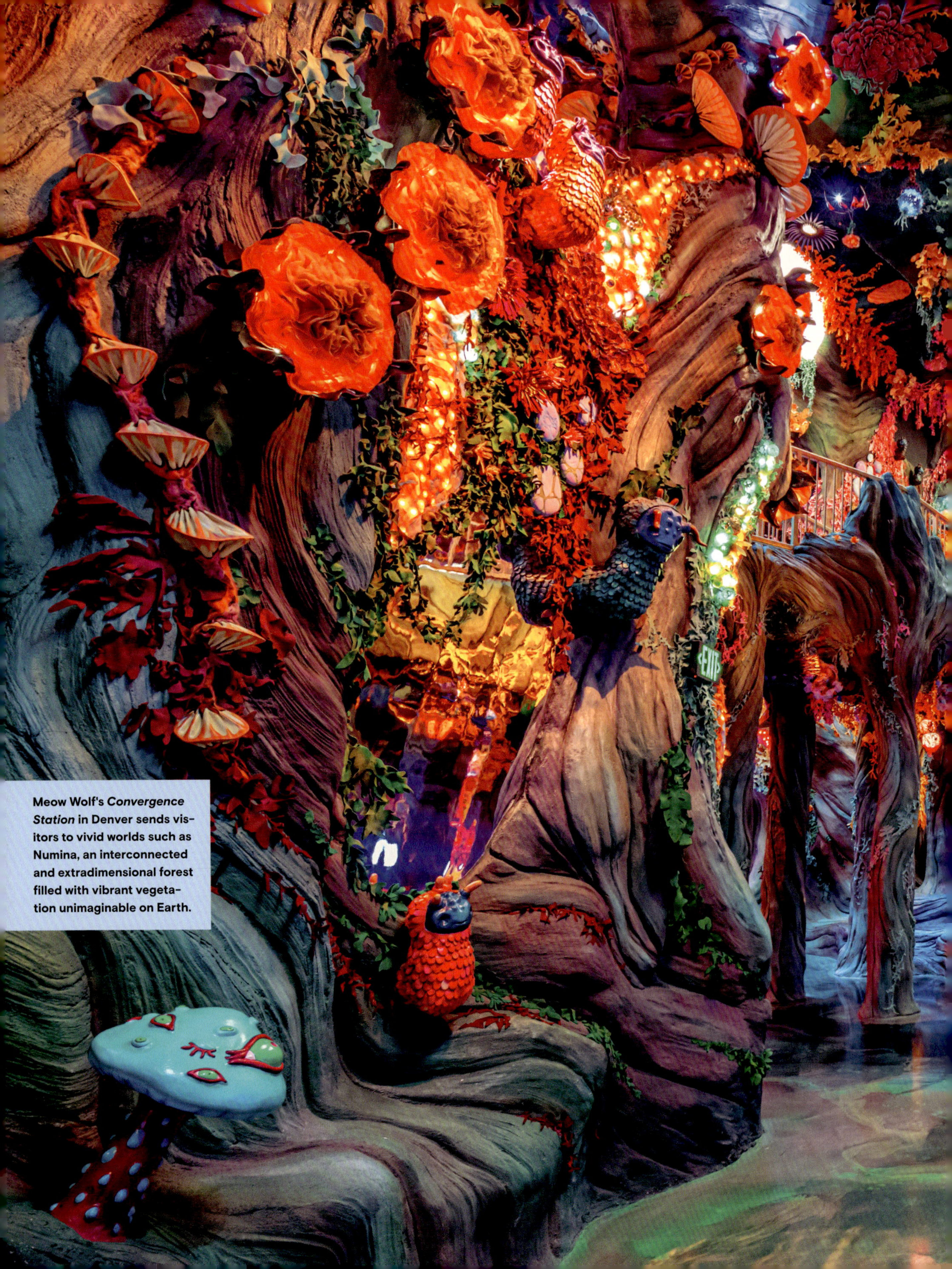

Meow Wolf's *Convergence Station* in Denver sends visitors to vivid worlds such as Numina, an interconnected and extradimensional forest filled with vibrant vegetation unimaginable on Earth.

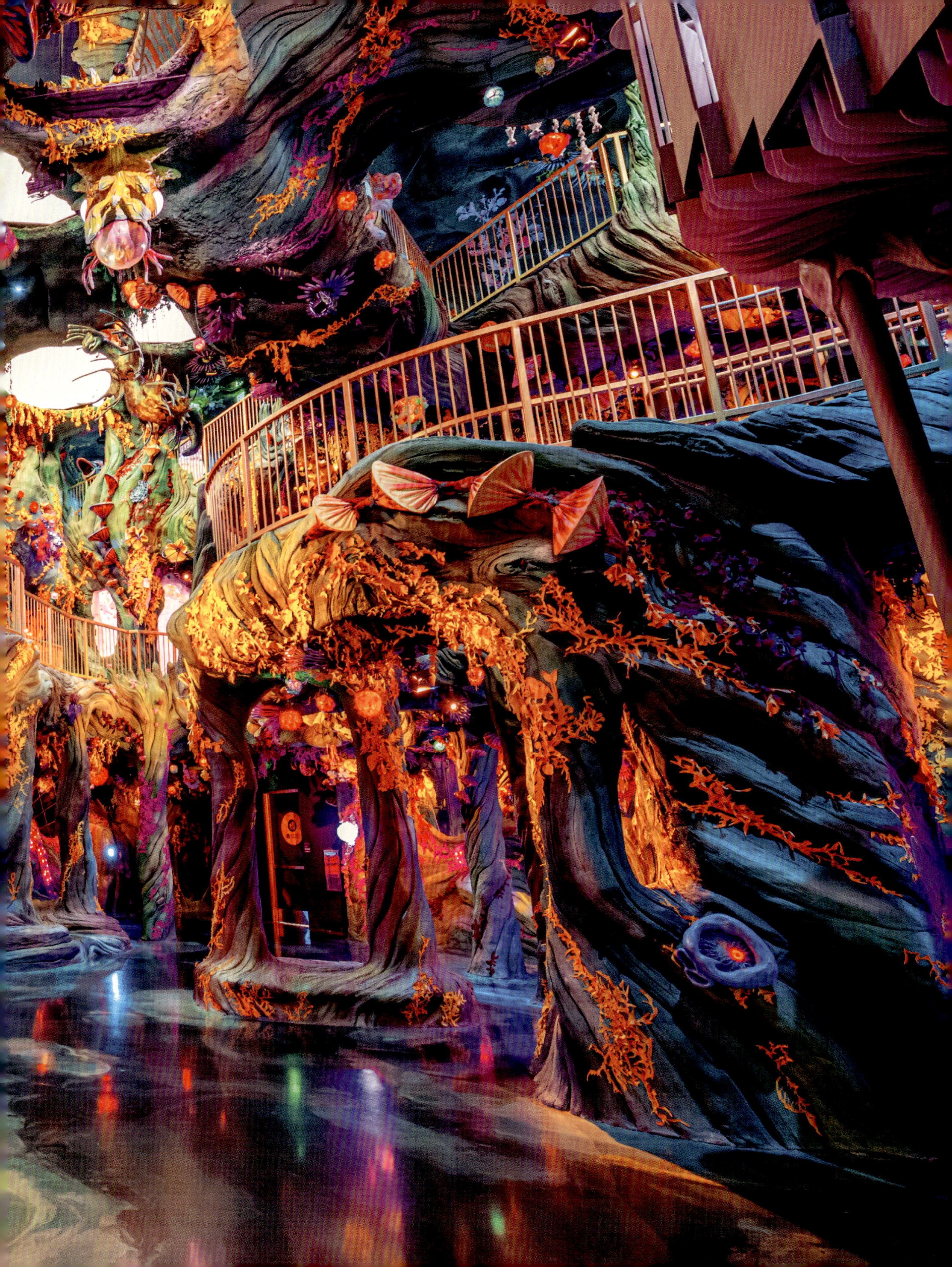

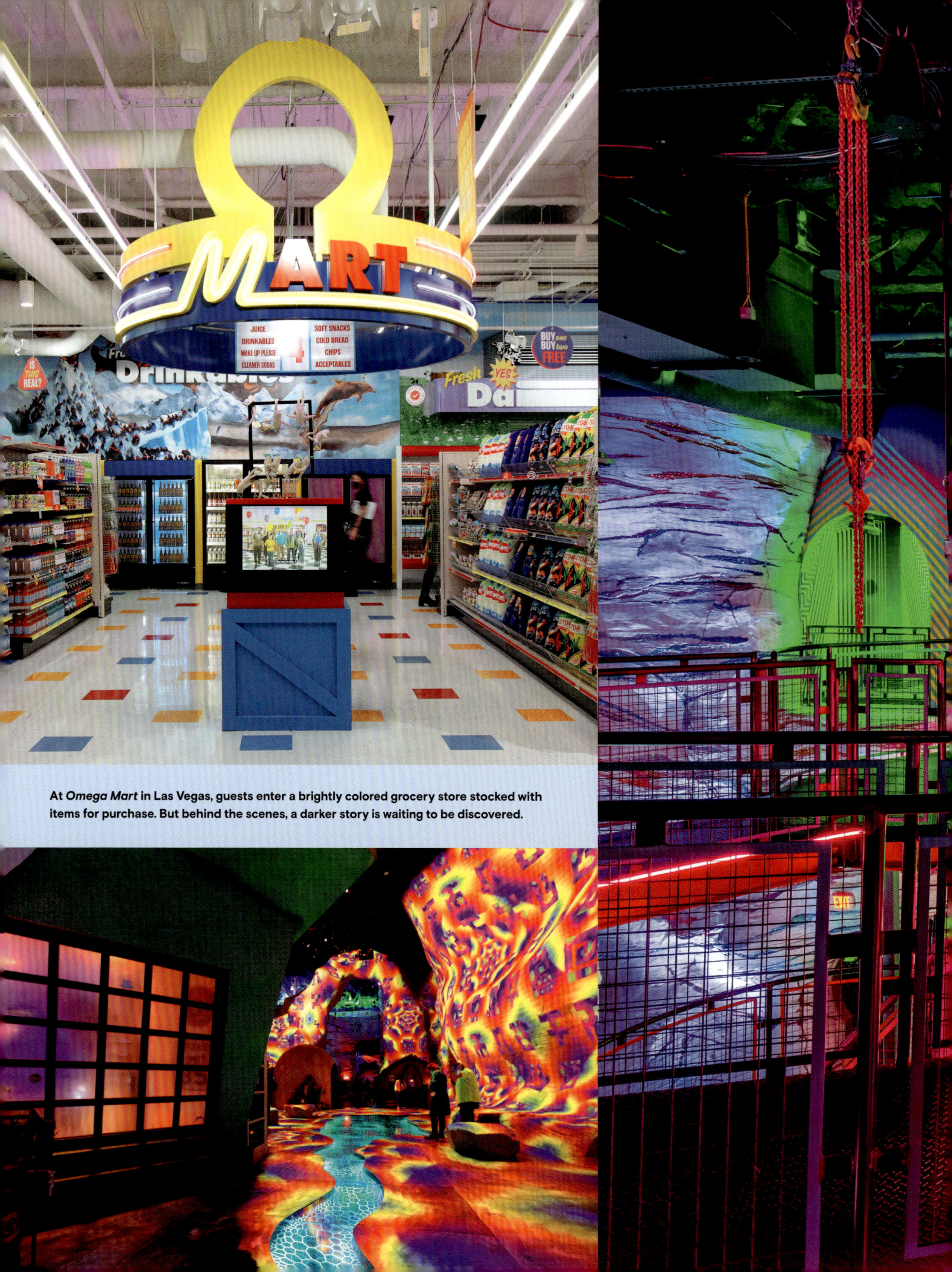

At *Omega Mart* in Las Vegas, guests enter a brightly colored grocery store stocked with items for purchase. But behind the scenes, a darker story is waiting to be discovered.

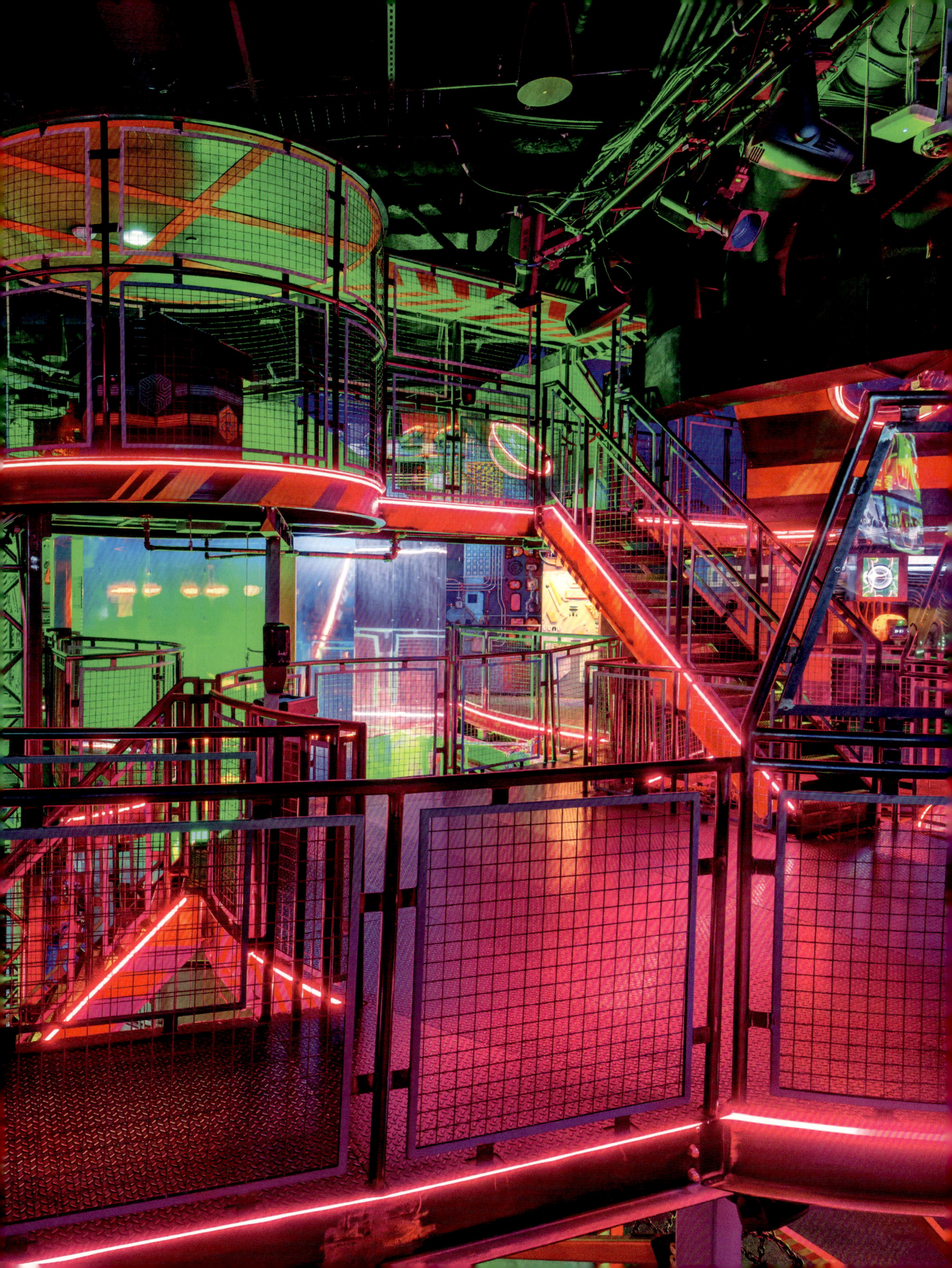

SECRET CINEMA

Founded in 2007 by Fabien Riggall, Secret Cinema fulfills every cinephile's dream: to step through the screen into a seamless, full-scale re-creation of an iconic film world and become part of its story. It all starts with the arrival of a mysterious invitation, containing no information except for a time, place, and dress code. When you show up at the indicated location, you'll have only an inkling of the story that's about to unfold—you may find yourself among the inmates in *The Shawshank Redemption*, recruited as a spy by MI6 in *Casino Royale*, or mingling with bohemians and cabaret performers in *Moulin Rouge!*, to name just a few of their adaptations. Whatever the production may be, though, you can rest assured that you're in for something spectacular.

Secret Cinema's calling card is their commitment to making each adaptation feel as realistic and immersive as possible. From movie musicals to period dramas to sci-fi flicks, they build out locations from former warehouses or London's Olympic Park in great detail, then fill them with both actor-led and audience-driven performances. Each night for anywhere between twenty and sixty nights, crowds as large as 5,000 participants and upwards of eighty actors spend several hours living as the film's characters: dressing, playing, and even eating and drinking as if they were really inside the cinematic world. The centerpiece of each show is, of course, a screening of the film in question, enhanced by the collective sensation that you're experiencing real-life movie magic.

Although Secret Cinema began as advertised—that is, a secret reserved for a devoted following who spread its gospel mainly through word of mouth—it wasn't long before shows were selling out and Hollywood took notice. Studios such as Disney, Universal, and Paramount started to approach the company to create unique, interactive productions that build excitement around upcoming films. By giving fans the coveted opportunity to live within their favorite movies rather than just passively watch them unfold, Secret Cinema went from staging productions in abandoned London warehouses to creating bespoke immersive shows for some of the biggest IP owners in entertainment.

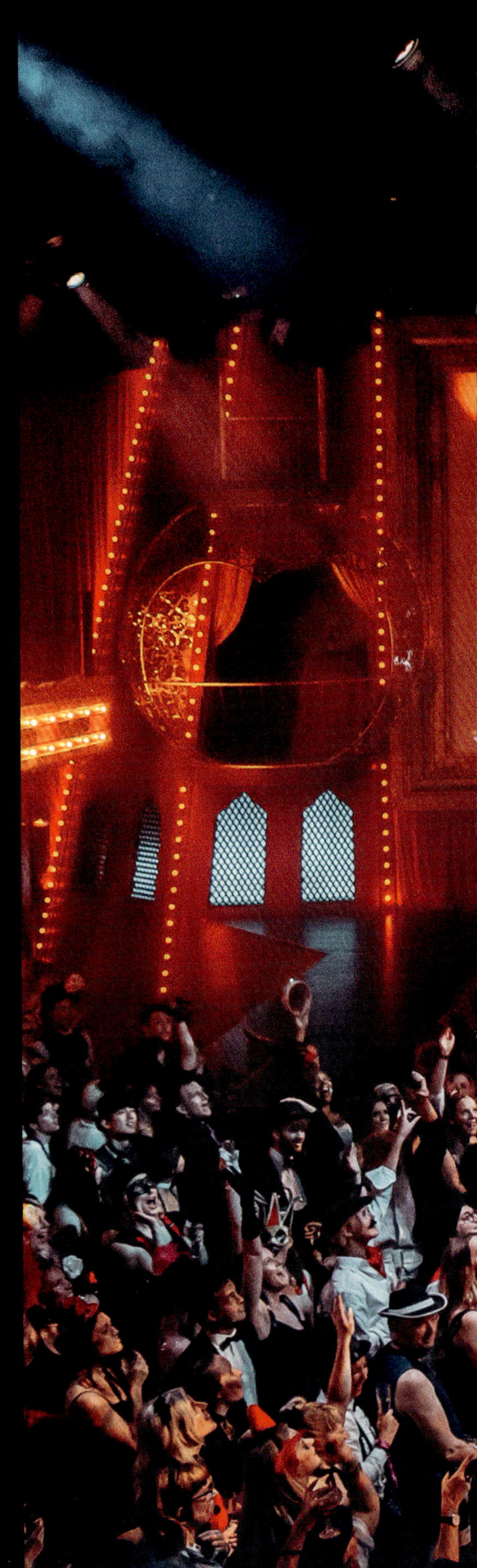

Secret Cinema productions like *Moulin Rouge!* welcome guests into an astonishing cinematic world, featuring sets, costumes, performances, food and drink, and more.

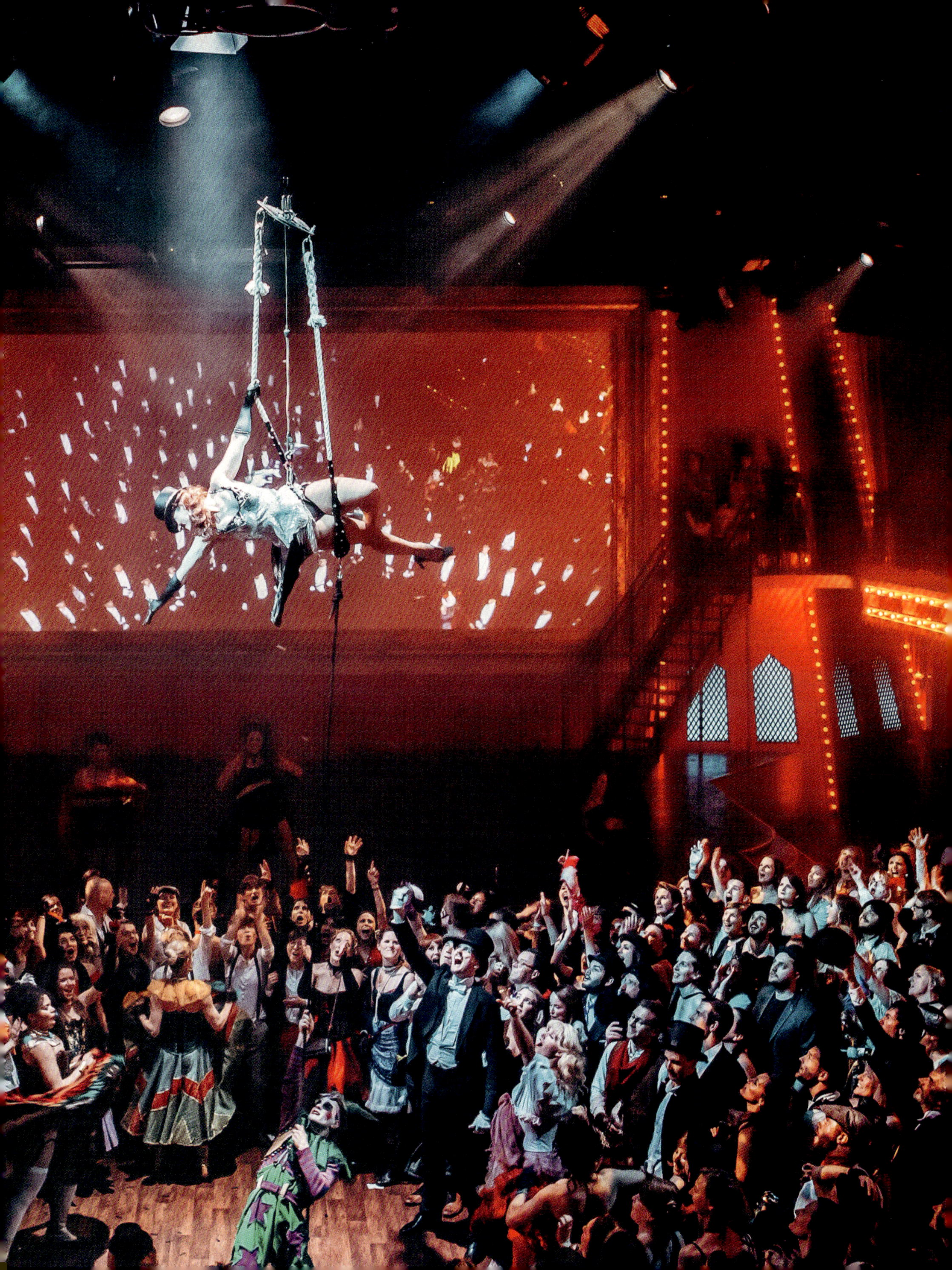

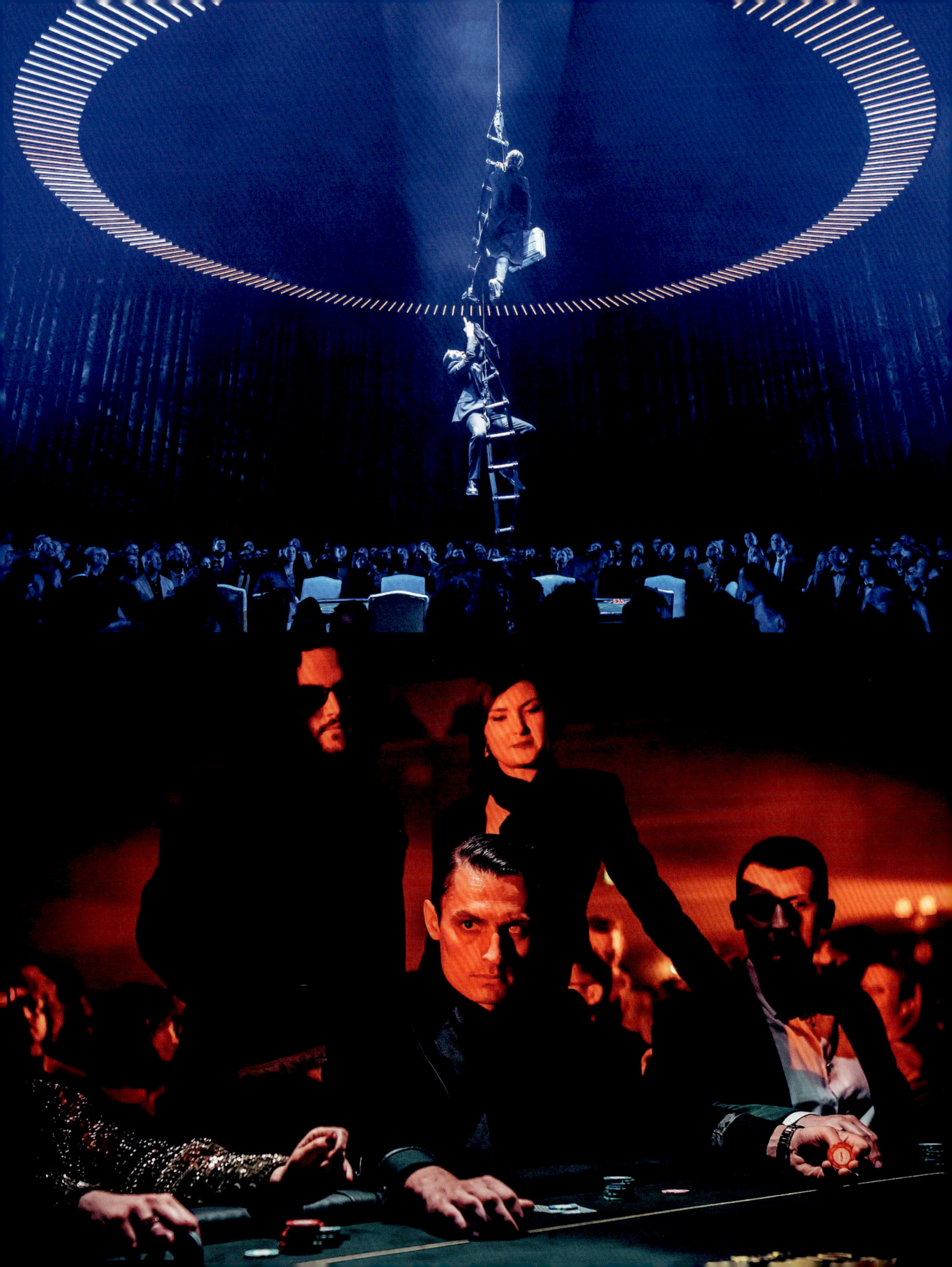

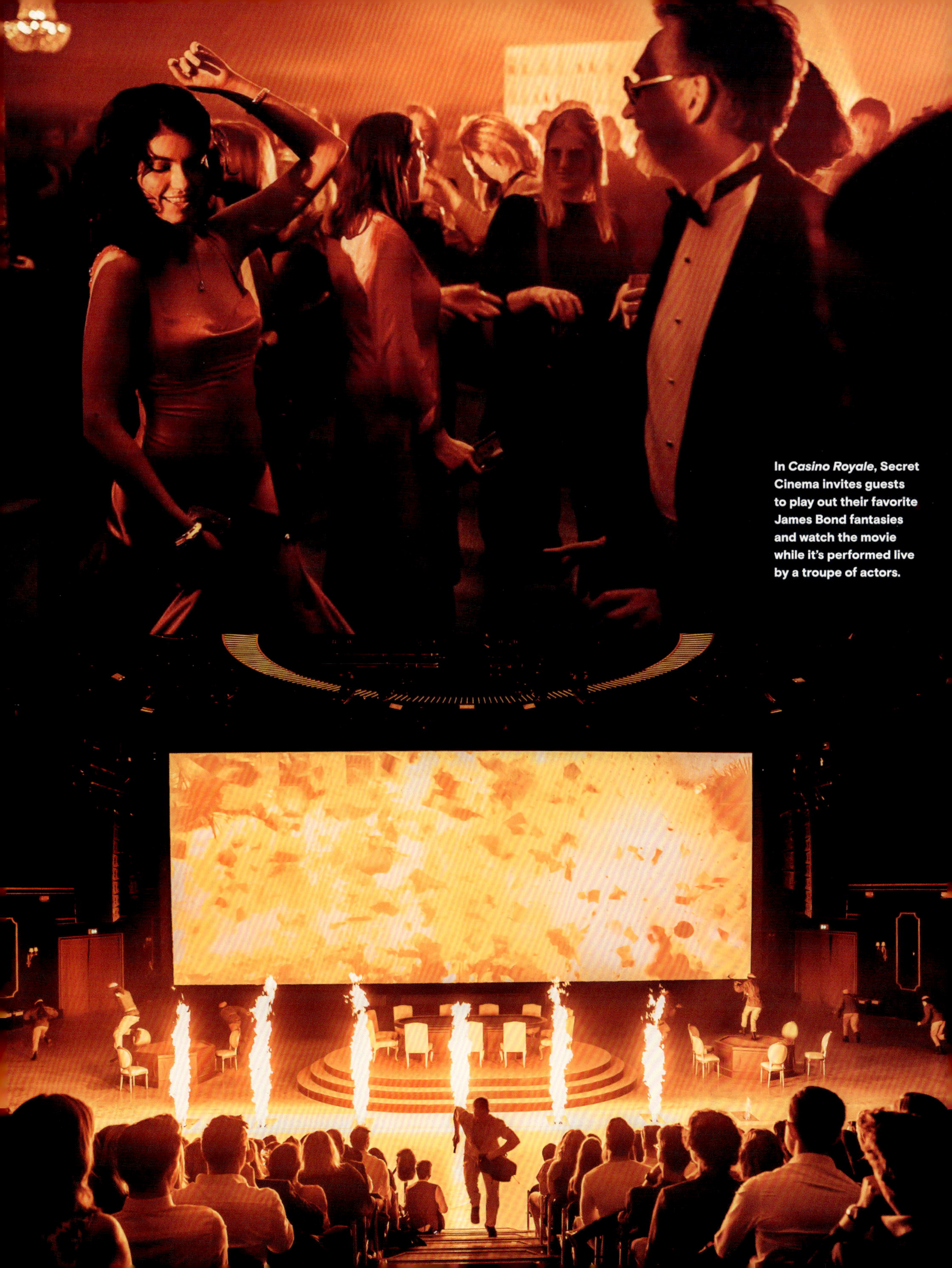

In *Casino Royale*, Secret Cinema invites guests to play out their favorite James Bond fantasies and watch the movie while it's performed live by a troupe of actors.

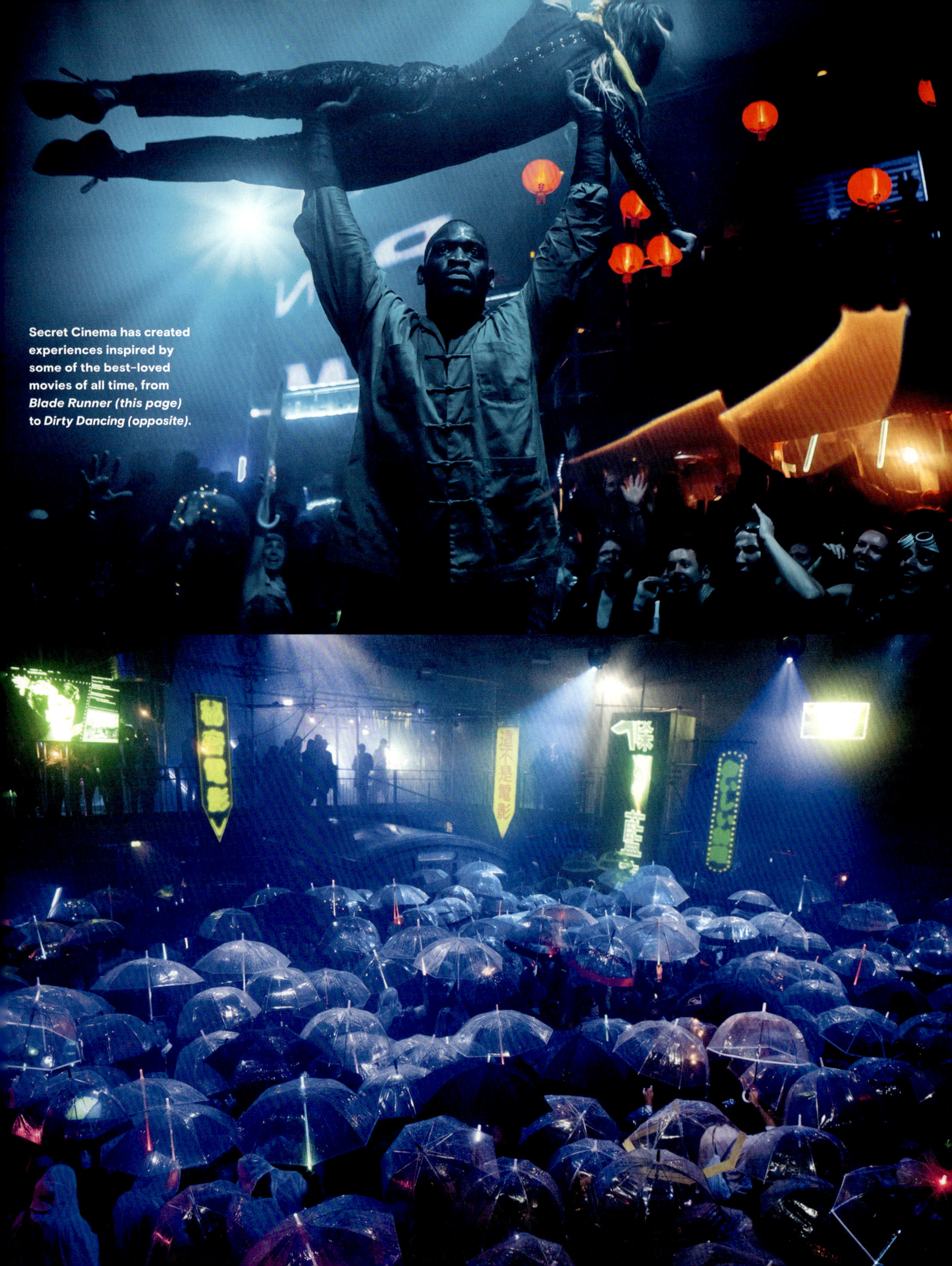

Secret Cinema has created experiences inspired by some of the best-loved movies of all time, from *Blade Runner (this page)* to *Dirty Dancing (opposite)*.

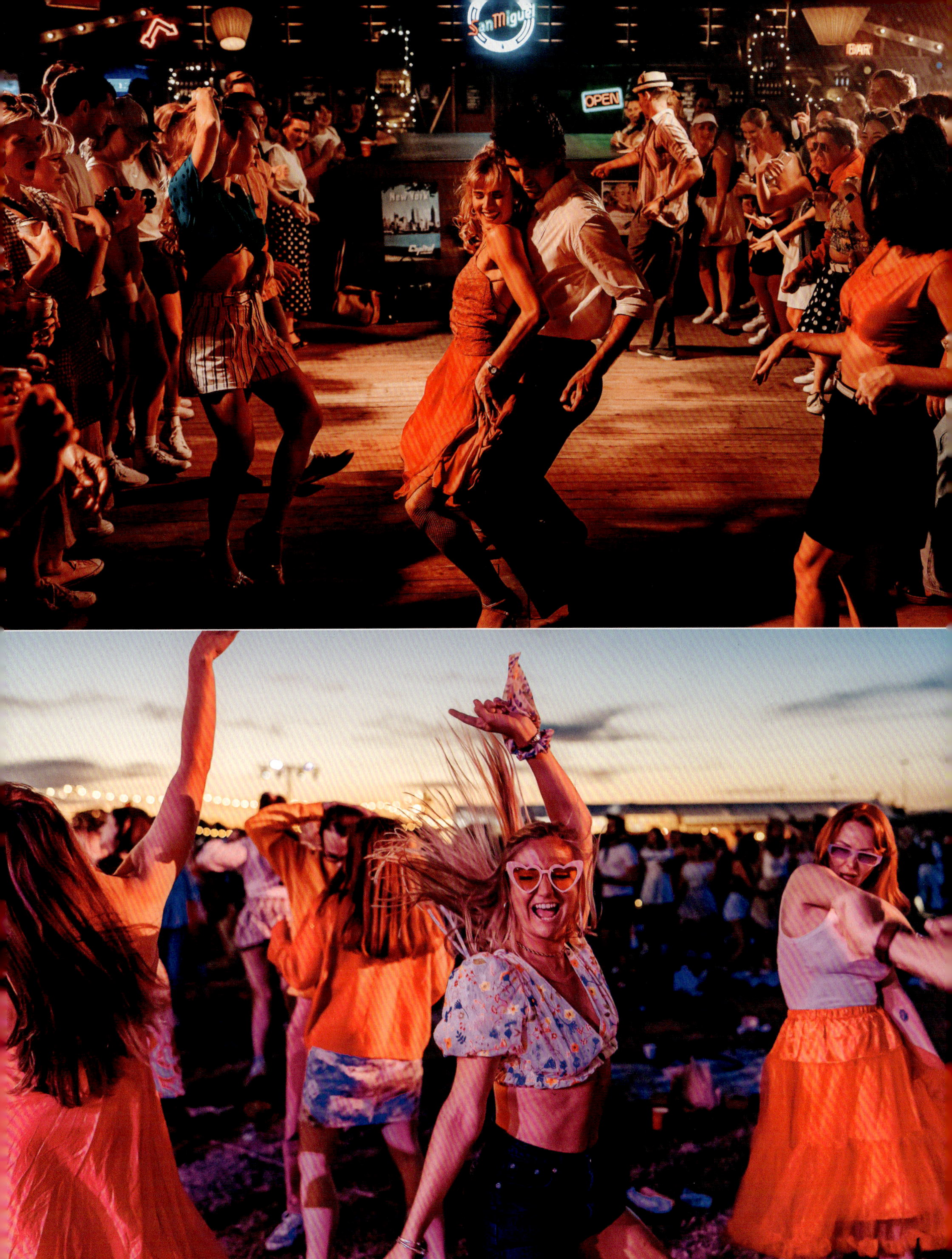
San Miguel
OPEN
BAR
New York

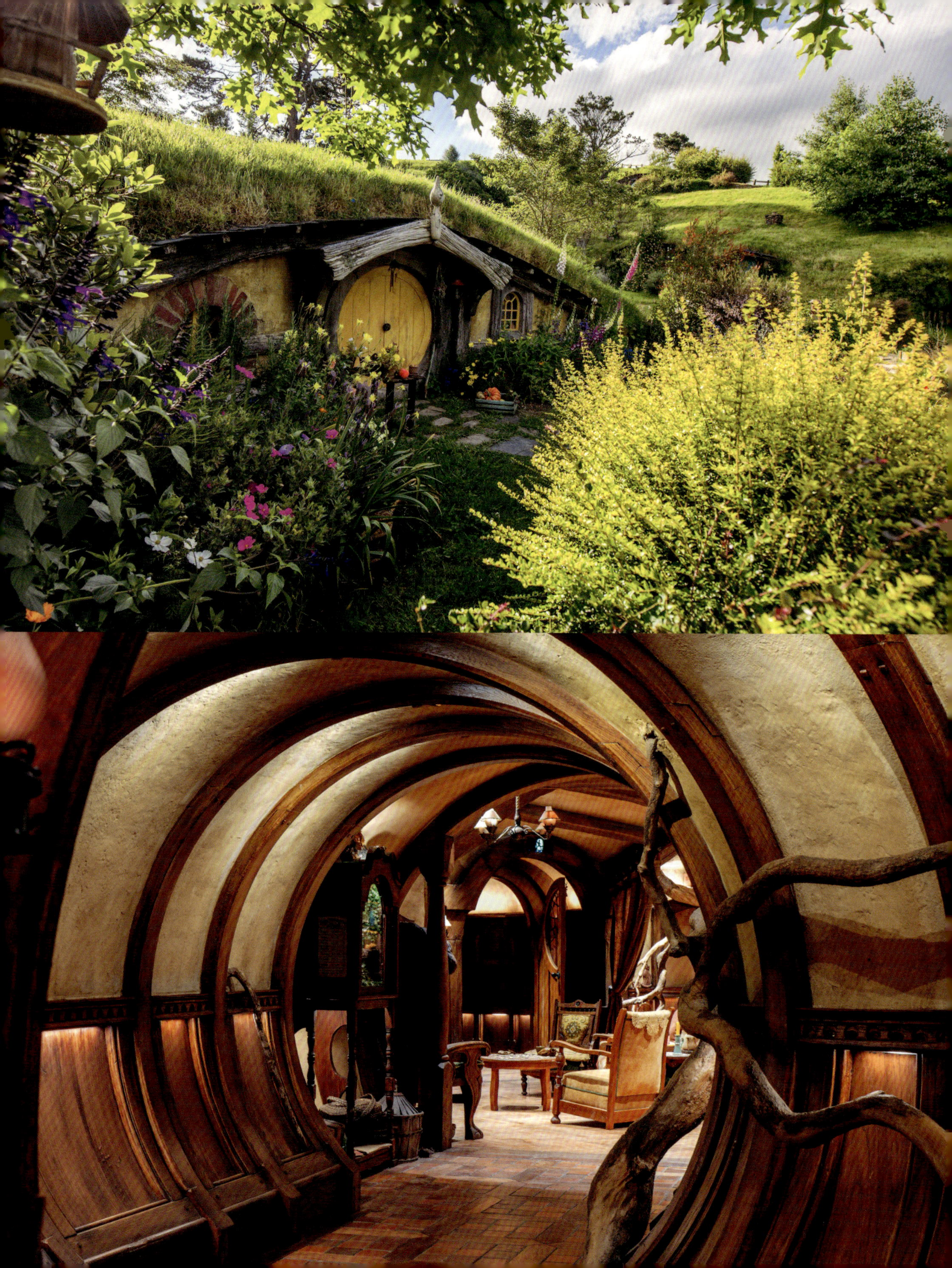

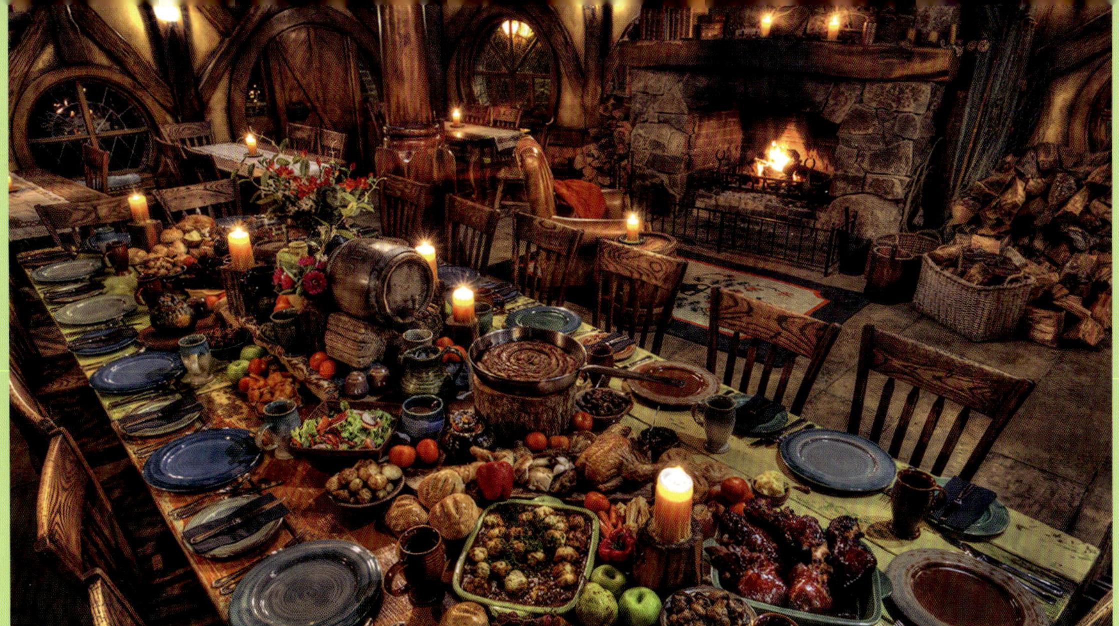

HOBBITON MOVIE SET

Nestled in the rolling hills of New Zealand, the Hobbiton Movie Set invites visitors to step into the enchanting world of Middle-earth as seen in Peter Jackson's iconic film trilogy, *The Lord of the Rings*. Surrounded by pristine, lush landscapes, Ian Alexander's 1,250-acre farm was a natural choice to stand in for the peaceful, rustic Shire. Initially a temporary movie set, Hobbiton was transformed into a permanent attraction after filming concluded—and subsequently became one of New Zealand's top tourist destinations, drawing more than 500,000 visitors annually.

Hobbiton is far from ordinary. It offers a world-class immersive experience that captivates guests by engaging all of their senses. Walking the winding paths of the hills, a typical tour group is greeted by the comforting scent of a cozy fire wafting from hobbit-hole chimneys, as if a hobbit were actually at home. Feeling the wooden doors and grass beneath their feet, visitors appreciate nature and history, two key hobbit values. Further along the journey, one can admire a beautiful, rambling community garden planted for the season. The tour concludes at the Green Dragon Inn, with a tasting of housemade Southfarthing brews to round out the experience.

Attention to detail and world-building is central to the Hobbiton Movie Set experience. Set pieces are carefully aged and painted by hand; paths in front of hobbit holes are maintained to appear authentically worn. Visitors are encouraged to explore and discover unique details on their own: bread for sale at the baker's house or hives of bees surrounding the beekeeper's abode. Tour guides can personalize each experience, tailoring the tour to match specific interests. These efforts create the sense that Hobbiton is an active, living community, much more than just a movie set. As visitors satisfy their curiosities, they become part of that community.

Though the creators of Hobbiton want visitors to dive deeply into the details, they also subtly curate the experience to prevent overstimulation. Some hobbit holes invite you inside for further exploration, while others simply contribute to the village ambiance. At sites offering more to explore, paths widen to encourage guests to step aside and pause. Various sized hobbit holes provide playful photo opportunities, allowing visitors to imagine themselves as either the tall wizard Gandalf or a hobbit. These thoughtful touches are Hobbiton's own form of movie magic, inviting people to actively engage in the experience.

Hobbiton is not only an opportunity for fans to immerse themselves in a real-life version of a fantasy they know and love; it is a destination that enchants anyone who visits. Whether you arrive at the Hobbiton Movie Set with a vast knowledge of Middle-earth or merely a sense of curiosity, you will depart having truly experienced the captivating charm of the Shire.

Transformed from an iconic film set into a popular tourist destination, Hobbiton allows guests to immerse themselves in the most luscious, idyllic corner of Middle-earth. They can peer into hobbit holes or pop by the Green Dragon Inn for second breakfast.

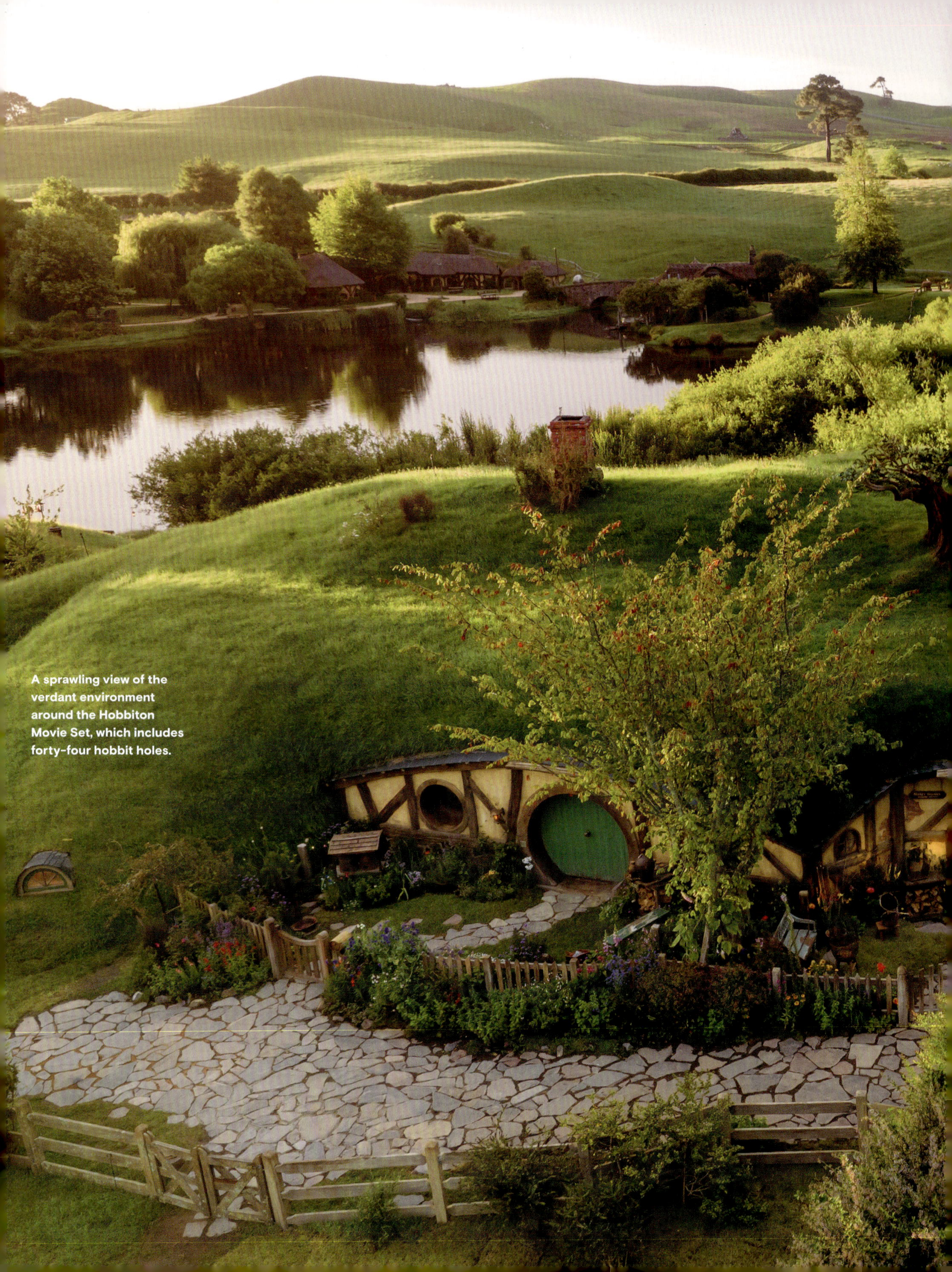

A sprawling view of the verdant environment around the Hobbiton Movie Set, which includes forty-four hobbit holes.

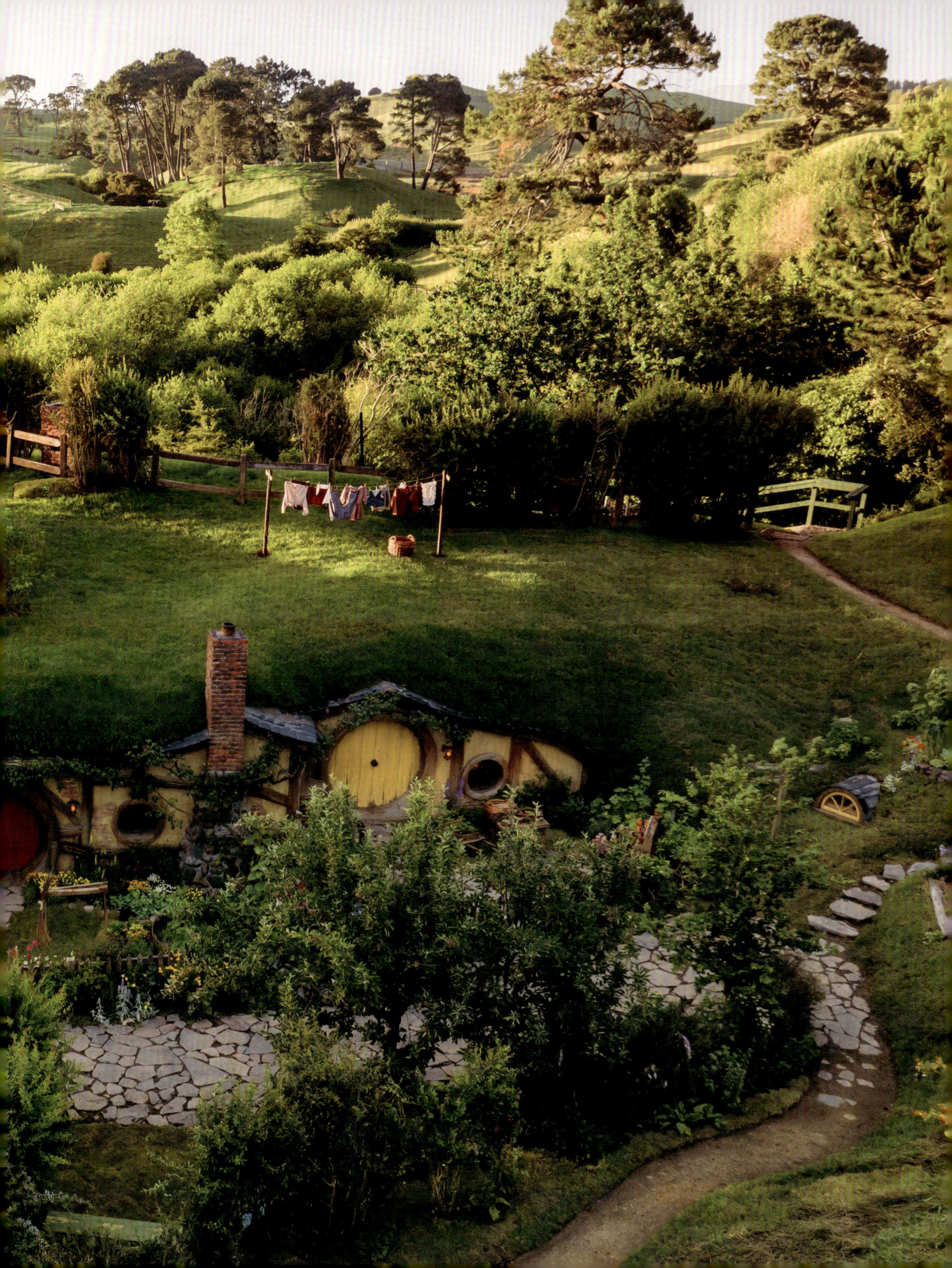

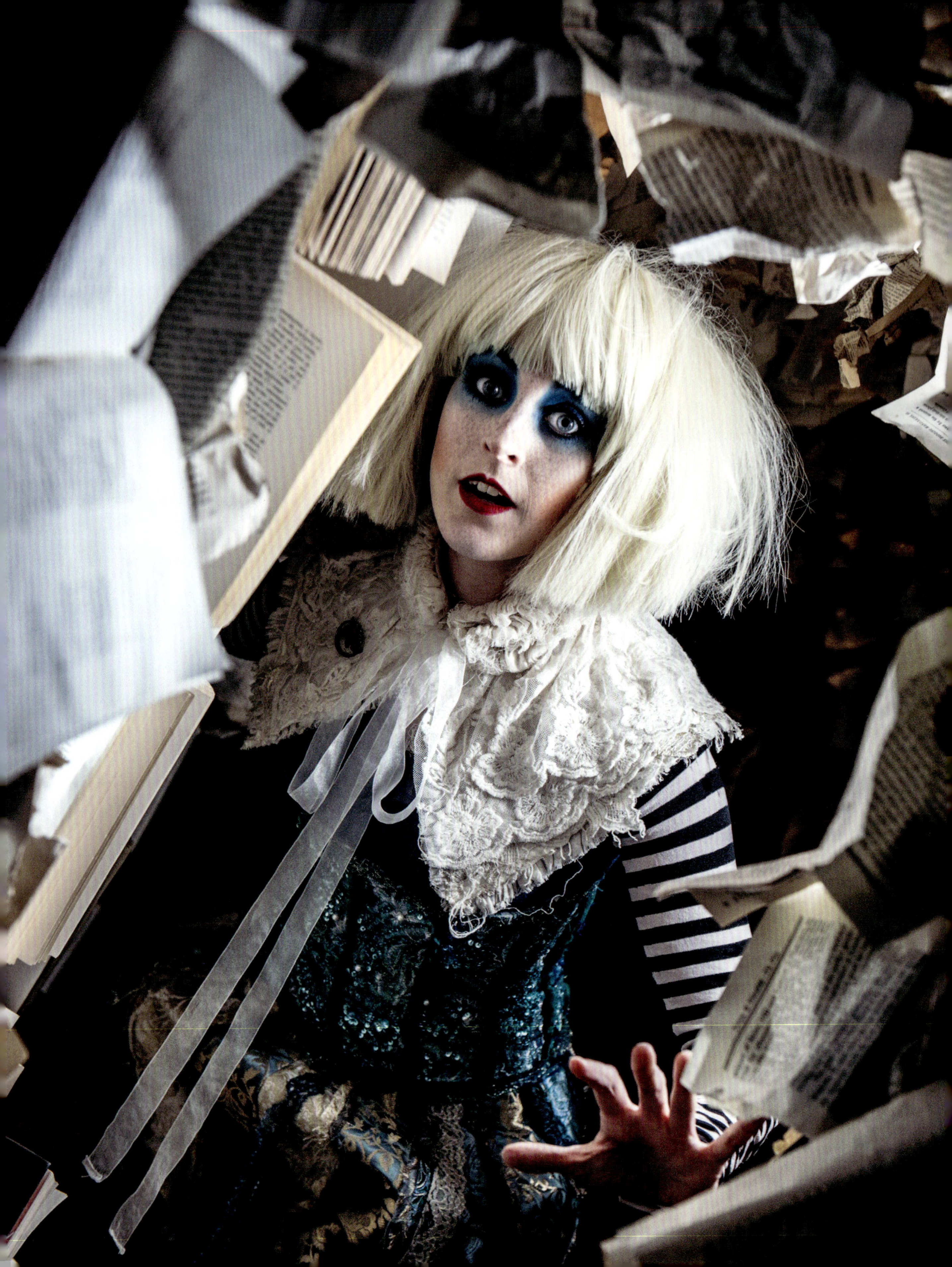

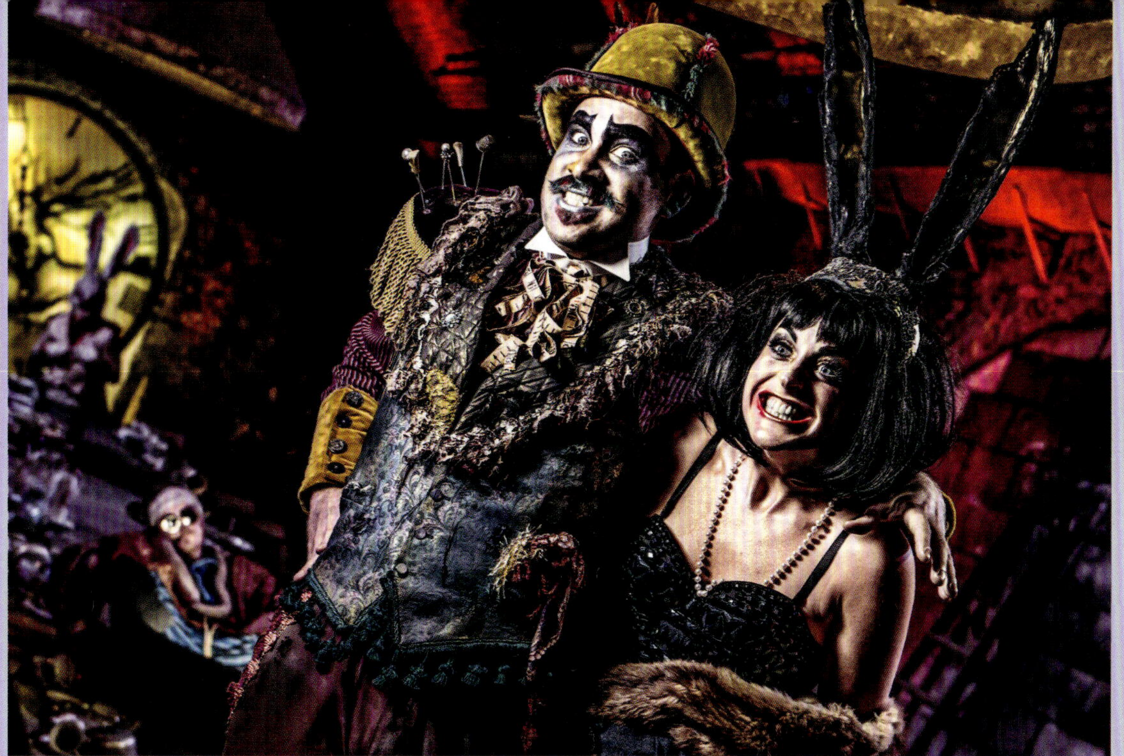

ALICE'S ADVENTURES UNDERGROUND

London-based company Les Enfants Terribles' *Alice's Adventures Underground* is the immersive-theater equivalent of a Mad Tea Party: sumptuously designed, playfully interactive, and delightful at every fast-paced turn. From the moment you choose between "eat me" and "drink me," you're tumbling down a rabbit hole filled with kooky characters in wild costumes, eccentric puppets, enchantingly detailed sets, and the controlled chaos that the story is so well known for. Multiple distinct story paths, based on your choices and the luck of a card draw, give the sensation that there's an entire complicated world stowed beneath the surface.

You'd be right, in fact—there are complex machinations happening just out of sight that make this Wonderland possible. First staged in 2015, *Alice's Adventures Underground* has undergone years of development in various venues to make it into the well-oiled machine that is slated to reopen soon under London's Waterloo Station. Meticulous timing of lights and musical cues, careful choreography, and a sophisticated computing system to keep it all on track are key to making *Alice's Adventures Underground* a whirlwind experience that's seamlessly immersive, resource-efficient, and full of surprise and delight. Groups of up to sixty people enter the show every fifteen minutes, after which they are split into four subgroups—hearts, clubs, spades, and diamonds, of course—with the same thirty-some actors performing on a loop throughout. The organization and pulsing of audiences means that the show is able to accommodate a healthy number of customers while preserving the personal and intimate feeling of a much smaller performance.

In the words of Les Enfants Terribles' creative director, James Seager, "In immersive theater, what the audiences don't get to see is as important as what they do get to see." That's especially true for a show that's as ambitious as *Alice* in both scope and scale. Giving each audience member a sense of agency and embodied interaction in a living, breathing world while maintaining high throughput is no easy feat. It takes a little bit of mad genius—which, fortunately, there's no shortage of with Les Enfants Terribles.

Les Enfants Terribles draw on their background in theater with their traditions of elaborate costumes, makeup, sets, lighting, music, and even puppetry to transform their immersive version of *Alice in Wonderland* into an unforgettable adventure.

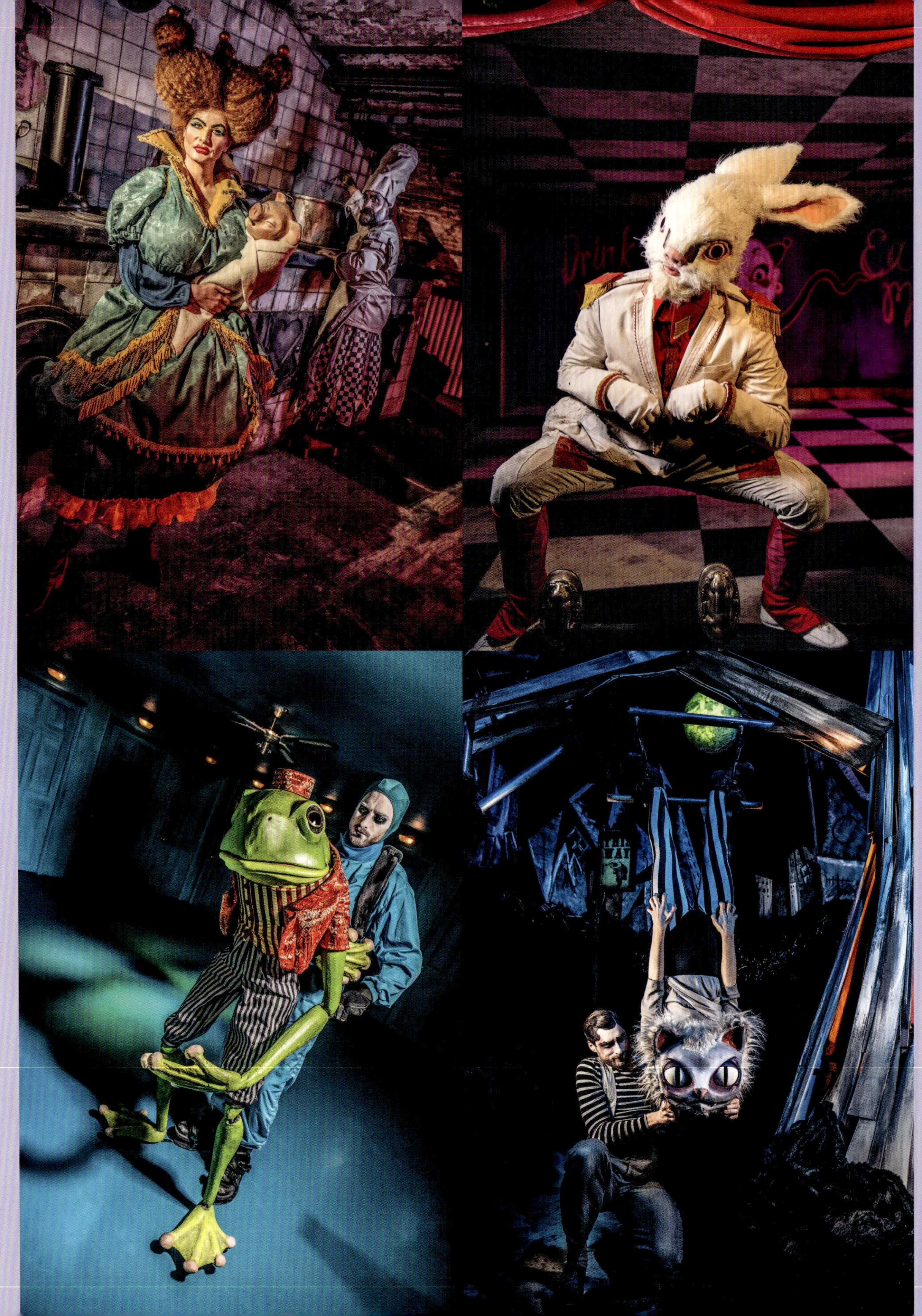
Drink

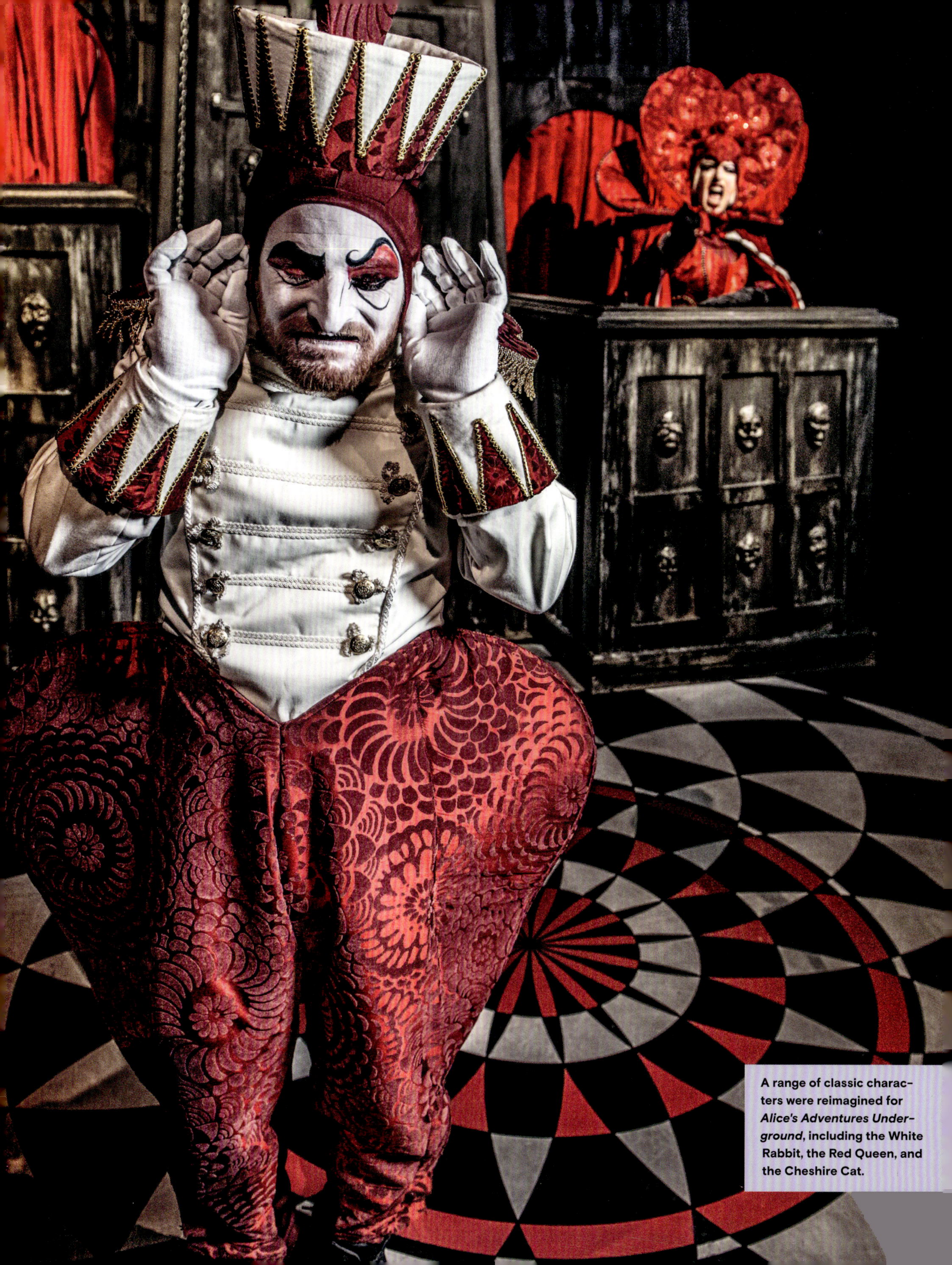

A range of classic characters were reimagined for *Alice's Adventures Underground*, including the White Rabbit, the Red Queen, and the Cheshire Cat.

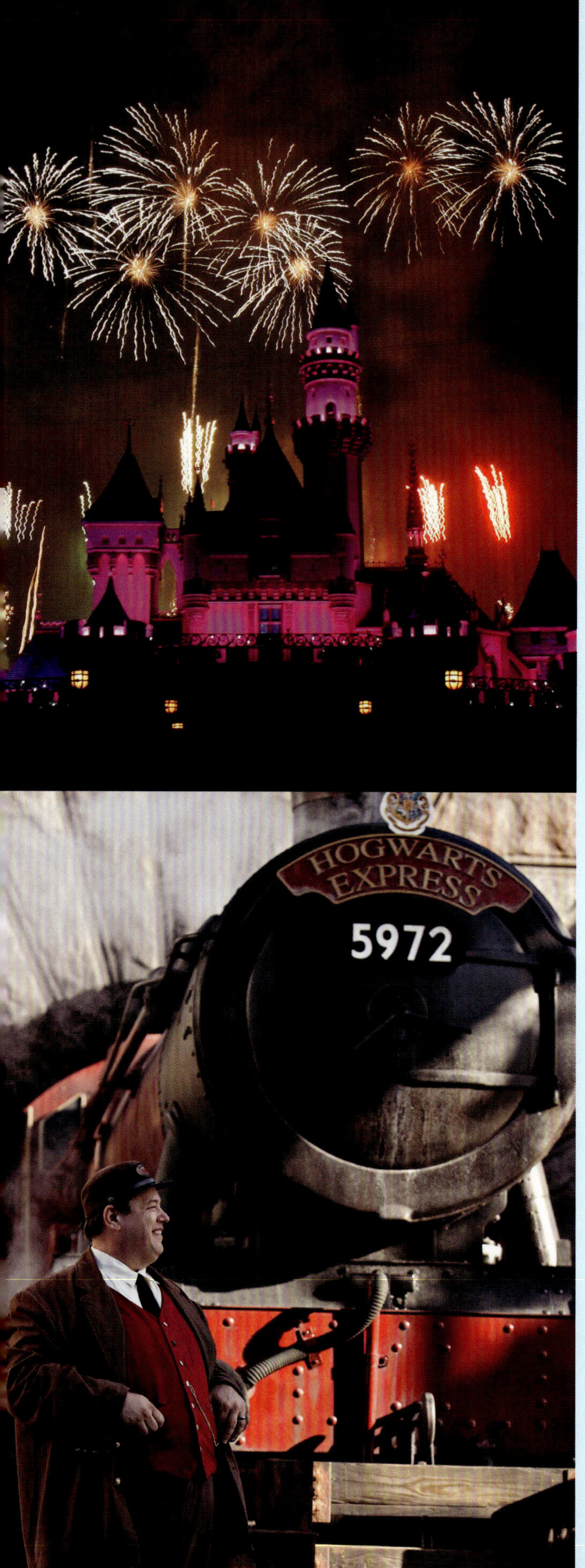

THEME PARKS

Theme parks are among the first and most successful examples of living stories, led by industry giants like Disney, Universal, and SeaWorld. When Disneyland opened in 1955, it revolutionized entertainment by defining the modern theme park—a place designed not only for thrills but also for storytelling. Unlike traditional amusement parks, theme parks use rides, shows, and immersive environments to bring beloved intellectual properties to life so visitors can experience them firsthand. According to pioneering theme-park designer Scott Trowbridge, the founding goal of the Disney Imagineers was to create "the tools and technology to allow a stronger personal connection to [Disney's stories], to find ways to create experiences that allow people to get closer to characters, to be more immersed in the stories, and to travel to places they couldn't possibly be going, but somehow they are."

Today's theme parks have perfected this kind of immersion, thanks in large part to advanced technology that enables them to be more interactive, embodied, and multisensory than ever. With the help of innovations like RFID chips, infrared cameras, state-of-the-art robotics, and more, theme parks are able to make magic happen. At the Wizarding World of Harry Potter at Universal Orlando Resort, for example, even Muggles can try their hand at being a wizard with an interactive wand. With a flick of the wrist, visitors can cast spells that open curtains, turn on lights, and make feathers levitate. At Pandora—The World of Avatar at Walt Disney World's Animal Kingdom, the Avatar Flight of Passage ride lets parkgoers experience the sensation of soaring through Pandora on the back of a banshee. Rounded screens that stretch beyond your peripheral vision and motion-synchronized seats fully immerse you in the sights and sensations of the journey. As you weave through the jungle, dive off waterfalls, and skim across the ocean's surface, the thrill feels as real as if you were truly flying.

***Clockwise from above:* Fireworks illuminate Sleeping Beauty Castle at Disneyland; in Diagon Alley at Universal Orlando's Wizarding World of Harry Potter, visitors are immersed in familiar locations and events from the book and film series; the conductor of the Hogwarts Express greets guests.**

Theme parks also amplify their storytelling through multisensory world-building. The Wizarding World

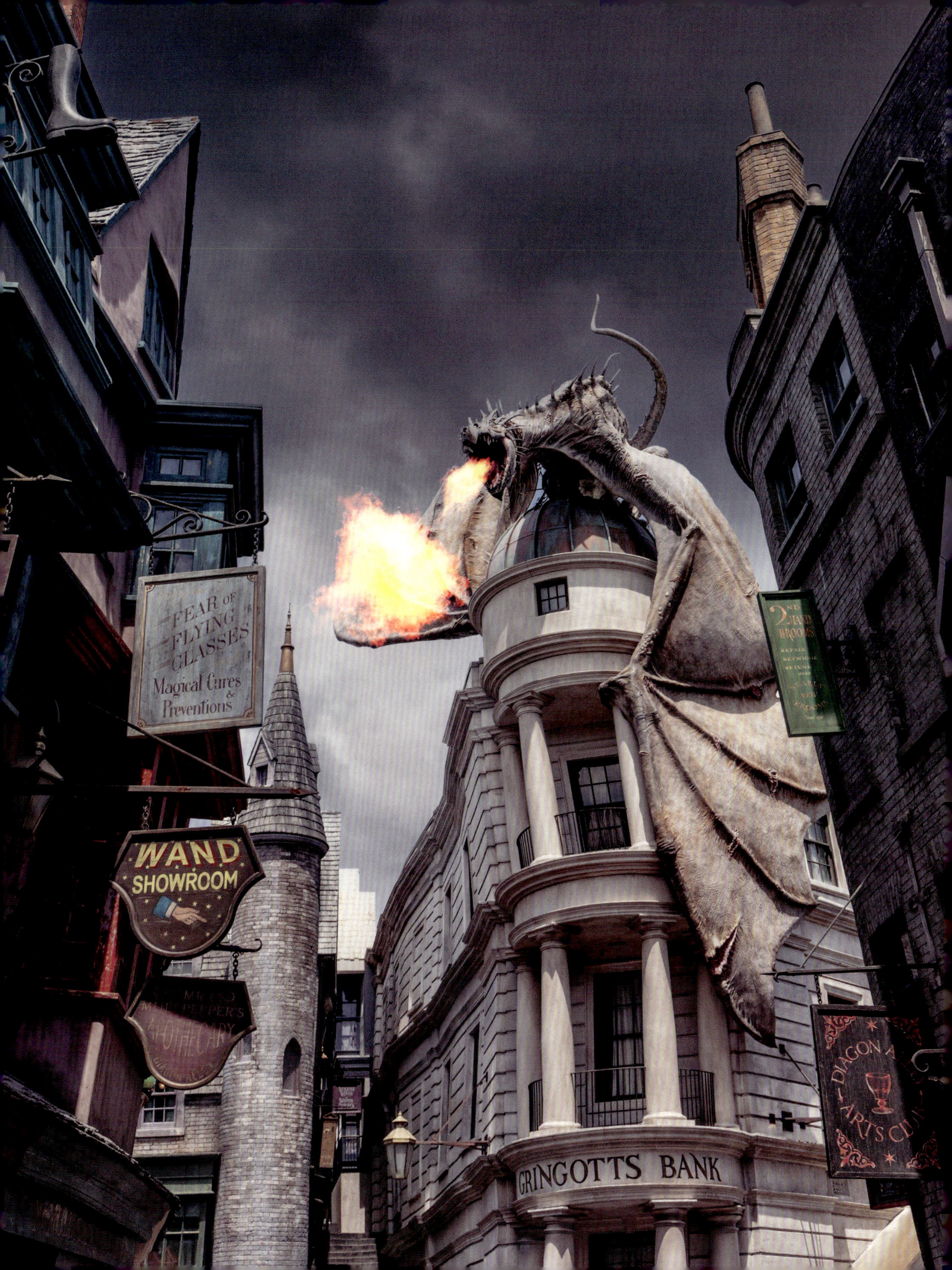

FEAR OF FLYING GLASSES
Magical Cures & Preventions
WAND SHOWROOM
GRINGOTTS BANK

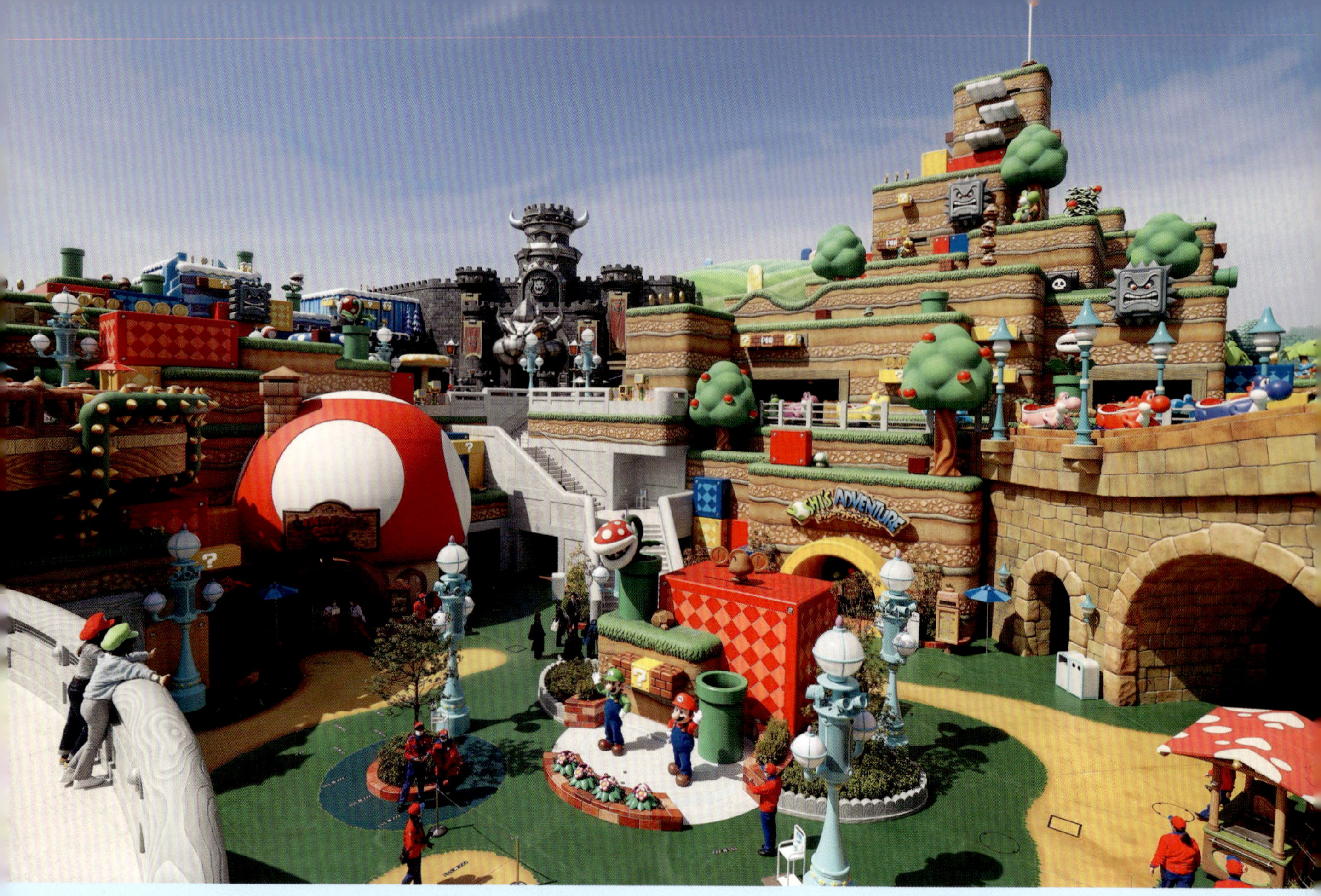

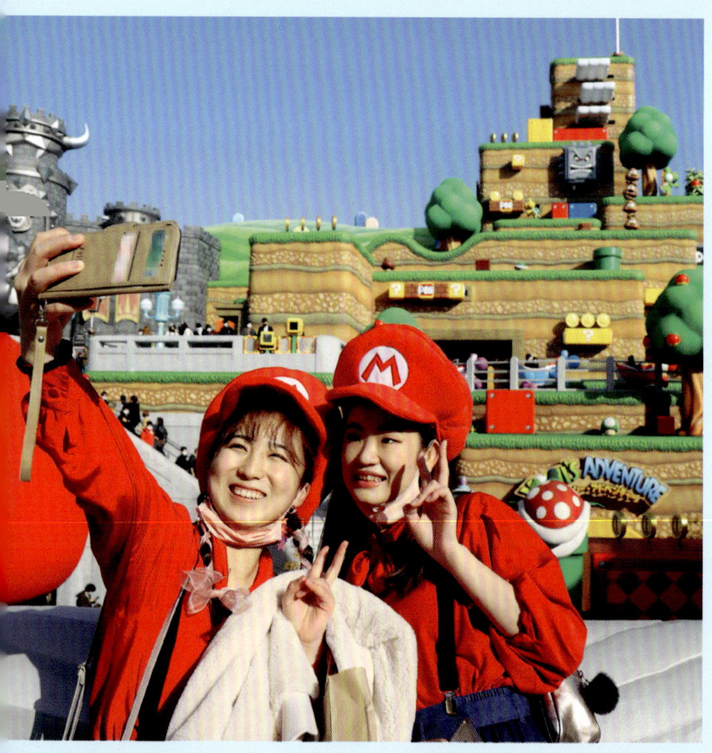

offers live shows, themed food, and rides that bring the *Harry Potter* universe to life. Visitors often arrive in wizarding costumes, enhancing the feeling of being in a town full of wizards and witches. In Pandora, the Na'vi River Jouney takes guests through bioluminescent caves and a vibrant rainforest alive with the sights and sounds of exotic creatures. These parks spare no expense in creating vividly detailed and realistic worlds, making them as expansive as real villages, complete with world-specific sights, scents, textures, and food.

This page: **SuperNintendo World in Osaka, Japan, where fans can explore the Mushroom Kingdom and other locations from the popular video-game franchise.** ***Opposite:*** **Guests take in alien wildlife and bioluminescent plants at Pandora—The World of Avatar at Walt Disney World Resort in Florida.**

The allure of theme parks is clearly a powerful one: In 2023, the world's top twenty-five drew 244.6 million visitors—a 23 percent increase from the previous year and a near-complete return to pre-pandemic attendance levels. Guests come not just for thrilling rides but also to create lasting memories with family and friends, forging deep personal connections to the rich stories these parks bring to life.

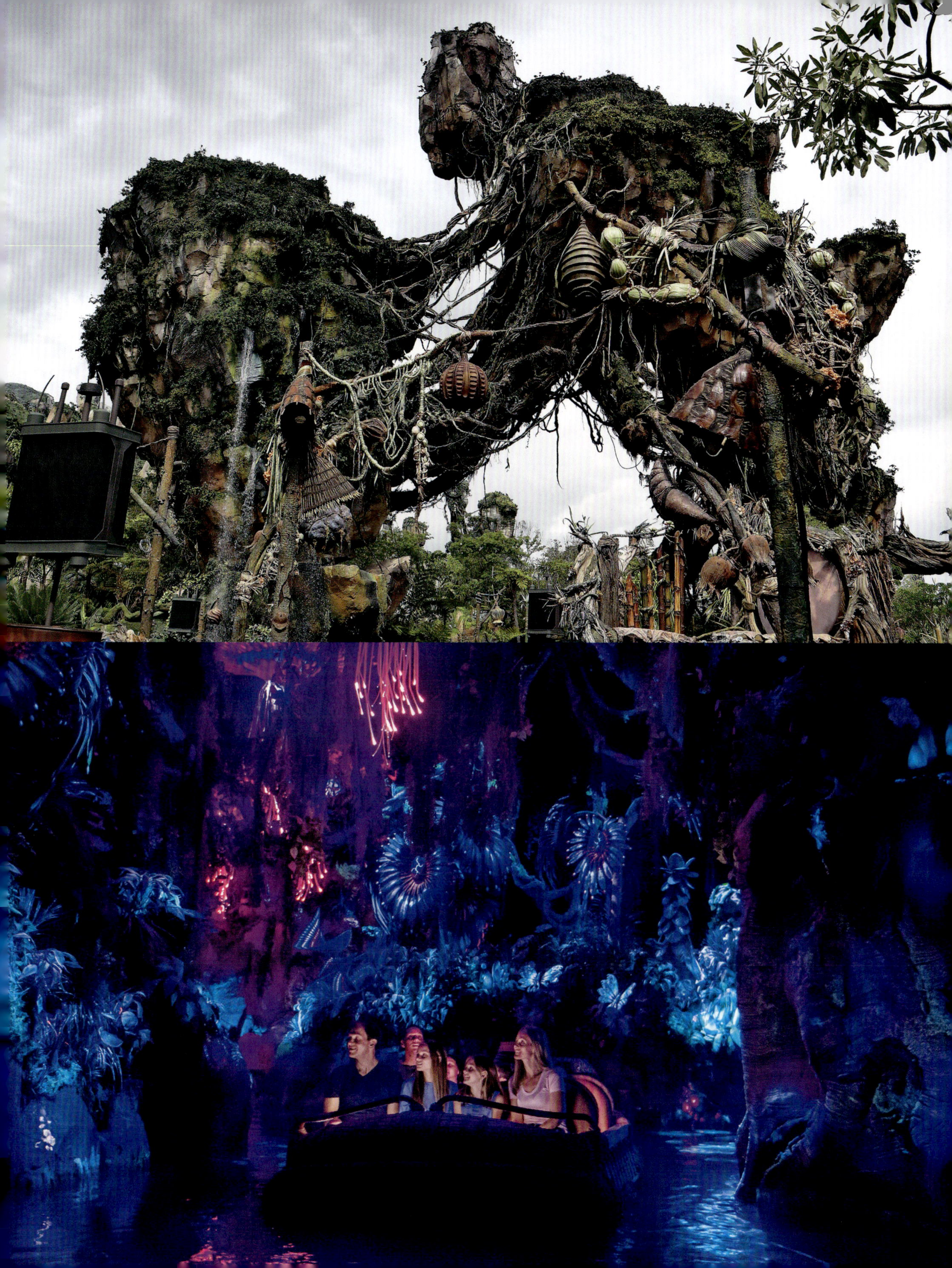

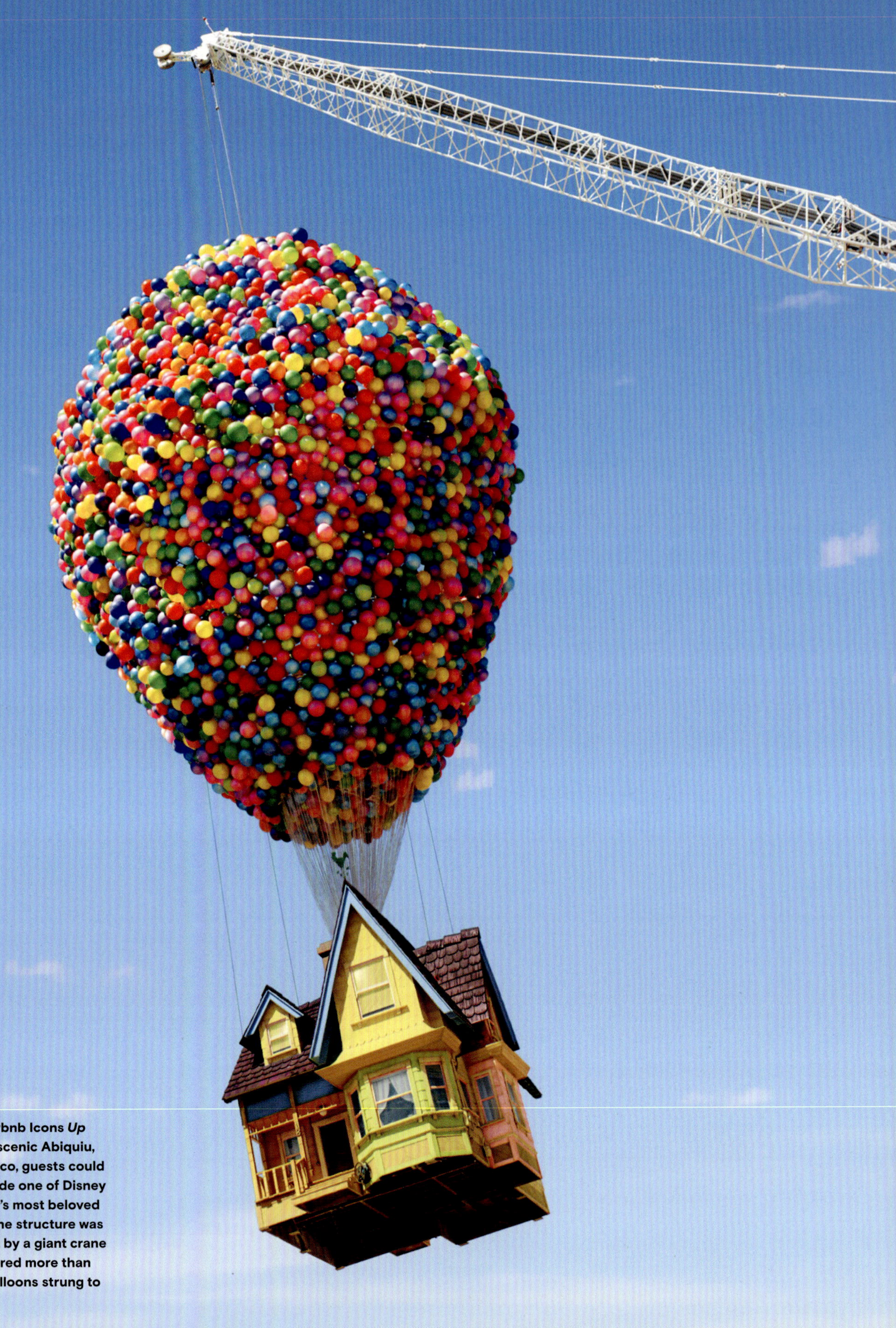

At the Airbnb Icons *Up* house in scenic Abiquiu, New Mexico, guests could sleep inside one of Disney and Pixar's most beloved homes. The structure was held aloft by a giant crane and featured more than 8,000 balloons strung to the roof.

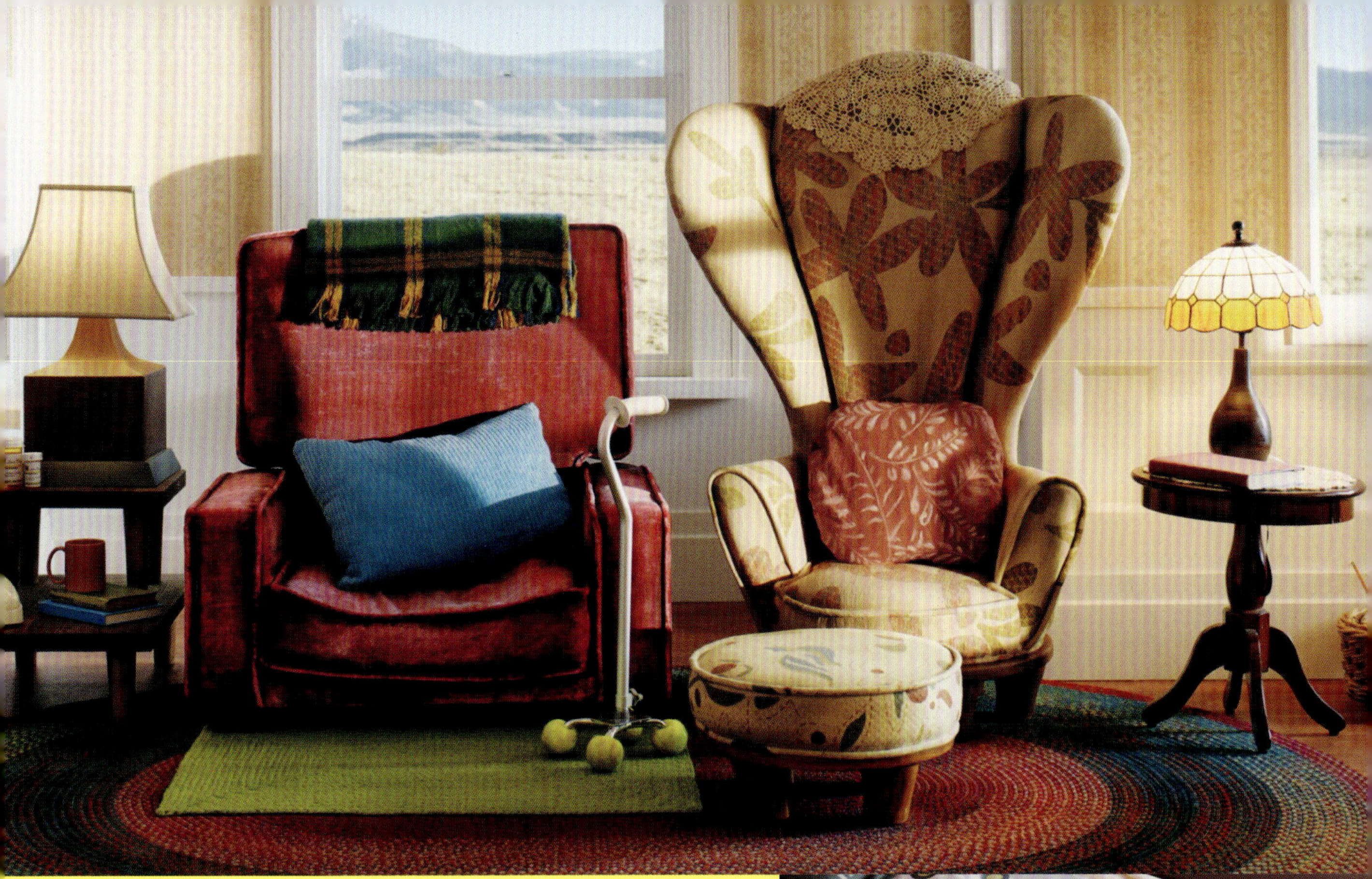

AIRBNB ICONS

The iconic house from Pixar's *Up* was, briefly, not confined to the beloved animated film; it could, from May to July 2024, also be lived in. In Abiquiu, New Mexico, more than 8,000 colorful balloons suspended (with the help of a crane) a remarkably accurate replica of Carl and Ellie's whimsical home fifty feet in the air. Invited guests could stay overnight in this incredible replica, which they could also watch soaring up in the sky. Details from the movie, like the creaky wooden floorboards, the pictures on the walls, and Ellie's adventure book, brought the experience to life. Guests could take in the view from the breakfast nook, sleep in Carl and Ellie's cozy bed, and discover playful artifacts from their fictional life.

While Airbnb's original business model has thrived and continues to do so, today's travelers crave more than just a place to sleep—they want an experience. Enter Airbnb Icons, which offers wildly unique and exciting travel experiences where visitors can embark

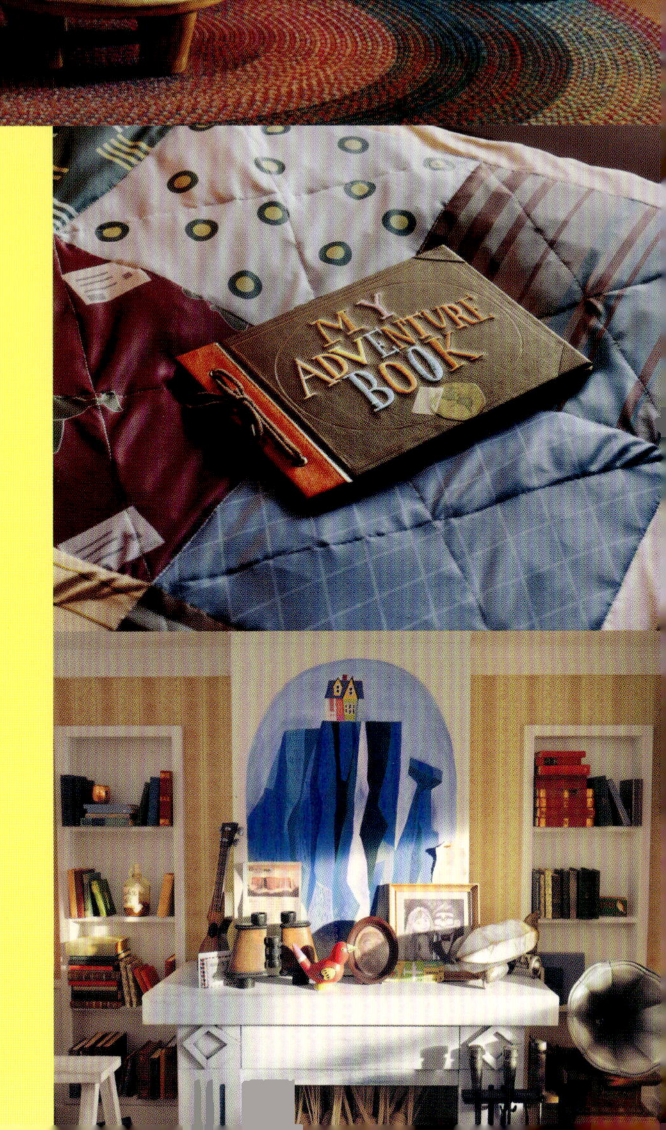

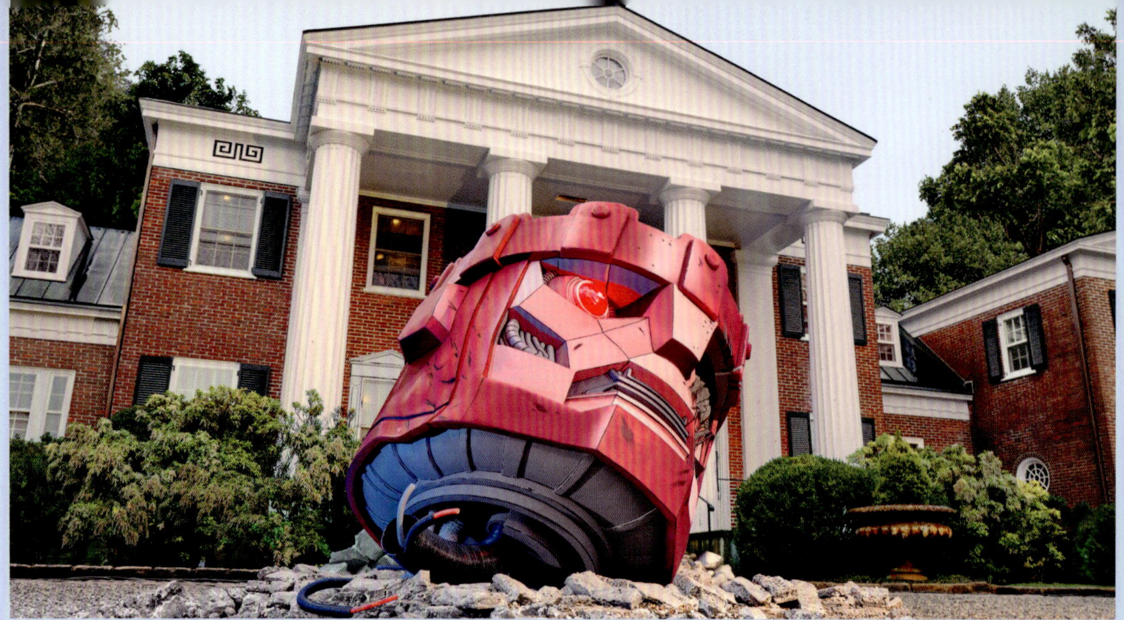

At the Airbnb X-Mansion in Westchester County, fans of the comic-book and movie franchise morphed into mutant trainees at Professor Xavier's Institute for Higher Learning, with the chance to take part in trainings, lab experiments, and secret mission briefings. Rooms were painted to mimic a 2-D comic-book look and featured more than a hundred pieces of unique *X-Men* paraphernalia.

on adventures inside their favorite fictional worlds. Brian Chesky, Airbnb's cofounder and CEO, explains that "Icons take you inside worlds that only existed in your imagination—until now."

The *Up* house was just one of eleven elaborate Icons that Airbnb announced in 2024. Guests could also spend a few nights at the X-Mansion from *X-Men* in New Castle, New York, where every surface in the house was painted by hand to look 2-D. Visitors felt like they had stepped into a comic book as they dressed up in the costumes of their favorite characters, took combat lessons from professional stunt coordinators, and encountered visiting X-Men. In Malibu in 2023, they could find the famed Barbie DreamHouse, where Barbie left Ken in charge of renting out his room. With perfect replicas of pools, pink floats, and dance floors, Ryan Gosling's iconic character hosted this special overnight stay.

Airbnb currently places its Icon experiences front and center, allowing guests to apply for a stay directly from the app. Selected winners receive a digital golden ticket to these "story-cations" for free, or at most $100. To amplify the excitement, Airbnb has also invited numerous social-media influencers, who then share their experiences on Instagram and TikTok. Chesky calls it "a new era" for the company, emphasizing that Icons establish Airbnb as fantastical "destinations" in their own right rather than just places to stay. People are eager to live and adventure within rich story worlds when they travel, and Airbnb is making their dreams come true.

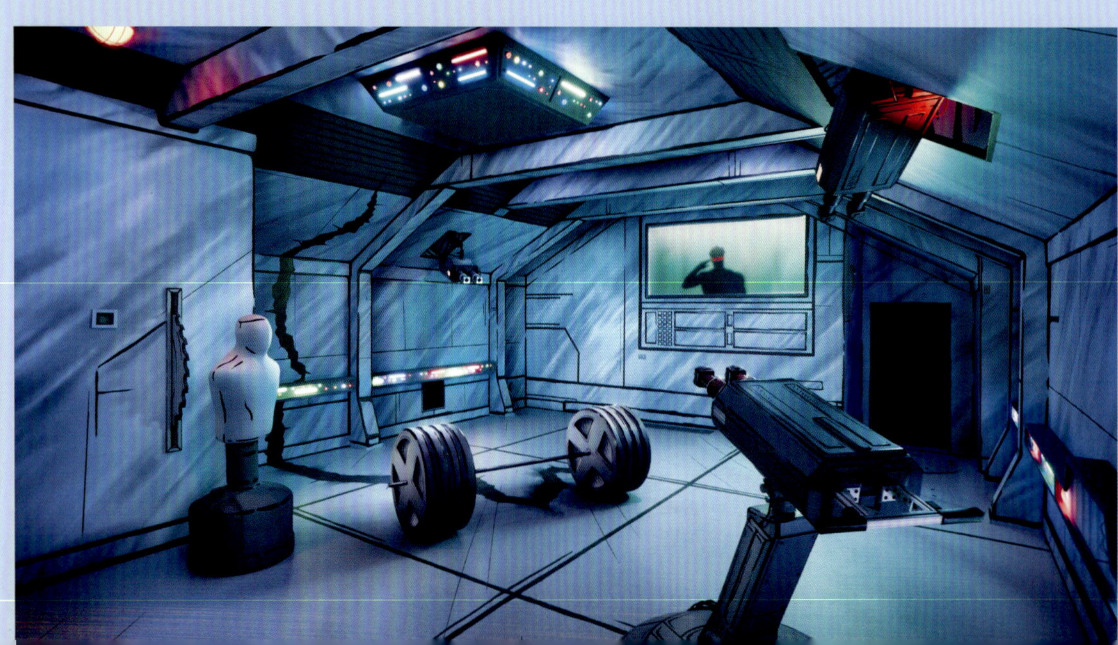

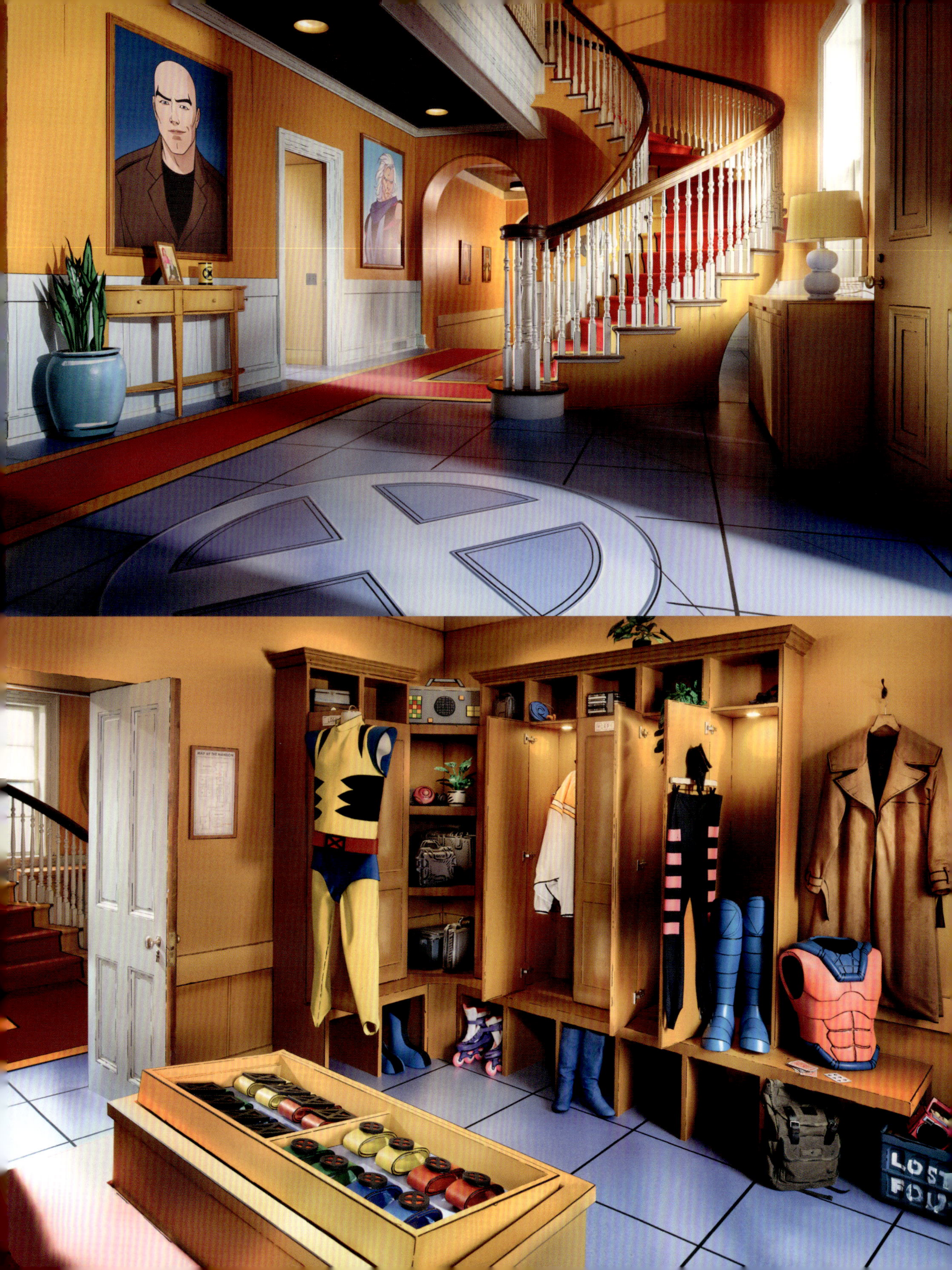
MAP OF THE MANSION
LOST
FOU

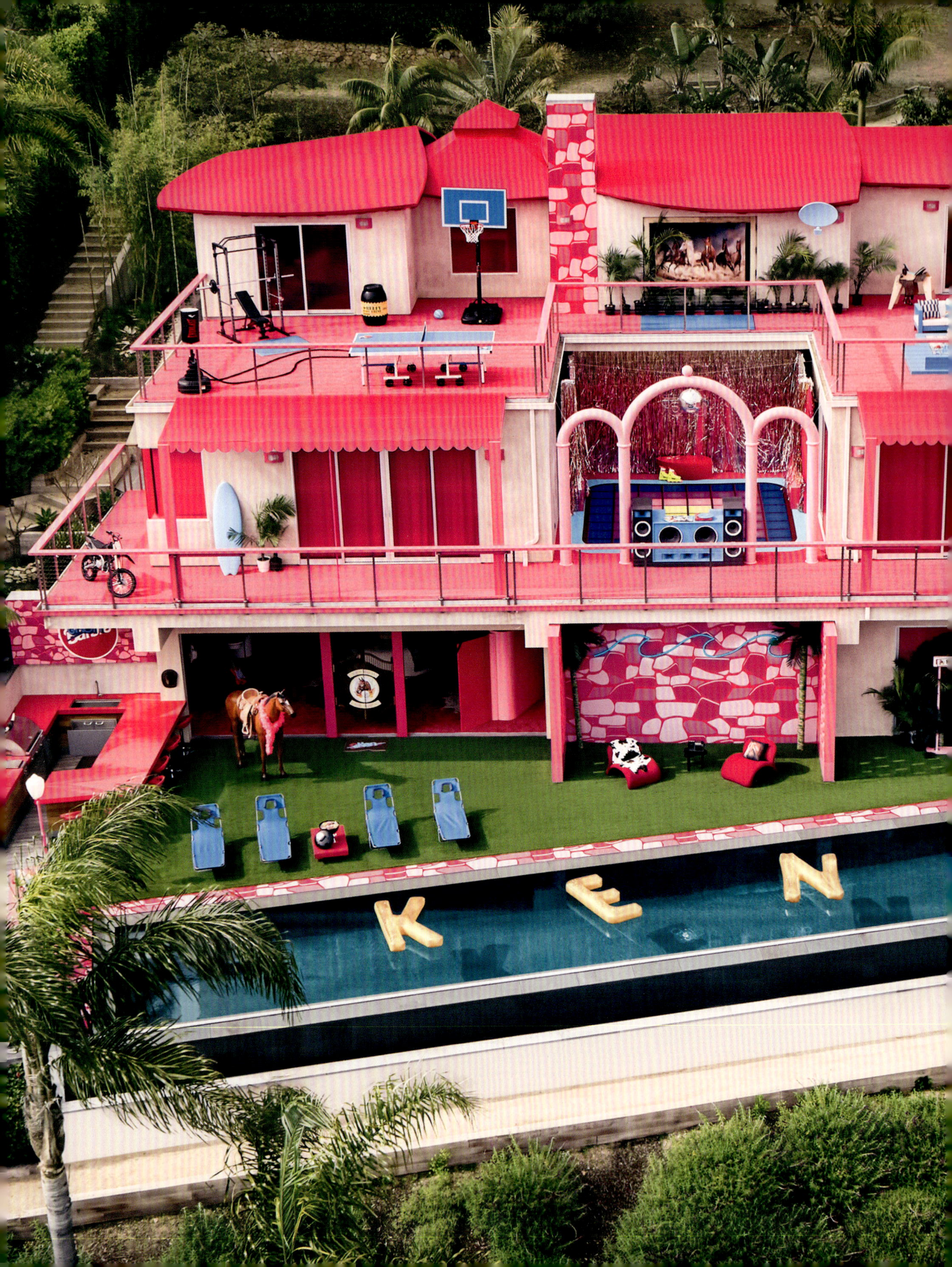
K E N

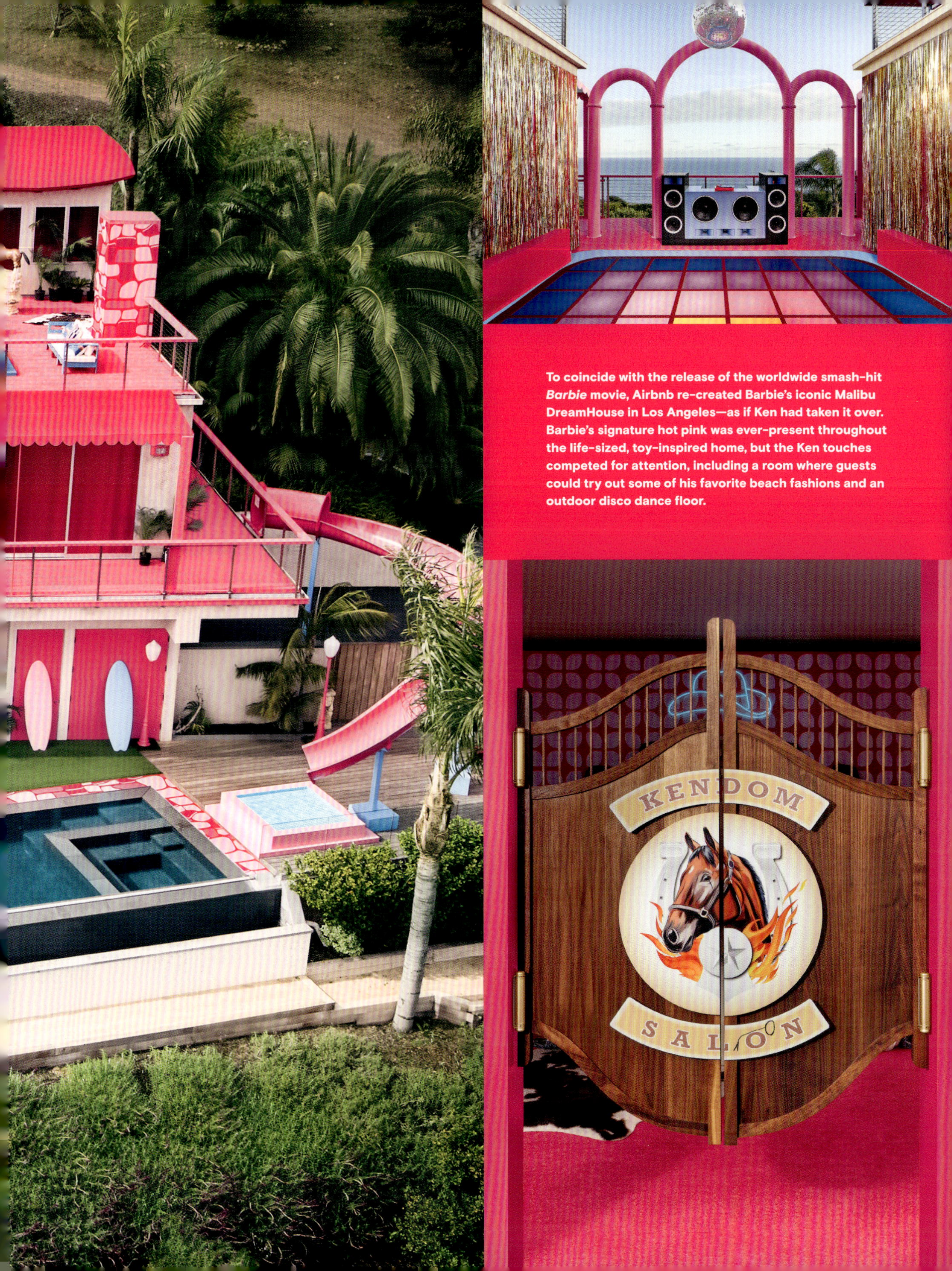

To coincide with the release of the worldwide smash-hit *Barbie* movie, Airbnb re-created Barbie's iconic Malibu DreamHouse in Los Angeles—as if Ken had taken it over. Barbie's signature hot pink was ever-present throughout the life-sized, toy-inspired home, but the Ken touches competed for attention, including a room where guests could try out some of his favorite beach fashions and an outdoor disco dance floor.

IMMERSIVE ART

If you ask a person on the street to think of an example of "immersive entertainment," chances are the first thing their mind will go to is *Immersive Van Gogh*. This was the original (launched in 2008) and still one of the most popular art exhibits that use projection mapping to envelop a large space. Vivid and dramatic artworks are brought to life on the walls and floors surrounding guests. Unlike in traditional galleries, the works aren't small, still, and framed on a wall, but larger than life, free, and full of movement and animation. Often located in grand interior spaces and accompanied by music, these experiences are designed to give visitors a feeling of awe and wonder, as if they are stepping into the world of the paintings.

Exhibits of this kind have become so popular that you can now find variations in cities across the globe. The selection of artists ranges from Frida Kahlo to Claude Monet to Pablo Picasso, while some non-art shows focus on subjects such as astronomy and wildlife. The number of companies and venues that specialize in these exhibits has grown as well, including Lightroom, Culturespaces, Frameless, lilililili, Lighthouse Immersive, and Artechouse.

The reason for the proliferation of these immersive exhibits has to do in part with the underlying business model. Their appeal, based on the power of the experience coupled with the name recognition of these artists, is broad enough that they can attract large audiences. Lighthouse Immersive's website boasts that they have sold more than seven million tickets since 2019; the Van Gogh experience produced by Exhibition Hub and Fever clocks in at a reported five million visitors since 2017; and Culturespaces, based in France, says it gets five million guests per year at their exhibitions. Because these shows tend to be hosted in venues spacious enough for the art to expand to spectacular sizes, they can also accommodate many visitors per showing—for example, the maximum capacity for Culturespaces' *Atelier des Lumières* in Paris is 850 people, and that's on the smaller end for their venues. Additionally, aside from the initial expenses to create the presentations and purchase the equipment, the operating costs are relatively low—there's no need for live performers, large staffs, or elaborate sets.

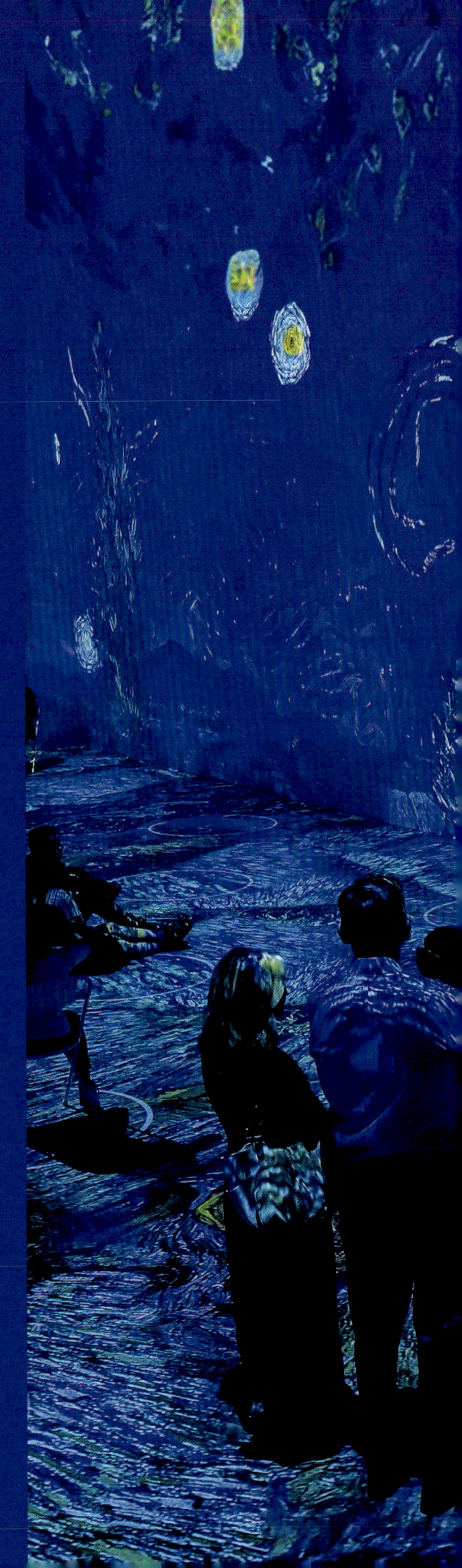

Visitors within *Starry Night* at Lighthouse Immersive's Van Gogh exhibition.

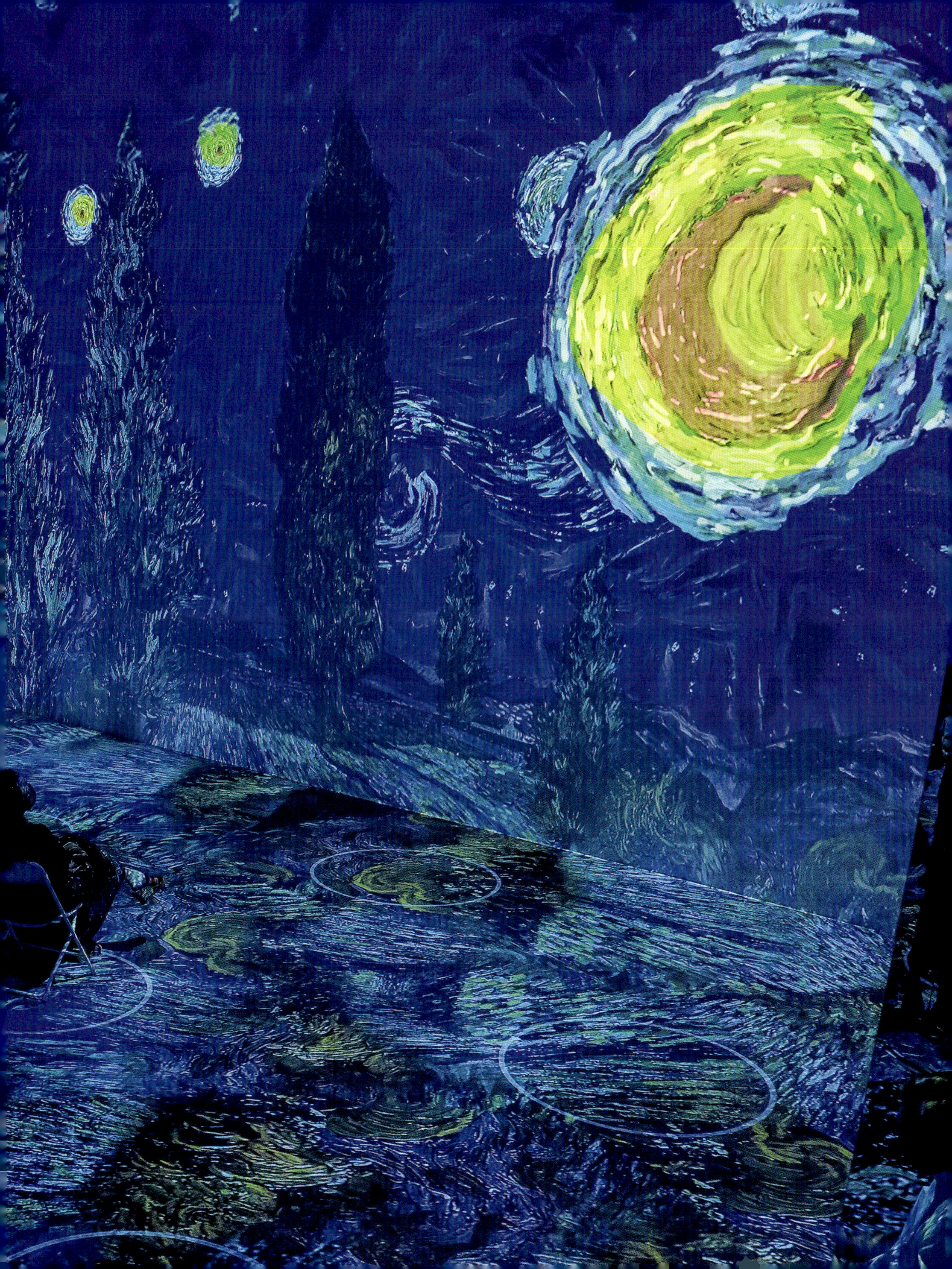

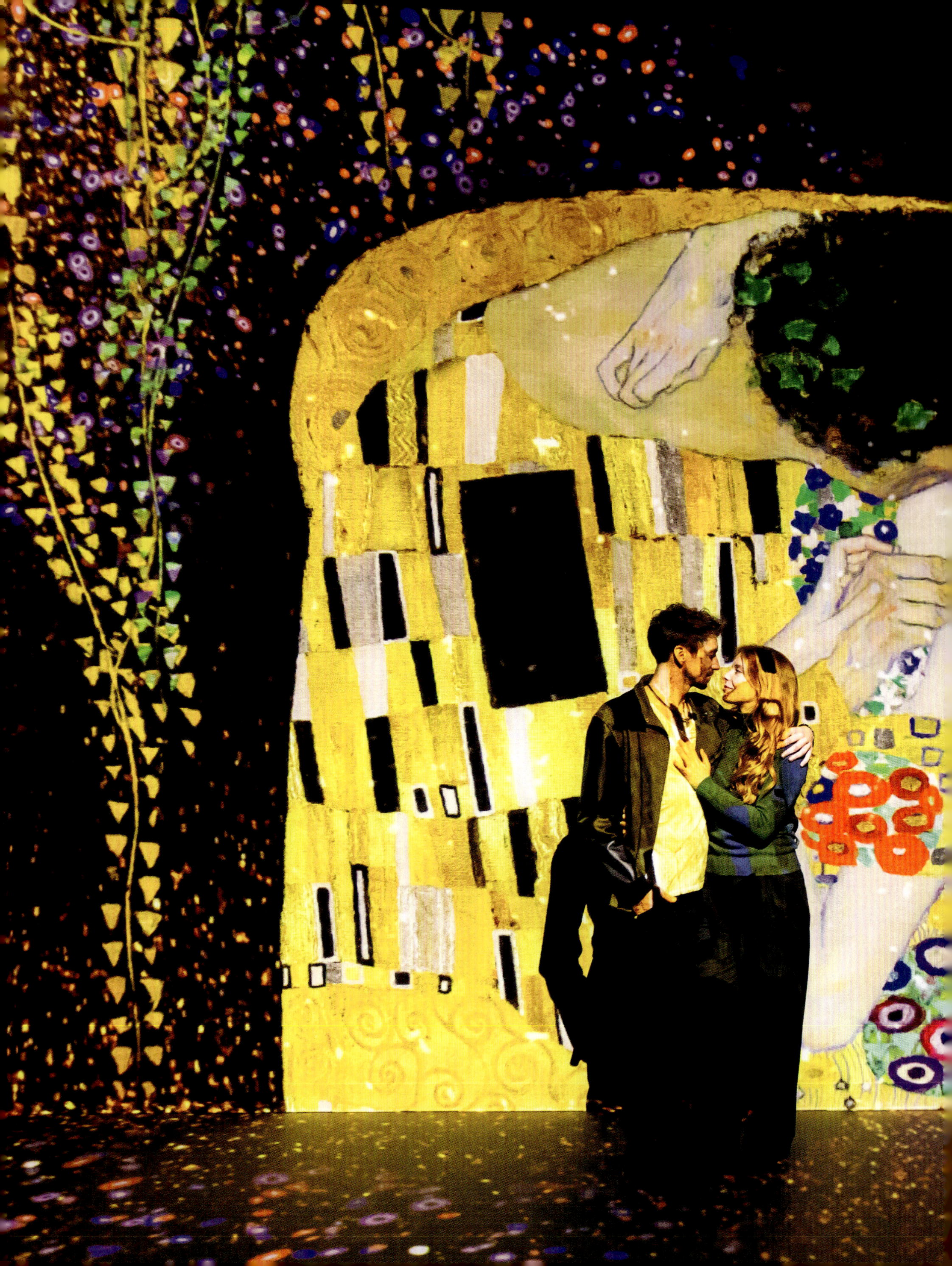

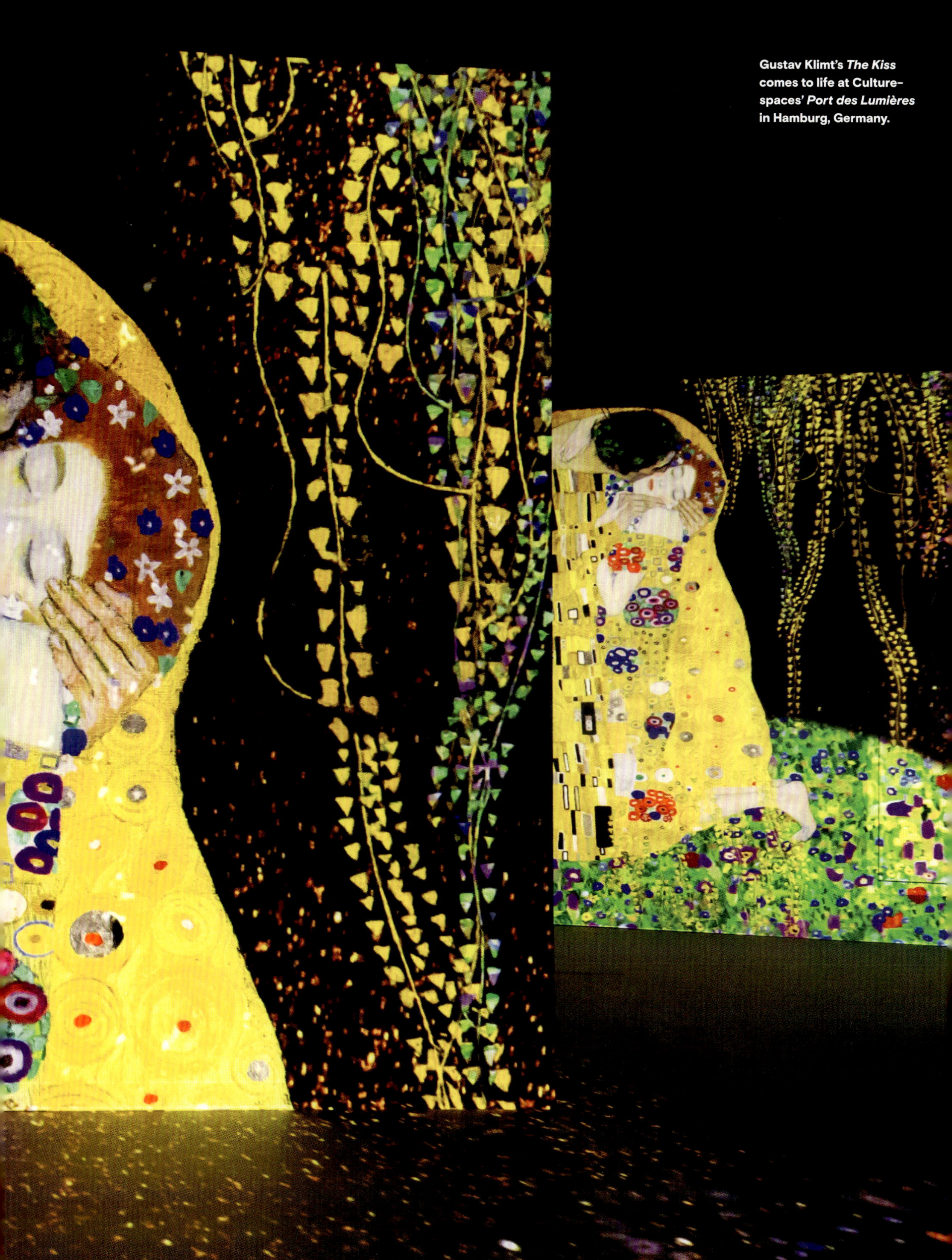

Gustav Klimt's *The Kiss* comes to life at Culturespaces' *Port des Lumières* in Hamburg, Germany.

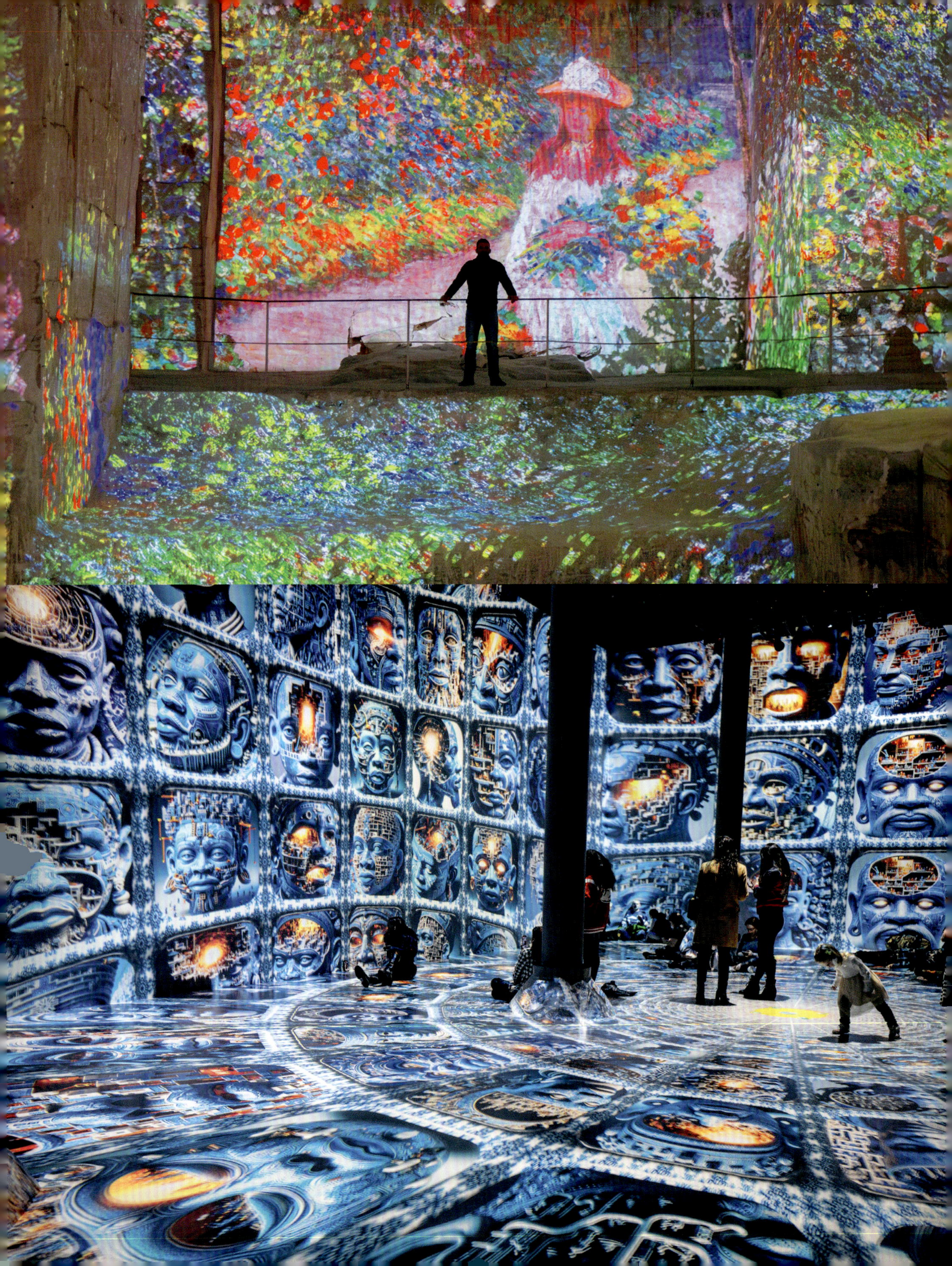

In order to continue innovating on the format, certain operators are looking to enhance their projection art shows with more storytelling. London's Lightroom, for example, collaborated with renowned painter David Hockney to design an exhibit on his work featuring his own commentary. In another exhibit, *The Moonwalkers*, the company worked with Tom Hanks to create an immersive documentary about moon exploration.

These art exhibits solve one of immersive storytelling's biggest challenges: creating an experience that's both emotionally resonant and economically viable at scale. As new artists come to this form, it will continue to evolve, attracting more and more audiences who are hungry for experiences that are spectacular and awe-inspiring.

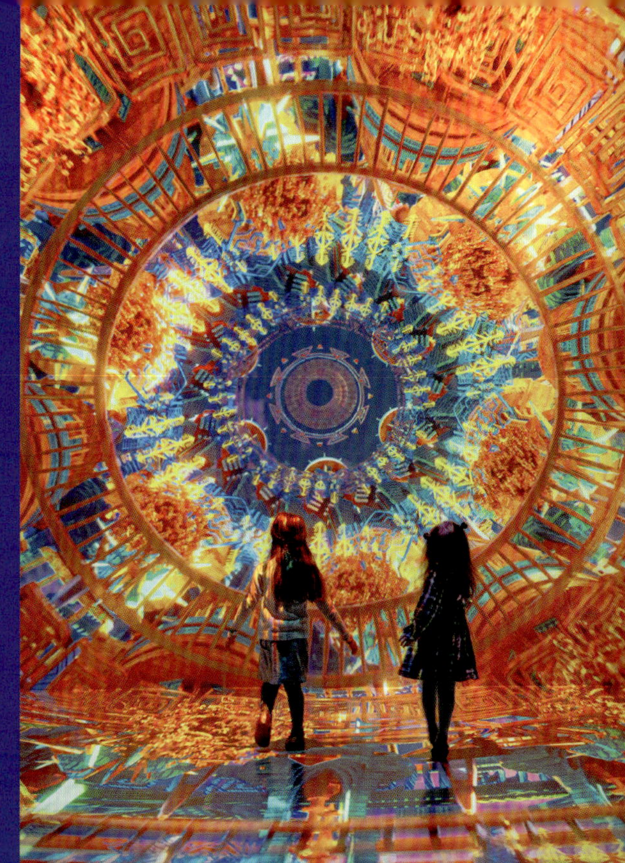

***Clockwise from left:* A visitor to Culturespaces' *Carrières des Lumières* surrounded by a Monet painting; Artechouse's *Ase: Afro Frequencies* exhibition, featuring the art of Vince Fraser and poetry by ursula rucker; Artechouse's original exhibit *Timeless Butterflies* invites guests into a world bursting with color and movement; another scene from *Ase: Afro Frequencies*.**

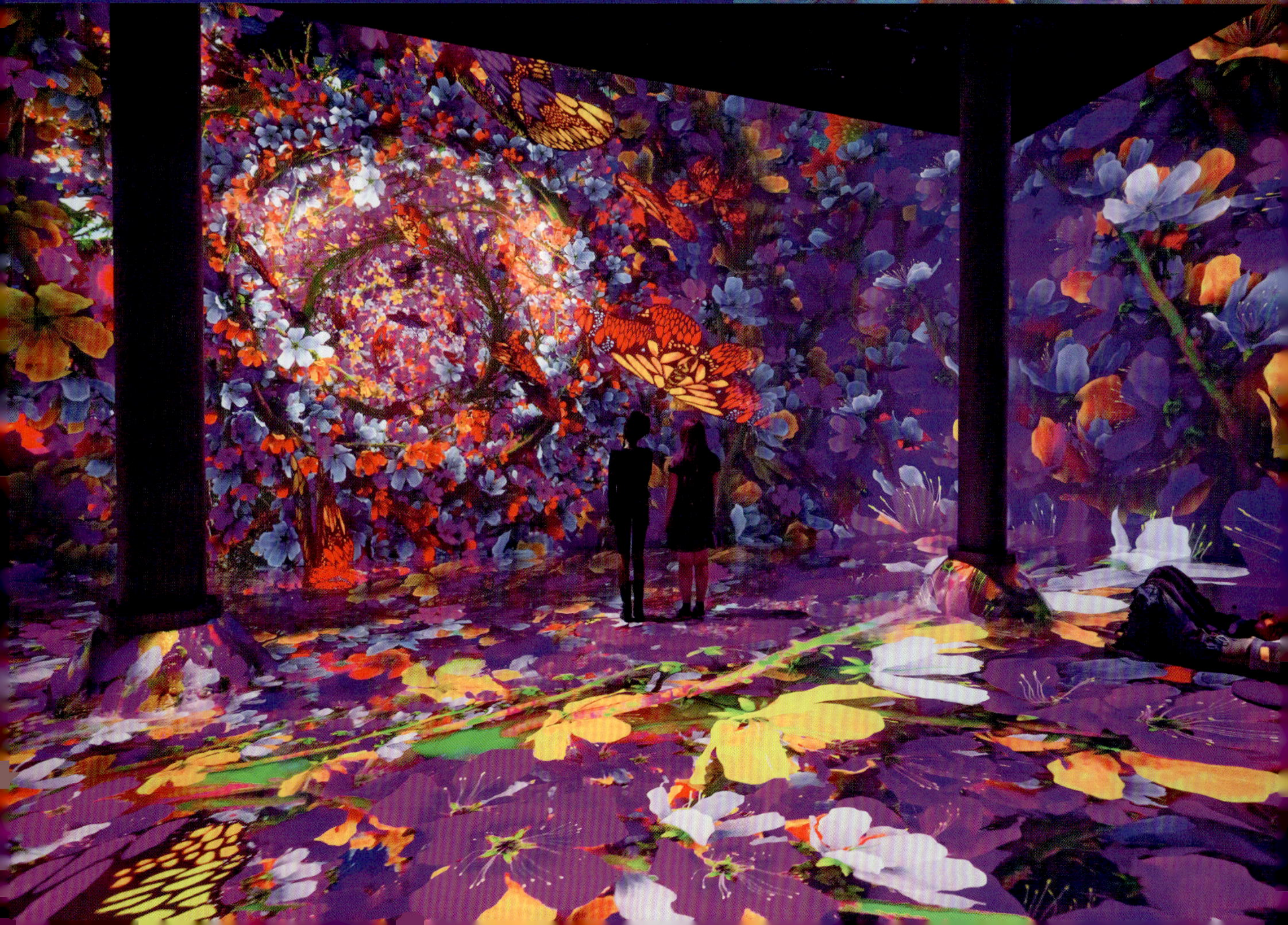

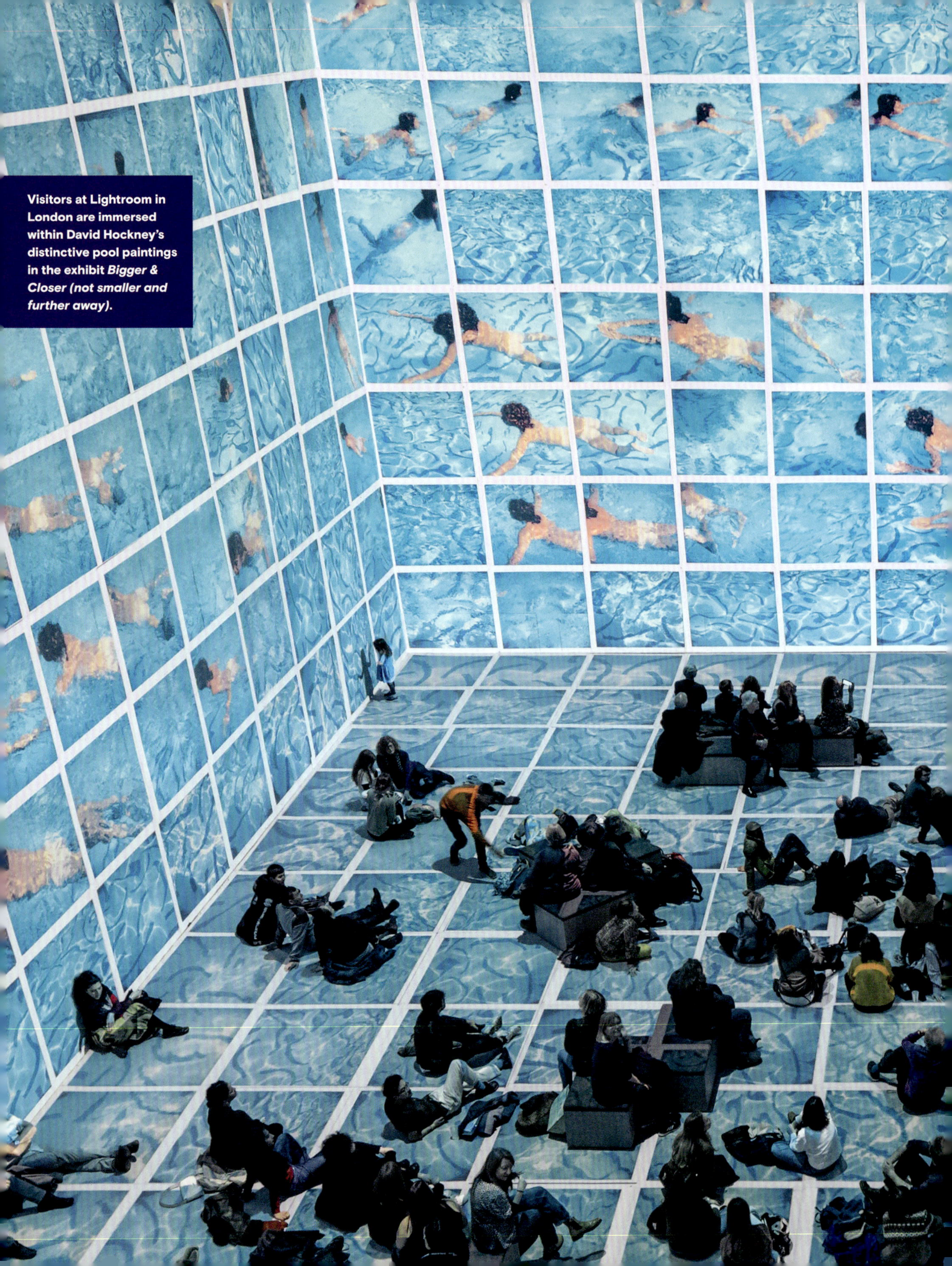

Visitors at Lightroom in London are immersed within David Hockney's distinctive pool paintings in the exhibit *Bigger & Closer (not smaller and further away)*.

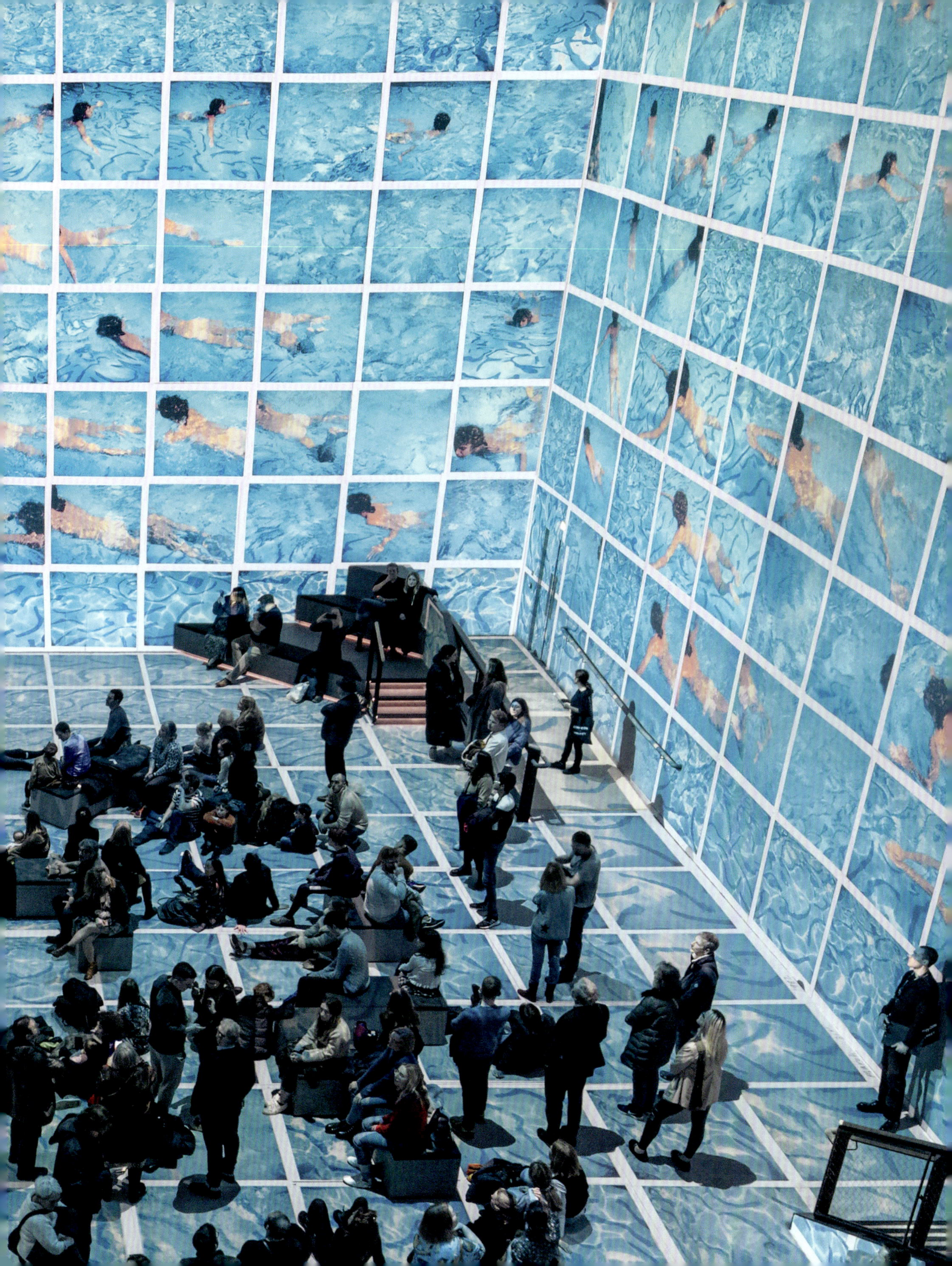

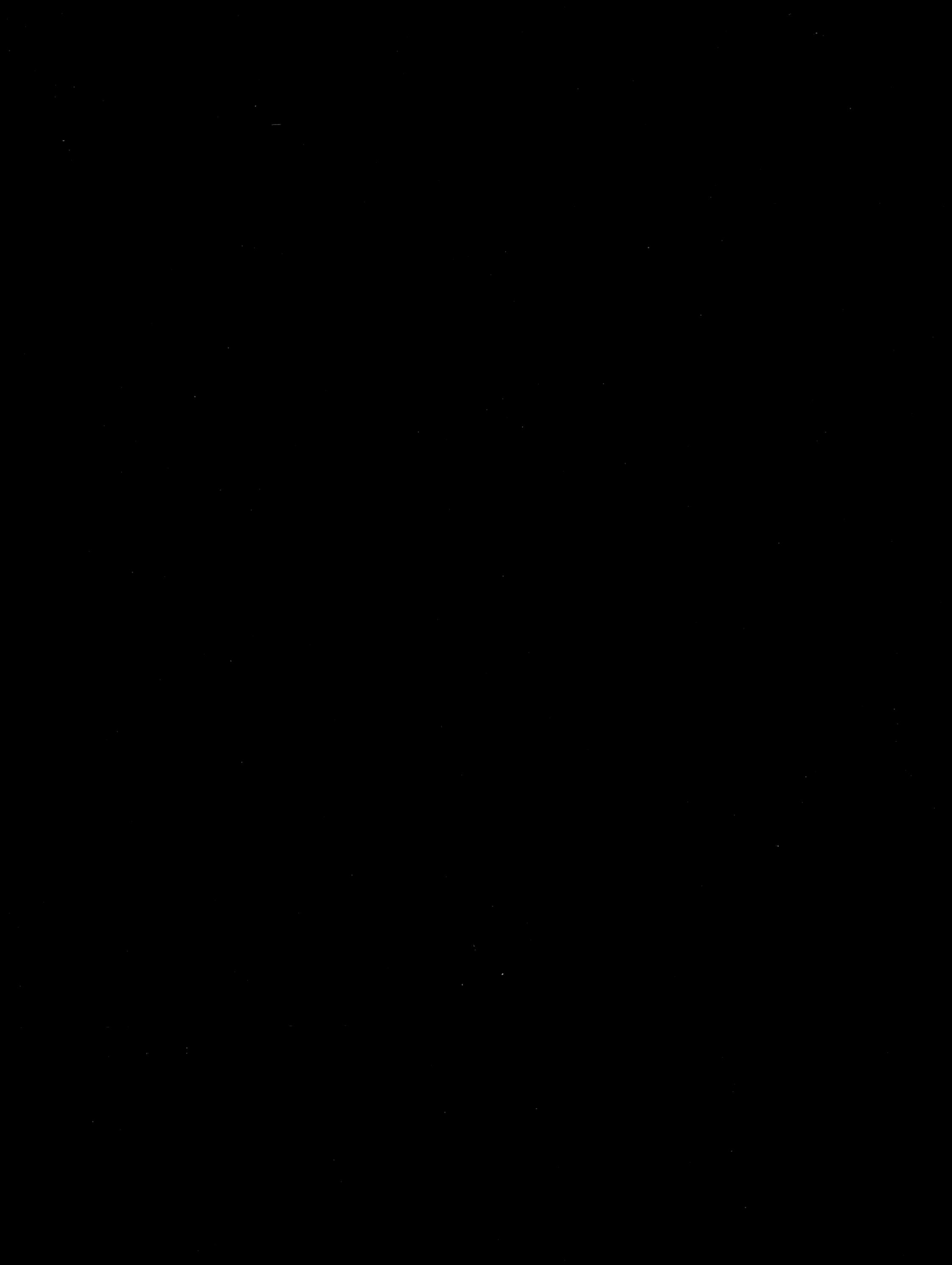

THE FUTURE OF STORYTELLING

IS

EMBODIED

The author with Ouannii, a character aboard the *Star Wars: Galactic Starcruiser* experience.

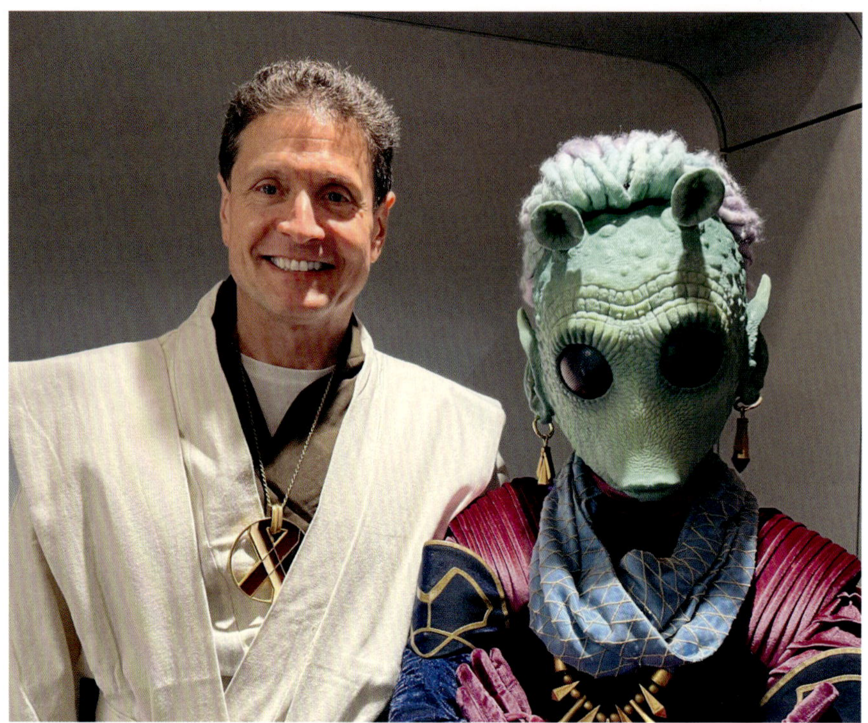

My father was a fencer. He took up the sport late, in college, and initially wasn't very good. But he kept at it, and in April 1970, at the age of thirty—shortly after I turned five—he defeated the world's top-ranked fencer in the prestigious Martini Epée Challenge. Two years later, he represented the United States in the 1972 Olympics in Munich.

Many of my most vivid memories from childhood are of watching Dad fence. I barely recall ever seeing him lose. He could get four touches behind in a five-touch bout and he'd still come back to win. In 1972, he won his second consecutive U.S. National Championship in epée while fencing with a sprained ankle. To me, he was invincible. Every kid likes to imagine that their dad is Superman; mine, I was certain, really was.

Naturally, I picked up a sword as soon as I could, and fencing quickly became a focal point of my young life. Then, not long after Dad competed in the Olympics, something happened that united my burgeoning passion for fencing with my equally intense passion for science fiction and superhero stories: In 1977, George Lucas released *Star Wars.*

Like millions of other moviegoers, I was immediately hooked. Suddenly, my fencing training took on a fantastical element: I saw myself as Luke Skywalker studying the art of lightsaber combat and my dad as the training master, Obi-Wan Kenobi. I threw myself into the sport with ever-greater gusto. In 1981, when I won my second consecutive Junior Olympics championship, my father—my greatest hero—stepped up to the podium and placed the gold medal around my neck. It was and remains one of the proudest moments of my life.

After college, when my book-publishing business started to take off, I stepped away from competitive fencing. I continued to fence for fun in my spare time, though, and never quite let go of my Jedi fantasy. So when, just a few years ago, I walked into the lightsaber training room in Disney's *Star Wars: Galactic Starcruiser* (see p. 202) and was handed a lightsaber, I was more than just up for the challenge. I had been training for this moment my entire life.

For those unfamiliar: *Galactic Starcruiser* was a short-lived but extraordinary offering in the world of living stories. For two full days, a group of friends and I lived in a massive, shockingly convincing model spaceship along with more than 400 guests and their dressed-in-character staff. We adventured in costume; we ate meals that looked straight out of Mos Eisley Cantina; we watched stars, ships, and planets float by outside our cabin windows. It was brilliantly crafted, extremely nerdy (in the best sense of the word), and wildly fun. And for an exhilarating half hour in the ship's lightsaber training room, I lived a dream I had been harboring since childhood.

Though my lightsaber's blade was covered with a plastic sheath (explained as a protective measure to keep me and my fellow trainees from getting hurt), in every other way this thing was *real*. Lifting it, I could feel the weight of its hilt, the subtle texture of its metal engravings against my fingertips. At a signal from the instructor, I powered it on and it came to life, its laser blade emerging with the trademark electric hum I had been waiting to hear for forty-five years. Then we were in training, and as I swung the blade back and forth to parry laser blasts fired from a device mounted on the wall nearby and felt the force of each impact thrumming through the hilt, I could also feel the beating of my own heart, an internal gauge of both the physical exertion and the sheer thrill of the moment. I was more than a little proud when one of my friends, watching nearby, remarked, "Wow...Charlie's really good at this!"

Ultimately, the lightsaber training experience was tangential to *Starcruiser*'s larger story. For me, though, it was a peak experience. It wasn't only the realization of a lifelong fantasy; it was also a physical reenactment of themes that had animated my earliest memories.

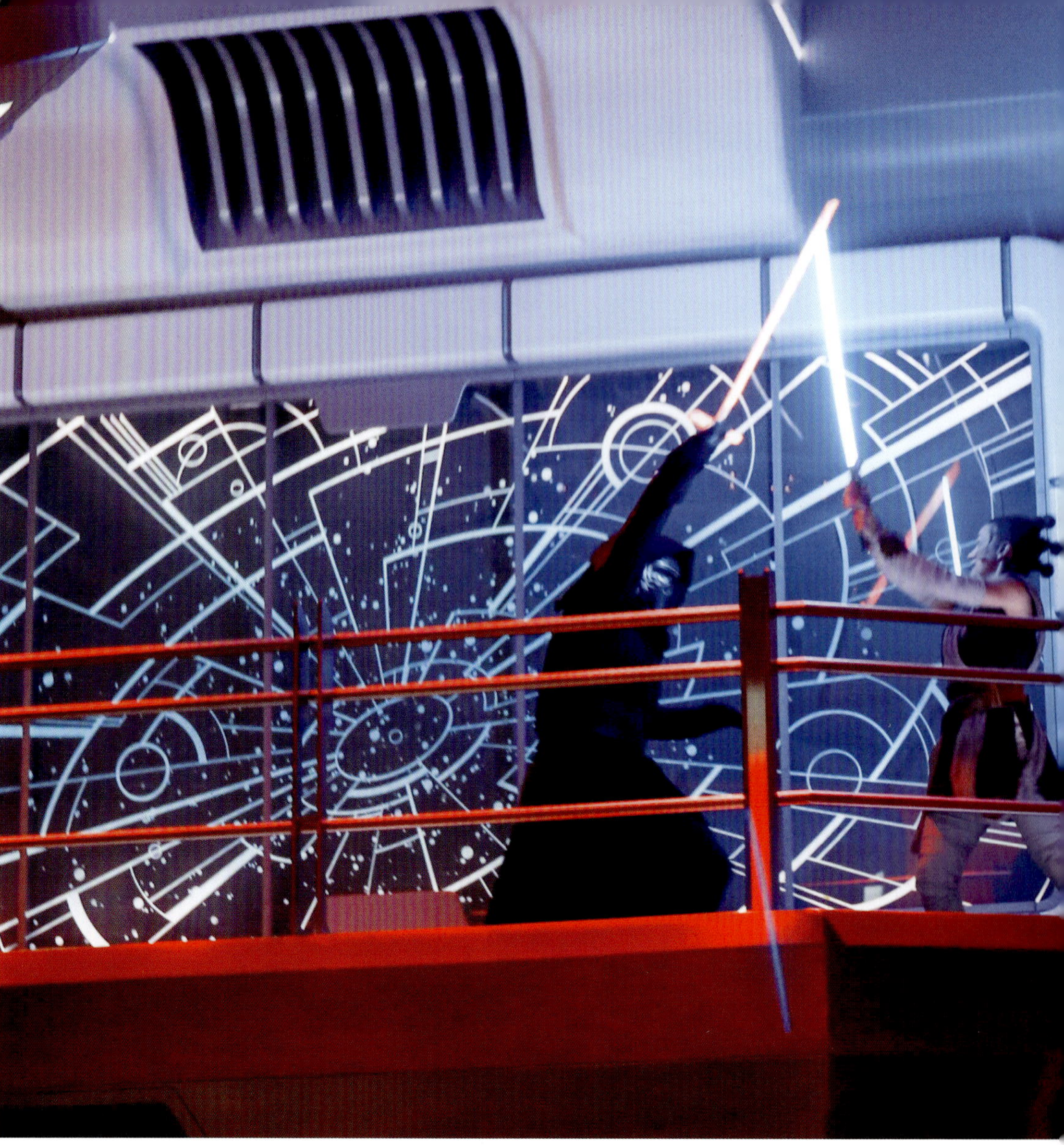

We think often of the images that define our lives: the wedding photos, the kids' birthday parties, the family vacations. But what of the movements, the textures, the feelings? For me, wielding a blade is one such movement. It connects me to my childhood, my love for my father, my passion for competition, my pride in my physical abilities. In that brief lightsaber training exercise, the story of *Galactic Starcruiser* became one with *my* story. It was a physical experience I will never forget.

Although it was open for only a little more than a year, *Galactic Starcruiser* was groundbreaking in the way it engaged not only the actience's eyes and ears but also their entire bodies. I've begun referring to this feeling of being physically present in the work as "embodiment." But it's not as simple as mere presence. A truly embodied

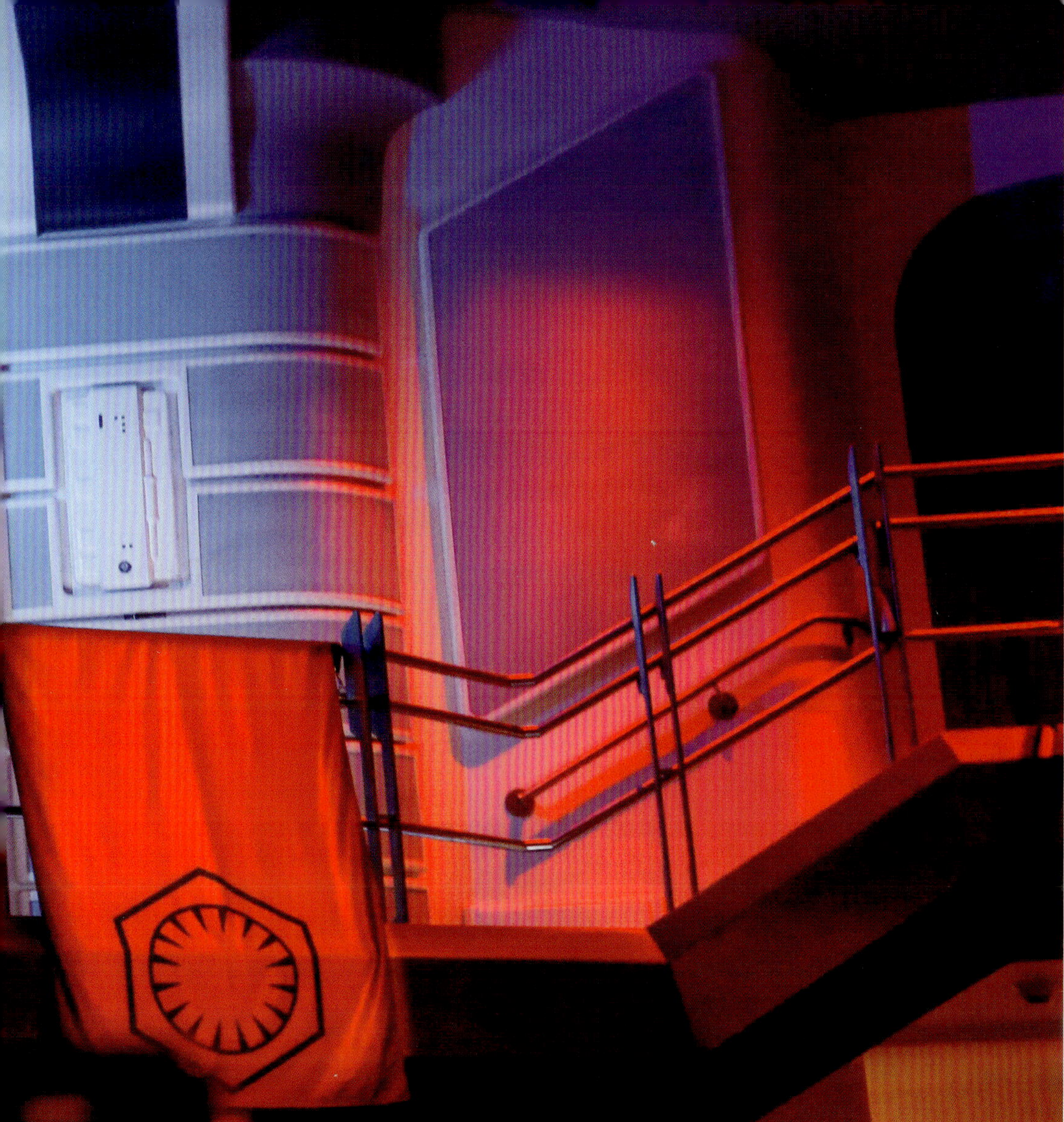

Kylo Ren and Rey faced off in a lightsaber battle aboard Disney's *Star Wars: Galactic Starcruiser*.

living story won't just engage your hands, feet, ears, and eyes; it will engage every one of your senses, even ones you're unaware of—like the perception of your heartbeat or your internal temperature. Embodiment pushes living stories to new planes of possibility. I believe embodiment is a new storytelling technique that creates a complex web of experience, emotion, and memory: It gives living stories the power to transport your whole self to other worlds. Think about the way the texture of bark against your fingers makes you nostalgic for the childhood experience of climbing a tree in a way that a simple image of a tree does not. Or the way the smell of the ocean wafting through your car window as you speed along a coastal highway carries a special excitement, separate from its sight. This is how embodiment works—it tells a story to the body by engaging every sense.

TELLING STORIES TO THE BODY

The first time I got a taste of what an embodied living story could be like was in 2013, when I experienced a VR prototype by "Godmother of Virtual Reality" Nonny de la Peña, Peggy Weil, and co-director of the Barcelona Event Lab, Mel Slater. Set in an interrogation room in Guantánamo Bay, it was part of a series of VR stories that de la Peña called "immersive journalism." These prototypes envisioned a new way to use technology and gaming platforms to convey news, documentaries, and nonfiction stories.

Participants in de la Peña's prototype sat in a chair with their hands clasped behind their backs. Through the VR headset, they saw an avatar, imprisoned in an interrogation room, mimicking their head movements and breathing rhythms. Throughout, the sound of dialogue based on the transcript taken from a real Guantánamo Bay interrogation played as if it were coming from the next room. Another related project by de la Peña and Weil, *Gone Gitmo*, taught users about the unlawful detention of Guantánamo prisoners by having the virtual interrogator ask participants if they'd like to call their parents or lawyer, or ask why they were being detained, and then denying each request. The effect was one of total hopelessness.

The experience de la Peña created was technologically simple, yet it went far beyond the conventions of film. It featured little interactivity and the bare-bones animated visuals necessitated by a shoestring production budget. Its impact, however, was profound. When I interview de la Peña about the work, she says, "When we asked people afterward how their body felt—even though you could see them being filmed, sitting up with their hands behind their back—they reported that they were hunched over in a stress position, and they expressed fear that they were going to be interrogated next.... They had a connection to the scenario that I had not been able to achieve in documentary or print journalism."

Because participants' bodies were put in relatively submissive postures during the scene, they were able to experience a sliver of the stress and fear a real prisoner in that situation may have felt. In this way, de la Peña's work was groundbreaking in its ability to engender empathy through an embodied immersive experience. She went on to tackle many other important topics, like poverty, hunger, and war, using her immersive journalism methods and was honored with a Peabody Award for her impact. De la Peña's work has demonstrated how embodied living stories can affect real social change.

STORING MEMORIES IN THE BODY

Why do embodied living stories feel so emotionally powerful for those who experience them? For an explanation, I turned to science writer Annie Murphy Paul. In her book *The Extended Mind*, Paul presents a growing body of research that suggests that thinking and feeling, processes once thought to occur solely in our brains, are in fact heavily influenced by our bodies and environments. She offers up studies that demonstrate that movement can improve memory, that emotions are partially constructed from bodily sensations, and that physical involvement in complex situations improves comprehension and recall of the action taking place. The book isn't explicitly aimed at storytellers, but for me, reading it was a watershed moment. All the beliefs that I've long held intuitively about the power of immersive, embodied storytelling suddenly gained the backing of rigorous scientific inquiry.

When I think about my experience with de la Peña's work, one of the things I remember most vividly is the sense of terror and helplessness that came with being made to assume a submissive posture—sitting in a chair with my hands behind my back. The encounter was fictional, and yet those emotions felt real, powerful, *visceral*. Where did they originate from? Common wisdom might hold that the fear came from the environmental stimuli—the harrowing interrogation audio and the cage I was being held in. This conception is essentially brain-centric: It implies that the fear originates in the brain and the body responds accordingly. But a review of psychological literature suggests that the true sequence of events is precisely the opposite: Emotions originate in the body and then the brain processes and labels them. I felt afraid and helpless because *my body* was in a fearful posture.

Embodiment doesn't only affect the emotionality of an experience. It can also make it more memorable.

In fact, this idea isn't particularly new: As Paul notes in *The Extended Mind,* psychologist William James proposed it over a century ago, writing, "Common sense says, we lose our fortune, are sorry and weep; we meet a bear, are frightened and run; we are insulted by a rival, are angry and strike...the more rational statement is that we feel sorry because we cry, angry because we strike, afraid because we tremble." As Paul writes, "The body produces sensations, the body initiates actions—and only then does the mind assemble these pieces of evidence into the entity we call an emotion."

She refers to the sensations of the body as the "ground floor" of emotional construction. It follows, then, that if storytellers are able to get in on this ground floor, to build up emotions throughout the body, they stand to create richer and more resonant experiences. This helps explain why I recall the emotions I felt in de la Peña's work and so many other embodied stories I've experienced so vividly: because my whole body was brought into the emotional development of the piece. But as I learned in *The Extended Mind,* there's another factor at work here as well that's helped lodge these experiences so powerfully in my memory. Embodiment doesn't only affect the emotionality of an experience. It can also make it inherently more memorable.

Paul relates the story of a group of actors who had worked on a play. Five months after the end of its run, researchers found that the actors still remembered many of their lines that had been accompanied by some kind of movement or gesture; conversely, they had forgotten most of the lines they had delivered while standing still. Summarizing the results of this study as well as further research on the connection between movement and memory, Paul writes,

"Linking movement to the material to be recalled creates a richer and therefore more indelible 'memory trace' in the brain." She goes on to demonstrate that even if the movement in question isn't a direct enactment of the information (like an actor gesturing while they deliver a line) but is simply related to the information and occurs at the same time as it's being conveyed, it still measurably improves later recall.

Taken as a whole, the insights of *The Extended Mind* suggest that involving the body in a story experience may present special opportunities for emotional impact, and perhaps even make the experience more memorable. But if the body is this rich, often untapped resource of emotional connection and memory-making, how do we best make use of it? In what language do we tell stories to the body?

THE LANGUAGE OF LIVING STORIES

Though the medium of filmmaking is well established today, when it was first invented no one quite knew what to do with the motion-picture camera. Early filmmakers treated it more like a tool for capturing theater—keeping the camera stationary, positioning it at a medium distance from the action, avoiding close-ups—than a new paradigm. It wasn't until directors began experimenting with the unique capabilities of the film camera that the medium truly came into its own.

The screen is the canvas of cinema; by learning to creatively utilize the camera to maximize the emotional resonance of the stories projected on that screen, early filmmakers brought the medium into its golden age. In a living story, the canvas is the audience

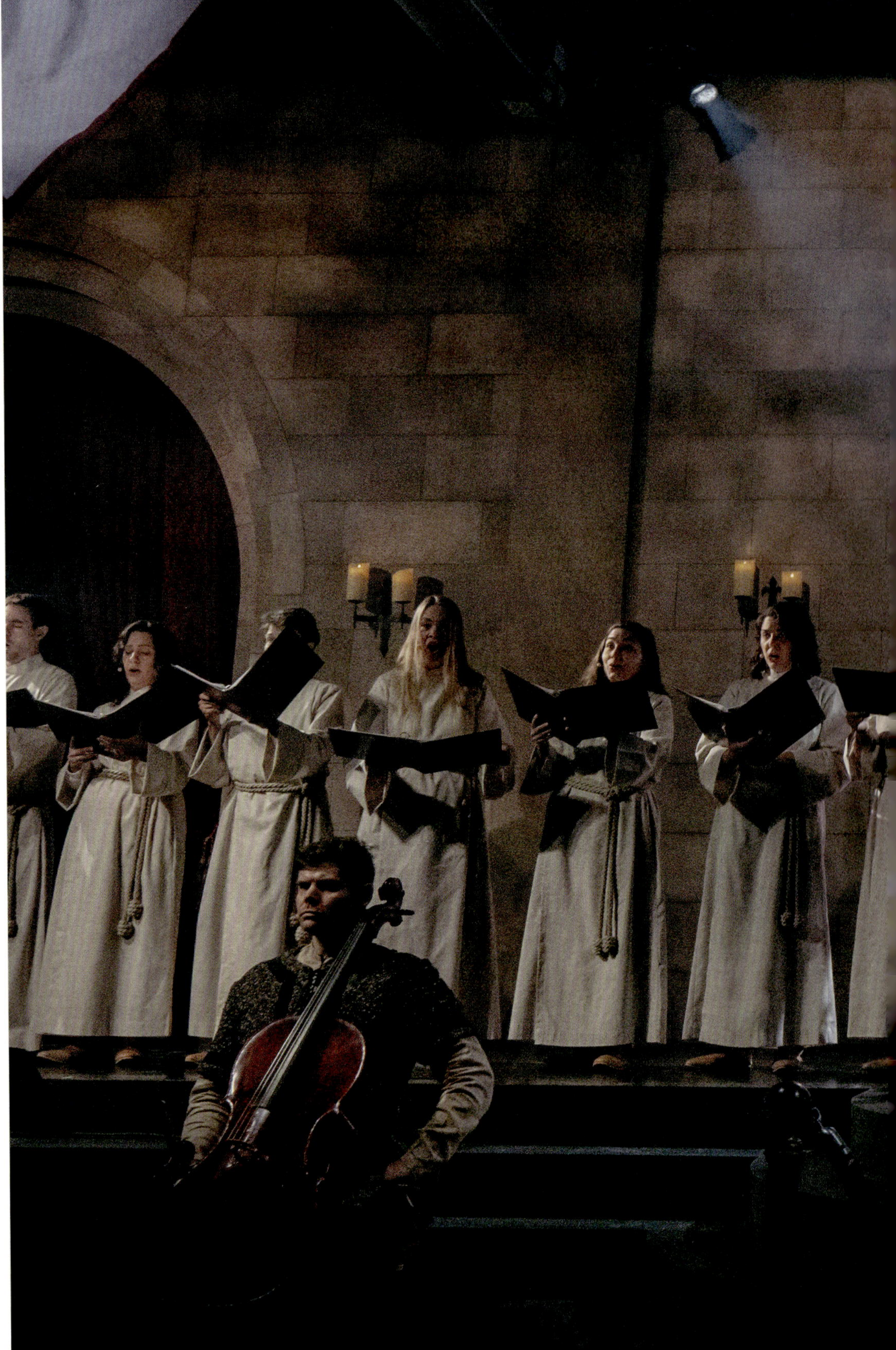

Giant Spoon's "Bleed for the Throne" activation at South by Southwest tapped into multiple senses—not just sight and sound but also smell and touch—to immerse audience members in the world of *Game of Thrones*.

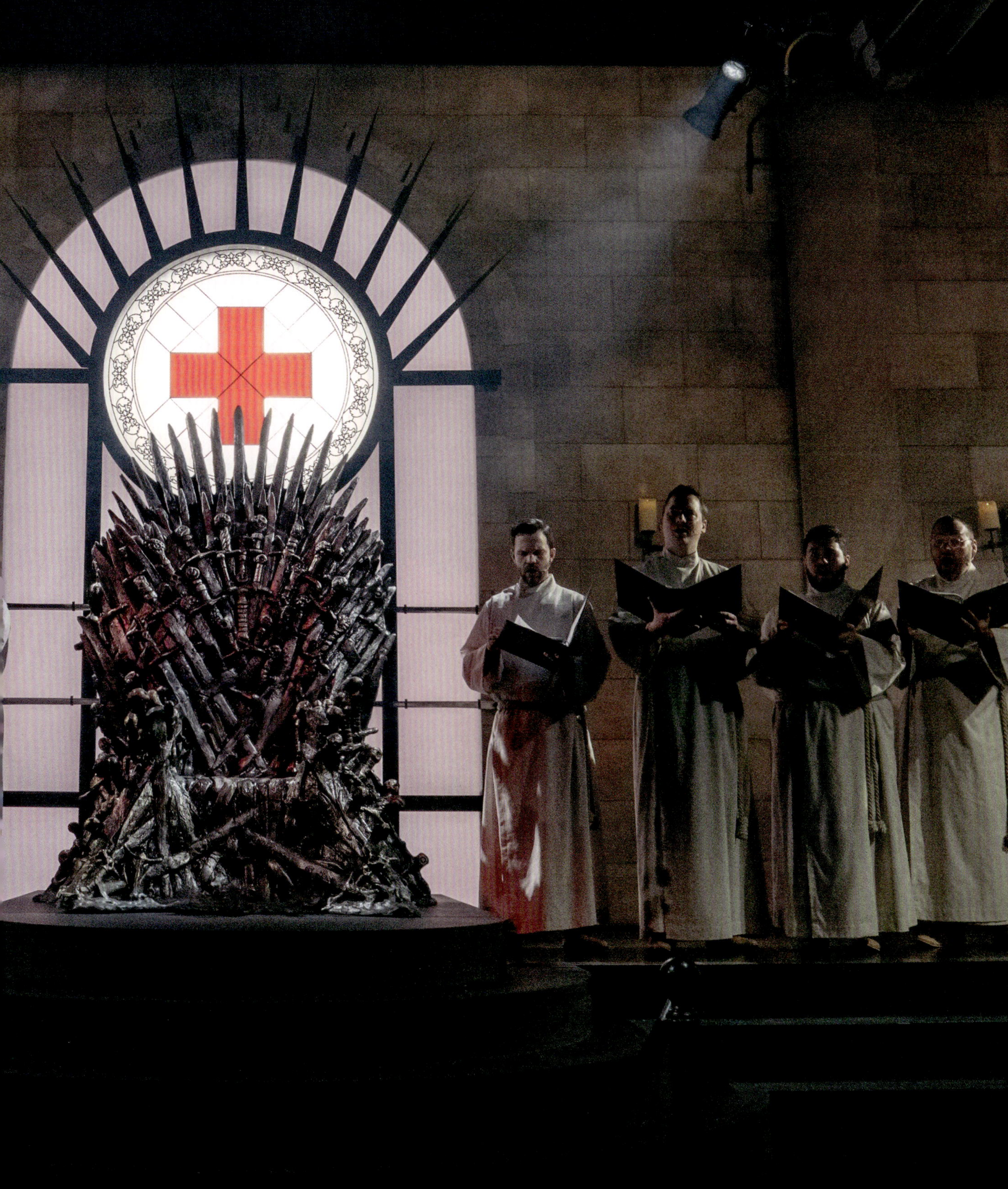

itself, and the story should be projected not only onto the eyes and ears of each audience member, but into, onto, and throughout their entire bodies. By telling them holistically, to the body, the brain, and all the senses, we will create stories with the full depth of lived experiences. But to use embodiment effectively as a tool of storytelling, we need a creative "language" of the body—comparable to the language of cinema.

The best living storytellers are keen observers of their own bodies. Like all artists, they embrace the power of observation so that they can identify the everyday details that others often miss.

As a painter might spend time wandering out in the world, seeking inspiration from nature, or a writer might sit in a café and jot down overheard conversations, so too should an aspiring creator of living stories be attuned to their everyday physical reactions. This is because even simple physical gestures, like raising a glass for a

There's evidence that aside from creating emotions in their own right, bodily sensations can color our perceptions of the world around us.

toast and giving someone a hug, inspire deep emotion. Such actions become enmeshed in and symbolic of a complex web of emotional threads. Similarly, a repeated action can be complicated or recontextualized throughout the course of a narrative. Perhaps you have to regularly water a plant that you received as a gift from a friend, but as your relationship with that friend changes, the action of watering the plant takes on new meaning.

There's evidence that aside from creating emotions in their own right, bodily sensations can color our perceptions of the world around us. A study published in the October 24, 2008, issue of the journal *Science* found that participants who were given a warm cup of coffee to hold were more likely to judge others as generous and caring than those who were asked to hold an iced coffee. From an embodied narrative perspective, we might say that the temperature of the mug functioned like lighting in a film, where a trustworthy character might be depicted in full light and a villainous one cast in shadow.

Consider de la Peña's prototype. Would the participants have feared their impending interrogation had their hands not been behind their backs? The best living storytellers are on a mission to discover the evocative bodily sensations, movements, and positions that spur emotions, then learn how to deploy them effectively in immersive stories.

To be sure, sensory stimulation alone is not enough. In fact, if creators aren't careful, too much sensory stimulation can ruin an otherwise strong piece. In 1960, for example, the film *Scent of Mystery* released various odors into the audience that aligned with the onscreen happenings through a technology the creators called Smell-O-Vision. Rather than enhancing the film, the odors overwhelmed and distracted the audience. Those seated at the front of the theater were bombarded with a loud hissing noise when the odors were released into the air, and those on the balcony sniffed loudly because they barely reached them. The goal of living stories is not to provide more sensory information—it's to place the audience directly into the world of the story and enhance their emotional experience of it.

Let's contrast *Scent of Mystery* with a successful use of smell in a living story. Marc Simons, cofounder of ad agency Giant Spoon, discovered the impact that smell could have on immersive experiences while working on a *Game of Thrones* activation at South by Southwest in Austin in 2019. "We were running a blood drive," he recounts. "'Bleed for the Throne' was our motto. So people would give blood, and afterward they would walk into a church experience we had created with the Iron Throne up front and an actual chorus singing about their dedication to it." But during the planning, as Simons and his team walked through the space, they could tell that something was missing. They didn't want people to feel like they were walking through a set piece of a church. They wanted to suspend reality; they wanted their visitors to *be in a church*. Eventually, they realized that what was missing was scent: If they intended for this to be a church and not just look like one, the space needed to smell like a church. So they purchased incense and wafted it through the space, creating another layer of reality. "It took you out of walking the streets of Austin," Simons says, "and put you in this mindset that told every one of your senses that this was actually a church." For him, achieving that full sensory immersion is pivotal. "If you can suspend the reality of whatever's going on outside—Comic-Con, or South by Southwest, or whatever else—you create this bubble where people's minds are entirely open to listening and hearing and understanding your message."

Simons found a sensory touchstone that established a connection between the audience and the narrative. Taste can serve the same purpose. But even the five senses we're most familiar with

EXTENDED SENSES

Beyond the best-known five, researchers believe that there could be as many as thirty-three senses. A selection of those that are most relevant to living stories is included below.

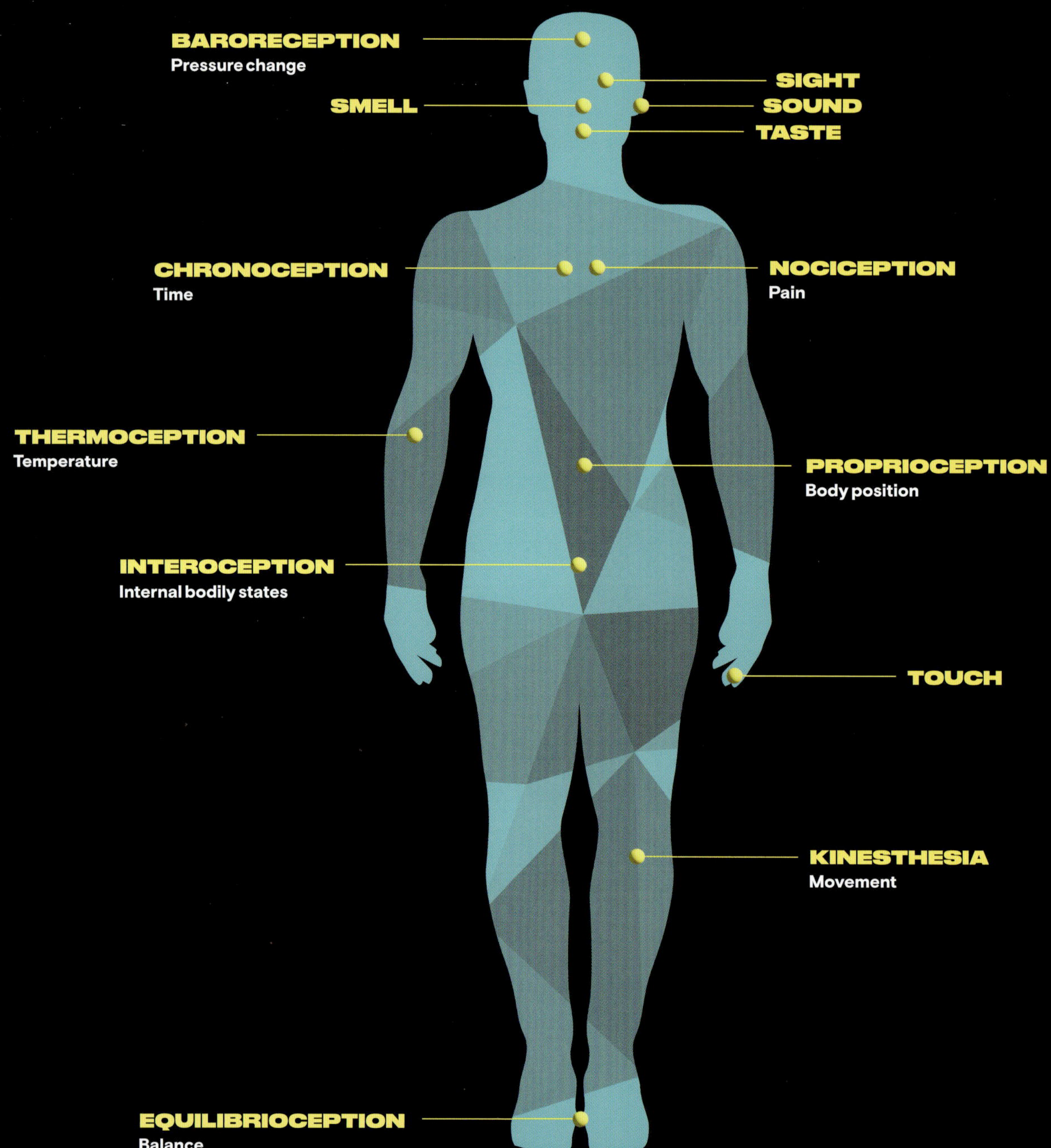

are just the start: Today, psychologists estimate that humans possess anywhere from eight to thirty-three senses, allowing us to perceive things like the temperature of our surroundings (thermoception), the positions of our bodies in space (proprioception), and our own internal biological processes, such as our heartbeats (interoception). Engaging this robust spectrum of sensory experience offers new and potent pathways for building emotion through immersive storytelling.

This is the power of living stories: They can connect us with our deepest selves, just as my experience on the *Galactic Starcruiser* stirred up cherished memories of fencing with my father. Traditional media—which we observe while sitting in the same position, staring at a screen for hours—can't deliver this feeling of embod-

We didn't evolve to sit still on the couch. We evolved to run, jump, dance, climb, crawl, search, discover, feel. In other words, we evolved to be actively and directly involved in the rich sensory experience of the world around us.

iment. A diverse "media diet" in today's world may feed the brain, but it does nothing for the body; in fact, much of modern society as a whole seems oriented toward detaching us from our bodies in favor of our brains.

We didn't evolve to sit still on the couch. We evolved to run, jump, dance, climb, crawl, search, discover, feel. In other words, we evolved to be actively and directly involved in the rich sensory experience of the world around us. Educators learned long ago that the best way to teach students isn't always to have them sit at desks and memorize diagrams of biological processes, but instead to let them enact those processes themselves, or study them in the field. It's time for storytellers to take the same step forward and begin to use the full depth of human experience as their canvas. In doing so, they can create richer stories, deeper emotions, and lasting impact.

CAMP

Since 2018, CAMP has been at the forefront of redefining both retail and play through its stores and immersive experiences. Founding CEO Ben Kaufman says that CAMP's rotating offerings solve the "what should we do today?" question by giving families a place to go on a real adventure: "What we've done at CAMP is combine play, product, and programming into this ritualistic destination that's attempting to do for families what Starbucks did for professionals."

At any of CAMP's nine vibrant locations, kids and their families step inside what appears to be a typical toy store. But soon they stumble upon a hidden magical door, revealing a whimsical world where they are part of an unfolding journey. Whether it's beloved franchises from companies like Disney, Paramount, and DreamWorks or a CAMP original concept, families encounter a wealth of activities. They can interact with characters, explore inventive, larger-than-life environments, take part in group sing-alongs, and engage in a variety of games. The experiences at each CAMP change throughout the year, encouraging guests to return and discover the next story that awaits them.

CAMP experiences are ticketed and timed, functioning like shows in a theater. Kaufman says, "We actually think of ourselves more as an operator of venues and less as an operator of stores. Our stores are basically just theaters that change the show about every four months. Like any theater, there's merchandise for sale. But the main reason why you visit the theater isn't the merchandise, it's the show." CAMP presents opportunities to purchase merchandise throughout, seamlessly integrating them into the story. Instead of being just generic items on a shelf, these products are extensions of the stories themselves, physical tokens of vivid memories shared by kids and their families.

Through its inventive approach, CAMP has transformed retail into an immersive experience where visitors don't just shop—they create meaningful family moments. With its unique combination of merchandise and ticketed live events, CAMP demonstrates that people are happy to spend on making magic together.

When guests enter CAMP, it looks like a high-end children's toy store, but once you go through the magical door, it becomes an immersive playground for kids and parents filled with actor-led performances, games, and arts-and-crafts projects. The themed "shows" are based on popular IP such as *Bluey*, *Encanto*, and *The Little Mermaid*.

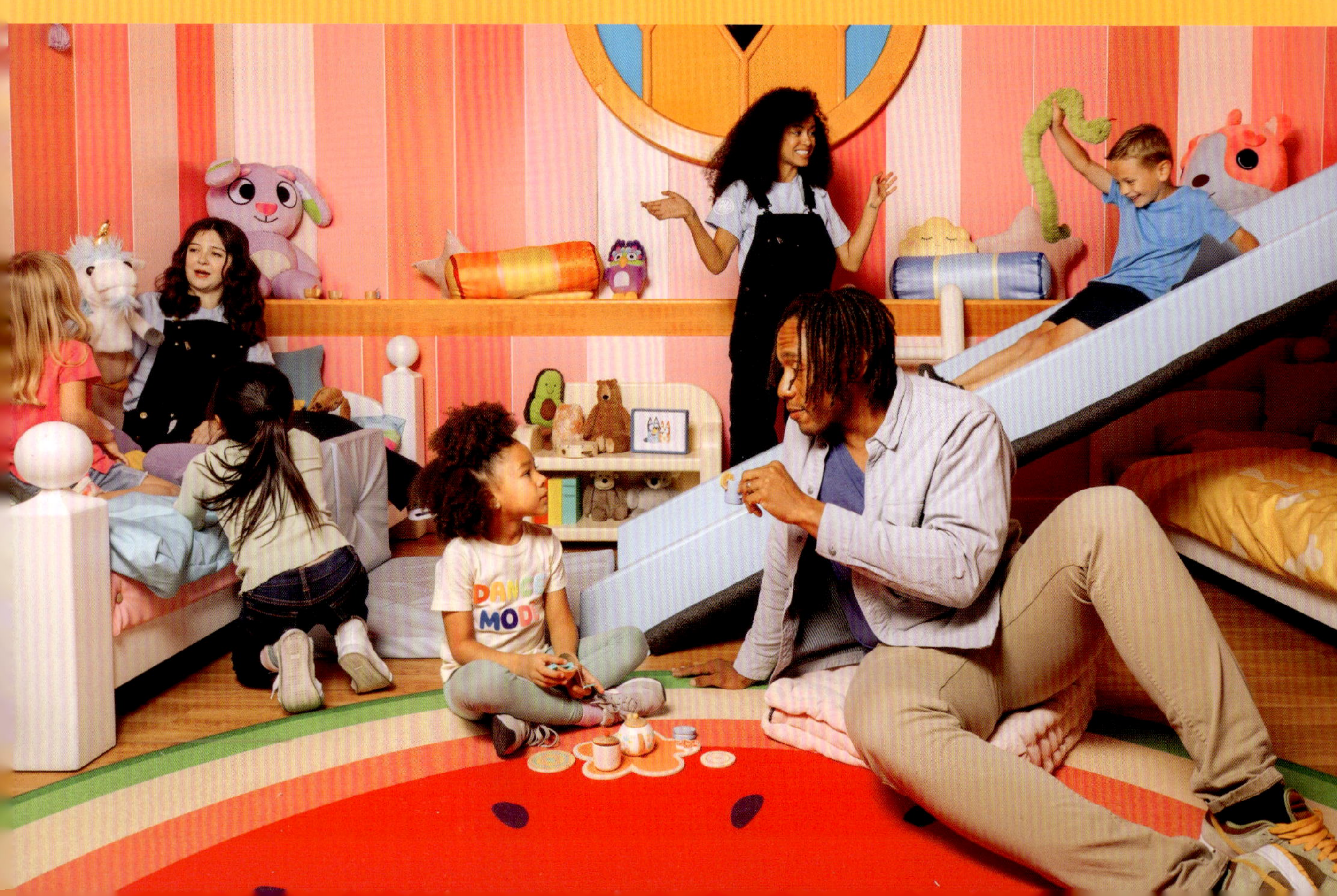

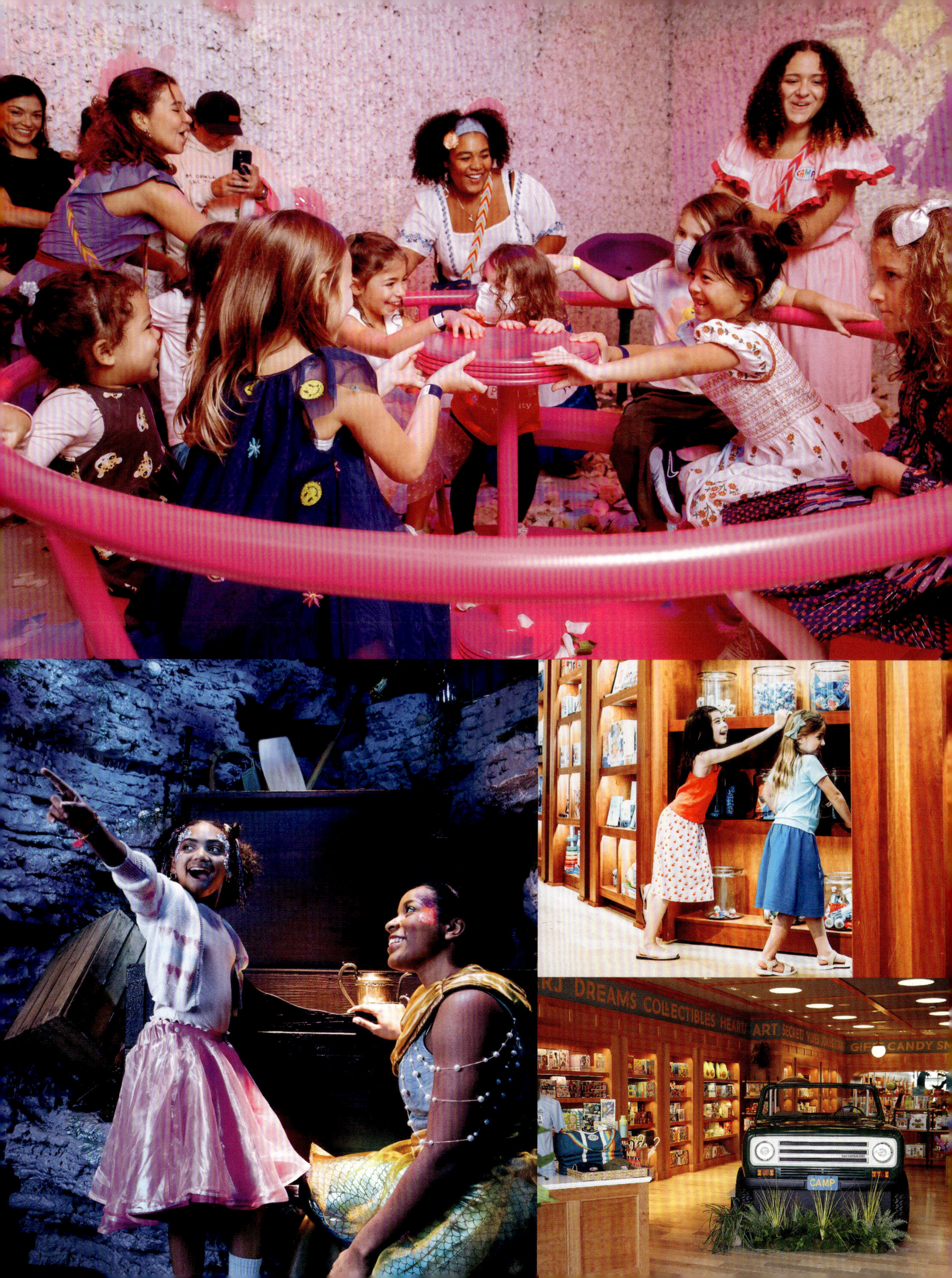
DREAMS COLLECTIBLES
ART
CANDY
CAMP

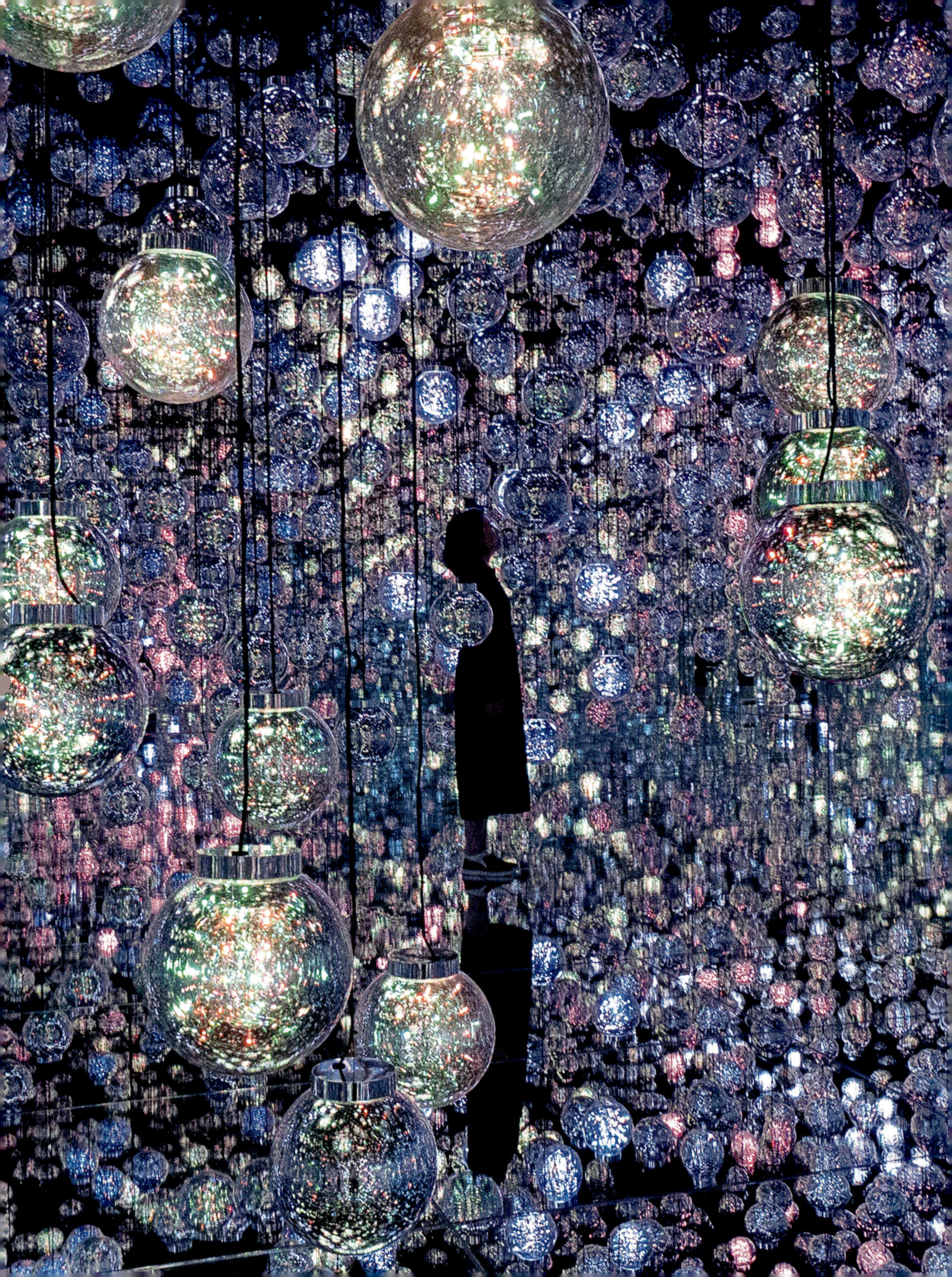

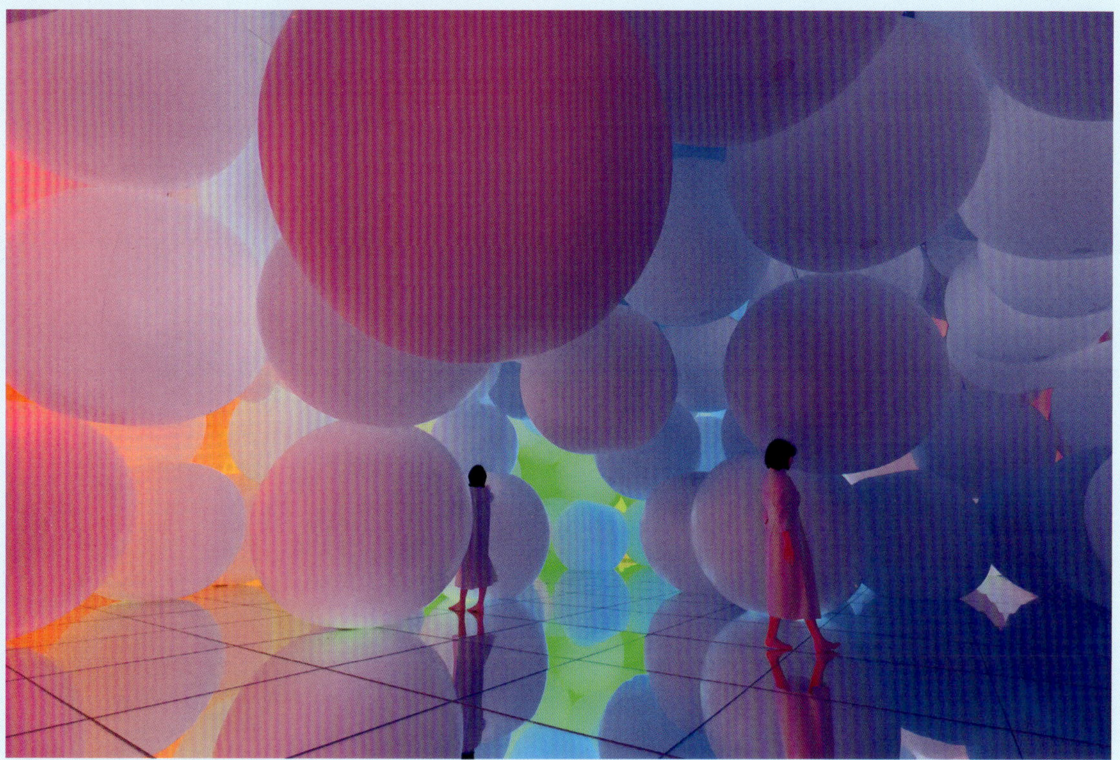

TEAMLAB

Based in Tokyo, international art collective teamLab, founded in 2001, consists of artists, architects, animators, programmers, engineers, mathematicians, and other interdisciplinary specialists. The group came together to explore and ultimately dissolve the boundaries between art and science, nature and technology, self and other. Inspired by natural forms and the endless possibilities of digital media, the group is creating some of the most unconventional art experiences the world has ever seen—and some of the most popular.

teamLab's large-scale exhibitions and museums are best described as ecosystems: Rather than being confined to frames on walls, their artworks of dynamic light and sound expand to fill the spaces they inhabit. Some are not even limited to one room, wandering the galleries like living beings; others still travel from venue to venue, originating in one city's teamLab show only to appear in another on the opposite side of the globe. Many works are designed to be responsive—on the walls, waterfalls made of light part to your touch, and flowers bloom on the floor where your feet land. With certain pieces constantly changing or responding to interactions from guests, the experience there feels alive and eternally evolving, making it inviting for repeat visitation.

teamLab's worlds push their concepts to extend infinitely and positively in every direction. The scale of their museums feels unmatched: Large venues and open floor plans lend credence to the feeling that you really are in an endless space. You're welcome to touch almost anything you see, and the art flourishes in your presence. Multisensory experiences where you can wade through water populated by digital fish or bat around huge luminescent balls give you permission to play and bask in a renewed freedom. It's a vision of a different kind of reality—one where nature, humanity, and technology coexist peacefully and harmoniously.

Above: Visitors can interact with huge, colorful spheres in "Expanding Three-Dimensional Existence in Transforming Space." _Opposite:_ Getting lost inside "Bubble Universe" from teamLab's _Borderless_ exhibition in Azubadai Hills in Tokyo.

Compare that freedom with the formality of the traditional art museum, and it's not hard to see why teamLab is so in demand. They offer something new and magical that's also thoughtful and purposeful, with a profound message about our oneness with nature. What they've made is a new type of artistic experience—one that sheds all borders and embraces embodiment, agency, and awe.

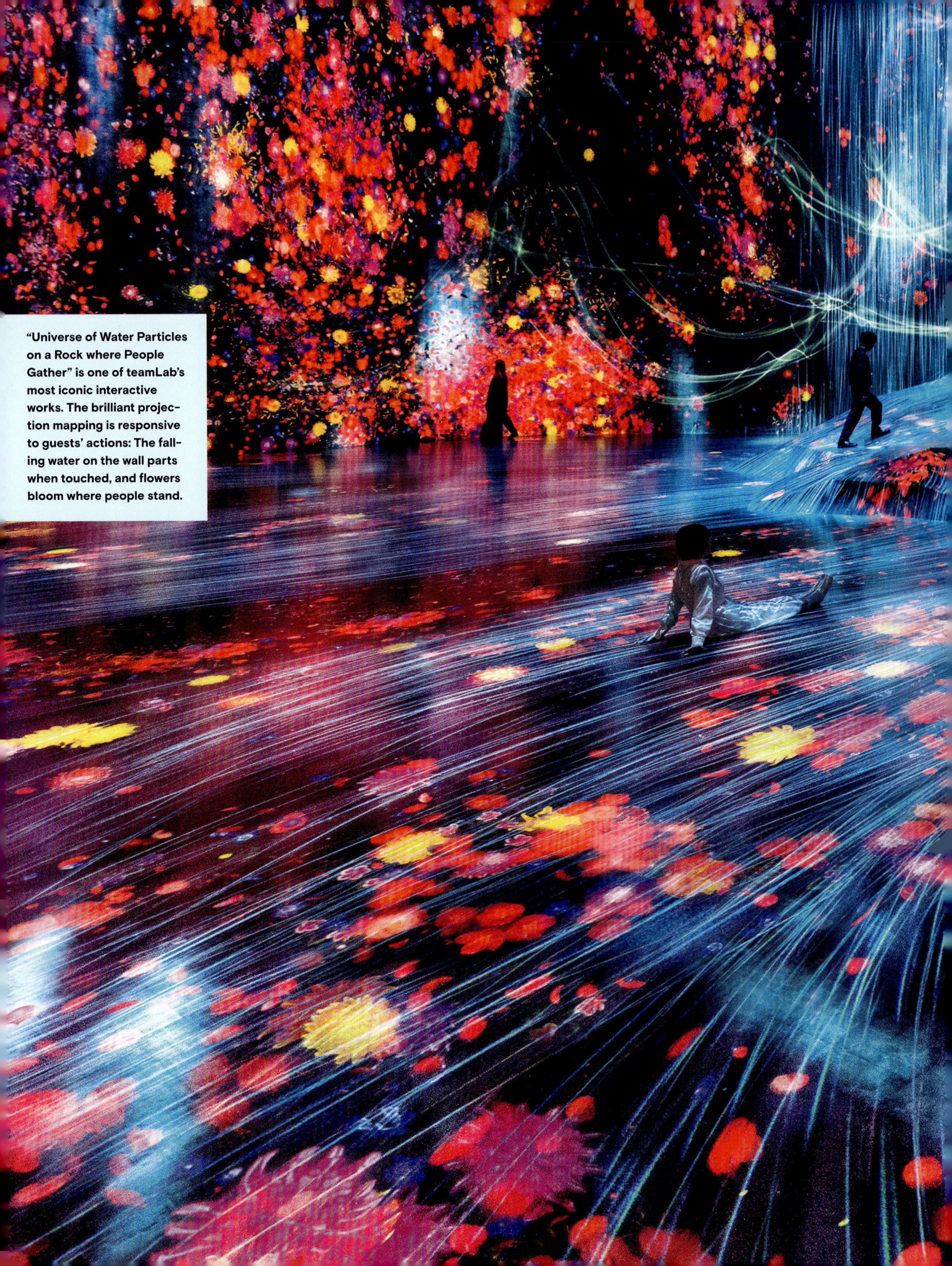

"Universe of Water Particles on a Rock where People Gather" is one of teamLab's most iconic interactive works. The brilliant projection mapping is responsive to guests' actions: The falling water on the wall parts when touched, and flowers bloom where people stand.

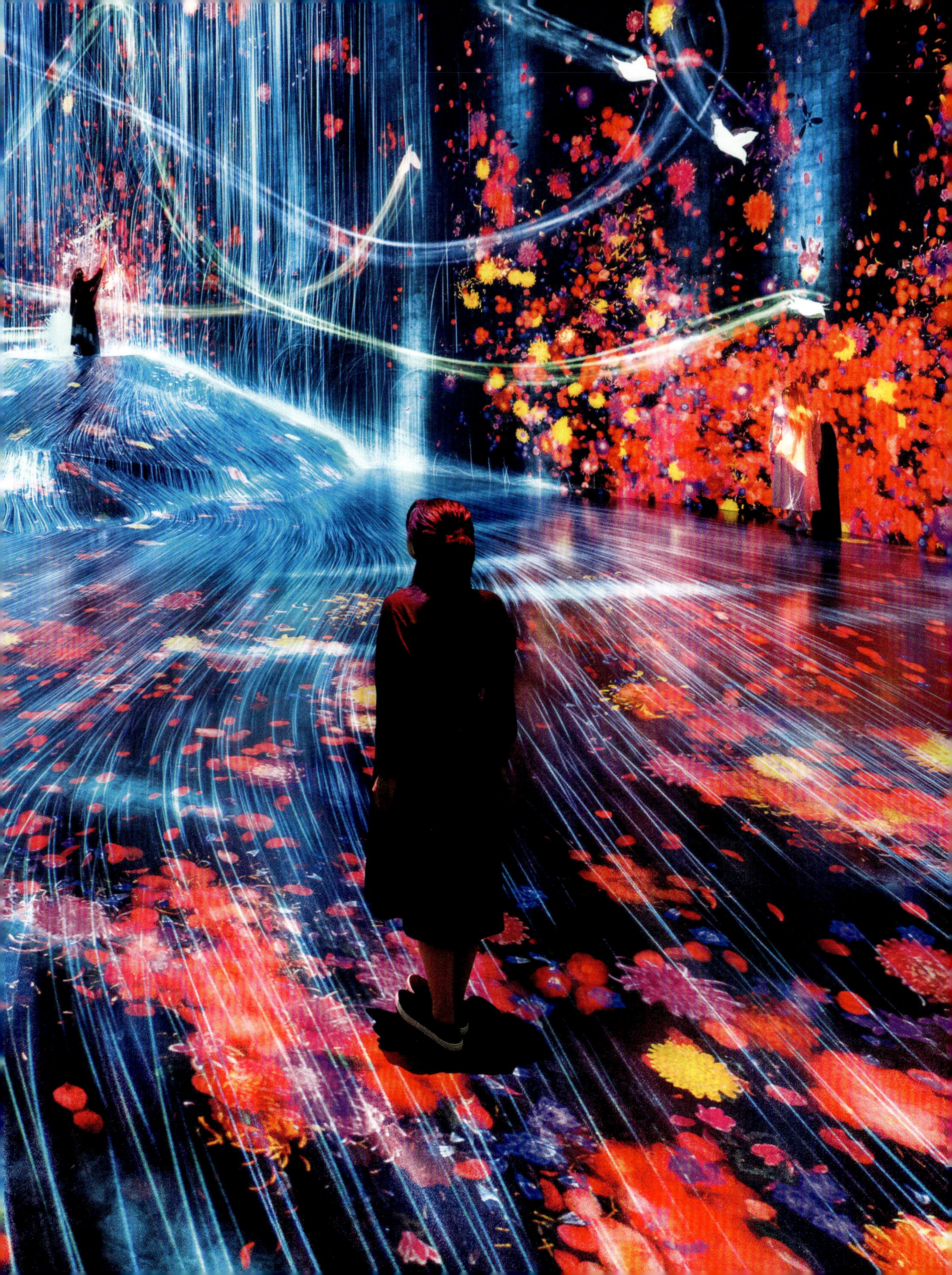

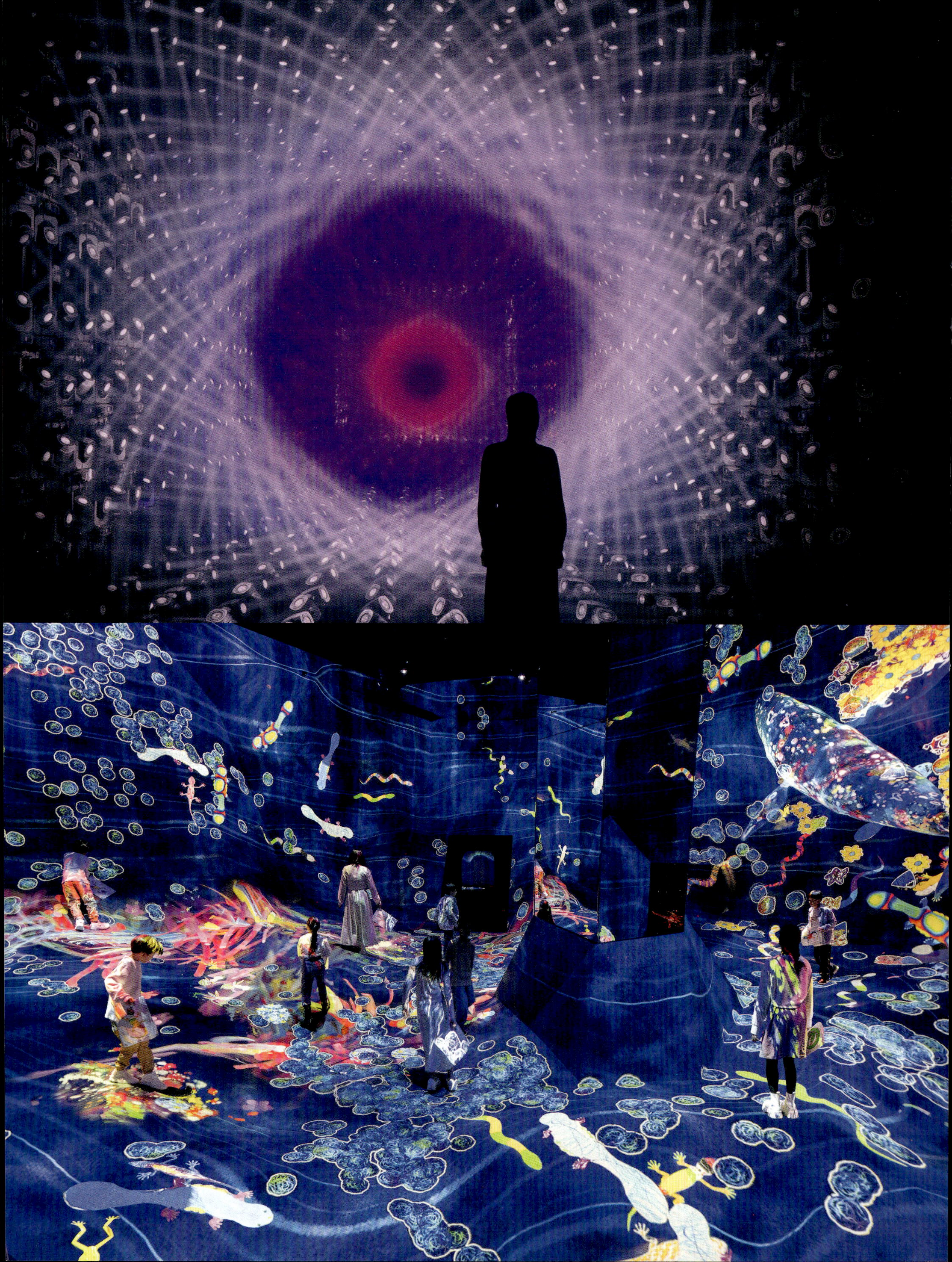

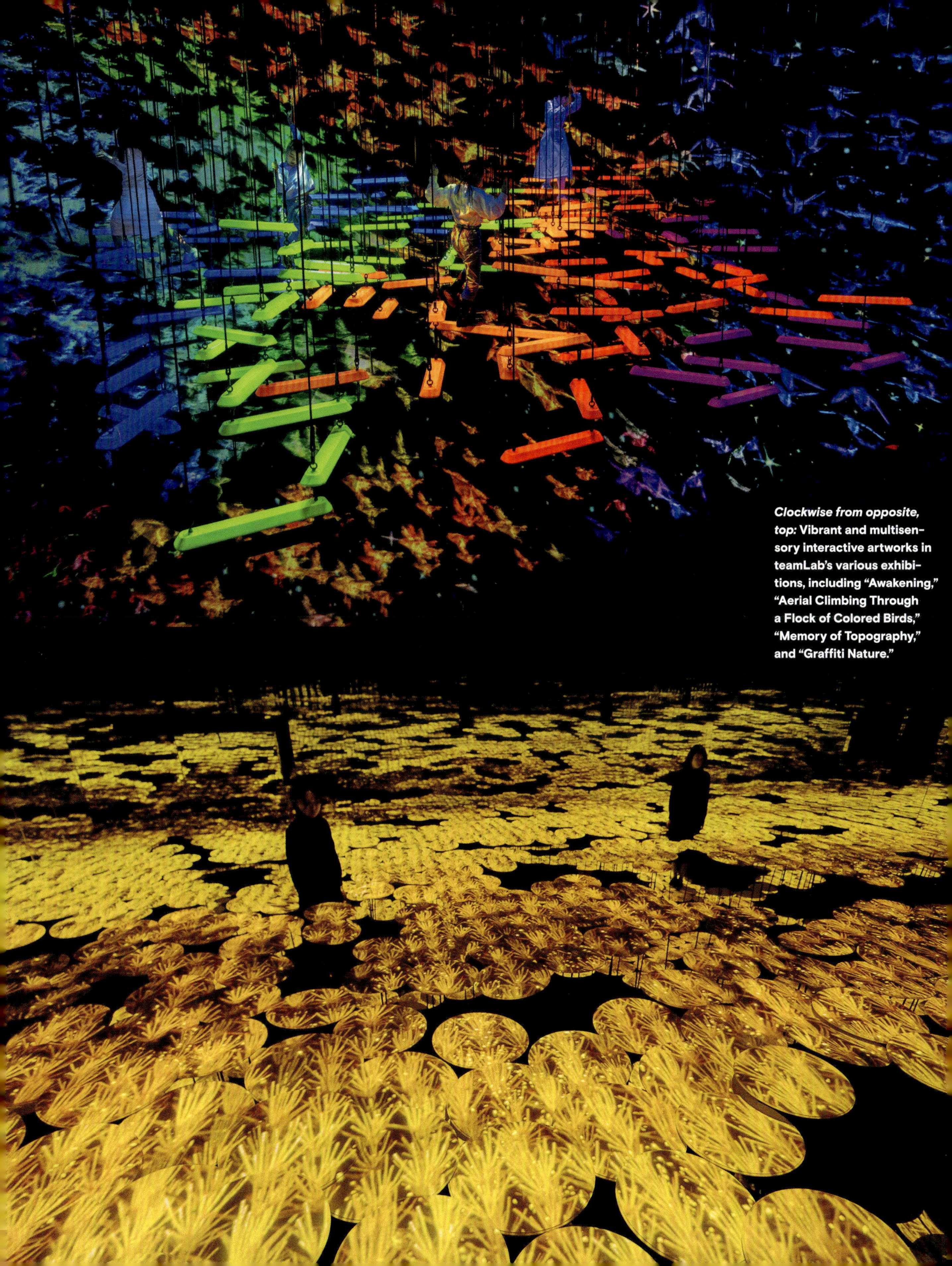

Clockwise from opposite, top: **Vibrant and multisensory interactive artworks in teamLab's various exhibitions, including "Awakening," "Aerial Climbing Through a Flock of Colored Birds," "Memory of Topography," and "Graffiti Nature."**

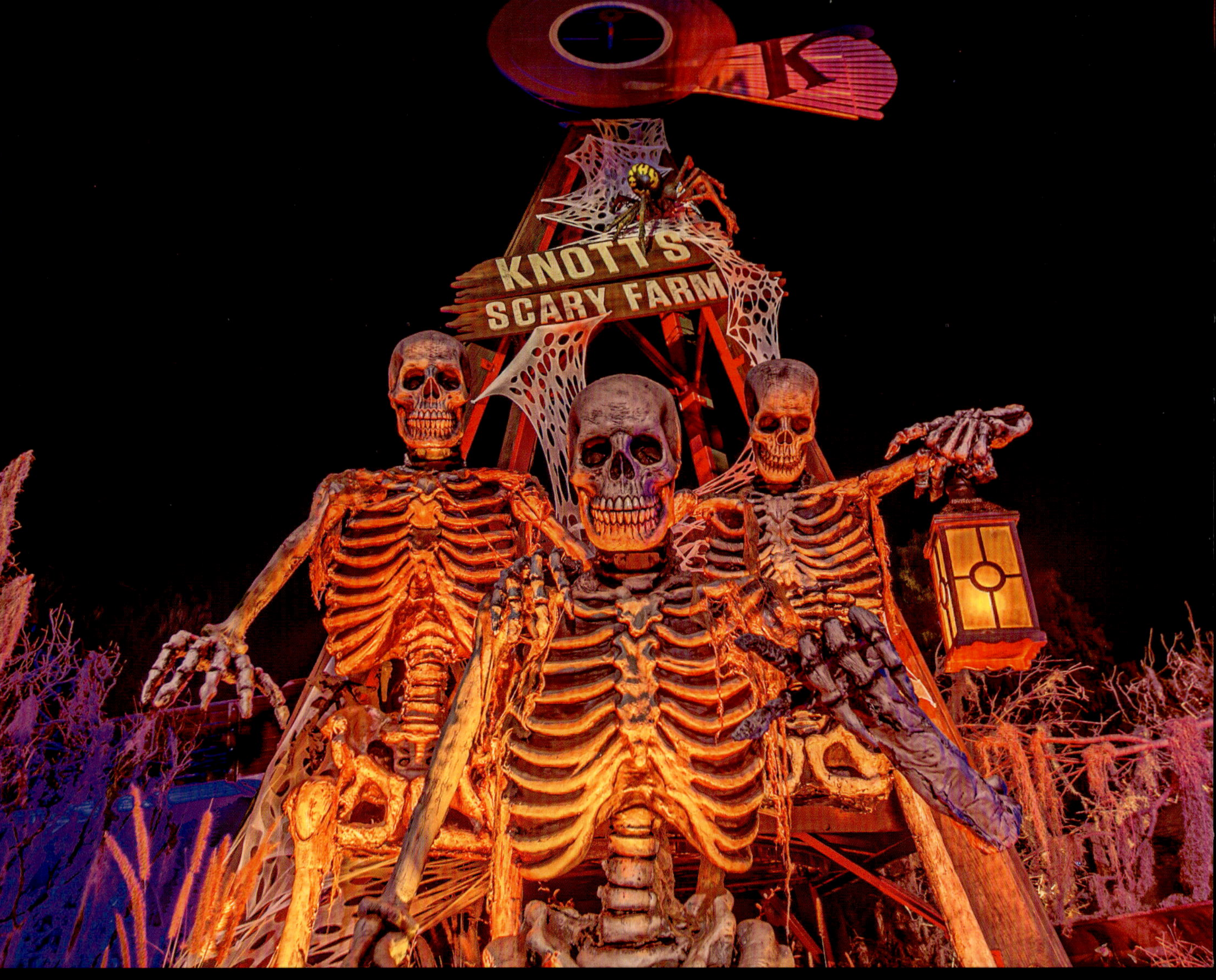

KNOTT'S SCARY FARM

Knott's Scary Farm is a long-standing Halloween tradition that transforms the Knott's Berry Farm theme park into 160 acres of sinister attractions including wandering monsters, haunted houses, and "scare zones."

Since 1973, people have sought bone-chilling experiences at Knott's Scary Farm in Buena Park, California. Each Halloween season, amusement park Knott's Berry Farm transforms its 160 acres into a sprawling realm of never-ending nightmares, featuring more than a thousand actors. As the oldest and longest-running Halloween takeover of a theme park, Knott's Scary Farm has set the standard for elaborate, large-scale haunted attractions.

Knott's Scary Farm was the first theme park to expand the haunted-house concept to an entire haunted park. In addition to the typical rides (revamped to fit the Halloween theme), the seasonal event contains "scare zones," which are described as "vast and encompassing zones that submerge you in a symphony of terror." Here, you can encounter roaming monsters and navigate ominous mazes. From the Ghost Town Streets to the Forsaken Lake, each scare zone is fully developed through elaborate set design and entertainment technology. These areas are further brought to life by surprise interactions with actors who are transformed through movie makeup techniques and elaborate costumes, as well as performances

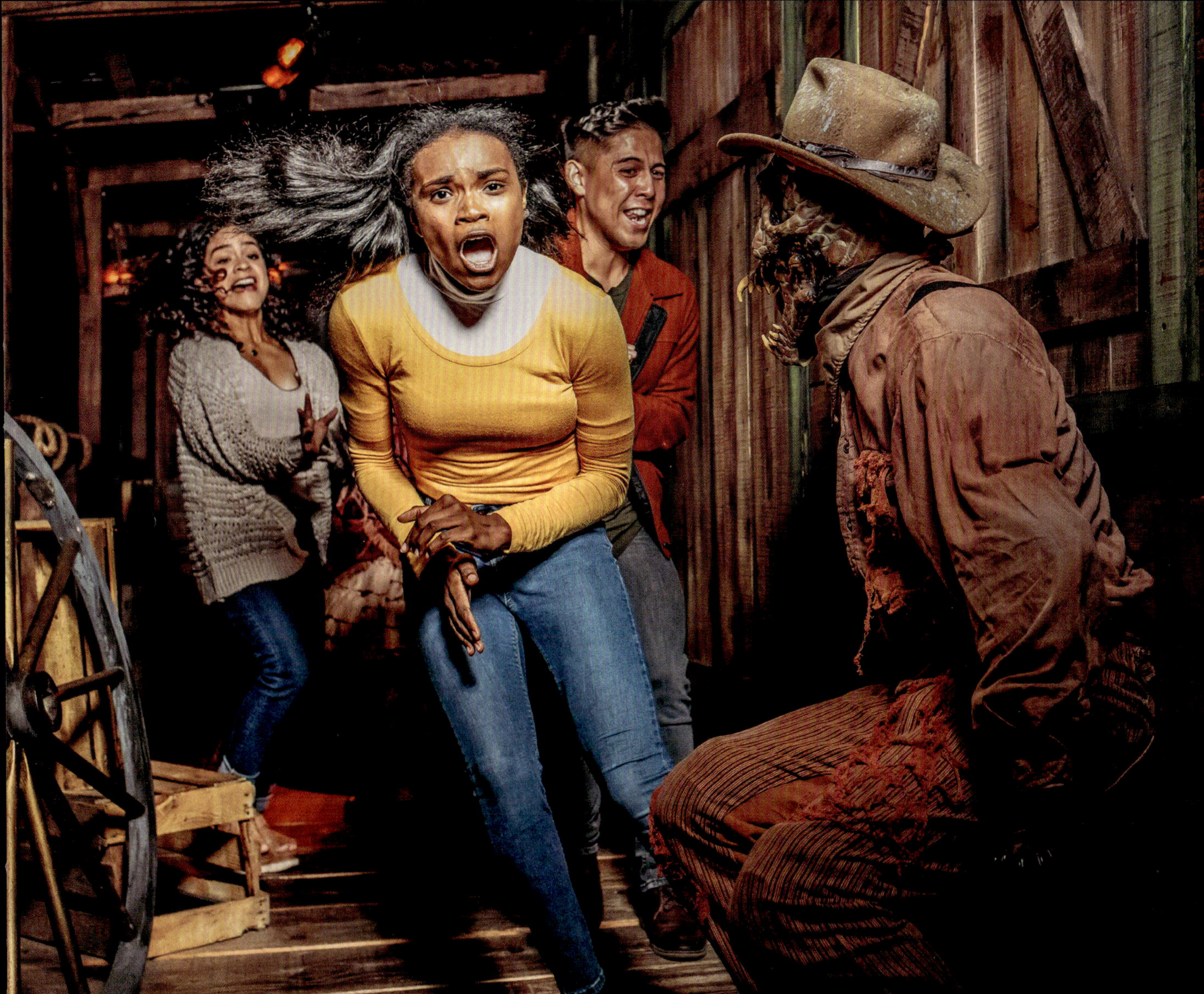

based on carefully crafted storylines and scripts. Visitors can also enjoy various live shows that incorporate song, storytelling, satirical cultural commentary, and more.

Knott's Scary Farm represents a scaled-up evolution of the American haunted-house tradition, elevating what was once a do-it-yourself genre of attraction to new heights. Haunted houses were among the original location-based immersive experiences, first emerging during the Great Depression, when families began creating horror-filled houses to occupy kids and teens on Halloween. In 1969, Disneyland opened its Haunted Mansion, solidifying the place of haunted houses in the American cultural canon. Four years later, Knott's Berry Farm launched its first Halloween theme-park takeover.

Soon similar events, known as "mega haunts," began cropping up across the country at Six Flags, Disneyland, Universal Studios, and more. With larger spaces and higher budgets, these haunts have become far more sophisticated than their predecessors. Every aspect of the experience, from food and beverage to thematic development, is meticulously crafted.

Haunted attractions are a unique case study in immersion because they revolve around fear. Unlike other attractions, they tap into the human fascination with controlled fright, which provides a profound sense of being fully engaged in the moment. Visitors experience heightened physical sensations that can be thrilling and cathartic, as well as strengthen social bonds. Year after year, Knott's Scary Farm demonstrates the timeless appeal of fear-based immersive experiences.

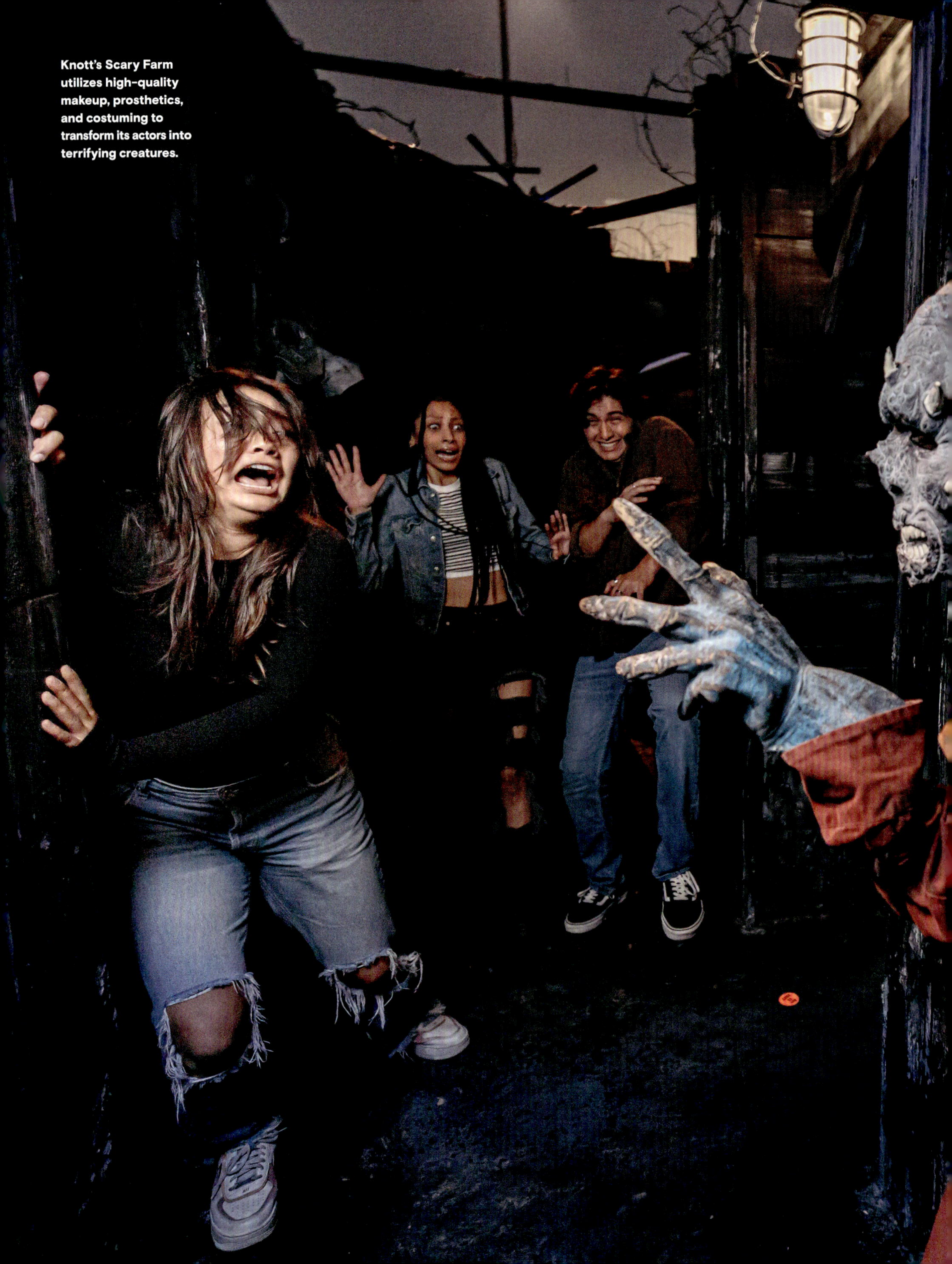

Knott's Scary Farm utilizes high-quality makeup, prosthetics, and costuming to transform its actors into terrifying creatures.

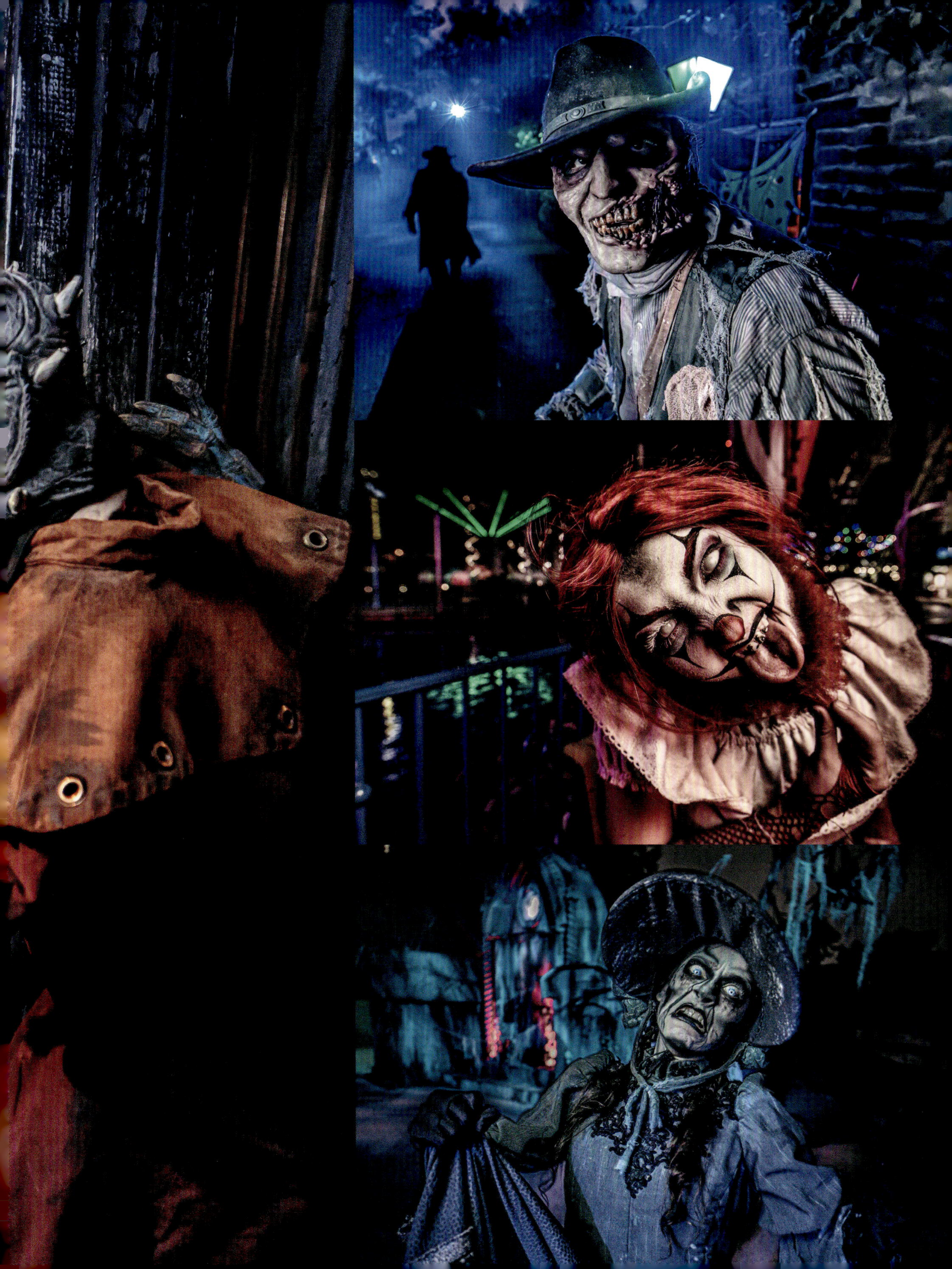

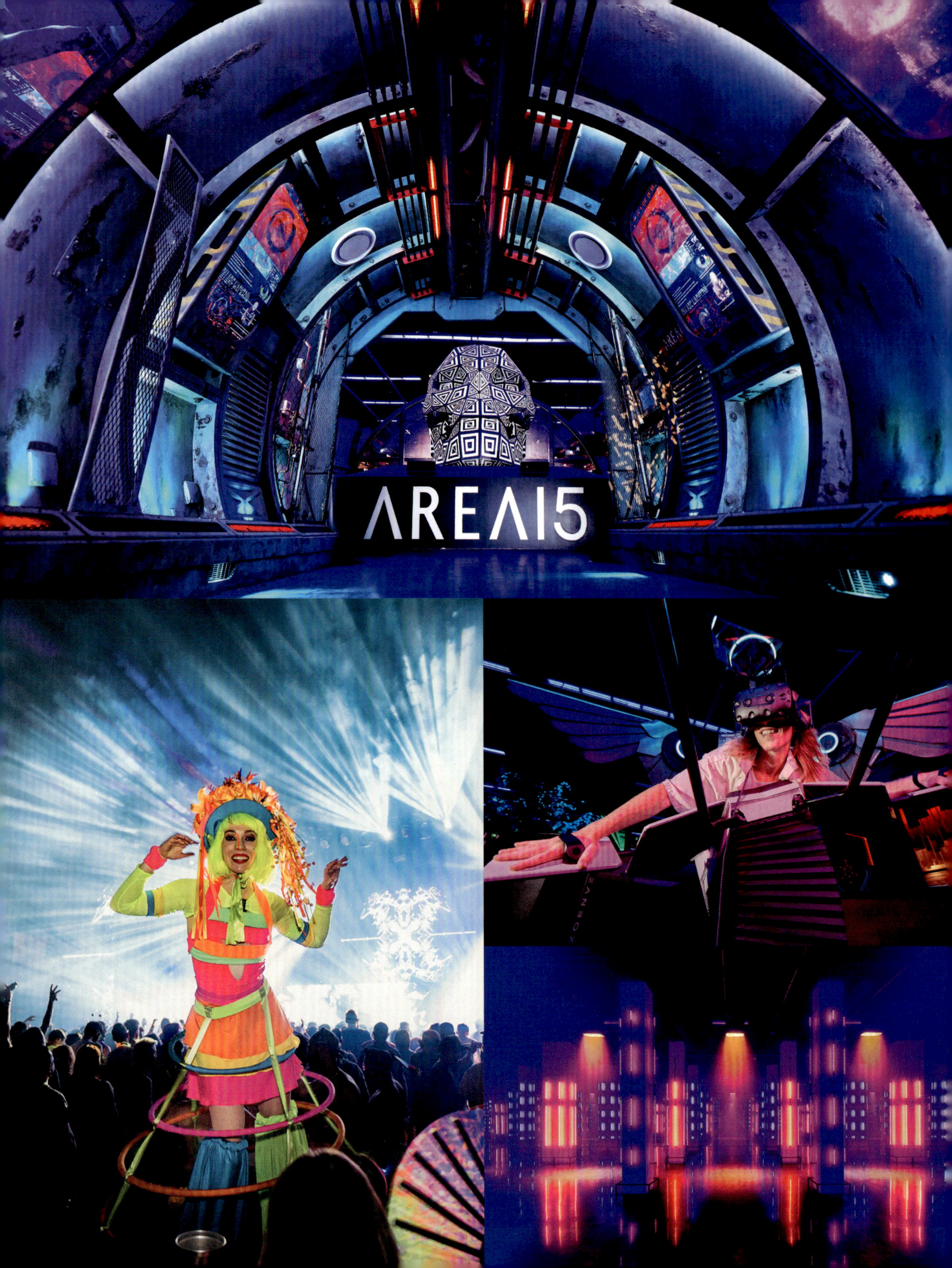
AREA15

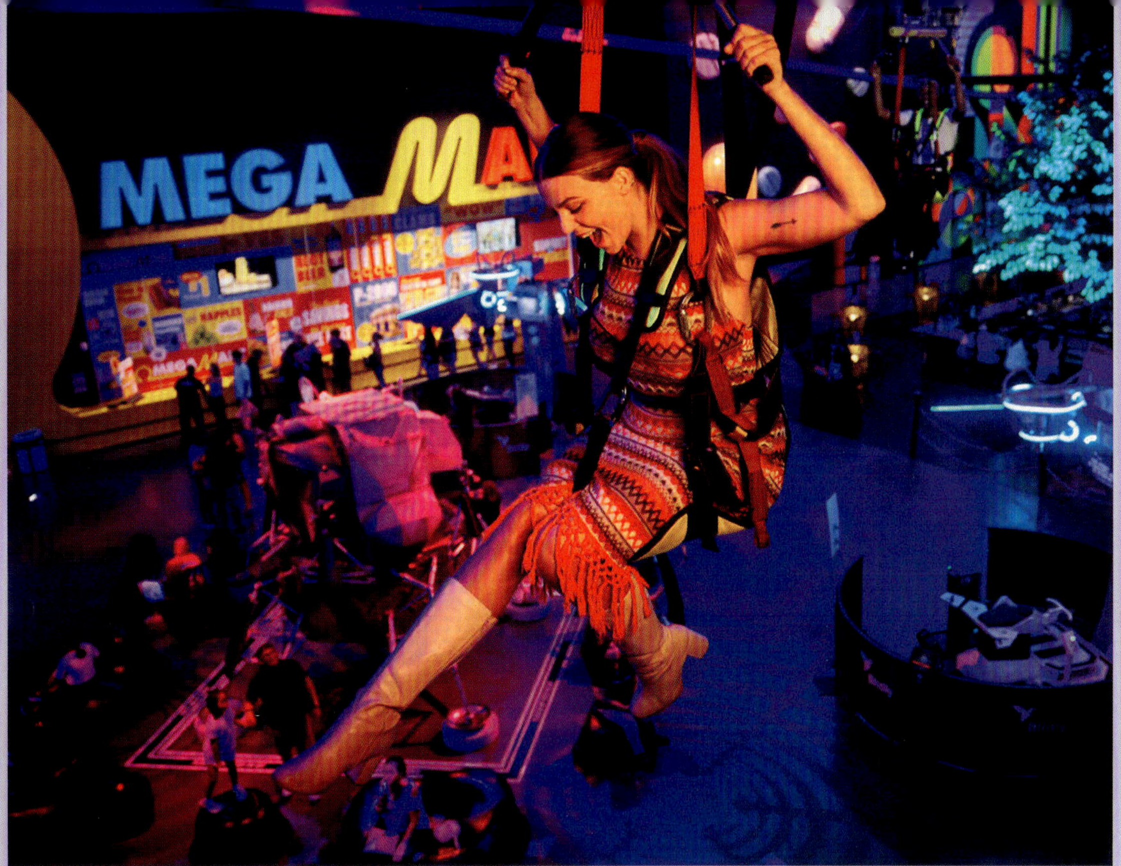

AREA15

AREA15 is a new kind of entertainment venue located just off the Las Vegas Strip. A self-described "immersive entertainment and events district," it revels in being an art-filled "wanderland" of sensory overload that offers a wide variety of experiential entertainment concepts in one place.

Inside, a plethora of experiential offerings await: the elaborate and mind-bending "grocery store" *Omega Mart* from art collective Meow Wolf; the playful and psychedelic *Wink World* from one-time AREA15 "director of content and cool sh*t" and former Blue Man Group member Chris Wink; the *John Wick* experience, full of action-packed missions and cinematic environments; an infinity of intriguing lights and sounds at Museum Fiasco; different competitive-socializing experiences, from axe-throwing to AR-enabled dodgeball to a tech-infused driving range; and numerous retail and dining options. On top of it all, AREA15 features Burning Man-style art installations inside and out and regularly hosts events such as raves and corporate gatherings. Each of the curated components of AREA15 is distinct, yet they all share an ambitious vision and attention to detail, with the goal of collectively transforming the space into a destination.

And a destination it certainly has become: More than thirteen million people have visited AREA15 since it opened, approximately a third of whom are locals to the Las Vegas area. With such success after only four years, AREA15 is adding even more experiential art and entertainment. Their plans include Universal's *Horror Unleashed*, a 100,000-square-foot immersive horror attraction; a flagship location for the colorful and interactive Museum of Ice Cream; and a brand-new space-themed experience from Felix & Paul Studios, *Interstellar Arc*, that welcomes guests into the twenty-sixth century.

AREA15 was created as a home to something that you can't find anywhere else: a "wondrous mash-up" of concepts that invite you in and push the boundaries of what art and entertainment can be. Their success shows that gathering these experiences together in one place can lead to something truly exciting: a multisensory mecca where people come from all over to immerse themselves in the unexpected and escape the ordinary.

Clockwise from opposite, top: **The entrance to AREA15, featuring the psychedelic skull sculpture *Shogyo Mujo* by BARTKRESA studio; a woman soaring over "The Spine," the central hub of AREA15, on roller glider Haley's Comet; a visitor trying out VR flying simulator Birdly; inside of the light and sound experience *Museum Fiasco*; a performer at the Neon Dream party hosted in AREA15's event space.**

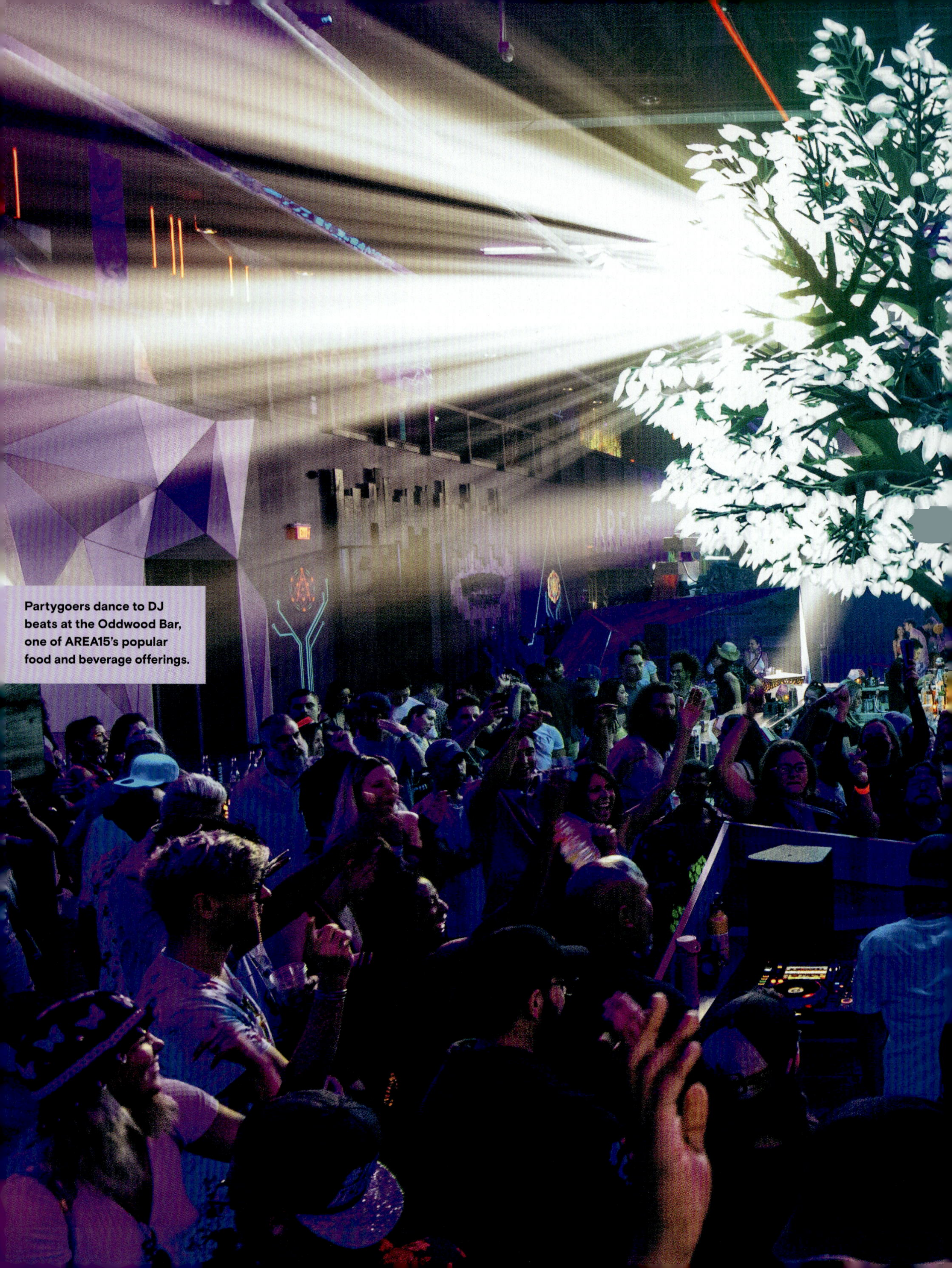

Partygoers dance to DJ beats at the Oddwood Bar, one of AREA15's popular food and beverage offerings.

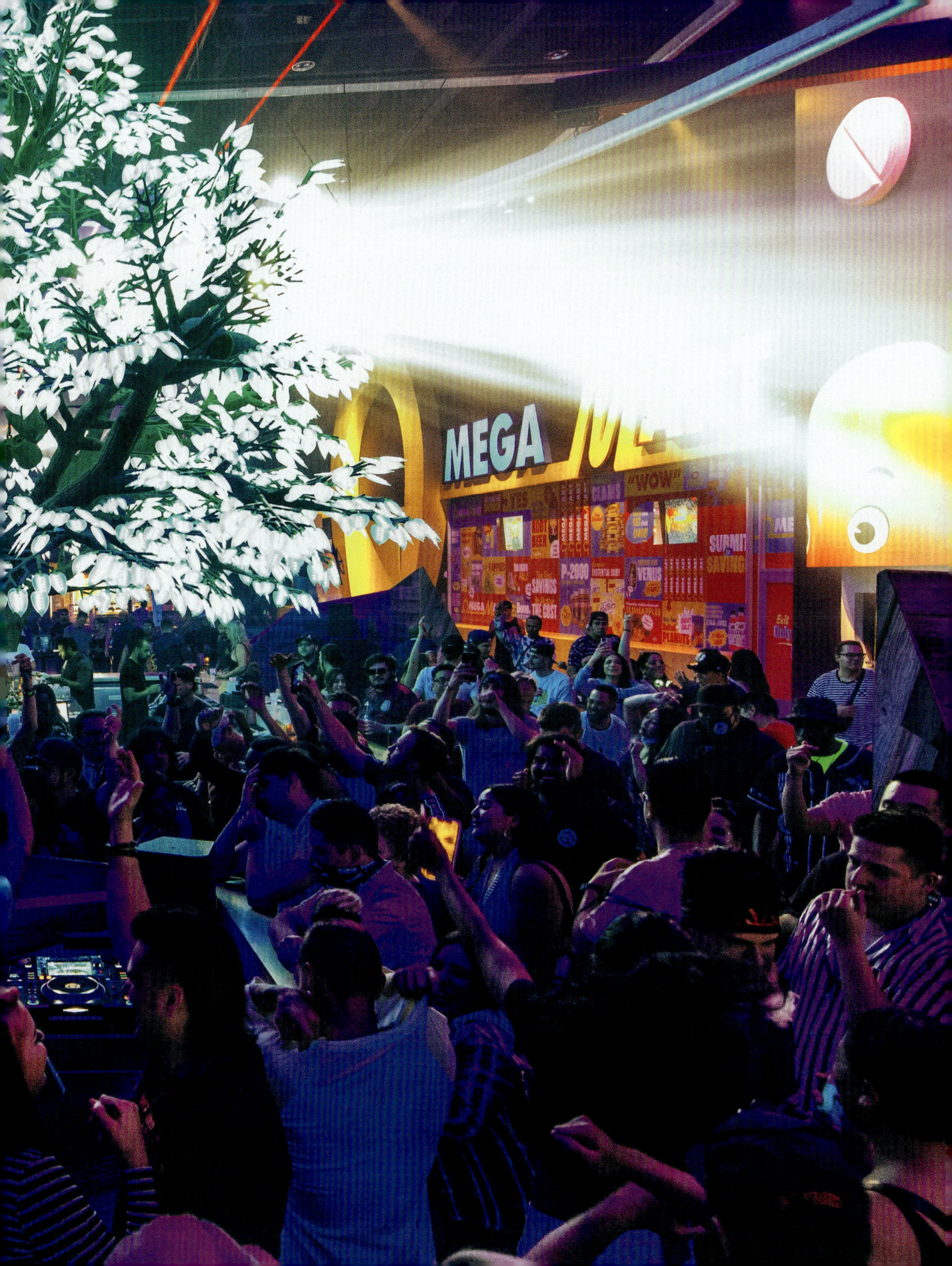
MEGA
"WOW"

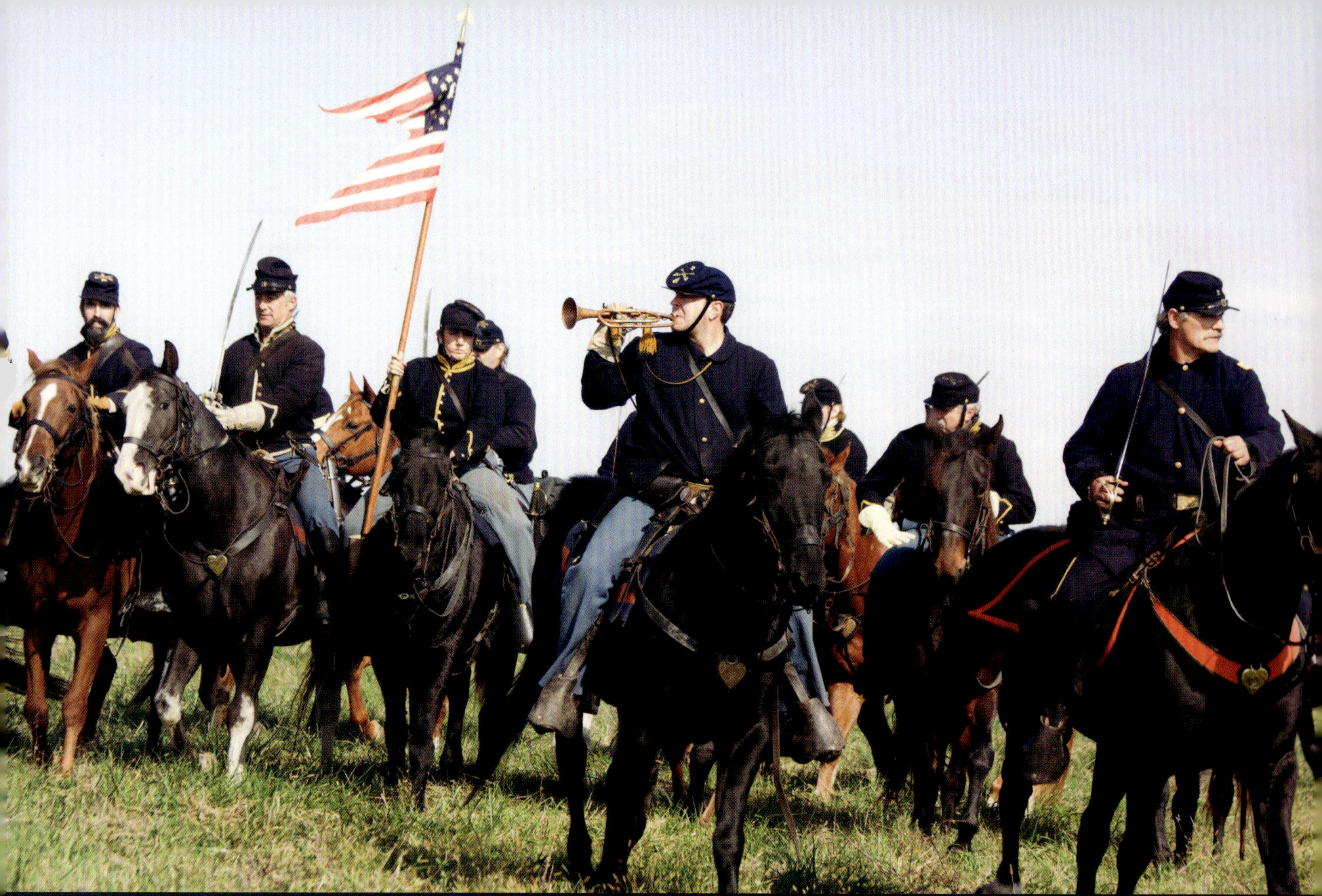

CIVIL WAR REENACTMENTS

Countless "living history" events take place globally each year: fairs, festivals, and gatherings that re-create historical episodes to varying degrees of authenticity, ranging from broad eras (as with Renaissance fairs), to the conditions at certain locations, to specific military engagements. One of the most prevalent forms of living history in the United States is the American Civil War reenactment. Though episodes from the war have been reproduced since the conflict was still ongoing, modern reenactments began in the 1960s and grew in popularity through the '80s. (One notable re-creation of the Battle of Gettysburg in 1998 involved between 15,000 and 30,000 participants and about 50,000 spectators.) Today, more than a hundred Civil War reenactments are staged across the country annually, usually over the course of a weekend.

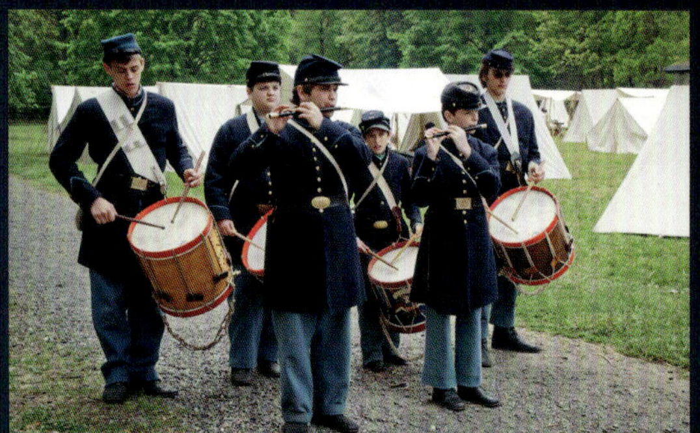

Historical reenactments provide participants and spectators alike with a uniquely embodied educational experience. Some Civil War reenactors take authenticity seriously, committing to sleeping, eating, and speaking as much like their historical counterparts as possible during the events. They might take pains to wear period-accurate clothing and wield genuine weapons to further increase their immersion. Others may be less committed to precision and more to approximating the physical experience of battle—charging, shooting, and even pantomiming death—in order to feel closer to real soldiers who fought and died. Audiences, too, learn from watching reenactments, from military strategy to the minutiae of daily life in a war camp. Data and stories, indicating numbers of casualties or battle conditions, become easier to comprehend in this form, even when scaled back for practicality.

Civil War reenactments are also highly collaborative social events; participants work together and with audiences to reconstitute history in a way that enhances everyone's understanding of it, even as the events themselves get further away in time. Reenactors are often professional or amateur historians who make themselves available to spectators to give context and answer questions about what they've seen play out. Repeat attendees get to know one another and bond over a shared love of history, creating a community with a common purpose.

The future of Civil War reenactments is currently in question. Detractors have various criticisms: Some find that they glorify violence; others argue that they whitewash elements of America's past, particularly slavery, thus perpetuating harmful myths about the war; still others point to the lack of diversity among reenactors, leading to historical inaccuracies. To proponents, however, these physical retellings are important to the conservation of memory, and never more so than in the midst of heated debate over whose memories deserve to be preserved. (For example, Black reenactors have endeavored to represent perspectives that have been widely neglected.) While the general popularity of reenactments has waned in the past few decades due to shifting political perceptions and rising costs, there remains a committed contingent that continues to gather, muskets and bayonets in hand, to make history live again.

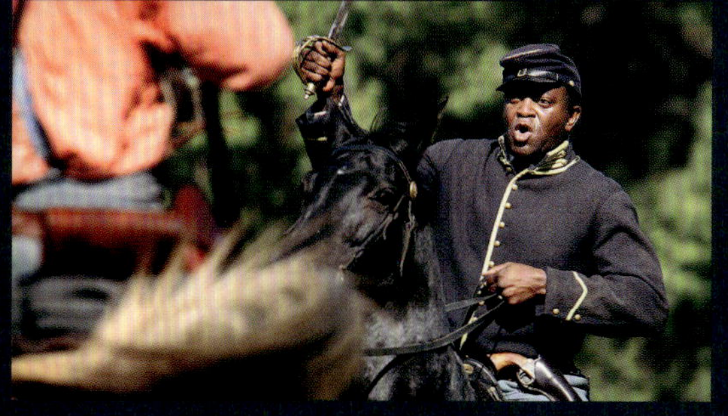

Every year, tens of thousands of Civil War reenactors gather to re-create episodes from the historical conflict, from military bands to cavalry charges.

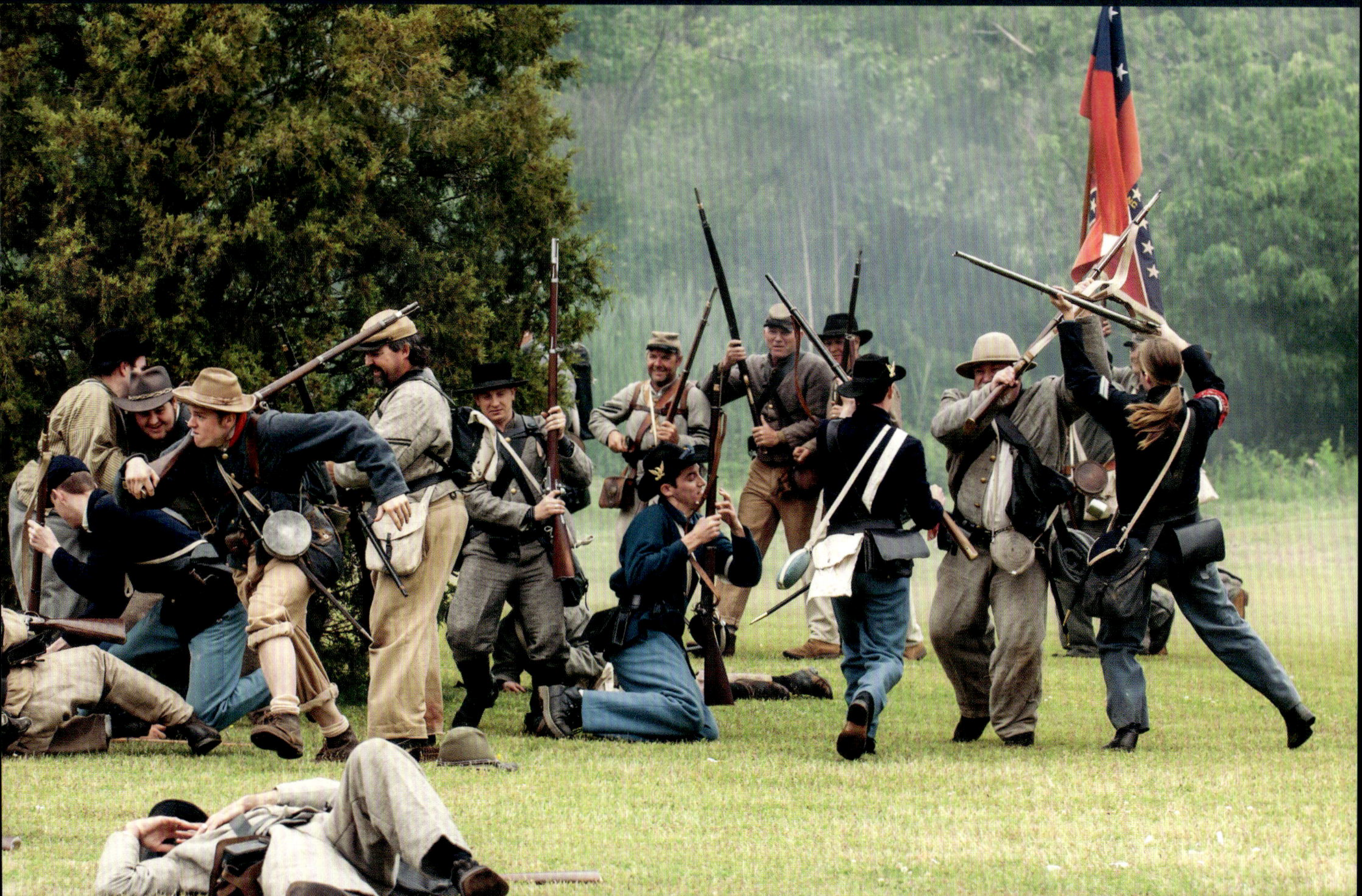

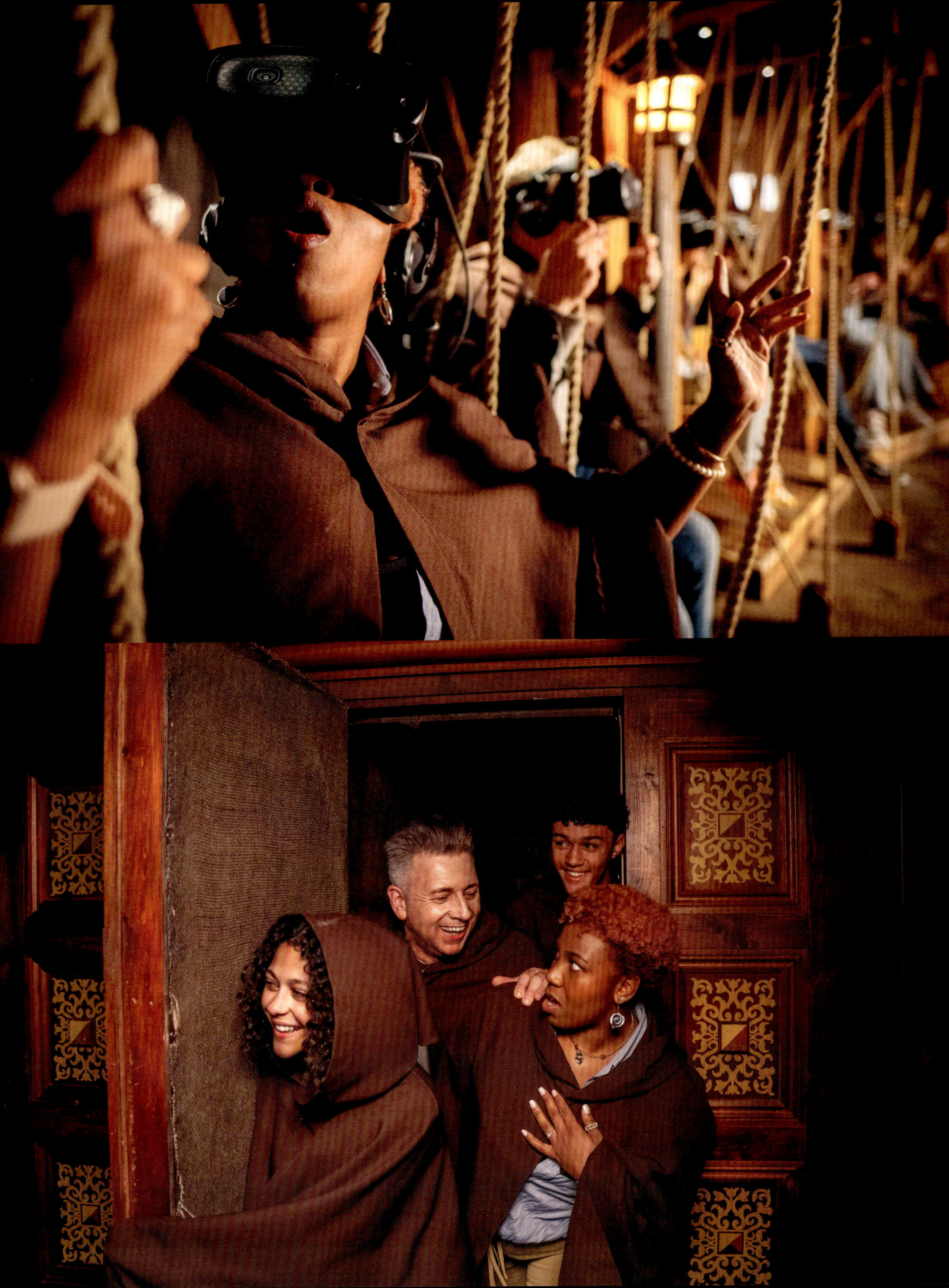

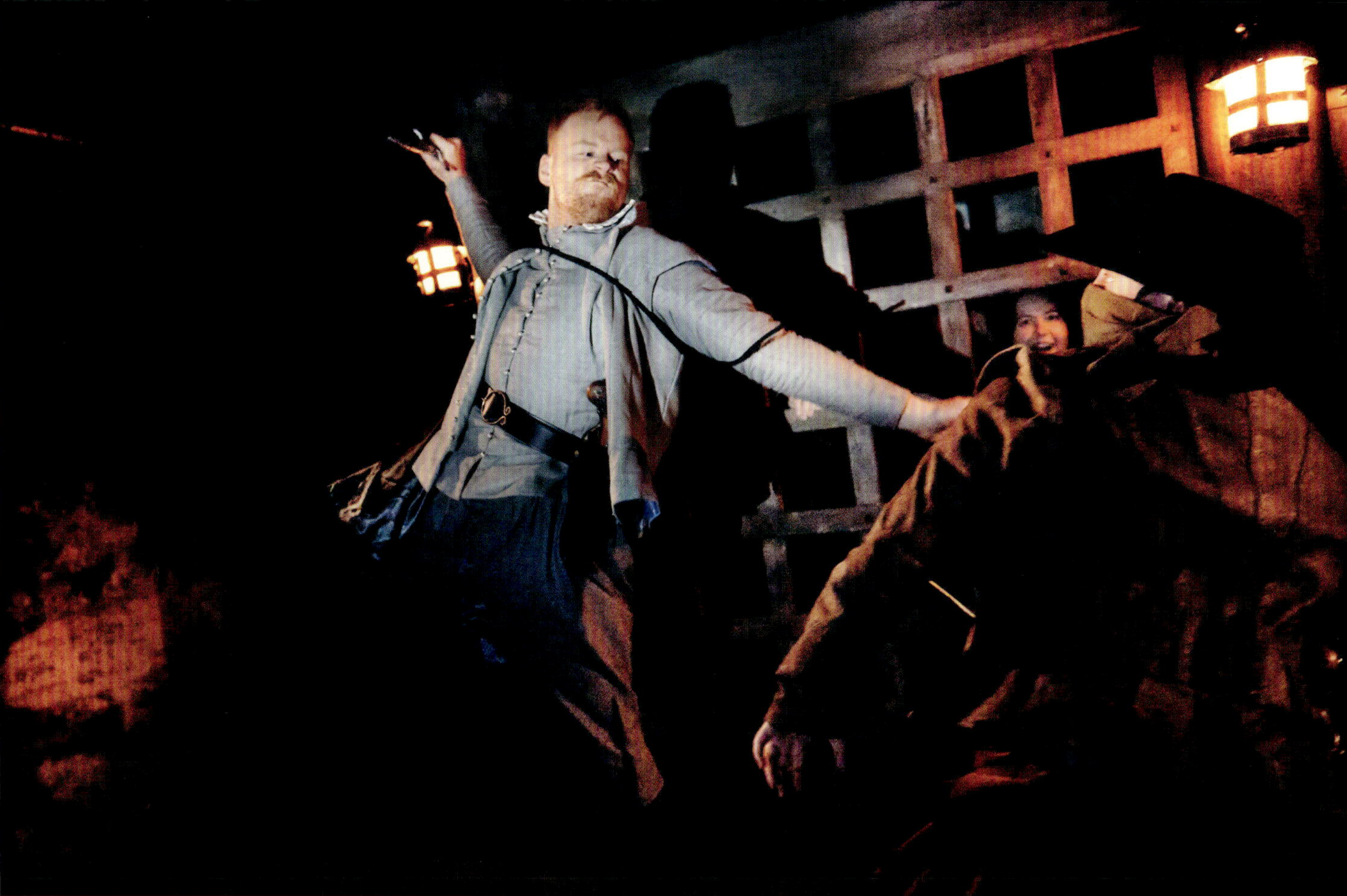

LAYERED REALITY

Founded in 2017 by Andrew McGuinness, Layered Reality is an immersive entertainment company that fuses physical, theatrical, and digital techniques to create social, fun, and memorable experiences. Their 2018 proof of concept, *SOMNAI*, transported participants into the world of dreams through a combination of live theater and virtual reality. That prototype led to the development of *Jeff Wayne's The War of the Worlds: The Immersive Experience*, an experiential adaptation of the 1987 album musical (itself adapted from H.G. Wells's seminal novel) that would go on to receive a Thea Award for Outstanding Achievement and become London's longest-running immersive show. From 2022 to 2025, Layered Reality collaborated with Historic Royal Palaces to stage *Gunpowder Plot*, an immersive production in the Tower of London's Tower Vaults that took audiences back in time to 1605 to infiltrate the infamous conspiracy. Their latest creation, *Elvis Evolution*, set to open in 2025, will take visitors on a journey through Elvis Presley's life and legacy using cutting-edge technology like augmented reality and generative AI.

The approach that Layered Reality takes to immersive entertainment is, as the name suggests, layered. On the first layer, their productions make use of physical sensations—everything from smell to temperature to movement—to create an embodied experience of the story. *Jeff Wayne's The War of the Worlds* has participants clambering through obstacles, sliding down slides, even feeling the "pinch" of a Martian machine; in *Gunpowder Plot*, audiences sat on swings to simulate rappelling from the Tower of London and climbed into a rocking boat that gave the sensation of sailing down the Thames. According to McGuinness, these moments of embodiment are subtle but essential: "The multisensory

Clockwise from opposite, top: **Participants in *Gunpowder Plot* sat on swings with VR headsets on, simulating a rappelling experience; a fight scene unfolding in front of the crowd; audience members, dressed in capes, interacted and conspired with cast members, who improvised accordingly.**

nature definitely adds to the memory making....With our experiences, people won't be consciously aware of the sensory elements that help to place them in the world, making them feel like they're actually a participant and gone to a different place. Elements like temperature or aroma—those sorts of elements are really important because they make you believe you are living in the story."

Images from *Jeff Wayne's The War of the Worlds*, clockwise from opposite, top: A performer instructing a participant to look through an old-fashioned camera; a scene from inside the VR portion of the experience; audience members marvel at the sights available to them through VR; a cast member and participants in discussion about their next move.

The next layer involves elements of theater: costumed actors, immersive sets, props, and special effects that give weight to the feeling of truly stepping into another world. The performers are an integral part, leading small groups of guests through the experience and reinforcing the sense of aliveness as they interact and improvise with the audience. Film-quality sets lend each production an impressive and authentic look and feel, and sophisticated sound and lighting systems allow for powerful immersion as well.

Finally, Layered Reality incorporates digital technologies in order to make their productions feel awe-inspiring. Virtual-reality headsets are used so audiences can witness things that would otherwise be impossible, such as Martian fighting machines from the vantage point of a hot-air balloon in *Jeff Wayne's The War of the Worlds*, or zip-lining over London in 1605. Augmented reality, projection mapping, and volumetric holograms are also used to enhance the productions—while remaining integrated as seamlessly into the physical experience as possible. In keeping with Layered Reality's dedication to staying on the cutting edge, *Elvis Evolution* will use artificial intelligence to reconstruct key moments from the King's life based on thousands of personal photos and home videos from his estate.

With these three layers working in concert, Layered Reality is able to create living stories that are truly unique, powerful, and unforgettable. "Ultimately, we're in the memory business," explains McGuinness. "At the end of the year, we want to be on the list of our visitors' most memorable experiences."

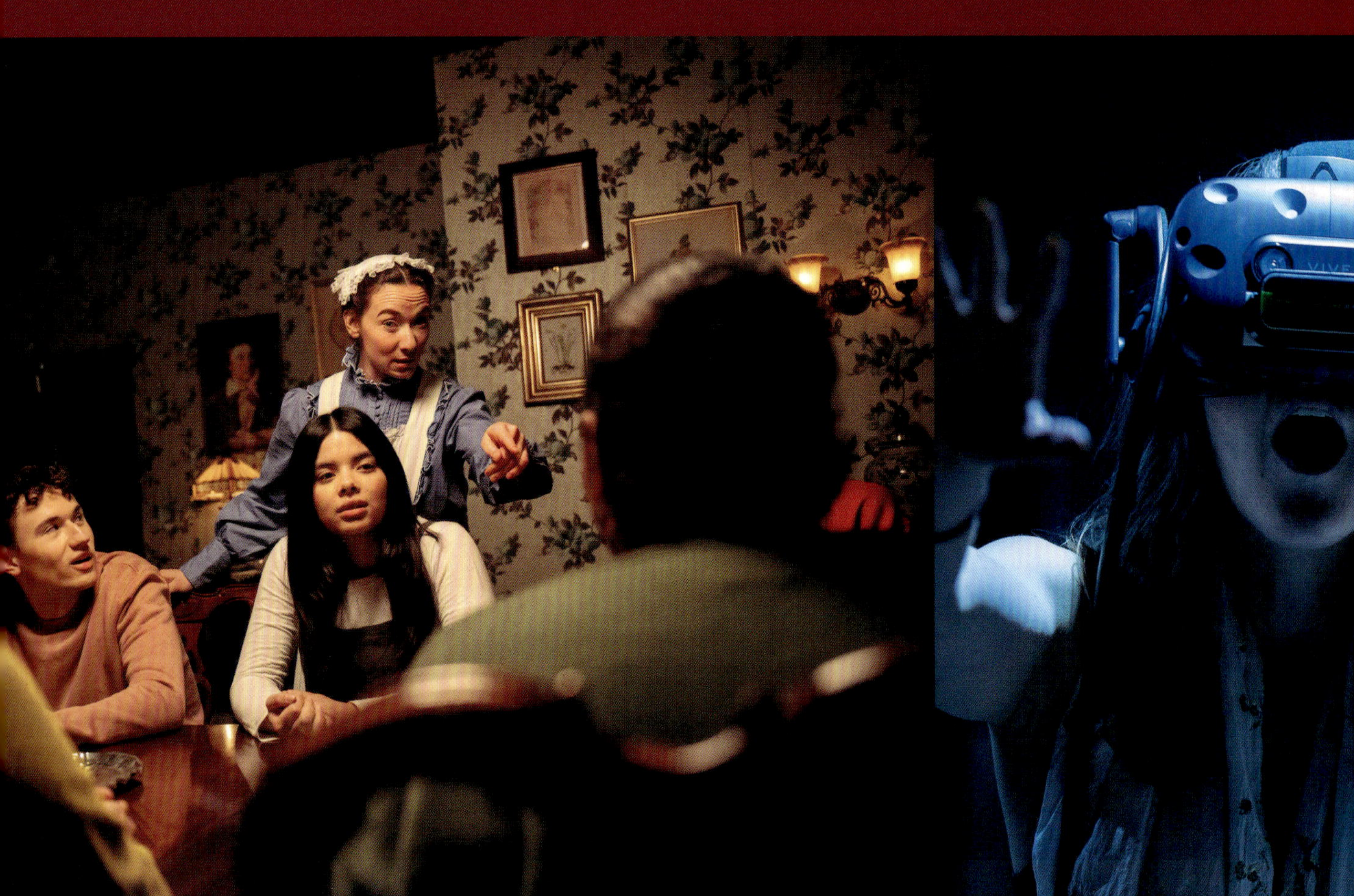

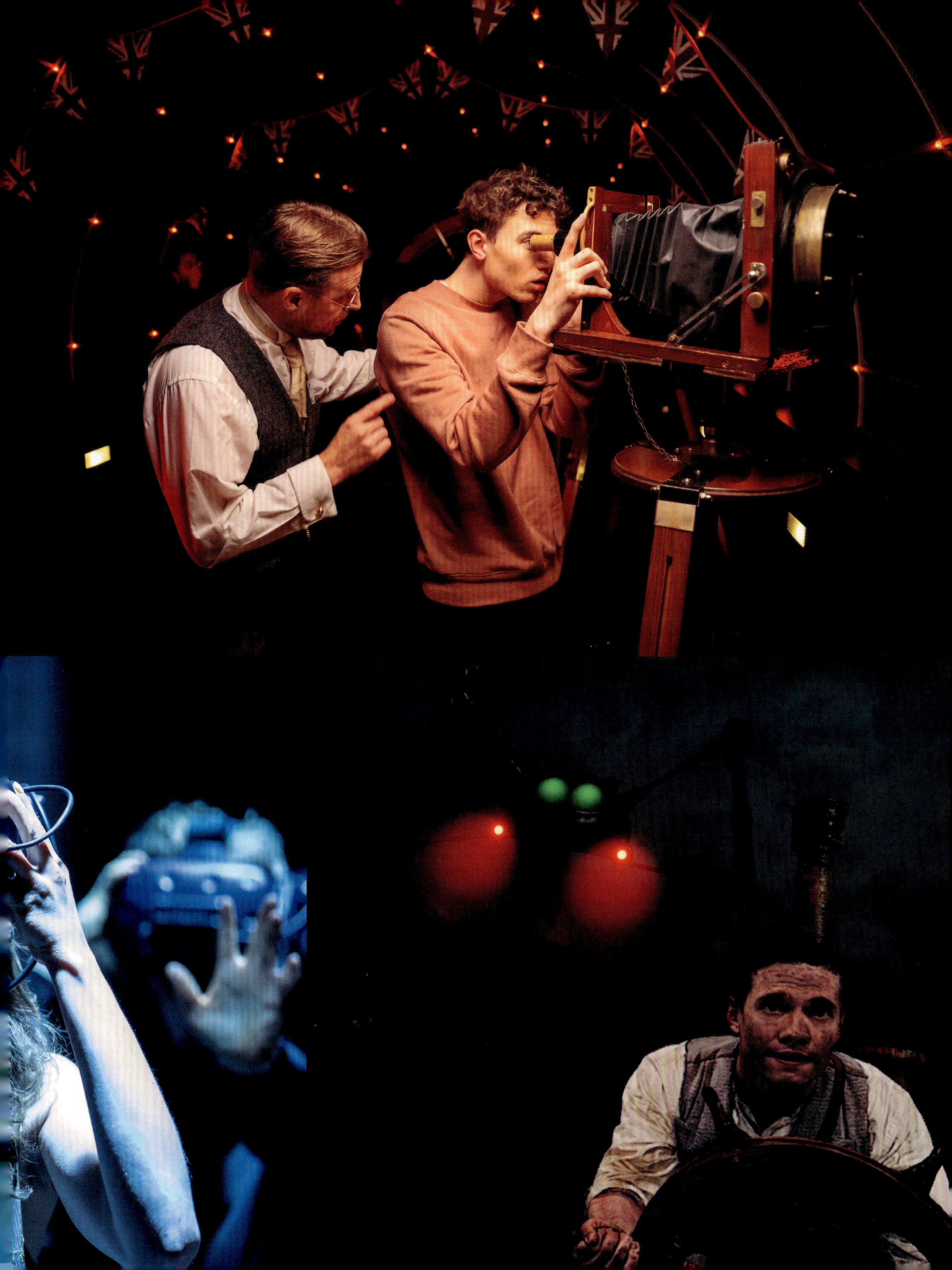

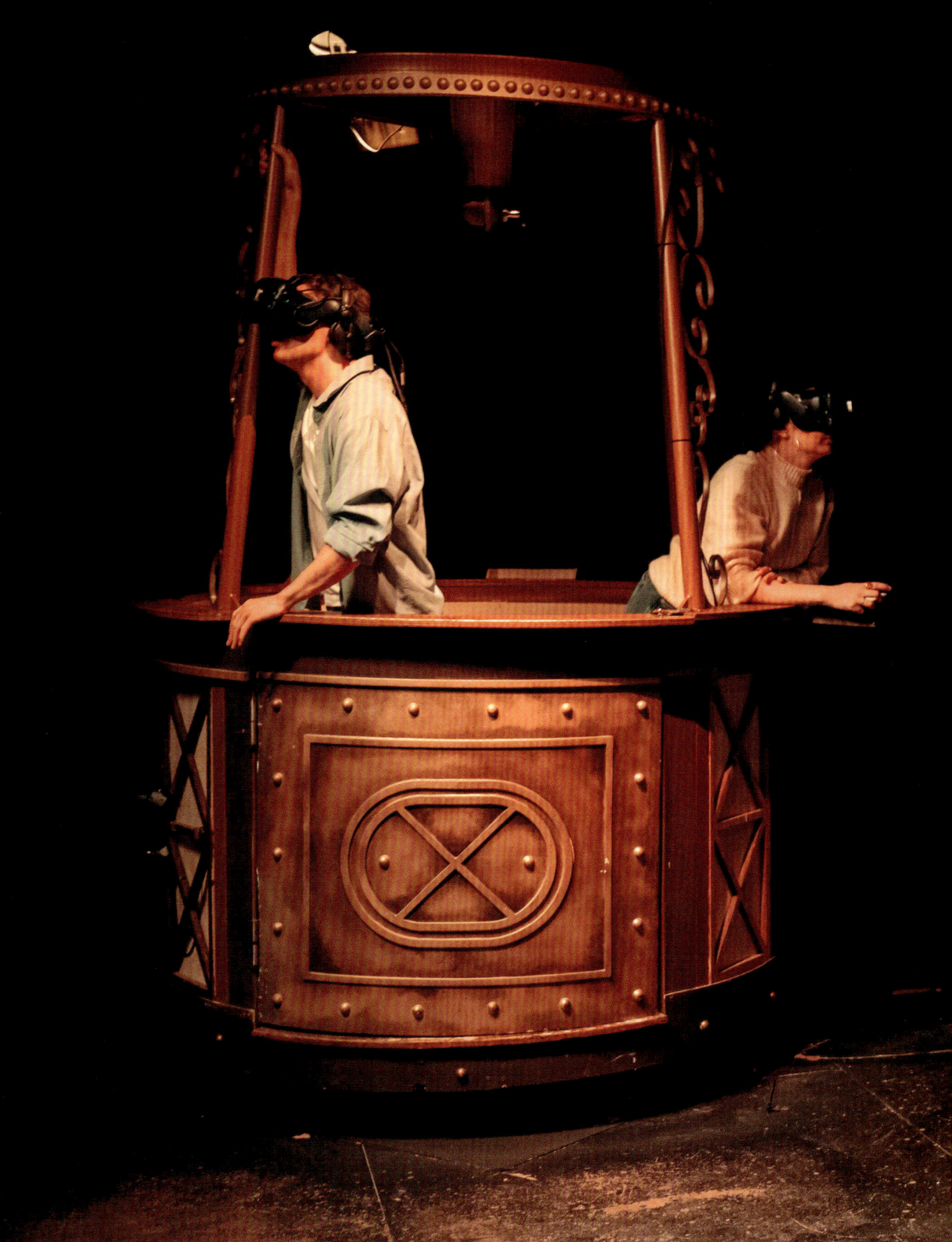

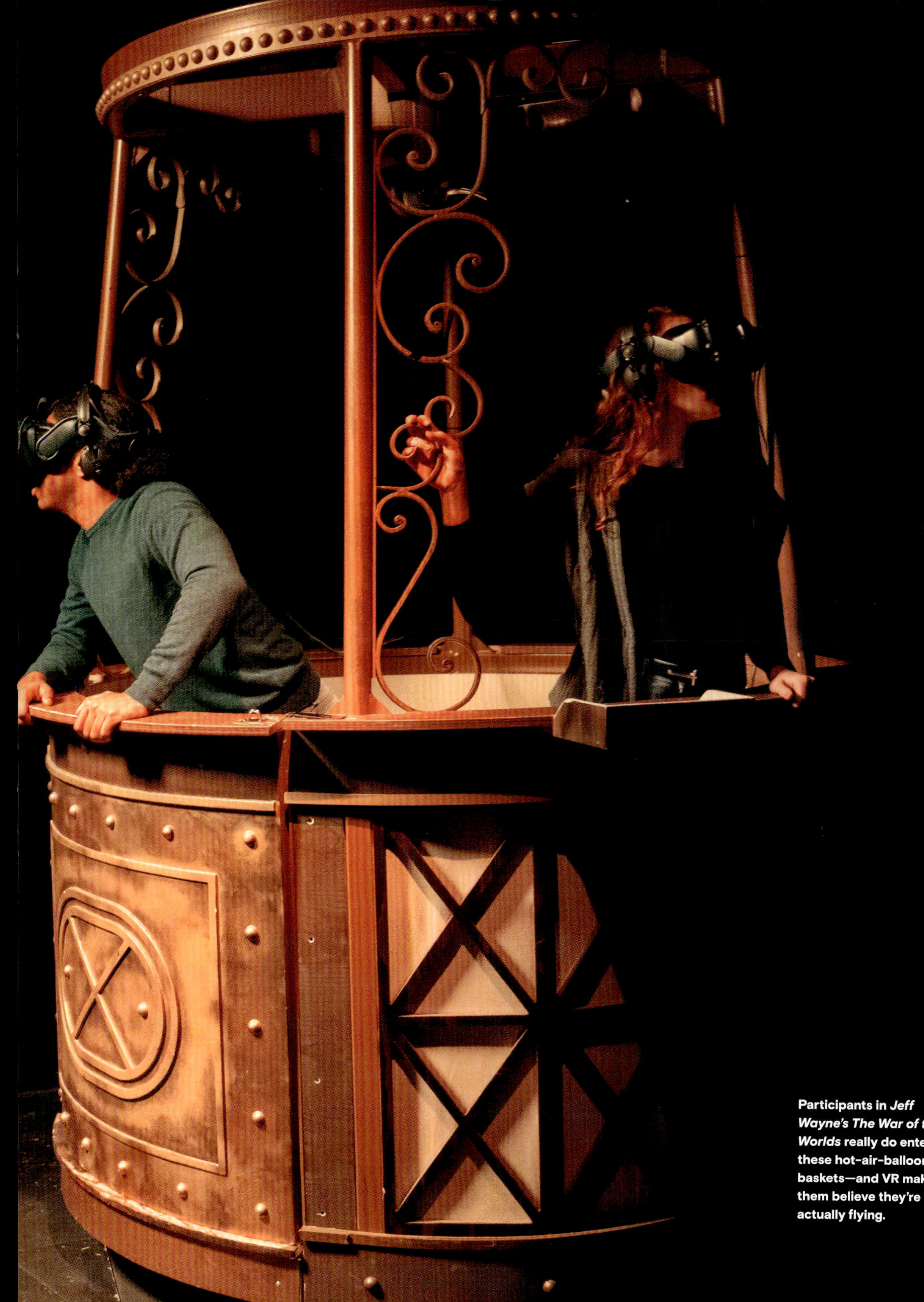

Participants in *Jeff Wayne's The War of the Worlds* really do enter these hot-air-balloon baskets—and VR makes them believe they're actually flying.

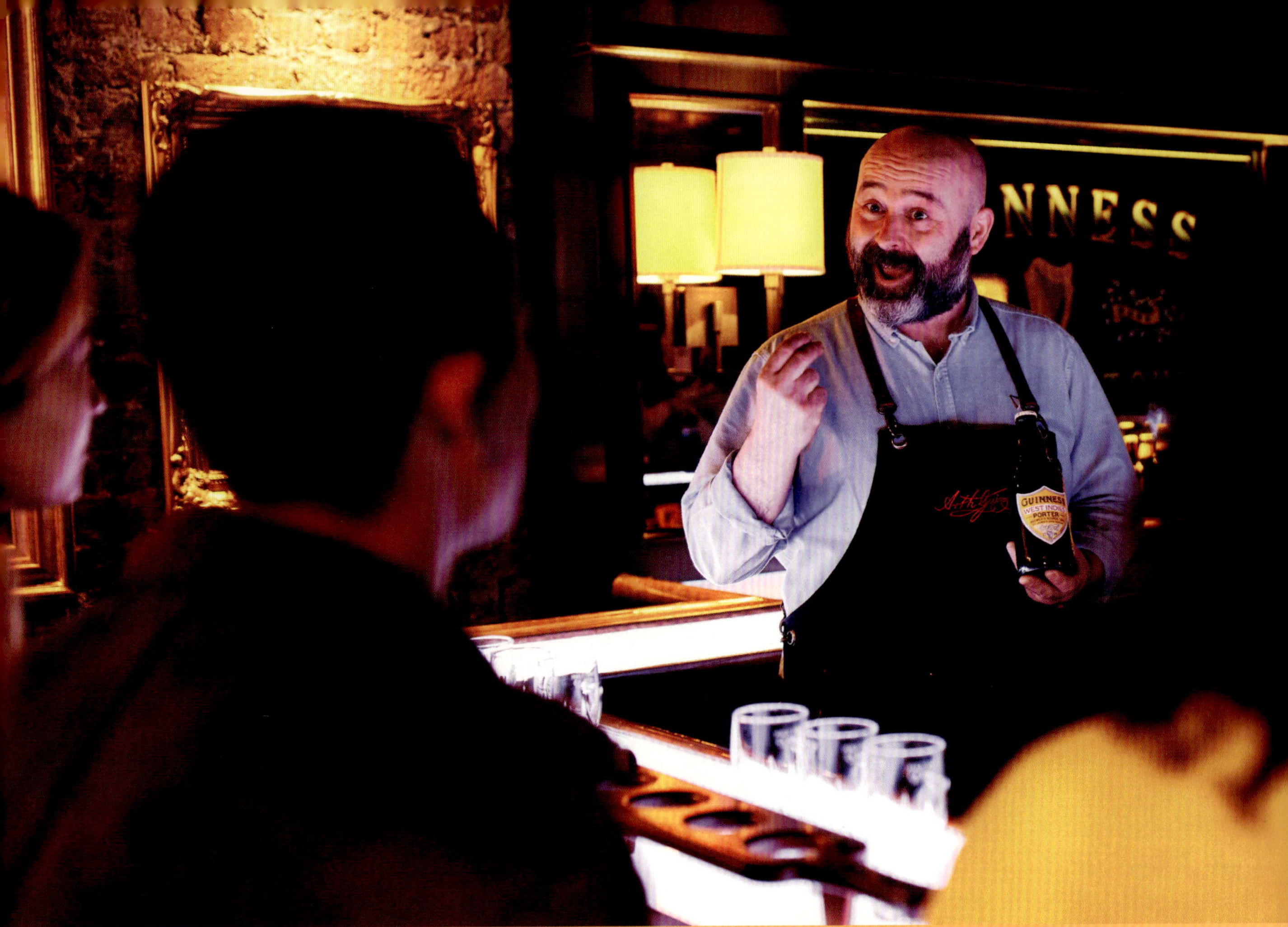

CORPORATE EXPERIENTIAL

For years, brands have sought to create experiences that turn customers into fans. Some consumer-facing companies conduct factory tours, for example, with the idea that a peek behind the curtain at how your favorite products are made will give you a new appreciation for them. Others curate history museums dedicated to their brand, aiming to educate and cultivate a bond with visitors around their origin stories. However, today's consumers expect more from their go-to companies: They're looking for ways to engage authentically and form connections with the products and services they use; they're looking for methods of expressing themselves and having more personalized experiences; and they're looking for communities of like-minded people. More than just a mere transaction, they want to build genuine, meaningful relationships with their favorite brands.

Above: **A guide at Guinness Storehouse shows visitors how to pour the perfect pint.** ***Right:*** **The "Stoutie" is Guinness's name for a customized pint with your selfie printed in the foam.**

The companies that understand this desire are creating location-based experiences that go way beyond traditional retail. These permanent locations introduce guests to the brand's world, offering tastings, interactive exhibits, educational classes, and other activities that immerse visitors in the company's story through a variety of senses. Take Starbucks's Roasteries, for example: upscale locations not only to enjoy premium coffee and baked goods but to witness the roasting process firsthand, to learn about high-end coffee-making techniques, to refine your palate through tastings, and to have a

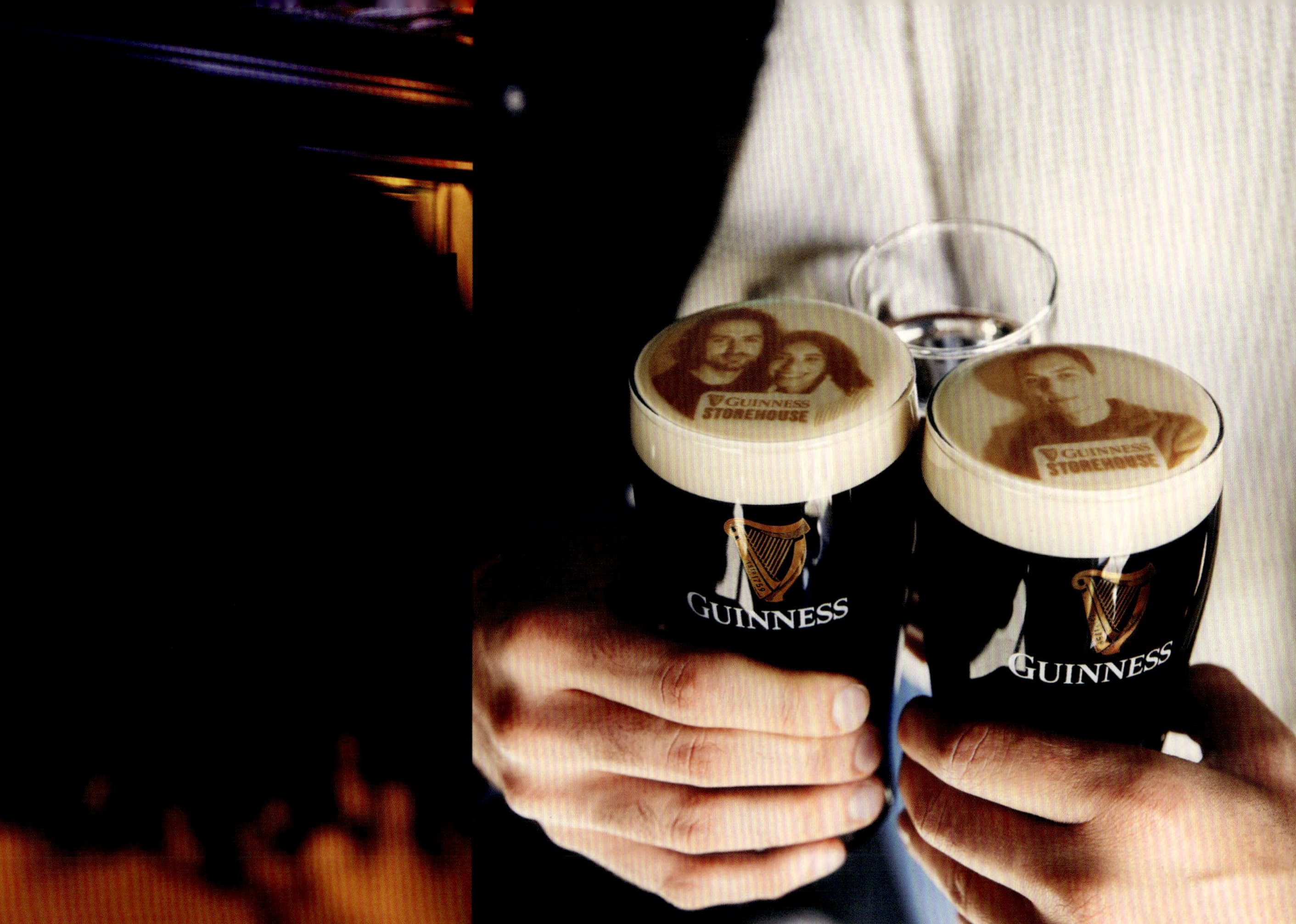

place to relax and build camaraderie. Or Lululemon's experiential stores, where wellness and community are just as important as shopping—visitors can take an assortment of fitness classes in the "sweat studio," grab a healthy bite at the "fuel bar," and connect with other fans of the brand in dedicated coworking and community spaces.

Giving people the chance to live out a brand's values and purpose is another distinguishing element. Vans's experiential House of Vans venues hosted musicians, art exhibits and workshops, and even "bowl sessions" in indoor skateparks, providing sites for their customers to express their true selves and find fellow action-sports, music, and street-culture enthusiasts. These programs allowed guests to interact and engage with the brand in ways that were fun, embodied, and meaningfully tied to its identity.

Finally, the opportunity for personalization differentiates these brand experiences from their predecessors'. Whether it's making custom-printed M&M's at the M&M Store in New York City, designing a custom pair of sneakers at the Nike House of Innovation, or printing your own likeness in the foam of a pint at the Guinness Storehouse, these special opportunities to co-create with the company enable guests to show who they are, and in doing so form a deeper connection with the product.

The best examples of location-based brand experiences feel like unique offerings worthy of an additional entry fee. Their popularity has only increased as they've become more immersive: The Guinness Storehouse, for one, welcomed 1.65 million visitors in 2024, a 10 percent increase from the year prior; in 2023, Nike and Lululemon both saw a greater year-over-year increase in foot traffic compared with traditional sportswear outlets, per location analytics firm Placer.ai. Visitors are drawn to these experiences because they're more than transactional points of sale; rather, they're designed to foster a positive relationship with the company and a compatible community through ample opportunities for education, self-expression, and socialization based around a brand.

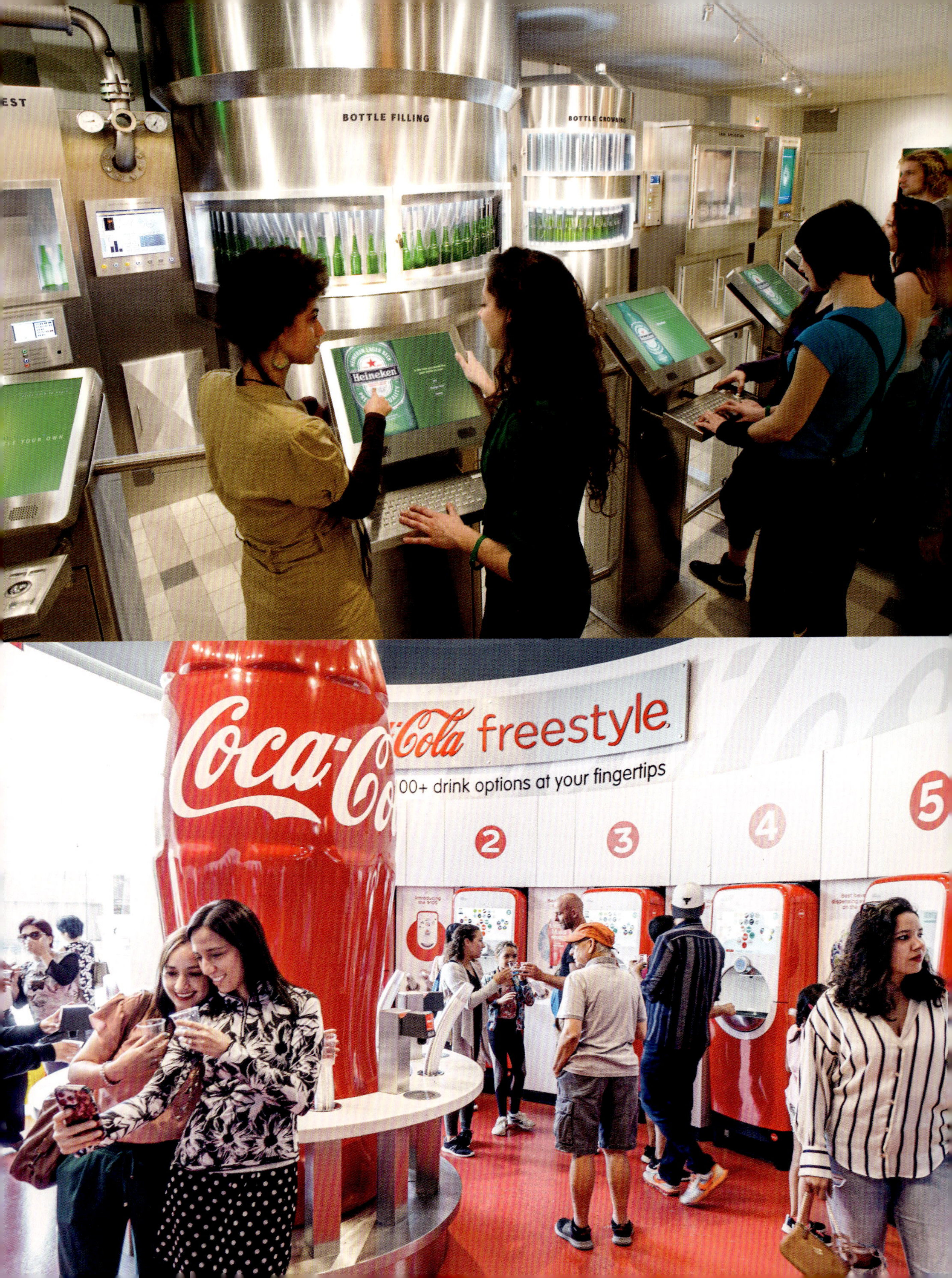
BOTTLE FILLING
BOTTLE CROWNING
Heineken
Cola freestyle
00+ drink options at your fingertips
2
3
4
5

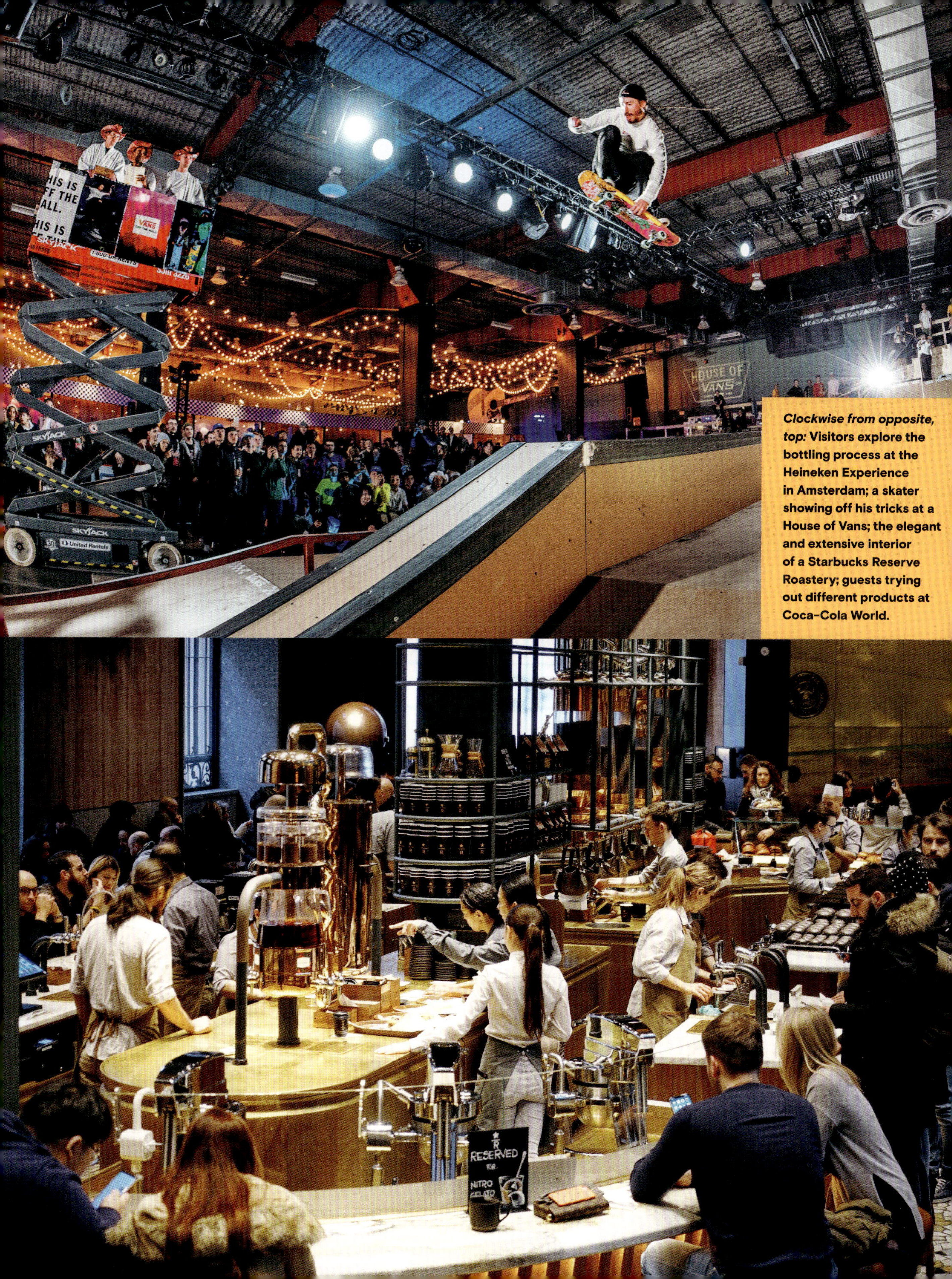

Clockwise from opposite, top: **Visitors explore the bottling process at the Heineken Experience in Amsterdam; a skater showing off his tricks at a House of Vans; the elegant and extensive interior of a Starbucks Reserve Roastery; guests trying out different products at Coca-Cola World.**

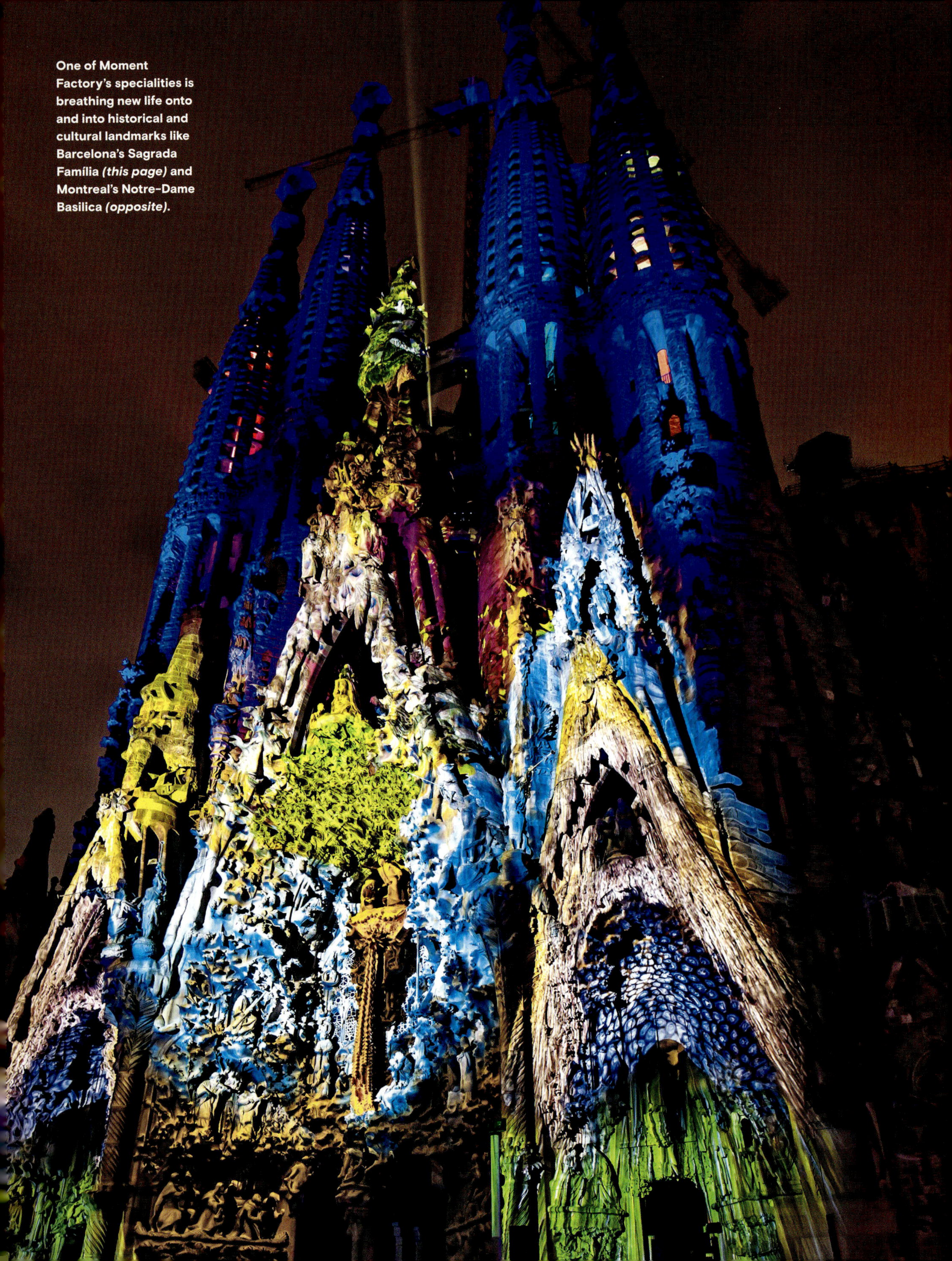

One of Moment Factory's specialities is breathing new life onto and into historical and cultural landmarks like Barcelona's Sagrada Família *(this page)* and Montreal's Notre-Dame Basilica *(opposite)*.

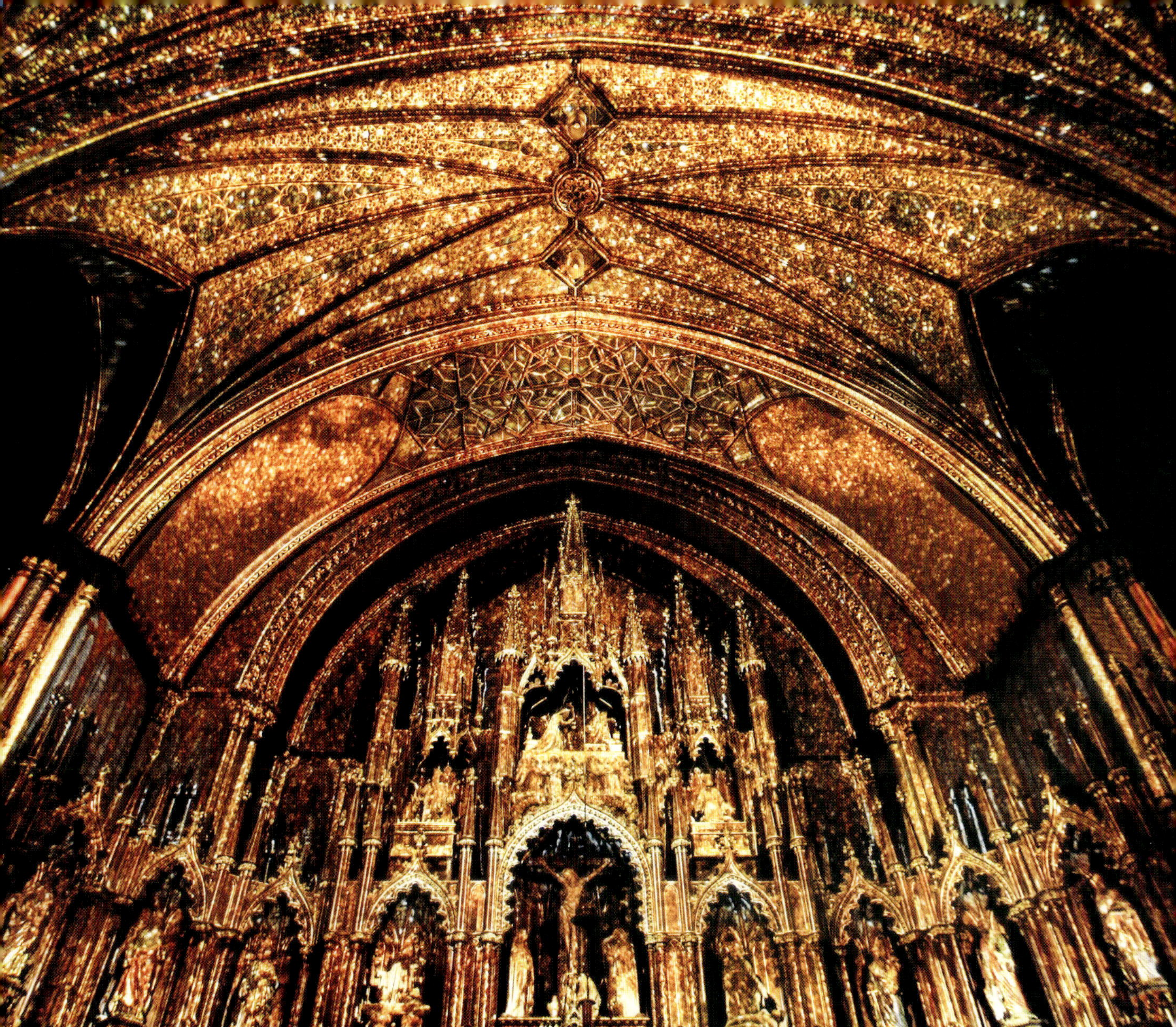

MOMENT FACTORY

"We do it in public" is the provocative motto of Montreal-based multimedia studio Moment Factory, founded in 2001 by Sakchin Bessette and Dominic Audet. What this means is that public spaces are their canvases for creating connection: From concert halls to historical monuments to the natural world, Moment Factory is dedicated to turning these locations into sites for "digital campfires," or tech-enabled places of wonder where people gather and tell stories.

Moment Factory began in Montreal's rave scene, enlivening musical acts with stunning multimedia visuals. Since then, they've expanded to creating custom experiences and installations for live performances, brand activations, cultural sites, transportation hubs, and more. Masters of transforming audiences' emotional experience of space and time through light and sound, the studio has worked with musicians like Billie Eilish, Phish, and Madonna; brands like FIFA, Moët & Chandon, and Sony; and landmarks like Barcelona's Sagrada Família and the Notre-Dame de Reims Cathedral in France.

In addition to their custom programs, Moment Factory has produced thirty-four original creations that have sold more than seven million tickets in twelve countries as of 2025. Among these experiences are the AURA shows: indoor experiences that use pixel-precise projection mapping and epic orchestral scores to highlight the artistry and history of heritage sites in a new way—and by doing so, reinvigorate tourism. Since 2017, AURA at the Notre-Dame Basilica in Montreal has attracted more than 225,000 visitors a year and earned a Thea Award for Outstanding Achievement, among other honors.

Elaborate, colorful, and animated projections exquisitely mapped onto a building's architecture and synchronized to music are the defining features of Moment Factory's AURA shows.

Among Moment Factory's other innovative original offerings are their Lumina night walks, where immersive storytelling goes beyond the confines of man-made architecture and into the great outdoors. In twenty locations across Asia, Europe, and North America, the night walks

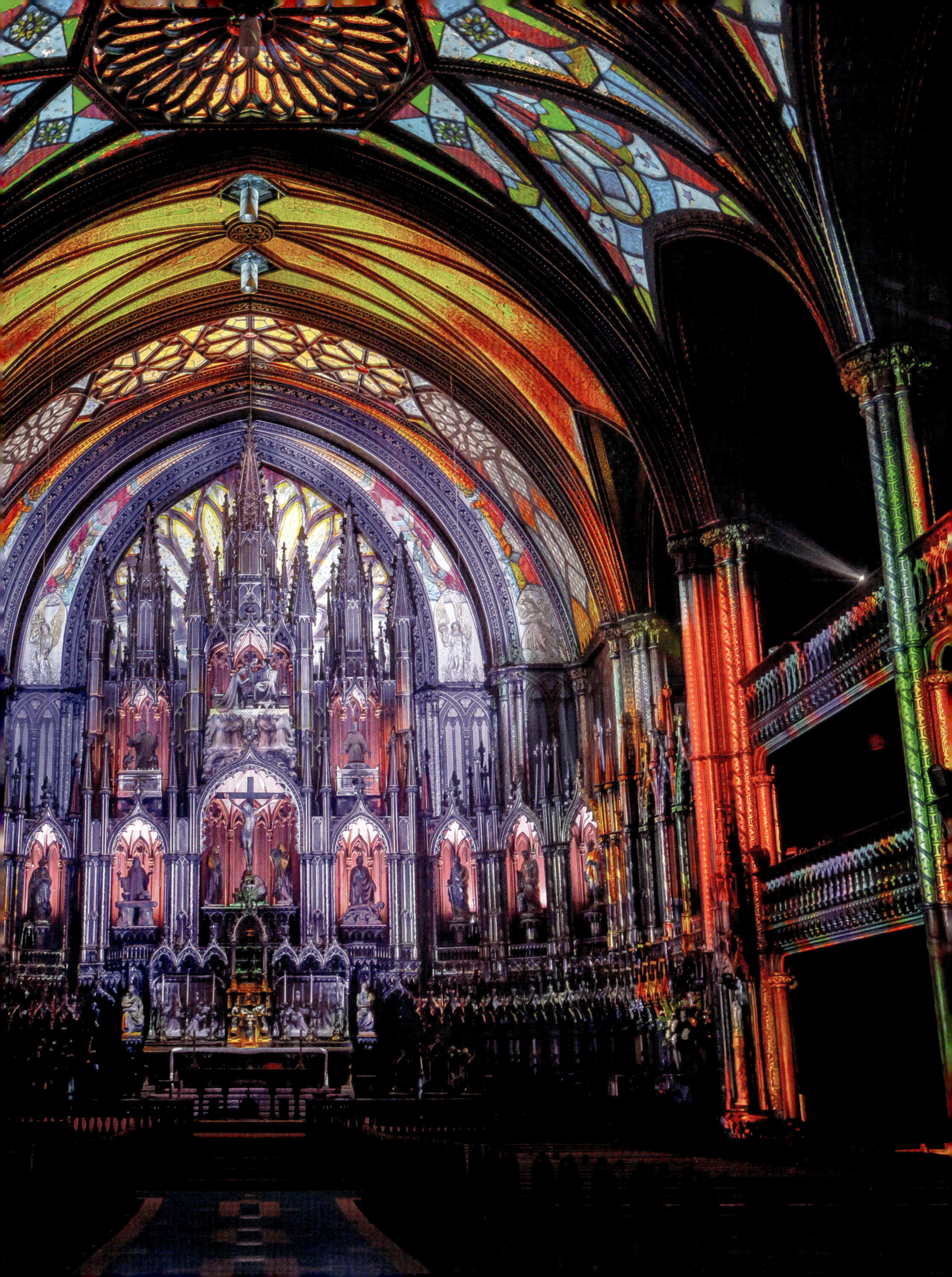

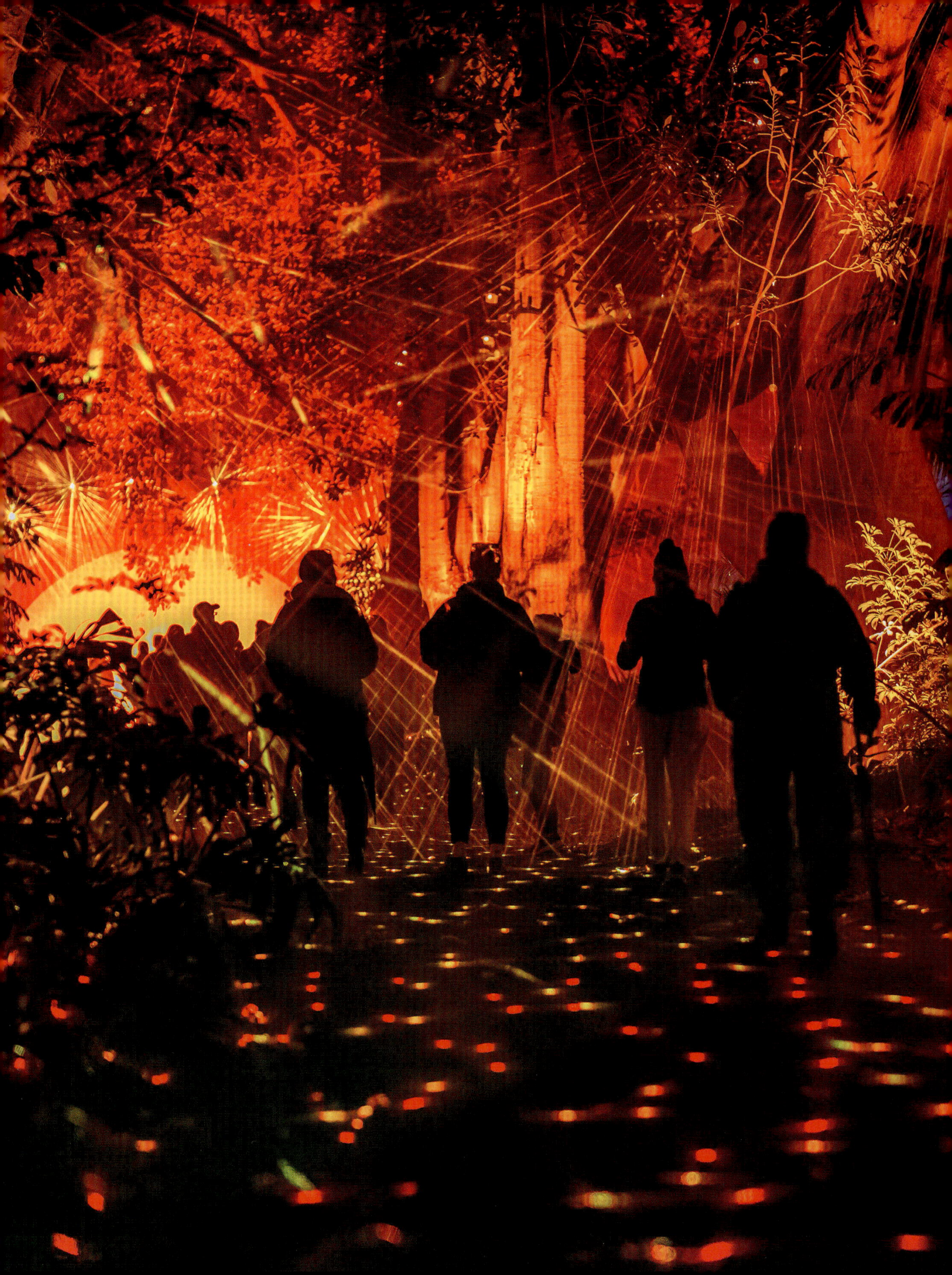

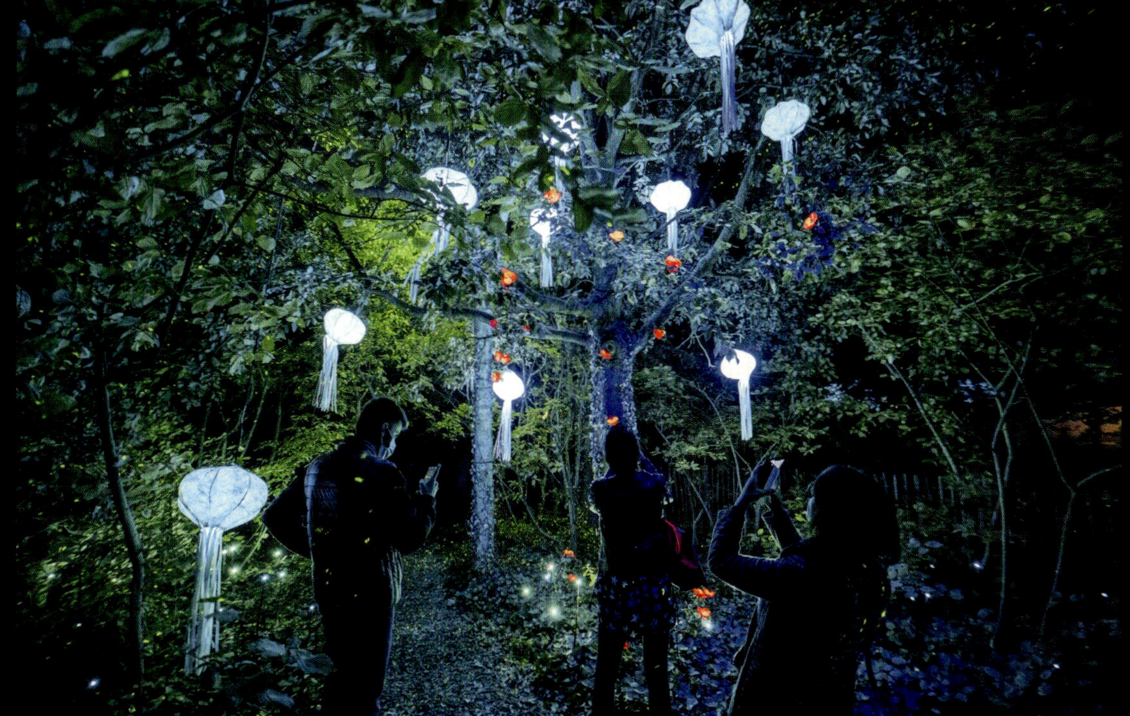

have elevated natural beauty through immersive, multimedia effects. Light and scenographic installations, projection mapping, original soundtracks, and layers of emotionally resonant storytelling transform outdoor spaces that aren't typically used after dark into multisensory journeys that feel like walking through a fairy tale. Many Luminas also incorporate interactive elements to give visitors more ways to connect to the stories and to one another, such as reactive walking sticks in Nova Lumina, projections that respond to visitors' songs and touch in Lumina Borealis, and colored wristbands that unlock photo opportunities in Rainforest Lumina. These innovative nighttime activities have proved invaluable for attracting tourism, in one case even contributing to an 1,800 percent increase in traffic to the region. While nature is filled with countless stories, they've never been revealed like this: by the light, warmth, and human connection generated by a digital campfire.

Lumina night walks integrate lighting, special effects, original music, and storytelling into immersive and participatory outdoor experiences, guiding visitors on enchanted journeys through nature.

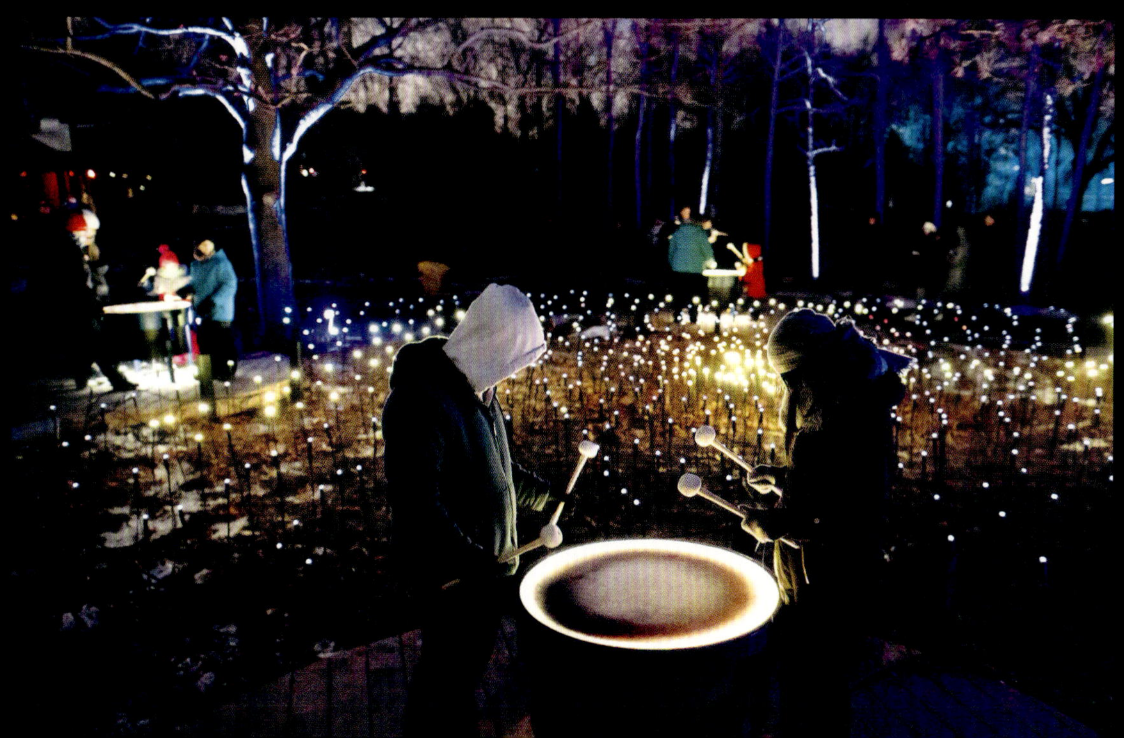

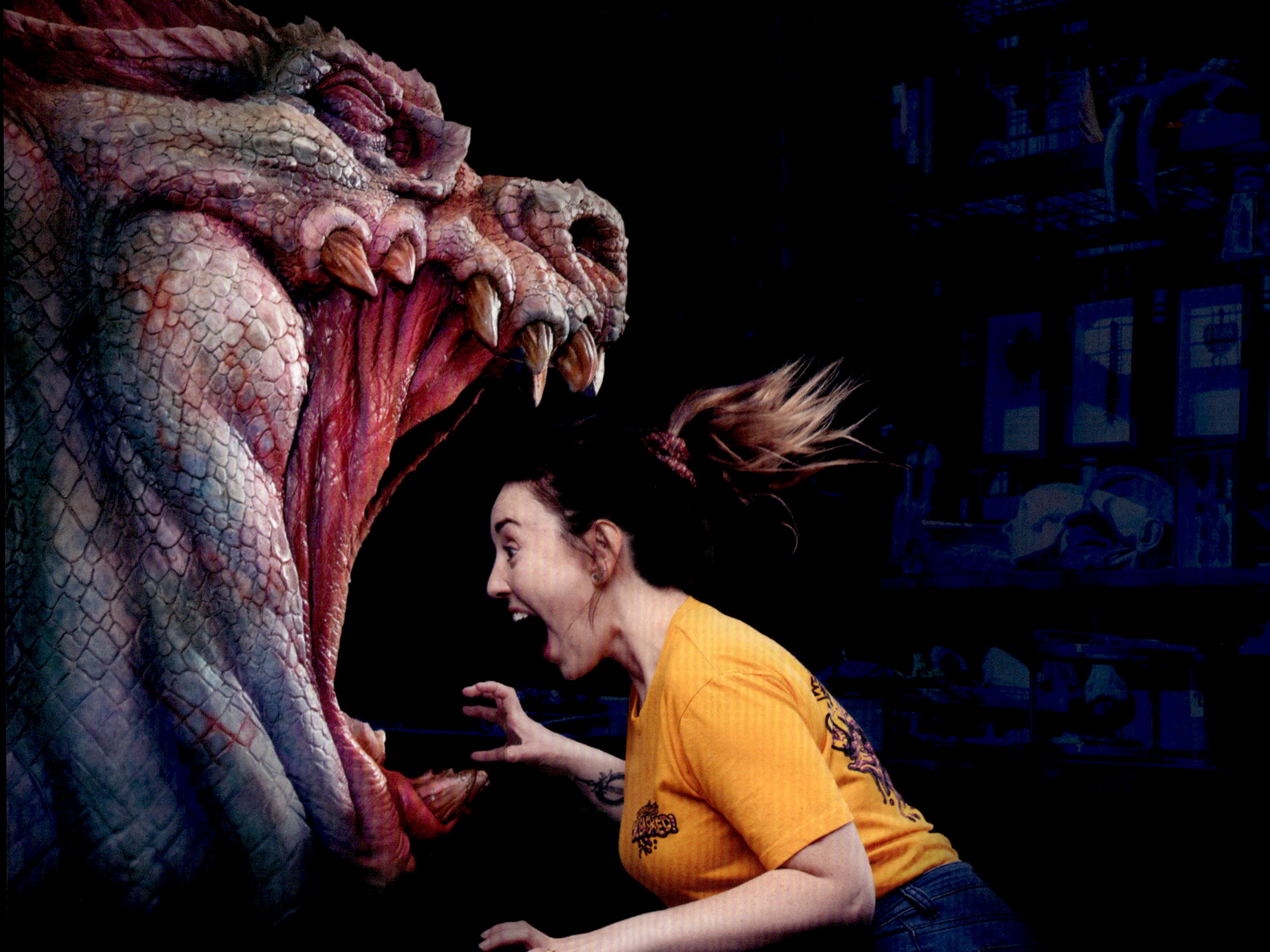

WĒTĀ WORKSHOP UNLEASHED

Founded in 1987 by Richard Taylor and Tania Rodger, the award-winning creative-services company now known as Wētā Workshop has created stunning practical and special effects for more than a hundred movies. The New Zealand-based studio has lent their creative brilliance to countless iconic films like Peter Jackson's *The Lord of the Rings* trilogy and his adaptation of *The Hobbit*, James Cameron's *Avatar* films, and *Blade Runner 2049*. Along the way, they've won five Academy Awards, four BAFTAs, and three Thea Awards for their outstanding work. After seeing Wētā Workshop's creations on the silver screen, many a moviegoer has wondered: How do they make that movie magic?

Wētā Workshop Unleashed answers that question in the form of a magic-carpet ride through a world of imagination and creativity. Part studio tour, part hands-on education, and part immersive experience, this is a supremely imaginative representation of what goes on behind the scenes with some of the world's best-known designers and producers of stunning visual effects. The journey through this fictionalized, fantastic version of Wētā Workshop's headquarters takes you into three elaborate cinematic worlds (a

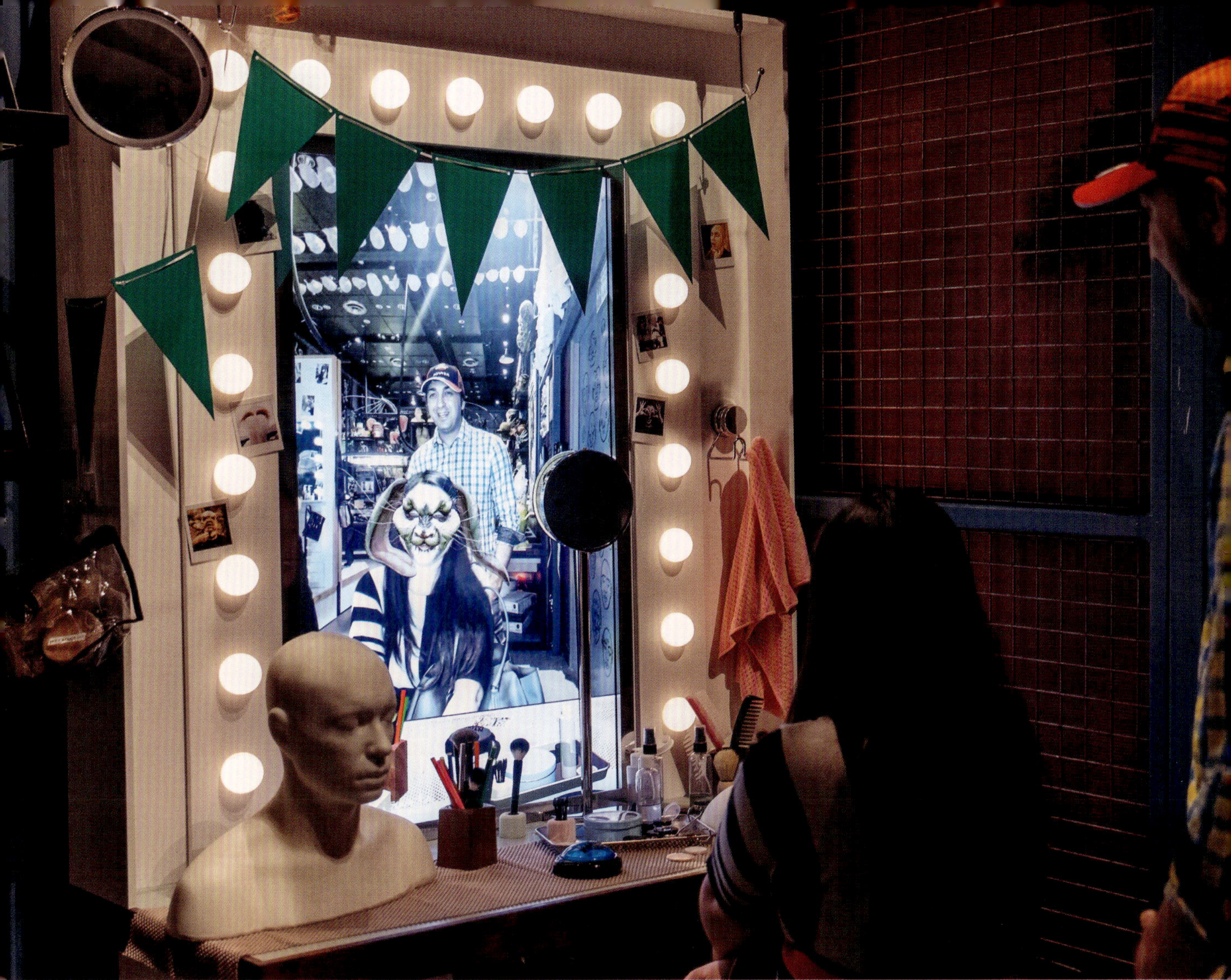

creature feature, a fantasy adventure, and a sci-fi flick, all dreamed up specially for the experience) to learn about the real-life processes behind making film and TV come to life.

Wētā Workshop's creative specialities are many—they design ultra-realistic armor, weapons, creatures, miniatures, props, costumes, prosthetics, vehicles, and more—and the tools of their trade are explored in a vibrant environment that makes you feel as though you're in a movie just as much as you're working on one. You'll walk through an animatronics department that resembles a mad scientist's lab, an art studio where you get shrunk to the size of a miniature, a manufacturing hall complete with a smithy and a throne room, and a soundstage under the gaze of a huge alien robot.

But while the narrative and sets are embellished, the lessons are real and practical. Wētā Workshop Unleashed is not just a fun tour but also a celebration of craft and a vehicle for teaching the next generation. Each "film" and department includes detailed panels illustrating the steps of the creative process as well as a host of interactive elements intended to give you a feel for the actual work, from puppeteering creatures to tracing character designs on a lightboard to molding plasticine sculptures. Wētā Workshop Unleashed pays tribute to the artistry of special effects by getting guests fully involved in unleashing their own creativity.

***Above:* An augmented-reality mirror gives a guest a monstrous makeover. *Opposite:* One of the many interactive stations, where visitors can experiment with creating different monster noises inside the mouth of the beast itself.**

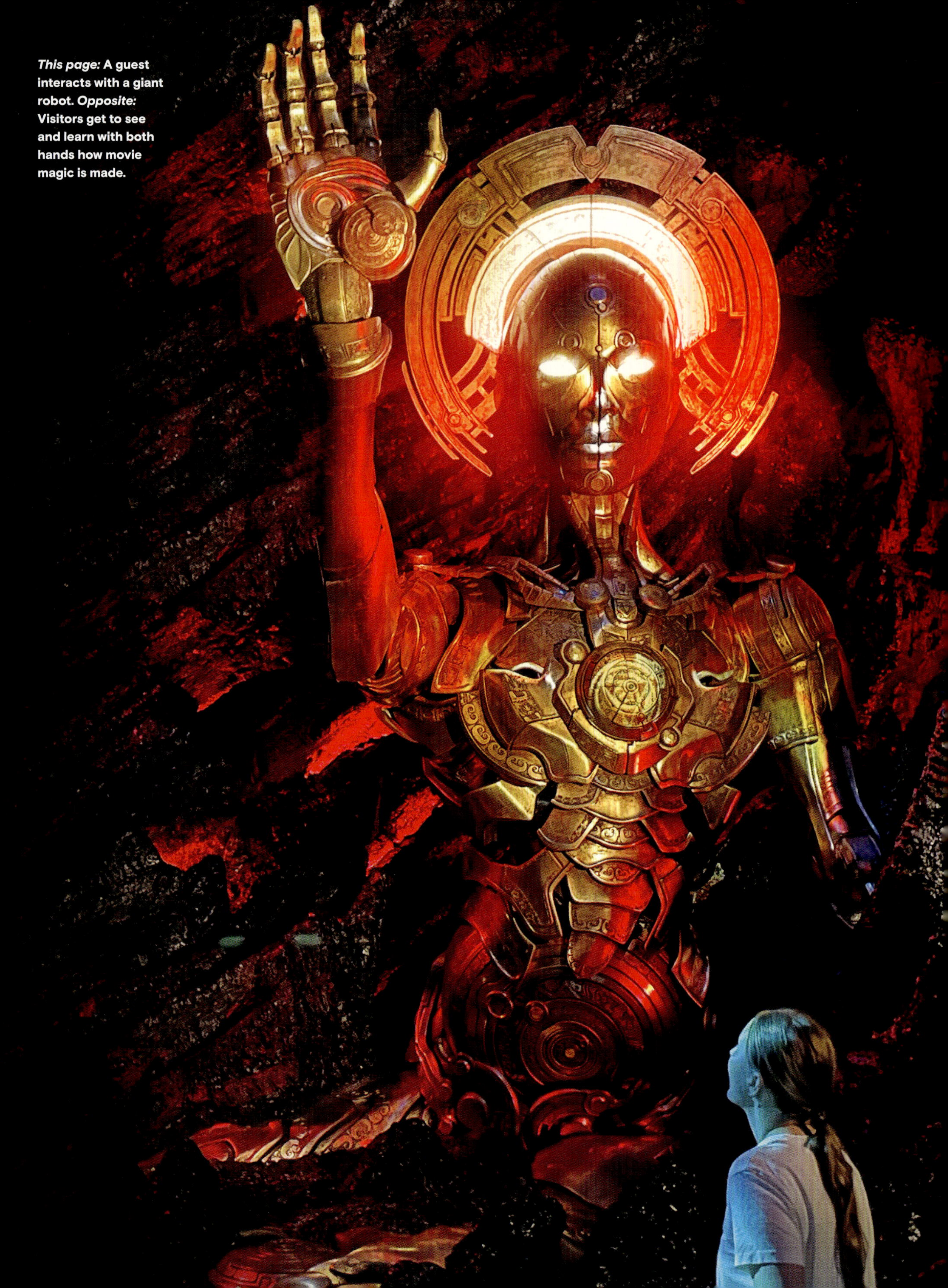

This page: A guest interacts with a giant robot. *Opposite:* Visitors get to see and learn with both hands how movie magic is made.

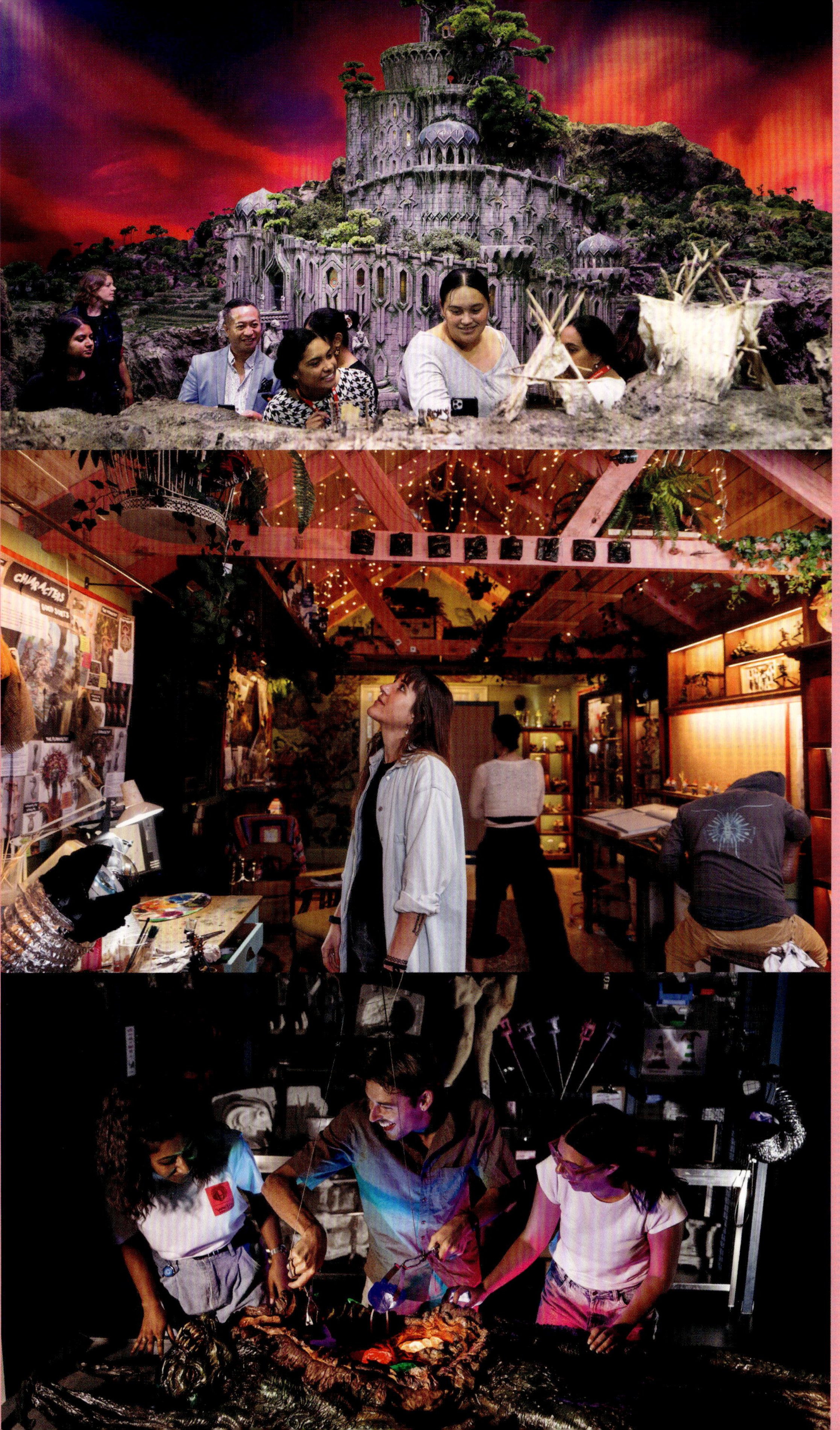

4

THE FUTURE OF STORYTELLING IS RESPONSIVE

Almost every night when my son, Daniel, was a little boy, he wanted me to tell him bedtime stories. While there were books we both loved, what he most enjoyed was having me come up with stories "from my head" about Sparky, a character not so loosely based on him, and turn things that had happened to Daniel during that day or week into grand Sparky adventures. Now and then Daniel would interject, asking how Sparky reacted to something that he himself had experienced. I tried my best to mix the real with the imagined. Recognizing himself in the story, knowing that this story I was weaving was made for him and him alone: That's what made it truly special.

For most of us, stories that respond to our lives and our environments were only possible at bedtime, exclusively written and performed by Mom and Dad. Then we grew up watching television and films, where the story unfolds before us as we observe. We learned that stories are scripted for our consumption—and forget we ever wanted more.

But the appeal of being personally addressed still runs deep. We respond energetically to being called—in fact, a study conducted in 2005 shows that infants as young as five months can start to tune out a room full of noise if they hear their own name. We're more engaged

When stories are able to adapt to the preferences and actions of each participant, the actience feels seen and recognized, and thus stories that are responsive become more meaningful and intimate than stories produced for anonymous mass audiences.

when we feel individually recognized, not generic or anonymous. The more personalized, the more meaningful the experience. We learn better when a teacher adapts to our individual learning style, and we like when the bartender at the local pub knows our favorite drink without our having to order it.

Over the course of my career, I have seen how energized people get when a story responds to them for the first time. And it makes sense. Who wouldn't be compelled by a narrative experience created precisely for them, and to some extent *by* them?

I call this storytelling phenomenon "responsiveness." When stories are able to adapt to the preferences and actions of each participant, the actience feels seen and recognized, and thus stories that are

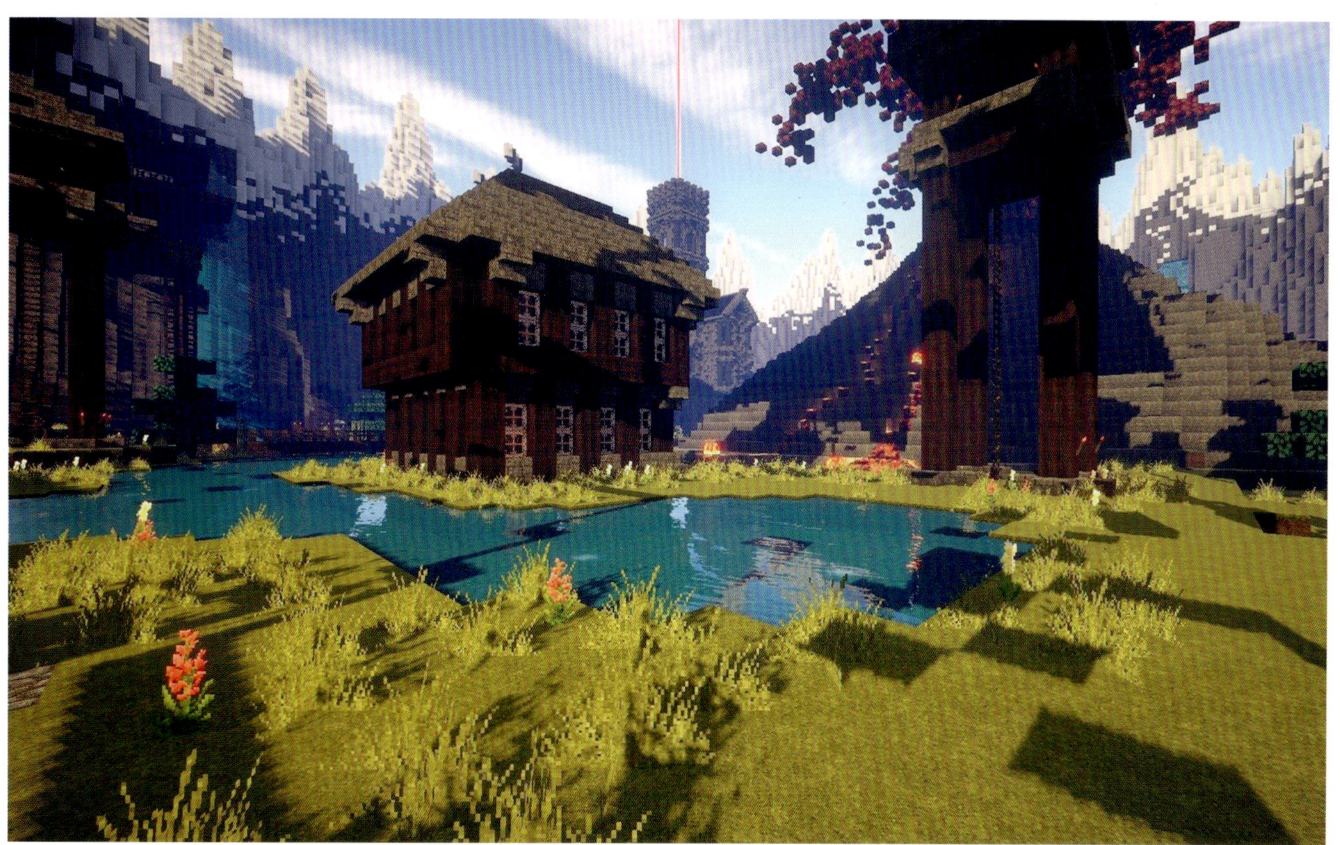

There are myriad ways that ***Minecraft*** lets players customize their experience—they can build unique environments, create personalized adventures, or even design their own mini games.

responsive become more meaningful and intimate than stories produced for anonymous mass audiences. The more the story responds to the participant, the more engaged the participant becomes, contributing more of themselves—their likes, dislikes, and ideas—to the experience. In this way, responsive stories can evolve to reflect the character of each individual.

You've likely already experienced an element of responsiveness in your entertainment consumption. For example, computer games and video games such as *The Sims*, *Second Life*, and *Minecraft* respond to player choice in real time. You can express your personal taste by customizing avatars and environments. The increased responsiveness has made these games extremely popular, with people investing huge numbers of hours in personalizing, building in, and playing them. Their appeal was not lost on Netflix's then-CEO Reed Hastings, who noted that "we compete (and lose to) *Fortnite* more than HBO."

But what about stories? Can they also adapt in real time based on the audience's likes, dislikes, current mood, and even daily activities? The exciting truth is that creators are beginning to take people's desires for stories that employ responsiveness to heart, and new technology is making it possible.

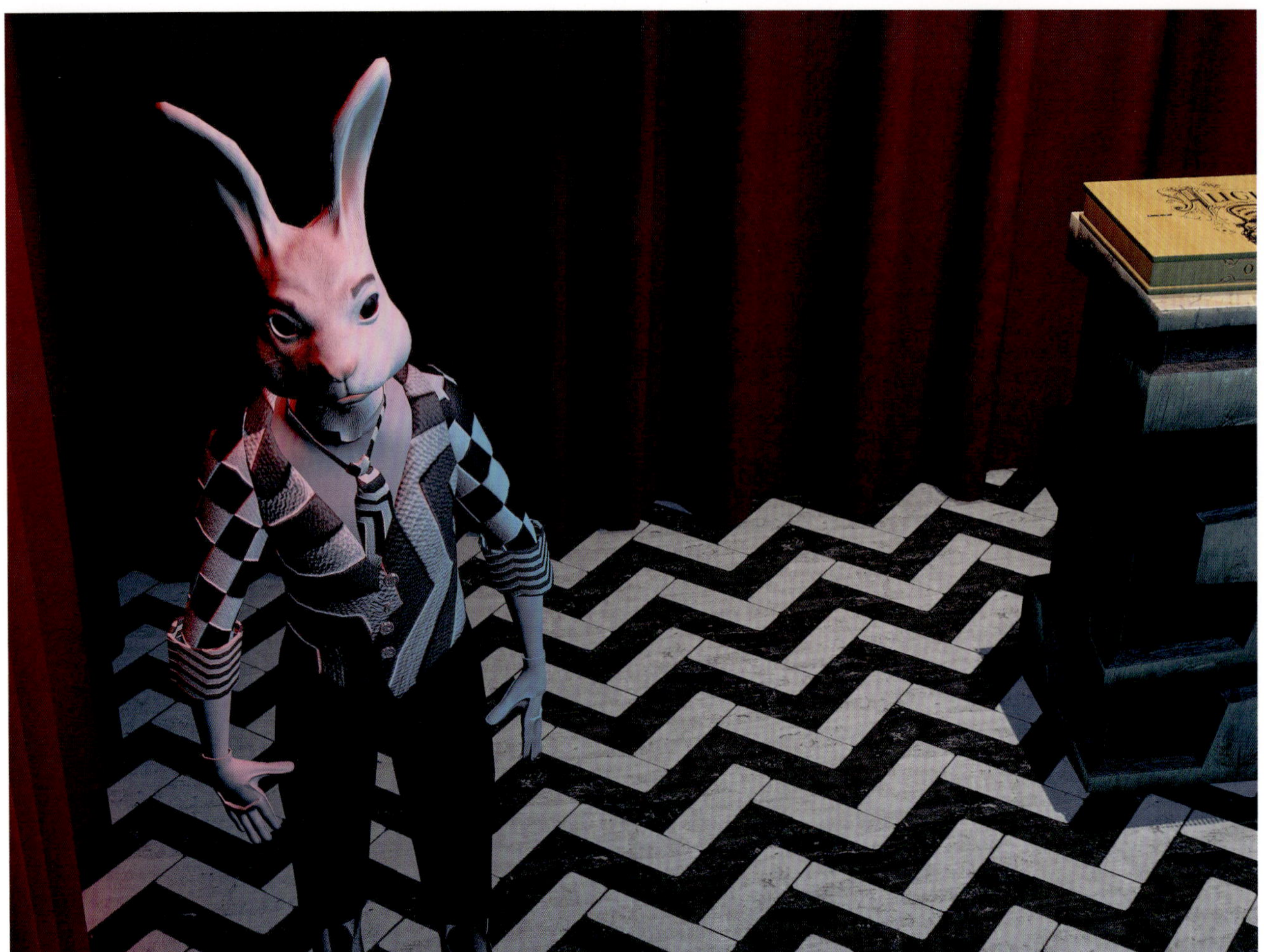

The animated White Rabbit in *Alice, the Virtual Reality Play* could interact with participants in real time as it was being puppeted by an unseen actor.

REPARTEE WITH A RABBIT

One of the earliest and most memorable examples of true responsiveness in a living story that I ever experienced was *Alice, the Virtual Reality Play*. In 2017, DV Group, a French digital and VR innovation studio, presented *Alice* at our Future of StoryTelling Summit at Snug Harbor Cultural Center on Staten Island (see p. 290). At the beginning of the experience, I put on a VR headset—something I have done dozens of times—and looked down at my now-animated hands. But what followed was a series of encouters I will never forget.

When an animated, adult-sized rabbit—the White Rabbit from Lewis Carroll's *Alice's Adventures in Wonderland*—reached out and tapped my shoulder, I could physically feel his hands. Yes, I was really being touched by an animated character.

"Come now, Alice!" said the Rabbit, in a proper British accent. "We're late, we're late, for a very important date!"

We were in an animated underground room, and the Rabbit began to question me. *What was my favorite pudding? (Bread.) Animal? (Puffin.) Color?* To my last answer, the Rabbit scoffed. "Purple?! Wait until I tell the Queen! She'll have a thing or two to say about that!"

The Rabbit asked me to curtsy—"You're meeting the Queen!"—then immediately deemed my attempt inadequate. "Lower—lower! Who taught you to curtsy? You curtsy like a boy!"

I laughed at the heckling—until the Rabbit asked me to sing.

I hesitated. I don't like singing, certainly not in front of others. I cannot carry a tune. The Rabbit nudged me some more; again I demurred. But the Rabbit would not take no for an answer, so after some further hesitation, I began to sing the first thing that popped into my head: "Tiny Dancer" by Elton John.

I wasn't two bars in before the Rabbit was once more ridiculing me—first, over my choice of music ("That's a silly song!"), then my performance. ("Oof! *Now* I see why you didn't want to sing...so off-key!")

Again, I laughed. And again I tried, knowing the musical result would not improve yet wanting to show I was game. I would never have imagined I would work so hard to impress an animated character. Or that I might get personally roasted by one.

There were other remarkable interactions, such as when I picked up an animated slate and, again, felt its actual physicality—its weight, its rough texture—then wrote on it with an animated stick of chalk.

Then came a misbegotten adventure in what looked like an English garden. Humpty Dumpty sat on a brick wall and asked, in a Cockney accent, if I could please catch him if he jumped. "Yes," I assured him and moved closer to the wall, positioning my hands just beneath him. "Are you absolutely *sure* you'll catch me?" Another assurance from me—and in the next moment he jumped but somehow fell between my hands, splattering on the floor. A genuine sense of guilt and failure, even slight horror, came over me.

Then, a third Carroll creation, the Cheshire Cat, escorted me through a forest and encouraged me—in a different English accent from the others—to pluck an animated mushroom from the ground and eat it. I reached down, again felt its solidity, and placed it on my tongue. It tasted like meringue, sweet and delicious.

When the "reality play" was over, I realized I had crossed another boundary in the world of living stories. I had lived a hybrid moment—part real, part computer-generated, as if I had entered the movie *Who Framed Roger Rabbit*. What had long been an abstraction had now turned tactile. For the first time, I had interacted with a virtual character in a virtual world, yet I had physically touched and even eaten something that appeared animated, all *in real time*. It felt like magic. As far as I knew, no living story had accomplished the seamless blending of analog and digital at this level before.

I was fortunate to have the creators show me how it was done. One actor, with an obvious gift for voices, had played all three characters—the Rabbit, Humpty Dumpty, and the Cheshire Cat—in a motion-capture suit. He wore a head rig equipped with a camera and a light that projected on his face so that his human expressions would be transferred in real time onto the readable expressions of the animated characters. A digital director at a computer sat in the corner of the space, almost like a DJ at a club, controlling the atmospherics of each environment: animation, lighting, background music, all of it cued in real time on a keyboard. A third participant, nicknamed "the Ninja," made sure that the cables of my tethered VR headset did not tangle or obstruct my motion; when I reached for the slate or mushroom, the Ninja ensured that the real object was placed where I was reaching so that I could grab it. The final effect made me feel as if I were a character in the classic Disney animated film adaptation of *Alice in Wonderland*—except that instead of just following the script, I got to help write it myself.

For the first time, I had interacted with a virtual character in a virtual world, yet I had physically touched and even eaten something that appeared animated, all *in real time*.

Alice, the Virtual Reality Play was an exhilarating glimpse of a story responsive to me, to my actions, my strengths, my weaknesses. In that snappy, specific exchange over my bad singing, the Rabbit was alertly reacting to my performance, almost as if we were in an improv skit together. I felt challenged to raise my game, to improvise better, to be funnier, quicker, more honest. The Rabbit's aliveness made me feel even more present, more engaged, pushed me to be more resourceful. Stepping into this story world, I was discovering what I was truly capable of—more boldness, if not musicality.

If I felt seen and heard and understood (if also slightly mocked) because I had acknowledged that I liked purple, did not know how to curtsy, and sang off-key, imagine if a virtual character could eventually understand me on a whole other, deeper level. How exciting would it be to go down that rabbit hole?

Alice was incredible—though it was only made possible because three skilled people were right there, in that same physical space, helping it all go smoothly. I left wanting all of my stories to be responsive like that but thinking that would never be a reality given the costs. But now I realize it can be—and at a scale larger than I could have ever envisioned.

RESPONSIVENESS AT SCALE

Over the years, there have been gallant attempts at allowing audiences to decide how stories will unfold, such as the *Choose Your Own Adventure* book series in the 1970s and the standalone "Bandersnatch" episode of the Netflix series *Black Mirror* in 2018; however, neither of these was entirely responsive but rather a pre-written or pre-filmed branching narrative decision tree that the audience got to choose their way through.

The real revolution will come when the narrative can adapt and be created in real time—and we're just now on the threshold of having the technology to do that.

Rockstar Games has been a pioneer in using emerging technology to design responsive storytelling. In 2018's *Red Dead Redemption 2*, each of the more than a thousand NPCs (non-player characters) has its own personality and the capacity to "remember" past events, leading to hundreds of different outcomes based on player choice. For example, if you come across a highway robbery and decide to intervene, you'd better watch out for those thieves next time you travel that road. Similarly, the victim of the robbery will act kindly toward you if you meet them again in the game. *Grand Theft Auto VI*, scheduled for a 2026 release, will build on the realism and nuance of *Red Dead Redemption 2*'s NPC intelligence with new, generative-AI-powered tools. Where players were once limited to entering certain buildings or areas usually for the purpose of furthering the plot, advances in AI allow for generated interiors, dramatically increasing the number of buildings players can enter and explore, and more realistic NPC behaviors that aren't programmed in advance.

The next top entertainment company—the one that will be as big as, or bigger than, Disney/Pixar—will be on the front lines of fully personalized, immersive storytelling.

These recent advancements in gaming AI caught the attention of venture-capital firm Andreesen Horowitz, which in 2022 launched a $600 million effort dedicated to gaming start-ups called Games Fund (with a second $600 million round announced in spring 2024). Games Fund provides funding for game studios and invests, among other things, in research for AI, VR, and other immersive tech that's pushing gaming to new frontiers. Gaming is already a multibillion-dollar industry. Games Fund sees potential for highly responsive, personalized gaming to be even bigger, with capabilities that extend far beyond console and PC gaming and into the entertainment industry at large.

New technologies will also make responsive stories economically viable. The popular "Bandersnatch" experiment on *Black Mirror* was intriguing, fun, and novel—but the creation process was expensive and grueling. The crew reportedly produced more than five hours of footage to account for the episode's various endings, making the budget and production timeline double that of a standard *Black Mirror* outing. The project was so complex, admitted the showrunners, that it was like making "four episodes at the same time." AI video generation models like Sora, Dream Machine, and Character-1 can help solve this problem by enabling the near real-time creation of realistic, dynamic content. With these models filmmakers can generate complex scenes, environments, and characters with minimal manual input, significantly reducing production costs and time. In July 2024, Hedra Labs released its first version of an AI creation suite that allows users to generate ninety-second videos of original characters with expressive human faces and voice acting in sixty seconds. As this technology improves, it will pave the way for more personalized living stories, as AI can create content tailored to individual preferences or user interactions. The future potential of these models could revolutionize the entertainment industry, combining the cinematic quality of the movies with the immersive, interactive nature of video games to produce something entirely new.

The next top entertainment company—the one that will be as big as, or bigger than, Disney/Pixar—will be on the front lines of fully personalized, immersive storytelling. "Pixar, Disney, and Marvel were all able to create memorable worlds that became part of their fans' core identity," Jonathan Lai, general partner at Games Fund, writes. "The opportunity for the next Interactive Pixar is to leverage generative AI to do the same—to create new story worlds that blur the lines between traditional storytelling formats, and in doing so, create universes unlike any we've seen before."

Beyond AI creation suites, emerging tools for assessing user data points promise even more opportunities for personalization. What if living stories could base the characters, plot, setting, and soundtrack

A character created with Sora, OpenAI's image- and video-generation software.

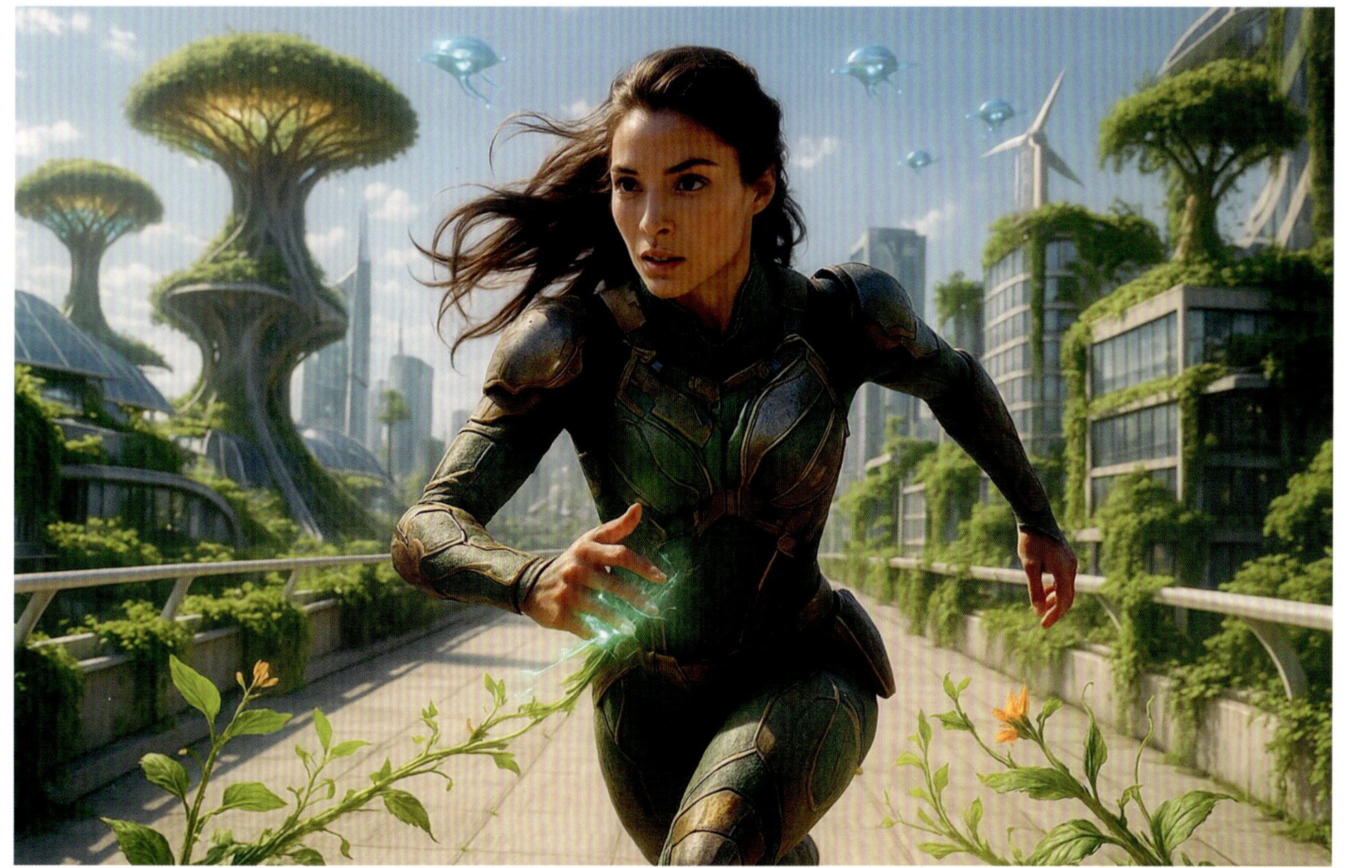

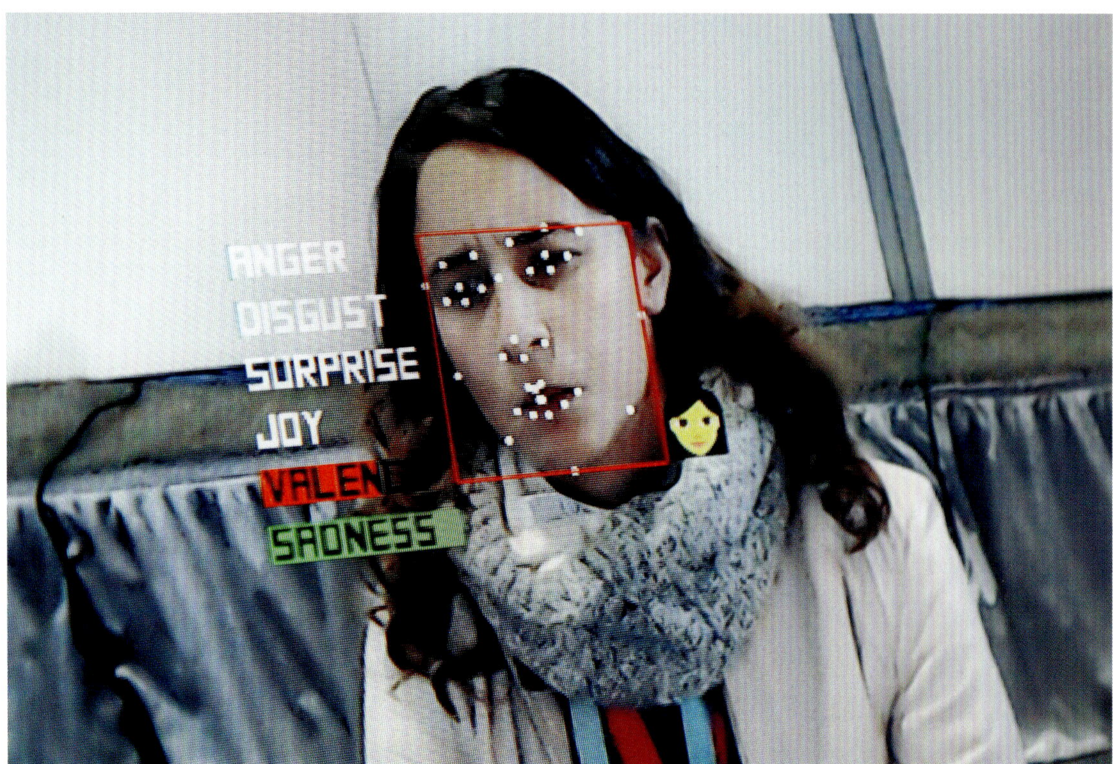

A demo of emotion-detecting technology created by Affectiva, a software company working on AI that can "read" human emotions by analyzing facial and vocal expressions.

on your digital footprint—just as retailers present you with product recommendations based on your previous choices? By mining our digital history, these tools can determine our interests, preferences, behavior patterns, personal history, current physical surroundings, and so on. Imagine two people going through the same immersive experience: A person who regularly watches rom-coms, listens to pop music, shops for perfume, and posts creative photos of their outfits on social media will have a very different story journey from someone who likes horror, heavy metal, and fantasy novels. We may be on the threshold of a world in which every aspect of an immersive story is individually tailored to the experiencer.

But the possibilities for responsiveness do not end there. With the advent of technology known as "affective computing," living stories may eventually be capable of going a step further by responding to your emotions in the moment.

Affective computing involves "reading" (with the aid of a camera or wearable such as a smartwatch) facial expressions, gestures, heart rate, pulse, body temperature, and more, to infer your real-time responses to stimuli. Affective computing technology already goes far beyond the ability to read a sad facial expression or determine your level of excitement based on perspiration. According to Rosalind Picard, head of MIT Media Lab's Affective Computing Group, "We can [tell] if your heart is racing...from a neutral expression using an ordinary camera on your laptop or phone. We can read from a neutral face if your breathing is becoming irregular and showing signs of stress." Affective computing technology's ability to pick up on the subtlest of bodily reactions creates limitless possibilities for in-the-moment responsiveness. Picard's lab laid the groundwork for the founding of the company Affectiva, which specializes in technology called "Emotion AI." Emotion AI is a machine-learning-based software that can detect complex human cognitive and emotional states. It is multimodal, meaning it measures the whole body to get a complete picture of how you're feeling and responding to stimuli right then and there. CEO Rana el Kaliouby cofounded Affectiva out of a need to bridge the gap between technology and our humanity, seeking an answer to the question "What if our technology could understand us better and connect with us in a more empathetic and relevant manner?" With this data, AI-powered living stories would have the ability to know, like an intimate friend, how we're feeling in the moment—and how to respond.

By combining our emotional data with generative AI, storytellers could create experiences that evolve based on the actience's real-time emotional states. Feeling upbeat? The story and characters will reflect your chipper mood. Or if you had a particularly bad day, the AI could create a dramatic, moodier arc for you to experience. Whatever the feeling, the merging of these technologies could create deeply personalized, emotionally resonant experiences, with content that feels more responsive and connected to the actience's inner world.

Inevitably, AI tools will gain access to more and more inputs both in real time and from past experiences: all the places we've been, the people we've met, the books, TV, and films we've enjoyed, the music we love, our favorite photos and apps, and on and on. The next generation of virtual characters will evolve to reflect us, with storylines responsive to our actions, moods, interests, and personality.

We, the passive audience, watch and hear movies, plays, TV shows—often gripping stories that have the power to move us emotionally. How much more will we be moved when we, the actience, have *helped create* the story, one featuring our preferences, passions, peculiarities? One that responds meaningfully to our cues, and that we then respond to in turn?

Right now we can only achieve this level of intimacy in storytelling if Mom and Dad are doing the writing and producing. But I believe that with the inevitable leap in computing power, we may soon see a future where the intimacy with which we tell bedtime stories will be reproducible for everyone.

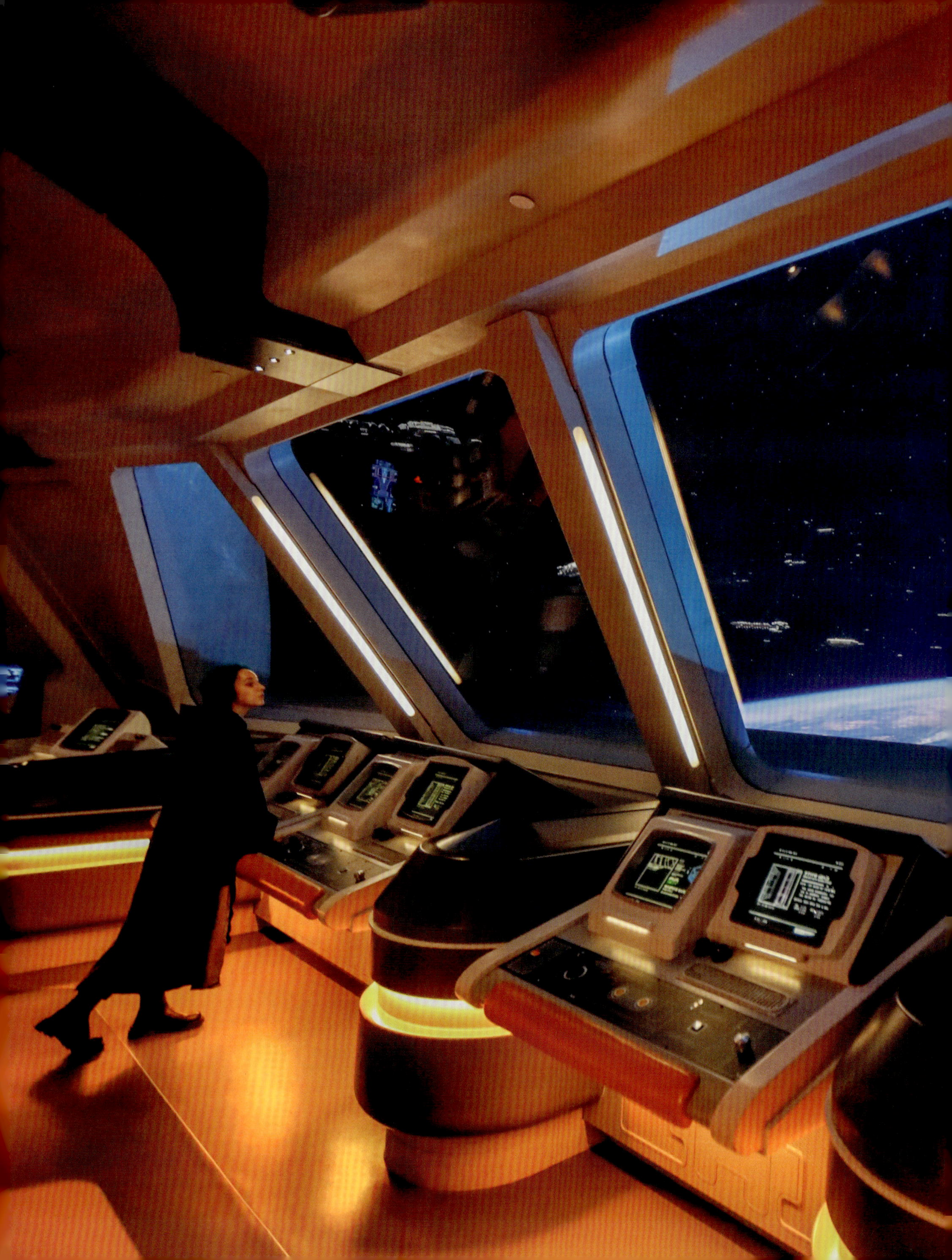

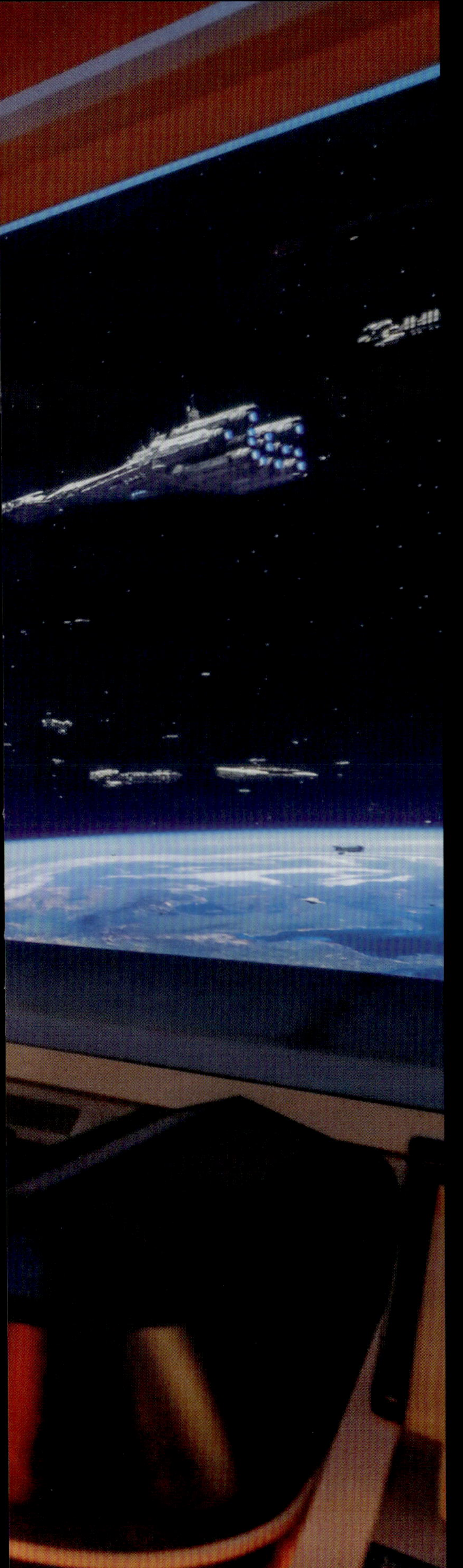

STAR WARS: GALACTIC STAR-CRUISER

In 2022, Disney's most ambitious experiential concept to date touched down at the Walt Disney World Resort in Florida: the *Star Wars: Galactic Starcruiser*, a first-of-its-kind, multi-day immersive experience that offered an adventure to another world.

Guests' personal *Star Wars* story began at the spaceport, where they boarded the *Halcyon*, an intergalactic cruise ship, for a two-night luxury voyage to the stars. From the moment of arrival, they were completely immersed in the world of *Star Wars*. Staff were decked out in full costume and makeup, with backstories at the ready to round out their characters; well-known figures from the beloved franchise like Chewbacca and Rey began to appear and interact with the voyagers; the food was straight out of a galaxy far, far away, with unusual colors and textures to evoke alien cuisine. Every room on the ship—from the bridge to the luxury dining hall to the engine room and each of the 100 guest rooms—was meticulously designed and built in a retrofuturistic-yet-luxurious style befitting the films' aesthetic. Each one of these rooms was filled with in-world activities, from learning to navigate the ship to having a drink at the bar to droid racing. Everything was so carefully calibrated that travelers could see the stars and planets outside of each porthole change with the movement of the ship each day. Die-hard fans came prepared, decked out in full cosplay and ready to live out their dreams of forty-eight hours in the *Star Wars* universe—and the *Galactic Starcruiser* delivered that experience many times over.

A guest gazing out at a simulated starscape from the bridge of the *Halcyon*

In the narrative, the *Halcyon* is celebrating its 275th anniversary. It's discovered that members of the Resistance are stowaways, after the journey is interrupted by the arrival of the First Order. Every traveler's trip was different thanks to a variety of activities and interactions that could change the trajectory of their personal story depending on their choices. In addition, a custom-built app allowed participants to communicate with characters, discover secrets and hidden objects, and embark on special missions. (Guests could also simply enjoy blue

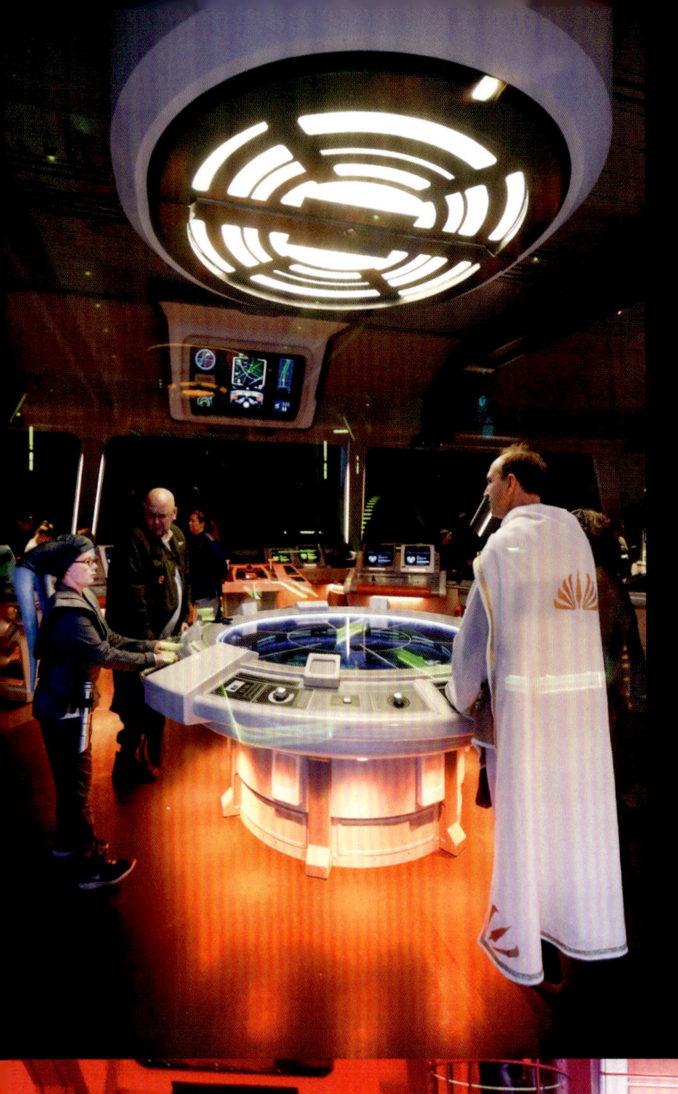

milk and a holo-Sabacc card game in the lounge, if so desired.) Even more individualized and highly detailed spaces on the ship opened as the story progressed. Travelers could choose to align themselves with the Resistance and their narrative experience would differ from that of someone who pledged their allegiance to the First Order. At several points, all passengers would congregate in the main hall to watch dramatic scenes play out between the heroes and the villains, who moved the main plot forward.

Star Wars: Galactic Starcruiser attempted to do something that no other experience had done before. A major entertainment company, leveraging an extremely popular IP, put forth an immersive-theater-meets-live-action-role-play concept that brought together story, technology, entertainment, dining, and hospitality unlike anything previously seen in this galaxy. Thanks to the level of world-building, the technology, the number of actors and performers, the quality of food and accommodation, and the opportunity to fulfill lifelong fantasies, many fans came away feeling like the experience and the memories were priceless. Sadly, the *Galactic Starcruiser* made its last voyage in September 2023, but it truly set a new standard for living stories.

Travelers on the *Galactic Starcruiser* lived their own *Star Wars* stories for three days and two nights, taking part in activities and meeting characters from the world of the franchise.

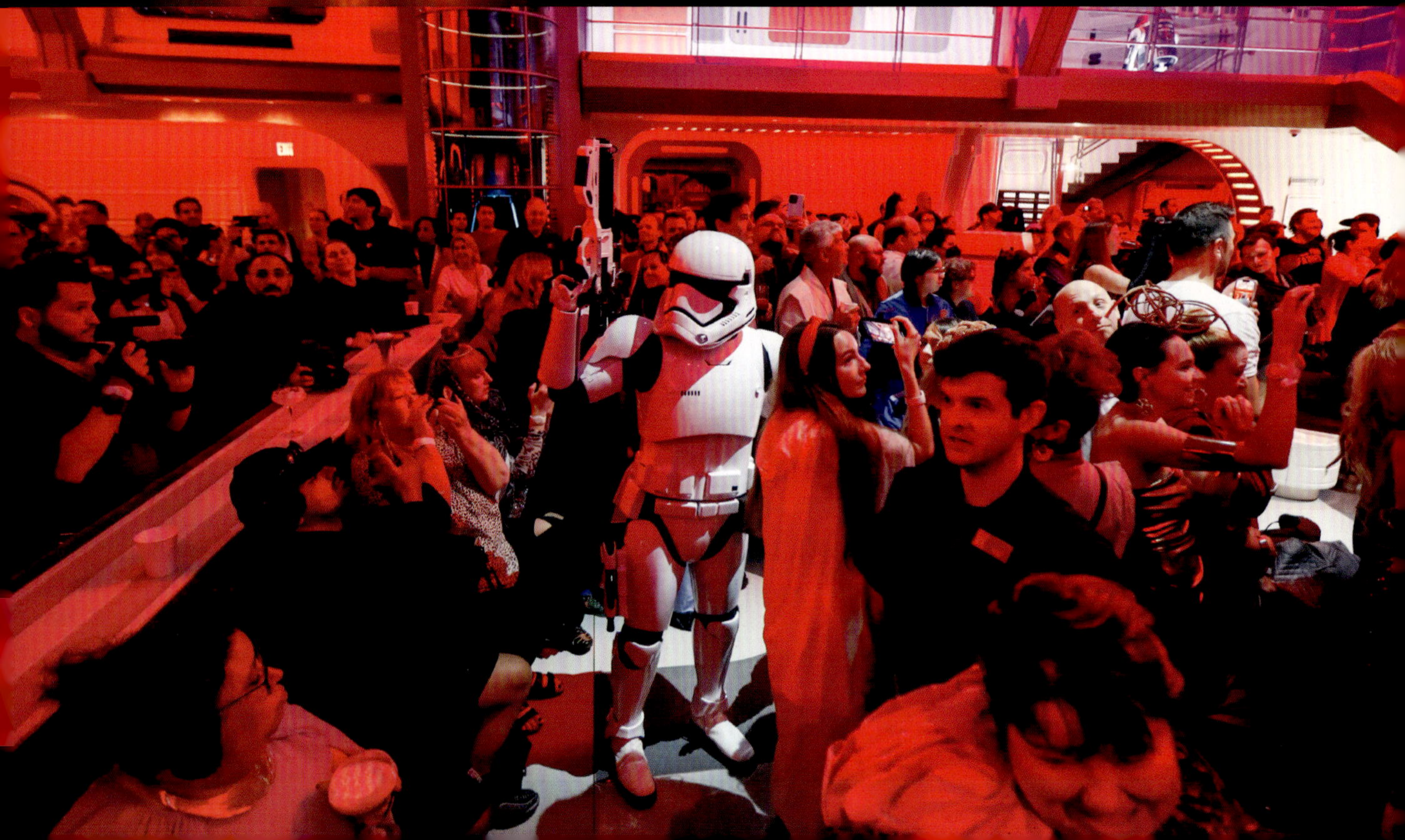

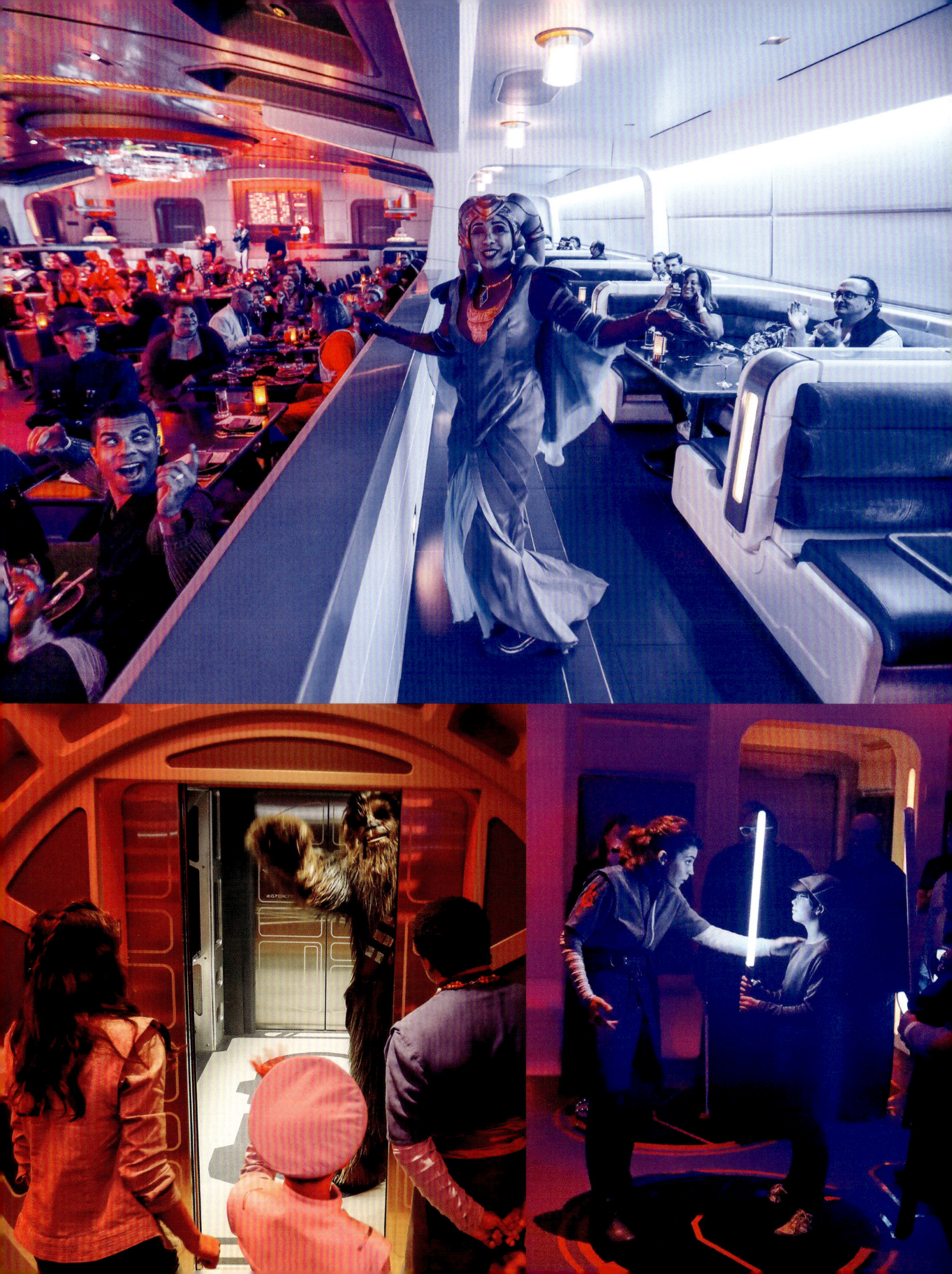

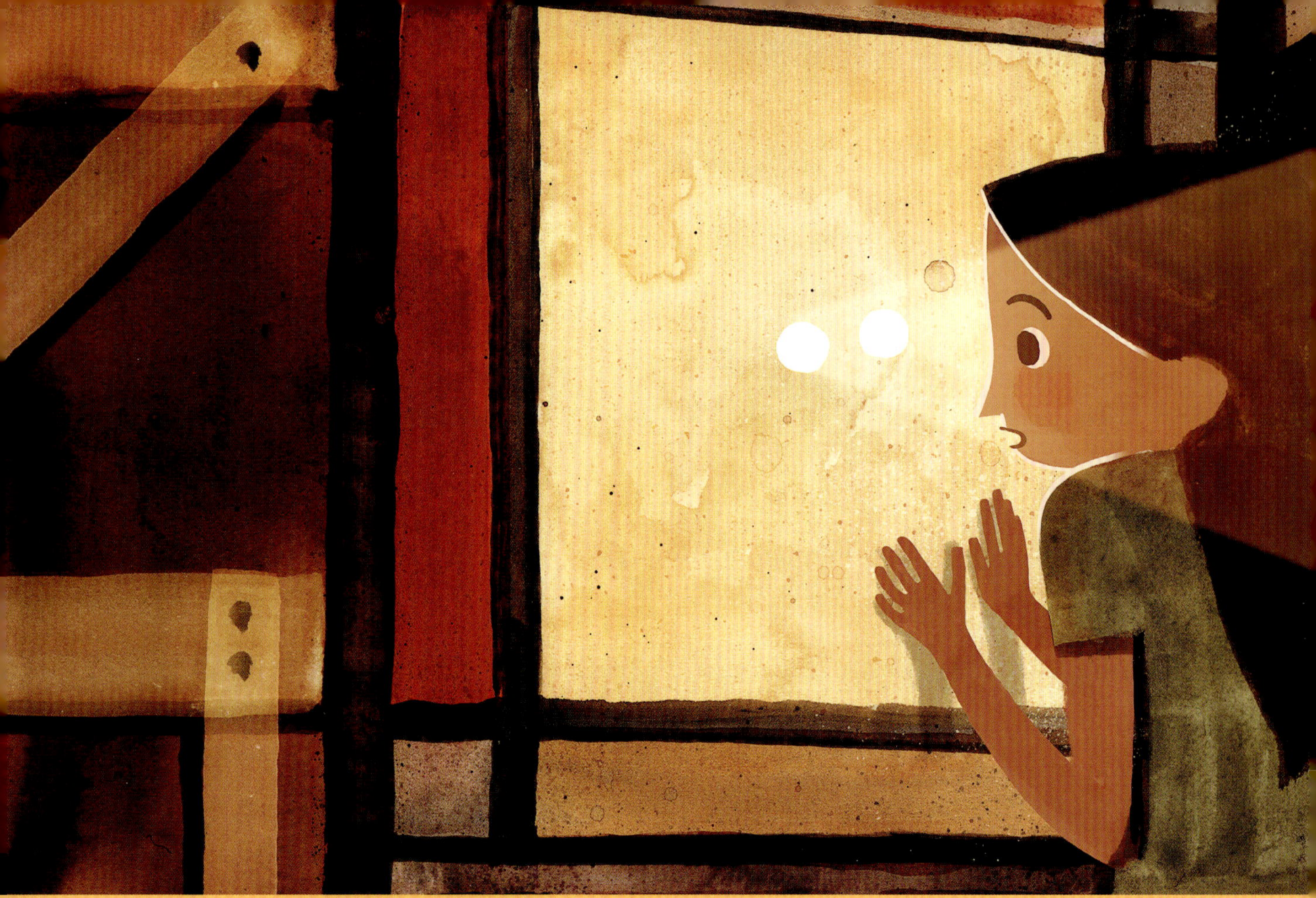

WOLVES IN THE WALLS

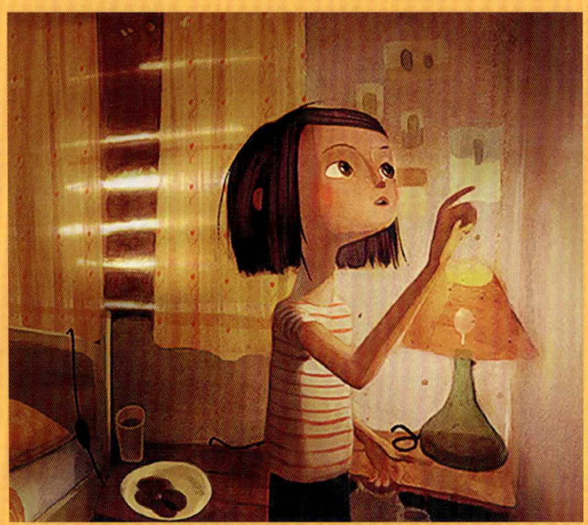

"You hear them, don't you?" asks Lucy, the protagonist of the virtual-reality fable *Wolves in the Walls*. Lucy invites you into her home to search for clues that reveal the truth about the sounds in the walls. Over the course of this extraordinarily interactive story, you get to know her personally and come to care for her.

Developed by Fable Studio with collaboration from Third Rail Projects, *Wolves in the Walls* is a groundbreaking example of responsiveness. One of the first projects to make such effective use of an interactive virtual character, it earned a Peabody Award in 2022 and a Primetime Emmy Award for Outstanding Achievement in Interactive Media in 2019.

The magic of *Wolves in the Walls* lies in the bond you form with eight-year-old Lucy. At the beginning of the story, no one in her life believes her, so she draws you into existence with a crayon. While other characters remain oblivious to you, Lucy sees you, resulting in a connection that grows as the story unfolds. This connection is the key to the experience's emotional impact. According to co-creators Pete Billington and Jessica Shamash,

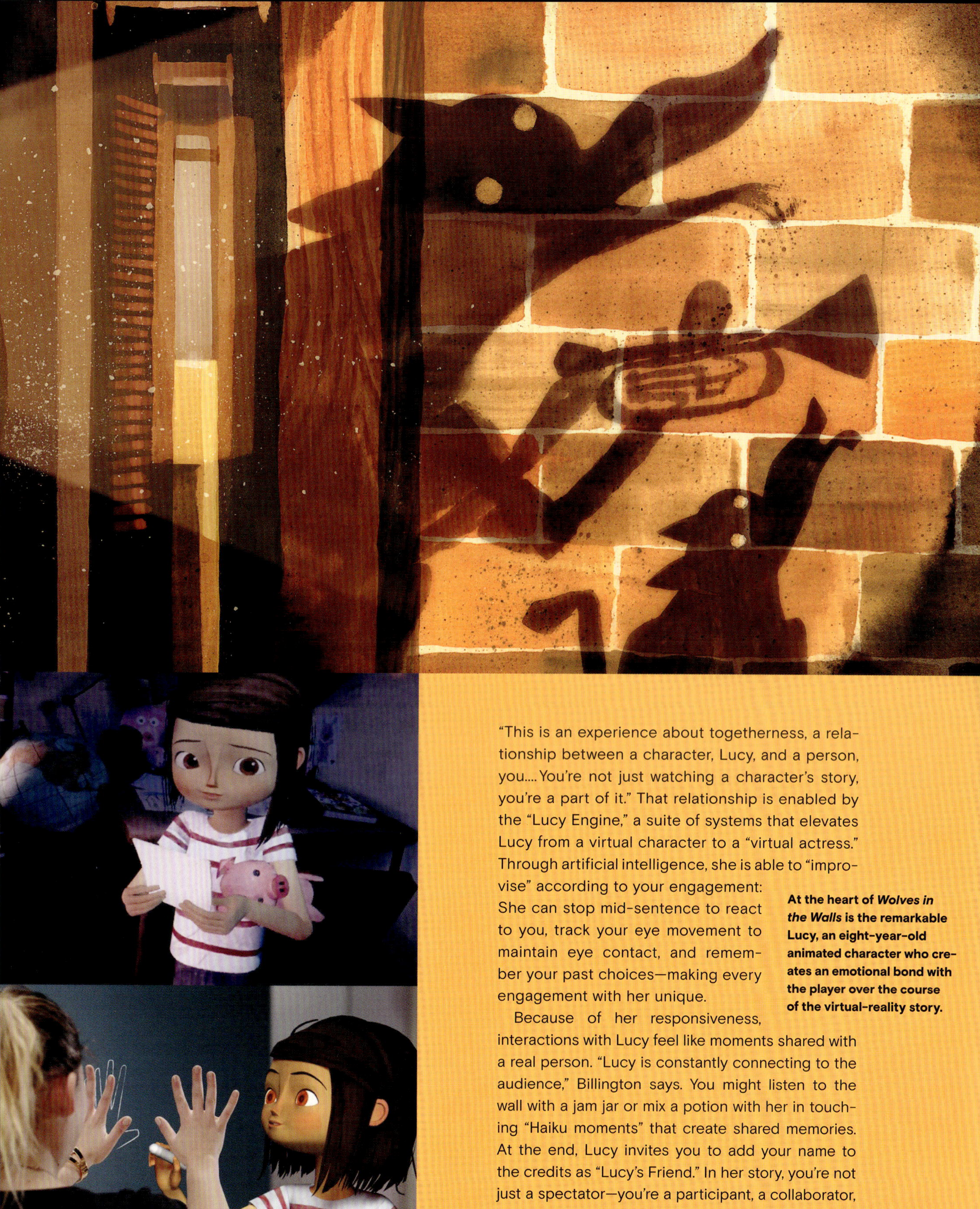

"This is an experience about togetherness, a relationship between a character, Lucy, and a person, you.... You're not just watching a character's story, you're a part of it." That relationship is enabled by the "Lucy Engine," a suite of systems that elevates Lucy from a virtual character to a "virtual actress." Through artificial intelligence, she is able to "improvise" according to your engagement: She can stop mid-sentence to react to you, track your eye movement to maintain eye contact, and remember your past choices—making every engagement with her unique.

At the heart of *Wolves in the Walls* is the remarkable Lucy, an eight-year-old animated character who creates an emotional bond with the player over the course of the virtual-reality story.

Because of her responsiveness, interactions with Lucy feel like moments shared with a real person. "Lucy is constantly connecting to the audience," Billington says. You might listen to the wall with a jam jar or mix a potion with her in touching "Haiku moments" that create shared memories. At the end, Lucy invites you to add your name to the credits as "Lucy's Friend." In her story, you're not just a spectator—you're a participant, a collaborator, and a companion.

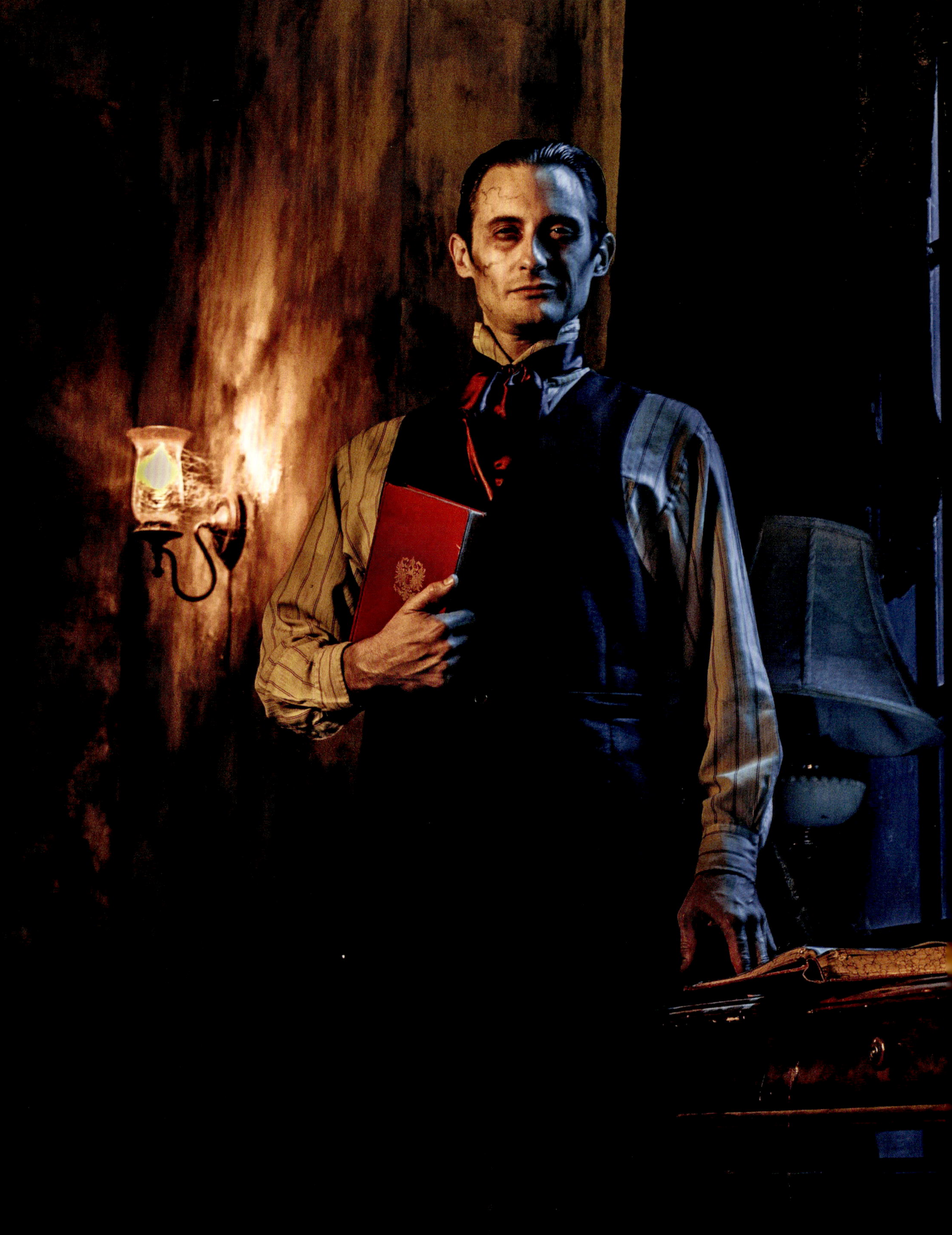

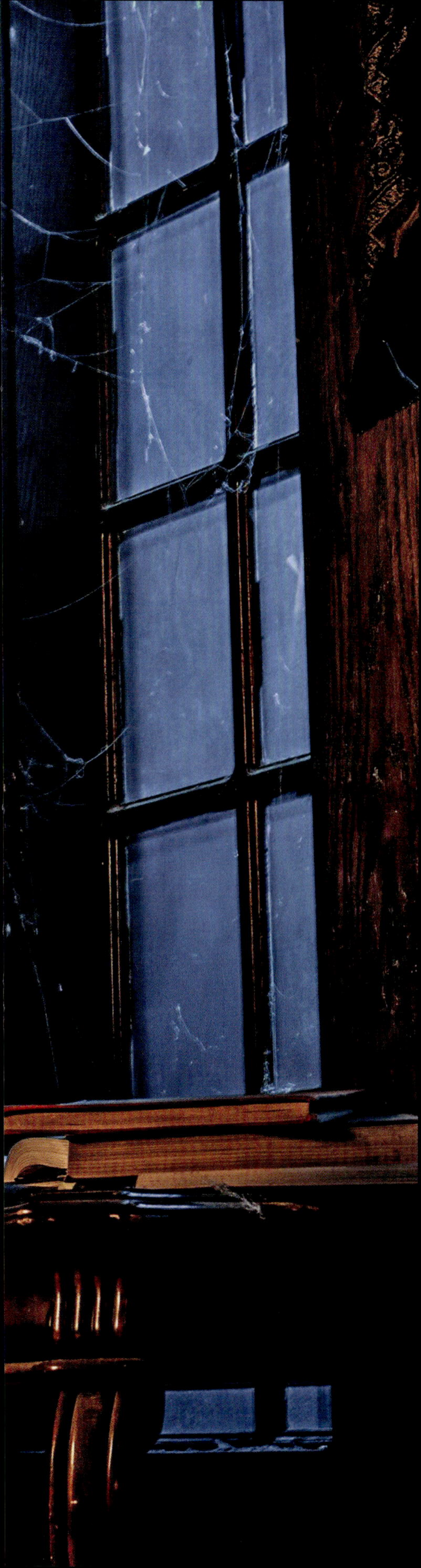

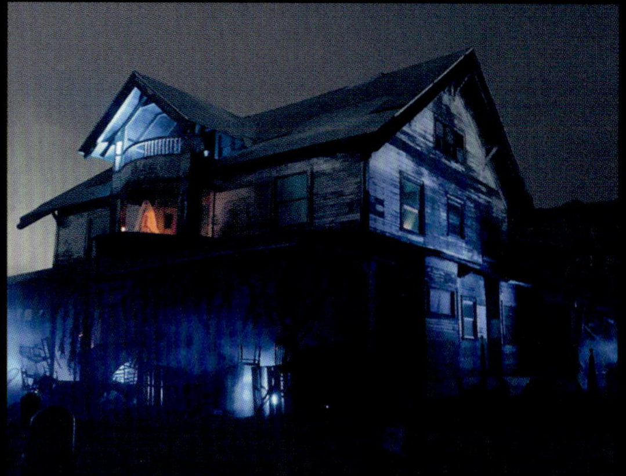

DELUSION

Fear reaches new heights at Los Angeles-based immersive horror company Delusion, which transcends the typical haunted-house concept by blending compelling storytelling, audience participation, and cinematic-level production techniques. Crafted primarily by writer, director, and stunt coordinator Jon Braver, Delusion unveils a brand-new experience nearly every September, giving fans something to look forward to each Halloween season.

***Clockwise from left:* One of the vampiric characters from *His Crimson Queen*, Delusion's 2016 production; the company's main venue from 2021 to 2023, the historic Phillips Mansion in Pomona, California; a character from 2023's *Nocturnes and Nightmares*, Ruth, reading a note aloud to the gathered audience.**

Braver draws on the surrounding Hollywood community to assemble exceptional teams of practical-effects and makeup artists, stunt performers, sound designers, and more. These teams ensure that all the senses are engaged throughout, creating a visceral and immersive adventure.

Another strength of Delusion's strategy is tailoring the experience to its specific location, such as an abandoned house or school. As Braver explains,

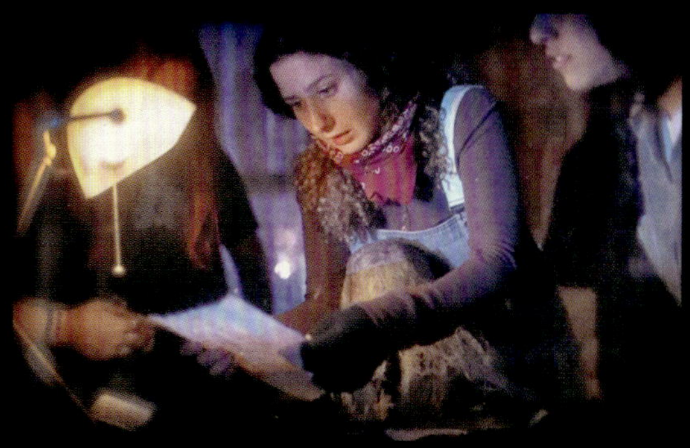

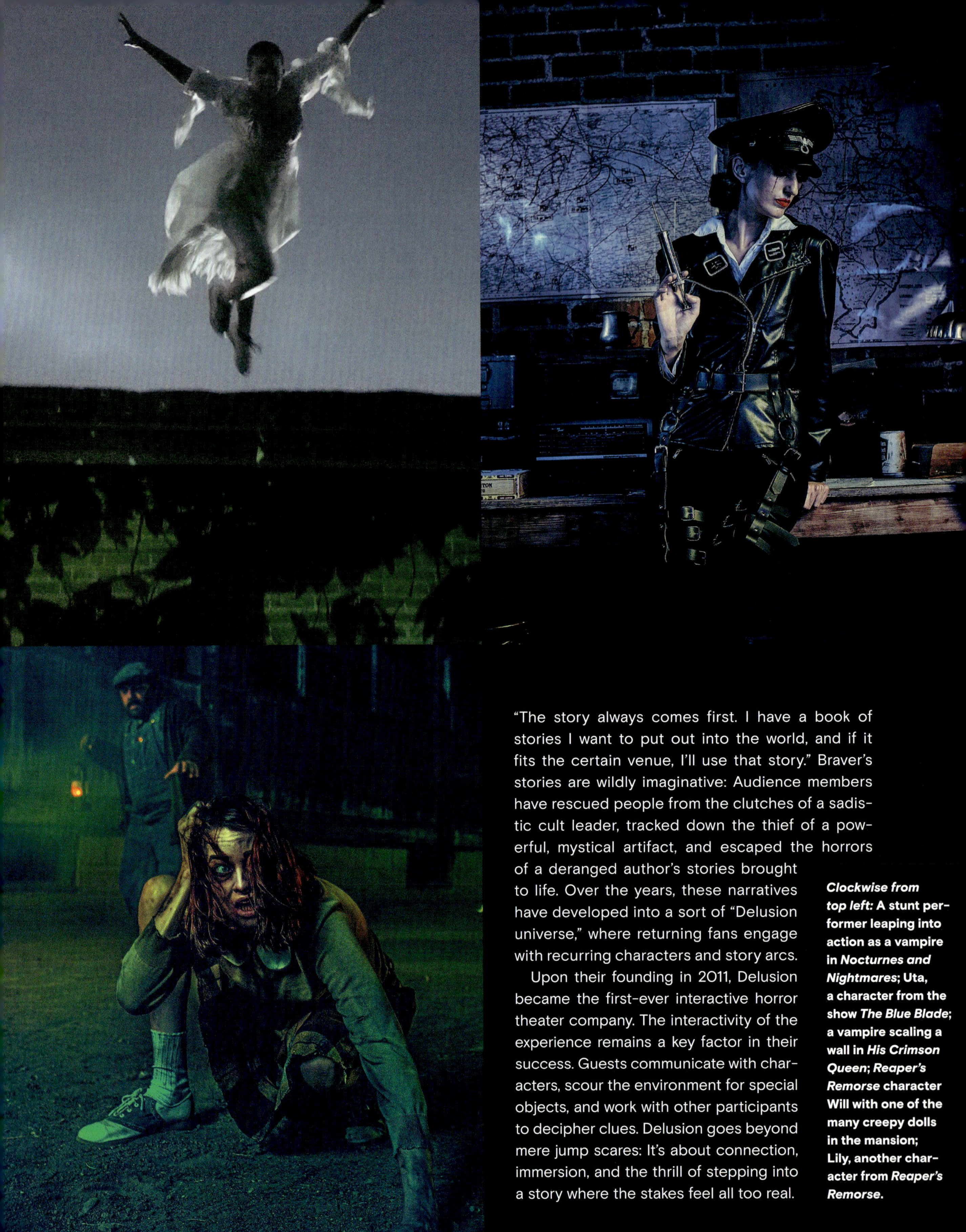

"The story always comes first. I have a book of stories I want to put out into the world, and if it fits the certain venue, I'll use that story." Braver's stories are wildly imaginative: Audience members have rescued people from the clutches of a sadistic cult leader, tracked down the thief of a powerful, mystical artifact, and escaped the horrors of a deranged author's stories brought to life. Over the years, these narratives have developed into a sort of "Delusion universe," where returning fans engage with recurring characters and story arcs.

Upon their founding in 2011, Delusion became the first-ever interactive horror theater company. The interactivity of the experience remains a key factor in their success. Guests communicate with characters, scour the environment for special objects, and work with other participants to decipher clues. Delusion goes beyond mere jump scares: It's about connection, immersion, and the thrill of stepping into a story where the stakes feel all too real.

Clockwise from top left: **A stunt performer leaping into action as a vampire in *Nocturnes and Nightmares*; Uta, a character from the show *The Blue Blade*; a vampire scaling a wall in *His Crimson Queen*; *Reaper's Remorse* character Will with one of the many creepy dolls in the mansion; Lily, another character from *Reaper's Remorse*.**

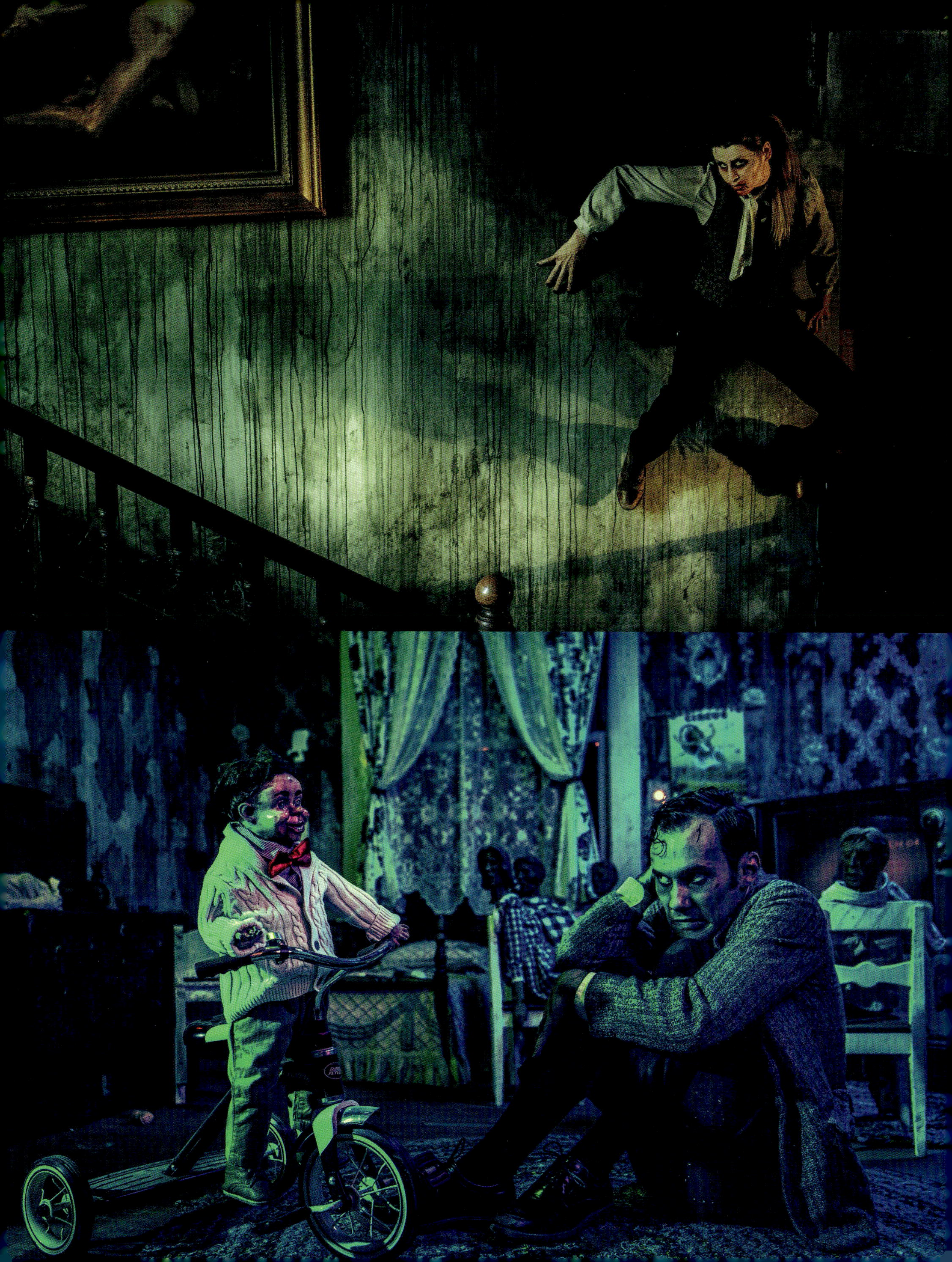

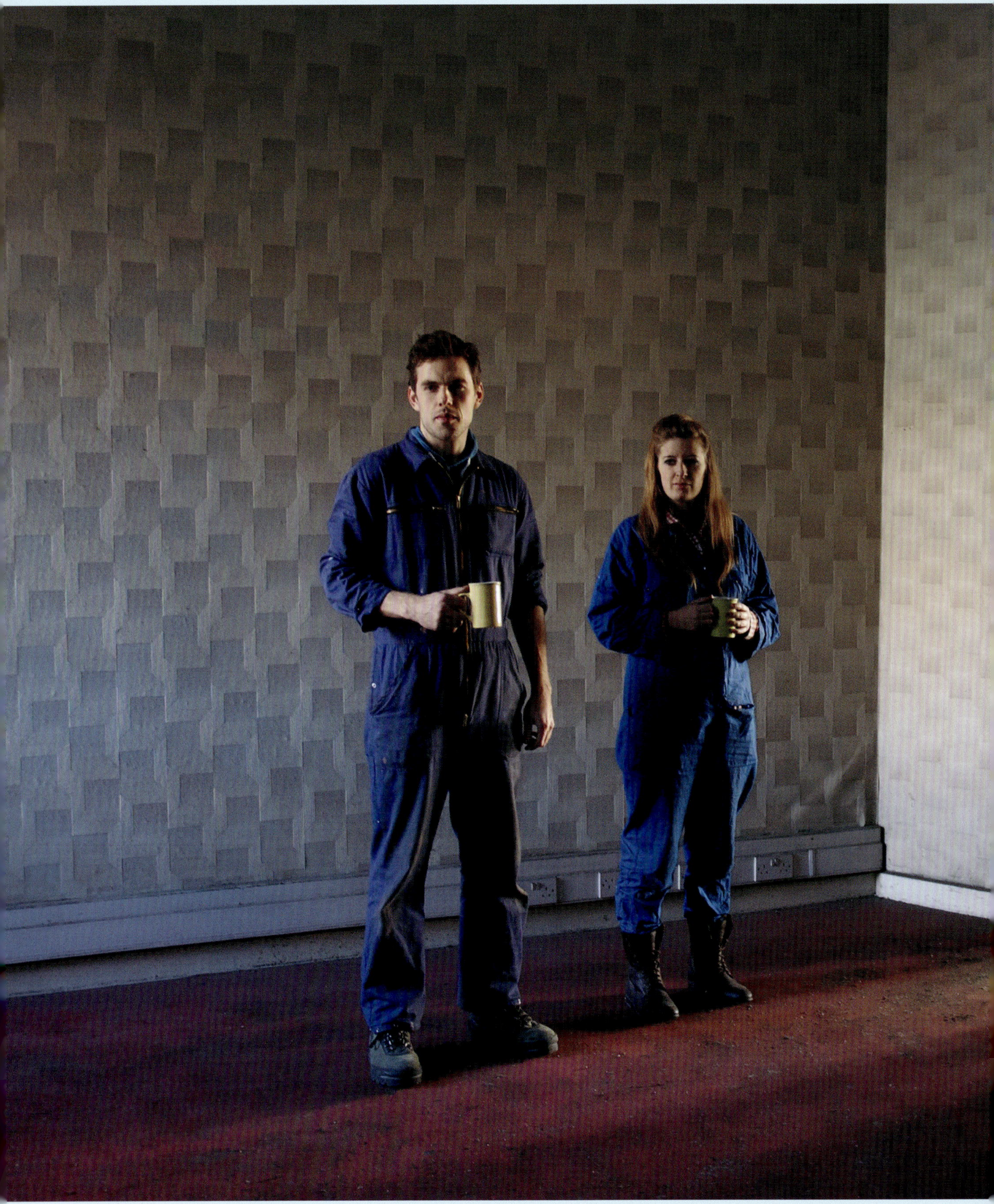

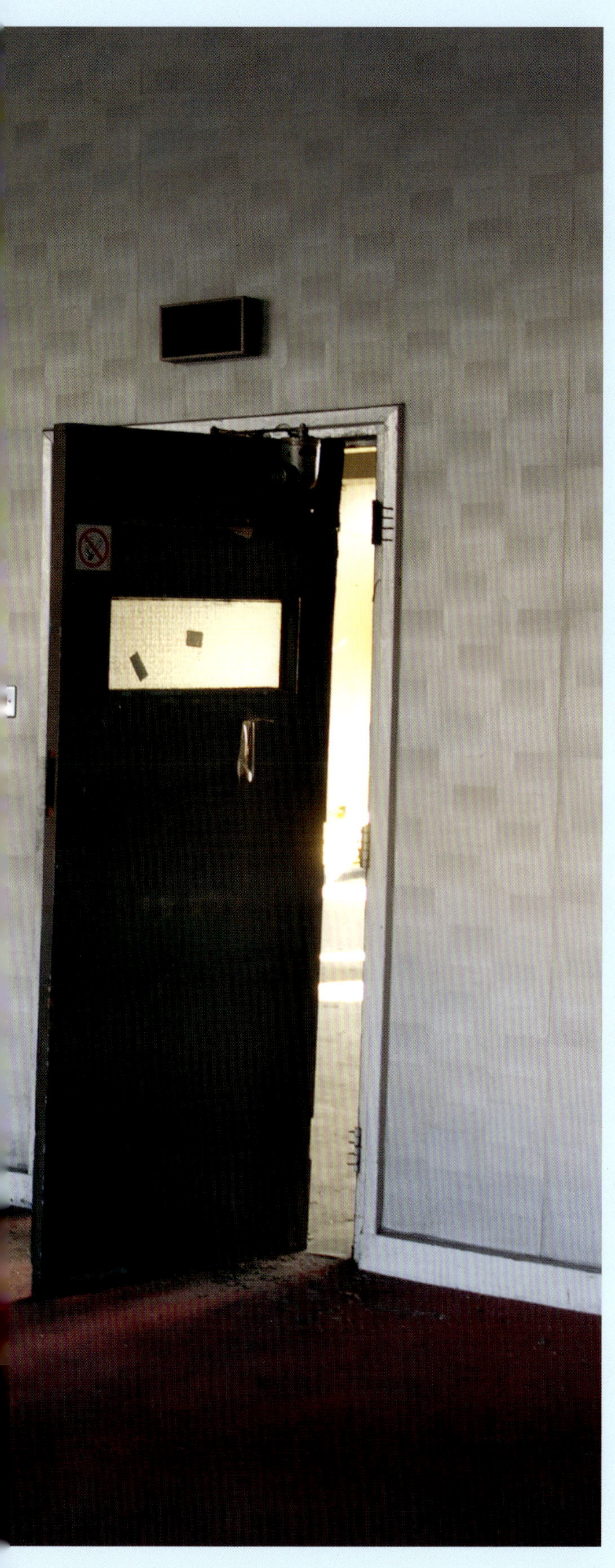

YOU ME BUM BUM TRAIN

You Me Bum Bum Train is a once-in-a-lifetime experience that sends you hurtling through a whirlwind of inconceivable scenes, each one with you as the star. Over the course of the sixty-minute journey, you play many different characters as the sole participant—or "passenger"—in elaborate scenarios brought to life by hundreds of live actors and meticulously crafted sets. How you respond is up to you, and the unfolding action evolves according to the choices you make. While the specifics are kept secret (all passengers are sworn to secrecy), those who have taken part say it is "exhilarating," "transformative," and "life-changing."

The experience ignites a sense of childlike wonder as you find yourself in scenarios you thought you could only dream of—some wildly surreal, some disarmingly mundane. The attention to detail is so precise that it feels less like acting and more like living flashes of many different lives. With no script and no one to follow, you're forced to think on your feet, respond in the moment, and trust your instincts. That challenge can be surprisingly empowering—it reminds you that you have the agency to live however you want.

Morgan Lloyd and Kate Bond, founders and creators of *You Me Bum Bum Train*.

Behind the scenes, the story of *You Me Bum Bum Train* is just as extraordinary. Founders Kate Bond and Morgan Lloyd created the show in 2004 as a series of London-based pop-ups. As it became even more elaborate and developed, it attracted a cult following. When the ticket lottery (you can only get a ticket by entering and winning) reopened in 2024 after an eight-year hiatus, more than 120,000 people applied within the first minute. With only one passenger admitted at a time and tickets priced at $100, the show remains a true labor of love. Several thousand volunteers—many of whom joined simply to help it exist, even if they never got to "ride" themselves—have come together to create this remarkable production. Their selfless dedication speaks to the profound impact of the experience and the community it inspires.

If you're lucky enough to board *You Me Bum Bum Train*, you'll never forget it. The immense amount of work, care, and creativity behind it make it one of the most legendary immersive experiences of all time.

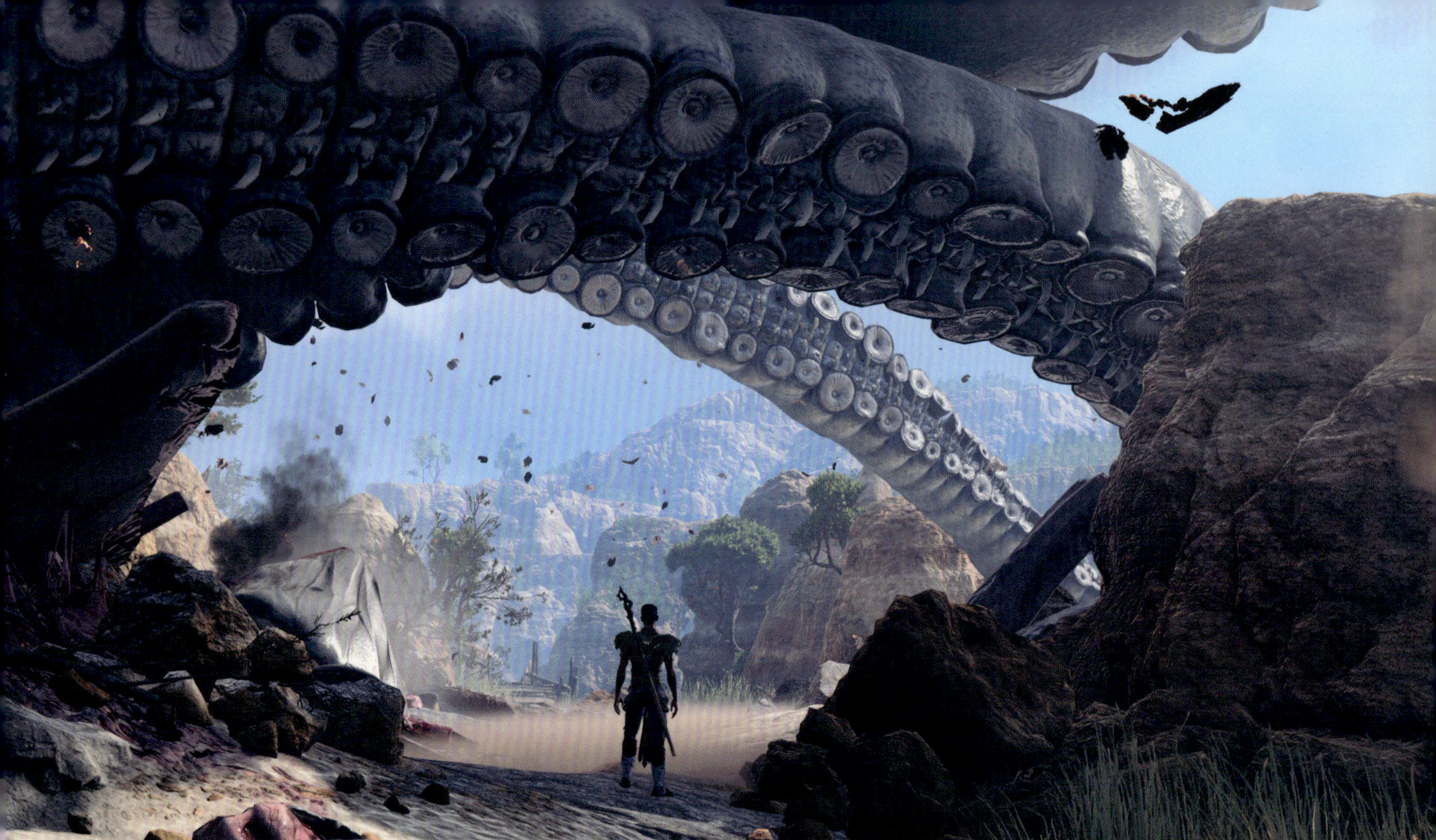

BALDUR'S GATE 3

More than fifty years after its release, *Dungeons & Dragons* (or *D&D*, for short) remains a hugely popular staple of role-playing games (RPGs). About 85 million people have played it, and it earned $1.17 billion dollars for publisher Wizards of the Coast in 2024—a staggering number for a game that originally came out in 1974. With the advent of video games, digital RPGs attempted to replicate that success for single players. However, when it comes to allowing players unlimited freedom and creativity, they have struggled to keep up: The capabilities of preset code and existing hardware can only go so far compared with games that are actively facilitated by human participants. A video game that could approximate the limitless possibilities of *D&D* remained out of reach—until Larian Studios released *Baldur's Gate 3*.

Based on the *D&D* IP, the game draws heavily from the fifth edition of its tabletop incarnation, reproducing its mechanics almost exactly. Players begin by creating their character, selecting from an impressive array of races, classes, and backgrounds. From there, they're dropped right into the Forgotten Realms—one of fans' favorite *D&D* settings—and given near absolute freedom. While the overall story goals and main characters are consistent between playthroughs, the manner in which players achieve those goals or form relationships with those characters is more or less up to them.

Unlike in other video games, where players might have one path forward or at most a handful of potential solutions, challenges in *Baldur's Gate 3* can be tackled in a myriad of ways. Just like in *D&D* (or indeed in real life), you can face conflicts head-on with guns blazing, use diplomacy and charm to win people over, sneak around and employ subterfuge, or even sometimes ignore the issue altogether. Each approach is acceptable and can be undertaken through a wide variety of skills, items, and dialogue options. It's an incredible achievement on the part of the developer to not only allow for such creativity—which requires keen foresight and complex systems to successfully anticipate and execute—but also reward ingenuity through unique and interesting outcomes that mean no two playthroughs are exactly alike.

The choices that players make don't take place in a vacuum. The rich world of *Baldur's Gate 3* is

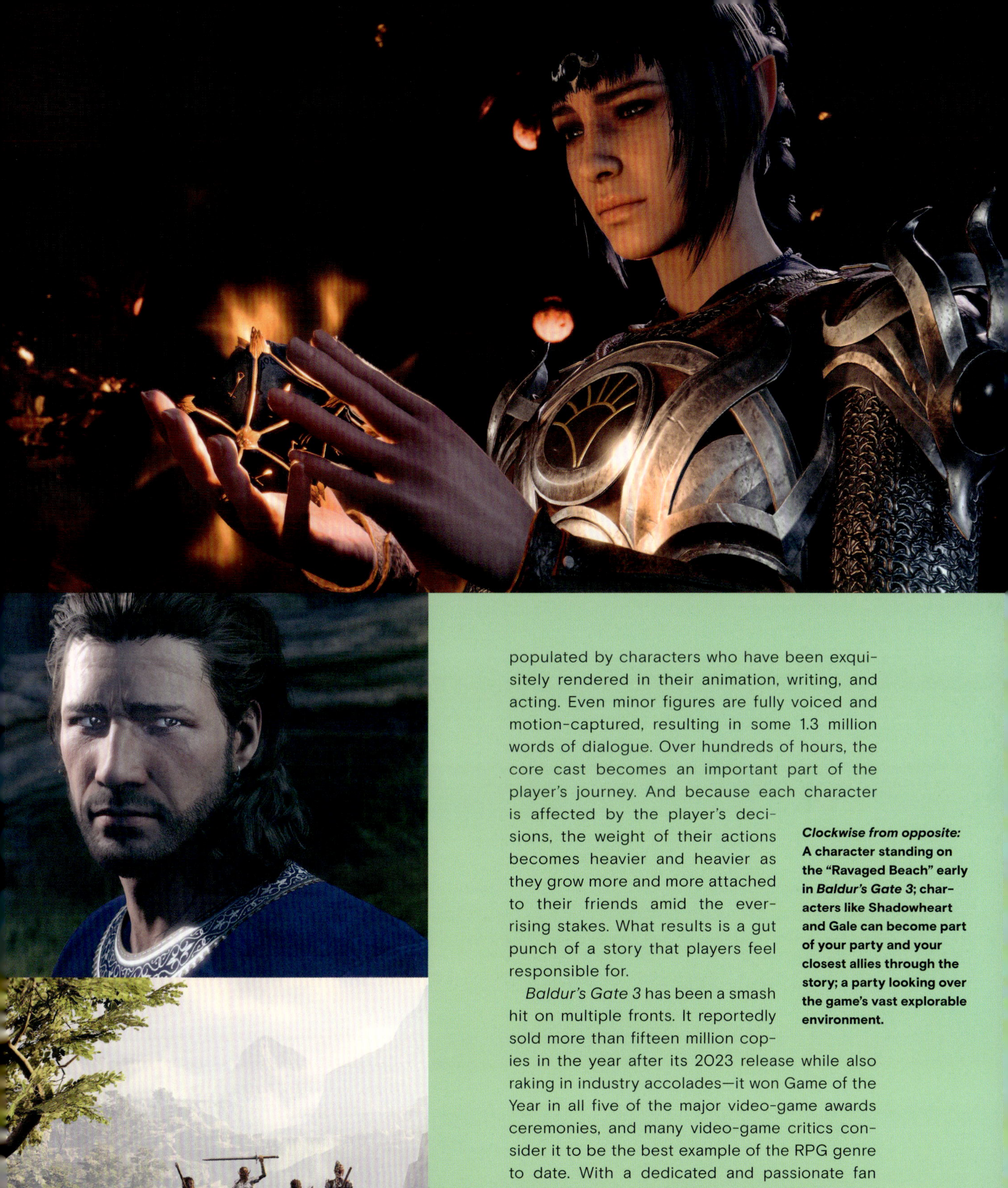

populated by characters who have been exquisitely rendered in their animation, writing, and acting. Even minor figures are fully voiced and motion-captured, resulting in some 1.3 million words of dialogue. Over hundreds of hours, the core cast becomes an important part of the player's journey. And because each character is affected by the player's decisions, the weight of their actions becomes heavier and heavier as they grow more and more attached to their friends amid the ever-rising stakes. What results is a gut punch of a story that players feel responsible for.

***Clockwise from opposite:* A character standing on the "Ravaged Beach" early in *Baldur's Gate 3*; characters like Shadowheart and Gale can become part of your party and your closest allies through the story; a party looking over the game's vast explorable environment.**

Baldur's Gate 3 has been a smash hit on multiple fronts. It reportedly sold more than fifteen million copies in the year after its 2023 release while also raking in industry accolades—it won Game of the Year in all five of the major video-game awards ceremonies, and many video-game critics consider it to be the best example of the RPG genre to date. With a dedicated and passionate fan base that continues to play and replay it, *Baldur's Gate 3* will almost certainly be remembered as a game changer.

JOHNNIE WALKER PRINCES STREET

The brewery tour has become an archetype of the beverage industry. Countless beer, liquor, and wine brands now give customers an opportunity to visit their facilities, taste their product, and hopefully leave with a fond impression of the company. But from an experiential standpoint, the offering has stagnated: After all, once you've seen one fermentation chamber, haven't you seen them all? What do these experiences offer for repeat visitors? How could they better capture the hearts—and taste buds—of those who aren't already aficionados?

In 2021, whiskey giant Johnnie Walker unveiled their answer to this challenge: Johnnie Walker Princes Street in Edinburgh, Scotland. Located in the shadow of the iconic Edinburgh Castle, this experience isn't a conventional distillery tour or whiskey tasting but rather a multisensory celebration of Scotland and a master class in personalization.

Scotch has a reputation for being an acquired taste—a reputation that Johnnie Walker Princes Street aims to defy by inviting visitors to discover the whiskey that suits them best. The first step of the Journey of Flavor is to complete a short quiz on a tablet: On a scale of 1 to 5, how do you feel about chili peppers? Fresh rosemary? Vanilla bean? The quiz is only a handful of questions and takes less than five minutes to finish, but it's designed to specifically tailor the entire ninety-minute experience to your preference.

Behind the scenes of this questionnaire is a sophisticated system powered by artificial intelligence, which compares your answers to an extensive database of smells and tastes in order to determine your particular "FlavorPrint." With that, you receive a recommendation of one of six profiles—fruity, spicy, creamy, fresh, malty, or smoky—to match your palate. From then on, the drinks you'll be offered will correspond to this profile, greatly increasing the chance that you'll find a libation you love. This AI personalization makes it possible for anyone to discover a passion for scotch, even and especially those who previously thought they didn't like it, weren't drinking it "properly," or it wasn't "for them" (as is the case for many younger people and women).

Visitors embark on a multisensory journey through Johnnie Walker's four Scottish brand homes: distilleries with distinct histories and flavor profiles.

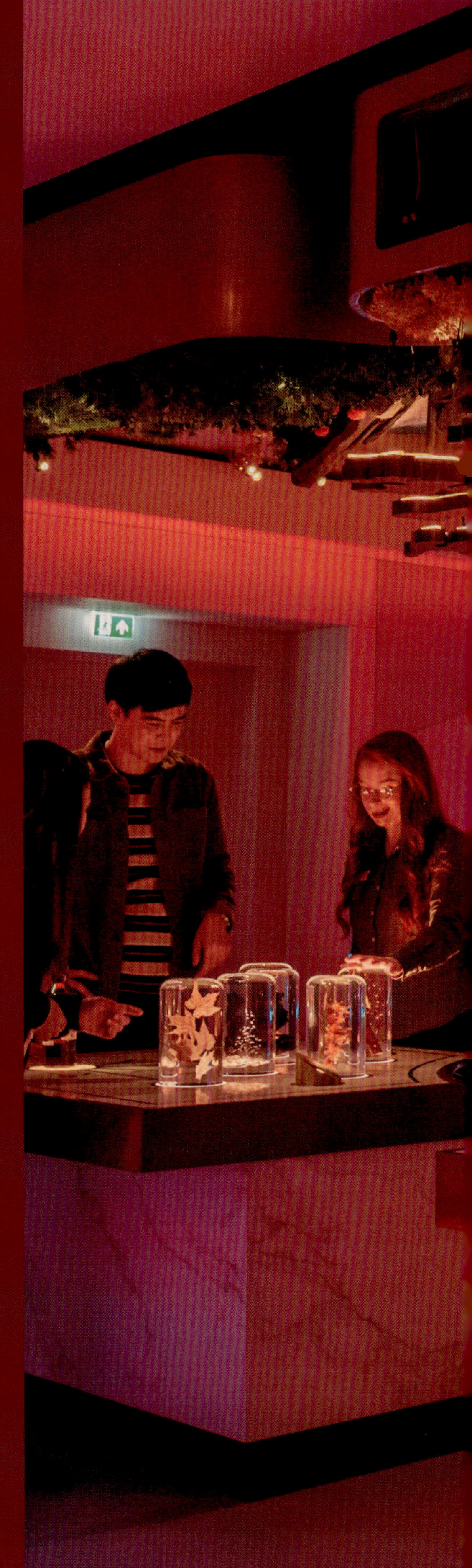

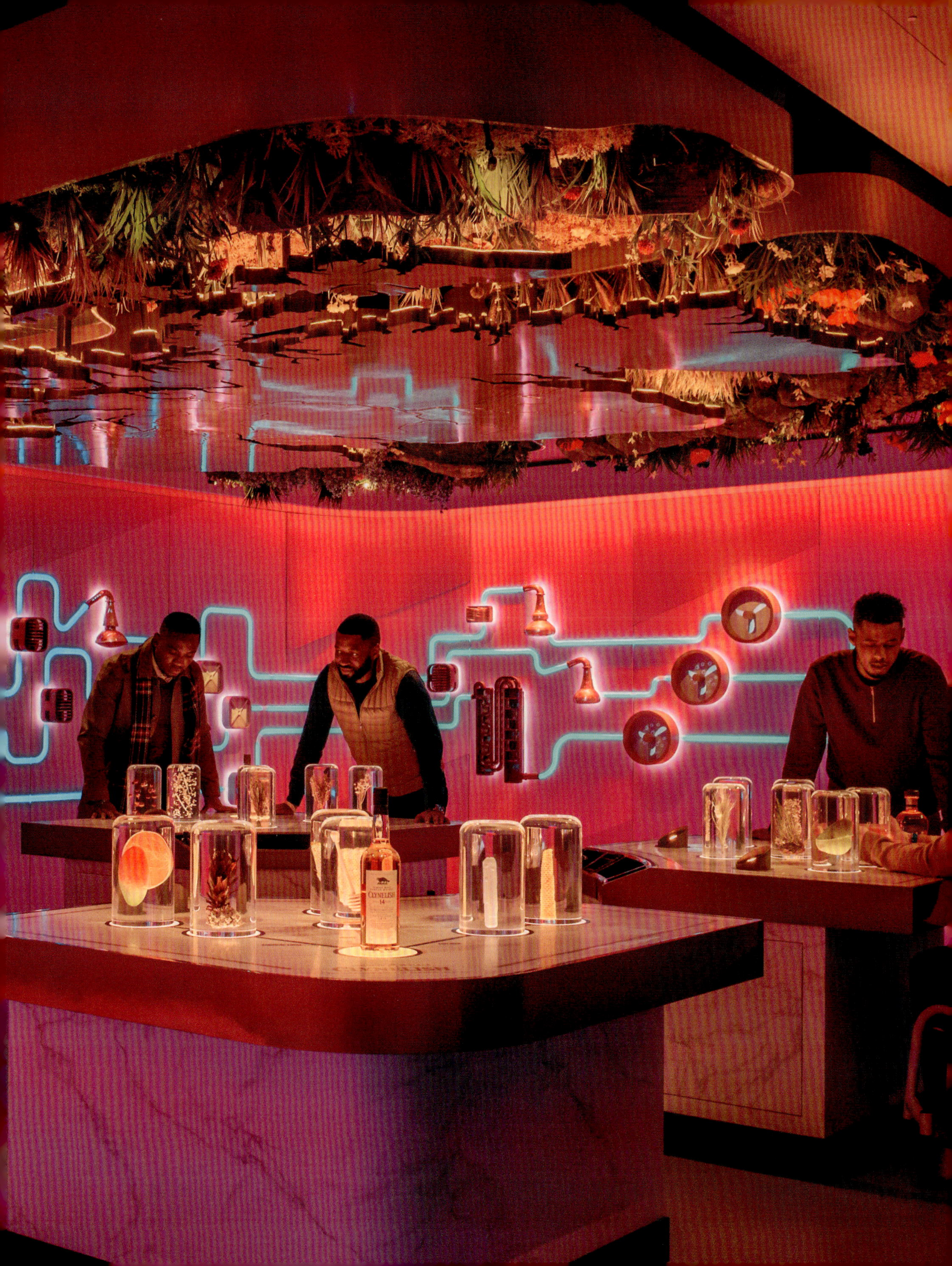
CLYNELISH
14

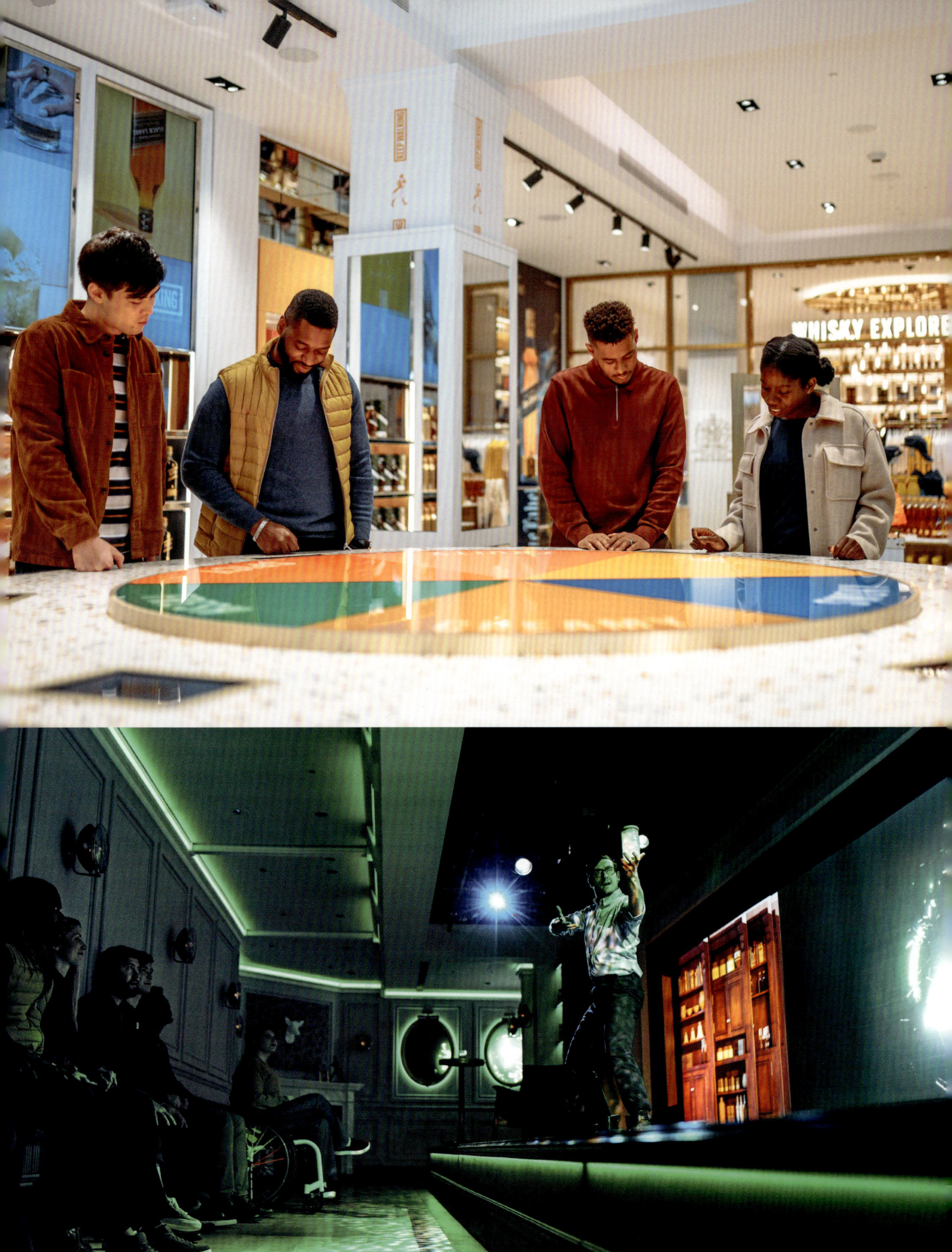
WHISKY EXPLORE

Clockwise from opposite, top: **Visitors' taste profiles are identified at the beginning of the experience through a series of questions; Johnnie Walker Princes Street is located in a historic building in Edinburgh's city center; the Explorers' Bothy, home to a unique culinary experience that pairs the brand with specially crafted bites; raising a toast with drinks based on personal preferences; a tour guide brings the history of the brand to life.**

Once you have your profile, you embark on a voyage through the history of Johnnie Walker and its home of Scotland. Engaging multimedia experiences and multiple tastings transport you via flavor, scent, sound, and visuals to the four brand homes: Glenkinchie in the Lowlands, Clynelish in the Highlands, Cardhu to the northeast, and Caol Ila in the southwest. The qualities of each Johnnie Walker whiskey are inextricable from the terroir in which it was produced, a fact emphasized in exceptional fashion by STIR, the premium culinary experience found in the Explorers' Bothy on the top floor of Princes Street. The Four Corners pairing menu, for example, drives home the uniqueness of Johnnie Walker to Scotland by serving blends from each brand home alongside small plates inspired by the flavors of their region.

By the end of your time at Princes Street, you'll have not only a better understanding of Johnnie Walker, Scotch whiskey, and the country's natural environment but also a better understanding of your own tastes and preferences (and, perhaps, a new favorite cocktail). Through leveraging next-generation technologies to create a personal bond between you and the brand, Johnnie Walker Princes Street sets the standard for experiences that are authentically engaging and immersive.

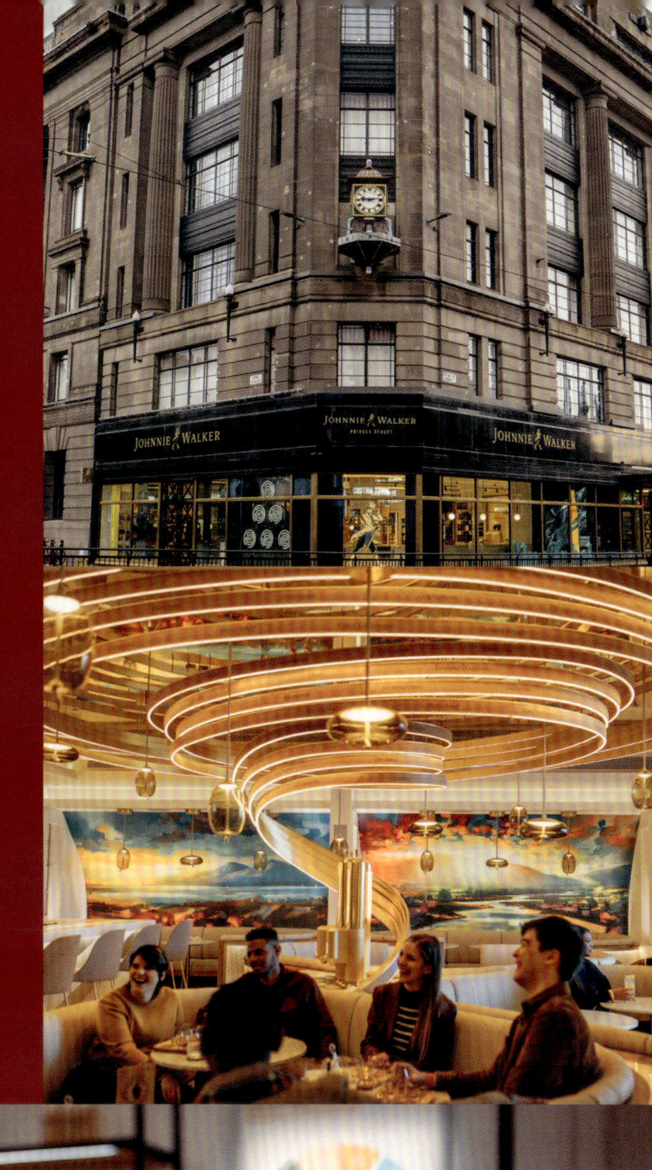

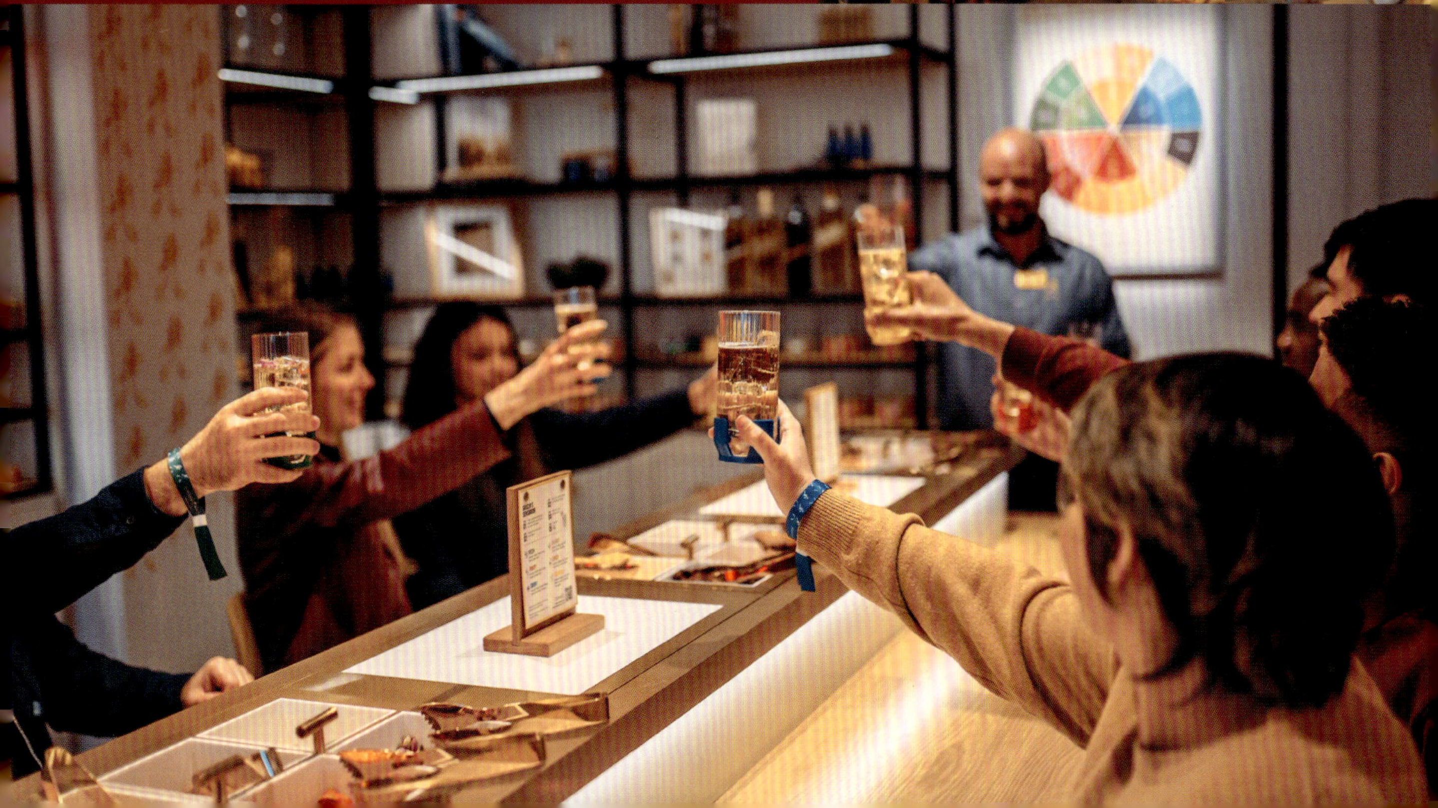

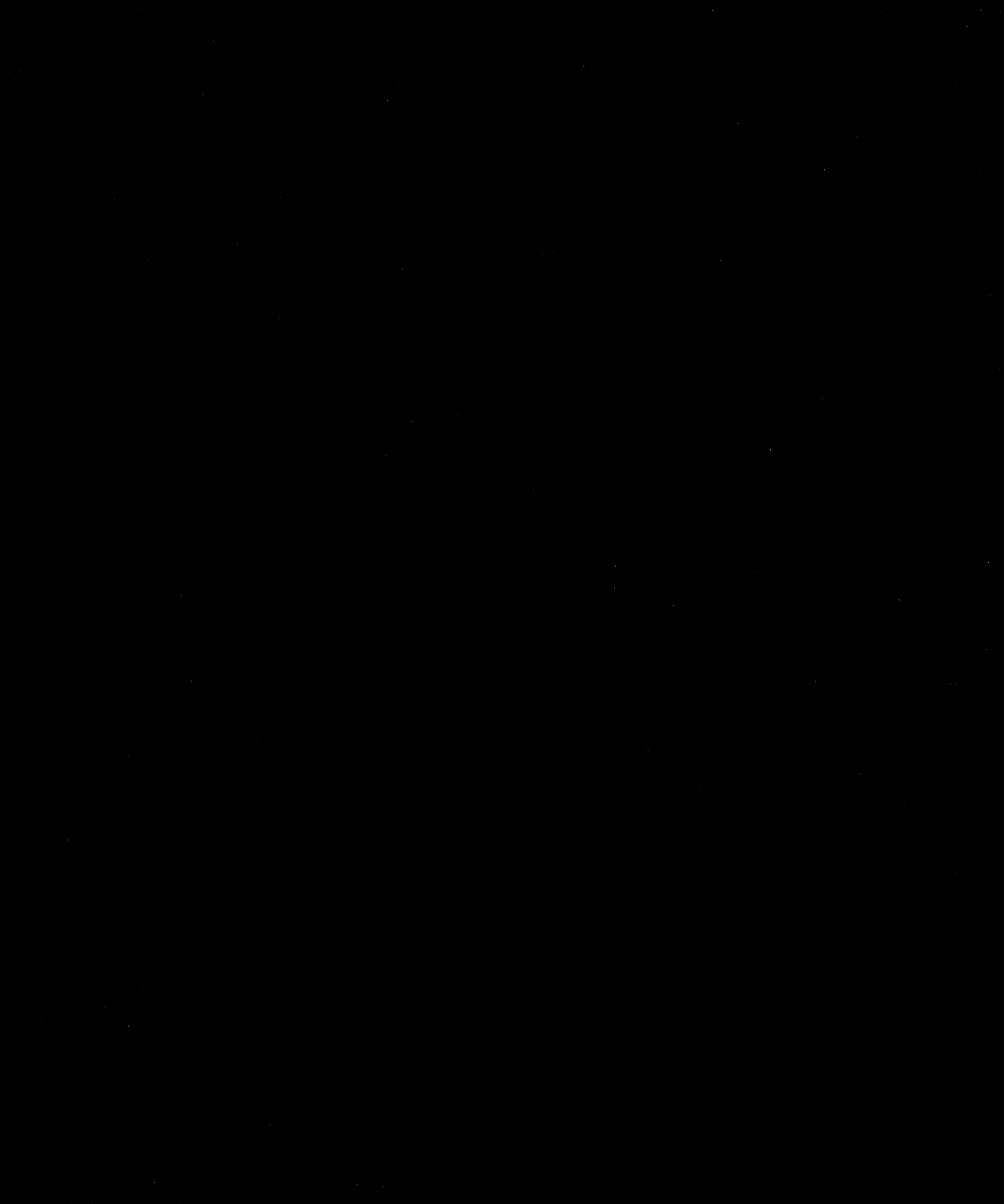

5

THE FUTURE OF STORYTELLING IS SOCIAL

In January 2025, I took a trip to Amsterdam to experience Victor van Doorn's latest escape-room masterpiece, *The Alchemist.* Escape rooms, as you may know, are not solo endeavors—they usually require three to eight people to solve (see p. 242). I've done dozens of escape rooms in my life—sometimes with strangers, other times with friends or family. For this experience, I was joined by my two good buddies and fellow escape-room fans Andrew and Brent. Together, we ventured up to the third floor of the beautiful, historic building in Amsterdam where *The Alchemist* is located.

After waiting for several minutes in the antechamber, we were approached by a disheveled, jittery secretary who ushered us into a vestibule area. "You've got to help," he said, as he took Andrew by the shoulders and looked searchingly at each of us. "The ritual—it failed. Mary's spirit is stuck in the room—the planets are moving so quickly—not much time left..."

"Whoa, whoa," I responded. "Slow down and explain."

We learned that a 400-year-old alchemist, Mary, had been studying for years to complete a powerful, complex ritual that would disintegrate her physical form and allow her spirit to ascend to another realm. But she had done it wrong, without the necessary circle of support, and now Andrew, Brent, and I had to help finish the ritual before the planets moved out of alignment. This clear, urgent goal immediately gave us a common purpose.

The secretary practically pushed us from the vestibule into the alchemist's study, a reveal that was nothing short of breathtaking. We entered a dimly lit, wood-paneled study with a ceiling so high I couldn't quite make out the top. As I looked around, I saw a large chalkboard with inscrutable equations, magical-looking objects, quirky mechanical inventions, and a gorgeous stained-glass window. But there was little time for marveling, as Andrew and Brent had already started on the first task: turning the lights on.

"Move this lever on three," Andrew said. We each grabbed a lever on the far wall and flipped them up simultaneously, and the lights came on, illuminating the stunning floor-to-ceiling bookshelves and a large, hexagonal altar in the middle of the room that had been shrouded in darkness a moment before. It was a simple task to solve, but the room instantly rewarded our collaboration and boosted our confidence as a group.

We proceeded to tackle other challenges, working through their increasing difficulty with good teamwork and a lot of banter. One task in particular leaned heavily on our communication skills: Standing on the balcony level, I worked on solving a puzzle that revealed a series of numbers. The numbers, I realized, corresponded with six large gamelan bells—three on the balcony and three below me on the first floor. Brent ran up to the balcony so that he and Andrew could hit the numbered bells in the order I called out—which resulted in a lovely, resonant melody. I was struck by how naturally we had each assumed our roles. Like the music we created, we were now acting in harmony.

The completion of the bell song turned on three enormous spotlights on the balcony level. Andrew, who was below, joined Brent and me as we each moved to a spotlight and trained the beams on a large crystal on a wooden table below us. As the beams connected, the crystal came to life, emanating light, and engraved a symbol in the center of a flat rock with a laser. It was a magnificent moment of synchronization that reminded me of a special effect in an *Indiana Jones* movie.

By the time we made it to the finale—a spectacular scene where the three of us held hands around an altar as Mary's spirit was released from the room—Andrew, Brent, and I felt more connected than ever—and bonded by our shared sense of having collaborated to accomplish something meaningful.

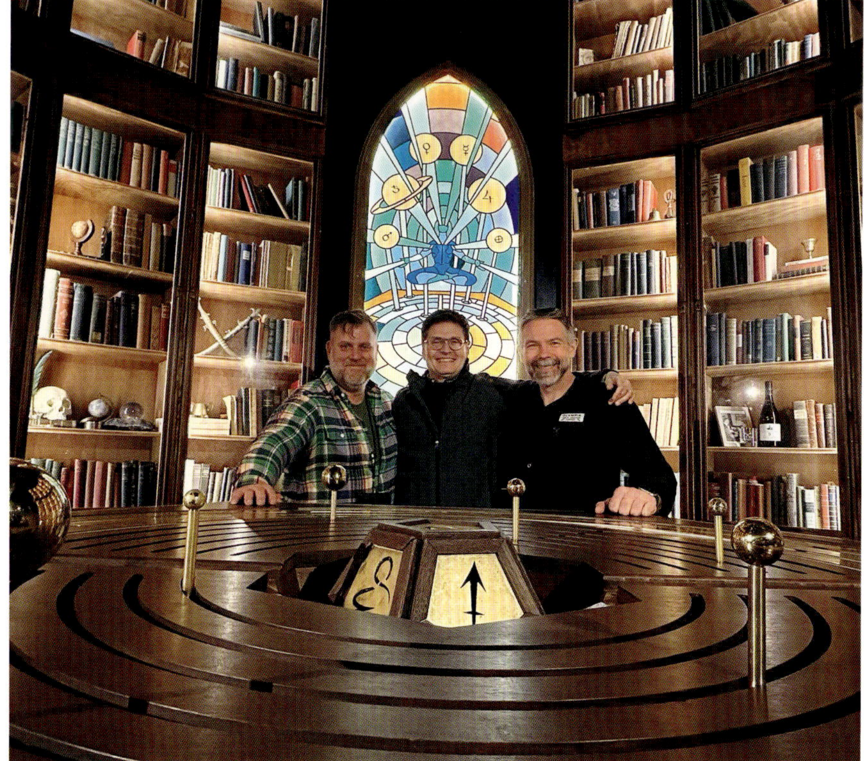

The author and his friends celebrate their accomplishment after completing *The Alchemist*.

Living stories have the power to bring us together in this specific way. When we think of social experiences, we might think of going for dinner or a beer with friends. That's a fun time, but it doesn't provide the same kind of collaboration that living stories can. If Andrew, Brent, and I had just gone to a pub, we might have had a nice conversation, but the alchemy of *The Alchemist* was that it gave us a common purpose, taught us to work together, and made us feel like heroes.

What I love most about escape rooms is how they acknowledge and reward our deep-seated, human desire to play and work together. *The Alchemist* relied on our teamwork skills to unlock the story; if we hadn't been able to collaborate, we wouldn't have gotten to experience how the story ended. This is how humans work, too—if we don't share, we miss out.

In fact, we evolved as a species to be social animals. We're happiest when we share experiences with one another. It follows, then, that we're also happiest when we're creating and engaging in our stories together.

A team working together on a puzzle at *The Alchemist* in Amsterdam.

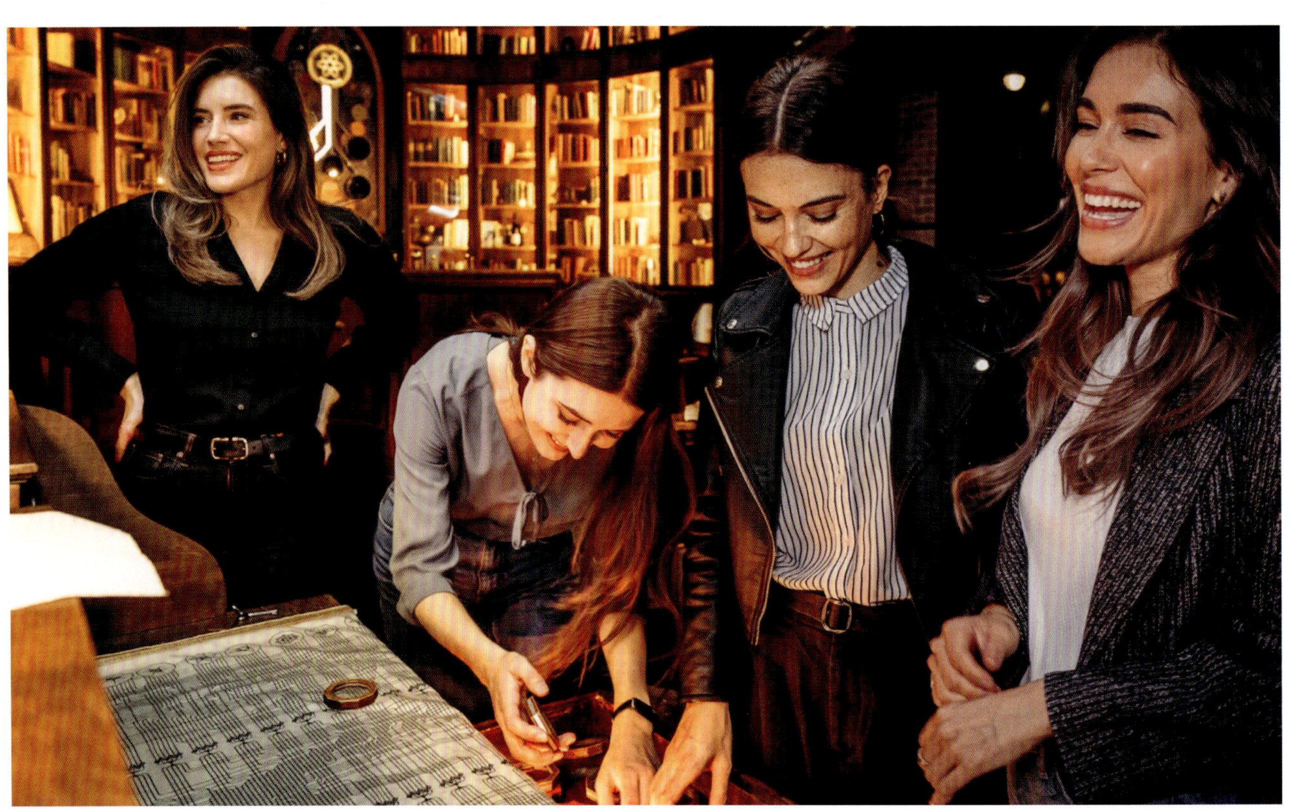

SHARING STORIES HELPS US SURVIVE —AND THRIVE

It's no secret that stories are the key to strong social ties: They help us communicate, build trust, and empathize with one another. Historically, stories have even helped entire groups of people survive worst-case scenarios.

We first shared stories, or at least recounted our immediate experiences, out of necessity. These stories gave us a better chance of survival: "I walked by that cave with my friend and he got eaten"; "I told others my story, and those who listened avoided that cave; those who didn't got eaten." The ones who survived—and passed on their genes—were the ones who listened to stories. In this way, we've literally evolved to be storytellers and story listeners.

It's no secret that stories are the key to strong social ties: They help us communicate, build trust, and empathize with one another.

Master storyteller and thirty-year Hollywood veteran Brian McDonald, the author of a seminal book on storytelling, *Invisible Ink*, illustrates the importance of stories to our survival with his own story about the Moken, a semi-nomadic people who have lived on the islands off the coasts of Myanmar and Thailand for hundreds of years.

The Moken depend on the fish, crustaceans, and sea cucumbers they catch from hand-built canoes, and their homes are built on stilts in the water. Over the millennia, they developed an oral tradition, passing down stories and legends from generation to generation.

These stories focused on the sea and captured their collective experience and wisdom. One legend tells of "the Laboon," "the wave that eats people," and how, before it arrives, the sea recedes.

On December 26, 2004, a massive earthquake struck off the coast of Sumatra, triggering a tsunami that killed more than 225,000 people across the region. The Moken legend of the Laboon, according to a story on the news program *60 Minutes*, bore "an astonishing resemblance to what actually happened on December 26."

On the day of the tsunami, Saleh Kalathalay, a Moken elder and fisherman, witnessed the sea rush out. Knowing the story of the Laboon, he sounded the alarm long before any waves arrived. "The young people called me a liar," he told *60 Minutes*. "I said, we've told a story of the wave since the old times. But none of the kids believed me. I grabbed my daughter by the hand and said, 'Child, get out of here or you'll die.'"

They and others fled their water homes to high ground long before the first wave reached them. Many on the island died, but all the Moken people survived, though their village was destroyed.

The legend of the Laboon did not endure for thousands of years and dozens of generations because it gave instructions on how to avoid tsunamis. It lasted that long because it was a riveting story that was handed down. Yet key survival information was embedded in the narrative. Thousands of years after its conception, it literally saved the Moken.

Similarly, in his book *The Songlines*, novelist and travel writer Bruce Chatwin recounts aboriginal song-myths passed down for thousands of years that speak of mountains, lakes, and other geological formations. The descriptions of geography and terrain aren't just quaint folk poetry—they're maps, verified by modern satellite imagery and archaeological explorations. The songlines guided people of the time to water in periods of drought and taught them to safely traverse vast expanses of land. In fact, it's believed that the aboriginal song-myths mapped out the Australian continent long before European settlers arrived.

These ancient stories prove that our species is hardwired to share. But it's not just for literal survival purposes that we do so. Studies show that human beings are driven to share with others partly because of the emotional payoff. A 2014 Yale study concluded that "experiences were more intense when shared," according to authors Erica Boothby, Margaret Clark, and John Bargh. We trade stories not simply out of necessity but for the sheer joy of it. When we share our burdens and our victories, we deepen our social ties to one another and to the world as a whole.

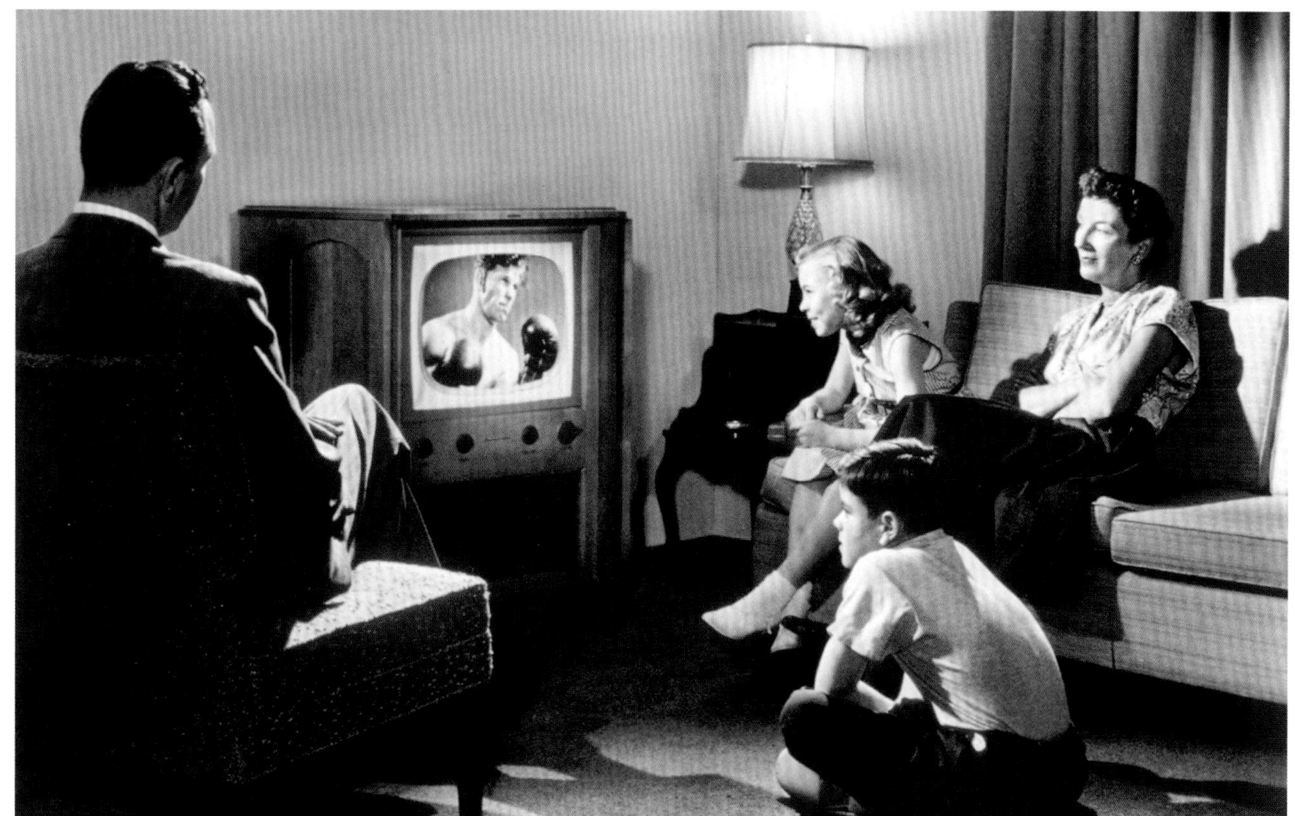

By the mid-1950s, more than half of the households in America had a television, and the average person was watching between four and five hours a day.

NO MORE BOWLING ALONE

If we get so much joy out of sharing, it's no surprise that when social-media platforms emerged more than twenty years ago, they exploded in popularity. When given the opportunity to divulge every moment of our lives, we took it. While social media has connected us in ways that were previously unfathomable, it can also—ironically—be isolating. In fact, it wasn't too long ago that we did so many more things together, in person. Kids played kick the can, cops and robbers, make-believe, and hide-and-seek, which taught them important social skills. Religious affiliation was far greater, so people gathered weekly in houses of worship. A big deal was made when a new neighbor moved in. Bowling leagues, bridge clubs, and knitting circles boomed.

Increasingly over the past several generations, though, something changed, a tear in the social fabric eloquently captured in Robert D.

Putnam's classic, *Bowling Alone: The Collapse and Revival of American Community*. He observes that between 1980 and 1993, league bowling decreased by a staggering 40 percent—even though the total number of *individual* bowlers rose 10 percent. He argues that this statistic—among many other indicators of low civic engagement—has deep social significance. People were still bowling, but they were choosing to do it alone, forgoing the social benefits of leagues.

What caused this declining civic engagement—or what Putnam calls "vanishing social capital"? With the ubiquity of the television, the computer, and finally the smartphone, the need to play together, learn together, even *be* together for our enrichment and amusement slowly but surely eroded. We spent less time in groups, less time outdoors. People didn't even bowl alone anymore—they quit altogether. While many of us do still venture to the theater to watch a movie, even this has been in decline for two decades. We are a society of passive, solo media consumers, isolated by the very technology that was supposed to connect us. When we don't participate in communal experiences, when we fail to engage with our fellow man, we become antisocial—and this leads to divided, low-trust societies full of lonely people. If this sounds familiar, it's because it is. When he wrote *Bowling Alone* in 2000, Putnam predicted much about our current situation. What he didn't predict was just how isolated—and how divided—we would become.

Living stories invite us to come together again, not to passively consume media in a quiet room but to think, play, and wonder together.

The good news, Putnam writes, is that this problem is not irreversible. If we leaned away from our social nature because technology made it easy to do so, then the problem could be solved, in part, by building tools for two-way, less passive, more intimate stories. Living stories invite us to come together again, not to passively consume media in a quiet room but to think, play, and wonder together. Perhaps it's no coincidence that Meow Wolf's *House of Eternal Return* in Santa Fe (see p. 98), one of the most popular and pioneering living stories, was literally built in an abandoned bowling alley.

THE ANTIDOTE TO ATOMIZATION

Video games, once thought to be the domain of the solo player, have become vibrant platforms for social connection. In the 1990s and early 2000s, multiplayer co-op games like *Quake, Halo,* and *Call of Duty* exploded onto the scene, turning the once solitary act of console and PC gaming into something that required synchronized, real-time teamwork. A more recent example is the award-winning *Baldur's Gate 3* (see p. 214), whose elaborate co-op experience mimics the mechanics of a game historically played in person: *Dungeons & Dragons*. MMORPGs (massively multiplayer online role-playing games) like *World of Warcraft* allow for even greater social reach, as players from all over the world can come together to collaborate on quests, tackle in-game challenges, and form guilds. In fact, many guilds run on schedules that require members to log on at the same time every week, leading to lifelong relationships. I know of at least one person who met their spouse through a *World of Warcraft* guild!

Video games are in many ways a precursor to immersive, in-person living stories. In-person experiences take the social aspects, world-building, and mechanics of co-op gaming and bring them to life. They also bring us physically together, which, as Putnam notes, is vitally important to the health of our society. Escape rooms in particular have become a popular way to socialize in real life. *Room Escape Artist* reports that escape rooms have grown from a dozen facilities in the United States in 2014 to approximately 2,000 in 2024. In other countries, they have seen even more rapid growth in a shorter period. According to Chinese event ticketing platform Meituan, the number of escape rooms in China expanded from 2,400 in 2019 to more than 45,000 in 2021.

Competitive socializing (see p. 238) is another rapidly flourishing industry that prioritizes social connection. It combines food and drink with gamified, immersive activities where guests aren't passive diners but rather players and collaborators. Experiences such as the ones offered by Puttshack (mini golf), Formula 1 Arcade (driving simulation), Level99 (virtual arcade), Flight Club

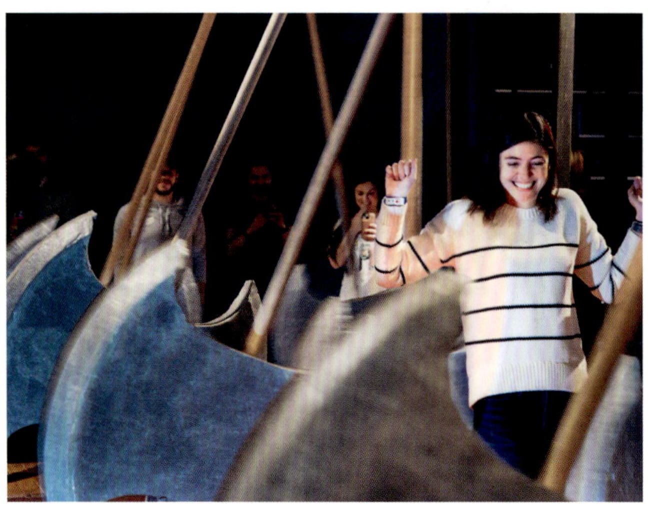

A visitor dodges obstacles on the Axe Run at Level99, located in the Natick Mall outside Boston.

(darts), and other food and beverage concepts are reinventing bars as preferred after-work hangout spots. According to research conducted by Cushman & Wakefield, competitive-socializing concepts have grown 386 percent since the beginning of 2021. Their ability to bring people together shows that technology is not the problem, and in many ways is the solution. And such social experiences answer a plea by Putnam, who wrote wistfully in the year 2000: "I challenge America's media moguls, journalists, and Internet gurus, along with viewers like you (and me): *Let us find ways to ensure that by 2010 Americans will spend less leisure time sitting passively alone in front of glowing screens and more time in active connection with our fellow citizens. Let us foster new forms of electronic entertainment and communication that reinforce community engagement rather than forestalling it.*"

Our challenge going forward is to create—at scale—many more new forms of entertainment that make us bond in person again.

MASTERS OF SOCIAL STORYTELLING

One of the most memorable communal experiences I've ever had was during a living story I participated in a dozen years ago in London at an event produced by Secret Cinema (see p. 104). The entertainment company, founded in 2007 by Fabien Riggall, is known for creating live, immersive experiences related to films, but it keeps the details—as advertised—secret.

Weeks before the date of the event, a "court summons" arrived in my mailbox, with a date to appear at a certain location at a certain time. I was to come dressed in a suit.

When I arrived on the appointed date at the courthouse, I was joined by a group of fifty others who had also been summoned. We were led into a courtroom, where one by one we stood before the judge.

"Charles Melcher," the judge pronounced from his bench when it was my turn, "I find you guilty as charged, and sentence you to ten years' incarceration." The others met the same, or worse, fates.

As we were led out of the courtroom, another wave of fifty doomed individuals entered.

Outside, police loaded us onto a prison bus, its windows blacked out, with an armed guard in the front. We couldn't tell where we were going, but after about fifteen minutes we slowed and stopped. We were ushered off the bus into a large courtyard, enclosed by twelve-foot concrete walls topped by barbed wire, surrounding a large brick building. More buses pulled in behind us, disgorging more groups of well-dressed convicts. The head guard and the warden appeared to "welcome" us. After the latter delivered a speech laying down the law and telling us "how things work in my house"—a reference to the film the experience was based on—he steered us into the experience in waves.

We were hustled inside the building, into a gymnasium, where we were each handed a gray prison uniform and a bag, each with a number on it. We were told to strip to our underwear, don the uniform, and place our personal effects into the bag. We were then taken through the showers, where we watched naked prisoners be doused with lyme.

We passed a cell where a guard shoved a prisoner against the wall, then a second guard did so, this time much harder. I began to feel afraid.

Finally, we came to a long row of empty cells. I was led into one of them—alone, like everyone else, it appeared—and the cell door clanged shut.

Wherever this was all leading, it was *not* what I had expected. It may have been entertainment, but the experience was nerve-wracking and frightening.

After some time alone in my cell, I was escorted to the prison cafeteria. I took my partitioned metal tray, waited in line, accepted the slop loaded into each of the tray's small compartments, and found a seat at one of the long tables. Many of the prisoners ate in silence, but I struck up a conversation with a young man and woman sitting across from me. I arrived at the experience alone and was relieved to

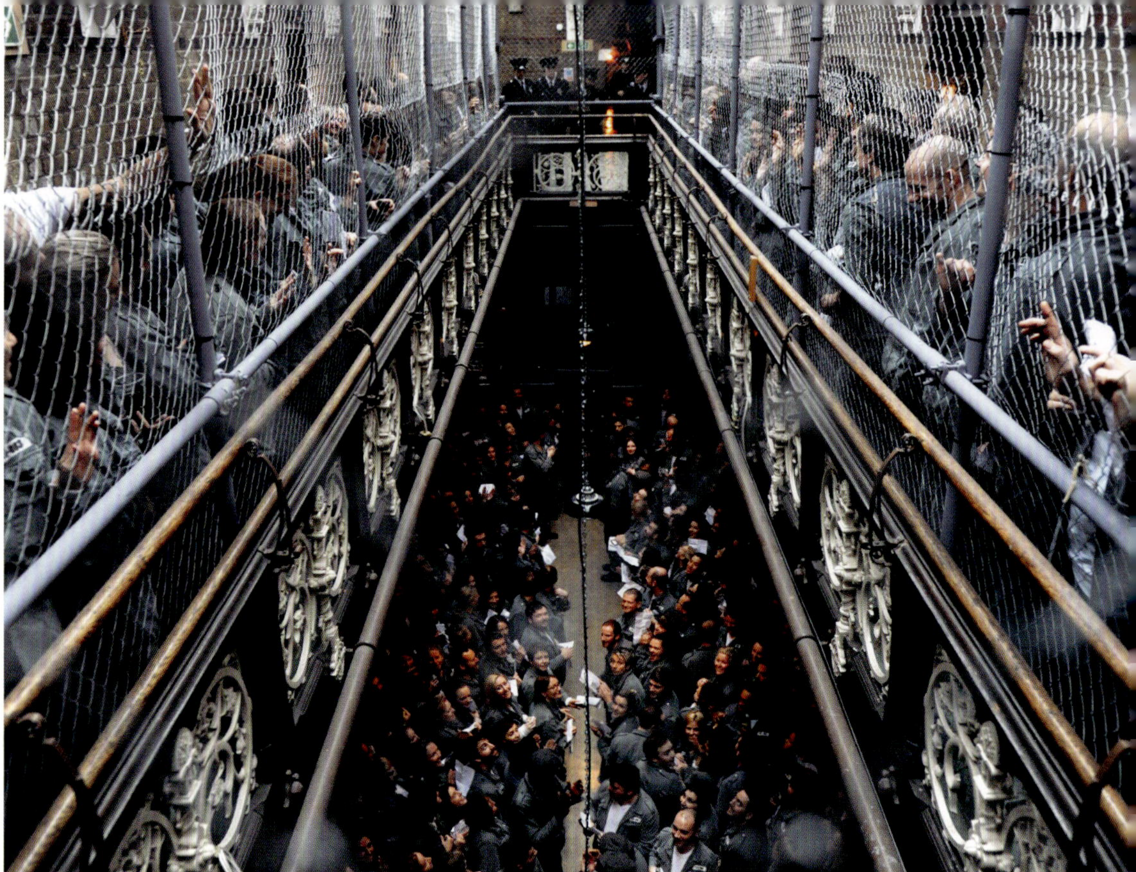

Prisoners gathered in Secret Cinema's production of *The Shawshank Redemption*.

make new friends. We agreed that the gray meat we'd been served was overdone, the rest at least edible. Even trivial conversation helped maintain some sense that normal reality existed outside these walls.

After our meal we had half an hour of unsupervised time, so I explored the prison. I passed some work rooms, including one where they were making candles. I stopped in the chapel to hear a chaplain deliver a sermon to several pews of prisoners. I paused at the entrance to the laundry room, observing guards attempt to untangle two prisoners. People gathered near me to watch. The guards gradually got the upper hand, then smacked the prisoners across the head with their clubs, doing far more damage than the prisoners had done to each other. I moved on and encountered the young man and woman I had talked to in the cafeteria. He leaned in and whispered, "The library. Knock three times on the window. When it opens, say 'Rita Hayworth.' They'll slip you a beer."

I nodded, thanked him, and followed him to the library. That beer tasted so good.

A horn sounded over the PA, instructing us to return to the cellblock area. When we'd all assembled, we watched the approach of the warden a level above us, his menacing steps clanking on the metal walkway. He stopped, studied us with contempt, and began bellowing a stern lecture. Just a few seconds in, from the PA system, came the strains of opera—an aria. I recognized it was from Mozart's *The Marriage of Figaro*. The warden's eyes went wild with rage at the interruption.

"Silence!" he yelled from the balcony.

The music persisted. And then someone in our crowd began to sing along.

It was a simple, tentative voice. The warden's look turned murderous, as he scanned the crowd to locate the offender. Another prisoner began to sing, and another, and another, as the warden tried impotently to silence us. Before I knew it, I was singing too, along with everyone, what seemed like all 400 of us singing together, drowning out the warden's berating. We overwhelmed his voice with ours, in defiance of him and also as a gesture of freedom, of strength. It was an empowering, even beautiful moment. I no longer felt alone.

A phalanx of guards appeared, each looking disgusted, and hustled us all back to the gym, where we were directed to sit in one of the folding chairs set out in rows. At the front of the gym, a guard yanked on a ring to pull down one of those old-fashioned movie screens. The lights went off. A projector behind us started up. The screen filled with white light. A movie began.

The Shawshank Redemption.

We had been living in the world of the film for the previous two hours.

It was just about a perfect ending to the ordeal. I had started out alone, been locked up alone, and left with a sense of genuine connection to my fellow inmates. When we had all joined in song, I'd felt the power of a collective voice, literally. I left feeling more human, even uplifted by the experience.

It was the first time I'd been through an immersive story capable of creating that level of unity among the audience. In hindsight, it makes sense. We're social animals. Living stories provide a vibrant new way for us to experience things together. Aside from the simulated reality, my Secret Cinema adventure felt special because I faced this unsettling environment with others, feeling similar things, at the same time. It was a metaphor, in a sense, for life. By myself, I felt empty, anxious, and afraid. It was only when I joined that chorus that I began to feel safe—even powerful.

Like everything else in life, stories are better when shared.

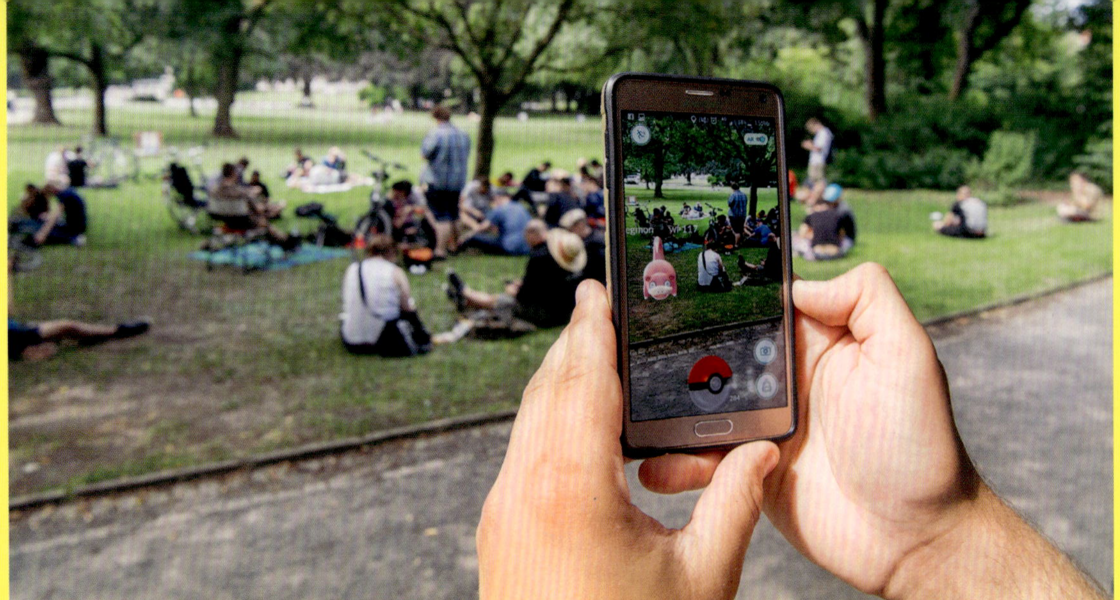

POKÉMON GO

The summer of 2016 was unlike any other—people around the globe were heading outside in historic numbers. They were taking long walks, serendipitously meeting up with friends and making new ones; it felt like a magical moment of world peace. *Pokémon GO*, an augmented-reality mobile game developed by Niantic in collaboration with Nintendo and the Pokémon Company, had taken the world by storm. Based on the beloved Japanese media franchise Pokémon (which includes trading cards, video games, films, and an animated series), the app uses AR to place virtual versions of the colorful, collectible monsters in the real world, allowing players to capture, train, and battle them. It remains an astounding success as the most popular and profitable AR app of all time, grossing an estimated $7.9 billion in revenue in seven years, more than 230 million players at its peak, and still ninety-plus million players per month worldwide.

Pokémon GO **is a global phenomenon that encourages people to play and explore outdoors.**

Pokémon GO was built on the belief that AR can strengthen our connection to the analog world. According to Niantic founder John Hanke, he and his team were initially inspired by the thought of turning the planet itself into a playing surface, à la classic board games. Of their first experiment in this concept, *Ingress*, Hanke says, "The idea was pretty simple: What if that game board was just the planet?... That map is the starting point, and then rather than moving characters around with the joystick, the idea was you *are* the character." Niantic began developing games that invite users to explore the world through location-based gameplay. In *Pokémon GO*, players have to traverse their neighborhoods to find Pokémon in various real-world locations. PokéStops and Gyms, where players battle and train their Pokémon, are tied to public art installations, landmarks, and popular gathering spots. By encouraging people to meet up there, the game fosters interest in places they may not have previously known about.

In addition to the spontaneous interactions that occur in these spaces, team membership strengthens social bonds. Players join one of three teams, each with a unique philosophy and mascot, creating playful and competitive alliances. The community that subsequently developed became so strong that Niantic began to organize annual *Pokémon GO* Fests: events where fans can come together to meet each other, play together, and share their love for the game. These festivals have been a massive hit, attracting hundreds of thousands of players in cities across the globe, from New York to London to Osaka and beyond. *Pokémon GO* also encourages physical activity with features like the Buddy System and Adventure Sync, which reward players for walking and spending time outdoors.

Pokémon GO is a remarkable example of the merging of digital and analog to inspire real-life adventure and social bonding. The thoughtful game design leads players to explore their local communities and co-create their own stories with friends. The game's legacy is not just in its success but in its ability to bring people together and encourage them to engage with the world around them in new and meaningful ways.

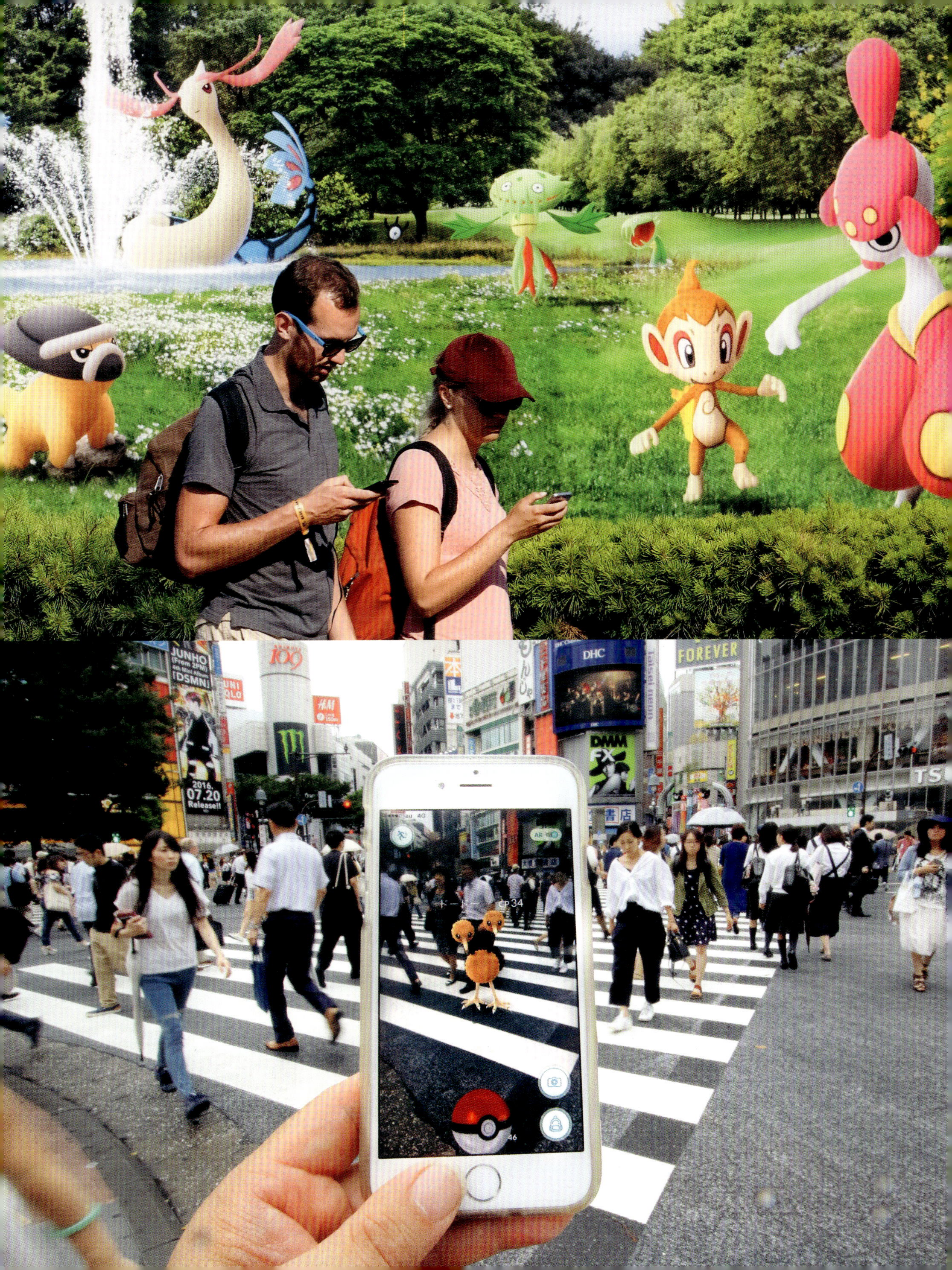
JUNHO
2016. 07.20 Release!!
109
H&M
DHC
FOREVER
DMM FX

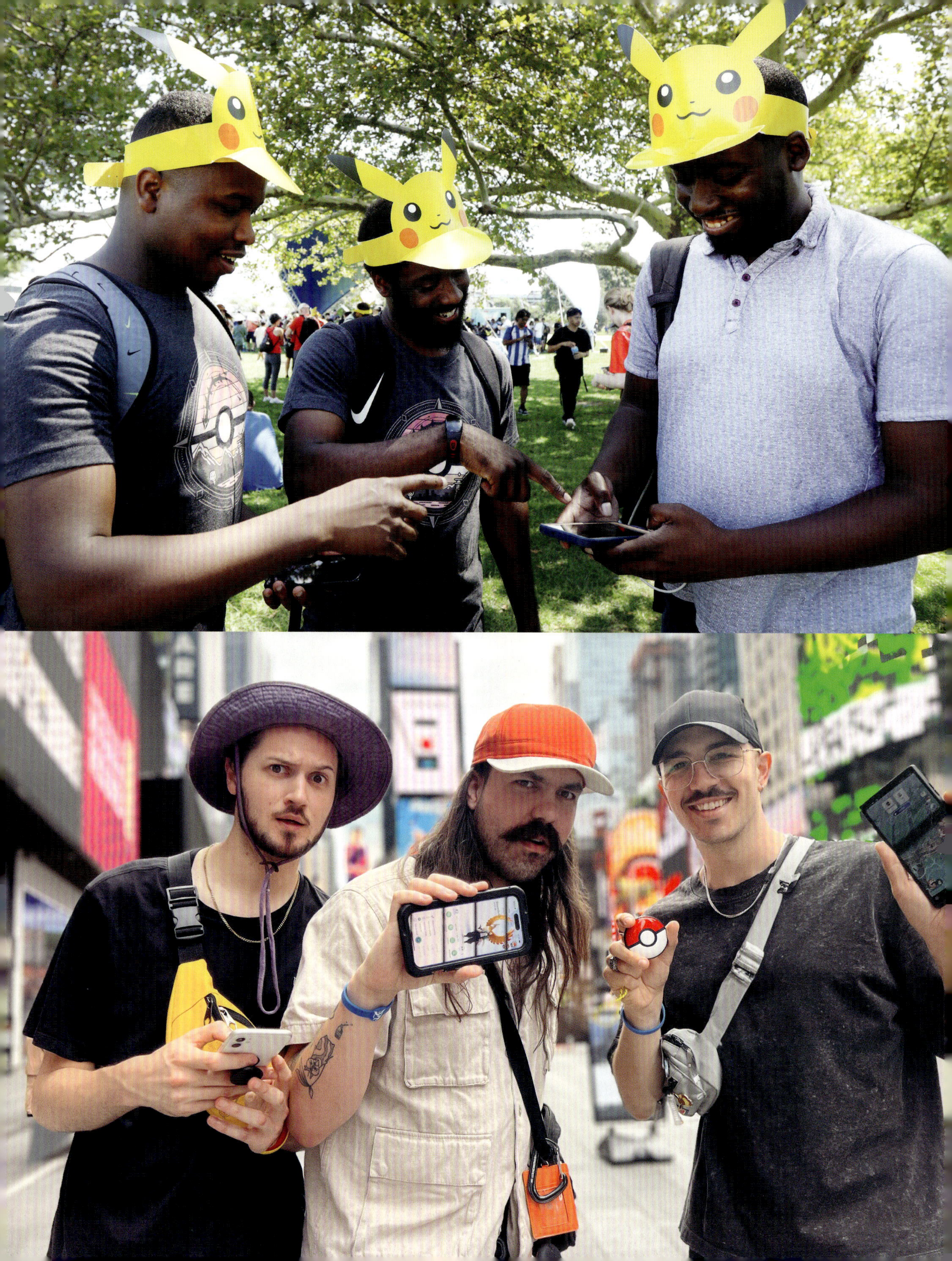

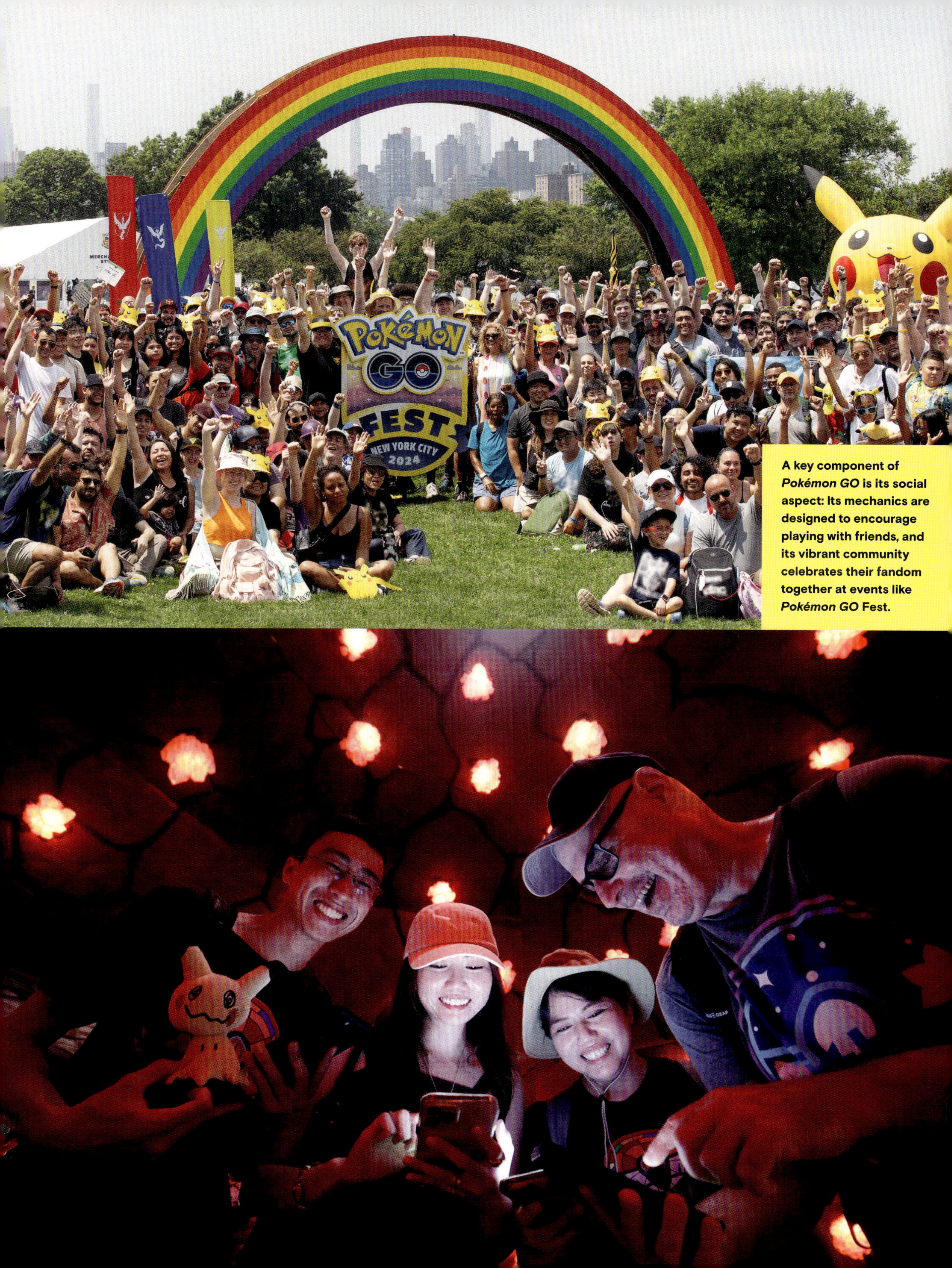

A key component of *Pokémon GO* is its social aspect: Its mechanics are designed to encourage playing with friends, and its vibrant community celebrates their fandom together at events like *Pokémon GO* Fest.

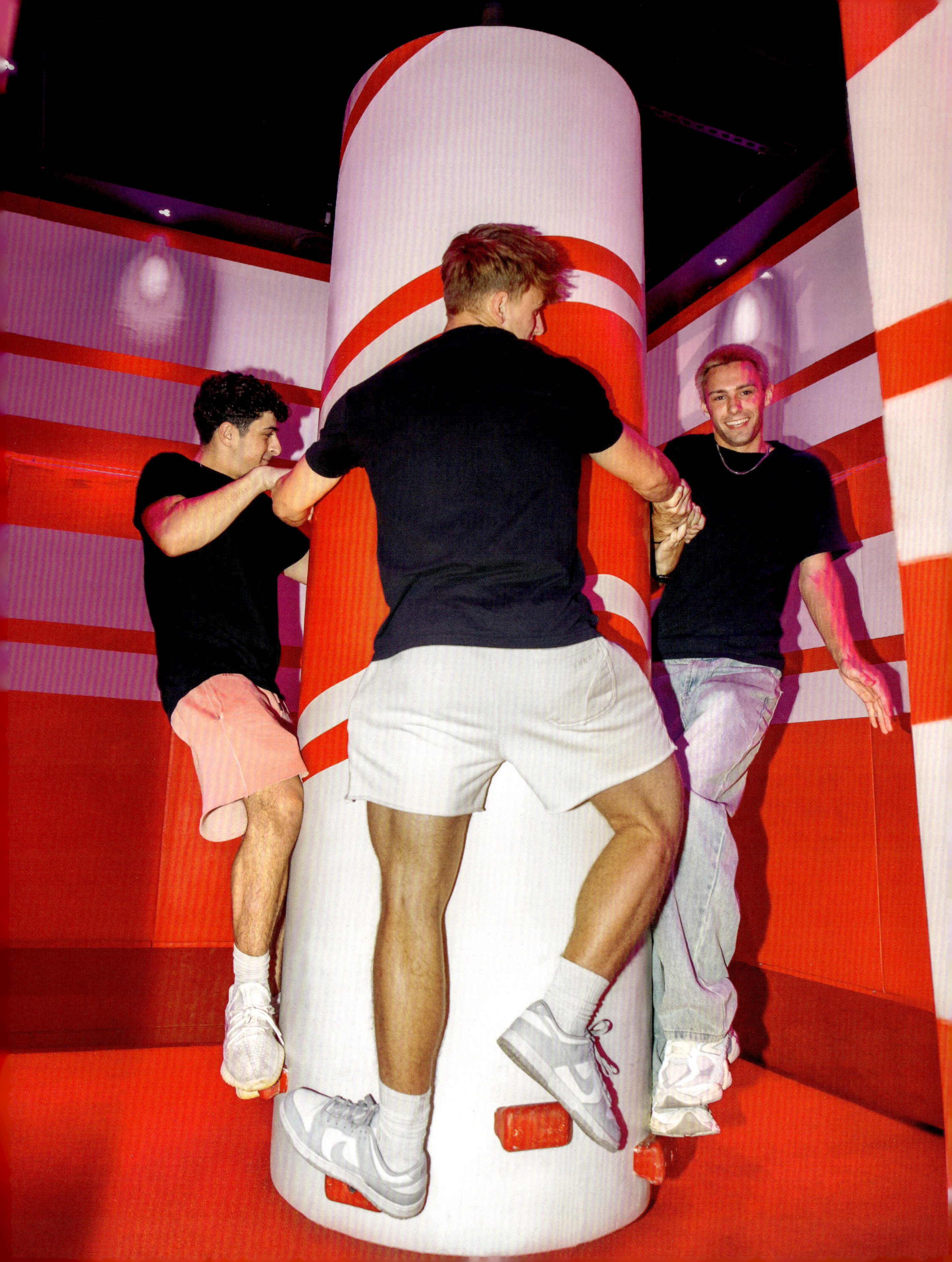

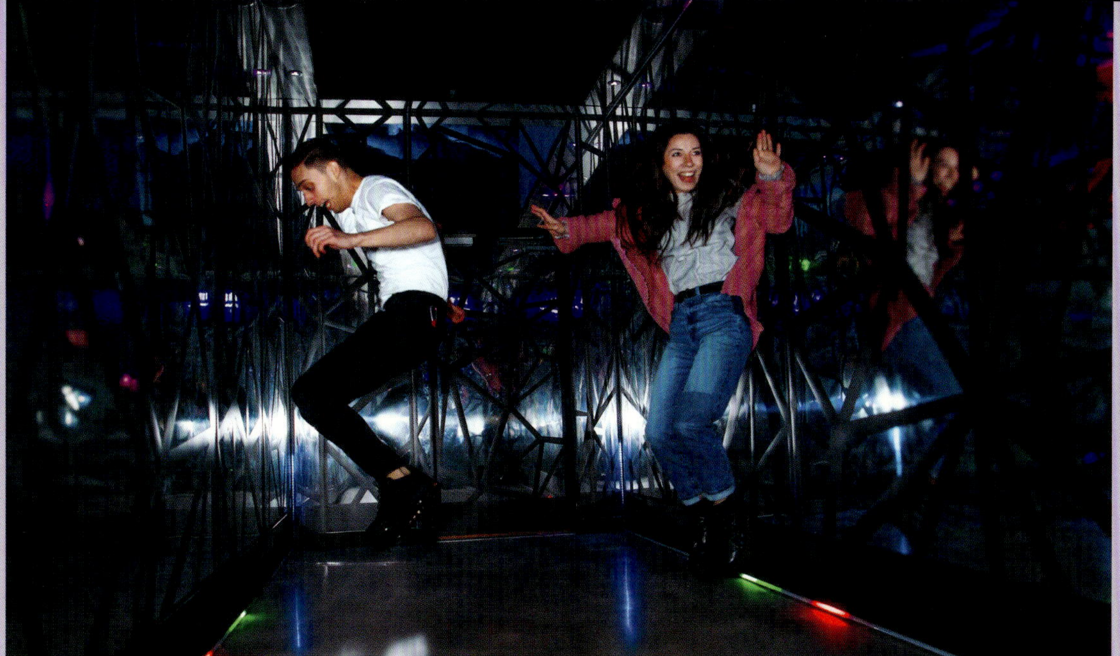

COMPETITIVE SOCIALIZING

Imagine the cool ambience of a bar combined with glitzy, high-tech versions of classic social games you already love. As you compete with friends in a reimagined game of mini golf, axe-throwing, or table tennis, you also enjoy premium food and drinks. Welcome to the world of competitive socializing, an energizing new sector of the leisure market. As part of a growing trend mixing entertainment with food and beverage, competitive socializing offers engaging activities when people go out, blending social interaction with playful challenges.

The industry has seen tremendous growth, especially post-pandemic. According to Cushman & Wakefield, competitive-socializing concepts have expanded by 386 percent since the beginning of 2021, and per real estate services company JLL, they now comprise 32.1 percent of mall tenants offering leisure activities in the U.S. Consumer preferences drive this growth; in one survey, 42 percent of Millennial restaurant-goers said entertainment options influence their dining choices. Although these venues can be costly to develop and build, the investment pays off as consumers spend on entertainment, food, and beverages. Competitive socializing also has great potential for repeat visitation, with KAM research indicating that U.K. customers visit such venues an average of 1.2 times per month. Furthermore, the game-centered design of the venues makes them suitable for various audiences, from work colleagues to couples to families.

Success in this sector often involves enhancing the experience with state-of-the-art technology. As Adam Breeden, the founder or cofounder of six of the most successful competitive-socializing companies, says, "I can certainly vouch for the fact that bringing technology into these businesses is the game changer." For example, the golf experience that Breeden cofounded, Puttshack, uses golf balls with integrated computers for automatic scoring, and F1 Arcade's cutting-edge full-motion racing-simulator technology physically mimics the thrilling intensity of controlling an ultra-high-speed engine. Another of his endeavors, the competitive-darts experience Flight Club, has invested in advanced systems like "darts vision," which tracks darts and provides instant replay as well as automatic scoring.

The popularity of competitive socializing reflects a broader shift in the entertainment industry. In the post-pandemic world, people have a heightened desire for social connection. Rather than simply dining out, they now seek interactive experiences where food and drinks are a bonus—and competitive socializing delivers on all fronts.

Groups cooperate and compete in Level99's physical challenges, such as dodging lasers in Museum Heist *(above)* and staying on the turning pole in Sugar Twist *(opposite)*.

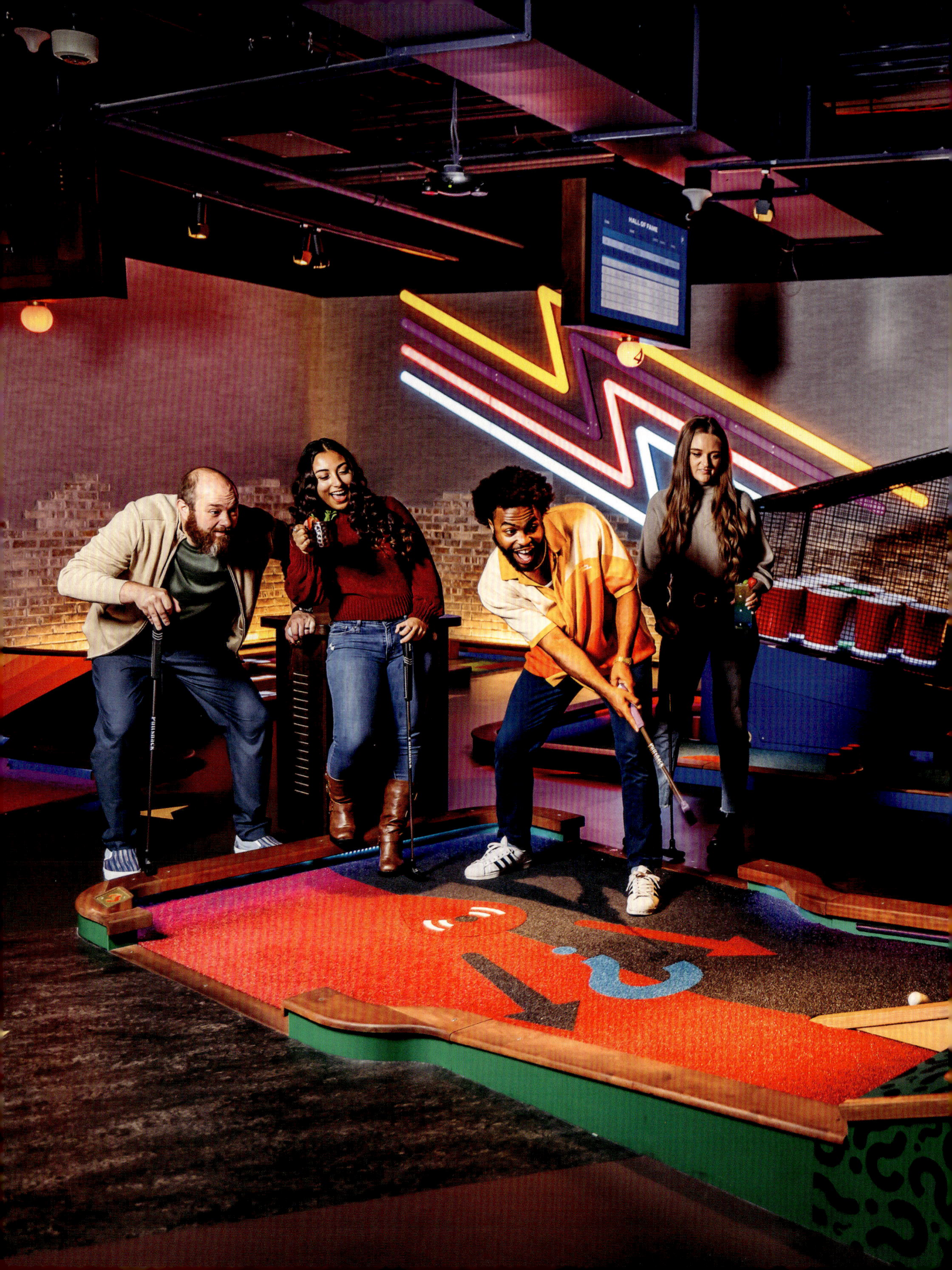
HALL OF FAME

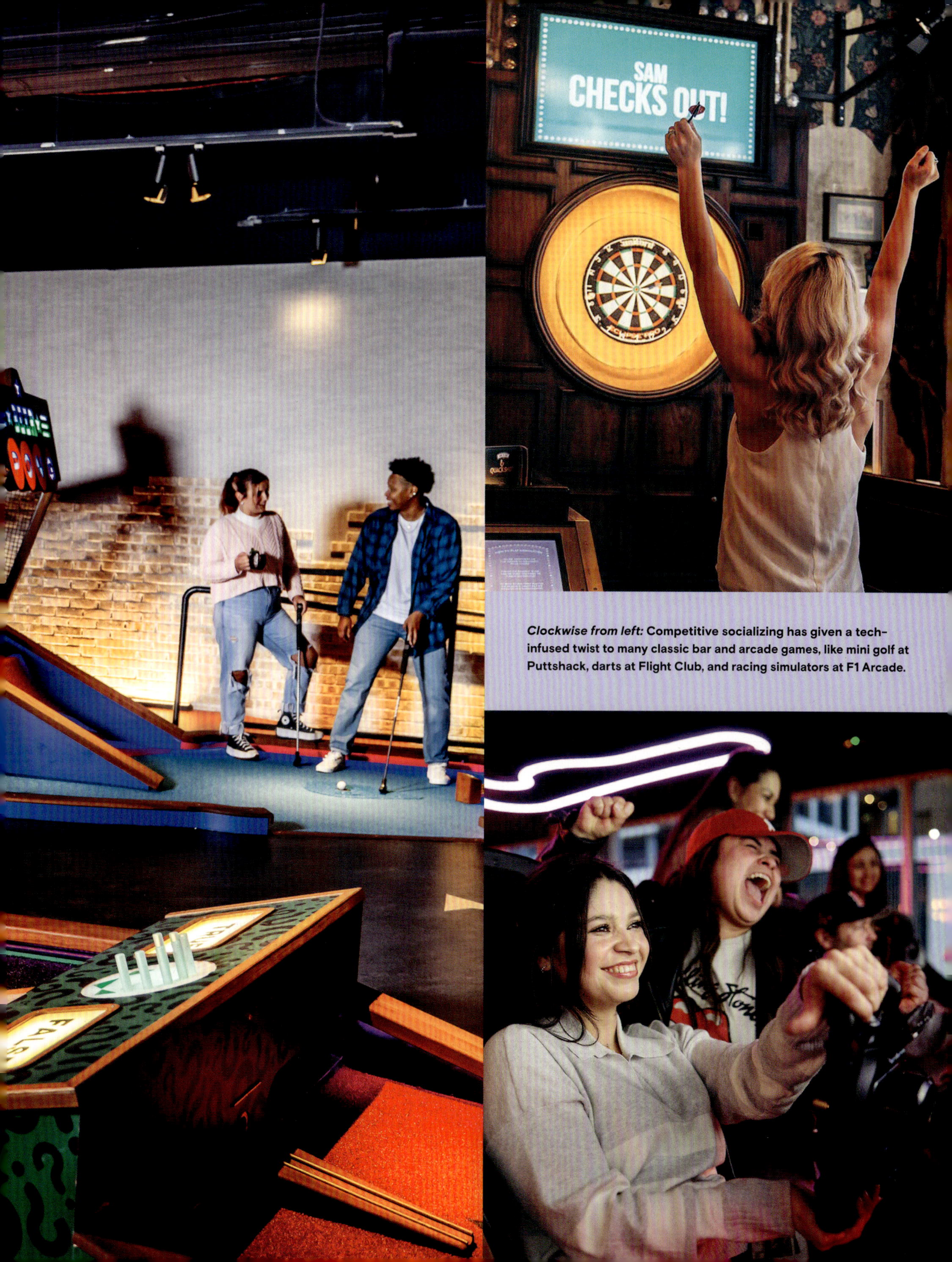

Clockwise from left: **Competitive socializing has given a tech-infused twist to many classic bar and arcade games, like mini golf at Puttshack, darts at Flight Club, and racing simulators at F1 Arcade.**

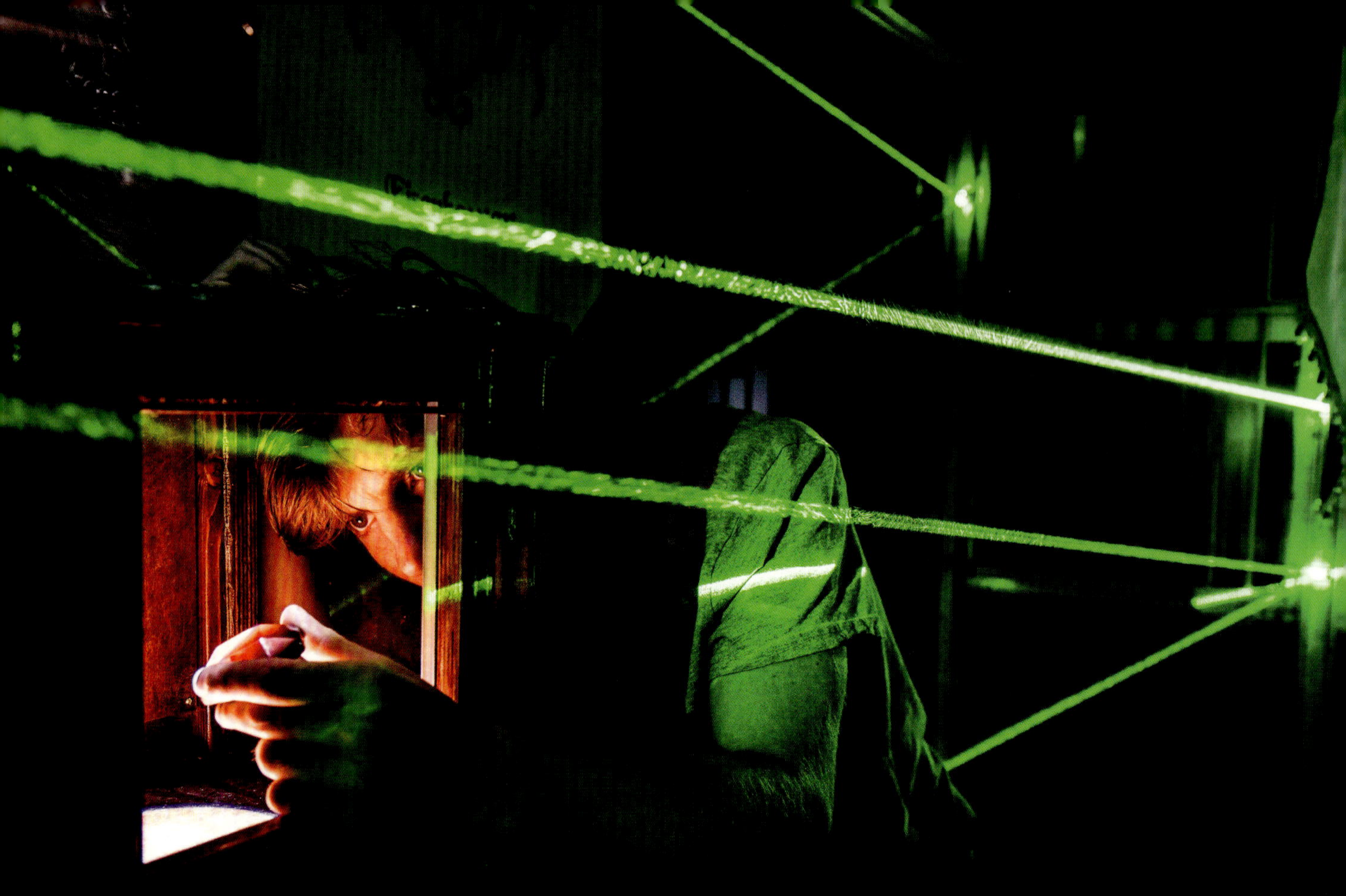

ESCAPE ROOMS

When you combine the mental stimulation of a puzzle, the interactivity of a game, the physicality of a LARP, and the social appeal of a trivia night, you get the ultimate pastime: the modern escape room. The idea of an interactive puzzle room centered on the concept of unlocking a door to "escape" (also known as an escape game or an escape-the-room game) originated in Japan in 2007, descended from text-based and then point-and-click adventure games of the 1980s and '90s. Before long, the craze had spread throughout Asia and to the rest of the world, eventually evolving into the industry of today, valued globally at more than $9 billion in 2024.

As the popularity of escape rooms has exploded, what began as singular puzzle rooms requiring only some general code-cracking know-how and a clock to beat have become something much more complex and sophisticated in design and production value. Some now feature technological enhancements that allow supervising Game Masters to adjust the difficulty level in real time or provide hints to help players succeed; others boast movie-level set design and professionally trained live actors to enhance immersion. Occasionally, "escape room" is a misnomer—you may, in fact, need to unlock several rooms, making the experience more of an "escape complex." And more and more, escape rooms are crafting compelling narratives to elevate the emotional stakes and further motivate players. In fact, many of the best escape rooms are more akin to 3-D story games.

But the biggest driver of escape rooms' growth isn't that they're infused with tech, or have authentic

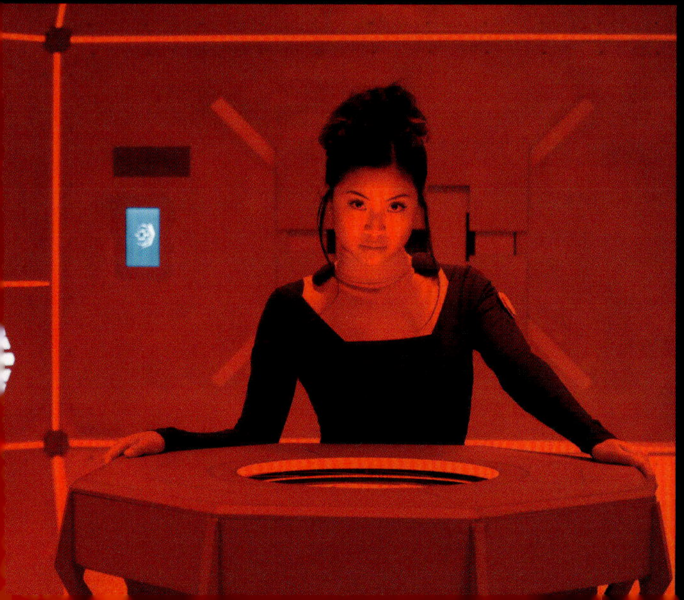

trappings, or even show their burgeoning potential for storytelling. Rather, it's that they handily fulfill our innate desire for social problem-solving. As human beings, we're hardwired to form coalitions to accomplish tasks, so it's no wonder that an environment designed specifically to facilitate—and indeed require—cooperation scratches a particular itch. Escape rooms offer that opportunity to collaborate and play in a way that's fun, engages both our minds and bodies, and gives us a sense of camaraderie and accomplishment by overcoming challenges together.

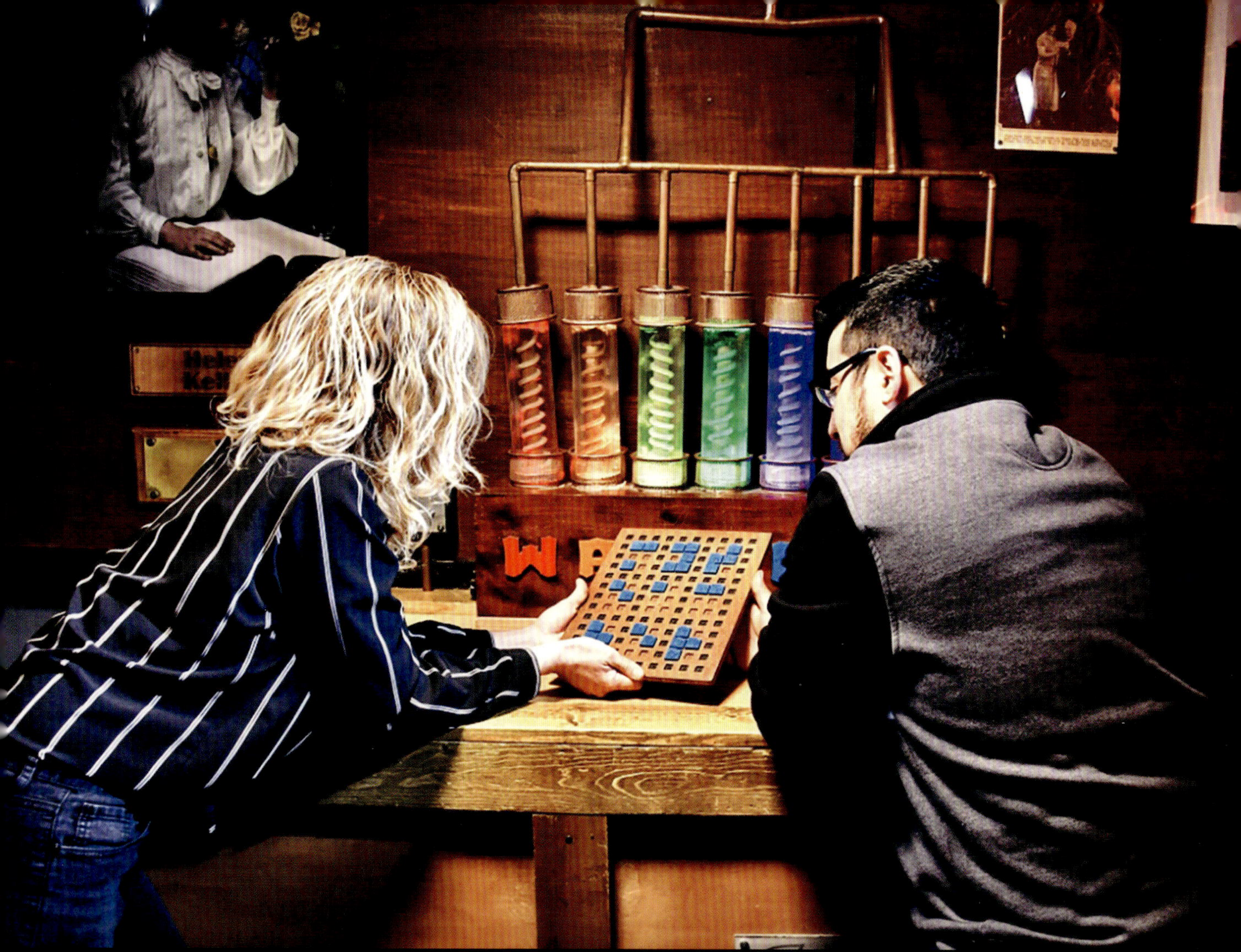

Clockwise from opposite: **A participant carefully removes the prize in Sherlocked's *The Vault*, a heist-inspired escape experience in Amsterdam; two people work together to solve a puzzle in the *Great Houdini Escape Room* at Palace Games in San Francisco; a scene from *The Dome* in the Netherlands, voted as one of the world's top escape rooms.**

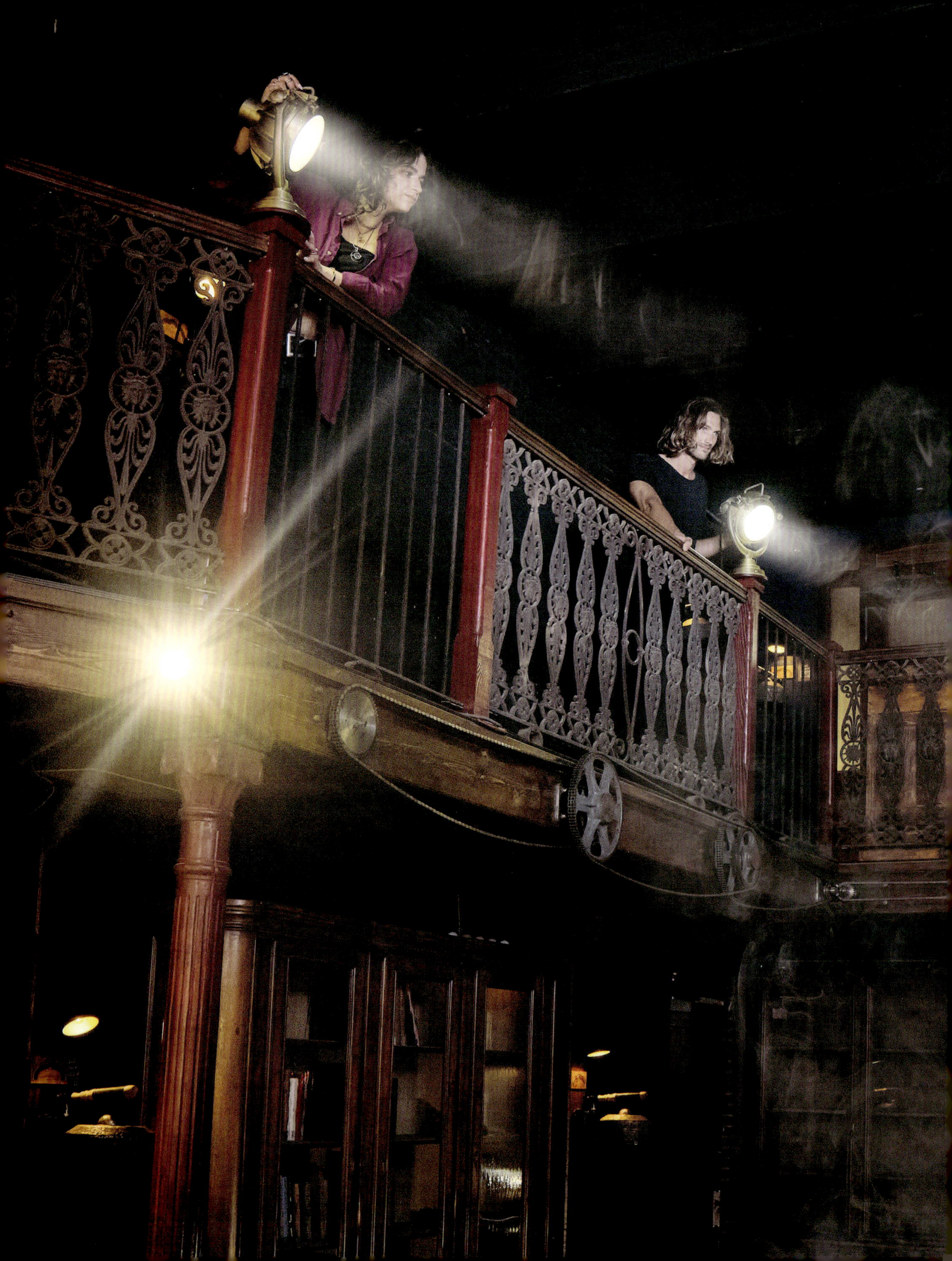

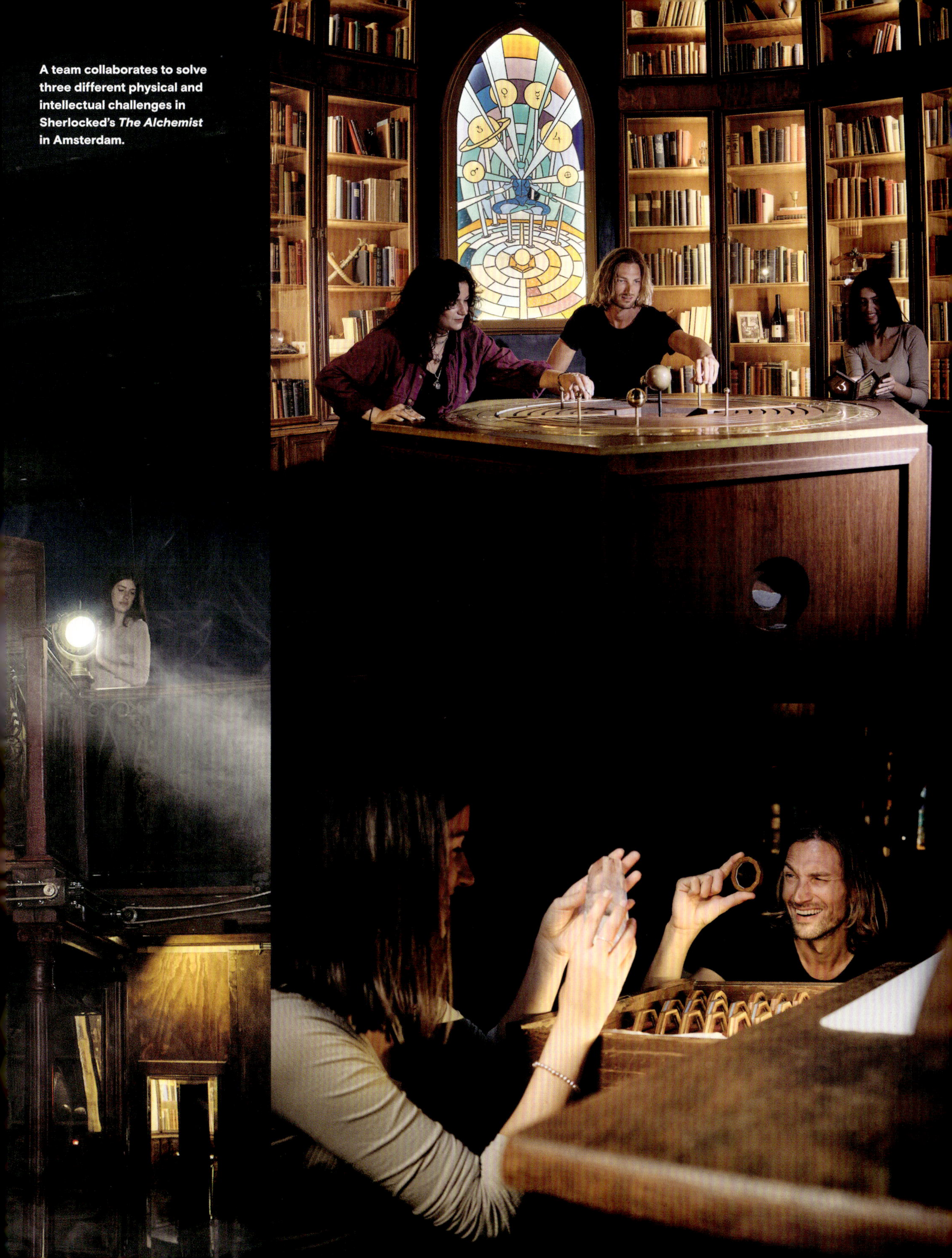

A team collaborates to solve three different physical and intellectual challenges in Sherlocked's *The Alchemist* in Amsterdam.

MUSEUM OF ICE CREAM

Launched in 2016, Museum of Ice Cream is a pioneering force in the world of experiential museums. Visitors can expect to be engaged by its many eye-catching interactive elements, from swimming pools of sprinkles to jungles of hanging bananas. The museum embraces a playful spirit, with its website even asking, "Ready to rediscover your inner child?"

With five locations across the United States and one in Singapore as of early 2025, each MOIC features multiple "magical playscapes," each tailored to its city. In New York, guests ride the "Celestial Subway," a bright-pink train complete with NYC maps and stops at "Graham Central Station," "Skybecca," and "Starlem." In Chicago, the Jelly Bean Room pays homage to the iconic Cloud Gate sculpture, welcoming people into a space filled with every jelly-bean flavor imaginable. Across all locations, common staples include play spaces with slides, carnival games, and, of course, chances to snack on scoops of ice cream. While some rooms offer ice-cream-related facts, the museum focuses less on the history of the treat and more on the sense of joy it evokes.

Everything about MOIC is meticulously designed with ice cream lovers in mind. From whimsical pastel colors and imaginative decor to larger-than-life installations, each room is crafted to awaken the senses and inspire a sense of wonder. The museum invites guests of all ages to play, laugh, and rediscover the simple joys of childhood through interactive spaces that celebrate the magic of ice cream. Whether they're families, groups of friends, or anyone else looking to indulge their sweet tooth and inner child, visitors are encouraged to create joyful memories together.

With more than a million visitors to date and a wave of other venues adapting its innovative business model, MOIC has made a lasting impact on the experience economy—proving that when you lead with fun, creativity, and a love for ice cream, people will follow.

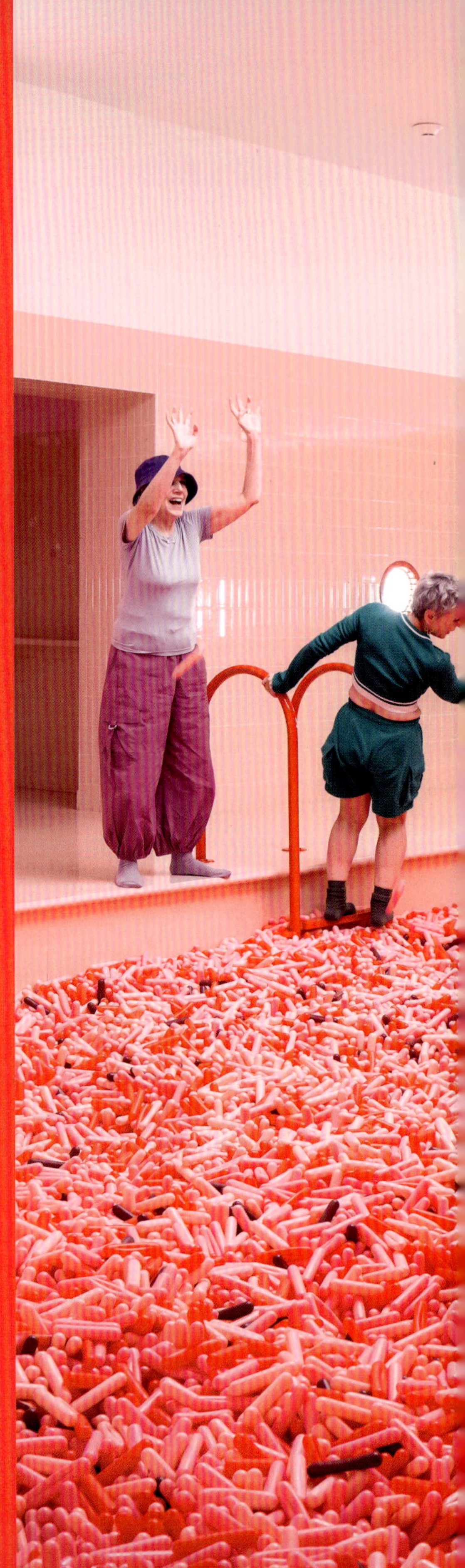

Guests slide into the Museum of Ice Cream's sprinkle pool.

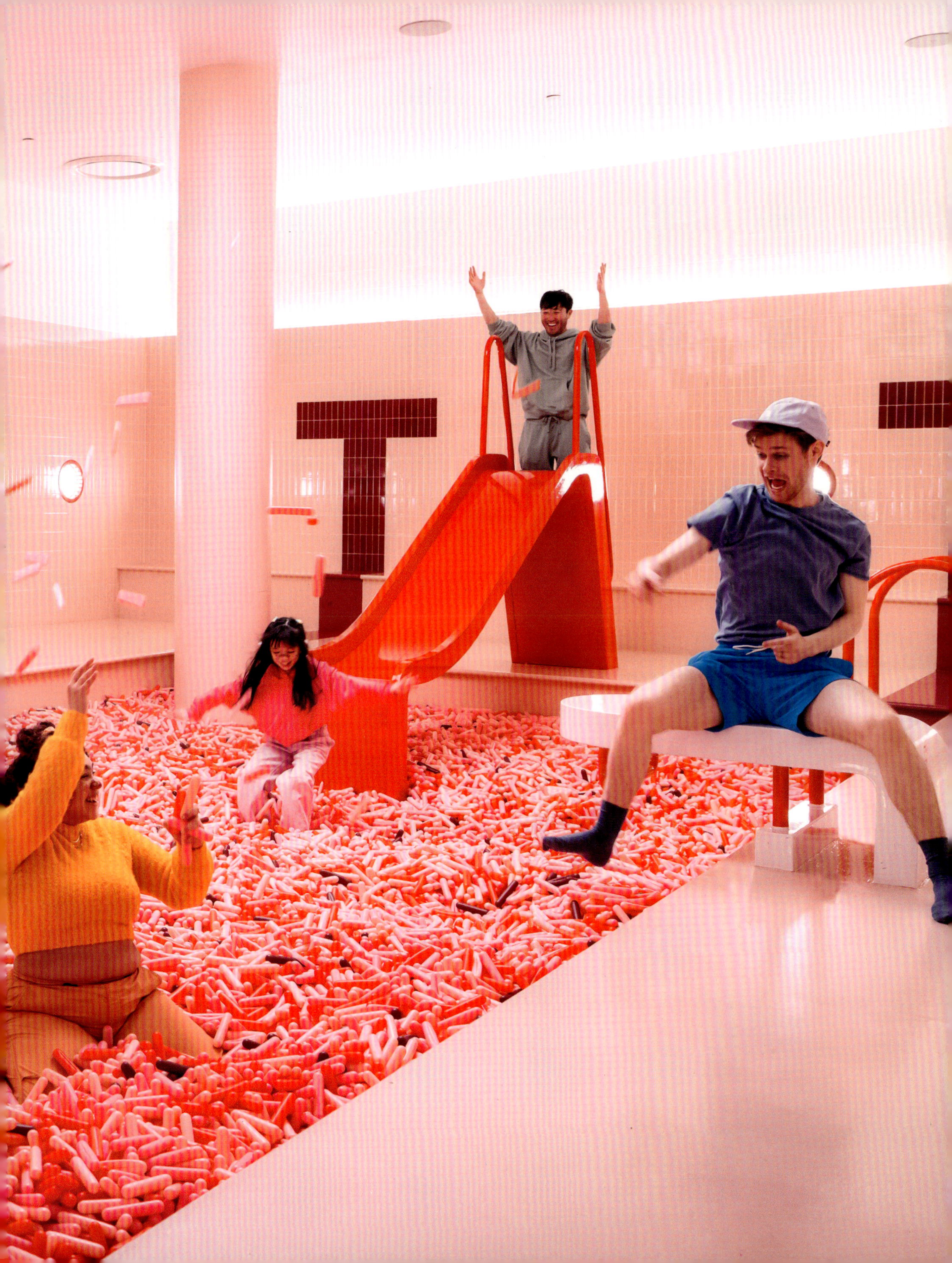

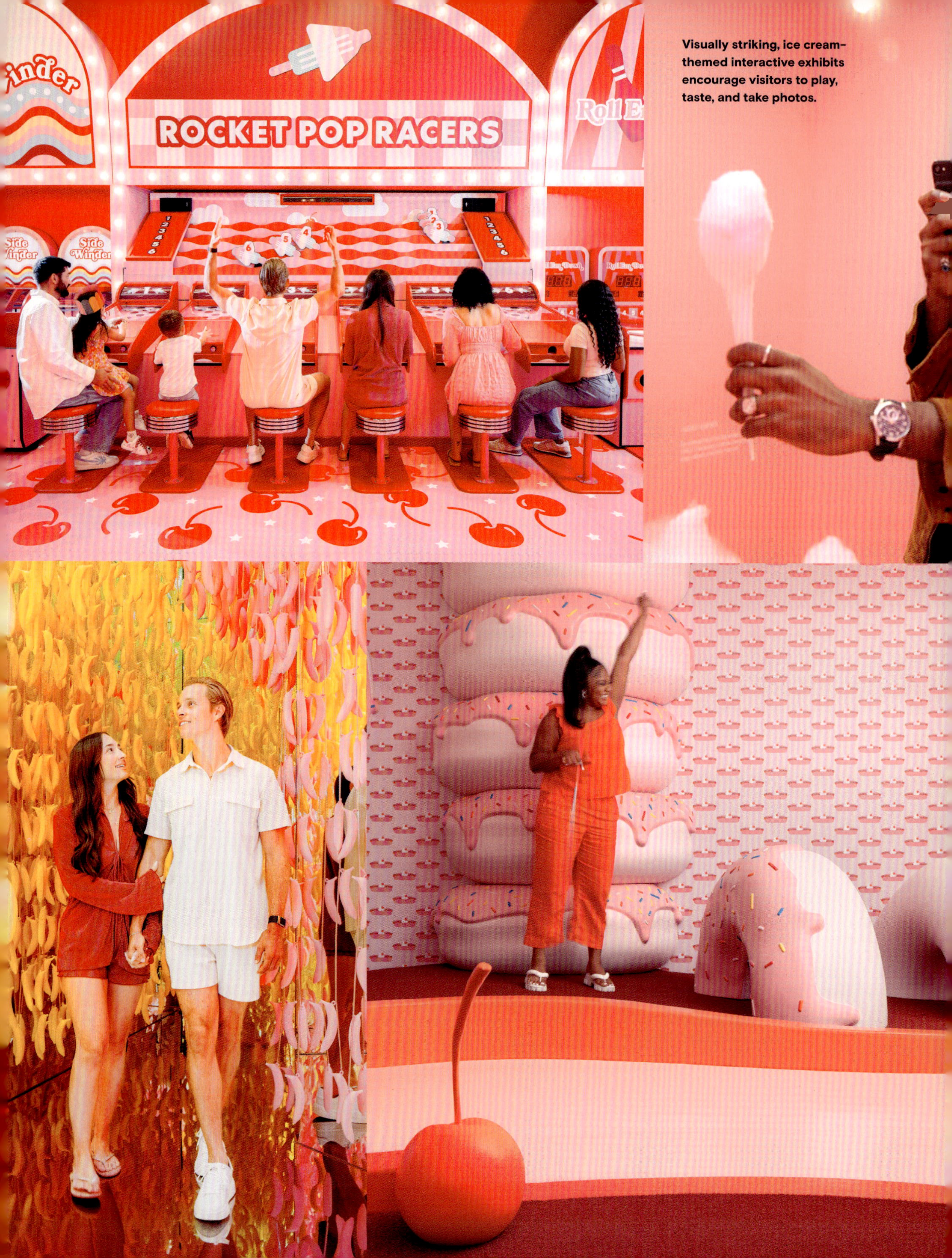

Visually striking, ice cream-themed interactive exhibits encourage visitors to play, taste, and take photos.

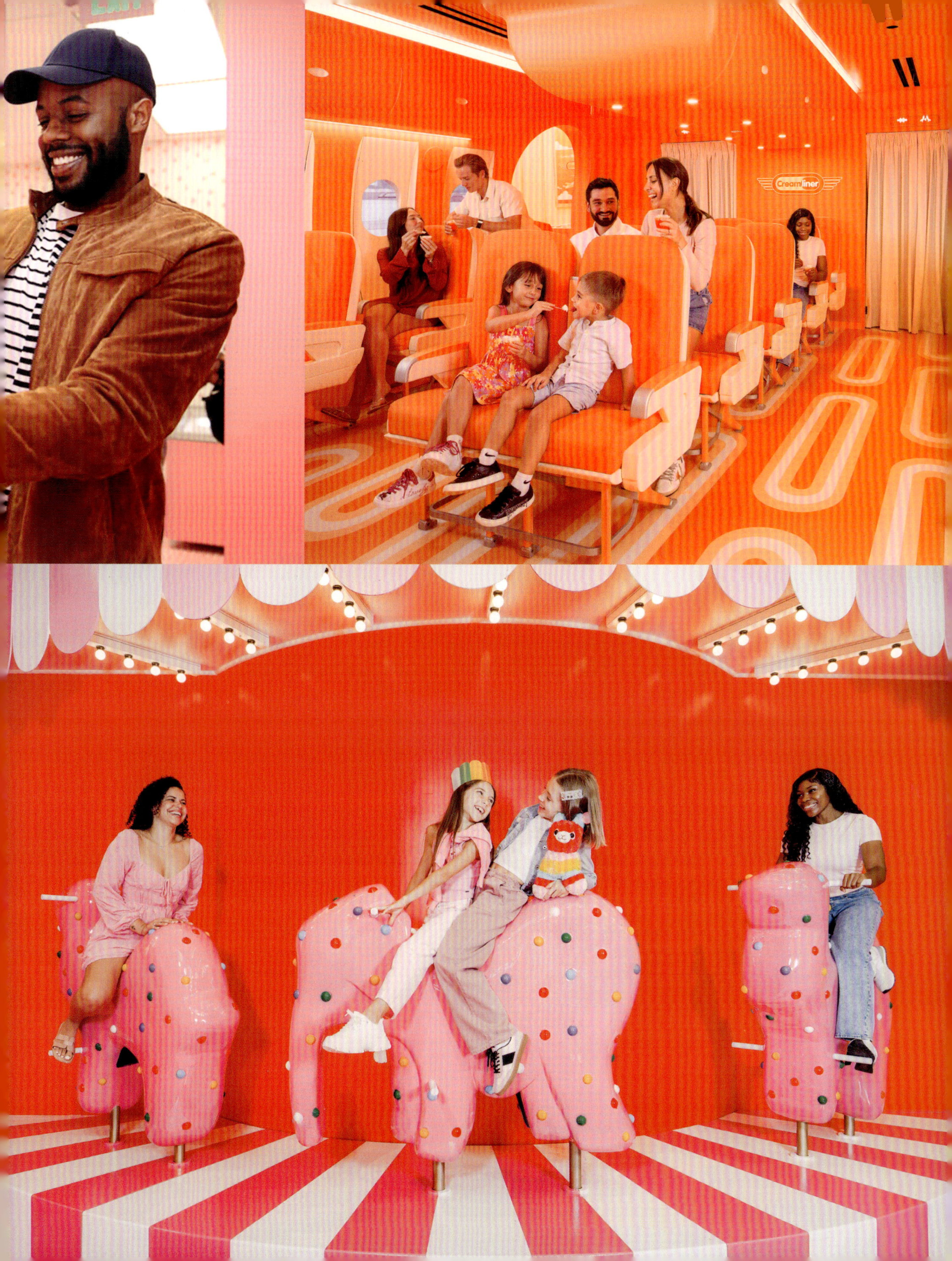
Creamliner

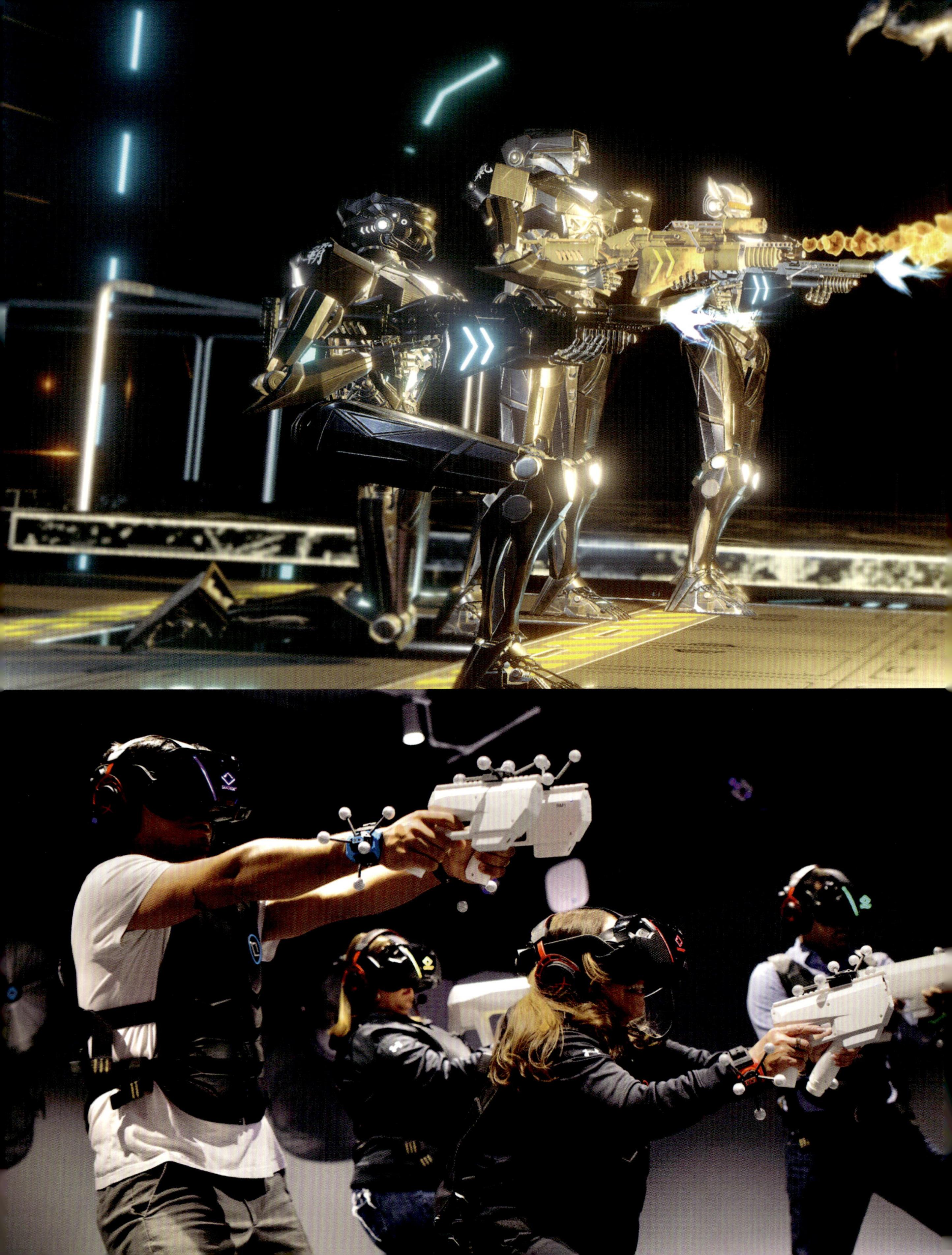

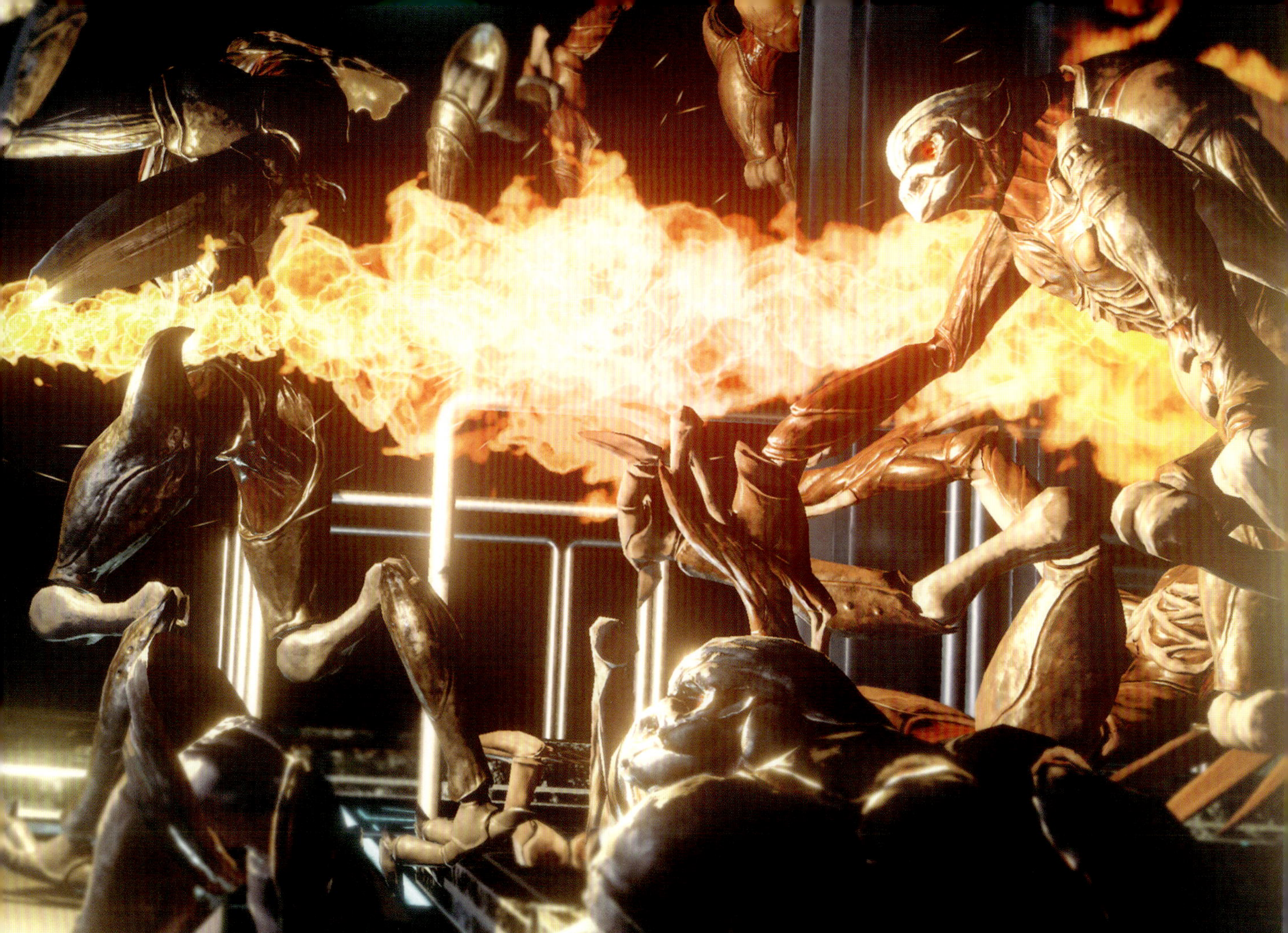

SANDBOX VR

At the intersection of embodied storytelling and gaming stands Sandbox VR: one of the fastest-growing location-based virtual-reality start-ups in the world as of 2025. Its story began in 2016, when game developer Steven Zhao decided to try to create something akin to a real-life *Star Trek* holodeck. The idea snowballed from there, raising more than $60 million in investments from Silicon Valley VCs as well as names like Justin Timberlake, Katy Perry, and Kevin Durant. Today, with more than fifty-seven locations worldwide in cities from San Francisco to London to Shanghai (and more on the way), Sandbox has become one of the most successful and widespread examples to date of an in-person experience that turns VR gaming into a social activity.

The core concept is simple: You and your friends can embody video-game heroes. At Sandbox, up to six people, decked out in VR headsets, haptic backpacks, and motion-capture wearables, can step into a shared virtual world for a variety of specially designed experiences. Its patented technology combines full-body motion capture and haptic feedback to provide a much higher level of immersion than is possible at home. Your avatar responds to your motion in real time, so in order for your character to dodge obstacles, fire weapons, and complete challenges, you must physically act yourself—thus increasing your sense of truly being in the game.

Sandbox currently offers several exclusive experiences, all developed in-house by their own studio. Their classic games, like *Amber Sky 2088* and *Deadwood Valley*, take the form of first-person shooters, complete with an array of peripherals like prop guns that function as your weapons in-game. Newer offerings, like the

Armed with virtual-reality headsets and motion-capture sensors, participants take on team challenges like repelling invading aliens in *Amber Sky 2088*.

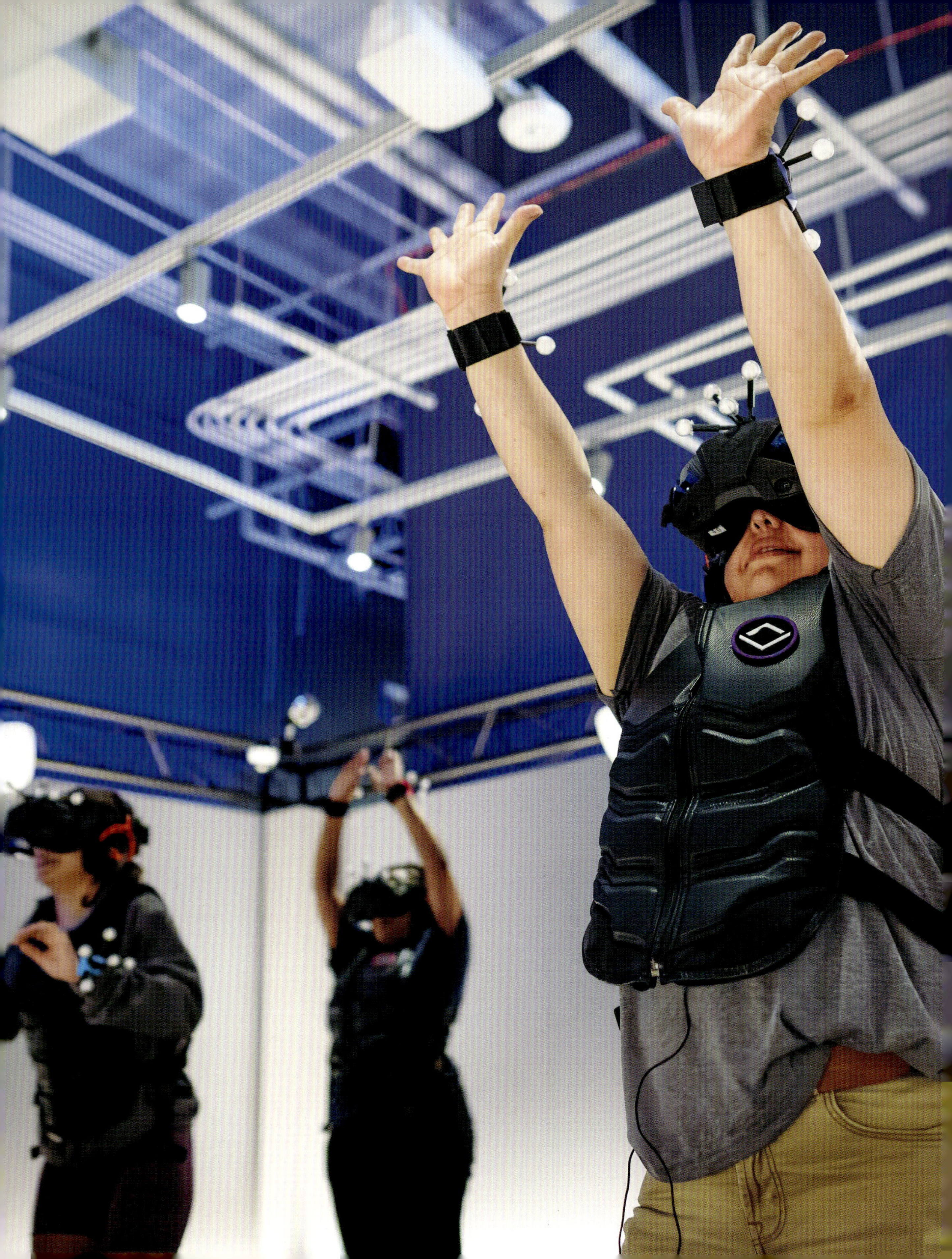

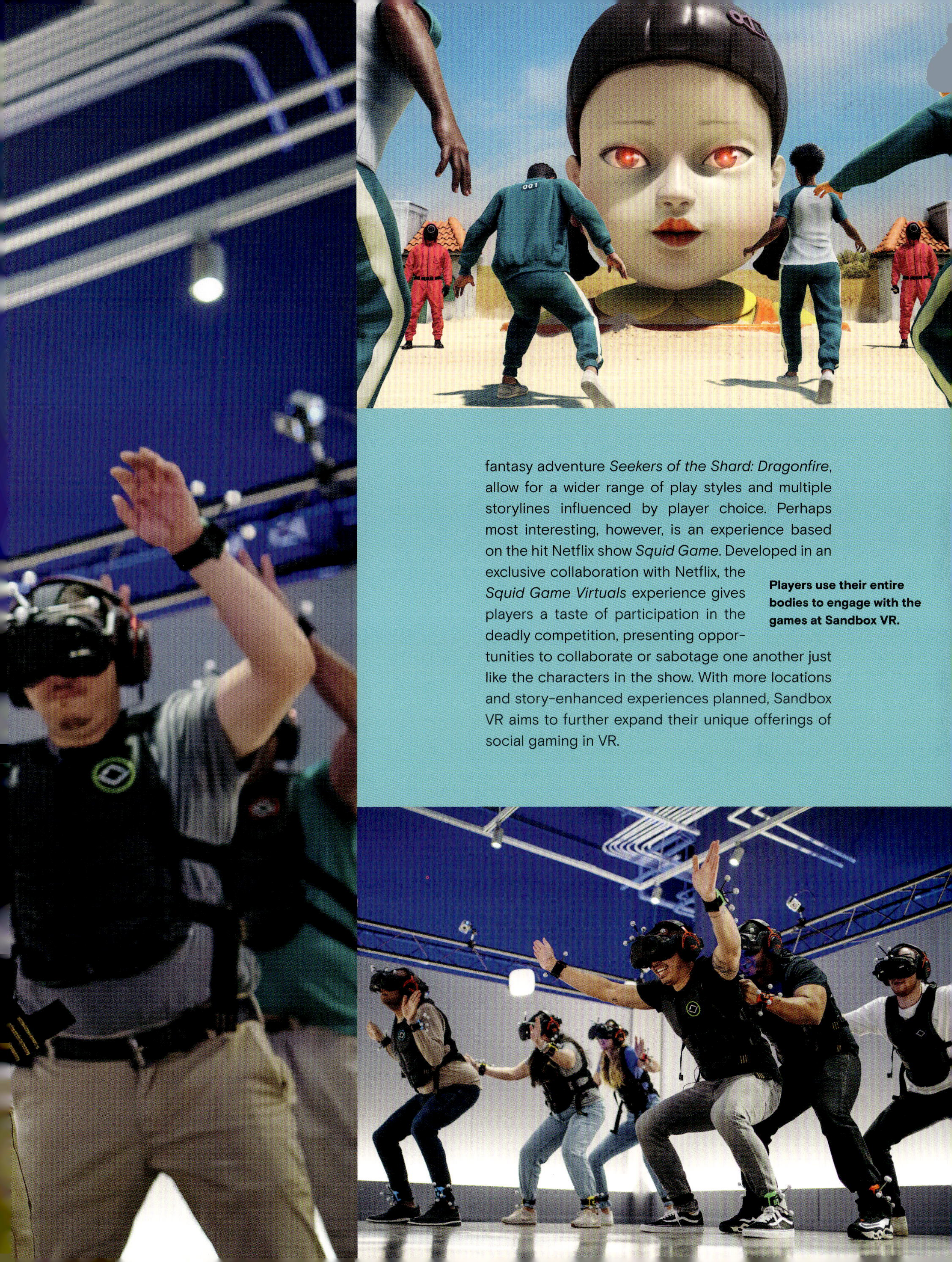

fantasy adventure *Seekers of the Shard: Dragonfire*, allow for a wider range of play styles and multiple storylines influenced by player choice. Perhaps most interesting, however, is an experience based on the hit Netflix show *Squid Game*. Developed in an exclusive collaboration with Netflix, the *Squid Game Virtuals* experience gives players a taste of participation in the deadly competition, presenting opportunities to collaborate or sabotage one another just like the characters in the show. With more locations and story-enhanced experiences planned, Sandbox VR aims to further expand their unique offerings of social gaming in VR.

Players use their entire bodies to engage with the games at Sandbox VR.

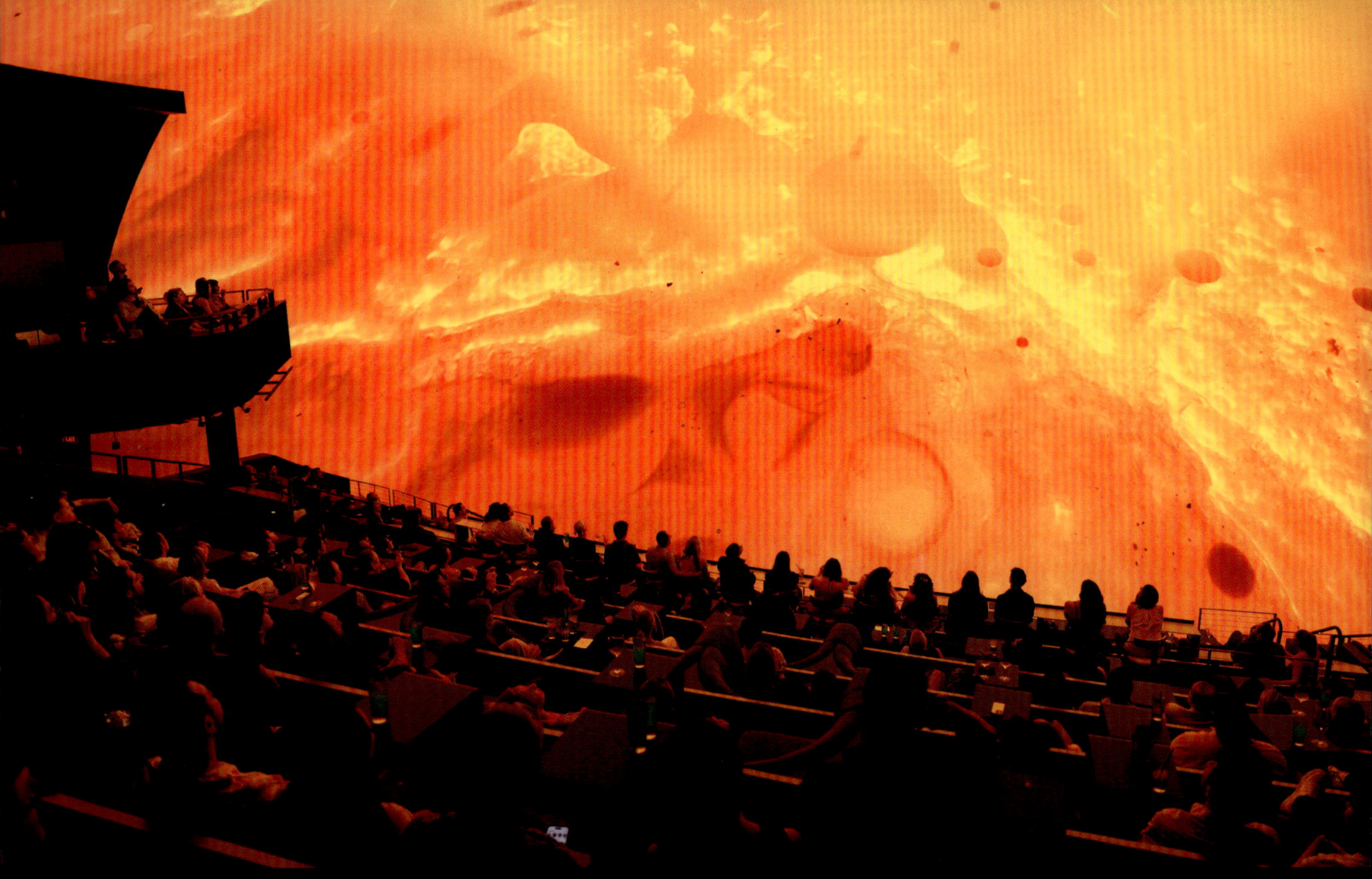

COSM

Cosm is revolutionizing the way we experience sports, entertainment, and arts by creating immersive venues that prioritize shared experiences. Their eighty-seven-foot diameter, 180-degree LED dome features ultra-high-resolution displays, drawing you into the action with stunning clarity and realism. Whether it's a live sporting event, a breathtaking Cirque du Soleil performance, or a journey through the history of the earth, the experience is visually immersive and larger than life. The first Cosm venues opened in 2024 in Los Angeles and Dallas, each with a capacity of 2,000 people. Since those openings, the company has raised an impressive $250 million as part of its plan to build an additional fifty venues across the country.

***Clockwise from above:* Guests are immersed in Cosm's domed-shaped screen watching Ricardo Romaneiro's *Liquidverse*; *Orbital* from Guy Reid and Planetary Collective; and Nancy Baker Cahill's *Seek*.**

In their quest to redefine the fan experience, Cosm introduced what they call "Shared Reality": delivering the immersive quality of virtual reality without the isolation of a headset. The dome's 8K+ resolution LED displays wrap around the entire audience, enveloping every person in the content. Socialization lies at the heart of the experience; visitors can share a drink at any of the several bars, order food and eat on comfortable seating inside the dome, or take in the fresh air on the outdoor deck. All of these features make Cosm a vibrant social hub.

While the programming spans a broad range of content, the sports content stands out as one of Cosm's most popular. They've partnered with NBC Sports to bring audience favorites into Shared Reality, including NBA basketball, NHL hockey, UFC mixed martial arts, and Premier League soccer. Using cutting-edge technology, Cosm captures and broadcasts events live in high-quality video, even providing views that fans wouldn't normally get from a TV broadcast—from courtside, the end zone, or even in the gameplay among the athletes—giving fans the ultimate sports-bar experience.

As Cosm continues to expand across the country, the company is poised to become a player in the future of live sports and entertainment. This isn't just a place to watch; it's a place to *experience*, together.

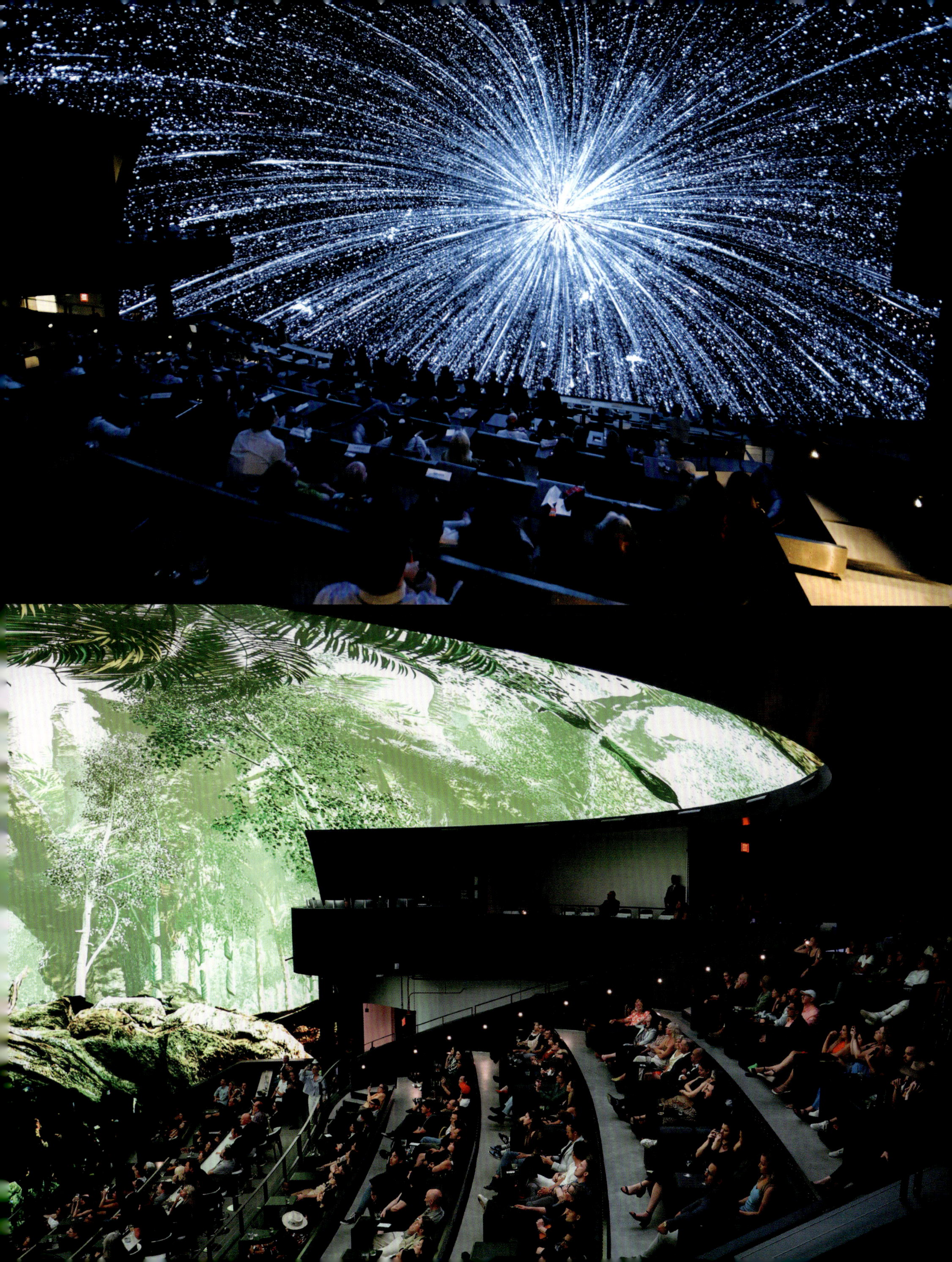

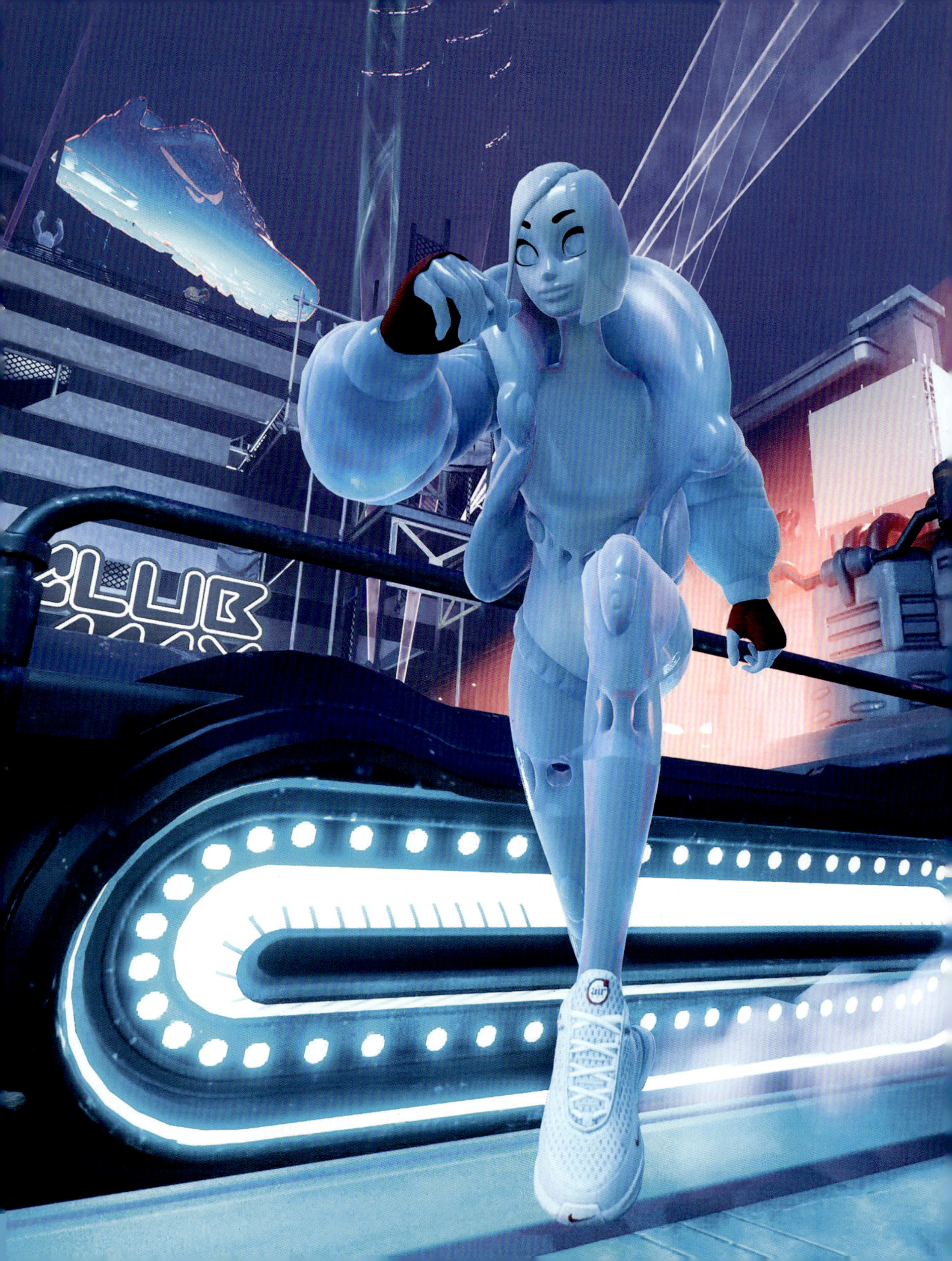
CLUB

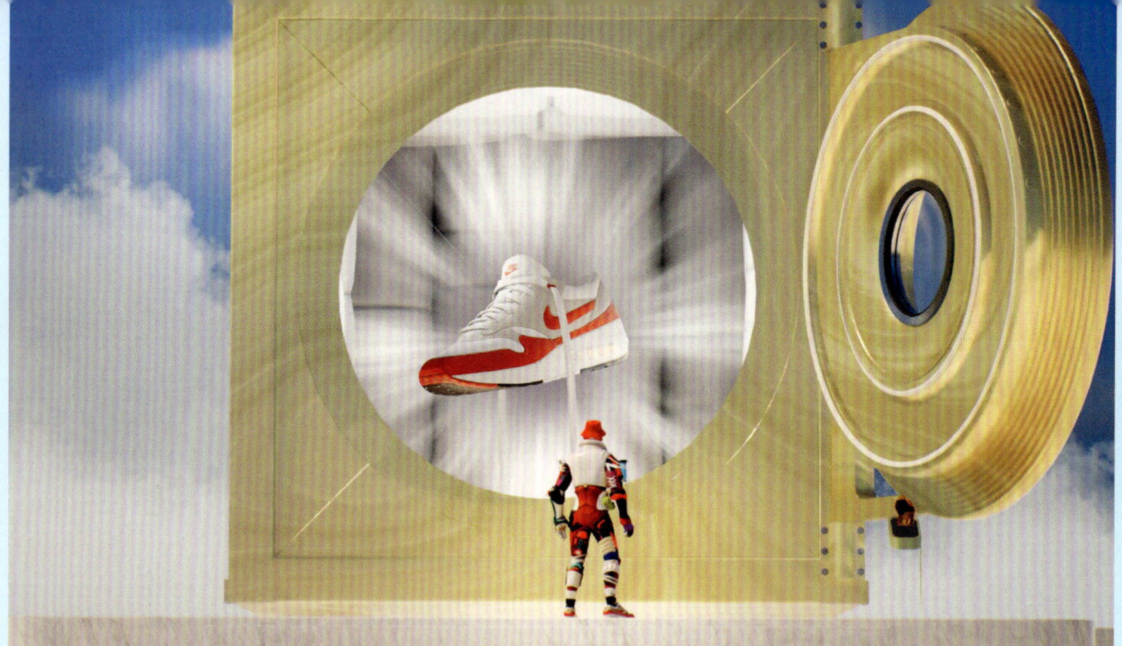

NIKE AIRPHORIA

Maxxed Out Max ***(above)*** **and Airie** ***(opposite)*** **are the two main characters of Air Max City in Nike's** ***Airphoria*****, a story-driven game built in** ***Fortnite*****.**

In 2023, Nike and *Fortnite* introduced *Airphoria*, a groundbreaking collaboration between Nike's Air Max brand and Epic Games' innovative Unreal Editor for *Fortnite* (UEFN). As one of the first brands to leverage UEFN, Nike created an imaginative, story-driven gaming experience in *Fortnite* where players embarked on a virtual sneaker hunt alongside up to four friends. This landmark event showcased both UEFN's innovative capabilities and Nike's forward-thinking marketing strategies to 3.1 million users. Over its first seven-day run, *Airphoria* was played more than 5.1 million times, with each session averaging twenty-two minutes. This success strengthened Nike's connection with fans, redefined brand engagement, and reshaped traditional marketing approaches.

Building on the legacy of their iconic Air Max sneaker, Nike developed Air Max City, a futuristic *Fortnite* world where every detail—from manhole covers to an Air Max 97-inspired train—was painstakingly designed to bring the Air Max story to life. Players set off on a quest to recover stolen sneaker "grails" taken by Maxxed Out Max, an original *Airphoria* character.

With *Airphoria*, Nike ventured into a new frontier for personalized brand engagement and self-expression: the virtual world. Players could purchase and equip *Fortnite* "skins" of *Airphoria* characters, as well as customize their digital sneaker-shaped Air Max backpacks by combining skins from other intellectual properties, creatively blending beloved brands and characters to showcase their individuality. More than twelve million virtual sneakers were collected during the event, making it the largest sneaker drop in history. These *Fortnite* skins and accessories signaled the beginning of a new revenue stream for Nike: virtual products that could be individualized and therefore made all the more valuable.

The personalization opportunities didn't stop there. With UEFN's new technology, players could create their own content within the *Airphoria* world, scripting and filming videos that they could then post on social media. By integrating Nike's assets into their designs, fans became co-creators in telling the story of the brand's evolving identity, deepening the relationship between Nike and its community.

Additionally, by making a virtual world where people from all over could play together, *Airphoria* offered an engaging social experience where sneakerheads collaborated and competed to have the most stylish avatars. *Fortnite*'s virtual live event capabilities elevated *Airphoria* into a shared cultural phenomenon, breaking barriers of accessibility and redefining how brands connect, play, and co-create with audiences. *Airphoria* exemplifies how personalized, social virtual worlds can enhance brand identity and create meaningful, memorable interactions that resonate well beyond the screen.

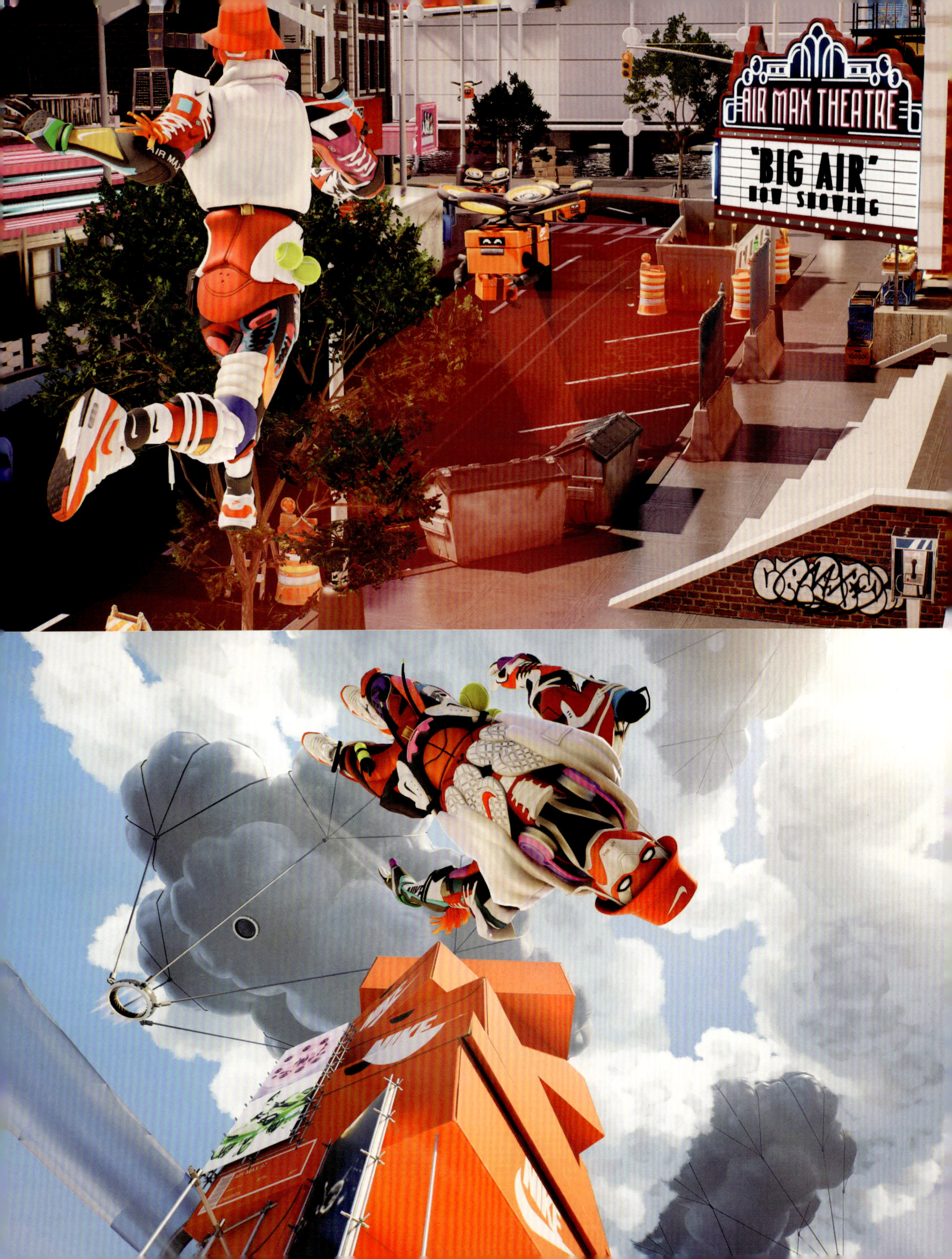
AIR MAX THEATRE
'BIG AIR'
NOW SHOWING

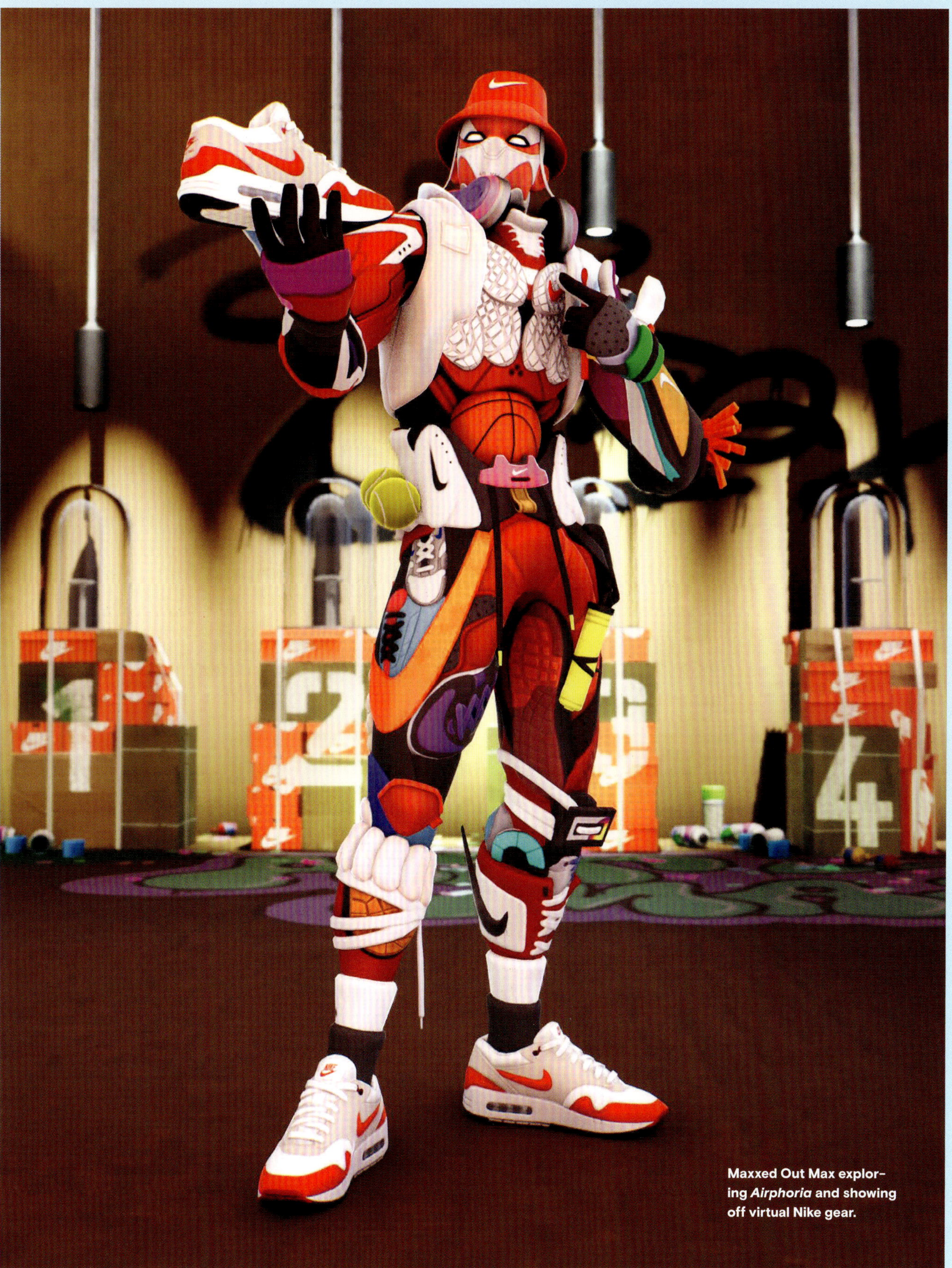

Maxxed Out Max exploring *Airphoria* and showing off virtual Nike gear.

THE FUTURE OF STORYTELLING

IS

TRANS-
FORMATIVE

Laura Espino wakes up in a tent. She doesn't know exactly where she is, only that she's an hour or so by car outside San Francisco. She unzips the flap and finds a beautiful, serene countryside, the dew just beginning to lift from the grass under the warming morning sun. Nearby she spots a herd of goats, and among them, a man on his hands and knees, pulling weeds. She recognizes him: Abraham. She steps out of the tent and walks over to him, and he looks up at her with a smile. Wordlessly, she kneels down and begins pulling weeds alongside him.

Twelve years earlier in 2000, Laura, then fourteen, had boarded a plane with her mother and left Argentina for the United States. It had been painful to say goodbye to the places and communities that had formed her life up to that point, but as the rhythms of her new life took hold, she found that the even deeper loss was that of her own identity. In Argentina she had been a voracious reader, a lover of language and creativity, fascinated even at a young age by the linguistic experiments of Jorge Luis Borges. But as she and her mother struggled to make a life as a pair of undocumented immigrants in the United States, her former passions were replaced by the harsh reality of constantly working to stay afloat. Even worse, she found that language, which she had once loved for its creative possibilities, was now a barrier: Who in this new country, through the cloudy window of her imperfect English, would truly be able to see her and know her as she knew herself?

This anxiety persisted over the years, even as she reached fluency, graduated from college, and began teaching English to other recent arrivals to the country. And as she worked tirelessly to master the language, her long-ago love for its creative uses faded further and further into her past—until, on a late summer day in 2012, Laura received an email that sparked a memory.

A friend had forwarded her a call for volunteers to help create an avant-garde interactive theater performance. The piece, created by a group called Odyssey Works, had a unique conceit: It would be written and performed solely for an audience of one person. Reminded of her old love of Borges, Laura filled out an application. Shortly after, she received a response from the group's founder, Abraham Burickson. He didn't want Laura to help create the piece; he wanted her to be its subject in a production created just for her.

After some initial reluctance, Laura agreed, and in the weeks that followed, she filled out extensive questionnaires and went through multiple rounds of interviews with Odyssey Works members. They mined deep into her past, searching for the themes that ran throughout her life—her difficulties with English, her long-dormant passion for creativity, a driving urge to find meaning in her lived experiences—and even interviewed her friends and family members to complete the picture. One of the group's guidelines is that they're not ready to stage the performance until one of their members has dreamed about the subject.

After this initial period of activity, several weeks went by with little word. And then, one Saturday, Laura woke up to a text instructing her to arrive at the Fifth Avenue Marina in Oakland, California, at 10 a.m. The performance was about to begin.

Starting from the marina, Laura proceeded through a series of "scenes," moving throughout the Bay Area with guides who spoke to her about subjects like literature, film, and creativity and gave her cryptic assignments such as checking out preselected books from a local library. At first, she was baffled by the experience, anxious about whether or not she was responding correctly, whether she was "playing the role" that she was supposed to play. She struggled to find the meaning in it all.

Then came a pivotal moment: Laura was handed off to a guide who spoke to her in a language she'd never heard before. She realized then that her desire to find the precise meaning in everything going on was hopeless, and from that point forward, she relaxed into the experience, accepting it as it came.

Soon after, she opened her bag to find that the book she'd been carrying with her was losing its words. Many appeared faded on its

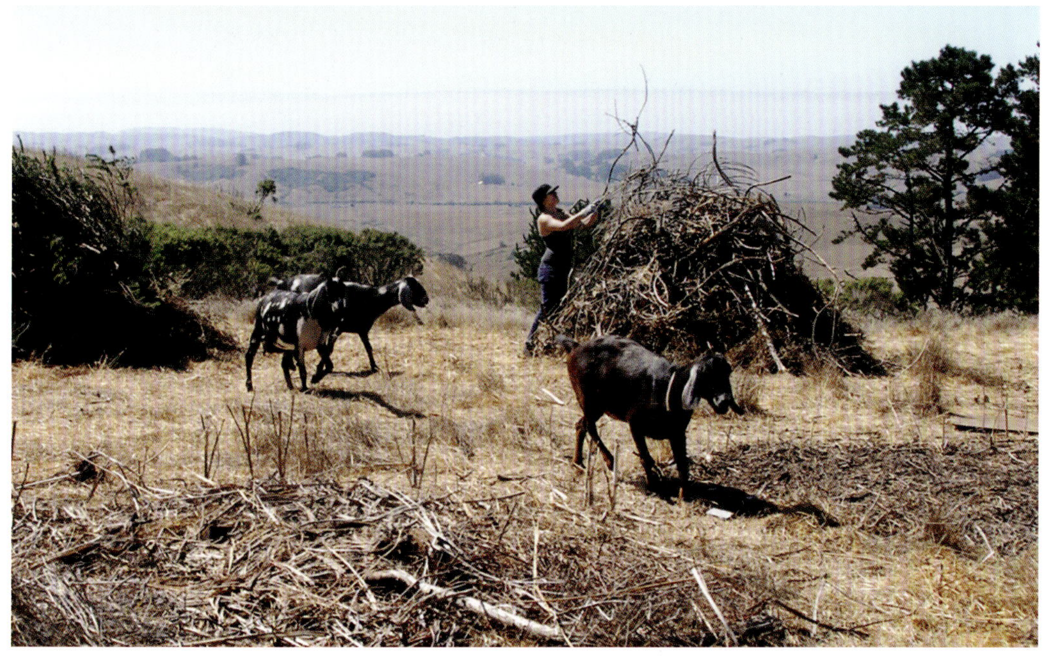

Laura Espino during her Odyssey, which was created just for her.

pages; some had disappeared entirely. Similarly, the words began fading from her interactions: When she met a man who, earlier in the day, had spoken to her while cutting and splicing strips of film, he remained silent, and all she heard was the sound of scissors cutting film strips, seemingly emanating from the room all around her.

Laura, too, stopped speaking. As one of her guides drove her out into the darkening Sonoma countryside that evening, she didn't say a word, instead sitting in companionable silence with this person who, she realized, knew more about her than almost anyone else.

It was a watershed moment for her, reminding her that she could be present with others in non-linguistic ways, refreshing her passion for creativity, and helping her better understand the threads that ran throughout her life, connecting the person she had been growing up in Argentina with the person she was now.

In the morning, she would pull weeds with Abraham. She wouldn't have spoken in almost twenty-four hours.

To this day, Laura thinks back on the experience often. It was a watershed moment for her, reminding her that she could be present with others in non-linguistic ways, refreshing her passion for creativity, and helping her better understand the threads that ran throughout her life, connecting the person she had been growing up in Argentina with the person she was now. "It helped me a lot to integrate myself," she says, "and feel more grounded in who I was becoming." In fact, she considers it among the most powerful experiences of her life, comparing it to her plane ride to the United States at age fourteen: "I remember that plane ride being transformative in a lot of ways. It's become a memory like that...even though I've been really moved by other live performances I've attended as an audience member, they just don't compare."

THE VALUE OF EXPERIENCE

When I was nearing my fiftieth birthday, I spent a great deal of time fretting about the best way to celebrate what felt like such a major milestone. Then, one day, a good friend gave me a piece of advice that has stuck with me ever since: She told me to "invest in making memories." So instead of buying myself something nice or throwing a big party that would likely have faded into a blur, I invited a group of my closest friends to spend a weekend enjoying the outdoors, eating well, and spending quality time together. The memories we made that weekend still put a smile on my face every time I look back on them. To this day, I've kept that advice close to my heart—whenever I can, I invest in making memories.

This mindset, of prioritizing experiences and memories above consumption and possessions, is a shift I've noticed among many of my friends. But it's not just us: In the past thirty-odd years, there has been a vast cultural movement toward emphasizing those memories and experiences and acknowledging the great value they bring to our lives.

Economists B. Joseph Pine II and James Gilmore were among the first to identify this trend with their 1999 book, *The Experience Economy*. This massively influential text inspired the careers of many of the storytellers I've written about in these pages and had a major impact on my own. Living stories are an outgrowth of the trend they described: that of consumers increasingly valuing experiences over goods and services.

In *The Experience Economy*, Pine and Gilmore describe a shift from traditional economic offerings, such as commodities and services, to *experiences* as the primary drivers of business.

When a café offers a pleasant environment for drinking the coffee it sells—maybe with some good music playing, a friendly barista to chat with, and a beautifully designed space in which to work or hang out with friends—it's offering an experience that goes beyond the mere sale of a commodity (coffee beans) or a service (a prepared cup of coffee). What you're truly paying for, when you visit that expensive coffee shop, is not just the high-quality cup of coffee but also the ambience of the café. You're paying to spend your time in a way you enjoy, and therefore the value of an experience is inherently more personal and customized than that of a commodity or service.

When they published *The Experience Economy* more than two decades ago, Pine and Gilmore were describing a ripplethat today has become a wave. Data from the U.S. Bureau of Economic Analysis analyzed by McKinsey & Company shows that by 2016, U.S. consumer spending on experiences was growing nearly four times faster than spending on goods; a 2019 study by ad agency Momentum Worldwide demonstrated that 76 percent of consumers preferred to spend their money on experiences rather than physical objects. Though these numbers understandably took a dive during the Covid pandemic, they have since come roaring back, with consumer spending on experiences in 2024 reaching record levels according to McKinsey.

Why do people seek out experiences? They are not assets in the traditional sense, cannot be resold, don't solve a problem or answer a need in the way that purchasing a vacuum cleaner or a haircut does. Some have speculated that the desire for experiences arises from a deeper desire to craft and reinforce a sense of identity in a rapidly changing world. Pine and Gilmore believe that "the value of experiences lies within [their recipients], where it remains long afterward." And in fact, studies have consistently shown that experiential purchases, as opposed to material ones, provide greater long-term happiness. Perhaps we are collectively coming to realize a fundamental truth: that it is the memories we accumulate, not the objects, that truly enrich our lives.

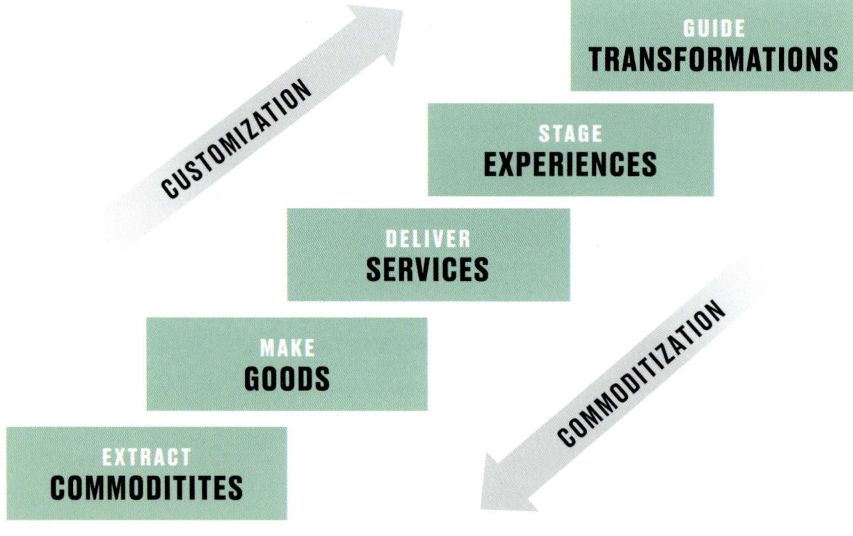

The progression of economic value as described by Pine and Gilmore in their seminal book, *The Experience Economy.*

FROM EXPERIENCE TO TRANSFORMATION

Within this framing of experiences as sources of richness, satisfaction, and personal growth, it would seem intuitive that the most valuable experiences are those that have some sort of lasting impact on our lives—that significantly and permanently expand our worldview or sense of self. And indeed, this is the final step in Pine and Gilmore's model of economic progression: When an experience is powerful and personal enough to truly change someone, it becomes a transformation. "People value transformation above all other economic offerings," Pine and Gilmore tell us, "because it addresses the ultimate source of all other needs: why the buyer desires the commodities, goods, services, and experiences he purchases." A great deal of our spending is already oriented toward transformation: We want to be smarter, healthier, happier, more confident, more effective, more fulfilled. Most of these transformations are impossible to buy—you can't simply pay to become smarter—but the business that provides transformation (a college, for example) can charge much more than the one that only gives you the tools (a bookstore).

Experiences have great power to be transformational when executed properly, in part because they are so intimately woven into the fabric of who we are. In the words of psychologist Thomas Gilovich, "We are the sum total of our experiences." And within the realm of experiences, living stories have the capacity to be especially potent drivers of transformation. This is because stories of all kinds are a means of passing on profound lessons; we've all heard others talk about books and movies that changed their lives, and many of us have experienced this ourselves. The fundamental difference with living stories is that, unlike all other story forms, we experience them ourselves rather than witnessing them from the outside; we are therefore more intimately connected with the messages and meanings they convey. If a story is a deep pool of meaning, then traditional, linear narratives offer us the opportunity to gaze into the pool and perhaps see our own reflections within it. Living stories, however, allow us to dive into the pool and swim around.

In his seminal book *The Hero with a Thousand Faces,* literary scholar Joseph Campbell argued that transformation is a near-universal theme of human mythology. Analyzing myths from around the world and throughout history, he found that the vast majority feature the same overarching structure: To put it simply, the hero of the story departs from their daily life into something new and different, encounters trials there, overcomes these trials through a process of personal growth and transformation, and then returns to their original life with new understanding. This narrative arc applies not only to myths but also to the vast majority of stories of all

By combining the emotional force of narrative with the immediacy of lived experience, living stories have the power to transform our perspectives.

genres. It should occur, too, in living stories—but here, each audience member plays the role of the hero, and so the heroic transformation is their own. By combining the emotional force of narrative with the immediacy of lived experience, living stories have the power to transform our perspectives.

In his famous saga *The Captive,* Marcel Proust wrote that "the only true voyage of discovery...would be not to visit strange lands but to possess other eyes, to behold the universe through the eyes of another, of a hundred others, to behold the hundred universes that each of them beholds..." Living stories have the remarkable ability to give us new eyes. In doing so, they can change how we see each other, ourselves, and the world around us.

CHANGING HOW WE SEE EACH OTHER

As the experience economy gained steam in the early 2000s, some began to recognize the profound transformational potential of designed experiences. One such group was a Hong Kong–based humanitarian aid organization called Crossroads Foundation (see p. 284). In 2005, the group was looking for a special way to commemorate their tenth anniversary, and they hit upon a bold idea: to create an experience where those with the most power in their community—local corporate and community leaders—would briefly "live the lives" of those with the least.

Inspired by the ancient Chinese proverb "I hear and I forget, I see and I remember, I do and I understand," Crossroads invited their participants to truly understand the lives of the least fortunate members of their community by spending twenty-four hours living in simulated slum-like conditions. The experience was intense and uncompromising: Participants slept in structures they had built from piles of debris, ate food scraps salvaged from garbage bags, and dealt with the pressures of day-to-day slum life, such as encounters with aggressive loan sharks.

Creating the simulation was a lot of work, but the organization's leaders assured their staff that they'd only have a ten-year anniversary every decade. What they didn't count on was the strength of the reaction from their participants. Many were stunned by the power of the experience and urged Crossroads to create more like it. Word spread, and soon enough the group was running simulations every week, covering a broad range of topics including blindness, water shortages, and HIV/AIDS. Starting in 2009, they began bringing a refugee-camp simulation, then known as A Day in the Life of a Refugee, to the World Economic Forum's annual meeting in Davos. The experience wasn't just effective for how it simulated living conditions in refugee camps but also for giving participants a small taste of the real-life struggles and emotions that refugees live through. Vaibhav Lodha, who experienced A Day in the Life in 2017, was shaken by an intense interaction he had when attempting to get medicine for his family from a soldier. "Do you have a daughter?" the soldier asked him. "Bring your daughter tomorrow and you'll get the medicine." One CEO who went through it commented, "Reading a thousand books would not have taught me what I learned in the past hour." Many described it as one of the most powerful and profound experiences of their entire lives. For almost all, it was likely the first time they had ever understood, in an embodied, multisensory way, what it was like to be anyone other than themselves.

When we expand our experiences to include those of another, we permanently change the lens through which we perceive them. In the words of another participant at Davos, after going through A Day in the Life, "you can never think of the issue in detached numbers and policies ever again." Crossroads director DJ Begbie views that participant sentiment as a success. "If you want to see people connected and then responding to global issues," he said in an episode of the *Future of StoryTelling* podcast, "the very first place that you have to start is helping them care. And once people care, then they walk away saying, 'Now what can I do? How can I help?'"

When we expand our experiences to include those of another, we permanently change the lens through which we perceive them.

Coincidentally, the very same year that Crossroads staged their first simulation, the film critic Roger Ebert, in his remarks upon receiving a star on the Hollywood Walk of Fame, coined the term "empathy machine" to describe movies. While watching a movie, he said, "I can live somebody else's life for a while. I can walk in somebody else's shoes...the great movies enlarge us, they civilize us, they make us more decent people."

As the Crossroads story demonstrates, the "empathy machine" label truly belongs to living stories—the ultimate empathy machines—the closest we will ever come to experiencing the world through the eyes, bodies, and emotions of others. More so than any other form, they allow us, to use Ebert's words, to "live somebody else's life for a while."

Many of the early examples of living stories that aimed specifically at transforming their audiences originated from similarly

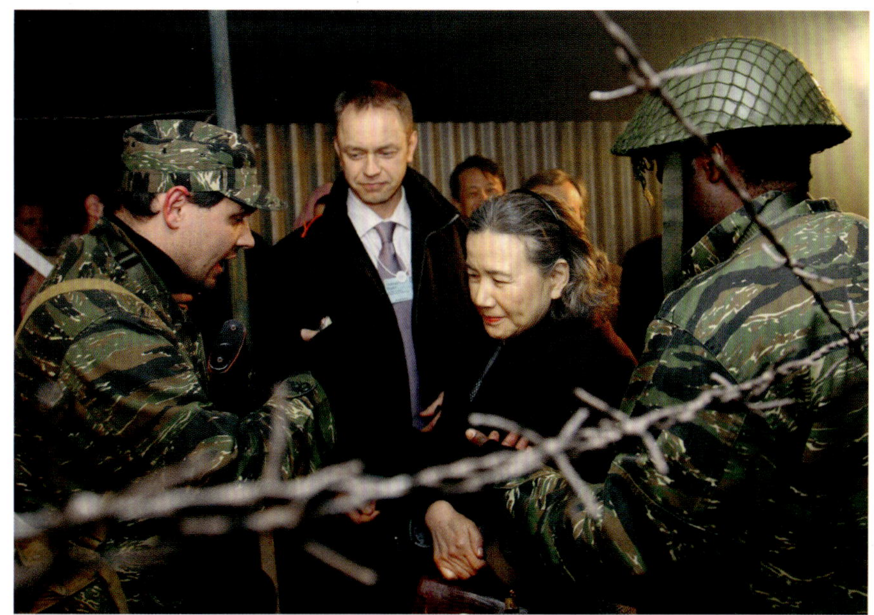

Participants are confronted by soldiers in Crossroads Foundation's A Day in the Life of a Refugee immersive simulation.

cause-driven mindsets, like Nonny de le Peña's Guantánamo Bay experience (see p. 142). It makes sense that when we think of building empathy and expanding our understanding of others, our first thoughts are often of activism. But despite the nobility of that impulse, it's only the beginning. As living stories continue to proliferate and diversify, we will each have opportunities to step into a vast array of other lives, increasing our understanding in all directions and deepening our connection with the great web of humanity.

Of course, what no medium so far invented can do is allow you to experience the actual inner life of another. Living stories can let us see into the lives of others with greater detail and immediacy than any previous form—even facing their decisions and feeling the weight of the potential consequences—but they can't let us *be* other people. So while they do have immense power to change the way we see and relate to our fellow humans, perhaps their even greater power is to change the way we see and relate to ourselves.

CHANGING HOW WE SEE OURSELVES

A quote often attributed to Meryl Streep is "Acting is not about being someone different. It's finding the similarity in what is apparently different, then finding myself in there." In other words, when we step into a role within a story, we don't change who we are—rather, we expand who we are in order to fit something new. One of the great gifts of living stories is that they encourage and promote this expansion.

If you go into a classroom of first graders and ask who can draw, who can sing, who can dance, they'll all raise their hands. But if you pose the same questions to a group of high school seniors, very few of them will believe they possess the ability to be creative and dramatic. As we move through life, our sense of who we *are* solidifies, with the unfortunate side effect that our sense of who we *might be* tends to narrow.

Sarah Lynne Bowman, an associate professor of game design at Uppsala University in Sweden and a founding member of the university's Transformative Play Initiative research group, believes that playing roles within interactive narratives can be a potent antidote to this narrowing. Through the TPI she has studied this potential extensively, with a specific focus on live-action role-playing, or LARP, in which participants gather and act out continuously evolving stories together (see p. 298).

Among the uninitiated public, LARP is often seen as mere escapism, conjuring images of adults dressed as knights and wizards pretending to fight each other with foam weapons. Bowman's early LARP experiences certainly fit that mold, at least to an outside observer: Her first was a LARP called *Vampire: The Masquerade*, in which players could choose to portray a vampire, werewolf, wraith, or mage. But as Bowman delved further into the world of LARP, she found that the stories being told within it are just as diverse as those of any other medium. In fact, there is an entire LARP subgenre, called Nordic LARP, that focuses on in-depth narrative and emotional development; these LARPs tend to feature little, if any, combat and function more like long-form improvisational theater than traditional gameplay. It was these immersive, emotional, character-driven LARPs that truly caught Bowman's attention, and as she played them, she found that she and her fellow players were deriving much more value from the experiences than their lighthearted trappings might suggest.

"If we're co-creating an entirely different social reality together, that's profound, just in and of itself," Bowman tells me. "Even if we're just doing it to laugh the whole time, or to roll dice and to kill monsters. The fact that we are able to say, 'Okay, for the next four hours, I'm going to be called this other thing, and my personality is going to be completely different, and we're going to live in a world where all sorts of magic is possible. And you're going to be the most important person on earth. You're going to save the earth.' To me, you can't say that that doesn't have an effect on the psyche." While writing her graduate school dissertation on the various functions of role-playing games, she found this to be true: Many players' lives were changed, in ways big and small, through their LARP experiences. Some of the most common outcomes were developing social and practical skills (the U.S. military uses LARP extensively in its training programs), establishing strong communal bonds, and exploring different sides of themselves.

Bowman has since dedicated her academic life to studying the transformative potential of role-play, and LARP in particular. One of its most powerful mechanisms, she has found, is identity exploration: By allowing us to step out of our established personal narratives, LARP opens our minds to possibilities for ourselves that we might not otherwise have considered. "Maybe someone's self-definition is 'I'm not a leader,'" she says. "A lot of people don't feel like they have that capability. But then all of a sudden, they're in this narrative framework where they're the king, and they're giving speeches and realizing, 'Oh, wait, I guess I could actually be a leader.' That is a profound shift that you can't get from less immersive experiences with less active, agentic roles."

Bowman refers to this identity expansion as "practicing different states of being," and she has found it to be a deeply profound experience—not only for the LARPers she has studied in her academic work but also for her personally. As someone who has struggled with anxiety all her life, she recounts her experience in a LARP called *Just a Little*

Lovin' about the AIDS crisis in the 1980s, role-playing as a character named Joanie with a more calm and confident disposition: "What I was wanting to find in that character was spiritual peace," she says. She discovered that by playing the character, she was able to feel that peace herself—a peace that had been markedly absent in her day-to-day life. She was able to remain calm even as, at a climactic moment in the narrative, her character faced imminent death. "This will sound weird," she admits, "but I was ready to die as Joanie. She was facing her own mortality, and she was totally at peace." This in itself was a powerful experience for Bowman, but the true learning, she explains, came when the scene ended and she stepped back out of the role. "I lost it," she says. "All that anxiety came crashing back in, all that 'Sarahness,' that construct of me that I didn't even realize I had been holding at bay. And I realized that's what I was holding all the time, that anxiety."

By stepping into another character, we may find opportunities to challenge not only the identities we build for ourselves but also those the world ascribes to us.

Playing Joanie helped Bowman recognize her anxiety as something separate from herself—something that, at times, she was able to put down. The peace she experienced as Joanie was part of the character she was playing, but it wasn't fictional. "That happened in my body," Bowman says, "so clearly I can go there. And each time I played her, it became easier."

By stepping into another character, we may find opportunities to challenge not only the identities we build for ourselves but also those the world ascribes to us. This occurs through a phenomenon known in the role-playing community as alibi: Within the "magic circle" of the fictional world, we have "alibi" to be something other than ourselves without consequences. We can engage in behaviors that might be outside our normal standards of conduct and in doing so challenge those standards.

Renowned experience designer and cofounder of the College of Extraordinary Experiences Paul Bulencea tells me about a particularly memorable example of alibi he witnessed at a LARP he designed in Abu Dhabi in 2016. Participants in the LARP were divided into five tribes inspired by the local history of the region, and members of the different tribes engaged in staged conflicts with foam swords throughout the experience. The magic circle of the LARP provided an opportunity for one woman, visiting with her family from Saudi Arabia, to step outside her normal social boundaries. "At that time," Bulencea explains, "women in Saudi Arabia were not allowed to run or to do sports. But when we were dividing up the group, she asked, 'Can I be in a different tribe from my husband? I want to chase him with the kids and beat him up!' I think that's a really simple and beautiful example of how games can break these strong social barriers and allow people to explore in a safe way, in an accepted way."

Bulencea suggests that the primary driver of identity exploration within living stories is their liminality. "If they're the good stuff, they create a liminal space," he explains. "And what happens within a liminal space is that your daily way of being and behaving is dissolved." In other words, living stories offer us the extremely rare opportunity to be someone other than ourselves.

Modern education has the tendency to narrow children's ideas of who or what they can be; living stories can counteract this narrowing by reminding us that "who we are" is whoever we have the capacity to imagine ourselves to be. And as Bowman points out, by this same token, living stories have the capacity to expand our sense of possibility not only for ourselves but for the world we inhabit. "It reveals to us that, on some level, we're all co-creating reality all the time," she tells me. "And if we're all co-creating reality all the time, then we can decide certain things together. That agency that we found in play, we can actually bring that back into the real world."

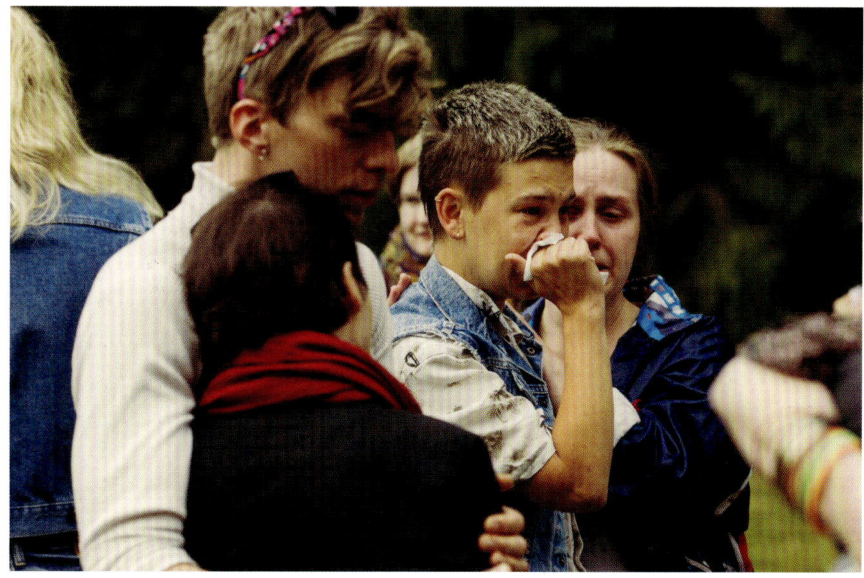

Participants overcome with emotion during the LARP *Just a Little Lovin'* in Finland.

CHANGING HOW WE SEE THE WORLD

In 2017, I experienced a living story that profoundly shifted my lens on the world around me. It was a six-hour Punchdrunk production called *Kabeiroi*, performed for an audience of just two and staged throughout the streets, buildings, and subway tunnels of London.

The experience began with an audio-guided walking tour that eventually led my friend Andrew and me to the British Museum. There, as we wandered past glass cases full of ancient Greek pottery and sculpture, the audio informed us that we were in fact looking at the recovered artifacts of an ancient Greek cult called Kabeiroi. It even hinted, at various moments, that the cult might still be in operation. And then, as we were exiting the building, something unexpected happened: We were standing at the top of the grand staircase that led down to the street, surrounded by throngs of people streaming in and out of the museum, when all of a sudden a woman slapped a note against my chest and then vanished into the crowd around us.

I was shocked to have had my personal space invaded—and so quickly that I never got a good look at who did it. As I scanned the crowd for her, it occurred to me that anyone I saw, any tiny detail of the world around me, might now be part of this story. It was like the city had suddenly come alive, and as we set off into the streets to follow the instructions on the note, I found that I was engaging with the world in a new way: deeply attuned to everything around me, taking in every detail, totally alert and engaged and, yes, immersed, in my surroundings. It was almost as though, after decades of more or less sleepwalking my way through life, I was now awake.

I was—in Proust mode—seeing the world with new eyes.

One of the simplest and yet most profound offerings of living stories is that they allow us to step out of our everyday lives, out of the world that at all other times we inhabit, and into something entirely different. There is a very specific feeling that often accompanies this experience: awe. Awe was the emotion I felt so powerfully when the woman slapped the note against my chest during *Kabeiroi* and I suddenly realized that the whole world surrounding me was now part of a story. I have felt it countless times while engaged in living stories, so much so that I consider it a hallmark of the medium.

In his book *Awe: The New Science of Everyday Wonder and How It Can Transform Your Life,* UC Berkeley psychology professor Dacher Keltner shares some of the surprising effects that awe can have on our psyches. “People who feel even five minutes a day of everyday awe are more curious about art, music, poetry, new scientific discoveries, philosophy, and questions about life and death,” he writes. But perhaps most striking is the effect awe has on our perceptions of ourselves in relation to the world. In Keltner’s words, when we experience awe, “our individual self gives way to the boundary-dissolving sense of being part of something much larger.”

Living stories break us out of our entrenched modes of being in the world, forcing us to see it, hear it, and sense it anew.

As cognitive scientist Andy Clark explains in his book *The Experience Machine,* the current reigning theory of perception dictates that rather than showing us the full sensory reality of our surroundings, our brain uses the smallest amount of information possible to build a predictive model of the world around us based on our past experiences. This is known as “predictive processing,” and it suggests that what we perceive as “the world” is in fact the output of the predictive model formed by our brains. By operating this way, the brain saves energy—but as we grow older and our “predictions” become more entrenched, they may lock us into limiting and potentially harmful perceptions and beliefs. Perhaps this is why, during my experience in Punchdrunk’s *Kabeiroi,* the world felt so new and refreshed: Shocked out of my normal model of perception, I very well might have been perceiving *more of the world,* just as I had when I was a child.

Living stories break us out of our entrenched modes of being in the world, forcing us to see it, hear it, and sense it anew. They place us in novel, unknown environments, often specifically designed to subvert our expectations and encourage exploration and discovery.

Both Felix Barrett of Punchdrunk and Vince Kadlubek of Meow Wolf mention this specifically while discussing their respective groups' work. "The goal is to slow an audience down so they're at a liquid pace, which you don't normally achieve in normal life," Barrett tells me. "So they're actually exploring in the same way as when they were children exploring their grandfather's attic."

Kadlubek generalizes this sentiment to all immersive environments. "There's plenty of opportunity for us to venture into the unknown in our everyday lives, but it's inherently dangerous to do so," he says. "Immersive experiences provide an environment where you can safely venture into the unknown."

Cognitive science suggests that the unknown is a powerful drug—one that has the ability to loosen our rigid modes of perception, making room for new ideas and beliefs. Confronting worlds different from our own may also remind us that ours is itself a construction. In the words of Sarah Lynne Bowman, "We're all co-creating reality all the time." As we return to our own reality after a powerful living-story experience, our senses refreshed and our stalwart beliefs temporarily hushed by encounters with the new and unknown, perhaps we may see ways to create it differently.

SETTING THE STAGE FOR TRANSFORMATION

Living stories have a profound capacity to change how we see and relate to one another, ourselves, and the world around us. But it can be tricky to design them in a way that specifically maximizes this transformative capacity, in part because transformation is so personal to each participant. In an open-ended, agentic living story, in which the audience's actions may vary widely and drive the narrative in unexpected directions, it's nearly impossible for any two attendees to have the same experience or come away with the same effect. According to Odyssey Works founder Abraham Burickson, "The problem with experience design is that we're not designing anybody's experience. What we're doing is creating the conditions under which certain experiences might be possible." By the same token, while a traditional storyteller is often concerned with finely crafting and portraying the transformations of their characters, the job of the living story creator is to create the conditions for their characters—i.e., the actience—under which such transformations might occur.

It may be appropriate, then, to think of the living story as in some sense "abstracted" storytelling. Traditional stories offer a linear account of related events that leads to a predetermined conclusion. Living stories are far less rigid; they are different for each actience member, and different each time they're experienced. Just as an abstract painting rejects direct representation and thereby opens itself to a vast array of interpretations, a living story invites its viewers to participate in the enactment of the narrative, allowing them to find meaning that is far more personal than any prescribed meaning could be. It is precisely in relinquishing narrative control that we create the conditions for deep actience engagement.

This deep engagement should be the goal of any storyteller working to create transformative living stories. When the audience engages deeply enough that the story they are experiencing becomes their story, their journey becomes the hero's journey, and the consequent transformation, too, is their own. And while there are countless approaches to plot, dialogue, and production design that can yield a deeply engaging story, there are two overarching conditions unique to living stories that set the stage for deep audience engagement: aliveness and safety.

"Aliveness" is a specific type of realism that the best living stories achieve, a realism not necessarily of plot but of experience. They *feel* real—alive—even if their visual design or the events taking place within them are outlandish. As Burickson tells me, "It's very hard to feel transformed by something, to feel really affected by something that is not alive."

Burickson describes aliveness as something akin to unpredictability. "Think about those great conversations with a new friend, or on a first date, where you're discovering something you didn't know," he explains. "That first moment in Meow Wolf where you walk in and—spoiler alert—you discover there's another world on the other side of that house. These are live moments. These are engagements with the unknown. They're very different from those troubling times when you feel like something is designed for you to do exactly what you're told to do."

Aliveness comes, in part, from good world-building. As Scott Trowbridge of Walt Disney Imagineering shared in Chapter 2, little details—such as the texture of a surface, the natural wear on an object that's supposed to feel old, the ambient sounds of the world around you—play an outsize role in making a story world feel real and alive. Things should never feel too perfect: An alive world has scratches and dings in it from having been lived in. But as Burickson tells me, aliveness also has to do with your agency within that world. When your movement through the story feels too planned out—"when you feel like something is designed for you to do in a prescribed way"—the sense of aliveness diminishes.

The twin quality that balances aliveness is safety, and it's critically important precisely because the best living-story experiences can be so engaging and all-encompassing: If an audience member becomes overwhelmed, they are likely to pull back and shield themselves rather than lean in and engage. Safety here means not only

An emotionally open and supportive environment, in which participants know that they are welcome to interact with the story without being judged or criticized, is crucial to achieving deep engagement.

physical safety, which is clearly essential, but also emotional safety. An emotionally open and supportive environment, in which participants know that they are welcome to interact with the story without being judged or criticized, is crucial for achieving deep engagement.

"The perception of safety allows the audience to lower their vigilance and surrender into the experience," Sarah Lynne Bowman tells me. As an example, she shares a cardinal rule for the LARPs she runs: "The door is always open. Meaning you can leave at any time, you can opt out at any time. Telling people that is one way that you can communicate to your audience that their experience is more important than the story." Somewhat paradoxically, by creating this exit opportunity, the storyteller also creates an environment in which the audience feels safe enough to engage freely.

CEMENTING TRANSFORMATION

I believe that as this new medium advances, the very best living stories will rank among the peak experiences of people's lives. They will offer actiences the opportunity to venture safely into powerfully alive, vibrant alternate worlds and realities, connect deeply with others, explore their own identities, and see the real world in new ways.

And yet, as all stories do, living stories end. The lights come up, you step through the final door, you power down the computer, the VR headset comes off—and you're back where you were before. You may have just had an incredibly significant experience, but more often than not, your feelings and epiphanies fade soon afterward. The reawakening I had during *Kabeiroi,* that profound sense of attunement to the world and all its wonder, is now only a memory. Thus the final question for the living storyteller attempting to offer a truly transformative experience becomes: How do we extend that transformation beyond the end of the story?

One experience that has created lasting transformations for thousands of people is Burning Man. Known to many as a psychedelic art festival, it should rightly be seen as one of the ultimate living-story experiences available today. What it lacks in structured narrative it makes back double in immersion: Visiting Burning Man is truly, and perhaps more so than any other experience I have had, like stepping into another world. It is a co-created, agentic, embodied, social, open-world adventure. And critically, when it comes to transformation, Burning Man allows you to take that world back with you. This occurs through a phenomenon known within the role-playing community as "bleed."

Coined by game designer Emily Care Boss, "bleed" refers to the process by which ideas, emotions, and values permeate the "magic circle" that separates the real world from the imagined one. One classic example of bleed is when LARPers feel so connected to their characters within the story that they continue to feel those characters' emotions after the LARP ends. Paul Bulencea, however, suggests that physical bleed may have even more lasting impact. He explains this

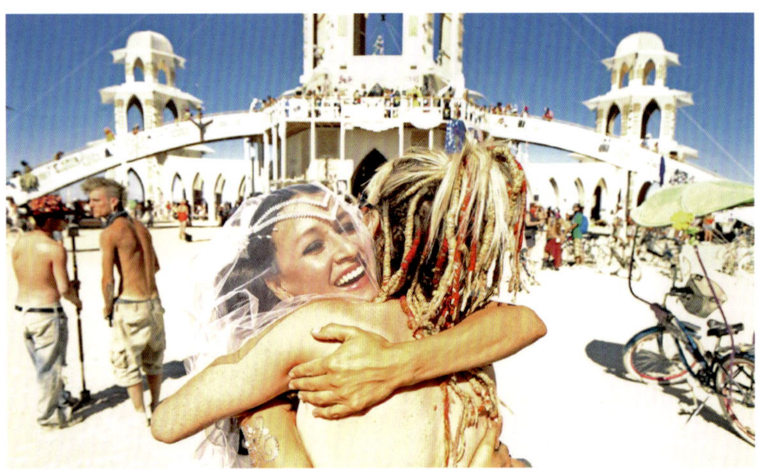

idea in the context of Burning Man, where the culture encourages attendees to wear outlandish outfits that would be uncommon in their normal lives. "If I'm going to Burning Man," Bulencea says, "I'm going to invest a lot of time into buying or creating those outfits. Afterward I might end up wearing some of them again. Wearing them will change how I behave, and it might give alibi to other people to start changing their clothing style as well." Thus the experimental, countercultural ethos of Burning Man "bleeds" out of the event into the world by way of the clothing.

Two Burning Man attendees embrace in front of a structure called the Temple of Transition.

This effect is not unique to Burning Man. Many LARPs also encourage players to make their own props and costumes. What's critical is that these physical mementos are not items purchased from the gift shop after the experience but rather authentic artifacts of the world of the story, offering a lasting connection to that world that is personal to the participant's specific experience within it. Even with experiences that don't involve audience-created props or costumes, storytellers should consider which pieces of the world—especially ones that play a role in the participant's journey—might be able to travel back out.

There is another and perhaps even more important way in which the transformations undergone within the story world can continue on in our lives beyond it, and this is through retelling. When we tell the story of our experience to others, we cement it in our own minds, give it shape and form that it may have previously lacked.

Recognizing the power of this process, a friend of mine, Matt Locke, describes a practice that he and his fellow LARPers call "frothing," referring to the frothy head on the pint of beer they consume at the pub after a day of play. Excited about their experiences, they take turns imparting the story of their own particular adventure. He says that it is in the retelling that the story becomes clear to the person recounting it. This way, he and his friends can form personal narratives that lend their memories of the experience greater staying power.

Almost every living-story creator I've spoken to agrees that the true key to cementing transformation lies not just in the experience itself, but also in what happens directly afterward. And they all emphasize the need to make space for the actience to process the experience together. In *The Experience Economy,* Pine and Gilmore label this step as follow-through. Bulencea refers to it as integration. Bowman calls it debriefing. But whatever the terminology, the concept is the same: The meaning of the experience is made in the retelling, when the story truly leaves the hands of the storyteller and enters the hands of the actience. It is in this process that the story becomes *their* story; *they* are the heroes; the transformations are *their own*.

ONWARD

Living stories can be powerful tools for transformation because they combine the emotional and imaginative power of narrative with the immediacy of lived experience. They allow us to create new realities and exist within them—and in the process see new possibilities for ourselves, our fellow humans, and the world we inhabit. But the truth is that we are only in the earliest stages of this burgeoning form, and even the best living stories today are just scratching the surface of the medium's full potential.

In the 1890s, when the earliest film experiments made by the Lumière brothers were competing with the literary works of H.G. Wells and Mark Twain, it probably would have been hard to believe that movies would ever match novels in artistic merit or popular appeal. And nearly a century later, when *Pong* came out in the same year as *The Godfather,* it would have been similarly hard to imagine that video games could ever truly compete with movies. Today, video games are far and away the most globally dominant entertainment industry, and we're at a new inflection point: Living stories are emerging and beginning to show their potential. I have been lucky enough to take part in many of the earliest experiments in this new media landscape. Some of them have fallen flat. Others have given me experiences I will never forget. I firmly believe that someday, not too far in the future, we will look back on the early 2000s and see the birth of a medium that left us, and our world, transformed.

CROSSROADS FOUNDATION

As the information age has shown, knowledge alone is not always enough to create change. We can read reports and sift through data on global issues—but without experiencing what people facing these challenges have actually felt, even the most compelling statistics can be lost. True empathy is a more powerful motivating force for change. But how can this kind of empathy be transformed into action?

For Hong Kong–based nonprofit Crossroads Foundation, the answer is found in experience. Their Global X-Periences are immersive simulations—detailed re-creations of real-life scenarios—that aim to foster an understanding of global issues. Global X-Periences cover a variety of topics, from poverty to HIV/AIDS to blindness, and are designed for a range of audiences, from families with children to government officials. Nearly 250,000 people have participated to date, including world leaders from the United Nations and executives from companies like Microsoft, Goldman Sachs, and Nestlé, plus other invitees to the World Economic Forum in Davos, where Crossroads ran the simulation annually for more than a decade.

It's one thing to learn about the global refugee crisis through a book, article, or film, but it's another entirely to take part in Crossroads' A Day in the Life of a Refugee simulation. The scenario unfolds in three phases: first, the onboarding phase, where participants are given an overview of the crisis and an identity card to help them play their role. Next comes the simulation itself. For two hours, they go through myriad experiences carefully modeled on the actual testimonies of internationally displaced people. They flee their village amid the sounds of explosions and gunfire, pick their way through

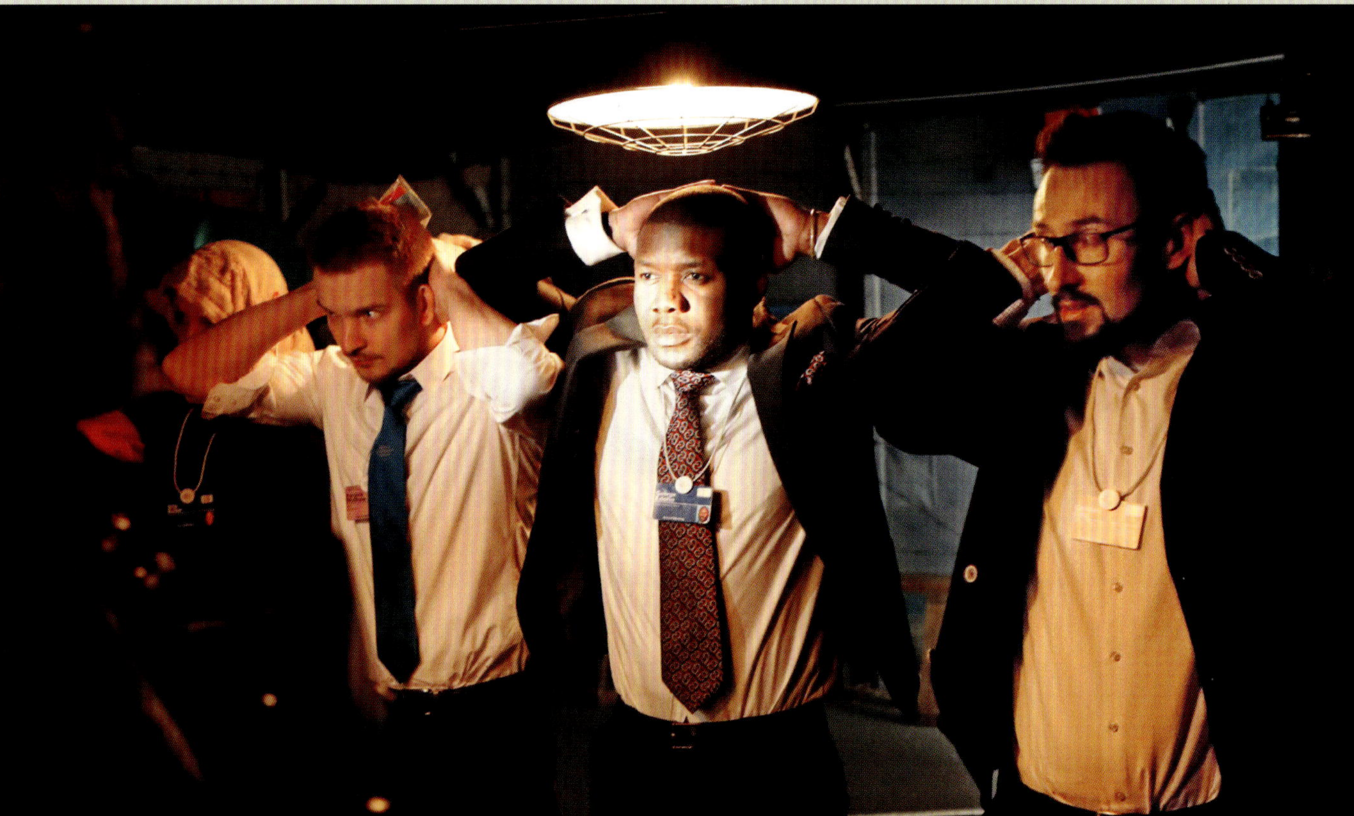

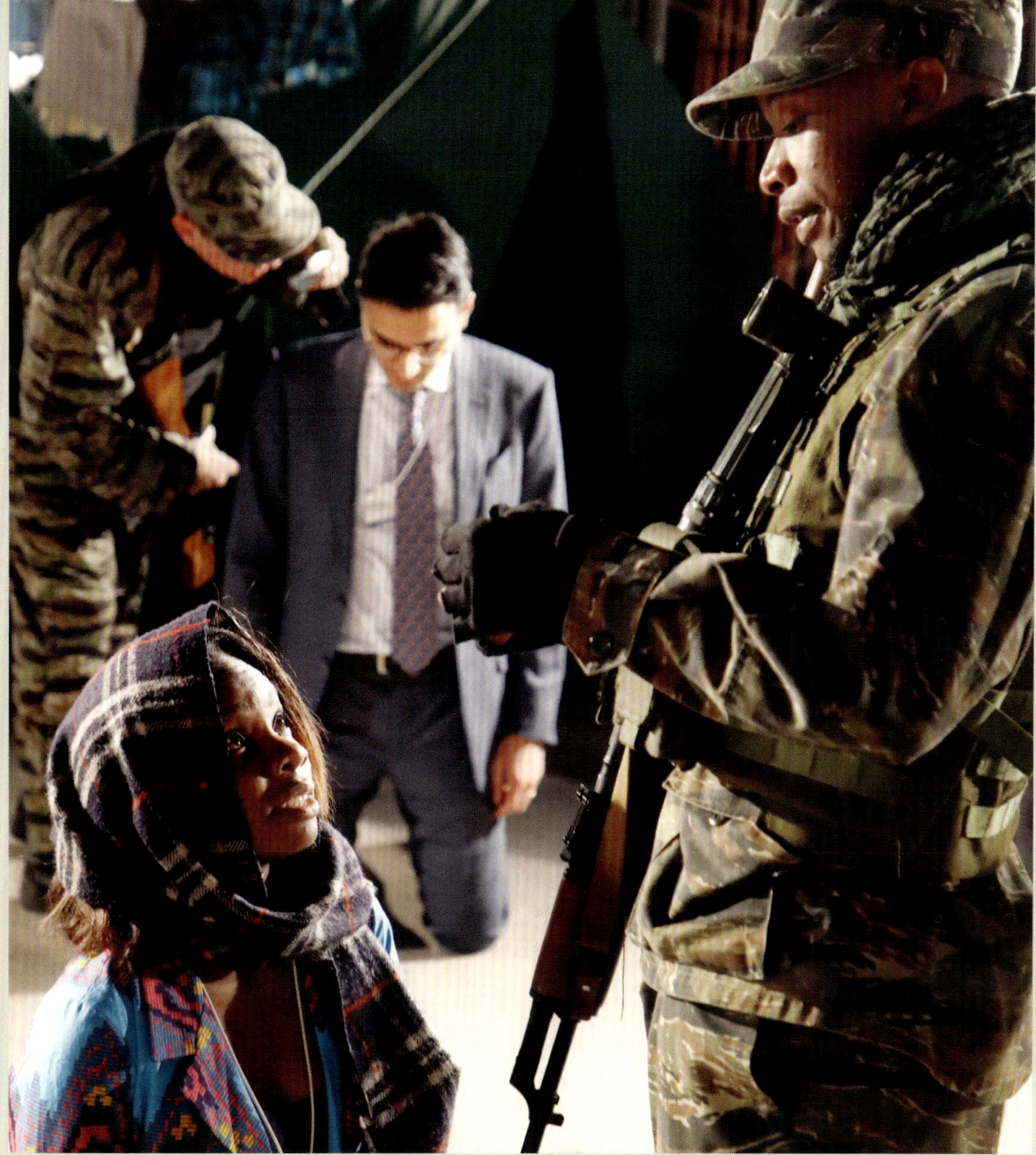

a minefield as quickly and carefully as possible en route to the nearest border, and make difficult choices to ensure their family's survival in the unforgiving conditions of a refugee camp marked by violence, deprivation, and loss.

Designed to evoke reality through sets, sounds, and live performances, this scenario intends to push participants just far enough out of their comfort zone to immerse them in the lived experience of actual refugees. You may know intellectually that the border crossing is only a simulation—but the emotions that arise when you're forced at gunpoint to hand over your jewelry, watch, and wedding ring are undeniably, viscerally real.

The impact that these immersive experiences have had on people is profound and transformative. According to Crossroads director DJ Begbie, some of the people who have participated in Global X-Periences have switched careers to focus on what they can do to help. Others have created new charities and programs, while others still have altered their company strategy in order to engage more meaningfully with global issues. These results are evidence that the empathy created by an embodied experience is a powerful driver toward sustained, purposeful change.

Participants play the role of refugees fleeing war in the A Day in the Life of a Refugee simulation, as they are corralled and screened by armed soldiers (played by real-life aid workers and refugees who themselves have had firsthand experience of displacement).

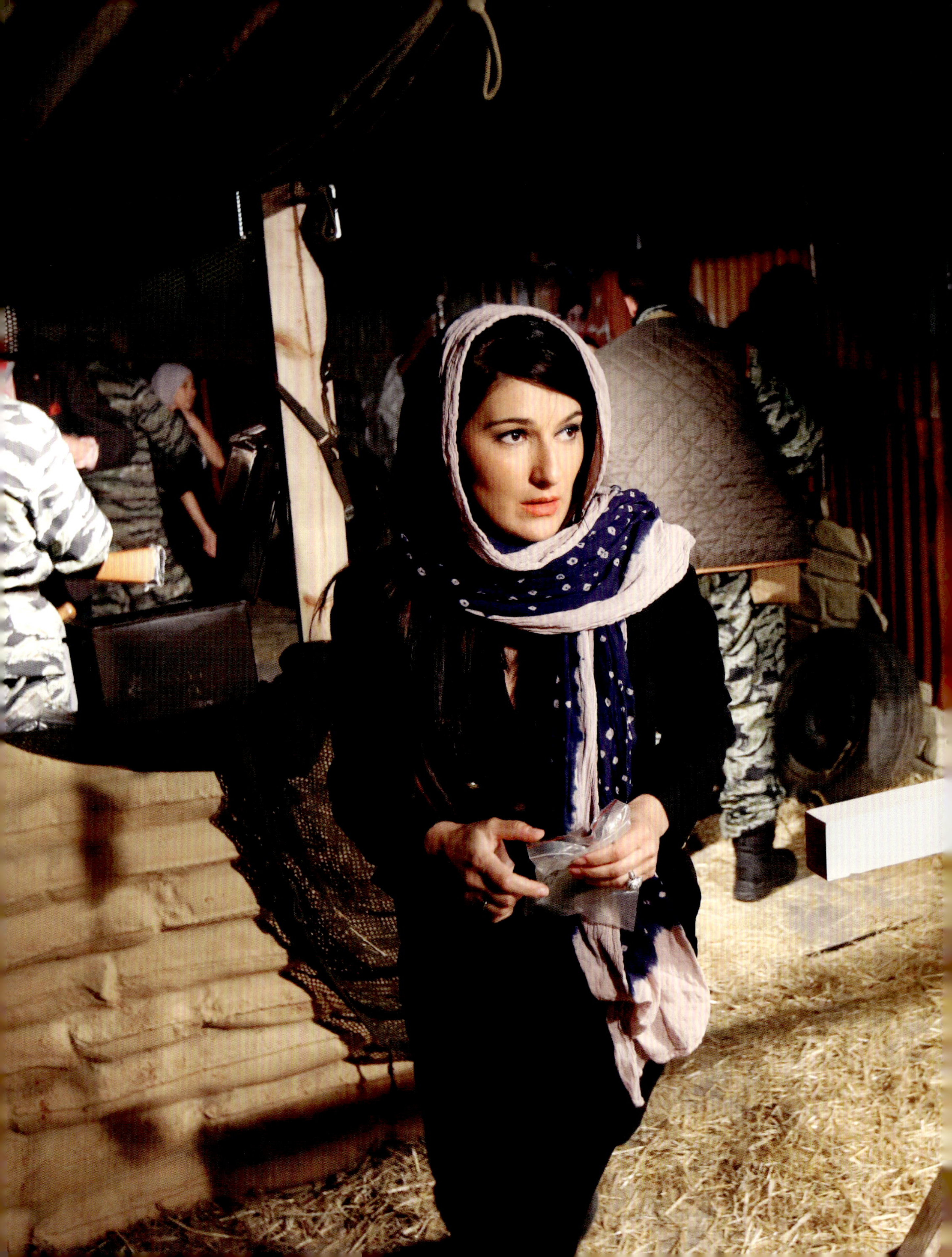

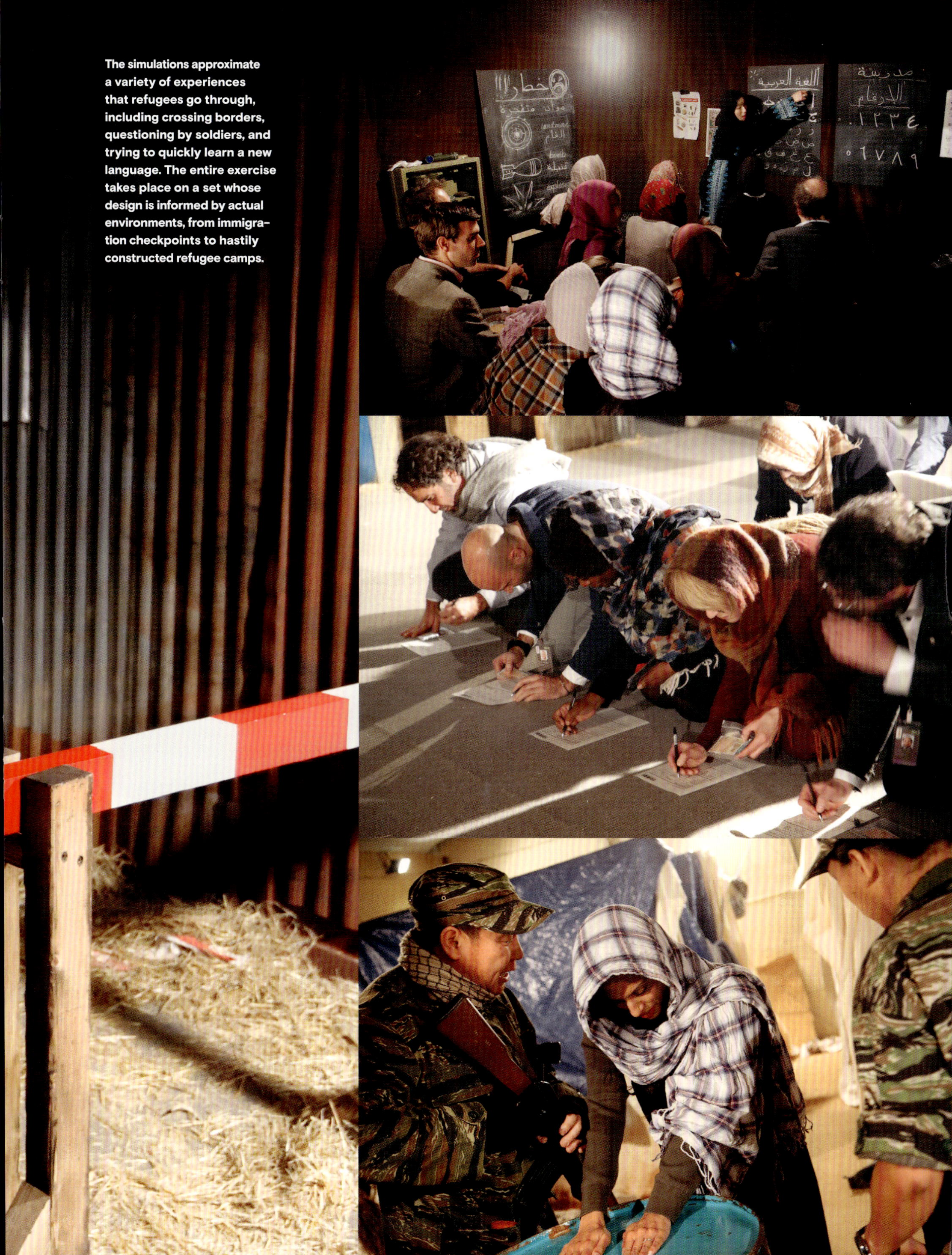

The simulations approximate a variety of experiences that refugees go through, including crossing borders, questioning by soldiers, and trying to quickly learn a new language. The entire exercise takes place on a set whose design is informed by actual environments, from immigration checkpoints to hastily constructed refugee camps.

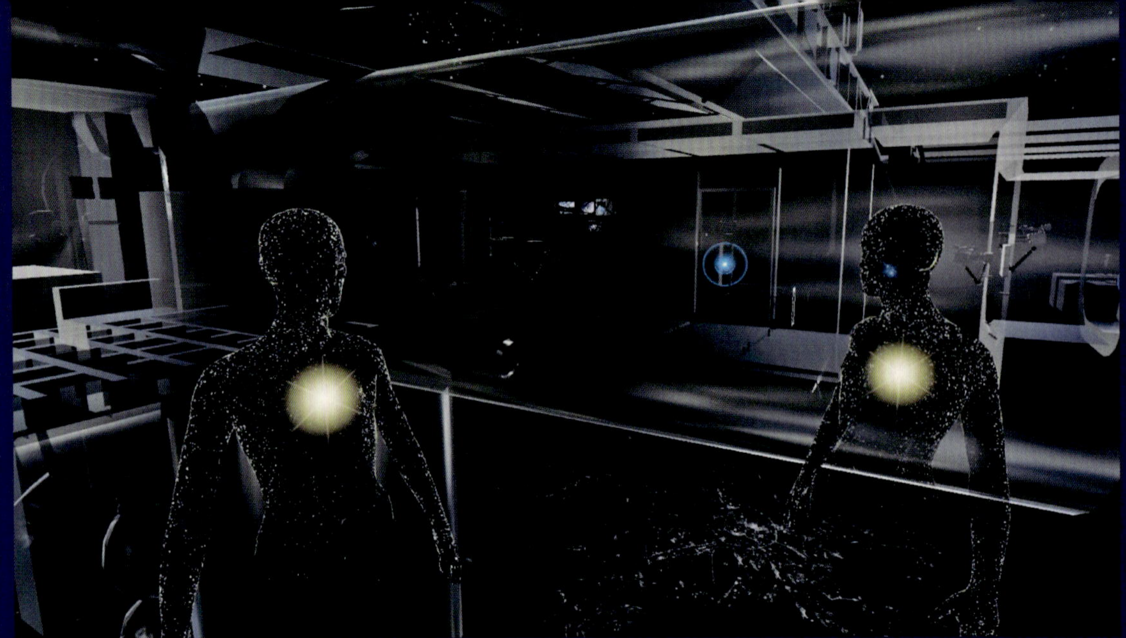

SPACE EXPLORERS: THE INFINITE

Montreal-based immersive entertainment company Felix & Paul Studios, founded by Félix Lajeunesse and Paul Raphaël, has been at the forefront of virtual-reality filmmaking for more than a decade—their 2014 piece, *Strangers*, is often credited as one of the first live-action VR films ever made. In the years since, they have continued to push boundaries, winning three Emmys and a Peabody Award for their VR pieces, including *The People's House* with Barack and Michelle Obama and *Miyubi*. Along the way, they've built a list of notable collaborators, among them Cirque du Soleil, LeBron James, and Wes Anderson.

In 2020, Felix & Paul Studios launched *Space Explorers: The ISS Experience*, a collaboration with NASA that documents the lives of astronauts aboard the International Space Station. The largest production ever filmed in space, it is the company's most ambitious project to date. Less than two years later, they unveiled *The Infinite*, a ticketed immersive exhibit that lets guests walk around a VR model of the ISS, where they can, at different points, unlock real footage of life on the station. The experience culminates in a spectacular VR spacewalk that gives visitors a taste of the "Overview Effect": the sense of awe, the preciousness of the planet, and the interconnectedness of all humanity that astronauts feel when looking down at Earth from approximately 250 miles above.

Clockwise from above: Inside the experience is a 3-D re-creation of the ISS, where other visitors' figures are marked by yellow orbs and VR video clips are activated by touching blue ones; a view from the first-of-its-kind virtual spacewalk, filmed outside the space station; guests in headsets explore the virtual space, while advanced-tracking technology prevents them from colliding with one another.

The technical accomplishments behind *The Infinite* are immense. For one, its state-of-the-art interaction system integrates the VR content from the ISS with a virtual space station that allows for six degrees of freedom; participants can look anywhere as well as move freely. Moreover, it solves one of the major challenges of VR entertainment so far: It has historically resulted in a very small throughput, as each guest needs to wear a headset. Felix & Paul Studios created an infrared tracking system that gives 1,200 people a day safe access to a 10,000-square-foot space, making *The Infinite* not only an achievement for the studio, but also a historic step forward for VR as a medium. Finally, the entire location-based experience can be packed up and moved to new markets: *The Infinite* has successfully opened in a dozen cities worldwide, from Montreal to Denver to Singapore and Shanghai. As of 2025, it is the world's largest interactive location-based VR experience.

Cinematic quality, artistic excellence, technological innovation, and an explorer's curious spirit: All of these define Felix & Paul Studios. They're true pioneers who have played a major role in innovating and elevating the art of immersive storytelling.

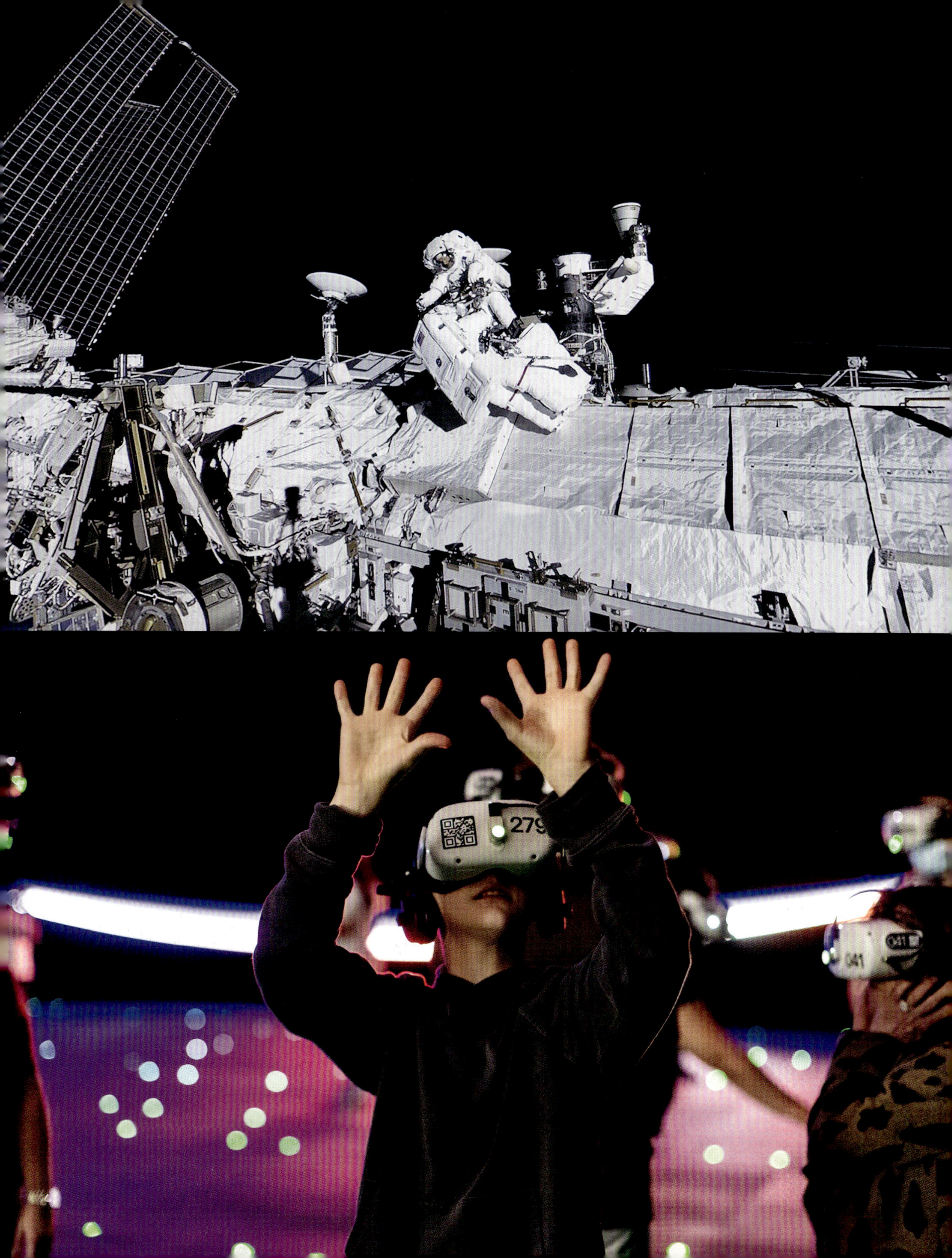
279
041

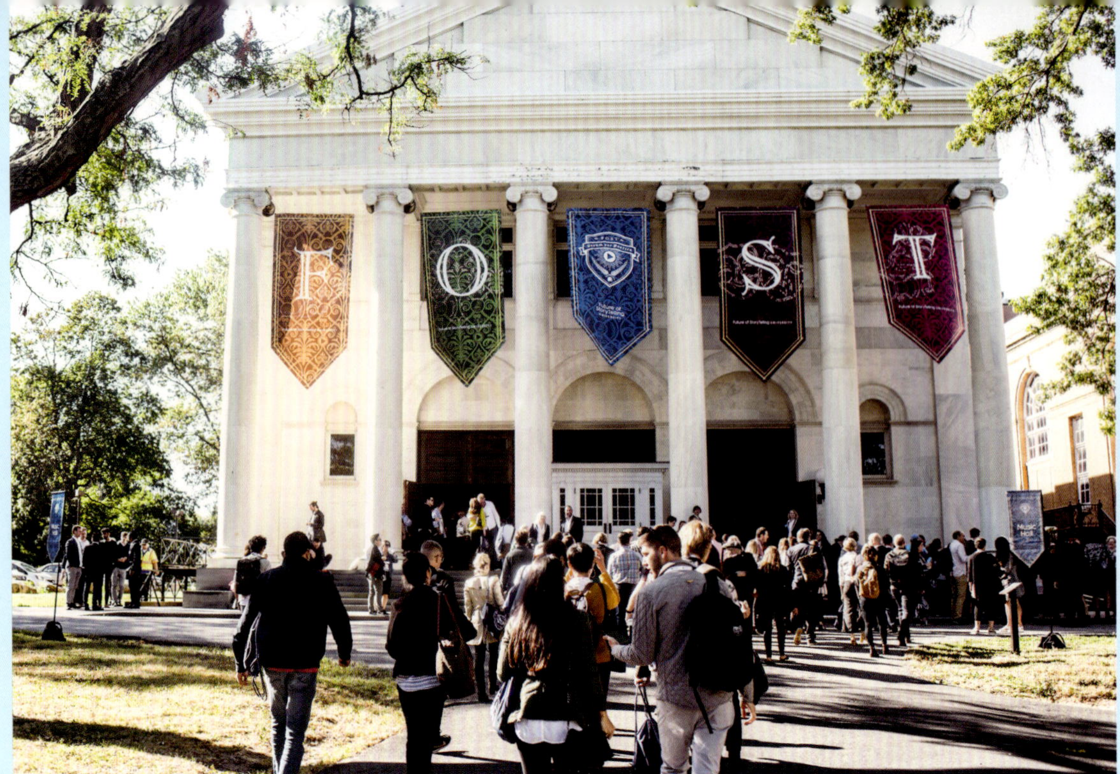

FoST SUMMIT

In the 2000s, the world of media was undergoing a profound transformation. Traditionally, different forms of media were siloed from one another; TV, publishing, theater, and other industries operated independently. With the advent of the digital revolution, the barriers between these industries began to break down as everyone started to work in the common language of zeros and ones. New forms of media emerged—mobile games, VR, podcasts, apps, and more. At the same time, the nature of the audience was changing. People no longer wanted to be passive consumers of media; they wanted to be active participants.

Clockwise from above: **The Snug Harbor campus, dressed up as "FoST University" for the 2017 immersive theme; a roundtable session taking place outside during the summit; a guest participates in one of the summit's many hands-on workshops; a student docent leading participants to their "classes" at FoST University.**

The Future of StoryTelling (FoST) Summit was created to explore the potential of this shifting media landscape. First held in 2012 at Snug Harbor Cultural Center on Staten Island, it brought together cutting-edge creatives, innovative technologists, and industry leaders from different storytelling fields with the intention of cross-pollinating and collaborating across disciplines. By forging these connections, the summit aimed to unlock new storytelling possibilities—perhaps even ushering in another renaissance in creativity.

To cultivate a new era of storytelling, the summit itself needed to reflect the ideas upon which it was built. More than just a traditional conference, it was designed to be participatory, embodied, and social. Rather than asking attendees to passively sit in a dark theater and be lectured to, FoST invited speakers to facilitate small-group roundtables where guests engaged in active discussion. Hands-on workshops where participants got their creative juices flowing—from puppetry to coding to aerial-drone photography—were designed to spark embodied learning and collaboration. These interactive sessions invited guests to connect not only with speakers but also with one another, creating more meaningful relationships than traditional networking typically affords. An interactive exhibit hall called the Story Arcade offered opportunities for attendees to try out cutting-edge technologies and meet their creators. Nightly live performances by next-generation artists reminded them of the emotional power of storytelling.

One of the most memorable elements of the FoST Summit was its metanarrative, a story that unfolded over the course of the conference. Each year, the summit took place within a new story world, complete with a full narrative arc with actors, sets, costumes, and more. Characters interacted with guests in surprising and enchanting ways, making it the first

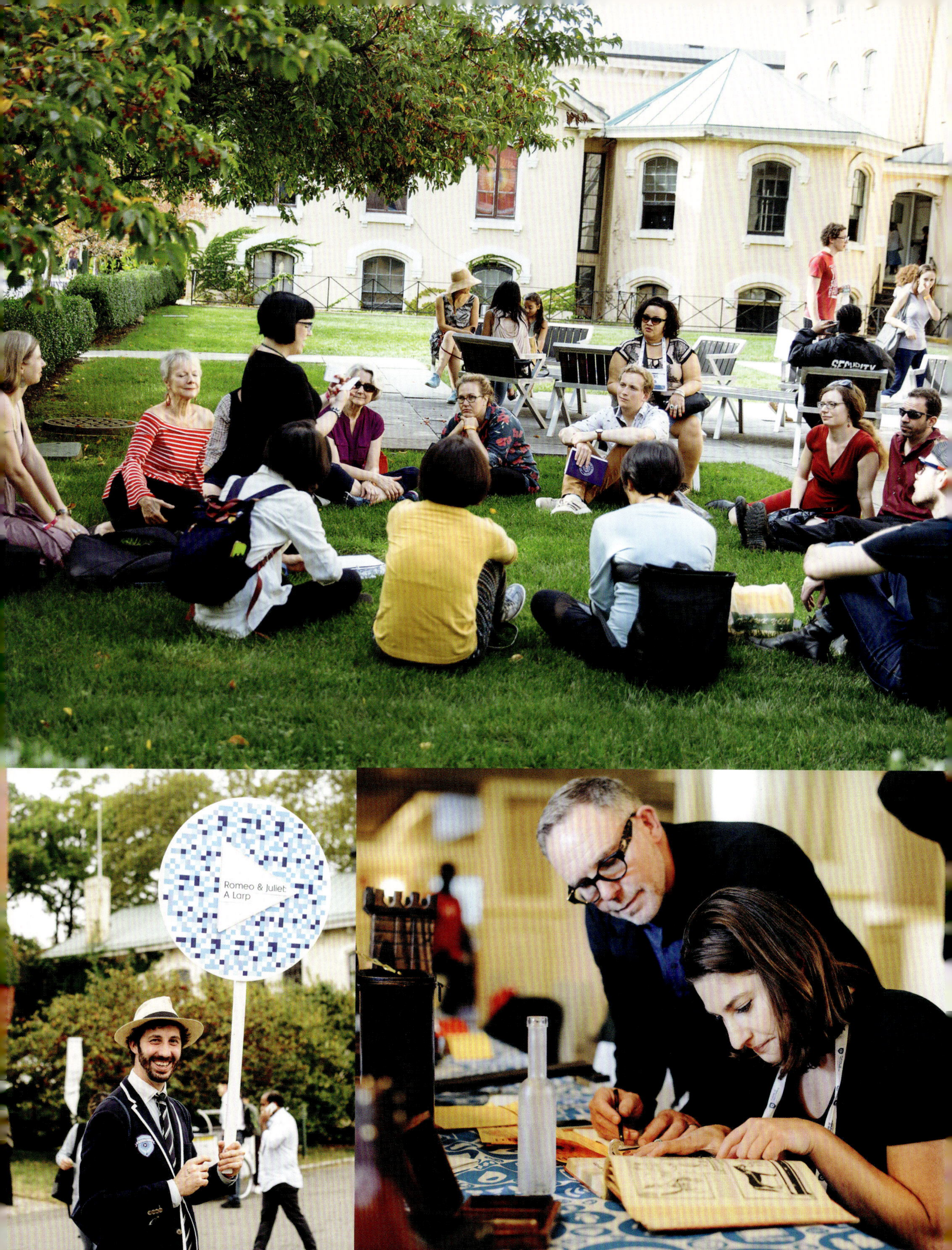
Romeo & Juliet
A Larp

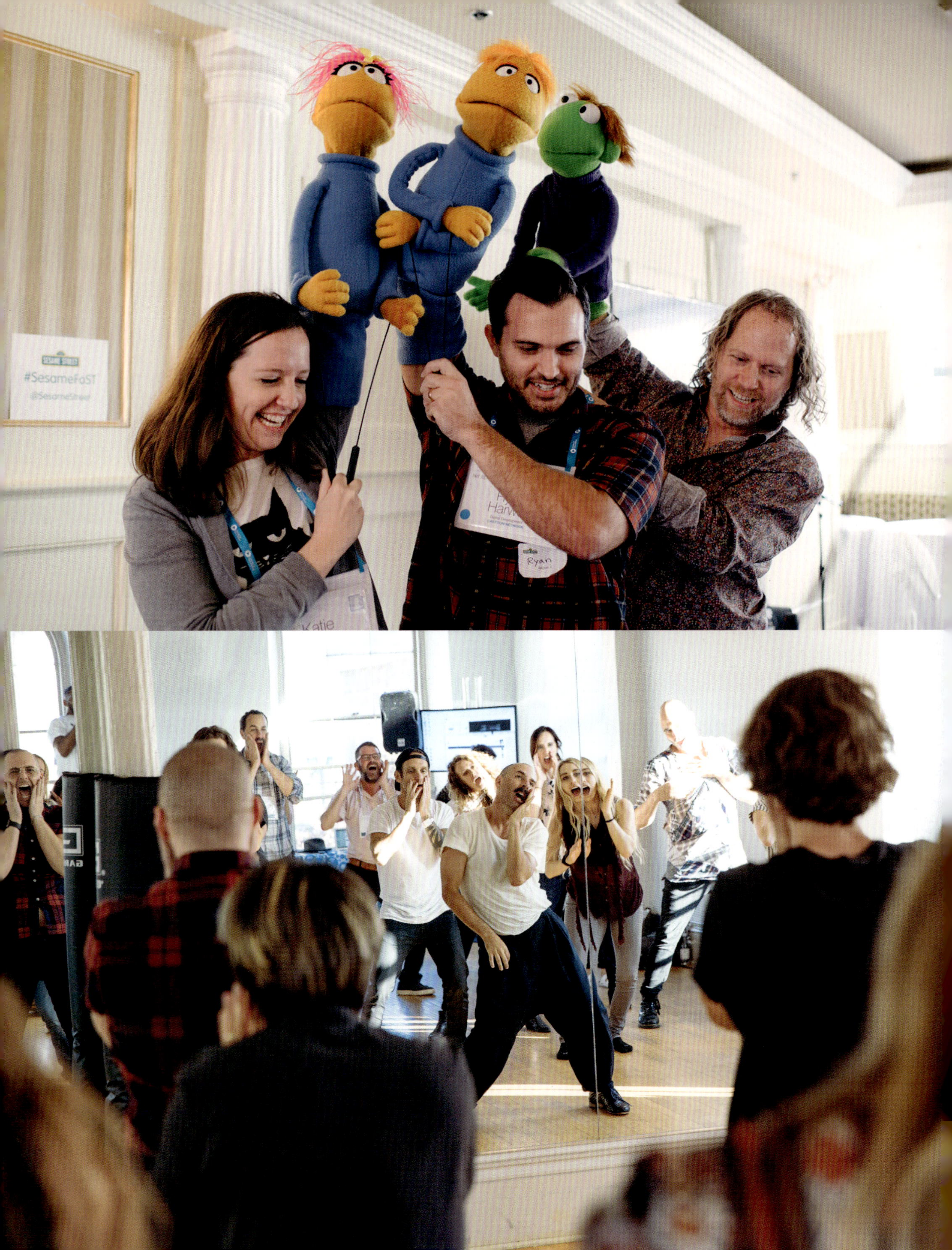
SESAME STREET
#SesameFaST
@SesameStreet
Ryan
Katie

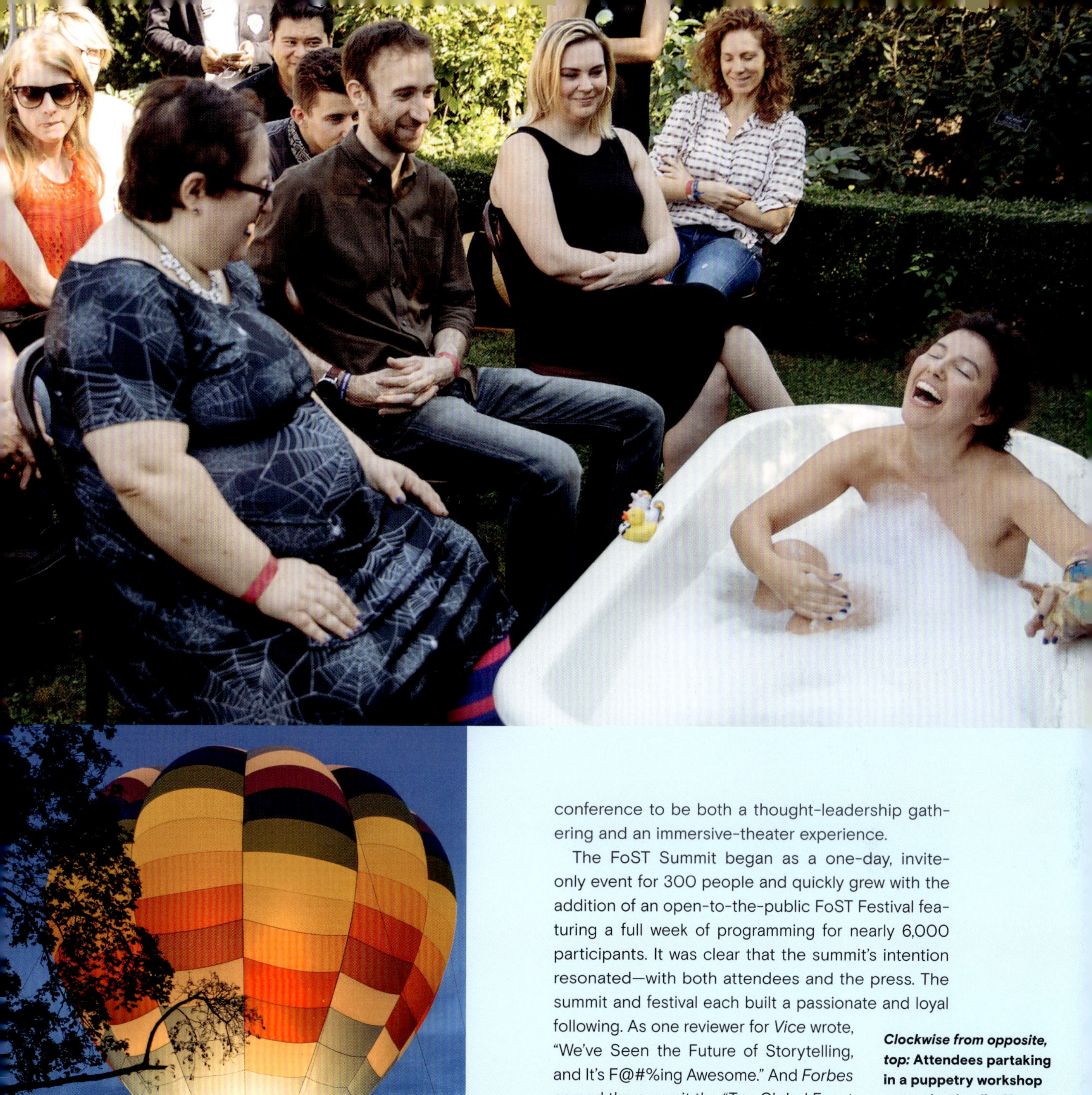

conference to be both a thought-leadership gathering and an immersive-theater experience.

The FoST Summit began as a one-day, invite-only event for 300 people and quickly grew with the addition of an open-to-the-public FoST Festival featuring a full week of programming for nearly 6,000 participants. It was clear that the summit's intention resonated—with both attendees and the press. The summit and festival each built a passionate and loyal following. As one reviewer for *Vice* wrote, "We've Seen the Future of Storytelling, and It's F@#%ing Awesome." And *Forbes* named the summit the "Top Global Event Getting Immersive Right."

The FoST Summit saw a vision of a future of storytelling that was impactful, delightful, and transformative—and set out to equip the next generation of storytellers with the tools, inspiration, and community they needed to see it through. It was both a creative incubator and a call to action, created to catalyze a new era of storytelling.

Clockwise from opposite, top: **Attendees partaking in a puppetry workshop put on by the Jim Henson Company; participants watching a performance of *Broken Bone Bathtub* by Siobhán O'Loughlin, transported from its usual bathroom venue to the Snug Harbor grounds; a hot-air balloon taking off on the final night of the 2017 summit; a movement class led by renowned choreographer Ryan Heffington.**

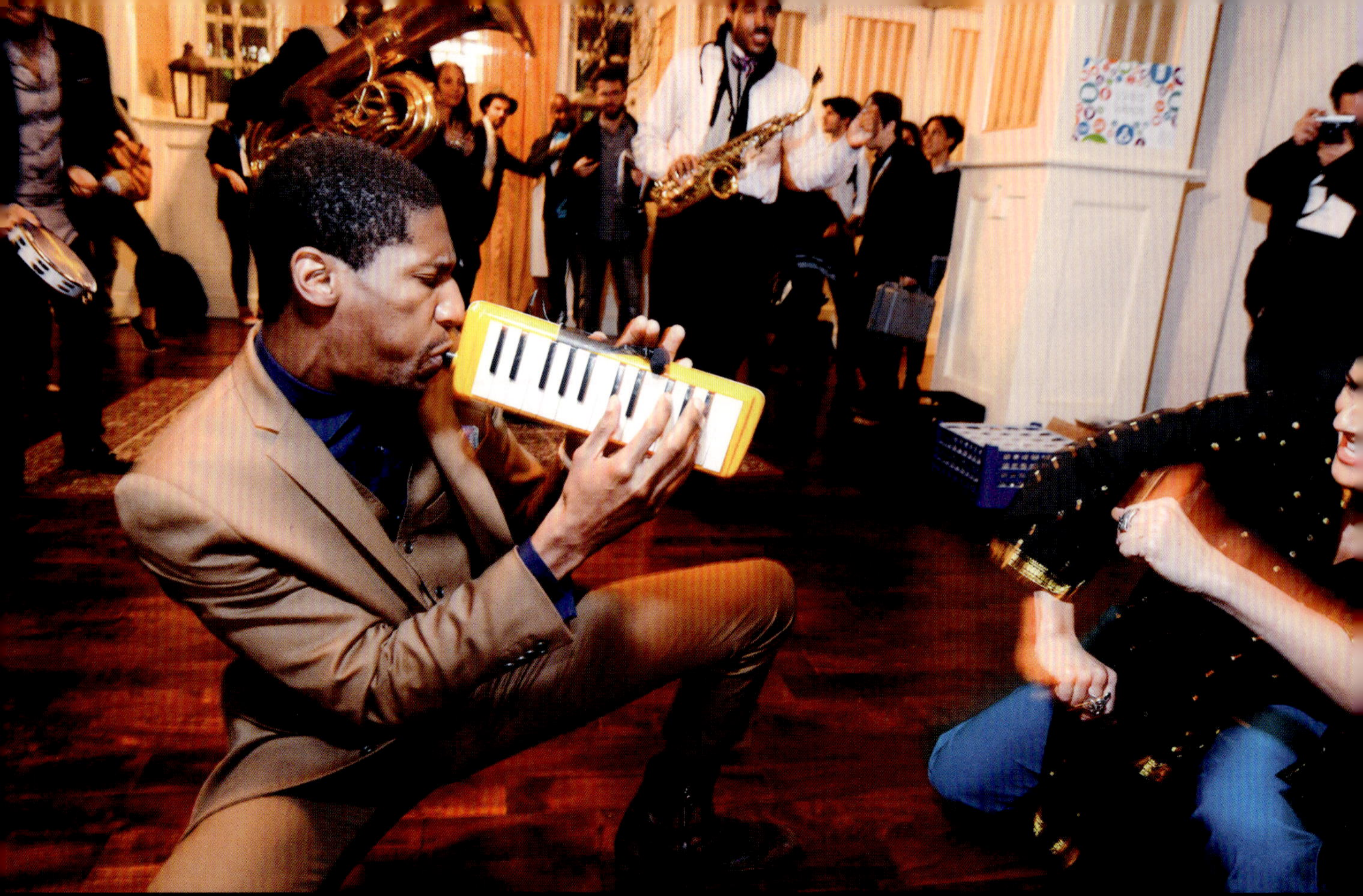

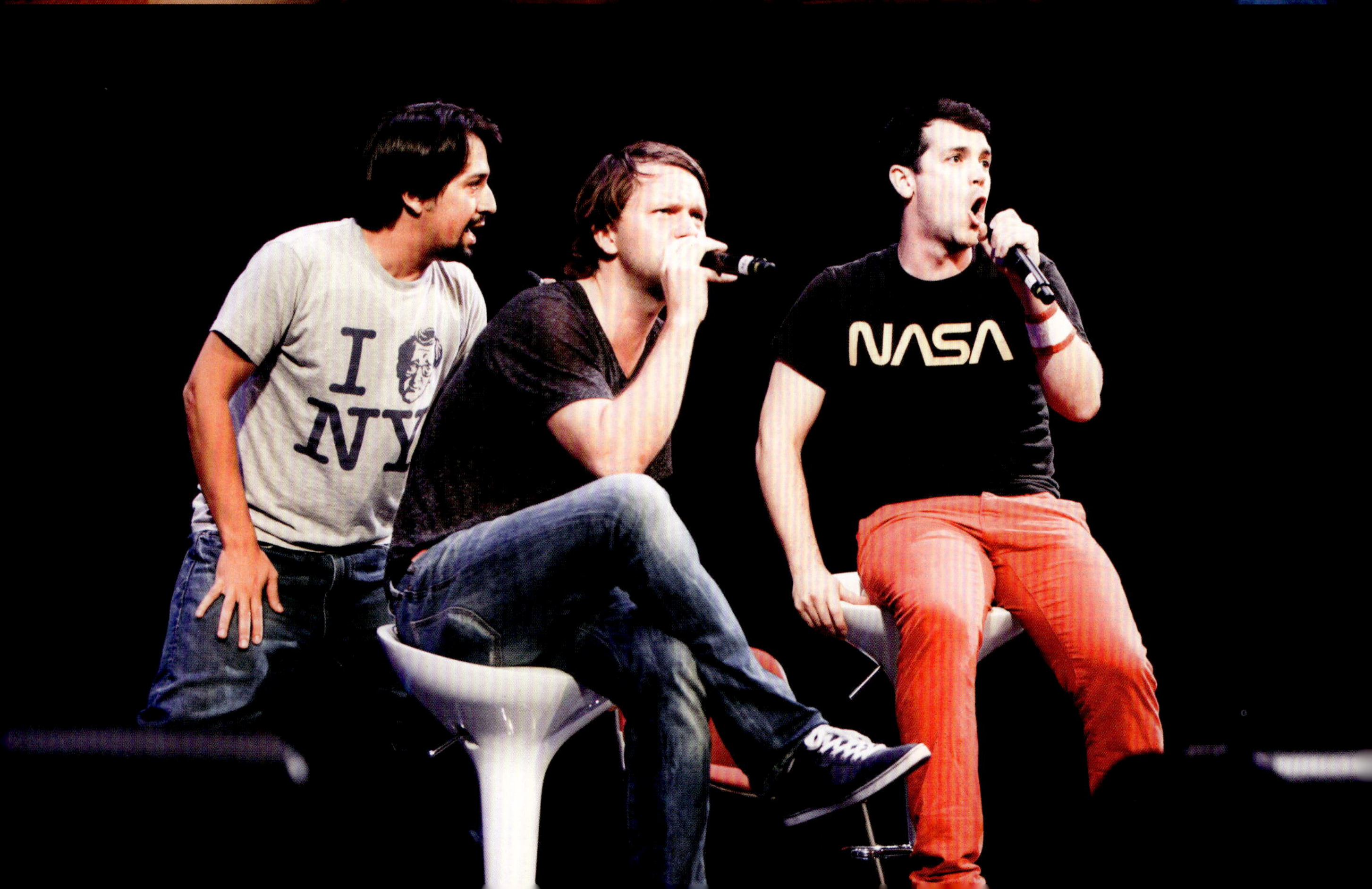

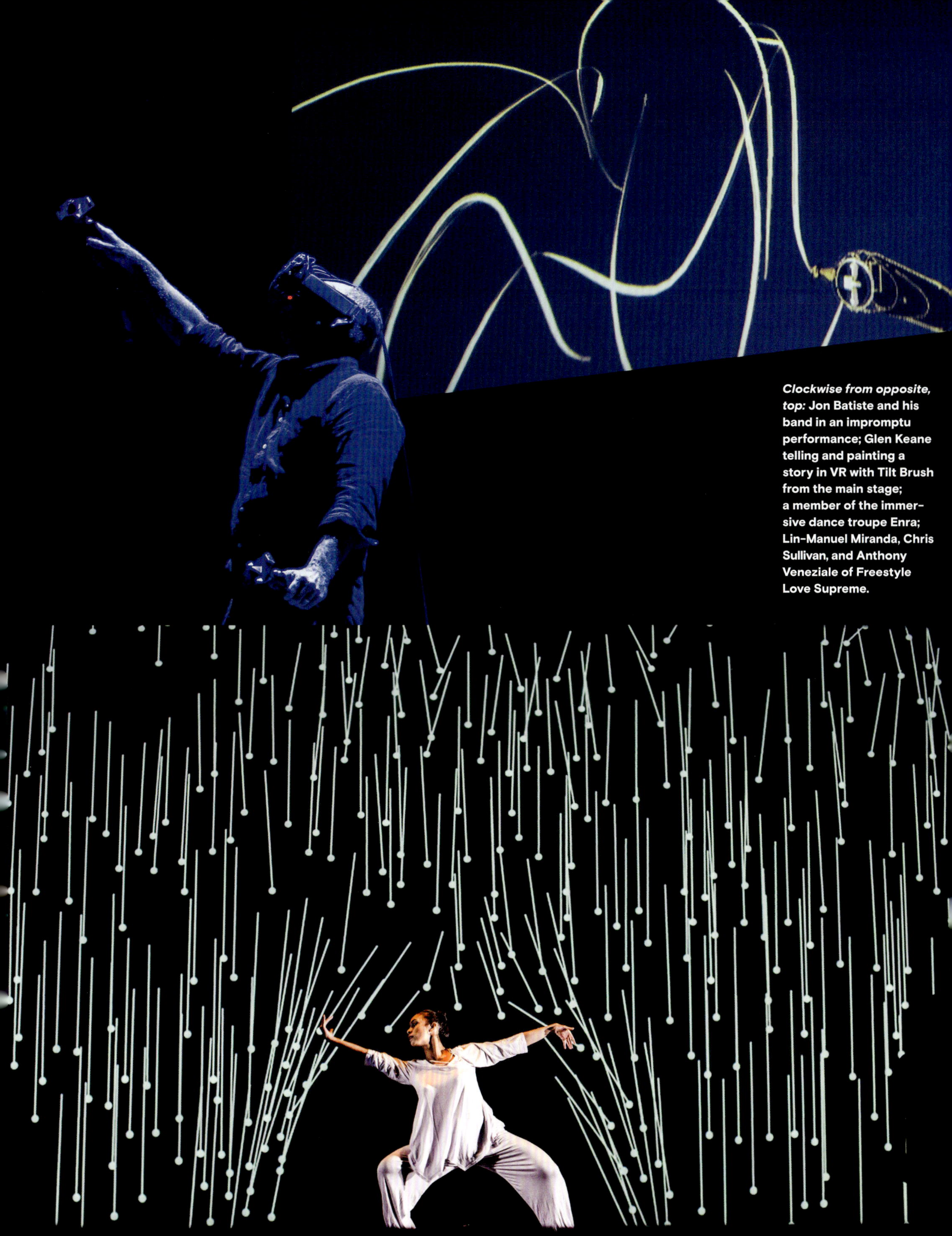

Clockwise from opposite, top: **Jon Batiste and his band in an impromptu performance; Glen Keane telling and painting a story in VR with Tilt Brush from the main stage; a member of the immersive dance troupe Enra; Lin-Manuel Miranda, Chris Sullivan, and Anthony Veneziale of Freestyle Love Supreme.**

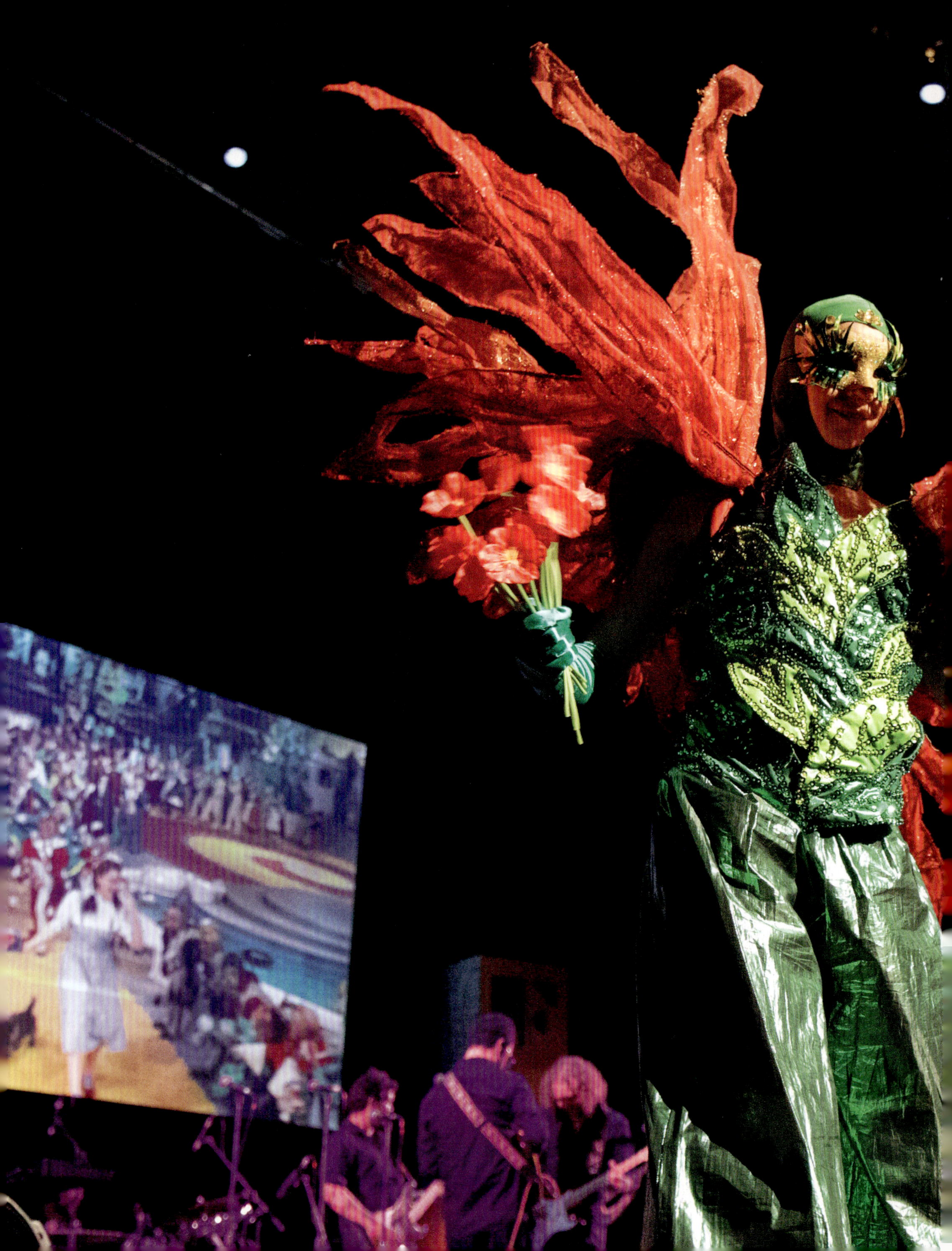

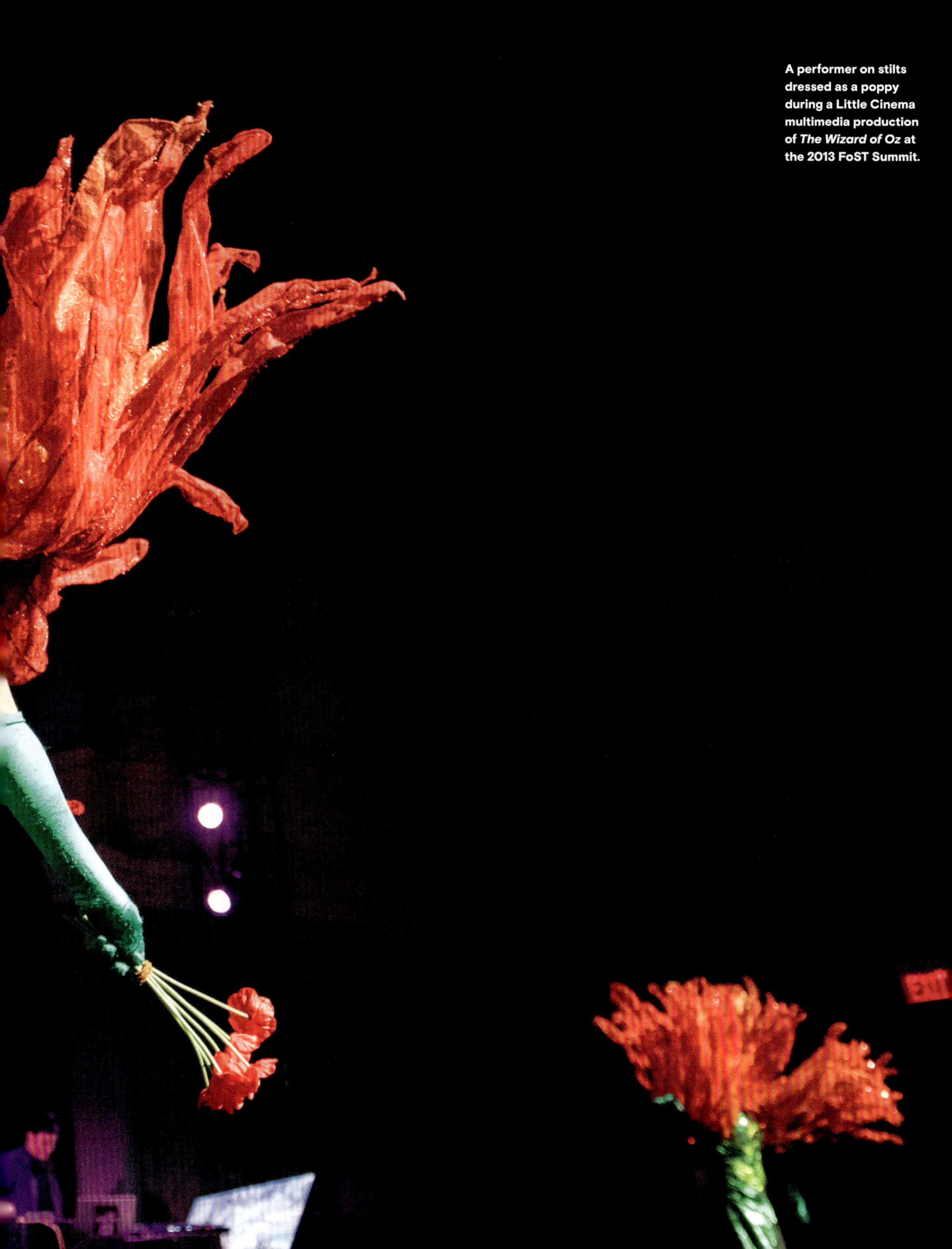

A performer on stilts dressed as a poppy during a Little Cinema multimedia production of *The Wizard of Oz* at the 2013 FoST Summit.

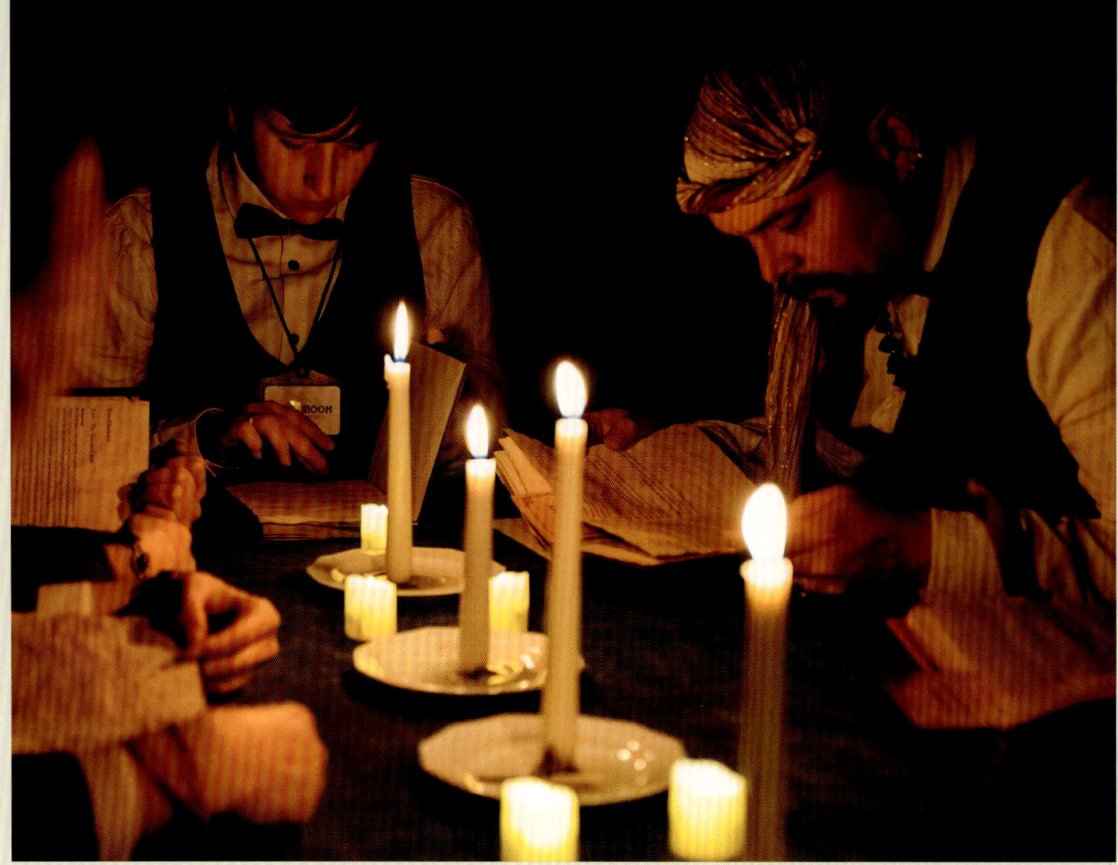

LARP

A zombie apocalypse. A college campus. The Wild West. A nuclear fallout shelter. New York City in the 1980s: A live-action role-playing (LARP) game can transport you to all of these places and more—and just might leave you changed by the time you return.

LARP's current form originated in the late 1970s and has long been portrayed by pop culture as a hobby for fans of sword-and-sorcery. Your generic idea of it may involve foam weapons, fake battles, and Renaissance-fair garb—but although that flavor of LARP is certainly a beloved mainstay, it by no means represents the entirety of the genre, which spans an incredible breadth and depth of collaborative, improvisational storytelling experiences. The only real limit is a group's collective imagination and goals: Many LARPs are meant to serve as a fun romp for a master archer or graceful elf, but others take on a more serious tone to foster greater understanding of historical moments or social issues. While a LARP's designers are responsible for setting the scene, finding a location, and establishing the rules, once the game begins, it's up to each individual player to decide on how they'll embody their character and interact with others. From there, the stories and adventures that unfold are co-created.

Above: Players in Chaos League's _Miskatonic University_ seek ancient and forbidden knowledge in a LARP inspired by the Cthulu Mythos. _Opposite:_ participants in _Demeter_, put on by Nordic LARP designers Sailing4Adventure, play out a Bram Stoker–inspired LARP on a traditional sailing ship.

LARPs can run anywhere from a few hours to several days. No two LARPs are exactly alike in setting, storyline, characters, mechanics, and so on. What they all have in common, however, is their emphasis on embodied and social role-playing. As opposed to role-playing in a tabletop or video game, LARPing cannot be done alone, and it must be done physically. Because you embody your character, you are the one doing any of their actions, not an avatar. If your character swings a sword, partakes in a dance, or argues or barters or bonds with others, you will be the one improvising the action and living the experience. When surrounded by fellow players who have mutually agreed to construct a story together, that experience becomes communal and powerful.

These core components have given LARP its staying power. It's not only an opportunity to step into the shoes of an interesting character but a chance to discover new things about yourself and others in a safe way. Maybe you would never volunteer to lead a charge against the enemy or sing in front of a crowd, but by playing someone who does,

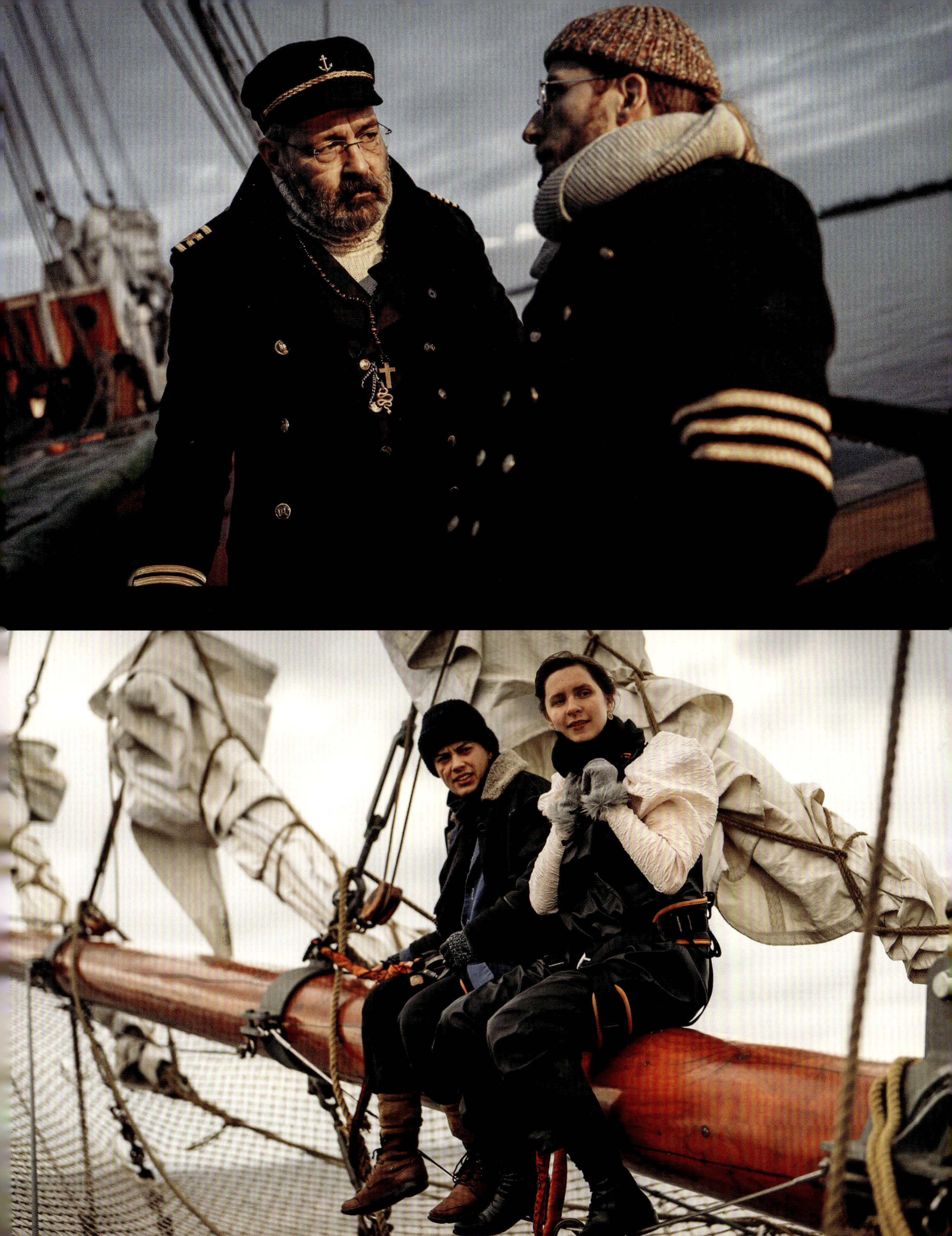

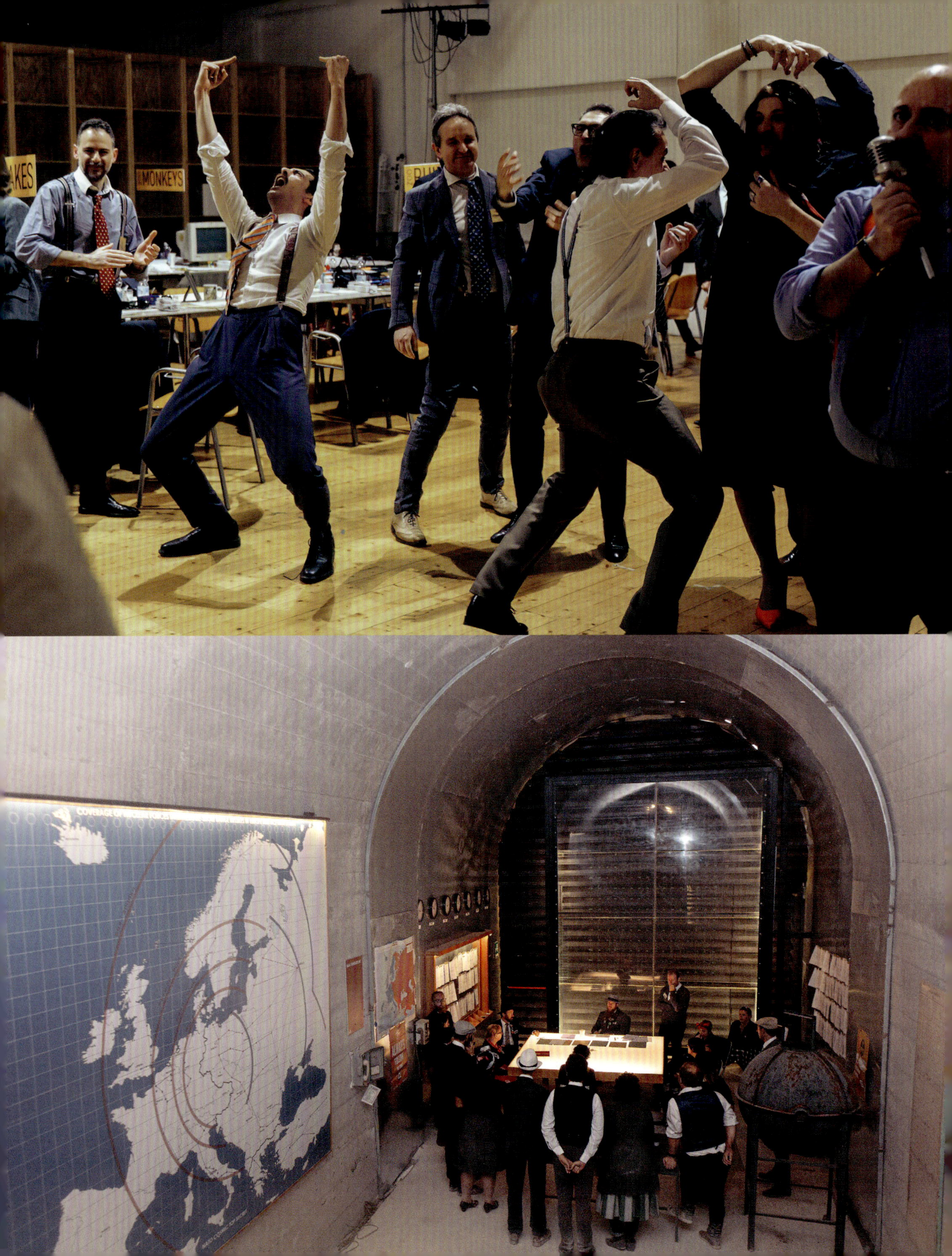
AKES
MONKEYS

you have the ability to see how it feels and be validated for it by a community. Of course, not everyone who participates in a LARP does so to try on new identities, but for those who are open to exploring the infinite possibilities of the self, the experience can be profoundly moving, even life-changing.

LARP has proved to have incredible longevity and an ever-widening appeal. It's no wonder, then, that major entertainment companies like Disney and Netflix are now incorporating elements of it into their location-based offerings. It's also an international phenomenon, with longstanding gatherings taking place in the U.S. and Europe and its popularity increasing in Asia, South America, and Africa. For many people, being able to change who you are for a period of time has a powerful allure. Participants may even find that a LARP changes them far after the game is over, opening them up to new experiences, new friendships, and new ways of thinking about themselves.

***Opposite:* Two Chaos League LARPs: *ZOO (top)*, a LARP where players become ruthless stockbrokers in the financial jungle of late-'80s Wall Street, and *Bunker 101 (bottom)*, a dystopian story set in an actual fallout shelter. *This page:* Participants immersed in their roles in the *Odysseus* LARP, a sci-fi survival story inspired by *Battlestar Galactica*.**

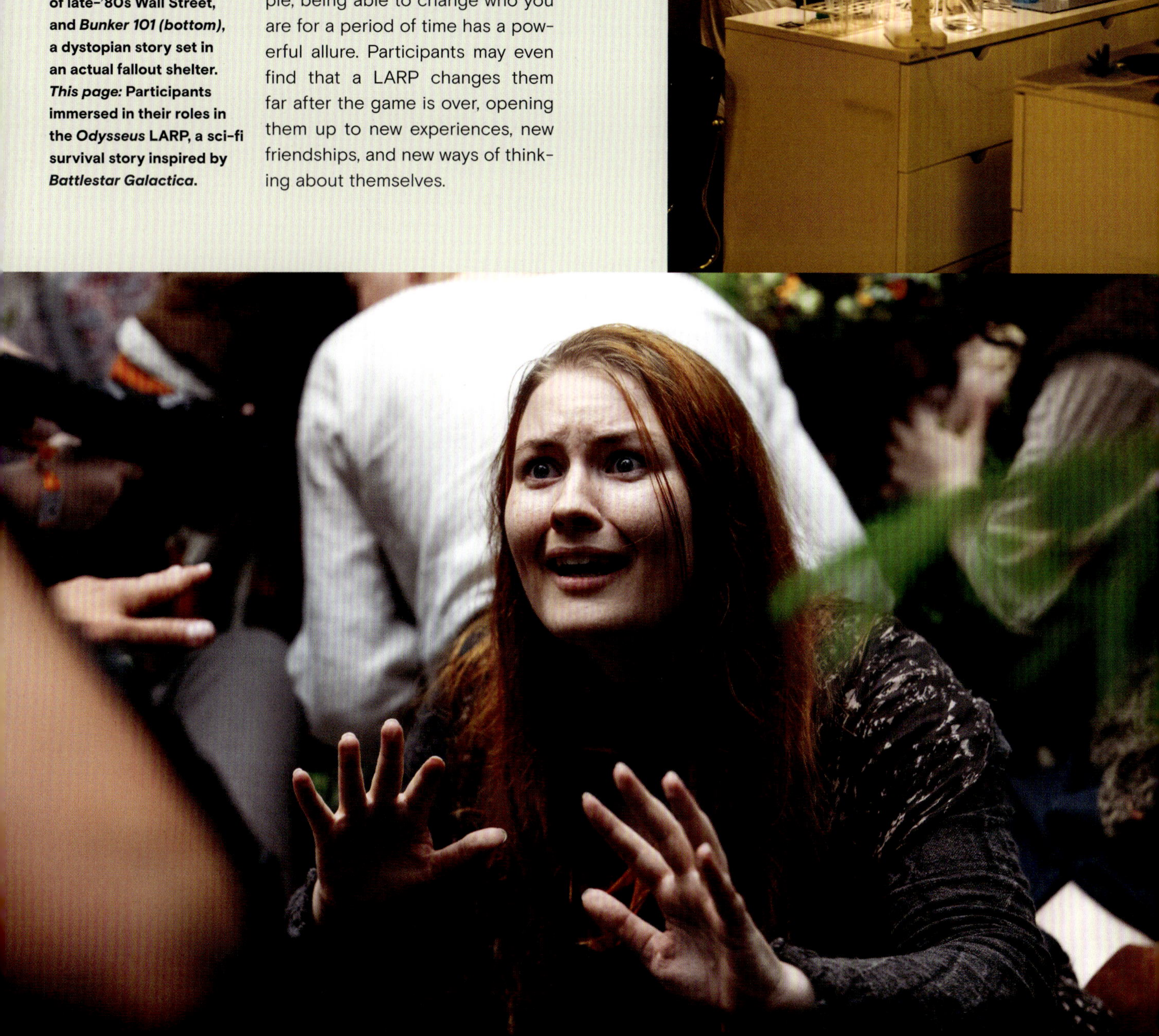

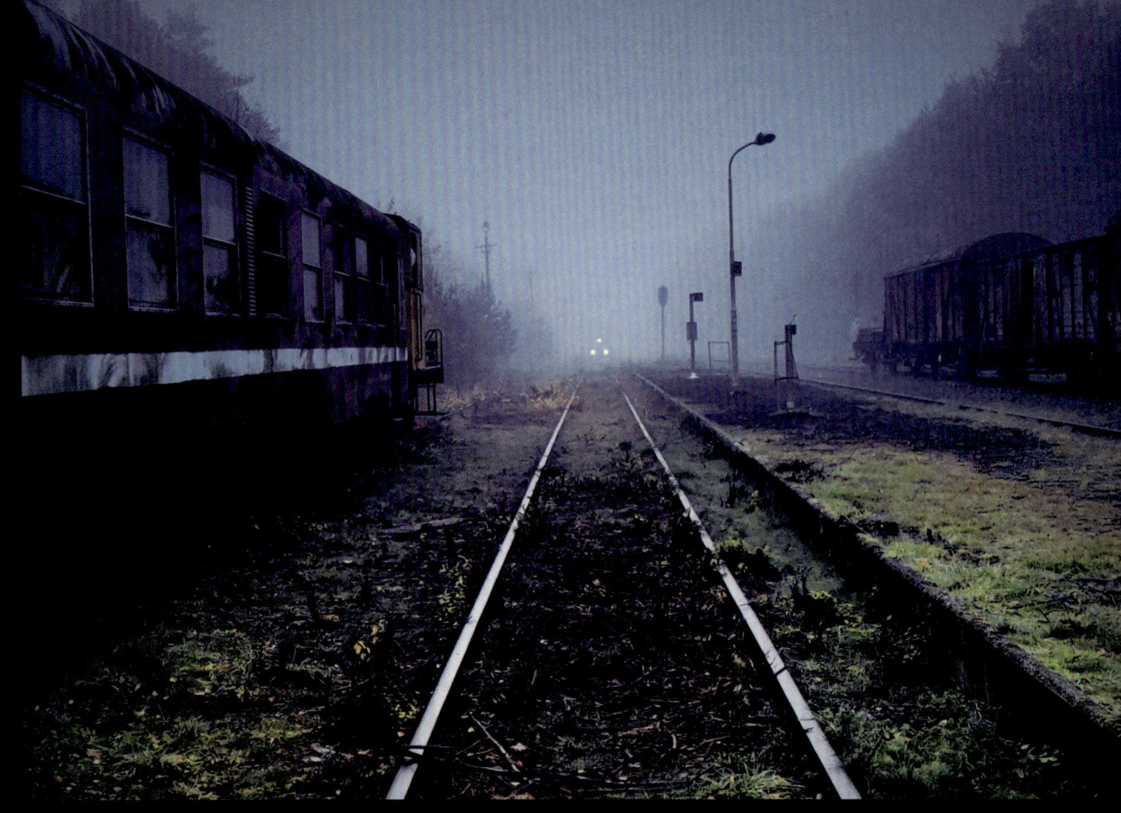

DEMISE OF THE GRICERS

At a disused railyard about an hour outside Brussels, fans of video games, horror films, escape rooms, and immersive theater can find an experience that welds all of these together into one extraordinary creation: *Demise of the Gricers*, a "real-life game" by Shiver Immersive. Designed for teams of four to six, this astonishing playable horror story takes world-building, interactivity, and embodiment to the next level—and serves as an unforgettable exemplar of a possible future of storytelling.

Above: **A view of the abandoned railyard where *Demise of the Gricers* takes place. *Opposite:* One of the murderous "gricers," or train cult members, who serve as the game's antagonists.**

Demise of the Gricers is built in a massive abandoned railyard that, as players soon discover, is overrun with members of a fanatic cult of trainspotters (also called "gricers"). Upon entering the game, participants are outfitted in blue coveralls, helmets, and kneepads, as well as several pieces of specially developed wearable tech—all of which help facilitate the very physical and tech-infused experience. Their objective is to complete missions and discover parts of the story while avoiding the eponymous enemies, played by live actors wearing welders' masks. For the next two to four hours, players explore the highly dynamic game environment, meet other characters, and, above all, try not to get caught.

According to creative director Jeroen van Hasselt, *Demise of the Gricers* was constructed with three main goals in mind: to utilize the special features of the old railyard—including real trains—at their disposal; to construct a game world that feels large and alive, as if it exists before you and persists when you're not there; and to design a real-life horror game around a unique mechanic. The first two goals are accomplished through careful attention to creating a singular and specific atmosphere full of apprehension. The trains and their surroundings are used to give players a range of experiences that they couldn't have anywhere else: from crawling under actual train cars to hiding from prowling gricers behind seats and in bathrooms to scaling and descending ladders while making their way through a three-dimensional landscape. Lighting and sound are used to great effect to heighten the drama and tension, with dynamic visuals and audioscapes designed to make the gricers feel all the more numerous and terrifying. The third goal is realized through the game's innovative yet intuitive mechanic:

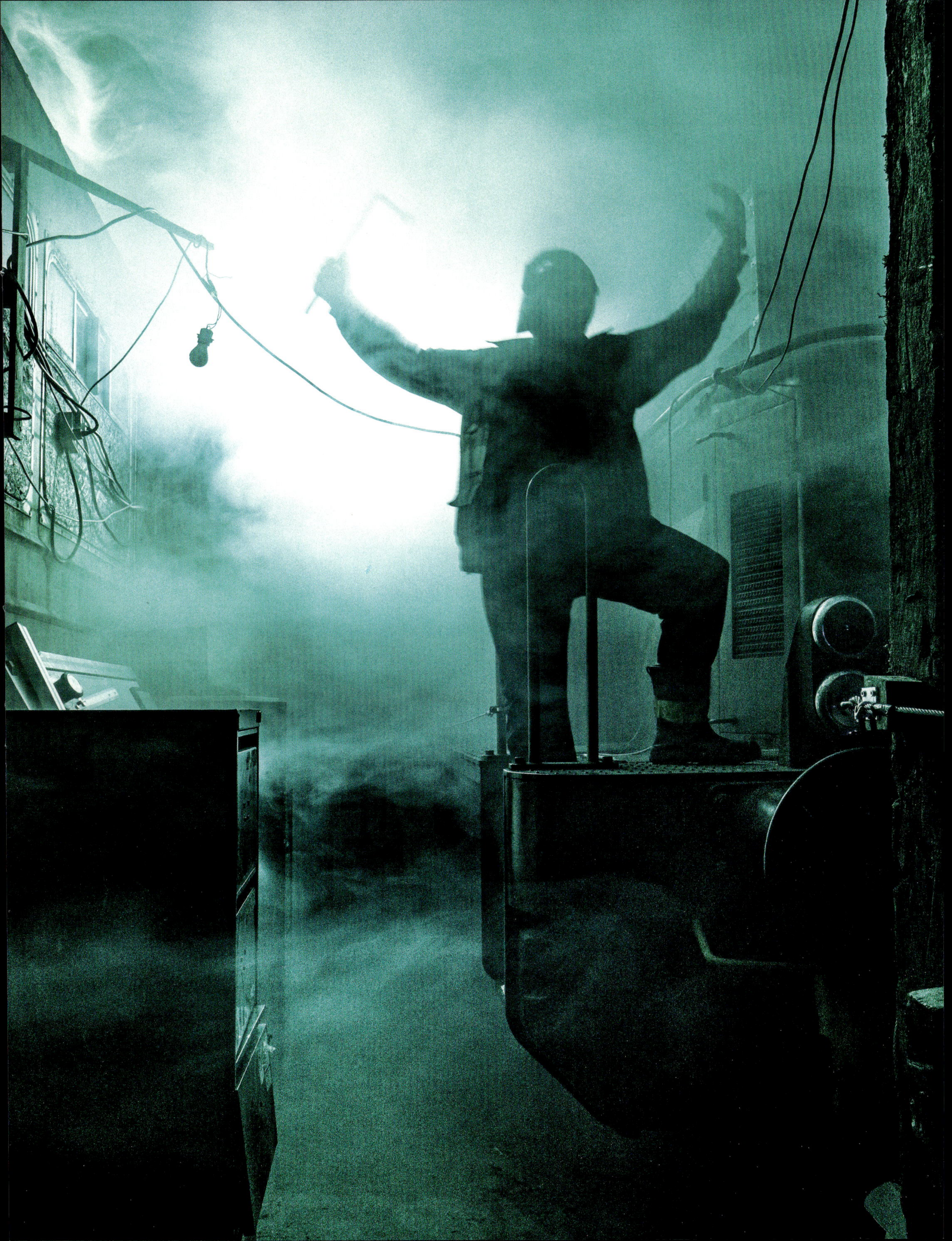

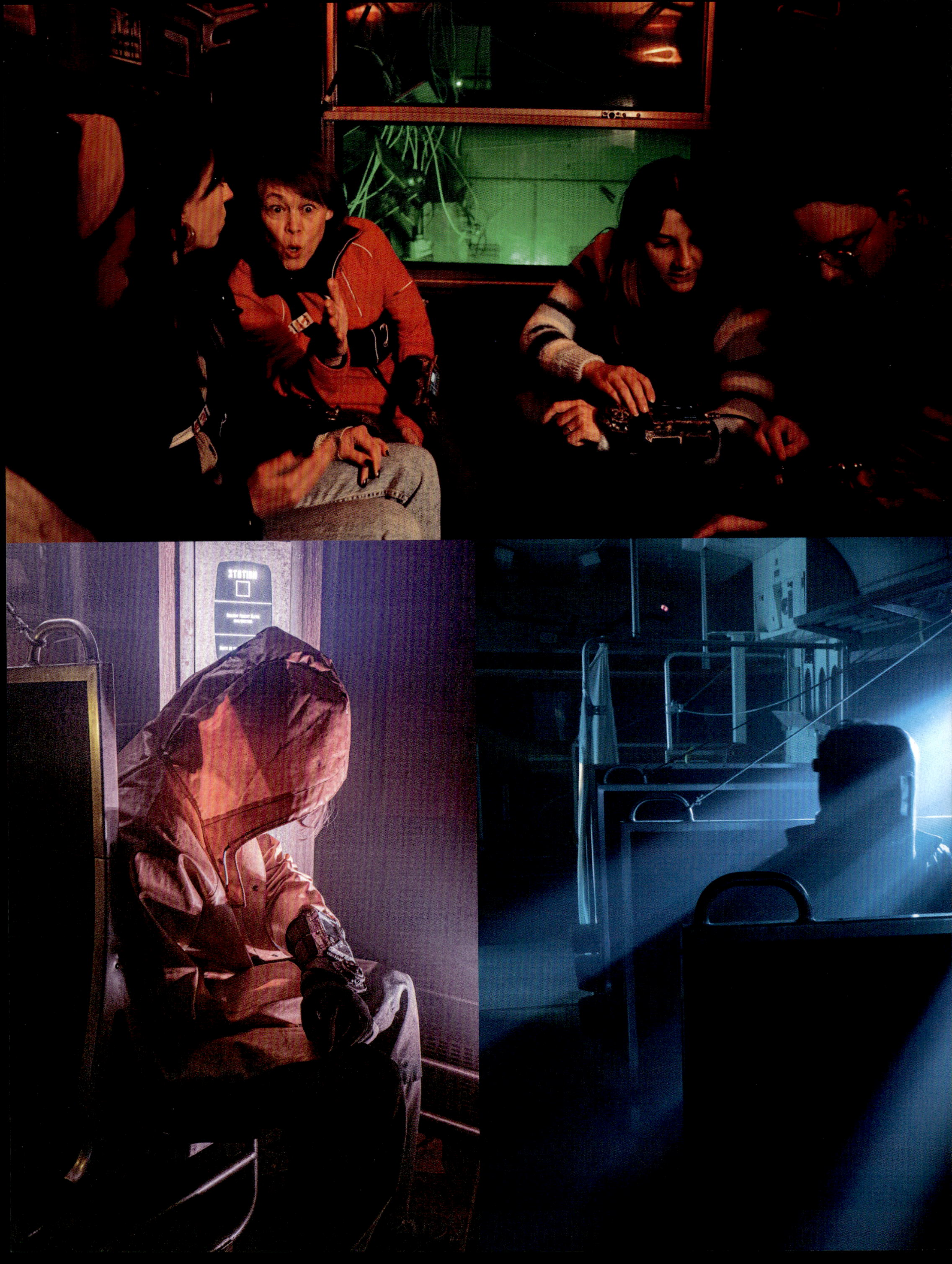
STATION

The eerie, intense environment of *Demise of the Gricers* was created through careful deployment of game mechanics, atmospheric lighting and sound, actors, wearable tech, and a dramatic real-world setting.

a literal lifeline. Players must physically clip onto a cable system that renders them "invisible" to their pursuers—but if they don't clip on in time, an alarm goes off, alerting enemies to their location. This innovative mechanic provides both safety and suspense, as players must quickly and carefully navigate the railyard to find the next clip-on point before the gricers arrive.

Demise of the Gricers merges game design, movie magic, live actors, physical sets, and a compelling story to create a truly visceral experience. As in any video game, players enter into its world, learn its physics and mechanics, and become invested in the story—but unlike any video game, this world is real. As a result, the stakes couldn't be higher. This new form of living-story adventure gives players an experience that they'll never forget, because they didn't just play a game—they lived it.

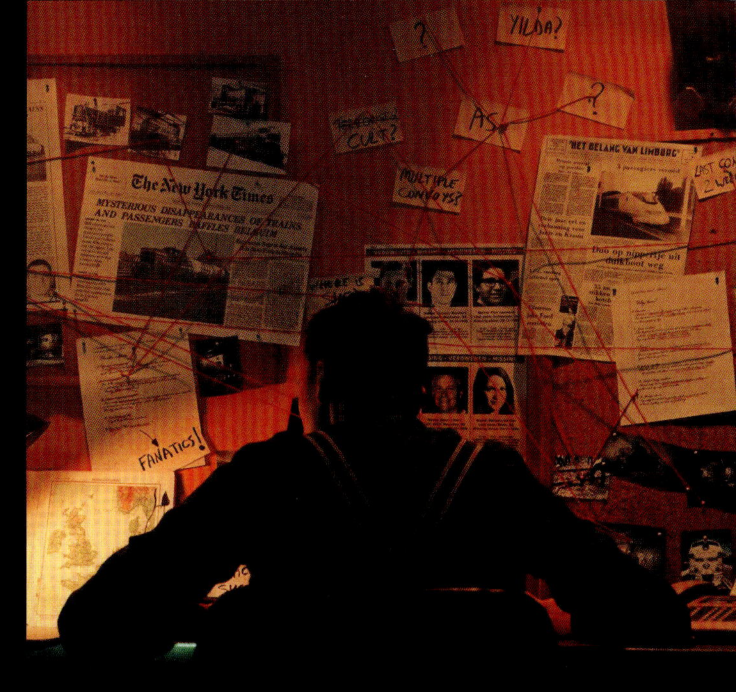

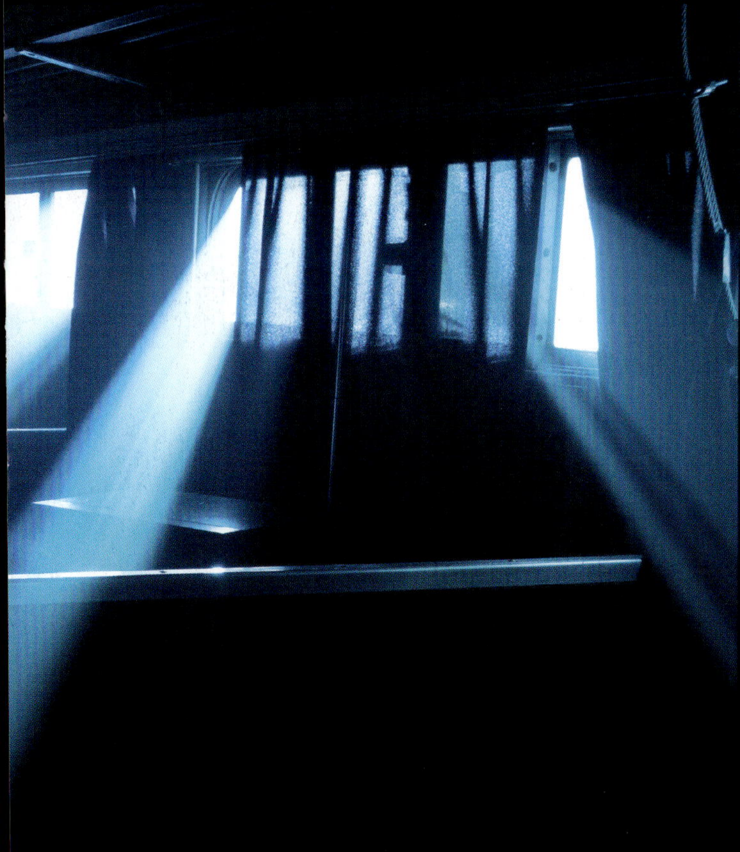

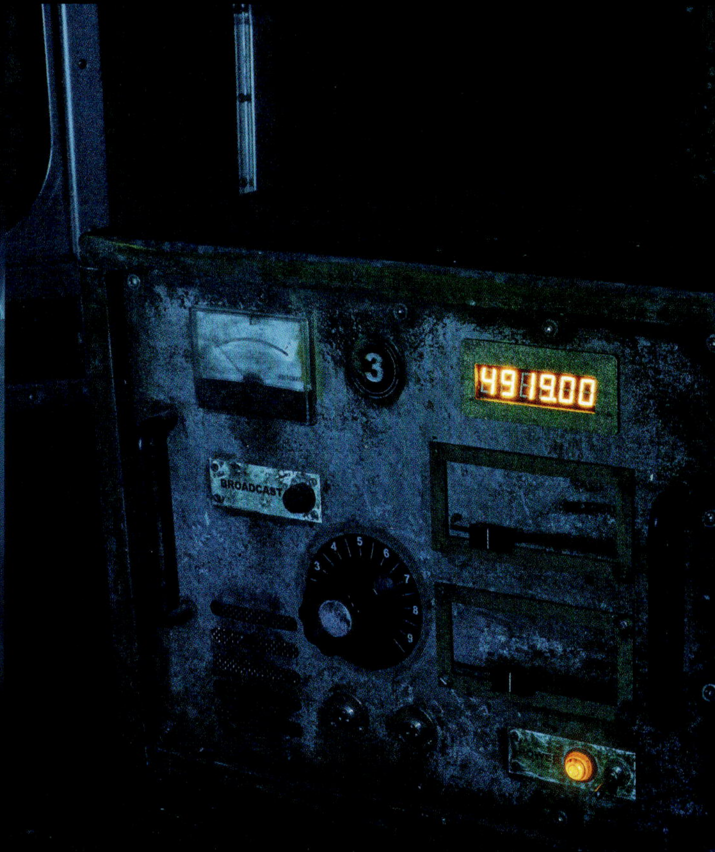

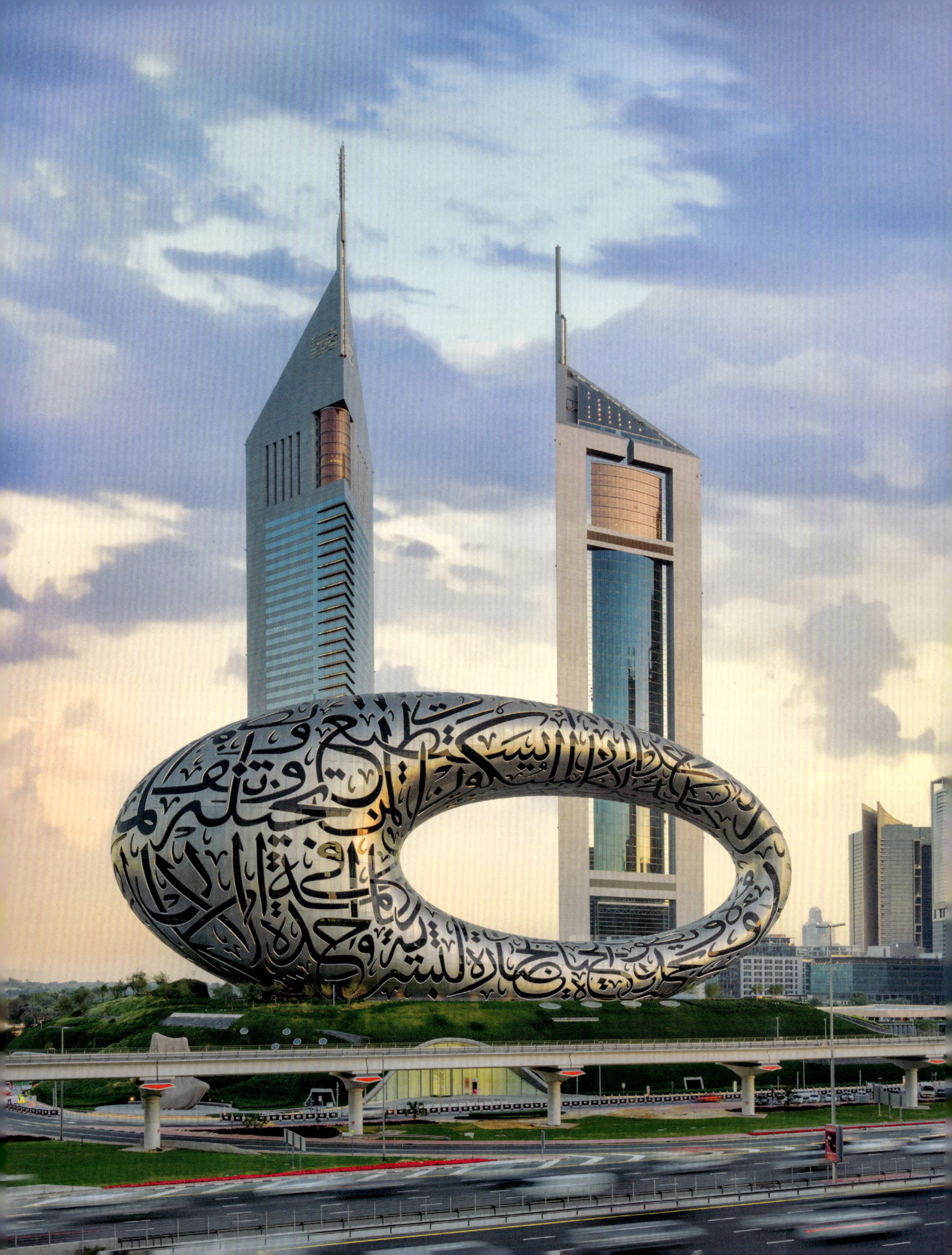

MUSEUM OF THE FUTURE

"The future belongs to those who can imagine it, design it, and execute it. It isn't something you await, but rather create." These translated words of H.H. Sheikh Mohammed bin Rashid Al Maktoum, vice president and prime minister of the UAE and Ruler of Dubai, adorn the exterior of Dubai's Museum of the Future and encapsulate its philosophy. Officially opened on February 22, 2022, the Museum of the Future is an immersive portal into life in the year 2071, when human innovation has made the challenges of our present into things of the past.

The exhibition at the museum is divided into five main parts, showcasing a series of interactive experiences (made in collaboration with creative studios such as Marshmallow Laser Feast, Superflux, and Framestore) intended to immerse visitors in the not-so-distant future. The journey begins with a trip in a space shuttle to the Orbital Space Station Hope and a series of experiences based on life in outer space. Moving downward, the next level is about preserving and enhancing biodiversity as a way to adapt and survive the climate crisis with a mixed-reality Amazon rainforest and the DNA Library, which imagines future applications for bioengineering. Al Waha—which means "The Oasis" in Arabic—is the third chapter, focused on health and wellness, where a series of sensory activities aim to ground visitors in mind, body, and spirit. The fourth level is called Tomorrow Today, which is about harnessing modern technology to help meet global challenges, and the fifth, Future Heroes, is focused on building future skills in young children.

Where most museums have a stiff focus on the past, the Museum of the Future has turned its gaze toward a brighter future; while many of today's stories are dystopian, it presents a distinctly optimistic view. These perspectives have been incredibly well received: As of 2024, the museum has already welcomed more than three million guests from 177 countries. Beyond the immersive exhibits, the Museum of the Future is intended as a global hub for intellectual discourse and exchange. In accordance with the vision of H.H. Sheikh Mohammed bin Rashid Al Maktoum, vice president and prime minister of the UAE and Ruler of Dubai, the Museum of the Future isn't waiting for the future to arrive—it's in the midst of inventing it.

The Museum of the Future features a unique columnless structure and a facade adorned with Arabic calligraphy. The building is shaped like a human eye looking toward the future, while the calligraphy, which doubles as windows, allows natural light to enter.

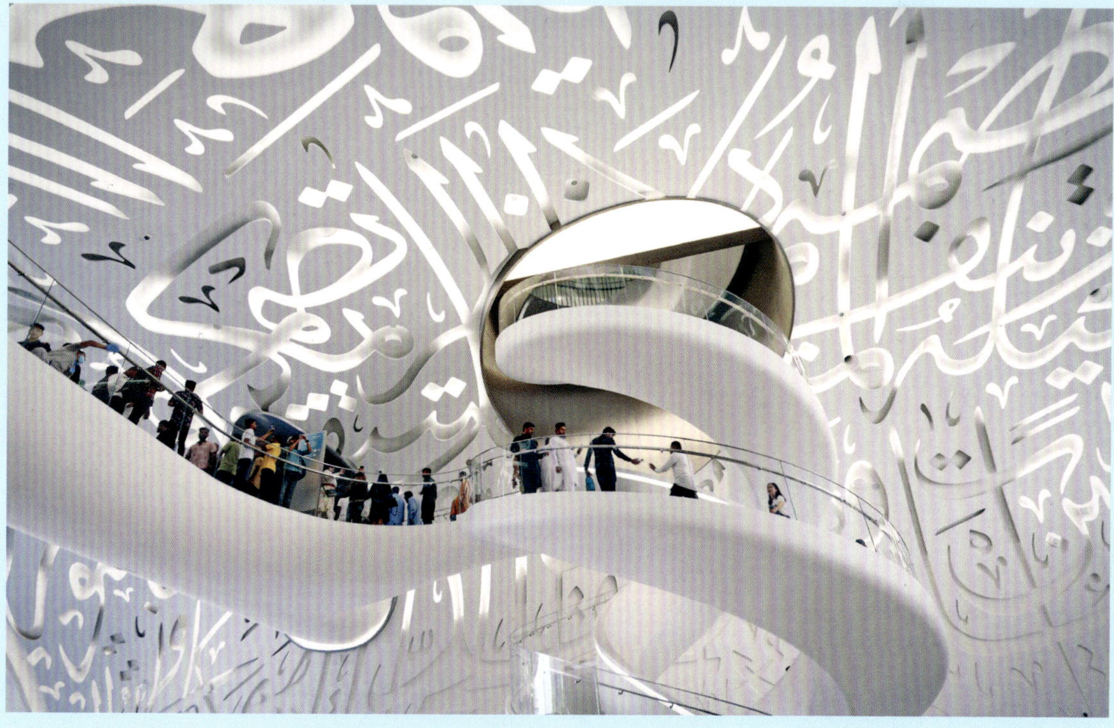

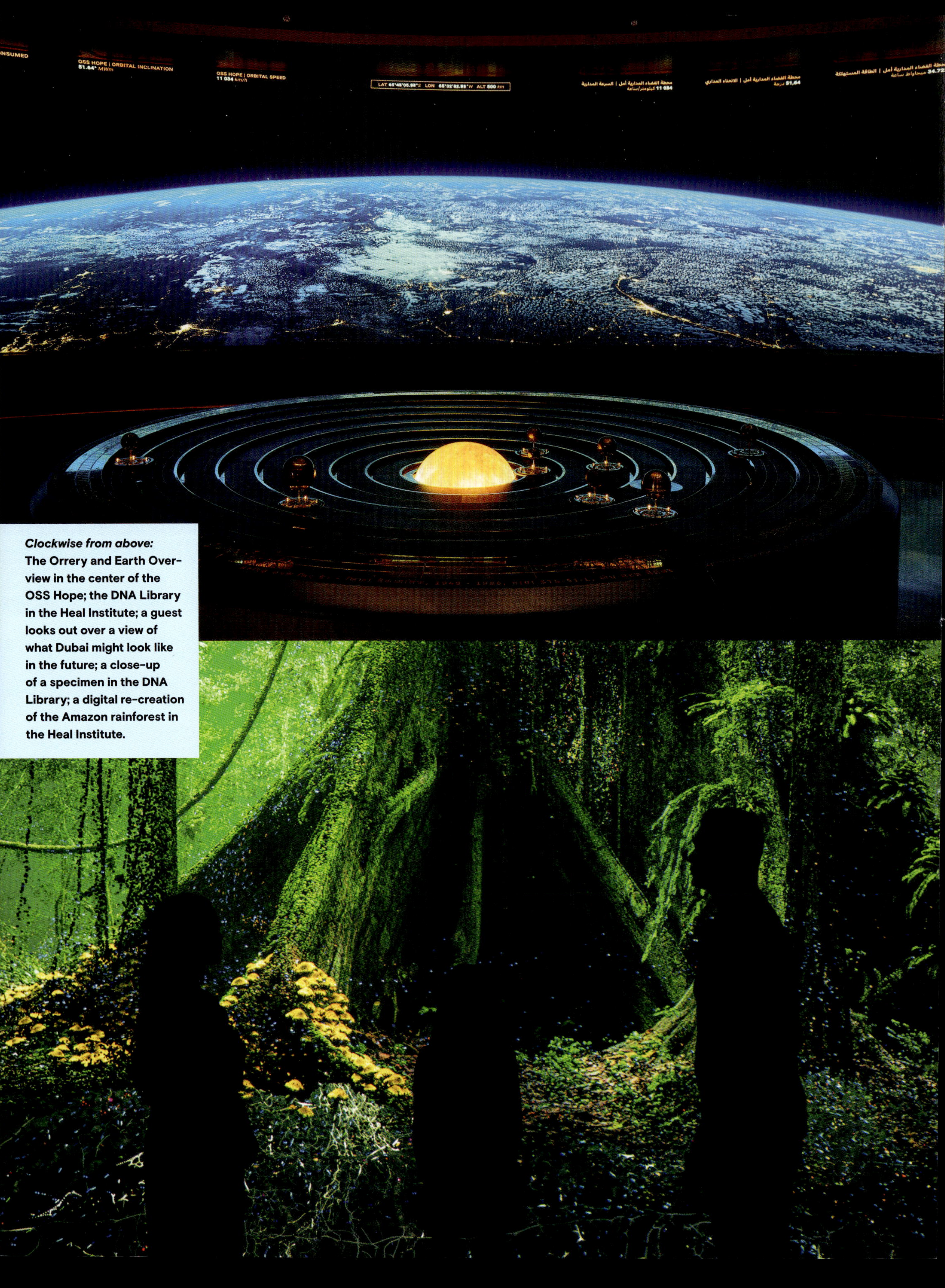

Clockwise from above: **The Orrery and Earth Overview in the center of the OSS Hope; the DNA Library in the Heal Institute; a guest looks out over a view of what Dubai might look like in the future; a close-up of a specimen in the DNA Library; a digital re-creation of the Amazon rainforest in the Heal Institute.**

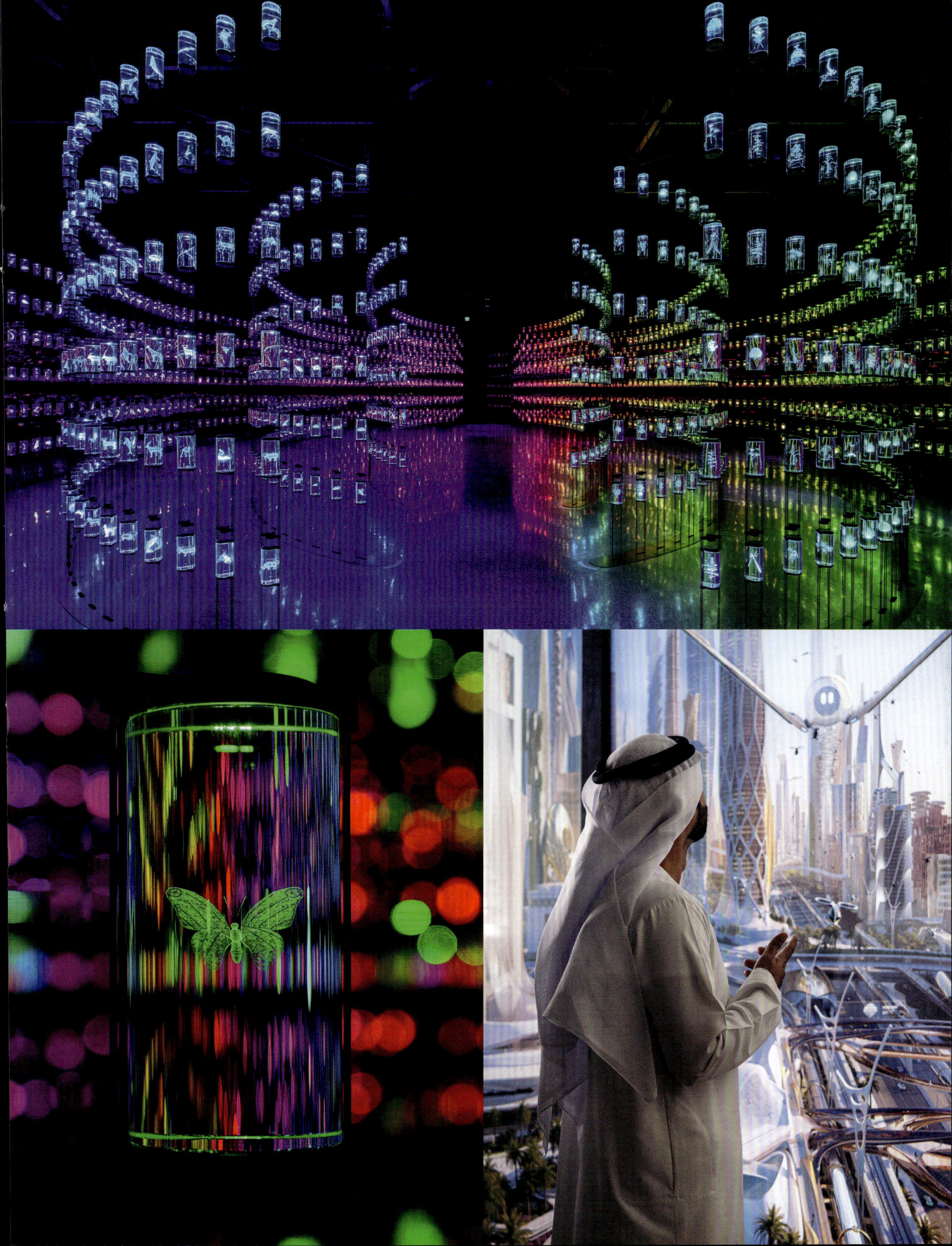

POSTSCRIPT

I've written a lot in this book about how living stories are the future of storytelling. But the truth is, the future is already here. The proliferation and success of so many agentic, immersive, embodied, responsive, social, and transformative experiences in recent years is evidence of their tremendous popularity. While still a young medium with substantial room for growth and improvement, living stories are already a profitable industry that regularly attracts large audiences and generates sizable profits.

Let's look at the numbers behind a few successful examples.

There's *ABBA Voyage*, a groundbreaking virtual concert in London by the Swedish pop group ABBA that features incredibly lifelike virtual "ABBAtars" of the band as they appeared in 1979. In its first year and a half, *ABBA Voyage* netted a staggering $270 million in revenue. It continues to routinely sell out every show with a 97.8 percent occupancy rate in its purpose-built 3,000-person arena.

Meow Wolf (see p. 98), the interactive art collective I've written about at length here, exists in five cities and is expanding to New York and Los Angeles over the next few years. Meow Wolf had an estimated ten million visitors in 2024 across its locations in Santa Fe, Las Vegas, Denver, Dallas, and Grapevine, Texas.

Fever, a discovery and ticketing platform for various experiences, including immersive ones, has seen a meteoric rise, with a valuation of an astounding $1.88 billion as of 2025. Fever operates in more than one hundred cities worldwide, producing and providing access to everything from pop-up art installations to aerial-drone concerts.

Planets TOKYO, the immersive art exhibit by teamLab (see p. 154), holds the world record for the most visited single-artist museum in the world, having welcomed 2,504,264 visitors between April 2023 and March 2024. At approximately $25 per ticket, that is a gross of more than $62.6 million from that one venue alone. The international collective, founded in 2001, has permanent exhibitions in Australia, Finland, Istanbul, Los Angeles, San Francisco, and New York.

Punchdrunk's *Sleep No More* (see p. 40), the award-winning immersive theater show that debuted in 2003 in London, ultimately expanded to Boston, New York and Shanghai; has had more than 5,000 performances for 2 million fans; and has grossed upwards of $240 million globally.

These examples—and others highlighted throughout this book—don't only emphasize the financial and cultural success of living stories. They also showcase the diverse mediums through which these experiences can come alive—from museums and art installations to concert and sports venues, escape rooms, immersive hotels, theme parks, video games, LARP events, and more—and affect industries beyond entertainment and gaming, like real estate, education, brand marketing, advertising, travel, hospitality, philanthropy, and museums. Living stories are flourishing across multiple touchpoints, offering something for everyone, regardless of interests or age. As the appetite for these types of experiences grows, so does the potential for innovation and expansion. With brilliantly talented creators making work that is attracting mass actiences and billions in investment dollars, there is so much more to look forward to as the industry continues to evolve. Living stories are pushing the boundaries of entertainment and storytelling in ways that were once reserved for science fiction—and they're transforming our cultural landscape in the process.

> Living stories are pushing the boundaries of entertainment and storytelling in ways that were once reserved for science fiction, and it's transforming our cultural landscape.

INTIMACY AT SCALE

Some of the most memorable moments in immersive theater, like my experience of auditioning for the role of the leading man in Punchdrunk's *The Drowned Man*, arise from one-on-one interactions between an actience member and an actor. These personalized, intimate experiences make for extraordinarily fun and lasting memories but are expensive and can be difficult to scale profitably. Successful examples of living stories have often had to make a trade-off between scale and intimacy. But with advancements in technology, I believe that we will soon be able to offer widespread access to responsive, individualized storytelling on a mass scale.

Breakthoughs in machine learning, wearables, display technologies, and spatial and distributed computing are rapidly pushing the limits of what's possible. But the biggest leap forward will come through generative AI. As discussed in Chapter 4, it will play a pivotal role in the development of living stories by enabling the creation of narratives and characters that actively engage with and respond to our tastes, preferences, and in-the-moment moods. As this powerful technology evolves, it will push living stories to new frontiers. Imagine a future in which you can experience an immersive living story in the comfort of your living room, or through Ray-Bans while wandering city streets. The potential for customization and interaction will make these experiences deeply personal for each individual, offering a level of engagement that traditional media can't match. And it will be able to do this at scale for millions of people at a nominal cost. We are on the verge of having the tools to create stories as responsive and intimate as the ones our parents used to dream up for us spontaneously at bedtime. And when that happens, living stories will become so engrossing, entertaining, and emotionally powerful that they will eclipse other forms of media in terms of popularity, profitability, and impact.

We are on the verge of having the tools to create stories as responsive and intimate as the ones our parents used to dream up for us spontaneously at bedtime.

This is a thrilling future to contemplate, but it comes with a caveat. What if living stories become so immersive, so widely available, and so responsive to our every desire that we never want—or have—to leave them? Could we become addicted to them at the expense of our real lives? As the medium evolves, it will be increasingly important for creators, investors, and developers to remain aware of the profound influence that living stories will have in our lives and to approach their development with a strong moral compass. As a comic-book reader and collector, I am reminded of Uncle

Ben's warning to Peter Parker: "With great power comes great responsibility." In the end, the stories we craft have the power to shape us and society—so we must use that power to build a future where these experiences enrich our lives rather than detract from them. As we say in my office, "Better stories for a better future."

LIVING STORIES CONNECT US TO OURSELVES AND EACH OTHER

In Chapter 1, I discussed anthropologist Michael Wesch's insights from his time in Papua New Guinea studying the oral culture of preliterate tribes. These communities "lived inside their stories—they were not things to be consumed but were platforms for connection, participation, spontaneity, mystery, immersion, and involvement." This is exactly what living stories do—they get at the root of what it means to connect to ourselves and each other.

Living stories counteract the disconnect many of us feel with the modern world in myriad ways. First, they get us off the couch—they give us the opportunity to be active, to reconnect with our bodies, and to learn new physical skills. Just as memorization and public speaking were important skills to master when stories were told orally, and the ability to read and organize information on the page was most useful when the written word came to dominate, living stories will favor participatory skills that engage us both mentally and socially: improvisation, collaboration, and communication.

Living stories also get us playing together, creating new friendships, deepening old ones, and strengthening our social and team-building skills. They help us empathize with one another and experience the world in new ways. They teach us more about ourselves as we react and respond to unique situations. They make us more playful, more imaginative, and more inventive. Perhaps most importantly, living stories give us unlimited opportunities for agency. By putting us in the driver's seat, they train us to take action, to better ourselves, to follow our dreams. By giving us the tools to influence the narrative, living stories encourage us to become more proactive and self-reliant. In this way, they do more than entertain—they teach us to live more fully and consciously, both within the story and beyond it.

Most of us have spent our entire lives passively consuming media, watching stories unfold without ever being able to influence their outcome. It's easy to see how that passive mindset might carry over into real life, leading us to believe that our actions can't make a difference in our own lives or in the world. But what if, from a young age, we were immersed in stories that we didn't just watch but actively participated in and co-created with others? What if every adventure, every challenge, was something we could solve together, where success was a product of collaboration, creativity, and action? Living stories don't just give us a sense of accomplishment during the experience—they show us that we have the power to make a difference in our own lives, and in the greater world as well.

Living stories don't just give us a sense of accomplishment during the experience—they show us that we have the power to make a difference in our own lives, and in the greater world as well.

I believe that living stories are the antidote to the apathy and isolation that so many people feel today. They prove that we can be the heroes of our own lives, not only as solitary figures but as part of a community. Rather than watching alone, we're going to *story* together. The future of storytelling will grant us the opportunity to see with new eyes, go on many adventures, and experience the world in wondrous ways, bringing us more in touch with ourselves and others. Living stories take us forward, yes, but also back, to something that feels more innately human. They help us become who we were always meant to be.

ACKNOWLEDGMENTS

This book is a record, recognition, and celebration of the relatively young medium of immersive experience. It's hard enough to tell great stories when you are working in an established medium. Now try to do it while you are simultaneously inventing the form, the language, and the business model. It is literally building the plane while you are flying it. I would like to start by acknowledging and thanking all of the brilliant creative people, the risk takers, the maverick makers, the artists with a dream, and the businesspeople who have supported and done their best to make it all make (dollars and) sense. To all of you, I tip my hat, pump my fist, and thank you from the bottom of my heart. You have invited me into your wondrous worlds, magical museums, and spectacular shows for some of the most enjoyable, unforgettable, and awe-inspiring experiences of my life.

Many people agreed to be interviewed for this book. They represent the top of their fields as creators, technologists, businesspeople, and thought leaders. Each was incredibly generous with their time, sharing their experience and knowledge openly and enthusiastically. To them I extended my deepest thanks: Ajaz Ahmed, Tim Alexander, Ignacio Bachiller, Felix Barrett, Jake Barton, DJ Begbie, Sakchin Bessette, Rohit Bhargava, Sarah Lynne Bowman, Paul Bulencea, Abraham Burickson, Brent Bushnell, Jon Braver, Danny Cannizzaro, Neil Carty, Jenova Chen, Will Dean, Winston Fisher, Fri Forjindam, Shari Frilot, Marian Goodell, Samantha Gorman, Trevor Guthrie, John Hanke, Alejandro González Iñárritu, Vince Kadlubek, Ben Kaufman, Takashi Kudo, Christian Lachel, Félix Lajeunesse, Oliver Lansley, Nick Lawhead, Matt Locke Greg Lombardo, Morgan Lloyd, Brian McDonald, Alex McDowell, Andrew McGuinness, Chris Milk, Annie Murphy Paul, Bryon Panaia, Tom Pearson, Nonny de la Peña, B. Joseph Pine II, Paul Raphaël, James Seager, Anil Seth, Marc Simons, Richard Taylor, Scott Trowbridge, Victor van Doorn, Jeroen van Hasselt, Jennine Willett, and Paul J. Zak.

I simply could not have completed this project without the thoughtful and diligent work of several talented researchers and contributing editors. At the top of that list is Luke Gernert, followed by Andrew Postman, Megan Wenerstrom, Helen Healey-Cunningham, and David E. Brown.

I have had the pleasure of working with the Melcher Media team on hundreds of books for clients, but this is the first one where I was the author, and I can say with certainty that there is no better group of talented craftspeople than this team to work with on a book. I owe them a tremendous debt of gratitude for putting up with me, and for helping to get this book finished and produced to the highest standards of quality. First and foremost to the gifted Megan Worman, Lauren Nathan, Madison Brown, and Charlotte Lamm for their calm and steady editorial direction, many valuable contributions, and long hours; to Bonnie Eldon and Susan Lynch for their skilled leadership and oversight of everything from contracts to the details of production; and to the rest of the Melcher Media and FoST teams, who contributed in a myriad of ways big and small: Thank you, thank you. I could not have done this without all of you.

Paul Kepple and Alex Bruce of Headcase Design brought virtuoso design and equanimity to the process. It has been a true pleasure to have worked with Paul and his team on many books over the years and an honor to have them work on this one.

A warm thanks also to Pedro Nekoi for his vibrant and layered illustration for the book's front cover.

A big heartfelt thank you to Lia Ronnen for seeing the vision and deciding to publish the book and throw the very sizable weight and talents of Artisan and Hachette Publishing Group behind the project. Special thanks also to my editor, Bridget Monroe Itkin, for her thoughtful feedback to the manuscript, and to the rest of the Artisan team for their contributions and stewardship.

I would like to extend my deepest gratitude and appreciation to the many people who participated in the journey that has been the Future of StoryTelling since its inception back in 2011. I would like to specifically thank a few whose support, advice, and contributions over the years have been especially meaningful: Jennifer Aaker, J. J. Abrams, Angela Ahrendts, Paola Antonelli, Margaret Atwood, Callie Barlow, Dan Barlow, Jess Bass, Sunny Bates, Bob Bejan, Teddy Bergman, Monica Bill Barnes, Yoni Bloch, Susan Bonds, Jeremy Boxer, Grace Boyle, Rob Bredow, Jessica Brillhart, Tim Brown, Jesse Burgum, Catherine Burns, Brent Bushnell, Wendy Calhoun, David Carey, Ronda Carnegie, Graydon Carter, Rahul Chopra, Marvin Chow, Marvin Chun, Beth Comstock, David Cowan, Jon Cropper, Scott Dadich, Dandy Punk, David Droga, Douglas Eck, Marc Ecko, Sarah Ellis, Frank Evers, Candice Faktor, Maureen Fan, David Fenton, Joel Fitzpatrick, Shari Frilot, Nickey Frankel, David Furnish, Meg Goldthwaite, Daniel Goleman, Al Gore, Kristin Gore, Christopher Graves, Brian Grazer, Jamie Gutfreund, Kris Hammond, Fox Harrell, Neil Patrick Harris, Mark Hodosh, Brian Hooks, Hugh Howey, Bjarke Ingels, Zem Joaquin, Bobby Jones, Julia Kaganskiy, Rana el Kaliouby, Maira Kalman, Jon Kamen, Glen Keane, David Kidder, Samantha Klein, Aaron Koblin, Robert Krulwich, Itamar Kubovy, Damian Kulash, Ari Kuschnir, Dawn Laguens, David Landa, Franklin Leonard, Kelly Leonard, Joe Lewis, Blanca Li, Shannon Loftis, Beau Lotto, Liz Luckett, Matt Luckett, John Maeda, Joe Marchese, Dominic Margetson, Jim Marggraff, Jacob Marshall, Peter Marx, Marc Mathieu, Alexis McGill Johnson, Tom Melcher, Lori Melichar, Tham Khai Meng, Pat Mitchell, John Morgan, Anne Mullen, Chris Murphy, Janet Murray, Sara Öhrvall, Ed O'Keefe, Todd Oldham, Karen Palmer, Richelle Parham, Bjarke Pedersen, Tom Perlmutter, Andrew Peters, Rosalind Picard, Maria Popova, Keri Putnam, Liza Garcia Quiroz, Yelena Rachitsky, Jade Raymond, Jonathan Reff, Charles Renfro, Fabien Riggall, Maria Rodale, Frank Rose, Philip Rosedale, Jay Rosen, Jane Rosenthal, Ivy Ross, Laura Roumanos, David Rowan, Kevin Ryan, Richard Sarnoff, Jeffrey Seller, Alexandra Shapiro, Tina Sharkey, Rachel Shechtman, Clay Shirky, Tiffany Shlain, Stephen Shore, Alan Siegel, Abby Skeans, Kevin Slavin, Nancy Smith, Rick Smolan, Scott Snibbe, Dee Solomon, Rob Sorcher, Julia Sourikoff, Barnaby Steel, Sarah Steele, Jimmie Stone, Stacey Tank, Darcy Troy Pollack, Baratunde Thurston, Jose Antonio Vargas, Michael Ventura, Benedetto Vigna, Laura Walker, Kevin Wall, Jamin Warren, Lance Weiler, David Weinberger, Mike Wesch, Polly Wiessner, Fred Wilson, Robert Wong, Sarah Wood, Tom Wujec, Todd Yellin, Devin Young, Lauren Zalaznick, Andrew Zolli, and Jeffrey Zurofsky.

Finally, and most importantly, I would like to thank my wife, Jessica, and my son, Daniel, for their support, wisdom, and unconditional love.

ABOUT THE AUTHOR

Charles Melcher is a creator, curator, and thought leader in the storytelling and technology space. He is the founder and CEO of Future of StoryTelling and Melcher Media.

Melcher's passion for immersive storytelling was evident from the time he first founded his book production company, Melcher Media, in 1993 with the motto "Reinventing the Way Stories Are Told." One of its first jobs was to create MTV Books, a publishing imprint that featured a series of interactive, cutting-edge titles like the award-winning *MTV Unplugged*. The company has continued to innovate and push the boundaries of the printed page, producing bestselling titles such as J.J. Abrams's *S.*, William McDonough and Michael Braungart's *Cradle to Cradle*, Lin-Manuel Miranda's *Hamilton: The Revolution*, Oprah Winfrey's *The Wisdom of Sundays*, and Kobe Bryant's *The Mamba Mentality*, among many others.

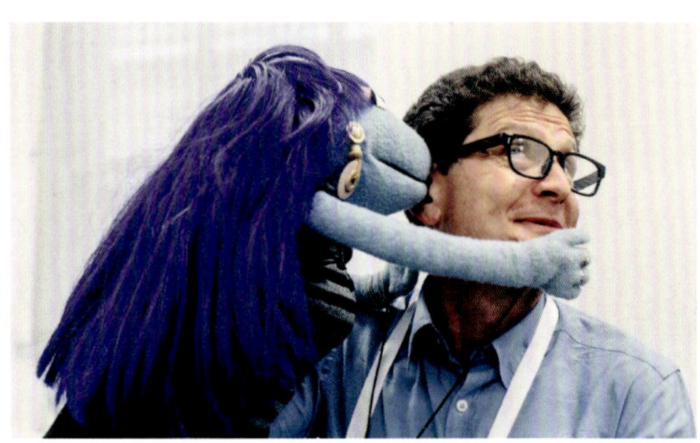

Melcher first worked with Vice President Al Gore on his bestselling book *An Inconvenient Truth*, and in 2011 they collaborated again on the company's first digital project, the interactive app *Our Choice*. The app was created in partnership with Push Pop Press, a software company of which Melcher was a founding partner. *Our Choice* was honored with a 2011 Apple Design Award, and that same year Push Pop Press was acquired by Facebook.

Melcher's successful foray into digital media led him to found the Future of StoryTelling (FoST) Summit in 2012, an invitation-only gathering focused on cutting-edge developments in storytelling and technology. FoST quickly grew to include a wide range of year-round activities, including an open-to-the-public festival. FoST continues to produce thought-leadership programming such as storytelling workshops, curated exhibitions, a monthly newsletter, *FoST in Thought*, and the biweekly *Future of StoryTelling* podcast. Today, FoST is also a multidisciplinary creative story studio

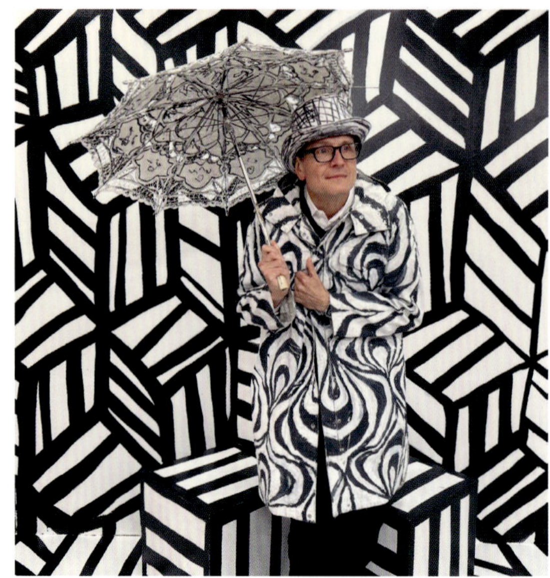

that produces award-winning projects for some of the world's most respected brands, institutions, and artists, including the first-ever VR spacewalk and tour of the ISS for Meta; an immersive experience for the opening of Apple's Carnegie Library flagship store in Washington, D.C.; and the curation and creation of 30,000 square feet of interactive exhibits and media for the Theodore Roosevelt Presidential Library.

Melcher is a frequent speaker on storytelling and technology and has presented at conferences and festivals such as SXSW, C2 Montréal, EY Innovation Realized, and the Milken Institute Global Conference. He also serves on the Photography Committee at MoMA and on the board of directors of the American Alliance of Museums and Punchdrunk International.

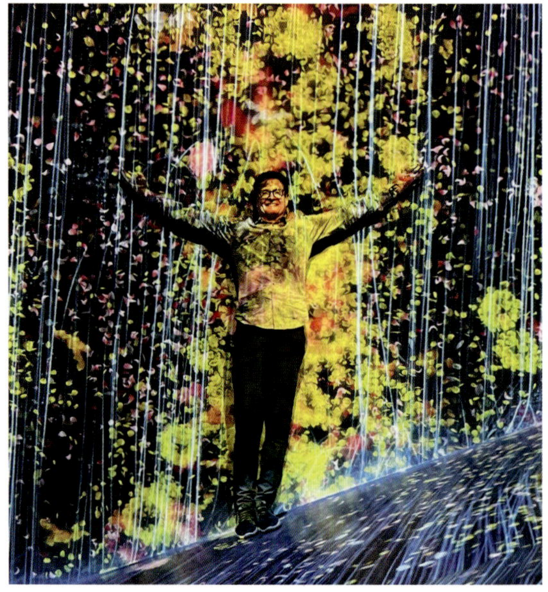

PHOTO CREDITS

Interior Credits

All photographs are copyright © their respective sources. 23: Emmanuel Lubezki; 34–35: Creative Commons; 38: Tender Claws; 40: Robin Roemer/Punchdrunk; 41: Brinkhoff/Moegenburg; 42–43: Julian Abrams/Punchdrunk; 44–45: Brinkhoff/Moegenburg; 46: Matt Flynn/Smithsonian Institution; 47: Local Projects; 48–49: Duhon Photography; 50–51 (top): Marcus Yam/The New York Times/Redux; 51 (bottom): Darial Sneed; 52–53: AKQA/Amazon; 54: Courtesy of Fever. STRANGER THINGS ™/© Netflix. Used with permission. Upside Down Pictures™ Monkey Massacre Productions 21 Laps™ Shawn Levy; 55 (top): © Netflix 2025. Used with permission; 55 (bottom): Courtesy of Fever. STRANGER THINGS ™/© Netflix. Used with permission. Upside Down Pictures™ Monkey Massacre Productions 21 Laps™ Shawn Levy; 56–57 (top and bottom): Courtesy of Fever. © 2025 Netflix. All rights reserved. BRIDGERTON and Netflix marks ™ Netflix. Shondaland mark ™ Shondaland. Used with permission; 57 (middle): Charley Gallay/Getty Images; 58–59: Courtesy of Fever. La Casa de Papel: ™/© Netflix. 2025. Used with permission; 60–63 (top): SON Studios; 63 (bottom): Gian Sapienza; 64–67: Courtesy of City Museum; 68: Painting and photo by Alexa Meade; 69 (top): Painting by Alexa Meade/photo by Mike Monaghan; 69 (bottom): Painting by Alexa Meade/photo by Ruby June; 70 (top): Painting and photo by Alexa Meade; 70 (bottom): Painting by Alexa Meade/photo by Mike Monaghan; 71 (top): painting and photo by Alexa Meade; 71 (bottom L–R): Painting by Alexa Meade/photo by Mike Monaghan; 72–75: Alistair Veyard; 79: Shannon Fanuko; 83: CBS Photo Archive/Getty Images; 86 (top): RSBPhoto1/Alamy Stock Photo; (bottom): Joni Hanebutt/Alamy Stock Photo; 89: Kate Russell/Courtesy of Meow Wolf; 91: Courtesy of thatgamecompany, Inc; 94–97: Courtesy of Giant Spoon; 98 (top and middle): Kate Russell/Courtesy of Meow Wolf; 98 (bottom): Josh Lane; 99: Karin Pezo/Alamy Stock Photo; 100: Atlas Media/Courtesy of Meow Wolf; 102: Kate Russell/Courtesy of Meow Wolf; 103: Atlas Media/Courtesy of Meow Wolf; 105: © Secret Cinema, Motion Picture © 2001 Twentieth Century Fox Film Corporation. All rights reserved; 106–107: @lukedyson/Luke Dyson/lukedyson.com/© Secret Cinema/CASINO ROYALE© 2006 Danjaq, LLC and United Artists Corporation. CASINO ROYALE, "007 Gun Logo" and related James Bond Trademarks, ™ Danjaq. All Rights Reserved; 108 (top): @lukedyson/Luke Dyson/lukedyson.com/© Secret Cinema/BLADE RUNNER and all related characters and elements © and ™ Warner Bros. Entertainment Inc. (s18) © 2018 Alcon Entertainment, LLC. All rights reserved; 108 (bottom): AI Overdrive/© Secret Cinema/BLADE RUNNER and all related characters and elements © and ™ Warner Bros. Entertainment Inc. (s18) © 2018 Alcon Entertainment, LLC. All rights reserved; 109: @lukedyson/Luke Dyson/lukedyson.com/© Secret Cinema/Dirty Dancing (R), TM & © 2022 Lions Gate Entertainment Inc. All Rights Reserved; 110–113: Hobbiton Movie Set; 114–117: Rah Petherbridge/Alice's Adventures Underground by Les Enfants Terribles; 118 (top): Robyn Beck/Getty Images; (bottom): Zuma Press Inc./Alamy Stock Photo; 119: Chris Chambers/Alamy Stock photo; 120: The Asahi Shimbun/Getty Images; 121 (top): Gustavo Caballero/Getty Images; (bottom): Handout/Getty Images; 122: Ryan Lowry; 123 (top): Ryan Lowry; 123 (middle): Ryan Lowry; 123 (bottom): Damien Maloney; 124 (top): Heather Sten; 124 (bottom); 125: Holly Andres; 126: Hogwash Studios; 127: Joyce Lee; 129: Lighthouse Immersive-San Francisco-MargoHawk2023; 130–131: Culturespaces/Fabijan Vuksic; 132 (top): Culturespaces/Vincent Pinson; 132 (bottom): ARTECHOUSE; 133: ARTECHOUSE: 134–135: David Hockney's Gregory Swimming, Los Angeles, March 31st 1982 in Lightroom. Courtesy of Lightroom, photograph by Justin Sutcliffe. © David Hockney; 138: Courtesy of Charles Melcher; 140–141: Los Angeles Times/Getty Images; 147: Courtesy of Giant Spoon; 150: Shannon Fanuko; 152–153: CAMP; 154: teamLab, *Bubble Universe: Spherical Crystallized Light, Wobbling Light, and Environmental Light - One Stroke*/teamLab; 153: teamLab, *Expanding Three-dimensional Existence in Transforming Space - Flattening 3 Colors and 9 Blurred Colors*/teamLab; 156–157: teamLab, *Universe of Water Particles on a Rock where People Gather, Flowers and People, Cannot be Controlled but Live Together – A Whole Year per Hour, Crows are Chased and the Chasing Crows are Destined to be Chased as well: Flying Beyond Border*/teamLab; 158 (top): teamLab, *Awakening*/teamLab; 158 (bottom): teamLab, *Graffiti Nature*/teamLab; 159 (top): teamLab, *Aerial Climbing through a Flock of Colored Birds*/teamLab; 159 (bottom): teamLab, *Memory of Topography*/teamLab; 160–163: Knott's Berry Farm LLC; 164 (top): Courtesy of AREA15 and BARTKRESA Studio; 164–167: Courtesy of AREA15; 170: Layered Reality Gunpowder Plot: A Tower of London Immersive Experience; 171: Layered Reality Gunpowder Plot: A Tower of London Immersive Experience/Mark Dawson Photography; 172 (bottom right): Layered Reality Jeff Wayne's The War of the Worlds: The Immersive Experience; 172 (middle): Marc Aspland; 173–175: Layered Reality Jeff Wayne's The War of the Worlds: The Immersive Experience; 176–177: Courtesy of Guinness Storehouse; 178 (top): BRC Imagination Arts; 178 (bottom): Jeffrey Isaac Greenberg 4+/Alamy Stock Photo; 179 (top): Ryan Lebel; (bottom): Michele D'Ottavio/Alamy Stock Photo; 180: Moment Factory, Ode à la Vie: Sagrada Família; 181–183: Moment Factory, AURA at the Notre-Dame Basilica; 184: Moment Factory, Light Cycles; 185 (top): Moment Factory, Oceana Lumina; 185 (bottom): Moment Factory, Terra Lumina; 186–189: Courtesy of Wētā Workshop Unleashed; 194: Courtesy of Atelier Daruma; 199: AI image generated with Sora; 200: UPI/Alamy Stock Photo; 202–203: Allen J. Schaben/Getty Images; 204–205: Allen J. Schaben/Getty

Images; 206–207: Fable Studios Inc; 208: Robert Kozek; 209 (top): Jon Braver; 209 (bottom): Fred Griessing; 210 (top left): Fred Griessing; 210 (top right and bottom left); 211: Robert Kozek; 212: Sean Raggett; 214–215: 2025 Larian Studios/2025 Wizards of the Coast; 216–219: BRC Imagination Arts; 223: Sherlocked; 227: Camerique/Alamy Stock Photo; 230: Sage Gallagher for Level99; 232: Secret Cinema/Laura Little; 233: Secret Cinema; 234: dpa picture alliance/Alamy Stock Photo; 235 (top): Friedrich Stark/Alamy Stock Photo; (bottom): Aflo Co. Ltd./Alamy Stock Photo; 236: © 2023 The Associated Press. All rights reserved; 237 (top): © 2023 The Associated Press. All rights reserved; (bottom): Marc Vollmannshauser for Niantic, Inc; 238–239: Sage Gallagher for Level99; 240 (top): Red Engine; 240 (bottom): Courtesy of F1 Arcade; 241: Puttshack; 242: Sherlocked; 243 (top): Palace Games; 243 (bottom): Roy Soetekouw; 244–245: Cijrille Kurvers; 246–247: Andrew Kelly for Museum of Ice Cream; 248 (top left): Chad Wadsworth for Museum of Ice Cream, (top right): Kelly Sullivan/Getty Images, (bottom left): Museum of Ice Cream; 249 (top and bottom): Chad Wadsworth for Museum of Ice Cream; 250–252: Courtesy of Sandbox VR; 253 (top): Courtesy of Sandbox VR. SQUID GAME ™/© Netflix. Used with permission; 253 (bottom): Courtesy of Sandbox VR; 254–255: Cosm Inc; 256–259: Courtesy of Nike, Inc; 263: Claire Woods; 271: Crossroads Foundation; 275: Kalle Lantz; 282: ZUMA Press, Inc/Alamy Stock Photo; 284–287: Crossroads Foundation; 288–289: Courtesy of Infinity Experiences - from the experience Space Explorers: THE INFINITE; 298: Chiara Marta Federica Sofia Cappiello/@chiaramfsofia_photo; 299: Oliver Facey/https://gallery.oliverfacey.co.uk/lrp; 300 (top): Alessandro Vizzarro/https://alessandrovizzarro.it/; 300 (bottom): Chiara Marta Federica Sofia Cappiello/@chiaramfsofia_photo; 301 (top): Ami Koiranen from the LARP Odysseus 2024; 301 (bottom): Tuomas Puikkonen from the LARP Odysseus 2024; 302–305: RLGB B.V. (tradename Entered); 306–309: All references to the Museum of the Future herein have been authorised and licensed by Museum of the Future LLC, the operator of the Museum of the Future, including all intellectual property rights therein; p. 307: Michele D'Ottavio/Alamy Stock Photo; 318: Courtesy of Charles Melcher.

Cover Credits

Main Cover: Andromeda Galaxy: Tony Rowell; woman sitting in wheelchair, man flying, girl on cloud, couple walking into refrigerator: Klaus Vedfelt; Man wearing glasses: izusek; Schoolbus: toos; Girl holding camera: BJI/Blue Jean Images; Man on slide: skynesher; Woman jumping: Tara Moore; Man in pink suit: ViewStock; Woman in blue shirt: amixstudio; Horror Cover: Vampire: film posters/Alamy Stock Photo; Moon: Ganapathy Kumar; Wolves/bats/castle: Everett Collection, Inc./Alamy Stock Photo; Spy Cover: snaptitude; Western Cover: INTERFOTO/Alamy Stock Photo; Comic Book Cover: Macrovector; Fantasy Cover: Sketch Master, ascrea; Historical Cover: Mouseion Archives/Alamy Stock Photo; Romance Cover: Adeela Parveen

This book was produced by

MELCHER MEDIA

124 West 13th Street
New York, NY 10011
melcher.com

Founder and CEO: Charles Melcher
VP, COO: Bonnie Eldon
Editorial Director: Lauren Nathan
Production Director: Susan Lynch
Executive Editor: Christopher Steighner
Senior Editor: Megan Worman
Assistant Editor: Madison Brown
Editorial Assistant: Charlotte Lamm

Lead Researcher and Contributing Editor: Luke Gernert
With additional editorial support from Andrew Postman, Megan Wenerstrom, Helen Healey-Cunningham, and David E. Brown

Designed by Paul Kepple and Alex Bruce at Headcase Design, headcasedesign.com

Main cover illustration by Pedro Nekoi

Special thanks to Chika Azuma, Alisa Cohen Barney, Michael Bass, Megan Carpentier, Laura Cray, Max Dickstein, Shannon Fanuko, David Gray, Carson Lee, Kevin Li, Grace Luckett, Sonia Menken, Carolyn Merriman, Nick Sexauer, Amy Snook, and Eitan Wolf.